Making
a Difference

D1503049

Making a Difference

Canadian Multicultural Literatures in English

Second Edition

Edited by Smaro Kamboureli

OXFORD
UNIVERSITY PRESS

OXFORD
UNIVERSITY PRESS

70 Wynford Drive, Don Mills, Ontario M3C 1J9
www.oup.com/ca

Oxford University Press is a department of the University of Oxford.
It furthers the University's objective of excellence in research, scholarship,
and education by publishing worldwide in

Oxford New York
Auckland Cape Town Dar es Salaam Hong Kong Karachi
Kuala Lumpur   ɔ City Nairobi
New   819.0808   ɔronto

Argentina Austria   MAK   ɔlic France Greece
Guatemala Hung   ɔrtugal Singapore
South Korea Swi   2007   Ukraine Vietnam

Oxford is   ɔrsity Press
in the   ɔntries

Published in Canada
by Oxford University Press

Copyright © Oxford University Press Canada 2007

The moral rights of the author have been asserted

Database right Oxford University Press (maker)

First published 2007

Library and Archives Canada Cataloguing in Publication

Making a difference : Canadian multicultural literatures in English / edited by Smaro
Kamboureli.—2nd ed.

Includes bibliographical references and index.
ISBN–13: 978–0–19–542288–7
ISBN–10: 0–19–542288–0

1. Canadian poetry (English)—Minority authors.   2. Canadian poetry (English)—20th century.
3. Canadian fiction (English)—Minority authors.   4. Canadian fiction (English)—20th century.
5. Minorities—Canada—Literary collections.   I. Kamboureli, Smaro

PS8235.M56M35 2006   C810.8'08   C2006–902693–9

Cover Design: Hye Kyong Son
Cover Image: Pattern of Spices/Imagesource/Firstlight

1 2 3 4 – 10 09 08 07
This book is printed on permanent (acid-free) paper ♾.
Printed in Canada

Introduction

As an anthologist and an anthology critic . . .

Making a Difference: Canadian Multicultural Literatures in English is the second edition of *Making a Difference: Canadian Multicultural Literature*, published in 1996. Why a new edition? Why indeed, since while still compiling the first volume, I had vowed to myself never to edit another anthology? It was not just the sheer labour involved that led me to make that, now broken, promise. Rather, it was the persistent ambivalence I felt—and still feel—about anthologies as a book genre.

At once a representation of a certain status quo—be it mainstream or not—and a response to it, an anthology *attempts* to offer a measure of existing conditions; often, it also attempts to announce or establish the emergence of new paradigms. I put *attempts* in italics precisely because an anthology, at least in my view of things, can only allege to accomplish what it sets out to do. Perhaps more than any other form of cultural production in general and literature in particular, anthologies are marked by the complex ways in which they operate as cultural instruments. Not only do they frame—you might even want to say arrest—what they represent, but by virtue of their strategies of restraint they inadvertently manipulate what they contain. They can function, then, as instruments of power, power in the sense that they have the potential to repudiate existing forms of knowledge and methods of knowing, while also performing (to use a Greek and Heideggerian term) as acts of *poesis* (making): 'a bringing forth', a revealing of something that was concealed.[1] So, even though anthologies reproduce original works, they have the potential to usher in something new. They can institute an instance of outing. In this respect, they become instruments of modernization. But, lest we forget what modernity's project involves, they inevitably also function as normalizing instruments. The value of the new—say, a new way of thinking about Canadian literature—lies, in part, in its aspiration to become the norm. Hence the function of anthologies as ambivalent mappings (and my discontent with them).

Anthologies operate as cultural instruments in a double way: as signs of their editors' praxis and rationales—rationales, 'as *rationes*', Timothy J. Reiss reminds us, '*become* instruments'[2]—and as objects applied to ends external to the anthologies themselves but internal to the cultural and public spheres within which they circulate. They are caught, then, in the fraught space between use-value and exchange-value—in the strict labour and economic as well as symbolic and cultural senses of these terms. How anthologies represent and/or produce value, as well as what that value entails, depends on the contexts within which they are disseminated and consolidated. They may be posited as instruments of valorization, but their particular uses as pedagogical and/or critical tools may misrepresent, be indifferent to, or cancel out their editors'

---

1 Martin Heidegger, *The Question Concerning Technology*, ed. David Farrell Krell, trans. William Lovitt (New York: Harper and Row, 1977), 294.
2 Timothy J. Reiss, *Against Autonomy: Global Dialectics of Cultural Exchange* (Stanford, CA: Stanford UP, 2002), 2.

intentions. Indeed, contrary to what some readers may think, the intentionality of anthologists is overestimated. Theirs is not the kind of authorial intentionality inscribed in single-authored books. While anthologists should claim responsibility for their choices and the reasons informing them, they cannot be held accountable for how the contents of their anthologies—or, for that matter, their introductions and headnotes—are read or taught. What's more, as Jeffrey R. Di Leo says, 'the radically contingent nature of the contents of anthologies, and conditions upon which those contents have been determined'[3] curtail and shape the anthologists' intentions, often against their best wishes.

These are not issues anthologists could easily delineate in an introduction. For example, it would take far too much space to fully explain my rationale for each author, let alone for the particular texts, that I have selected for this anthology. What Robert L. McLaughlin calls 'ugly practical concerns' play a major role in the composition of anthologies. His account of editing, *Innovations: An Anthology of Modern and Contemporary Fiction* (1998), is a telling example of some of the contingencies that influence anthologizing:

> Although it was clear that for the anthology to fulfill its purpose I would need to add more pieces, the page count was already prohibitively high: I would also have to cut pieces. I also had to begin exploring which of these pieces were in the public domain and for which I would need to acquire permission from the rights holders and how much they would cost. I had a limited budget for permission fees.[4]

This information does not appear in his editorial introduction but in a subsequent essay about anthologizing. Counting page numbers, while keeping in mind font sizes and other such technical parameters, not to mention dollar figures and the inclusion of certain texts because their length helps balance out the overall size of an anthology, is, perhaps, one of the most frustrating and mind-numbing tasks anthologists have to perform, yet a task that determines an anthology's contents. Nevertheless, most anthology readers rarely, if at all, find it necessary to remember that such 'ugly practical concerns' have a direct impact on the final product they review or teach. And when such information, an essential aspect of the materiality of anthologies, is discussed in an introduction, it is read, at best, as a mere symptom of defensiveness. The point here, however, is that these material conditions belong to the strategies of restraint that are part and parcel of anthologies as cultural instruments. And so does their condition as publishing commodities and pedagogical tools. How and where they are marketed, along with the various economies embedded in their production, and how and in what courses they are taught also impact on their instrumentality.

Anthologies may have the capacity to consolidate themselves as texts, but the ways in which they signify across multiple platforms and through different readers are contingent on factors beyond those directly related to their making. Thus, if instrumental-

---

3 Jeffrey R. Di Leo, 'Editor's Note', *symploke*, 8, 1–2 (2000), 5. See also his book, *On Anthologies: Politics and Pedagogy* (Lincoln, NB: U of Nebraska P, 2004).
4 Robert L. McLaughlin, 'Anthologizing Contemporary Literature: Aesthetic, Cultural, Pedagogical, and Practical Considerations', *symploke*, 8, 1–2 (2000), 96.

ity has a *disciplinary* function, as I think it does, then in order to understand the disciplinary role of anthologies, we should take into account at once the anthologists' goals and rationales and the institutional and material conditions within which anthologies are produced and read. Anthologies are products of complex mediation processes. While they are often cast as supplements, texts complementary to what already exists, the meanings and value attributed to their contents are, in part, the result of the cultural processes that instrumentalize them. In this context, the reasons of Gerald Graff's dismissal of anthologies are too hasty: 'one of the worst pedagogical results of literature anthologies', he says, is 'legitimating the primacy of literary texts and their supposed transparency, and obscuring the importance of criticism and interpretation (not even to mention theory) for the literature classroom.'[5] Contrary to Graff's argument, anthologies are often necessitated by the desire to delegitimate existing canonical formations; what's more, they are already the result of reading and interpretation, and reading them in the classroom can only involve an interactive and interrelational reading practice that should dispel any notion about the transparency of literary texts. Since anthologies, especially large ones, are never taught in their entirety, by reading and teaching them we produce new configurations of them. Anthologies may 'have consequences, and are grounded in commitments',[6] as Di Leo writes, but they are also malleable. Teaching an anthology, then, resembles the act of anthologizing; by selecting and recontextualizing the anthologized material, the teacher, too, becomes an anthologist. As the art and act of teaching, but also as the multi-circuited process that encompasses the cultural, institutional, and state apparatuses that fashion us as teachers, pedagogy brings together the cultural scene anthologies respond to with the scene of the classroom. As Di Leo puts it, '[a]nthologies are shaped by pedagogies, and pedagogies shape anthologies.'[7]

CanLit and Its Trauma of Belatedness

My remarks above answer my question 'Why a new edition?' only in a roundabout way, albeit a way that articulates why I view anthologies, including this one, as instances of what I called earlier ambivalent mappings. Part of this ambivalence entails the irony that while they are meant to fill in a gap, anthologies are invariably subjected to perpetual displacement. As soon as they appear, the clock starts winding down toward their obsolescence. Hence the need to offer a new version of the first edition. Simply put, a lot—yet also very little—has changed since the time the original edition of this anthology was conceived, edited, and published—a sound reason, it seems to me, to register through this second edition what has transpired in the ten-year interim between then and now.

---

5 Gerald Graff and Jeffrey R. Di Leo, 'Anthologies, Literary Theory and the Teaching of Literature: An Exchange', *symploke*, 8, 1–2 (2000), 113.
6 Di Leo, 5.
7 Di Leo, 4.

Making a Difference: Canadian Multicultural Literature was a response to the cultural and political climate surrounding its production period. The period between the mid-1980s and the mid-1990s was intensely characterized by specific manifestations of that trait Canadians want to believe is peculiar to them, anxiety about identity. Anxiety about the tensions between the dominant and minority cultures was hardly a new development at that time, but a certain confluence of events and circumstances marked the era in ways that continue to resonate today. Along with such milestone events in the political and social spheres as The Canadian Act of Multiculturalism and the Free Trade Agreement (both in 1988), the Meech Lake Accord and the Oka Crisis (both in 1990), the Charlottetown Accord national referendum (1992), the North American Free Trade Agreement (1993), and the Quebec referendum on independence (1995), major developments in the cultural sphere also marked that period. Lee Maracle's call, at the Third International Feminist Book Fair in Montreal, to white authors like Ann Cameron writing about Aboriginal subjects to 'move over' (1988), the formation of the Racial Minority Writers' Committee of the Writers' Union of Canada chaired by Lenore Keeshig-Tobias (1992), the heated dispute between Marlene NourbeSe Philip and June Callwood about the representation of minority authors at the PEN conference in Toronto (1989), the storm that followed the Royal Ontario Museum's exhibit 'Into the Heart of Africa' (1989–90), and the controversy that erupted about the Writing Thru Race conference in Vancouver (1994) that Roy Miki organized[8]— these events created a sharp awareness of what has been dubbed 'identity politics'. That the cultural terrain is intricately related to that of politics, and that history should not be seen as a silent archive that has been packaged away, was made apparent by the role Joy Kogawa's novel *Obasan* (1981) played in educating the Canadian public about the need to pursue the Redress of the Japanese Canadians' internment in the Second World War. Seeing, then, that period of the 1980s and 1990s as being shaped by the so-called 'identity wars' was—is—a reductive, if not condescending, response to the urgency these events brought about, namely the need to address the politics of representation. If anything, multiculturalism had already shown itself to be 'a strange-headed beast',[9] more often than not out of joint with daily reality, if not with itself, while institutional attempts to implement change consistent with racial and ethnic equality often became synonymous with tokenism.

The first edition, then, appeared at a time when difference—understood in the contexts of both indigeneity and multiculturalism—took hold of the Canadian imagination with great force. Through a body of literature spanning the twentieth century, *Making a Difference* attempted to reflect that such institutional structures as the nation and the literary canon were at best volatile constructs, heavily inscribed by ideologies that, under careful scrutiny, exposed the degree and ways in which the production and reception of literature written by so-called minority authors were managed—read

---

8 Information and critical material about these events, as well as other references in this Introduction and in the anthology to social and cultural events of relevance to its contents, appear on the website of Oxford University Press Canada under *Making a Difference*: www.oup.com/ca/he/companion/kamboureli.

9 Sanjay Talreja, 'Introduction', *Strangers in the Mirror: In and Out of the Mainstream of Culture and Canada*, ed. Sanjay Talreja and Nurjehan Aziz (Toronto: TSAR, 2004), x.

instrumentalized—by dominant culture. The diversity of material and of the political and cultural views of the authors included offered, at least as I read them, ample evidence that such developments in the 1980s and 1990s as Canada's official policy of multiculturalism and the policies that resulted from the Canada Council's Advisory Committee for Racial Equality in the Arts (1990) could not once and for all resolve the issues they endeavoured to address, let alone meet with consensus.

In the time that has elapsed since then, the 'face' of mainstream Canadian literature may have changed irrevocably, but the intricate and hard questions raised by the politics of difference and of representation persist. If I felt compelled in 1996 to comment on the fact that a number of the contributors to the first edition had already accrued national awards, made it into the curricula of postsecondary institutions, and been published by major presses, it was because 'Making a Difference [was] intend[ed] to reflect the changed—and changing—state of cultural affairs in Canada,' but above all because I saw the need to acknowledge that 'Canadian literature as an institution . . . [was] still not as diverse as it should [have] been.'[10]

Jo-Ann Episkenew's statement, published in 2002, that 'it is only a matter of time before works of Aboriginal literature begin to appear *regularly* in anthologies' alerts us to the belatedness that characterizes the makeover of Canadian literature. And this is not just a matter of simply paying attention to 'Aboriginal literature . . . knocking on the door of the Canadian literary canon'; what's at stake here, she argues, is '[t]he challenge that [scholars] face [in] finding something to say about these seemingly uncomplicated works of literature when they have been trained to look for and analyze complexities'. Not to mention, as she notes '[d]uring [her] most cynical moments', the fact that under pressure to declare 'specialization' and secure '[t]enure and promotion', academics 'must carve out an intellectual space' for themselves: 'If Shakespeare is our passion, our challenge is a large one; after all, it is hard to make a space for one's self in such an *occupied* area. Clearly, it is easier to find a space in an area that is new and unoccupied, one like the area of Canadian Aboriginal Literature.'[11] Episkenew draws attention to some of the ways in which this literature is instrumentalized.

Significantly, her rhetoric evokes colonialism not as a thing of the past or as a mere spectral presence haunting Canadian literature and criticism, but as a condition that is still present in institutional and critical practices today. The ironic inversion characterizing her use of rhetoric—it is Shakespeare studies that is an 'occupied area' and Aboriginal studies that is a field yet 'unoccupied'—discloses the complicities inscribed in the belatedness of Canadian literature's overhaul. Anxious about its own colonial genealogy and overly conscious of its growing pains before reaching its present stage of self-confidence and international recognition, what I referred to elsewhere as the phenomenon of 'cultural celebrity',[12] CanLit as an institution is defined, in part, by the trauma of its own belatedness, hence its obsession with belatedness. The celebratory

---

10 'Introduction' to *Making a Difference* (1996), xviii in this edition.
11 Jo-Ann Episkenew, 'Socially Responsible Criticism: Aboriginal Literature, Ideology, and the Literary Canon', in *Creating Community: A Roundtable on Canadian Aboriginal Literature*, ed. Renata Eigenbrod and Jo-Ann Episkenew (Penticton: Theytus Books, 2002), 53–4, my italics.
12 See my essay 'The Culture of Celebrity and National Pedagogy', in *Home-Work: Postcolonialism, Pedagogy, and Canadian Literature*, ed. Cynthia Sugars (Ottawa: U of Ottawa P, 2004), 35–55.

ways in which certain indigenous and diasporic writings have been embraced by mainstream culture, along with the preoccupation of a large number of Canadianists with things postcolonial and diasporic, testifies to how the belatedness complex operates.

This belatedness signals at once the ideology of liberalism that permeates Canadian society and culture and the institutional limits of Canadian postcolonial practices today. Greek Cherokee author Thomas King may have been invited to give the 2003 Massey Lectures and have his own CBC Radio program, and Haisla author Eden Robinson may have met with commercial success, but long-established indigenous writers like Stoh:lo Lee Maracle and Okanagan Jeannette Armstrong, and indeed the majority of Aboriginal authors, continue to be published only by small presses, a number of them Aboriginal. Still, in the last decade indigenous and diasporic writing has come to enjoy unprecedented visibility. But 'if the notion of "writers of colour" came into national literary consciousness as a marginal notation in the 1980s,' Ashok Mathur wrote in 2005, 'it is with considerable alarm that we should note the mainstreaming of many of these writers in that they have begun to represent CanLit in many quarters.' What does it mean, then, that, in Mathur's words, '[w]hat began as a brown wafer begging to be tasted has [now] become the body it once opposed'? He does not think that the 'marketability' of these writers 'is a necessarily bad thing', but, as he goes on to say, 'the flip side, when that work is being written about, being read, being sought, is that such consumption is driven by a market desire for a particular direction or focus.'[13]

The marketability of racialized authors may render the construct of minority writing obsolete, but it also reveals the instrumentality attributed to it. A symptom of CanLit's belatedness, the impetus that drives the marketability of indigenous and diasporic writing comes from the need to recognize those Canada had forgotten, an exercise in remembering that feeds Canadian liberal ideology and responds to the demands of global economies. This is the cultural scene that the second edition of this anthology, *Making a Difference: Canadian Multicultural Literatures in English*, attempts to address.

If the politics of cultural appropriation and the difficulties indigenous and diasporic writers confronted in getting published in Canada dominated the debates ten years ago, there is now, in these global and post-9/11 times, concern with different configurations of racialization and racism, namely, racial profiling and security measures, and with the impact global mobility and economies have on Canada, its culture, and its cultural industries. Despite this, the turmoil and vociferous arguments of that earlier period have, in some ways, been replaced by what I have called elsewhere 'sedative politics',[14] a politics that results from the feeling that Canadian culture has, at last, 'arrived'. The belatedness that characterizes this state of affairs, at least in my understanding of it, both acknowledges and circumvents the distant and recent past. It reveals what it holds back, it lets us get a glimpse of what it represses, but it also

13 Ashok Mathur, 'Transubracination: How Writers of Colour Became CanLit', in *Trans.Can.Lit: Resituating the Study of Canadian Literature*, ed. Smaro Kamboureli and Roy Miki (Waterloo: Wilfrid Laurier UP, forthcoming in 2007).
14 See Smaro Kamboureli, 'Sedative Politics: Media, Law, Philosophy', in *Scandalous Bodies: Diasporic Literature in English Canada* (Toronto: Oxford UP, 2000), 81–130, and 'Ethnic Allegories: From Designated Margins to Postmodern Multiculturalism', 131–74.

displaces the politics of race and difference and eludes any direct confrontation with its historical consciousness.

There is an ironic symmetry between Canada's self-image as a multicultural haven, a society that respects differences, and critics like Michael Butts, whose entry 'Multicultural Voices' in the *Encyclopedia of Literature in Canada* remains suffused with nostalgia for colonial history. Thus the Canadian state continues to cultivate its international reputation as a society welcoming to immigrants and refugees even as it screens out, for example, Roma refugees by strategically distinguishing between 'discrimination' and 'persecution', while Butts writes that '[*a*] *longside* Canadian "mainstream" literature is a literature created by the numerous ethnic groups that arrived after the first British and French settlers.'[15] ' "Mainstream" ' may be in scare quotes, but in his formulation the literature created by ethnic groups still belongs to the margins of CanLit, and the devastating impact of those settlers' arrival on the First Nations is still felt and demands to be redressed. The history of Canada and its culture has evolved, but its evolution perpetuates the model of Western modernity. Embracing 'otherness' may help promote indigenous and diasporic literatures, but many of the ways in which this gesture is being practised help promote the state's cultural capital. '[T]o read belatedly the traces of the colonial memory or to send the card back to a sender who may or may not happen to be there to receive it', Ali Behdad writes, 'does not *necessarily* constitute an oppositional praxis.'[16] It is with the political implications of this belatedness in mind that *Making a Difference: Canadian Multicultural Literatures in English* should be read.

The Difference a Title Makes

So, what is different in this second edition?

The initial table of contents I compiled for this edition was over 800 pages long. It included plenty of examples of Aboriginal oratory, early Aboriginal oral and written literature and a large number of recent authors, more pre-twentieth-century black authors, a larger representation of different diasporic groups, more essays and excerpts from memoirs. Considering the hard choices in compiling an anthology, I was pretty happy with that original list. But it would have been too expensive to produce, and thus to buy. Nor was I certain that such a long anthology would have been a better pedagogical text. Fashioning an anthology relies on the process of elimination, and so the final text is much shorter and thus substantially different than the one I had allowed myself to dream of. In trimming the original contents back, I kept in mind the feedback I had received from various readers—some of them anonymous—and my own sense of how to balance the material in terms of content, genre, style, gender,

15 Michael Butts, 'Multicultural Voices', *Encyclopedia of Literature in Canada*, ed. W.H. New (Toronto: U of Toronto P, 2002), 764; my emphasis.
16 Ali Behdad, '*Une Pratique Sauvage*: Postcolonial Belatedness and Cultural Politics', *The Pre-Occupation of Postcolonial Studies*, ed. Fawzia Afzal-Khan and Kalpana Seshadri Crooks (Durham, NC: Duke UP, 2000), 77.

sexual difference, cultural and racial backgrounds, and different pedagogical concerns and contexts.

Though not much longer than the first edition, *Making a Difference: Canadian Multicultural Literatures in English* includes a larger number of authors. Many of the original contributors remain the same, but different names also appear. Moreover, some of the texts by authors in the first edition have been replaced by other selections—either because of considerations of length or because of the need to maintain a balance between genres and styles. Moreover, while the first edition contained only poetry and fiction, the second one also includes a sampling of life writing, creative non-fiction, and essays. *Making a Difference* still attempts to represent a diversity of authors and writing styles across a long span of time, but it does so by beginning with examples of fugitive slave narratives. Opening not, as was the case with the first edition, with a white European male, F.P. Grove, who nevertheless remains included, but with the voices of two women and two men who arrived in Canada in the late 1800s to escape from slavery, the anthology suggests that it is not only difficult to establish a *formal* beginning for indigenous and diasporic literatures but also necessary to keep questioning the origins of CanLit as an institution. Accessing the archive of imperial and colonial history, these narratives allow us to return to that period and the legacy of its politics a critical gaze, a gaze that can hopefully translate its belatedness into the politics of today.

The principles I followed in composing the headnotes are the same as those I employed in the first edition. Whenever possible, by quoting from interviews, I tried to let the authors introduce themselves, but I did not, as I did the first time around, attempt to interview the contributors. While some of the headnotes on authors who appear in both editions have not changed, others have been updated. Although some readers and teachers whose feedback was solicited by my publisher and by me would have liked to see a section of 'questions and instructions' for use in the classroom, I have decided against it. This kind of material may be useful in certain courses, but, depending on the situation, it can function in too prescriptive a fashion. This anthology can be taught in different contexts and levels, and approached from different disciplinary perspectives to provide such instructions. I have opted, instead, to provide more background information about the contexts (cultural, social, and political) that inform the making of this anthology and about the contributors on the publisher's website for the book, www.oup.com/ca/he/companion/kamboureli.

The title, different from yet similar to that of the first edition, is a result of the compromise reached between my publisher's desire to keep the original title for marketing purposes and my intention to signal that what is at stake at this point of studying indigenous and diasporic writing is considerably different from what figured in the study of this literature ten years ago. The difference signalled does not refer necessarily to progress, but rather to the need to read recent and earlier Canadian writing from the vantage of the present, a present, however, mindful of its historical consciousness, of how its historicity itself has produced the power relations it strives to address. Whether these changes constitute major differences or not is up to the readers to decide.

Acknowledgements

Had it not been for the encouragement that came from Laura MacLeod, formerly with Oxford University Press Canada, I would not have been galvanized into action. I am grateful to Eric Sinkins, my editor at Oxford, for his sound advice and good cheer, and above all his infinite patience. Special thanks are due to a number of contributors—too many to mention all of them here—who, patiently and generously, answered my queries, as well as to the various colleagues who offered feedback on the first edition and recommendations toward the second one. Without the help of my research assistants this anthology would not have come to life; I am immensely grateful to all of them. I owe special thanks to Andrea Bennett and Mark McCutcheon—they were instrumental in helping get the project off the ground and keeping it going; Louisa Sorflaten was an exemplary assistant in the fall of 2006; and Ben Authers and Debra Henderson, who stepped in at the very last, and most hectic, stages of this project, worked with great enthusiasm, professionalism, and panache. Needless to say, I am singly responsible for any mistakes or omissions. The support and friendship of my colleagues Mark Lipton, Donna Pennee, and Jennifer Schacker made me feel less of a stranger in my new institution. Finally, my deepest thanks are due to Phyllis Webb and Roy and Slavia Miki for their ongoing friendship and intellectual companionship.

This project has been completed with the support of the Canada Research Chair Program.

Introduction to the First Edition

Making a Difference: An Anthology of Canadian Multicultural Literature at once celebrates what has been called minority literature in Canada and attempts to change our understanding of what minority literature is.

What makes this anthology of Canadian literature different is its gathering together of both poetry and fiction by authors who come from a wide range of racial, ethnic, and cultural backgrounds. Beginning with F.P. Grove and Laura Goodman Salverson, the first non-Anglo-Celtic writers to achieve recognition in Canada, and including First Nations authors, this anthology belongs to the genealogy of Canadian literature, a body of writings that come from a variety of traditions that used to be kept separate from the so-called main tradition.

One of my primary intentions has been to create a space in which contributors to the anthology might dialogue with each other, without suspending their differences. Through their poetry, their fiction, and their statements about their writing that are cited in the headnotes, this anthology enables these authors to speak with each other across boundaries that are marked by many differences. Be they differences of race, of ethnic origin, of gender, of place, of ideological affiliations, or of thematic concerns and aesthetics, they characterize this literature in remarkable ways. Each of the seventy-one contributors speaks in her or his particular accent. I use the word *accent* here not so much as the language marker announcing that the origins of someone—like me, for example—lie outside Canada, but rather as a sign of particularities, of differences that do not become absent or are not rendered silent. The writers in this anthology make a difference because, when read together, they invite the reader to consider the social, political, and cultural contexts that have produced Canadian literature in general and their work in particular. As a collage of voices, *Making a Difference* fashions an image of Canadian culture that reveals how we have come to our present moment in history.

This history speaks of arrivals and departures, trajectories whose starting points contain, more often than not, conflict. It is a history of the legacy of colonization, but also a history of the 'discovery' of Canada as a new home whose 'newness' constantly calls forth the spectre of the past, the nostalgic replay of other geographies. It is also a history of persistent attempts to compose a unified vision of Canadian culture against the reality and cultural understanding of many Canadians, a history that bursts at its seams. It is, in other words, a history haunted by dissonance. This history, which is paradoxically one of plenitude and of disquieting gaps, is what the subtitle of the anthology intends to evoke.

Canadian Multicultural Literature. In some respects, one word too many. For Canadian literature is, should be thought of as, reflecting the multicultural make-up of the country. That I feel compelled to spell this out, that I do so at a time when, for example, some of the contributors to this anthology have won some of the most coveted Canadian literary prizes, suggests that Canadian literature—Canadian literature as an institution—is still not as diverse as it should be. Prizes do not by themselves establish the literary significance of an author; still, they confer on authors a validity, they sanction the kind of affirmation that the Canadian literary establishment has long denied Aboriginal writers and writers of non-Anglo-Celtic back-grounds. *Making a Difference* intends to reflect the changed—and changing—state of cultural affairs in Canada.

◈ ◈ ◈

In explaining how I came to select and represent the writers included in this anthol-ogy, I can only begin by resorting to the cliché offered by other anthologists. No sooner is an anthology complete than it begins to address its own gaps; it can only exist within the ellipses it creates.

While working on this project, I remained profoundly aware of the fact that inclu-sion is synonymous with exclusion. The irony that an anthology of this kind is, in many ways, a response to earlier cases of exclusion informed my wish to compile an anthology that would represent Canadian writing while calling into question repre-sentation itself. In many respects, this is an impossible task, perhaps even a preposter-ous ambition. Yet, if I were to reconstruct what prompted me in the first place to compile this anthology, the questioning of representation would figure prominently as both one of my primary goals and one of my guiding principles. I believe that we reside forever within the realm of representation: we represent ourselves through lan-guage and through our bodies, but we also see ourselves represented by others. No image, no story, no anthology can represent us or others without bringing into play—serious play—differing contexts, places, or people.

Making a Difference attempts to question representation in a number of ways, per-haps most significantly by challenging the concept of minority. All the contributors, by virtue of their race and ethnicity, belong to the manifold 'margins' that the Canadian dominant society has historically devised. Yet, if we consider these authors in the various contexts that have produced their writing, it becomes apparent that 'marginalization', from an individual as well as a collective perspective, is impossible to define in any stable way.

These authors' experiences with Canadian publishers, the reception of their work, their personal histories in Canada, how they position themselves with regard to their cultural differences, the diverse treatment of their racial and ethnic groups by the Canadian dominant society, how (if at all) these experiences are translated into litera-ture—all these and other related issues argue persuasively to one conclusion: that the concept of marginality has no inherent meaning in itself. As Russell Ferguson says,

> When we say marginal, we must always ask, marginal to what? But this ques-tion is difficult to answer. The place from which power is exercised is often a hidden place. When we try to pin it down, the center always seems to be somewhere else. Yet we know that this phantom center, elusive as it is, exerts a real, undeniable power over the whole social framework of our culture, and over the ways we think about it.[1]

1 'Introduction: Invisible Center', *Out There: Marginalization and Contemporary Cultures*, ed. Russell Ferguson, Martha Gever, Trinh T. Minh-ha, and Cornel West (New York: The New Museum of Contemporary Art; Cambridge, MA: The MIT Press, 1990), 9.

Minority literature, then, is nothing other than a construct, an expression of the power and literary politics of any given time.

This is why we see in *Making a Difference*, for example, a writer like Lee Maracle alongside a writer like Michael Ondaatje. Maracle might be one of the most prolific and widely read Native authors, but she began her writing career by publishing her own books because no Canadian publisher would publish her. Ondaatje, on the other hand, has long enjoyed a national reputation and has recently achieved international status. Similarly, Marlene Nourbese Philip and Dionne Brand are often now included in courses on Canadian literature and have become the focus of recent critical studies, but their lives and writing careers clearly reflect the discrimination and racism they have encountered in Canada. In contrast, Evelyn Lau has had her work published by mainstream presses, and resists writing out of, or identifying with, her ethnic community. In a different way, Frank Paci has been writing fiction for years, but only recently, after the success of Nino Ricci's first novel, to which his work has been compared, has he become more widely recognized. Difference, then, is always a matter of intensity, and is weighed differently in given historical moments. Its meanings are variable, shifting, even provisional.

My selection of contributors was intended to reflect, in part, a counterreading of what we have come to call mainstream and minority literatures in Canada. Multicultural literature is not minority writing, for it does not raise issues that are of minor interest to Canadians. Nor is it, by any standard, of lesser quality than the established literary tradition. Its thematic concerns are of such a diverse range that they show the binary structure of 'centre' and 'margins', which has for so long informed discussions of Canadian literature, to be a paradigm of the history of political and cultural affairs in Canada.

I did not want this anthology to be an instance of tokenism, and this was yet another factor that has informed my selections. By holding onto what the 'otherness' of writers—be it ethnicity, race, or gender—is in relation to the dominant culture's self-image, tokenism assigns a single meaning to cultural differences. It masks the many nuances of difference. On the one hand, it homogenizes the diversity that multiculturalism is intent on embracing; on the other, it disregards the fact that a writer's identity and the meaning of a poem or a short story cannot be defined in any single way.

Since the late 1980s, in response to the currency that multiculturalism has achieved in the political, social, and academic arenas, anthologies, critical studies, and course syllabi have gradually begun to include authors who have been traditionally excluded from mainstream representation. These gradual and tentative changes have been necessary steps toward revising our understanding of what constitutes Canadian literature. Yet many of these attempts, however well intended, have resulted in further consolidating the minority position of the selected writers. Representing Canada's multiculturalism with a spattering of only one or two authors, making such writers visible only by viewing them as representative of their cultural groups, does virtually nothing to dispel the 'marginality' attributed to those authors.

I have attempted to avoid such pitfalls by considering the contributors to this anthology as Canadian writers, and not as representatives of cultural groups. The tendency to read multicultural literature through the racial or ethnic labels affixed to its authors more often than not reinforces stereotypical images of the authors themselves and of their cultural communities. Labels are vexing and sneaky things because they are intended to express a stable and universal representation of both communities and individuals. By implying that there is a specific essence, say, to the writing of First Nations authors, labels prematurely foreclose our understanding not only of the complexity inherent in individual communities but also of the various ways in which authors position themselves within their cultural groups and the Canadian society at large. As Jeannette Armstrong has written,

> First Nations cultures, in their various contemporary forms, whether an urban-modern, pan-Indian experience or clearly a tribal specific (traditional or contemporary), whether it is Eastern, Arctic, Plains, Southwest or West Coastal in region, have unique sensibilities which shape the voices coming forward into written English Literature.[2]

The particular relations of writers to culture, the complex contexts within which they write, are always inscribed in the literature itself. And this is the reason why this anthology is not organized by cultural groups.

Even when a community claims a writer as its spokesperson, or when a writer voluntarily takes on that role, she or he must write out of a space of difference. The difference is made by the writing act itself, by a writerly belief in language as an act of the imagination, by a faith in the power of language, irrespective of its forms and contours, to effect change, to make us perceive ourselves and those around us *otherwise*.

Roy Kiyooka once said that, for him, 'to survive in this culture was essentially a quest for language as the modality of power about which you could be present in the world.'[3] In searching for potential contributors, this is what I have looked for: how these writers make themselves 'present in the world', how they articulate their relation to language and to culture. That many authors in *Making a Difference* share the same cultural background is, in many respects, a fortuitous result of my selection process. That the writing of those who have a common heritage often echoes similar themes and just as often reflects different concerns, attests that cultural boundaries are porous, that cultural representation is contingent on the authors' singularity of imagination. No single form of literary representation can adequately reflect a community's complexity. Indeed, the variety of authors that come from and write about individual groups resists any notion of a sole authentic image of those communities.

Thus, both Himani Bannerji and Rohinton Mistry come from India, but their writing gestures toward different spaces. This reflects not only the richness and diversity of Indian culture, but also their individual sensibilities. Armin Wiebe, Sandra Birdsell, Rudy Wiebe, Patrick Friesen and Di Brandt are all known as Mennonite writers, but their Mennonite experiences are coded differently in their writing.

---

2 'Editor's Note', *Looking at the Words of our People: First Nations Analysis of Literature*, ed. Jeannette Armstrong (Penticton, BC: Theytus Books Ltd, 1993), 7.

3 As cited in Roy Miki, 'Inter-Face: Roy Kiyooka's Writing, A Commentary/Interview', *Roy Kiyooka* (Vancouver: Artspeak Gallery and the Or Gallery, 1991), 48.

Furthermore, it would be reductive to read their work only through the signs of Mennonite background and, as a result, ignore all the other elements that contribute to the complexity of their writing. Communities have a social and cultural coherence, but they are also characterized by fluidity. No constellation of literary images can singlehandedly mould a community's particular ethos. We must read the distinctive ways in which authors identify with, or resist, their communities in the context of other historical factors that permeate their work.

As Thomas King says, 'when we talk about Native writers, we talk as though we have a process for determining who is a Native writer and who is not, when, in fact, we don't. What we do have is a collection of literary works by individual authors who are Native by ancestry, and our hope, as writers and critics, is that if we wait long enough, the sheer bulk of this collection, when it reaches some sort of critical mass, will present us with a matrix within which a variety of patterns can be discerned.'[4] It is my hope that *Making a Difference* will have a similar effect, that its readers will develop an incremental understanding of who its contributors are and what they tell us about the history of our multicultural tradition.

My selection process has also been informed by my desire to represent Canadian multicultural literature by bridging the gap between established and emerging authors. Many contributors—like Austin Clarke, Joseph Skvorecky, Joy Kogawa, Aritha van Herk, M.G. Vassanji—have produced substantial bodies of work that have influenced both our overall appreciation of their writing and some of the ways in which we approach Canadian literature. Presenting these authors alongside, for example, Zaffi Gousopoulos and Corinne Allyson Lee, who have so far published only in literary magazines, or next to authors like Hiromi Goto, Yasmin Ladha, Nice Rodriguez, and Ashok Mathur, who have so far published only one book each, reflects my attempt to give the reader a broad view of what Canadian multicultural literature has to offer at this point in time.

My intention to represent Canadian multicultural literature while questioning the label of minority attached to it has also led to my decision to organize the contents of this anthology according to the birthdates of authors. This arrangement, I believe, affords the reader a historical overview while, at the same time, dispelling the notion that multicultural writing is only a recent phenomenon. I would like to stress that I am not offering *Making a Difference* as an anthology that claims to redress all the gaps of cultural difference in the Canadian literary canon. No anthology could purport to do that. Any anthology that intends to offer a historical overview can only function as an allegory of literary history, can only map out yet another narrative path by which we can enter that history. Like all anthologies, *Making a Difference*, too, has gaps, but what it does not include, I hope, is balanced by the various ways in which I have tried to remain alert to change and limits.

How we function as subjects of our own representations and how we figure as objects in the representations of others; how culture is defined and who implements

---

4 'Introduction', *All My Relations: An Anthology of Contemporary Canadian Native Fiction* (Toronto: McClelland and Stewart, 1990), x.

those definitions; what or who devises the boundaries that determine how cultural difference, be it celebrated or curtailed, is represented—all these questions have been central to the making of this anthology. In my selection process I was guided by the belief that multiculturalism disputes certain kinds of representation, the kinds that are built around the principle of sameness, of cohesiveness, of linear development.

The seventy-one contributors represented here are introduced by headnotes that include both biographical information and, with a few exceptions, comments by the authors themselves. Although there was no difficulty collecting material about the lives and writing careers of most of these contributors, in some cases gathering information proved to be a real challenge. This accounts for some of the inconsistencies that appear in the kinds of information and material provided. Furthermore, I have encountered some discrepancies in dates and other facts in the various sources that I have consulted. I have tried to resolve those problems to the best of my ability.

The authors' statements cited in the headnotes come from interviews, from their essays (included in the bibliography that appears at the end of this volume) or, in many cases, from comments written by the authors. Beyond the need to introduce the basic outline of individual careers, the headnotes are designed to let the contributors speak for themselves about their writing. I am, of course, responsible for the specific comments that I cite, and I am aware that I mediate these writers' own self-representations. But representation, as I have already tried to explain, is a matter of construction, always something that stands in for something else.

Some of the comments I cite address issues about which many of the contributors have often spoken. I have taken this to reflect a persistent concern on their part and on the part of their audiences, and thus I have included such comments. How they became writers, how they approach their subject matter, what they think of language or the function of literature are some of these issues. I have also included statements which show the diversity of the cultural and social spaces from which these writers come, and which demonstrate that Canada, historically and culturally, has been both a troubling and an exciting place to inhabit.

Thus while some of the contributors speak of their resistance to labels like ethnicity and of the relationship of their cultural origins to their writing, they do so in different ways. The narrative that emerges from these comments is, then, one of contradictions, of differences. What is consistent is the anxiety many of these authors share about any homogenous image of Canadian culture, their concern with the tendency of readers and the media to represent their identities and their writings in minority terms, irrespective of the power with which some of these minority spaces are invested today. Like the literature included in this anthology, these comments illustrate that the differences that permeate Canadian multiculturalism are not to be seen as barriers but as signs of complexity.

❖ ❖ ❖

The literature in *Making a Difference* offers different soundings of the social and cultural body of Canada. Since its beginnings, the making of Canadian literature has coincided, in many respects, with the making of the Canadian state. Far from being a Canadian phenomenon alone, this overlap shows how literature, like other cultural expressions, measures the pulse of a nation. What might be particularly Canadian, however, is the kind of anxiety that has continued to characterize both what Canadian literature is and what constitutes Canadian identity. This is not surprising since Canada as a state is, relatively speaking, new. And it also explains David Taras's claim that 'there has been throughout Canadian history a passion for identity.'[5] Few would dispute this. What is disputed, though, is the overwhelming tendency to define Canadian identity in collective and unifying terms, this despite, or perhaps because of, the legacy of colonialism and the overpowering evidence that Canada has always been a place of diversities—racial, ethnic, and linguistic.

The binary structure which *Making a Difference* attempts to dissolve, that of 'centre' and 'margin', is part and parcel of Canada's colonial history, of its attempt to construct a Canadian identity that is modelled after the image of the colonizers. This, too, is consistent with the patterns of colonialism elsewhere. For in the history of Western domination, the paradigm of 'centre' and 'margin', as Gyan Prakash writes,

> surfaces precisely at the point where the encounter with cultural difference is organized into the colonizer/colonized polarity, where the historicist notion of history gathers 'people without history' into its fold, and where the metropolitan culture speaks to the marginalized in the language of its supremacist myths.[6]

In Canada's colonial history, 'the encounter with cultural difference' was, for all intents and purposes, a non-encounter. The British and French colonizers saw themselves as settlers, as arriving in a land that was taken to be more or less empty. The presence, cultural differences, spirituality, and languages of the Aboriginal peoples, the people who live in what we now call Canada, were not seen as having any inherent value. The land they inhabited, and which they continue to inhabit, was deemed to be ready for the taking. And this remained the case for a long time.

Canadian history, until relatively recently, perpetuated this image of Canada as a land that was 'discovered', not a land that was colonized. As Olive Patricia Dickason says,

> Canada, it used to be said by non-Indians . . . is a country of much geography and little history. . . . How can such a thing be said, much less believed, when people have been living here for thousands of years? As [Aboriginals] see it, Canada has fifty-five founding nations rather than the two that have been officially acknowledged. . . . Canada's history has usually been presented not as beginning with the first Europeans, the Norse, who arrived here in about AD 1000, but with the French, who came . . . in the sixteenth century.[7]

---

5 'Introduction', *A Passion for Identity: An Introduction to Canadian Studies*, ed. Eli Mandel and David Taras (Toronto, New York: Methuen, 1987), 10.

6 *After Colonialism: Imperial Histories and Postcolonial Displacements*, ed. Gyan Prakash (Princeton, New Jersey: Princeton UP, 1995), 4.

7 *Canada's First Nations: A History of Founding Peoples from Earliest Times* (Toronto: McClelland and Stewart, 1992), 11.

The myth that Canada was 'discovered' was intended to hide the fact that what we now call Canada has always belonged to other peoples, peoples with their own distinct languages and cultures.

Jeannette Armstrong's comments in this collection indicate the unequivocal presence of the rich and diverse cultures of Aboriginal peoples. She grew up in the nurturing environment of 'a traditional family . . . with a long history', a history that includes 'the total purity of our language', the Okanagan language that has 'been handed down through thousands of years'. But her Okanagan people have been one of the First Nations groups fortunate enough to maintain their language. As Armstrong says,

> I remember as a teenager that I began to understand the value of being who I am, an Okanagan woman, a person who has been educated and taught things that other people did not have access to. Many of our people were coerced and brutalized for speaking their language and practicing their culture until their memory grew distant and dim.

The early constructions of Canada as a unified nation were synonymous with the kind of colonial practices that Armstrong talks about—the imposed invisibility of First Nations peoples through such institutions as residential schools.

Some legislation and empirical conditions might have changed since then, but the prevailing notions of Canada as a nation, of Canadian identity, and of Canadian literature are still sequestered within this legacy of colonialism. As Lee Maracle has said, 'Unless I was sleeping during the revolution, we have not had a change in our condition.'[8] In this respect, the circumstances of Maracle's protagonist in the story included in this anthology must be seen not only as isolated events taking place in the life of a single woman but as part of the continuum of Canadian history. As the narrator of the story tells us, Bertha's 'memory retreats to another time', a time when 'Bertha was not called Bertha', when the 'home' for which Bertha longs is a place that can be conjured up only through happy but also troubled memories:

> Home was a young girl rushing through a meadow, a cedar basket swishing lightly against dew-laden leaves [. . .] while her mind enjoyed the prospect of becoming . . . becoming, and the words in English would not come. She remembered the girl, the endless stories told to her, the meanings behind each story, the careful coaching in the truth that lay behind each one, the reasons for their telling, but she could not, after fifty years of speaking crippled English, define where it was all supposed to lead.

The stories that Bertha was told as a child were, are, part of the oral tradition of the First Nations peoples, the cultural heritage that the official history of Canada has systematically ignored. In the story, Bertha is defeated by the burden of her memories, by the ways in which she and her people have been disenfranchised. Yet the memory of her life, her attempt at 'whispering her sorrow in the gentle words of their ancestors', is passed on to a young girl.

8 'The "Post-Colonial" Imagination', *Fuse* 16, 1 (Fall 1992): 13.

This passing on, this linking of the past and the present with gestures that speak at once of cultural genocide and cultural pride, of elision and perseverance, forms part of the continuum of Canadian history. It is a continuum that persists against the gaps that mark the official history of Canada. This is the continuum within which Lee Maracle, like other First Nations authors, writes: 'I can spiral out into the world', she says, 'to reconceive of place. I can stretch time. I can erase the artifice of separation that divides today from yesterday and yesterday from tomorrow. In this place all time is the same time. In this place images speak reality-paint truth in believable pictures.'[9]

The various attempts over time to define Canada as a cohesive nation, to invent a homogenous Canadian identity—an identity minus the identities of the Aboriginal peoples, and later the identities of new immigrants—has not been the only pattern that has determined the course of Canadian history. Despite its aggressive tactics, the colonial construction of Canadian identity has not remained unchallenged. During the course of Canadian history there have always been attempts to redefine this construction of a cohesive identity, even to displace it.

Ironically, some of these challenges stemmed, and in a way continue to do so, from the very force and exploitative tactics through which the colonial establishment attempted to consolidate its position. The Chinese Immigration Act of 1923, following earlier discriminatory legislation against Chinese immigrants, which, with few exceptions, prevented the arrival of Chinese people in Canada, is one example among many that discloses the early perception of a dominant Canadian identity to be dominant only insofar as other identities were systematically kept out of or at the periphery of Canadian society.

The comments and the writing in this anthology by Jim Wong Chu and Sky Lee reinforce the fact that the inherited notion of a unified Canadian identity has only imaginative coherence. And as Sky Lee's first book, *Disappearing Moon Cafe*, suggests, this kind of imaginative coherence has not been a strategy employed by mainstream societies alone. As Kae, the novel's narrator, finds out, her Chinese-Canadian family harbours a secret—or many secrets—that hold the key to how a community might internalize the racism that constructs its position as 'other' to dominant society. Due partly to the Chinese traditions that they bring to Canada and partly to the pressures they experience in Vancouver, Kae's ancestors try to conceal the knowledge that their Chinese patriarch had a child, and a male one at that, with Kelora, a Native woman. Their elaborate attempts to maintain for a long time a pure image of their cultural origins has disastrous effects on the younger generations. Yet the novel also shows the importance of hidden histories, the need to disperse the notion of cultural authenticity. This is the kind of imperative that tells us that cultural identity, as Stuart Hall has put it, 'is a matter of "becoming" as well as of "being".'[10]

The homogenous image of Canadian identity, Canada as 'a white man's country', is still an image we have to come to terms with by rereading and rediscovering the histories hidden behind it. As Elliot L. Tepper writes,

9 'The "Post-Colonial" Imagination', 14.
10 'Cultural Identity and Diaspora', *Colonial Discourse and Post-Colonial Theory: A Reader*, ed. Patrick Williams and Laura Chrisman (New York: Columbia UP, 1994), 394.

the process of integrating a more complete history of Canada into public consciousness is at its earliest stages. . . . Settlement history in general seems to plod methodically, and haphazardly, from 'European' to French to British to Other, an enduring image which has been politically useful but empirically incomplete.[11]

Yet, the unified image of Canadian identity has always exhibited fissures and shown itself to be fragile, full of anxiety to maintain, and redefine, its tenuous hold on power. We have come to see the constitutional debates, the recurrence of which characterize the modern history of Canada, as a syndrome that has afflicted many Canadians with 'constitutional fatigue'. This should not prevent us from seeing what they really mean: that Canada is a state in continual process, in a constant state of re-vision. The Meech Lake Accord and the Charlottetown Agreement, under the aegis of Brian Mulroney's government, were two of the most recent attempts at 'nation building'. They instigated yet another round of talks and soul-searching about what Canadian means. Most recently, the 1995 Quebec referendum had, in different ways, the same effect. Such political events, and the many Royal Commissions that precede and follow them, point to one thing. The unity of Canadian identity is a cultural myth, a myth that can be sustained only by eclipsing the identities of others.

We are at a point now where the presumed uniqueness of Canadian identity is only that—a presumption. *Making a Difference* is testimony to the fact that we can no longer harbour the conceit that Canadian identity is homogenous.

◈ ◈ ◈

Beginning with the 1971 policy of multiculturalism, introduced by Pierre Trudeau, and later with Bill C-93, the 'Act for the preservation and enhancement of multiculturalism in Canada' legislated in 1988, we have entered a new and formative period in Canadian history, what we can call the multicultural stage of Canadian cultural politics. According to K. Victor Ujimoto, 'Canada was the first and only nation in the world to establish a Multiculturalism Act.'[12] This might be so, but it is interesting to remind ourselves how the official acknowledgement of Canada's multicultural heritage was framed.

The federal policy of multiculturalism was the result of the work of the Royal Commission on Bilingualism and Biculturalism, whose Report covers six volumes (1967–70), including one entitled *The Cultural Contribution of the Other Ethnic Groups* (1969). The Commission's 1963 mandate was, as reported in its 1969 volume, to 'make recommendations designed to ensure the bilingual and basically bicultural character of the federal administration', and to find ways of 'promoting bilingualism, better cultural relations and a more wide-spread appreciation of the basically bicultural character of our country and of the subsequent contribution made by the other cultures'.

11 'Immigration Policy and Multiculturalism', *Ethnicity and Culture in Canada*, ed. J.W. Berry and J.A. Laponce (Toronto: U of Toronto P, 1994), 97, 98.
12 'Multiculturalism and the Global Information Society', *Deconstructing a Nation: Immigration, Multiculturalism and Racism in '90s Canada*, ed. Vic Satzewich (Halifax, Nova Scotia: Fernwood Publishing, and Social Research Unit, Department of Sociology, University of Saskatchewan, 1992), 351.

The Report's recommendations led to the 1969 Canadian Official Languages Act. By establishing French and English as the official languages of the country, this Act further reinforced the notion that the French and the British were the two founding nations of Canada. Still, the Act did very little to appease Quebec's anxiety about the sovereignty of its culture (in 1977 French was declared the single official language in Quebec), and accomplished little more in the rest of Canada. In English Canada, many of the objections were voiced in the western provinces, where there is a long-standing resistance to bilingualism and where ethnic groups, at the time notably Ukrainian-Canadians, felt further marginalized by the Act.

Indeed, the 1971 White Paper, Trudeau's policy of multiculturalism, and the subsequent Bill C-93, which passed while Brian Mulroney's government was getting ready for the 1988 elections, did nothing to realign the colonial ideology of official history. The White Paper was intended to preserve the heritage of 'the other cultures'; it reiterated that there are two official languages, but stressed that there were 'no official cultures'. In a similar fashion, Bill C-93 declared that, 'whereas . . . English and French are the official languages of Canada', it proposes to 'recognize and promote the understanding that multiculturalism reflects the cultural and racial diversity of Canadian society', and promises 'to preserve, enhance and share their cultural heritage'. The 1971 policy does not mention the First Nations peoples, and the 1988 Act specifically excludes them. The Canada Clause of the Charlottetown Agreement intended to rectify this omission by acknowledging the status of cultures other than those of the two official languages, but the Agreement was rejected (not necessarily for reasons related to multiculturalism) in the 1992 referendum. These are just a few of the factors that led to the official policy of multiculturalism. The legislative Acts as well as the events and political agendas that have given rise to them register some of the recent ways in which Canadian identity has wavered from one form of representation to another.

It is apparent that the history of Canadian multiculturalism is not a simple, linear narrative. It is a narrative that has many beginnings, a narrative that unravels in many directions. No matter what narrative thread we resolve to follow, some of the inherited perceptions about Canada have been decidedly altered. The land we now call Canada was already multicultural, and multilingual, before the arrival of the first Europeans. As J. McGee shows in his *Loyalist Mosaic* (1984), even the United Empire Loyalists who settled Upper Canada consisted of diverse ethnic groups. And George Elliott Clarke, in his comments cited in this anthology, makes it clear the origins of the Black people in the Maritimes go back to 1783 and 1815, when the Black Loyalists and Refugees arrived in Nova Scotia. The fact that the Dominion Parliament introduced an Immigration Act in 1906 intended to control the influx of Asian immigrants to Canada is not only an example in a series of discriminatory practices that belong, in effect, to the history of Canada's multiculturalism, but is also further evidence that the cohesiveness of Canadian identity has always been imaginary.

But not everyone would necessarily agree with this position. Multiculturalism signifies different things to different people, and has not been embraced with the same enthusiasm by all Canadians. Indeed, as Vic Satzewich points out, if multiculturalism is under attack from some for being too successful in promoting cultural pluralism, it is ironic that it has also come under attack by others for not promoting enough pluralism. That is, the traditional critique of multiculturalism has been that it promoted only symbolic ethnicity, or those aspects of non-anglo ethnic cultures which did not threaten the anglo-saxon dominated status quo.[13]

For some Canadians, then, the tolerance they see multiculturalism advocating threatens their understanding of Canadian history and augurs against the development of a cohesive Canadian identity, which they think should be the goal of the nation. For others, it is the very notion of tolerance to which they object, for tolerance alone does not promise that those who have traditionally been constructed as 'others' will be able fully to practise who they are as individual subjects. Along the same lines, multiculturalism has been attacked for offering a policy of containment, a policy which, by legislating 'otherness', attempts to control its diverse representations, to preserve the long-standing racial and ethnic hierarchies in Canada. The question of preservation has also been tackled in a different way, for some Canadians believe that the mandate of Bill C-93 to 'preserve' and 'enhance' the cultural heritage of Canadians other than those of Anglo-Saxon and French descent tends to promote stereotypical images of their cultures, and advocates a kind of ethnocentrism that might further prevent their integration into mainstream society. Thus while multiculturalism is expected to facilitate the process of decolonizing the inherited representations of Canadian history, the literary tradition, and other forms of culture, it is also seen as essentializing race and ethnicity, namely assigning to racial and ethnic differences, as well as their various expressions, attributes that are taken to be 'natural', and therefore stable.

In the field of literature, many of the contributors to *Making a Difference* have played a direct or indirect role in shaping our understanding of these arguments. As for myself, I believe that within this complex web of historical changes, cultural differences, and politics there still remains the fundamental question of what constitutes Canadian identity. But in the 1990s this question has been reconfigured, and, I think, irrevocably so. For we can no longer afford to think of Canadian identity in singular terms. Its imaginary cohesiveness has already collapsed upon itself. Nor can we afford to cavalierly dismiss the current interest in cultural differences as a mere fad, or an obsession. The recognition of cultural differences in the 1990s marks yet another beginning in Canadian multicultural history, the beginning of an attempt to understand how distinct identities can converge and dialogue with each other within Canada, how boundaries of difference must be repositioned—not in relation to the signs of 'centre' and 'margins' but in relation to new and productive alignments.

Making a Difference: Canadian Multicultural Literature is an instance of such a dialogue. The writing and the comments of the contributors in *Making a Difference* help animate some of Canada's multicultural realities. Students reading this anthology will discover how Canadian multicultural literature tugs at the seams of the fabric that is

13 'Introduction', *Deconstructing a Nation*, 15.

Canadian culture. They will see that for these writers, and for many others who could not be included in this collection, who we are as Canadians is contingent upon how we move from one context to another, how we cross the thresholds of memories, how we embrace or, for that matter, keep away from the differences we encounter, how we negotiate our histories in the context of other histories.

These kinds of convergences and negotiations have been the focus of an abundance of publications about multiculturalism, immigration experience, and the issues that pertain to the First Nations peoples within such disciplines as sociology, anthropology, law, political sciences and education. Yet Canadian literary criticism has shown a belated interest in these issues. Since the late 1980s, however, the increased publication of ethnic and Native anthologies and bibliographies, the various conferences and gatherings of writers aimed at resisting both the stereotypical reception of their work and the way they have been, if at all, represented in curricula, and the fact that now both large and small presses publish authors once considered to be only 'minor', have dramatically altered the amount and kinds of critical response to their work. As Enoch Padolsky says,

> Twenty or thirty years ago literature in English Canada consisted primarily of writings by British-Canadian writers and a few individuals from a small number of Canadian ethnic minority groups (e.g., Icelandic, Jewish, Ukrainian). Today, Canadian literature reflects a much broader proportion of a changing Canadian society and both the number of writers and the group experiences represented have expanded dramatically. Not surprisingly, this increasing diversity is having an impact on the way Canadian literature is perceived, and a number of critical, theoretical, and institutional issues have arisen because of it. At the moment these issues are in the process of being absorbed into a literary critical scene which also reflects other kinds of theoretical and critical challenges (e.g., feminism, post-colonialism, new historicism) and though changes in Canadian literary scholarship with regard to ethnic minority writing are clearly in the wind, the resolution of these new issues still lies in the future.[14]

I have stressed the construction of identity as a primary concern in multicultural literature. But I am also arguing that the representation of the differences, as Padolsky points out, must not be seen exclusively in terms of the question of identity, no matter how identity is configured. The authors in *Making a Difference* write by following the trajectories of their imaginations, and these lead them along many and diverse paths.

❖ ❖ ❖

'The imagination has a history,' says Guy Davenport, a history 'as yet unwritten, and it has a geography, as yet only dimly seen.'[15] It is the imagination of the writers included in this anthology that others our perceptions of reality, that invokes the figure

14 'Canadian Ethnic Minority Literature in English', *Ethnicity and Culture in Canada*, 361.
15 *The Geography of the Imagination* (San Francisco: North Point Press, 1981), 4.

of identity, that shows their geographies and their communities, their concerns with love, family, gendered bodies, to be unlimited. Unlimited in that these writers show the histories of these spaces and images to be forever written, unlearned, revised, transplanted, invented. 'For', as Iain Chambers says, 'to write is, of course, to travel.'[16] Reading through the poetry and fiction of the seventy-one authors in this anthology is indeed like taking a journey. It is a journey that takes us to many places, but also a journey that takes many forms and shapes. As the narrator of Yasmin Ladha's story says, directly addressing us as readers, 'Between you and me, there is no glint of a badge. Badges are razor sharp. Between you and me, the ink quivers.'

Much of the writing in *Making a Difference* involves actual travel, the kinds of departures and arrivals that accompany people of any diaspora. Diaspora—the dispersal of a people around the world—necessitated as it is often by major historical upheavals, carries along with it seeds from the original land that help the people on the move and their descendents to root themselves in the new place. The experience of displacement, the process of acculturation or integration, the gaps between generations, the tensions between individuals and their communities—these are some of the themes that inform diasporic literature. Sustaining a link with the past, paying homage to histories that one cannot afford to forget—or perhaps writing out of what they know best, as some writers would put it—is another important feature of diasporic writing.

For example, the poetry included here by Rachel Korn, A.M. Klein, and Irving Layton is deeply rooted in the experiences of the Jewish diaspora. Within this context, the short story by J.J. Steinfeld is a literal dramatization of the Holocaust experience of the female narrator's mother. As she rehearses her role in her one-woman play, she both relives her mother's experiences and tries 'to escape the character' she plays. But she knows that, in many respects, this is not just a one-woman drama: the past, she admits, is also a 'tangible character' in the drama. Her acting is an acting out of the past, an attempt to come to terms with the demons of history. Both this woman and the female narrator of Helen Weinzweig's story are born in Radom, Poland, not a mere coincidence in the context of this literature, but a significant detail that helps us locate it historically. Art, this time painting, and movement between a marriage and a love affair are the ways in which Weinzweig's character attempts to deal with her memories.

In a different way, the fiction of Harold Sonny Ladoo and Arnold Itwaru directly addresses the places from which they come. They show their settings to be storied places, places layered with the impact of colonialism, colonial desire, and its detrimental effects, especially on women. The function of language as a means of control is Marlene Nourbese Philip's point of entry into her critique of colonialism. The different kinds of discourse that she uses in her poetry are aimed to reveal that tracing the genealogy of a self must also involve uncovering the genealogy of language, an issue that also characterizes Jamila Ismail's poetry.

Indeed, language—language not as a mere instrument of communication but language as that which constructs the articulations of ourselves—is a recurring concern for many of the writers in this anthology. The title of Dionne Brand's long poem, *No*

16 *Migrancy, Culture, Identity* (London and New York: Routledge Press, 1994), 10.

Language Is Neutral, sections of which appear here, makes it clear that any neutrality attached to language only helps to conceal the various gestures of elision by which representation operates. 'No / language is neutral seared in the spine's unravelling. / Here is history too,' she says. And if this history, as I read her, is structured like a language, it is because the 'grammar' of the black people's experiences that she writes about bears the unmistakable signs of enslavement: 'talking was left for night and hush was idiom / and hot core.'

Fred Wah's desire 'to touch the sight of the letter oral tactile', to chase his fleeting memories of his father's writing hand as it moves the 'silver, black, gold nib' of a pen across a page, to understand how language inhabits his body, is a desire that reflects our passage 'through the language of time'. He makes us aware of how we are, in a certain way, 'histographs', because the representations of ourselves reside in, and are always inscribed by, history, a concern manifested in different ways in Kristjana Gunnars's and Aritha van Herk's prose.

The writing act as a specific manifestation of language is another way in which language appears in this literature. Many of these poems and stories are, literally, scenes of writing, scenes in which we see a writer at work. In the journal entries that record Daphne Marlatt's first return to the place where she was brought up, she wonders how to 'get' everything 'down'. So we see her watching over her own writing act: 'How completely i learned to talk Canadian (how badly i wanted to). . . . Wonder how it sounds to you?' she says in a letter she writes back home. How to get everything down is the same question that seems to preoccupy the protagonist of Makeda Silvera's story, a black woman who tries to be a writer while also trying to fulfill most of the roles expected of a woman.

Pressures similar to those that Silvera's protagonist experiences permeate much of the writing in this anthology. The questions of how gender is constructed, how the representation of gender impinges upon desire and sexuality, how who we are as men or women relates to where we come from are addressed in various ways by such authors as Claire Harris, Mary di Michele, Di Brandt, Yes him Ternar, Sandra Birdsell, M.G. Vassanji, Ian Iqbal Rashid, Ven Begamudre, and Shyam Selvadurai. Ashok Mathur's story focuses these concerns on his protagonist's body, a body that is not transparent in that it cannot easily be read as male or female. Beyond questioning the conventional representations of gender difference, this story also brings to the fore one of the most significant issues in multicultural literature, that of racialization. Concern with racialization, the construction of images of ourselves or of others by relying on the loaded and biased ideological definitions of racial categories, one of the processes that leads to racism, surfaces in much of the writing in this anthology. Corinne Lee, Roy Miki, Joy Kogawa, and Himani Bannerji are some of the writers who directly address this issue.

If some of the writing in this anthology, as I have suggested, deals with themes that directly pertain to the diasporic experience, there are also authors here who write from a diametrically opposed experience: the knowledge of not having been separated at all from their lands, but having been systematically denied the right to their places and cultures. The writing of Beth Brant, Daniel David Moses, Thomas King, Jeannette Armstrong, and Lee Maracle, and many other First Nations authors and storytellers who could not be included here, is a reminder to other Canadians that we have all been travellers, that, somewhere in our personal or familial histories in the recent or distant past, we all belonged somewhere else. And what is most pertinent about this reminder is that the first foreign travellers who came here came under the pretence of coming to an empty land. At the end of Beth Brant's creation story, 'First Woman touched her body, feeling the movements inside. She touched the back of Mother and waited for the beings who would change her world.'

◈ ◈ ◈

Making a Difference: Canadian Multicultural Literature is a gathering of voices that offer the reader only a sampling of what Canadian literature is about today. Beyond my own attempt here to introduce some of the contexts and concerns of this literature, it is the task of the readers to discover for themselves what these authors invite us to share with them.

' "Cultures" do not hold still for their portraits,' says James Clifford.[17] *Making a Difference* is a living and changing portrait of Canadian literature, a portrait that invites the reader in as one of the subjects. We portray ourselves by reading together.

---

17 'Introduction: Partial Truths', *Writing Culture: The Poetics and Politics of Ethnography*, ed. James Clifford and George E. Marcus (Berkeley, Los Angeles, London: U of California P, 1986), 10.

Fugitive and Non-Fugitive Slave Narratives

The four narratives that follow come from *The Refugee: Narratives of Fugitive Slaves in Canada. Related by Themselves. With An Account of the History and Condition of the Colored Population of Upper Canada*, collected and prefaced by Benjamin Drew (1856), a white abolitionist from Boston. Reverend Alexander Hemsley and Mr and Mrs Francis Henderson belong to the large number of fugitives (no exact figure exists, but they were probably between 30,000 to 40,000) who found refuge in Canada through the Underground Railway, although 'refuge' should not be confused with the 'Paradise' Upper Canada was thought to be in relation to the United States at the time. These fugitives found freedom from slavery here, but not freedom from racism. Mr Henderson's statement, '[t]here is much prejudice here against us,' reveals that not all of these former slaves found Canada to be a real 'haven'. While someone like William L. Humbert stated unequivocally, 'I would rather die than go back,' and Ben Blackburn said that, being in Canada on July 4th, he 'felt as big and free as any man could feel', others like Mrs Francis Henderson expressed a wish to return to the United States, 'were [it] a free country'. Indeed, a large number of black Americans who had arrived in the 'Canadian Canaan' as refugees sought to repatriate after President Abraham Lincoln's Emancipation Proclamation Act in 1863, and especially after the end of the Civil War between the Union and the Confederate States of America in 1865.

Whether we read them as testimonials or oral narratives, brief memoirs or interviews, historical accounts or instances of the slave narrative genre, these four life stories may be brief, but they speak volumes both about slavery and about what it was like to be a black in Canada at the time. These narratives, as is the case with the 116 others in Drew's collection, should also be read in such contexts as the American Fugitive Slave Law (1850), the Radical Reconstruction period following the end of the Civil War, the complex history of the Underground Railroad, and the legislation and politics in the Canadian colony in that period. And as Sophia Pooley's narrative testifies, the reader should also remember that, while most blacks at that time came to Canada to escape slavery in the United States, slavery—in spite of many Canadians' belief to the contrary—was an institution, albeit not widely spread, in Canada as well. Neither the fugitive slaves nor the black settlers who began arriving in Upper Canada in 1791, nor the Black Loyalists who settled in Nova Scotia in the early 1800s, nor the Refugee Negroes (those blacks who moved to the Maritimes as a result of the 1812 War) were the first black people to come to Canada.

According to Robin W. Winks's history, *The Blacks in Canada* (1971, 1997), there were slaves in New France, both aboriginal and black, before the first recorded reference to Olivier Le Jeune—'the first slave to be sold in New France'—brought directly from Africa at the age of six. Le Jeune was still a '*petit nègre*' when he converted, but, as his teacher, after whom he was named, Jesuit missionary Paul Le Jeune, wrote, he spoke the blunt truth in retort to the statement that all people are equal in the eyes of the Christian God: ' "You say that by baptism I shall be like you: I am black and you are white, I must have my skin taken off then in order to be like you".' Olivier Le Jeune died a free man at the age of thirty.

This is not the right place to recite the history of slavery in Canada and of the beginnings of racism directed specifically against blacks (see Winks's study cited above), but mentioning a few facts about that early period is necessary in order to read these narratives in context. There were about 4,000 slaves, including both blacks and aboriginals, in the middle of the eighteenth century in New France, most of them living in or around Montreal. Upper Canada, through Lieutenant Governor John Graves Simcoe, was the first province to legislate against slavery in 1793, but this act did not free any slaves; instead, it considered free the fugitives who had arrived, and intended 'to prevent the further introduction of slaves'. Slavery remained legal until it was abolished in the British colonies by the Act of the Imperial Parliament in 1833, which came into effect a year later. 'The last known private advertisement for slaves appeared in Halifax in 1820, in Quebec in 1821. When John Baker, a Quebec-born mulatto, . . . died [a free man] in Cornwall, Ontario, in 1871, the last person to have lived as a slave in British North America was gone from the scene.' Nevertheless, the elimination of slavery in Canada should not be confused with any consistent attempts to eliminate racism. Indeed, as blacks settled in Ontario, the Maritimes, and across the Canadian West, racism became entrenched as a prevailing reality for them, as well as for other 'undesirables', by the beginning of the twentieth century. The closer Canada came to developing a sense of its 'identity' as a nation-state, the more fiercely it articulated, and officially so, its rebuff of blacks, First Nations peoples, and those it cast as 'Orientals', people from the Middle East, Asia, and Southern Europe.

While, then, the fugitive slave stories recorded by Drew exemplify the experience of many other black fugitives who left no written record, an experience that amounts to having found freedom on the Canadian side of the border, these stories also belong to the genealogy of race relations in Canada. These fugitive slaves crossed the border in different, yet equally risky, ways: through steamers and small crafts that

docked in Oakville or elsewhere in the Niagara River basin, by swimming across the Detroit River into Amherstburg and then walking through farms and the woods to such towns as Windsor (called Sandwich then), often having to hide for long periods, with minimal food, before they could make it through the border. Some never made it, while others were caught and turned back. Thus, while Alexander Hemsley became a preacher at St Catherine's Circuit with the African Methodist Church, and was ordained to the office of the elder in 1842, Sophia Pooley did not enter Canada as a freed slave. Hers is not, technically speaking, a fugitive narrative. Reportedly the first black woman to come to Ontario, she arrived circa 1778 as a slave sold to the Mohawk Chief of the Six Nations, Joseph Brant, who had other slaves as well. She lived close to what is now Burlington. If, as she said, 'I had no care to get my freedom,' it was because there was little a black woman could have done to survive on her own at the time on either side of the border.

Drew's book (now available in its entirety at http://docsouth.unc.edu/neh/drew/drew.html) is an immensely important document. Still, it behooves us to remember that it belongs to a tradition of narratives that, be they fugitive or not, were more often than not collected by white editors—'a black message . . . sealed within a white envelope' (John Sekora, 1987). In what follows, the comments inside square brackets and the footnote are Benjamin Drew's.

Sophia Pooley b. ca. 1771–d. after 1865

I was born in Fishkill, New York State, twelve miles from North River. My father's name was Oliver Burthen, my mother's Dinah. I am now more than ninety years old. I was stolen from my parents when I was seven years old, and brought to Canada; that was long before the American Revolution. There were hardly any white people in Canada then—nothing here but Indians and wild beasts. Many a deer I have helped catch on the lakes in a canoe: one year we took ninety. I was a woman grown when the first governor of Canada came from England: that was Gov. Simcoe.

My parents were slaves in New York State. My master's sons-in-law, Daniel Outwaters and Simon Knox, came into the garden where my sister and I were playing among the currant bushes, tied their handkerchiefs over our mouths, carried us to a vessel, put us in the hold, and sailed up the river. I know not how far nor how long—

it was dark there all the time. Then we came by land. I remember when we came to Genesee—there were Indian settlements there—Onondagas, Senecas, and Oneidas. I guess I was the first colored girl brought into Canada. The white men sold us at Niagara to old Indian Brant, the king. I lived with old Brant about twelve or thirteen years as nigh as I can tell. Brant lived part of the time at Mohawk, part at Ancaster, part at Preston, then called Lower Block: the Upper Block was at Snyder's Mills. While I lived with old Brant we caught the deer. It was at Dundas at the outlet. We would let the hounds loose, and when we heard them bark we would run for the canoe—Peggy, and Mary, and Katy, Brant's daughters and I. Brant's sons, Joseph and Jacob, would wait on the shore to kill the deer when we fetched him in. I had a tomahawk, and would hit the deer on the head—then the squaws would take it by the horns and paddle ashore. The boys would bleed and skin the deer and take the meat to the house. Sometimes white people in the neighborhood, John Chisholm and Bill Chisholm, would come and say't was their hounds, and they must have the meat. But we would not give it up.

Canada was then filling up with white people. And after Brant went to England, and kissed the queen's hand, he was made a colonel. Then there began to be laws in Canada. Brant was only half Indian: his mother was a squaw—I saw her when I came to this country. She was an old body; her hair was quite white. Brant was a good look-ing man—quite portly. He was as big as Jim Douglass who lived here in the bush, and weighed two hundred pounds. He lived in an Indian village—white men came among them and they intermarried. They had an English schoolmaster, an English preacher, and an English blacksmith. When Brant went among the English, he wore the English dress—when he was among the Indians, he wore the Indian dress—broadcloth leg-gings, blanket, moccasins, fur cap. He had his ears slit with a long loop at the edge, and in these he hung long silver ornaments. He wore a silver half-moon on his breast with the king's name on it, and broad silver bracelets on his arms. He never would paint, but his people painted a great deal. Brant was always for making peace among his peo-ple; that was the reason of his going about so much. I used to talk Indian better than I could English. I have forgotten some of it—there are none to talk it with now.

Brant's third wife, my mistress, was a barbarous creature. She could talk English, but she would not. She would tell me in Indian to do things, and then hit me with any thing that came to hand, because I did not understand her. I have a scar on my head from a wound she gave me with a hatchet; and this long scar over my eye, is where she cut me with a knife. The skin dropped over my eye; a white woman bound it up. [The scars spoken of were quite perceptible, but the writer saw many worse looking cicatri-ces of wounds not inflicted by Indian savages, but by civilized (?) men.] Brant was very angry, when he came home, at what she had done, and punished her as if she had been a child. Said he, 'you know I adopted her as one of the family, and now you are trying to put all the work on her.'

I liked the Indians pretty well in their place; some of them were very savage—some friendly. I have seen them have the war-dance—in a ring with only a cloth about them, and painted up. They did not look ridiculous—they looked savage—enough to frighten anybody. One would take a bowl and rub the edge with a knotted stick: then they would raise their tomahawks and whoop. Brant had two colored men for slaves:

one of them was the father of John Patten, who lives over yonder, the other called himself Simon Ganseville. There was but one other Indian that I knew, who owned a slave. I had no care to get my freedom.

At twelve years old, I was sold by Brant to an Englishman in Ancaster, for one hundred dollars—his name was Samuel Hatt, and I lived with him seven years: then the white people said I was free, and put me up to running away. He did not stop me—he said he could not take the law into his own hands. Then I lived in what is now Waterloo. I married Robert Pooley, a black man. He ran away with a white woman: he is dead.

Brant died two years before the second war with the United States. His wife survived him until the year the stars fell. She was a pretty squaw: her father was an English colonel. She hid a crock of gold before she died, and I never heard of its being found. Brant was a freemason.

I was seven miles from Stoney Creek at the time of the battle—the cannonade made every thing shake well.

I am now unable to work, and am entirely dependent on others for subsistence: but I find plenty of people in the bush to help me a good deal.

Reverend Alexander Hemsley b. ca 1795[1]

[The famous decision of Judge Hornblower, of New Jersey, some years ago, in a case of a fugitive, will doubtless be recollected by many readers. The narrative subjoined was given by the individual more immediately interested in that decision. Mr Hemsley is confined to his bed a great part of the time by dropsy. He is a very intelligent man, and his face wears, notwithstanding his many trials and his sickness, a remarkable expression of cheerfulness and good-will. His dwelling is clean and nice, and he is well nursed and cared for by Mrs Hemsley, a sensible, painstaking woman, the very impersonation of neatness. As it does not appear in the narrative, it may properly be stated here, that Mr Hemsley has lost two children by death, since his removal to St Catharines; their sickness, alluded to in the narrative, extending through three consecutive years. If any capitalist is looking about him for an opportunity to invest, I think he might profitably employ two hundred dollars in lifting the mortgage from Hemsley's house and garden. Rev. Hiram Wilson of St C. who has managed to keep himself free from the care of riches, by giving to the needy, as fast as he earned it, every thing which he might have called his own, will be happy, without doubt, to attend to the business without fee or commission. Apropos, of Mr Wilson,—we know 'there is that scattereth, and yet increaseth'. But in Mr W.'s case, it requires but little financial skill to perceive, that while 'scattering' to relieve the sick and suffering,—the fugitive and the oppressed,—to an extent sometimes fully up to the means in his hands, any 'increase' must come from those who may feel disposed to let their means assist his abundant opportunities of benevolent action. But to the narrative.]

1 Attempts to locate the birth and/or death dates of Reverend Hemsley as well as of Mr and Mrs Francis Henderson have been unsuccessful.

I was in bondage in Queen Anne County, Maryland, from birth until twenty-three years of age. My name in slavery was Nathan Mead. My master was a professor of religion, and used to instruct me in a hypocritical way in the duties of religion. I used to go to church on Sunday to hear him talk, and experience the contrary on Monday. On the Sabbath he used to catechize us, and tell us if we were good honest boys, and obedient to our master, we should enjoy the life that now is, and that which is to come.

My idea of freedom during my youth was, that it was a state of liberty for the mind,—that there was a freedom of thought, which I could not enjoy unless I were free,—that is, if I thought of any thing beneficial for me, I should have liberty to execute it. My escape was not owing to any sudden impulse or fear of present punishment, but from a natural wish to be free: and had it not been for near and dear friends, I should not have remained in slavery so long. I had an uncle who was a preacher. He had a good many boys. I confided to him that I wanted to leave, and would like to have his boys accompany me. He said he would not dare to tell his boys, for if we were to undertake it, and get caught, it would ruin us all. The fear of being caught was then, I think, a greater restraint than it is now. Now there is a different spirit in the slaves, and if they undertake to escape, it is with a feeling of victory or death,—they determine not to be taken alive, if possible to prevent it even by bloodshed.

I was accustomed to leave home every Saturday night to visit friends seven miles inland, and to return on Sunday night. One Sunday night when I had got back from my visit, I took leave of my friends, they not knowing what I intended, as I had often told them on the Saturday nights, in the same way, that I never expected to see them again. After I bade them farewell, I started for New Jersey, where, I had been told, people were free, and nobody would disturb me. I went six miles, and then ambushed. On Monday night, I went thirty-three miles, and found a good old Quaker—one [we omit the name, but it will be published one day]—with whom I stayed three weeks. At the expiration of which time, I went to Philadelphia. I made no tarry there, but went straight over into New Jersey. After a stay of two months at Cooper's Creek, I went to Evesham, where I resided eight or nine years, being hired and getting my money. No one disturbed me all this time. I heard that I had been pursued by the son of my master, but that not hearing from me he went back. I then received favorable offers to go to Northampton, and I removed there, taking with me my wife whom I had married at Evesham, and my three children. At Northampton I remained unmolested until October, 1836. Then some four or five southerners, neither of whom had any legal claim upon me, having found out that I had escaped from bondage, went to the executor of my old master's estate (my master having been dead six or seven years) and bought me running,—that is, they paid some small sum for a title to me, so as to make a spec. out of poor me. To make sure of the matter, they came about my house, pretending to be gunning,—meanwhile looking after my children, and appraising their value in case they could get them. This I know, for they promised a lawyer my oldest son, if he would gain the case.[2] They hung round my house from Wednesday to

2 Mrs H. was from Caroline Co., Md. Her parents were made free 'by word of mouth'—but as her mother had no free papers, it was feared that the daughter might be enslaved. She was enabled to avoid the danger by emigration.

Saturday morning, when, while it was yet dark, they surrounded my house. It was my usual way to open the door, put my shoes on, and go off to work. Just as I opened the door that morning, an officer of the town followed the door right in, put his hand on me, and said, 'You are my prisoner!' I asked him 'what he meant by that?' He said he had received a writ to bring me before the court of common pleas. I told him 'I have no master, but I will go with you.' I sat down to put on my shoes,—then the five southerners flung themselves upon me and put me in irons. Then one of them pretended to be a great friend to me. 'Now,' said he, 'if you have any friends, tell me who they are, and I'll go for them.' I showed him the house where my employer lived, and told him to step up there, and ask him to come to me immediately. He came, and commenced reproving the constable for being in so low business as to be arresting slaves for slave-hunters. 'Poor business!' said he. I told him I was afraid they were going to smuggle me off, without taking me before the judge. The constable then, at his request, pledged his honor, to take me safe to the court at Mount Holly. They put me in a carriage, handcuffed, between two armed men of the party. One of these had been a boy with whom I had played in my young days in Maryland. He was there to swear to my identity. On the way, he tried to 'soft soap' me, so as to get some evidence to convict me, when we got before the judge. But I made strange of him and of every thing he said, I wouldn't know him nor any of his blarney. At Mount Holly, the judge told me, that it was alleged that I had escaped from the service of Mr Isaac Baggs of Maryland,—and that, if that were proved I might be sure that I would be sent back. The judge being a Virginia born man, brought up in New Jersey, was found, like the handle of a jug, all on one side, and that side against me. The friends employed counsel for me, and by the efforts of my counsel, the trial was put off to Monday. On Monday, the case was called, and the other side had an adjournment of a week, in order to get an additional witness. I was imprisoned during the week. A brother of the former witness was then brought forward—one whom I had known when a boy. The two brothers, who were both mean fellows, as they appeared against me to get money, swore to my identity, and that they knew me to have been the slave of Isaac Baggs. My counsel were David Paul Brown, John R. Slack, George Campbell, and Elias B. Cannon. The trial was not concluded until the lapse of three weeks. Then the judge decided, that my wife was a free-woman and might remain with her children,—'but as for you, Alexander or Nathan, the case is clear that you were the slave of Isaac Baggs, and you must go back.'

Then Mr John R. Slack went up to the judge, and laid the writ of *habeas corpus* before him. The judge looked it over in quick time—his color came and went tremendously. He answered in a low tone of voice, 'I think you might have told me that you had that before.' The lawyer answered, 'We thought it would be time enough, after seeing how far your Honor would go.' A good old friend—one Thomas Shipleigh—had ridden forty miles to get that writ. On the next day the sheriff took me before Judge Hornblower; two of my counsel went also, and one of the other party. My oppressor planned to take me out of New Jersey on the route, as if we left the State, Judge Heywood's certificate would take effect. Our party, however, were wide awake, and kept within N.J., but they prepared bull-dogs (pistols) in case any attempt were made at carrying me off. When we arrived at the court, Mr Brainard Clark, my claimant's lawyer, in the course of his argument, stated what great expense the claimants had been to for jail fees, &c., 'even seventy dollars'. Judge H. answered, 'If it had been seven times seventy, it would create no sympathy in me for them,—we can't expect to pass away human liberty for a mere trifle,'—or words to that effect. It was concluded that I should be given into the custody of the sheriff until February term,—then to be brought before the supreme court at Trenton.

I remained in jail until the February term, about three months, as comfortable as a man could be, imprisoned, and with the awful doom of slavery hanging over his head. The case was then taken up by Hon. Theodore Frelinghuysen. The other side could not meet Frelinghuysen's argument. In about three weeks the court declared me a free man. I was then let out of jail; but as I had become so well known, my friends were afraid that my claimants would waylay and smuggle me, and thought I had better leave for the North, which I did. I travelled some two hundred miles, most of the way on foot into Otsego county, N.Y., where I gave out through fatigue. I was sick when I got there. Here I was joined by my wife and children. I remained here until navigation opened,—we were forty miles from the canal at Utica. Then, from visions of the night, I concluded that I was on dangerous ground, and I removed with my family to Farmington. Years before I had had visions of the road I was to travel, and if I had obeyed the visions, the trouble would not have occurred. I had dreamed of being pursued, and that they had caught me, and so it turned out. From Farmington, I went on directly to Rochester, where I remained but one night. My health was good, with the exception of my eyes, which were dim of sight and inflamed, owing to the change from imprisonment to exposure to pelting storms of rain and snow. I felt that my persecutors who brought this trouble on me were actuated by a demonlike principle. We embarked from Rochester, on board a British boat, *The Traveller*, for Toronto.

When I reached English territory, I had a comfort in the law,—that my shackles were struck off, and that a man was a man by law. I had been in comfortable circumstances, but all my little property was *lawed* away. I was among strangers, poverty-stricken, and in a cold country. I had been used to farming, and so could not find in the city such assistance as I needed: in a few days, I left for St Catharines, where I have ever since remained.

My master did not use to do much at buying and selling, but there was a great deal of it in his neighborhood. The unwillingness to separate of husbands and wives, parents and children was so great, that to part them seemed to me a sin higher than the heavens,—it was dreadful to hear their outcries, as they were forced into the wagons of the drivers. Some among them have their minds so brutalized by the action of slavery, that they do not feel so acutely as others, the pangs of separation. But there are many who feel a separation from their offspring as acutely as human beings can possibly feel.

Masters sometimes show respect toward some particular persons among their slaves. I was never an eyewitness to a punishment where a man seemed to inflict it in any spirit of kindness or mercy. I have heard of a merciful disposition at such times, but never witnessed it: as a general thing they would manifest malignant, tyrannical feelings. I have seen a woman who was in state of pregnancy, tied up and punished with a keen raw hide.

Contrasting my condition here with what it was in New Jersey, I say, that for years after I came here, my mind was continually reverting to my native land. For some ten years, I was in hopes that something might happen, whereby I might safely return to my old home in New Jersey. I watched the newspapers and they told the story. I found that there would be a risk in going back,—and that was confirmed by many of my fellow men falling into the same catastrophe that I did,—and the same things happen now.

When I reached St Catharines I was enfeebled in health. I had come to a small inferior place; there were pines growing all about here where you now see brick houses. I rented a house, and with another man took five acres of cleared land, and got along with it very well. We did not get enough from this to support us; but I got work at half a dollar or seventy-five cents a day and board myself. We were then making both ends meet. I then made up my mind that salt and potatoes in Canada, were better than pound-cake and chickens in a state of suspense and anxiety in the United States. Now I am a regular Britisher. My American blood has been scourged out of me; I have lost my American tastes; I am an enemy to tyranny. I would as lief meet serpents as some people I know of in the States. If I were to meet them, my fighting propensities would come up. To meet one here, I would not mind it; there I would be afraid of the ghost of a white man after he was dead. I am no scholar, but if some one would refine it, I could give a history of slavery, and show how tyranny operates upon the mind of the slaves. I have dreamed of being back on my master's farm, and of dodging away from my master; he endeavoring to get between me and the land I was aiming for. Then I would awake in a complete perspiration, and troubled in mind. Oh, it was awful! When you go back home, remember poor Joseph in Egypt.

I am now about sixty years of age, and have been lying sick about nine months. I have here a house and a quarter acre of land. I have had a deal of sickness in my family, and it has kept me comparatively poor: it would take two hundred dollars to clear my estate from incumbrances. Had it not been for sickness, it would have been paid for long ago.

I have served the people in the provinces as a minister in the Methodist persuasion for some twenty years. My pay has been little, for our people all start poor, and have to struggle to support themselves. My mind has ever been to trust the Lord. I have never prayed for wealth nor honor, but only to guide his church and do his will.

Francis Henderson b. 1822

I escaped from slavery in Washington City, D.C., in 1841, aged nineteen. I was not sent to school when a boy, and had no educational advantages at all. My master's family were Church of England people themselves and wished me to attend there. I do not know my age, but suppose thirty-three.

I worked on a plantation from about ten years old till my escape. They raised wheat, corn, tobacco, and vegetables,—about forty slaves on the place. My father was a mulatto, my mother dark; they had thirteen children, of whom I was the only son. On that plantation the mulattoes were more despised than the whole blood blacks. I often wished from the fact of my condition that I had been darker. My sisters suffered from the same cause. I could frequently hear the mistress say to them, 'you yellow hussy! you yellow wench!' etc. The language to me generally was, 'go do so and so'. But if a hoe-handle were broken or any thing went wrong, it would be every sort of a wicked expression—so bad I do not like to say what—very profane and coarse.

Our houses were but log huts—the tops partly open—ground floor,—rain would come through. My aunt was quite an old woman, and had been sick several years: in rains I have seen her moving about from one part of the house to the other, and rolling her bedclothes about to try to keep dry,—every thing would be dirty and muddy. I lived in the house with my aunt. My bed and bedstead consisted of a board wide enough to sleep on—one end on a stool, the other placed near the fire. My pillow consisted of my jacket,—my covering was whatever I could get. My bedtick was the board itself. And this was the way the single men slept,—but we were comfortable in this way of sleeping, *being used to it*. I only remember having but one blanket from my owners up to the age of 19, when I ran away.

Our allowance was given weekly—a peck of sifted corn meal, a dozen and a half herrings, two and a half pounds of pork. Some of the boys would eat this up in three days,—then they had to steal, or they could not perform their daily tasks. They would visit the hog-pen, sheep-pen, and granaries. I do not remember one slave but who stole some things,—they were driven to it as a matter of necessity. I myself did this,—many a time have I, with others, run among the stumps in chase of a sheep, that we might have something to eat. If colored men steal, it is because they are brought up to it. In regard to cooking, sometimes many have to cook at one fire, and before all could get to the fire to bake hoe cakes, the overseer's horn would sound: then they must go at any rate. Many a time I have gone along eating a piece of bread and meat, or herring broiled on the coals—I never sat down at a table to eat, except in harvest time, all the time I was a slave. In harvest time, the cooking is done at the great house, as the hands are wanted more in the field. This was more like people, and we liked it, for we sat down then at meals. In the summer we had one pair of linen trousers given us—nothing else; every fall, one pair of woollen pantaloons, one woollen jacket, and two cotton shirts.

My master had four sons in his family. They all left except one, who remained to be a driver. He would often come to the field and accuse the slaves of having taken so and so. If we denied it, he would whip the grown-up ones to make them own it. Many a time, when we didn't know he was anywhere round, he would be in the woods watching us,—first thing we would know, he would be sitting on the fence looking down upon us, and if any had been idle, the young master would visit him with blows. I have known him to kick my aunt, an old woman who had raised and nursed him, and I have seen him punish my sisters awfully with hickories from the woods.

The slaves are watched by the patrols, who ride about to try to catch them off the quarters, especially at the house of a free person of color. I have known the slaves to stretch clothes lines across the street, high enough to let the horse pass, but not the rider: then the boys would run, and the patrols in full chase would be thrown off by running against the lines. The patrols are poor white men, who live by plundering and stealing, getting rewards for runaways, and setting up little shops on the public roads. They will take whatever the slaves steal, paying in money, whiskey, or whatever the slaves want. They take pigs, sheep, wheat, corn,—any thing that's raised they encourage the slaves to steal: these they take to market next day. It's all speculation—all a matter of self-interest, and when the slaves run away, these same traders catch them if they can, to get the reward. If the slave threatens to expose his traffic, he does not care—for the slave's word is good for nothing—it would not be taken. There are frequent quarrels between the slaves and the poor white men. About the city on Sundays, the slaves, many of them, being fond of dress, would appear nicely clad, which seemed to provoke the poor white men. I have had them curse and damn me on this account. They would say to me, 'Where are you going? Who do you belong to?' I would tell them,— then, 'Where did you get them clothes? I wish you belonged to me—I'd dress you up!' Then I have had them throw water on me. One time I had bought a new fur hat, and one of them threw a watermelon rind, and spoiled the hat. Sometimes I have seen them throw a slave's hat on the ground, and trample on it. He would pick it up, fix it as well as he could, put it on his head, and walk on. The slave had no redress, but would sometimes take a petty revenge on the man's horse or saddle, or something of that sort.

I knew a free man of color, who had a wife on a plantation. The patrols went to his house in the night time—he would not let them in; they broke in and beat him: nearly killed him. The next morning he went before the magistrates, bloody and dirty just as he was. All the redress he got was, that he had no right to resist a white man.

An old slaveholder married into the family, who introduced a new way of whipping,—he used to brag that he could pick a 'nigger's' back as he would a chicken's. I went to live with him. There was one man that he used to whip every day, because he was a foolish, peevish man. He would cry when the master undertook to punish him. If a man had any spirit, and would say, 'I am working—I am doing all I can do,' he would let him alone,—but there was a good deal of flogging nevertheless.

Just before I came away, there were two holidays. When I came home to take my turn at the work, master wanted to tie me up for a whipping. Said he, 'You yellow rascal, I hate you in my sight.' I resisted him, and told him he should not whip me. He called his son—they both tried, and we had a good deal of pulling and hauling. They could not get me into the stable. The old man gave up first—then the young man had hold of me. I threw him against the barn, and ran to the woods. The young man followed on horseback with a gun. I borrowed a jacket, my clothes having been torn off in the scuffle, and made for Washington City, with the intention of putting myself in jail, that I might be sold. I did not hurry, as it was holiday. In about an hour or so, my father came for me and said I had done nothing. I told him I would return in the course of the day, and went in time for work next morning. I had recently joined the Methodist Church, and from the sermons I heard, I felt that God had made all men free and equal, and that I ought not to be a slave,—but even then, that I ought not to be abused. From this time I was not punished. I think my master became afraid of me; when he punished the children, I would go and stand by, and look at him,—he was afraid, and would stop.

I belonged to the Methodist Church in Washington. My master said, 'You shan't go to that church—they'll put the devil in you.' He meant that they would put me up to running off. Then many were leaving; it was two from here, three from there, etc.—perhaps forty or fifty a week. —— —— was about there then. I heard something of this: master would say, 'Why don't you work faster? I know why you do n't; you're thinking about running off!' and so I was thinking, sure enough. Men would disappear all at once: a man who was working by me yesterday would be gone to-day,—how, I knew not. I really believed that they had some great flying machine to take them through the air. Every man was on the look-out for runaways. I began to feel uneasy, and wanted to run away too. I sought for information—all the boys had then gone from the place but just me. I happened to ask in the right quarter. But my owners found that I had left the plantation while they had gone to church. They took steps to sell me. On the next night I left the plantation. At length I turned my back on Washington, and had no difficulty in getting off. Sixteen persons came at the same time—all men—I was the youngest of the lot.

I enjoy freedom as all other hard-working men do. I was broken up in Rochester, N.Y. by the fugitive slave bill.

There is much prejudice here against us. I have always minded my own business and tried to deserve well. At one time, I stopped at a hotel and was going to register my name, but was informed that the hotel was 'full'. At another time, I visited a town on business, and entered my name on the register, as did the other passengers who stopped there. Afterward I saw that my name had been scratched off. I went to another hotel and was politely received by the landlady: but in the public room—the bar—were two or three persons, who as I sat there, talked a great deal about 'niggers',—aiming at me. But I paid no attention to it, knowing that when 'whiskey is in, wit is out.'

Mrs Francis Henderson

I was born of a slave mother in Washington, D.C., and was raised in that city. I was to be set free at the age of thirty. When my old mistress died, I was sold for the balance of the time to an Irish woman. When I first went there, I was the only slave they had ever owned; they owned afterwards a man, a woman, and a male child. The man went out to get some one to buy him. He left word at the grocery: the grocer was not particular to report the one who would purchase him to the old man by himself, but let on before the folks. This provoked the Irishman and his wife, and as the old man was taking out ashes from an ash-hole, the master went down, and as the slave raised his head, the man struck him about the temple, with a long handled scrubbing-brush. The old man never spoke afterwards. I saw the blow struck. The old man died the next morning. An inquest was held. I was afraid, and told the jurymen I knew nothing about it. The white girl said the boss wasn't at home,—she swore a false oath, and tried to make it out that the old man fell and hit his head against the bake oven door. The man was bound over, not to put his hand on a servant any more. Mistress used to pinch pieces out of the boys' ears, and then heal them with burnt alum. She dared not do much to me, as my former owners were in the city, and would not suffer barbarity. Her husband was under bonds of two thousand dollars to treat me well. But she treated the others so badly that some of my friends told me I had better leave. —— —— was there then with some persons who were going to travel north with him, and I joined them and came away.

I like liberty, and if Washington were a free country, I would like to go back there,—my parents were there. There are many congressmen there that the slaves are not treated so badly as in other parts.

Pauline Johnson 1861–1913

SIX NATIONS RESERVE, ONTARIO

The first Native writer in Canada to be published, and published to high acclaim, Emily Pauline Johnson (Tekahionwake) was also perhaps the most popular female writer of that period. Despite this, or perhaps because of her popularity, her poetry and short fiction have often been rejected by critics for their sentimentality, and sometimes because she took on 'the role of serving as mediator between the Indian, particularly the Iroquois, and white worlds'. As she was straddling two different cultural heritages at a time when First Nations people were still thought to be a 'vanishing race', she had good reason to take on that role, albeit in ways that often fed the exoticization and other stereotypical representations of aboriginal people by the dominant white society.

Born to George Henry Martin Johnson, a Mohawk chief on the Six Nations Reserve, near Brantford, Ontario, and English-born Emily Susanna Howells, Johnson was brought up and educated in the fashion afforded to middle-class women at the time. After the success of her first public reading at a literary event in Toronto (1892), and with her family in financial straits following her father's death, she began performing her poetry on a regular basis. Eventually she hired a manager and was billed as 'The Mohawk Princess'. Critics have made much of her performative style, namely, beginning her program in a European-style ball gown and then, to recite the Native part of her program, changing into a Native costume 'of her own design' that included a fringed buckskin dress, 'a beaded headdress and moccasins'. Touring and addressing audiences that rarely, if ever, saw live performances or were exposed only to such productions as those of Shakespeare, and doing so during the '"golden age" of traveling entertainment in Canada', Johnson was both able to share her work with a wide North American audience and make, at least for a while, a decent living. 'The Song My Paddle Sings' was one of her poems memorized by many of her contemporaries, and beyond. Ill health forced Johnson to stop touring, and she settled in Vancouver, where she died.

Nature, paying homage to her Native culture—especially Native women—traditional Native stories, the impact of colonization on Natives, and the misunderstandings between the aboriginal culture and the white culture are the recurring themes in her poetry and fiction. Her publications include *The White Wampum* (1895), *Canadian Born* (1903), *Legends of Vancouver* (1911), *Flint and Feather* (1912), and *The Mocassin Maker* (1913).

A Squamish Legend of Napoleon

Holding an important place among the majority of curious tales held in veneration by the coast tribes are those of the sea-serpent. The monster appears and reappears with almost monotonous frequency in connection with history, traditions, legends, and superstitions; but perhaps the most wonderful part it ever played was in the great drama that held the stage of Europe, and incidentally all the world during the stormy days of the first Napoleon.

Throughout Canada I have never failed to find an amazing knowledge of Napoleon Bonaparte amongst the very old and 'uncivilized' Indians. Perhaps they may be unfamiliar with every other historical character from Adam down, but they will all tell you they have heard of the 'Great French Fighter', as they call the wonderful little Corsican.

Whether this knowledge was obtained through the fact that our earliest settlers and pioneers were French, or whether Napoleon's almost magical fighting career attracted the Indian mind to the exclusion of lesser warriors, I have never yet decided. But the fact remains that the Indians of our generation are not as familiar with Bonaparte's name as were their fathers and grandfathers, so either the predominance of English-speaking settlers or the thinning of their ancient war-loving blood by modern civilization and peaceful times must, one or the other, account for the younger Indian's ignorance of the Emperor of the French.

In telling me the legend of 'The Lost Talisman', my good tillicum, the late Chief Capilano, began the story with the almost amazing question, Had I ever heard of Napoleon Bonaparte? It was some moments before I just caught the name, for his English, always quaint and beautiful, was at times a little halting; but when he said by way of explanation, 'You know big fighter, Frenchman. The English they beat him in big battle,' I grasped immediately of whom he spoke.

'What do you know of him?' I asked.

His voice lowered, almost as if he spoke a state secret. 'I know how it is that English they beat him.'

I have read many historians on this event, but to hear the Squamish version was a novel and absorbing thing. 'Yes?' I said—my usual 'leading' word to lure him into channels of tradition.

'Yes,' he affirmed. Then, still in a half whisper, he proceeded to tell me that it all happened through the agency of a single joint from the vertebra of a sea-serpent.

In telling me the story of Brockton Point and the valiant boy who killed the monster, he dwelt lightly on the fact that all people who approach the vicinity of the creature are palsied, both mentally and physically—bewitched, in fact—so that their bones become disjointed and their brains incapable; but to-day he elaborated upon this peculiarity until I harked back to the boy of Brockton Point and asked how it was that his body and brain escaped this affliction.

'He was all good, and had no greed,' he replied. 'He was proof against all bad things.'

I nodded understandingly, and he proceeded to tell me that all successful Indian fighters and warriors carried somewhere about their person a joint of a sea-serpent's vertebra, that the medicine men threw 'the power' about them so that they were not personally affected by this little 'charm', but that immediately they approached an enemy the 'charm' worked disaster, and victory was assured to the fortunate possessor of the talisman. There was one particularly effective joint that had been treasured and carried by the warriors of a great Squamish family for a century. These warriors had conquered every foe they encountered, until the talisman had become so renowned that the totem-pole of their entire 'clan' was remodelled, and the new one crested by the figure of a single joint of a sea-serpent's vertebra.

About this time stories of Napoleon's first great achievements drifted across the seas; not across the land—and just here may be a clue to buried Coast-Indian history, which those who are cleverer at research than I, can puzzle over. The chief was most emphatic about the source of Indian knowledge of Napoleon.

'I suppose you heard of him from Quebec, through, perhaps, some of the French priests,' I remarked.

'No, no,' he contradicted hurriedly. 'Not from East; we hear it from over the Pacific, from the place they call Russia.' But who conveyed the news or by what means it came he could not further enlighten me. But a strange thing happened to the Squamish family about this time. There was a large blood connection, but the only male member living was a very old warrior, the hero of many battles, and the possessor of the talisman. On his death-bed his women of three generations gathered about him; his wife, his sisters, his daughters, his granddaughters, but not one man, nor yet a boy of his own blood stood by to speed his departing warrior spirit to the land of peace and plenty.

'The charm cannot rest in the hands of women,' he murmured almost with his last breath. 'Women may not war and fight other nations or other tribes; women are for the peaceful lodge and for the leading of little children. They are for holding baby hands, teaching baby feet to walk. No, the charm cannot rest with you, women. I have no brother, no cousin, no son, no grandson, and the charm must not go to a lesser warrior than I. None of our tribe, nor of any tribe on the coast, ever conquered me. The charm must go to one as unconquerable as I have been. When I am dead send it across the great salt chuck, to the victorious "Frenchman"; they call him Napoleon Bonaparte.' They were his last words.

The older women wished to bury the charm with him, but the younger women, inspired with the spirit of their generation, were determined to send it over-seas. 'In the grave it will be dead,' they argued. 'Let it still live on. Let it help some other fighter to greatness and victory.'

As if to confirm their decision, the next day a small sealing vessel anchored in the Inlet. All the men aboard spoke Russian, save two thin, dark, agile sailors, who kept aloof from the crew and conversed in another language. These two came ashore with part of the crew and talked in French with a wandering Hudson's Bay trapper, who often lodged with the Squamish people. Thus the women, who yet mourned over their dead warrior, knew these two strangers to be from the land where the great 'Frenchman' was fighting against the world.

Here I interrupted the chief. 'How came the Frenchmen in a Russian sealer?' I asked.

'Captives,' he replied. 'Almost slaves, and hated by their captors, as the majority always hate the few. So the women drew those two Frenchmen apart from the rest and told them the story of the bone of the sea-serpent, urging them to carry it back to their own country and give it to the great "Frenchman" who was as courageous and as brave as their dead leader.

'The Frenchmen hesitated; the talisman might affect them, they said; might jangle their own brains, so that on their return to Russia they would not have the sagacity to plan an escape to their own country; might disjoint their bodies, so that their feet and hands would be useless, and they would become as weak as children. But the women assured them that the charm only worked its magical powers over a man's enemies, that the ancient medicine men had "bewitched" it with this quality. So the Frenchmen took it and promised that if it were in the power of man they would convey it to "the Emperor".

'As the crew boarded the sealer, the women watching from the shore observed strange contortions seize many of the men; some fell on the deck; some crouched, shaking as with palsy; some writhed for a moment, then fell limp and seemingly boneless; only the two Frenchmen stood erect and strong and vital—the Squamish talisman had already overcome their foes. As the little sealer set sail up the gulf she was commanded by a crew of two Frenchmen—men who had entered these waters as captives, who were leaving them as conquerors. The palsied Russians were worse than useless, and what became of them the chief could not state; presumably they were flung overboard, and by some trick of a kindly fate the Frenchmen at last reached the coast of France.

'Tradition is so indefinite about their movements subsequent to sailing out of the Inlet, that even the ever-romantic and vividly coloured imaginations of the Squamish people have never supplied the details of this beautifully childish, yet strangely historical fairy-tale. But the voices of the trumpets of war, the beat of drums throughout Europe heralded back to the wilds of the Pacific Coast forests the intelligence that the great Squamish "charm" eventually reached the person of Napoleon; that from this time onward his career was one vast victory, that he won battle after battle, conquered nation after nation, and but for the direst calamity that could befall a warrior would eventually have been master of the world.'

'What was this calamity, Chief?' I asked, amazed at his knowledge of the great historical soldier and strategist.

The chief's voice again lowered to a whisper—his face was almost rigid with intentness as he replied:

'He lost the Squamish charm—lost it just before one great fight with the English people.'

I looked at him curiously; he had been telling me the oddest mixture of history and superstition, of intelligence and ignorance, the most whimsically absurd, yet impressive, tale I ever heard from Indian lips.

'What was the name of the great fight—did you ever hear it?' I asked, wondering how much he knew of events which took place at the other side of the world a century agone.

'Yes,' he said, carefully, thoughtfully; 'I hear the name sometime in London when I there. Railroad station there—same name.'

'Was it Waterloo?' I asked.

He nodded quickly, without a shadow of hesitation. 'That the one,' he replied. 'That's it, Waterloo.'

Frederick Philip Grove 1879–1948

RADOMNO, PRUSSIA

In his second book on Frederick Philip Grove, *FPG: The European Years* (1973), Douglas O. Spettigue says, 'There is still much too little known about our literary forefathers; it will take our joint efforts to do them justice.' The notion of Grove as one of our Canadian 'literary forefathers' was at the time a rare instance of claiming an immigrant author as a forefather of the Canadian literary tradition. Whether he is one of 'us', or a 'stranger', as Ronald Sutherland once called him, Grove has long been a major, albeit controversial, figure in Canadian literature. From the first book he wrote in English, *Over Prairie Trails* (1922), which chronicles his winter-time commuting as a teacher in Manitoba, and his first Canadian novel, *Settlers of the Marsh* (1925), to his later novel, *The Master of the Mill* (1944), Grove's writing has commanded critical attention ranging from exaggerated or qualified praise to rejection. He won the Lorne Pierce Medal in 1934, was elected a Fellow of the Royal Society of Canada in 1941, and received the Governor General's Award for his fictionalized autobiography, *In Search of Myself* (1946). This kind of recognition, however, did not lessen Grove's feelings of neglect.

Beyond the ongoing critical debates about the literary value of Grove's fiction, arguments about him have also revolved around his identity and origins. Until Spettigue resolved the mystery of 'who Grove really was', what we knew about Grove derived from his own autobiographical narratives, which proved to be largely fictional. Both in his writing and in his life, Grove kept reinventing his identity and origins. He was not, as he claimed to be, a Swedish national born in Moscow, nor was he the son of a wealthy landowner who, upon leaving Europe, emigrated first to Canada. And he was a novelist and a translator of literary titles before he became a writer in Canada.

Grove, a German national, was born Felix Paul Greve in Radomno, Prussia, a border town now in Poland. He was brought up and educated in Hamburg. Living in a style beyond his financial means, he had to borrow money, was charged with fraud, and ended up spending a year in prison. Failing to earn a living that would have allowed him to repay the debts he had accrued, Grove faked a suicide in 1909, and found his way to America. He was accompanied by Elsa Ploetz (aka Baroness Elsa von Freytag-Loringhoven, also a writer), whom he eventually abandoned somewhere in Kentucky before he came to Canada. Assuming the name Fred Grove, he worked as a schoolteacher in the Mennonite regions of Manitoba, where he began to write. He moved to Ottawa in 1929, and, a year later, to a farm near Simcoe, Ontario, where he made a failed attempt to raise cattle.

As was made obvious by the great success of his three lecture tours across Canada in 1928 and 1929, Grove's audience at the time was well aware of what his life choices and writing represented. In Margaret Stobie's words, 'Here was an ideal subject for the Canadian Clubs—an immigrant who had tried life in the United States, spurned it, and chosen Canada; a New Canadian who could give voice to the silent strangers, who could reveal their needs, trials, and dreams to their would-be helpers.' With public lectures such as 'Canadians Old and New' and 'Assimilation', Grove participated in the vigorous debates of the twenties about immigration. In a tone that was ironic and extremely confident, Grove chastised the 'old' Canadians for not making the 'newcomers . . . feel at home'. Acknowledging the values inherent in the literary traditions of immigrants, Grove passionately argued that, 'If assimilation means the absorption of one race by another, the absorbing race not to undergo any change by the process, then there is no such thing as assimilation.'

The struggles of early immigrants that Grove wrote about in epic and tragic terms, and the frankness with which he approached the living conditions of women immigrants, make his writing exemplary of many of the patterns that characterize immigrant experience. Interestingly enough, his characters rarely, if at all, reflect a nostalgia for their origins or a need to align themselves with other members of their ethnic group. For example, the itinerant life of Phil, one of Grove's invented selves, in *A Search for America* (1927), expresses a kind of individualism modeled after Rousseau and Thoreau, rather than a desire to assert ethnic difference; indeed, Phil is often indifferent to, if not contemptuous of, the other immigrants he encounters. This is not the case, however, in the short story that follows, where Niels, a character who is also the protagonist of Grove's *Settlers of the Marsh*, finds encouragement in the presence of another Swedish immigrant.

The First Day of an Immigrant

About six miles west of the little prairie town of Balfour, twelve miles south of another little town called Minor, hard on the bank of the Muddy River which gurgles darkly and sluggishly along, there lies a prosperous farm, a very symbol of harvest and ease. Far and wide the red hip-roof of its gigantic barn shows above the trees that fringe the river which hardly deserves that name, seeing that it is no more than a creek. The commodious, white-painted dwelling, with its roofed-over porch and its glassed-in veranda, however, reveals itself for a moment only as you pass the gate of the yard while driving along the east–west road that leads past it, a few hundred feet to the north; for the old, once primeval bush has been carefully preserved here to enclose and to shelter the homestead; and the tall trees, with their small leaves always aquiver, aspen leaves, while screening the yard from view, seem at the same time to invite you to enter and to linger.

The east–west road cuts right through the property, leaving the level fields, at least the greater part of them, three hundred and twenty acres, to the north, while the yard nestles to the south in a bend of the little river which, curiously, makes the impression as if it were introduced into this landscape for the sole purpose of enfolding this home of man. Beyond the river, there is the remainder of another quarter section the greater part of which serves as pasture. Huge, sleek, gaily coloured cows and frisky colts, accompanied by anxious mares, have at all times access to the black-bottomed water.

The gates to both sides of the road—the one leading to the yard, and the other, opposite it, to the fields—stand open; and a black track leads across the grey-yellow highway from one to the other. There, humus from the field is ground together with the clay of the grade into an exceedingly fine and light dust, perfectly dry, which betrays that many loads have already passed from the field to the yard.

It is a beautiful, crisp, and sunny morning of that reminiscent revival of things past which we call the Indian summer. A far corner of the fields, to the north-west, is bustling with the threshing crews. Engine and separator fill the air with their pulsating hum; and the yellow chaff of the straw comes drifting over the stubble and crosses the road and enters even the yard, threading its way through the trees which, apart from the trembling leaves, stand motionless, and through the entrance that winds in a leisurely way through their aisles. Slowly the chaff filters down, like fine, dry, light snow.

Now and then a wagon, drawn by heavy horses and heavily laden with bags of grain, passes slowly over the road; and every now and then an empty wagon—empty except for a pile of bags on its floor—rattles out in the opposite direction, going to the scene of operations in the field. From the gate a diagonal trail leads through the stubble to the engine; it is cut a few inches deep into the soft soil and worn smooth and hard by many haulings.

That happens just now; let us jump on at the back and go with the driver, an elderly, bearded man of unmistakably Scottish cast: broad-shouldered and heavily set, his grave, though not unpleasant face dusted over with grime and chaff. The wagon, being without a load, rattles along; the horses trot.

Twice the driver has to get out of the trail in order to let a load pass on its way to the yard. To the left, the ground now slopes down a grassy slough in which here and there a clump of willows breaks the monotony of the prairie landscape; no doubt this slough holds water in spring; but at present it is perfectly dry. At its far end, beyond the threshing outfit, an enormous hay-stack rises on its sloping bank.

Now we are in the field of operations. All about, long rows of stooks dot the stubble, big stooks of heavy sheaves. Hay-racks drive from one to the other, one man walking alongside and picking up the sheaves with his fork, pitching them up to another who receives and piles them on the load. Here the work proceeds in a leisurely, unhurried way which contrasts strangely with the scene ahead. The horses do not need to be guided; they know their work; a word from the man on the load is enough to tell them what is wanted.

We have reached the vibrating machines now, joined by a huge, swinging belt. But our Scotsman has to wait a few minutes before he can drive up to the spout that delivers the grain, for another teamster is filling the last of his bags.

Two or three hay-racks, loaded high with sheaves, stand waiting alongside the engine that hums its harvest song. The drivers are lazily reclining on their loads while they wait for those who are ahead of them to finish. They do not even sit up when they move a place forward; the horses know as well as their drivers what is expected of them. Here, the air is thick with chaff and dust.

The few older men in the crew set the pace; the younger ones, some of them inclined to take things easy, have to follow. Those who are alongside the feeder platform, pitching the sheaves, do not make the impression of leisurely laziness.

The engineer, in a black, greasy pair of overalls, is busy with long-spouted oil-can and a huge handful of cottonwaste. The 'separator-man' stands on top of his mighty machine, exchanging bantering talk with the pitching men.

'Let her come, Jim,' he shouts to one of the men, a tall, good-looking youth who works with a sort of defiant composure, not exactly lazily but as if he were carefully calculating his speed to yield just a reasonable day's work and no more; a cynical smile plays in his young, unruffled face. 'Let her come,' the separator-man repeats. 'Can't choke her up.'

'Can't?' challenges Jim's partner, a swarthy, unmistakably foreign-looking man.

And from the opposite side of the feeder-platform another foreigner, a Swede, a giant of a man, six feet four inches tall and proportionately built, shouts over, 'We'll see about that.' He is alone on his load, for, as usual, the crew is short-handed; and he has volunteered to pitch and load by himself.

And this giant, the Swede, starts to work like one possessed, pitching down the sheaves as if his life depended on choking the machine. The Ruthenian, on the near side, follows his example; but Jim, a piece of straw in the corner of his smiling mouth, remains uninfected. He proceeds in his nonchalant way which is almost provoking, almost contemptuous.

All about, the drivers on their loads are sitting up; this is a sporting proposition; and as such it arouses a general interest. Even the Scotsman follows proceedings with a smile.

But apart from these, there has been another looker-on. The outfit stands a few hundred feet from the edge of the slough which stretches its broad trough of hay-land slantways across this end of the field; and there, among some willows, stands a medium-sized man, with a cardboard suit-case at his feet and a bundle hanging from the end of a stout cane that rests on his shoulder. He is neither slender nor stout, five feet and eleven inches tall, and dressed in a new suit of overalls, stiff with new-ness, his flaxen-haired head covered with a blue-denim cap that, on its band, displays the advertisement of a certain brand of lubricating oil. His clean-shaven face is broadened by a grin as he watches the frantic efforts of the two men on their respec-tive loads. His is an almost ridiculous figure; for he looks so foreign and absurd, the more so as his effort to adapt himself to the ways of the country is obvious and unsuccessful.

But he watches idly for only a very few seconds. Then he drops bundle and cane and runs, circling the engine, to the side of the Swede. There he looks about for a moment, finds a spare fork sticking with its prongs in the loose soil under the feeder-platform, grabs it, vaults up on the load of the giant, and, without a word of explana-tion, begins to pitch as frantically as the other two. The loads seem to melt away from under their feet.

The grimy separator-man on top of his machine laughs and rubs his hands. His teeth look strangely white in his dust-blackened face; his tongue and gums, when they show, strangely pink, as in the face of a negro. 'Let her come, boys,' he shouts again, above the din of the machine, 'let her come. Can't choke her up, I tell you. She's a forty-two. But try!' From his words speaks that pride which the craftsman takes in his tools and his output. He looks strange as he stands there, in the dust-laden air, on the shaking machine; his very clothes seem to vibrate; and in them his limbs and his body; he looks like a figure drawn with a trembling hand.

A fixed, nearly apologetic grin does not leave the face of the unbidden helper. There is good-nature in this grin; but also embarrassment and the vacancy of non-comprehension.

The elderly Scotsman who came out a little while ago has meanwhile driven up to the grain-spout and is filling his bags. He keeps watching the newcomer, putting two and two together in his mind. And when his load is made up at last, he detaches himself from the group, casting a last, wondering look at the man who is pitching as if he were engaged on piece-work; for, when the Swede has finished his load, this stranger has simply taken his place on the next one that has come along.

Then the Scotsman threads once more the diagonal trail across the field, staying on it this time when he meets another wagon, for the man with the load, such is the rule, has the right-of-way; and finally, when he reaches the gate, he drives through it and across the road, and on into the welcome shade. For the length of a few rods the entrance leads through the gap between the huge, park-like trees, and then it widens out into the yard. Right in front stands the house, a large, comfortable, and easy-going affair with a look of relaxation about it, though, no doubt, at present nobody there has time to relax, for, red from the heat of the ranges, women are frantically preparing the noon-day meal for the many-mouthed, hungry monster, the crew. The huge and towering barn, painted red, occupies the west side of the yard; and beyond it, a smaller building—it, too, painted red—is the granary for which the load is bound.

In its dark interior a man is working, shovelling wheat to the back. He is tall, standing more than six feet high, broad-shouldered but lean, almost gaunt. His narrow face is divided by a grey moustache which, as he straightens his back, he rubs with the back of his hand in order to free it from the chaff that has collected in its hairs. He is covered all over with the dust of the grain.

When the wagon approaches, he looks out and asks, 'How many, Jim?'

Jim is backing his load against the open door. 'Twenty-four,' he answers over his shoulder.

The man inside takes a pencil suspended by a string from a nail and makes note of the number on a piece of card-board tacked to the wall. Thus he keeps track of the approximate number of bushels, counting two and a half to the bag.

Jim, having tied his lines to the seat, tilts the first of the bags, and the man inside receives it on his shoulder and empties it into the bin to the left. That bin is already filled to one third of its height.

Jim speaks. 'Got a new hand, Dave?' he asks.

'Not that I know of,' replies the man inside with a questioning inflection.

'Fellow came about an hour ago, climbed up on a load, and started to pitch. Good worker, too, it seems.'

'That so?' Dave says. 'I could use another man well enough. But I didn't know about him.'

'Looks like a Swede.'

'Better send him over.'

So, when Jim, the Scotsman, returns to the field, he shouts to the stranger, above the din of machine and engine. 'Hi, you!' And when the stranger turns, he adds, 'Boss wants to see you,' nodding his head backwards in the direction of the yard.

But the stranger merely grins vacantly and, with exaggerated motion, shrugs his shoulders.

The others all look at Jim and laugh. So he, shrugging his shoulders in turn, drives on and takes his place behind the wagon at the spout.

Two more hours pass by; and still the stranger goes on with his unbidden work. The sun, on his path, nears the noon. Meanwhile the stranger has been the partner of all the men who drive up on his side of the outfit: but only one of them has spoken to him, that giant of a Swede who was the first man whom he helped. This giant is clean-shaven and dressed with a striking neatness, yes, a rustic foppishness which shows through all the dust and chaff with which he is covered. He does not wear overalls but a flannel shirt and corduroy trousers tucked into high boots ornamented with a line of coloured stitching along their upper edge. Those of the others who address him call him Nelson.

'Aer du Svensk?' he has asked of the stranger. 'Are you a Swede?'

'Yo,' the stranger has replied in the affirmative.

And further questions have brought out the fact that he has just arrived from the east, on a through-ticket reading from Malmoe in Sweden to Balfour, Manitoba, Canada. 'You'll find lots of Swedes up there,' the agent had told him at home, at Karlskrona in Blekinge, whence he hails.

Nelson grins when he hears that tale. Three years ago, when he himself left Sweden, he was told the same thing; but when he arrived, he found that the Swedish settlement was small and considerably farther north. Thus he has become wise in the tricks of the steamship-agent's trade. 'Did the boss hire you?' he asks, speaking Swedish, of course, while they proceed with the work in hand.

'No. I haven't seen anybody yet. But I do want work.'

'Better see him at noon. What's your name?'

'Niels Lindstedt.'

'Come with me when the whistle blows,' says Nelson as he drives away.

The brief conversation has cheered Niels greatly.

'I am in luck,' he thinks, 'to meet a Swede right away, a friend to help me in getting started.'

In Balfour, where he had landed very early in the morning, he had almost lost courage when he had found that nobody understood him. But at the hardware store a man—the same who had made him a present of the cap he was wearing—had made signs to him as if pitching sheaves, meanwhile talking to him, tentatively, in short monosyllables, apparently asking questions. Niels had understood this sign language sufficiently to know that he was trying to find out whether he wanted work in the harvest fields; and so he had nodded. Next the hardware dealer had made clear to him, again by signs, that his clothes were unsuitable for work; for he had been dressed in a black cloth suit, stiff and heavy, the kind that lasts the people at home a lifetime, so strong that even years of wearing do not flatten out the seams. He had shown him the way to a store where he had acquired what he needed, till he thought that now he looked exactly like a Canadian. Then he had once more returned to the hardware store, and the friendly man had put him on the road, pushing him by the shoulder and pointing and shouting directions till he had picked up his suitcase and the bundle with the clothes he had been wearing and had started out. When, after a few hundred yards, he had looked back, the hardware man had still been standing at the corner of his street and nodding and waving his arm, for him to go on and on, for many miles. And he had done so.

Most of the men with whom he has been working are foreigners themselves. Niels knows the English or Canadian type sufficiently already to recognize that. Some are Slavonic, some German; though they, too, seem to have Russian blood.

Niels exults in the work. After the enforced idleness of the passage across the ocean and the cramped trip in the train, it feels good to be at work in the open. He wonders whether he will be paid for what he does. He is hungry, for he has had no breakfast; and so he hopes he will get his dinner at least. Probably, he thinks, that will be all he is entitled to. He has heard, of course, of the fabulous wages paid to the workingman in America. But possibly that is no more than idle talk. As hunger and the consequent exhaustion lay hold of him, he begins to view things pessimistically.

The size of the field about him dazes him. The owner, he thinks, must be some nobleman. Will a field one tenth, one fiftieth of the size of this one some day be within his own reach, he wonders? The mere thought of it sends him once more into a fury of work; again he pitches the sheaves like one possessed.

Then, suddenly, startlingly, the noon whistle blows from the engine; and when he sees Nelson, the giant, just arriving on top of a load of sheaves, he runs over and helps him to unhitch his horses.

'Come on,' says Nelson and starts off, running and galloping his horses, in order to snatch a ride on a hay-rack which is returning empty to the yard. The rack waits for them, and they climb on, Nelson leading his horses behind.

When the team is stabled in the huge barn where Niels looks about and marvels, the two go over to the granary and find Dave Porter, the boss. Dave looks Niels over and asks a few questions, Nelson interpreting for his new friend.

A few minutes later the newcomer is hired at current wages of four dollars a day till threshing is over; and if he cares to stay after that, at a dollar and fifty a day for plowing till it snows or freezes up. Niels gasps at the figures and has to recalculate them in Swedish money, multiplying them by four: sixteen and six Kroner a day! There must be a mistake, he thinks; he cannot have heard right. The wages must be for the week. But when Dave turns away and Niels asks Nelson, the giant laughs and says, 'No. No mistake.'

So they turn and walk over to the house for dinner.

Niels is quick to learn; and by the time he has had his dinner and gone over the yard with Nelson while they are waiting for the horses to finish theirs, he has picked up much of the new country's lore.

In the granary where they return Niels shows him the figures jotted down on the piece of card-board which show that already the huge bins hold eight thousand bushels of oats, four thousand of barley, and three thousand of wheat. Niels is awed by the enormity of these quantities. There is a strange sort of exhilaration in them. He merely pronounces the figures and has to laugh; and something very like tears comes into his eyes. Nelson chimes in with his throaty bass. No, Niels does not feel sorry that he has come out into this west.

Yet, when the horses are taken out again and the two new friends once more find room on an empty hay-rack, to return to the field, there is a shadow on his consciousness. At dinner, in the house, he has become aware of a certain attitude towards himself, an attitude assumed by those who were unmistakably Canadian. After all, this is not home; it is a strange country; and he is among strange people who look down upon him as if he were something inferior, something not to be taken as fully human. He does not understand that, of course. He has heard Jim, the cynical, good-looking young fellow say something to a number of the men who, like Niels himself, were apparently recent immigrants. Jim had contemptuously addressed them as 'You Galishans!' And it had been clear that they resented it. Niels does not quite see why they should; if they are Galicians, why should they mind being called by that name? But he also understands that what they really resent is the tone in which it was said.

He wonders as he looks about while the horses trot briskly over the stubble whether in a few years' time this country will seem like home to him, as apparently it does to Nelson, his newly-won friend.

And with that he turns his mind away from his critical thoughts and back to his dreams. He sees himself established on a small farm of his own, with a woman in the house; and he sees the two of them sitting by lamp-light in a neat little living room of that house while from upstairs there sounds down to them the pitter-patter of little children's feet—his own little children's, romping before they crawl into their snug little beds.

That is his vision: the vision that has brought him into these broad plains. And that vision is destined to shape his whole life in the future.

A.M. Klein 1909–1972

RATNO, UKRAINE

'The true poet is he who, nourished upon the ancestral heritage, yet—if only in the slightest—deviates therefrom. Rooted in the common soil, he turns his eyes to new directions.' These words by A.M. Klein capture the ways in which he practised his poetry: by immersing himself in his Jewish heritage while renewing it by showing how it relates to the larger humanistic tradition.

A.M. (Abraham Moses) Klein was born in Ratno, in what is now Ukraine, and immigrated to Montreal with his family in 1910. The orthodox Jewish milieu in which he was brought up and his solid Jewish education had a profound influence on Klein's belief in the role the poet has to play in his community. In his twenties he joined Young Judea, a Zionist youth movement, and later he became the associate director of the

Zionist Organization of Canada, acted as the editor of *The Canadian Zionist*, worked as a speechwriter for Samuel Bronfman, and was a contributing editor to *The Canadian Jewish Chronicle*. In 1949 his experiences on a research trip to Israel, Europe, and Northern Africa, commissioned by the Canadian Jewish Congress, led to his only novel, *The Second Scroll* (1951). Its complex and tightly structured narrative can be seen as a 'scripture' that comprises both the theological and secular histories of Klein's heritage, while evoking the modernist tradition as practised by James Joyce, a writer Klein admired and about whom he wrote.

A student at McGill University, he was associated with the *McGill Fortnightly Review* group of poets, and began publishing his poetry in both Canadian and American magazines. After he received his BA (1930), he studied law at the Université de Montréal, and practised law for many years. *Hath Not A Jew* (1940) and *Poems* (1944) announced his lifelong commitment to exploring the victimization of Jews and celebrating their rich tradition. *The Hitleriad* (1944), in its mock-epic style, is an indictment of Nazism that offers a satiric portrait of Hitler. *The Rocking Chair and Other Poems* (1945), which won the Governor General's Award, was highly acclaimed by critics and poets. Some of the poems in it, earlier published in the magazine *Poetry*, received the Edward Bland Prize, an award given by black Americans to poetry of social importance. This collection, focused as much on Jewish themes as on his Quebecois environment, expressed Klein's belief that there was much that the Jewish and francophone communities of Quebec shared at the time: 'a minority position; ancient memories, and a desire for group survival. Moreover the French Canadian enjoys much—a continuing and distinctive culture, solidarity, *land*—which I would wish on my own people.' At the same time that these poems bear the strong signature of Klein's background, they express a universalist vision both about the function of the poet and the ways in which history can be redeemed.

In 1954, after the first signs of a psychological illness, he stopped practising law, eventually stopped writing, and withdrew from the public life. In recognition of his major contribution to Canadian literature, Klein received the Lorne Pierce Medal in 1957. His work continues to attract attention as the Quebec Writers' Federation A.M. Klein Poetry Prize and the posthumous editions of his work testify. The latter include *The Short Stories of A.M. Klein* (1983) edited by M.W. Steinberg, *A.M. Klein: Literary Essays and Reviews* (1987) edited by Usher Caplan and M.W. Steinberg, and *A.M. Klein: The Complete Poems* (1990), 2 vols., edited by Zailig Pollock.

Autobiographical

I

Out of the ghetto streets where a Jewboy
Dreamed pavement into pleasant bible-land,
Out of the Yiddish slums where childhood met
The friendly beard, the loutish Sabbath-goy,
Or followed, proud, the Torah-escorting band,   5
Out of the jargoning city I regret,
Rise memories, like sparrows rising from
The gutter-scattered oats,
Like sadness sweet of synagogal hum,
Like Hebrew violins   10
Sobbing delight upon their eastern notes.

2
Again they ring their little bells, those doors
Deemed by the tender-year'd, magnificent:
Old Ashkenazi's cellar, sharp with spice;
The widows' double-parloured candy-stores   15
And nuggets sweet bought for one sweaty cent;
The warm fresh-smelling bakery, its pies,
Its cakes, its navel'd bellies of black bread;
The lintels candy-poled
Of barber-shop, bright-bottled, green, blue, red;   20
And fruit-stall piled, exotic,
And the big synagogue door, with letters of gold.

3
Again my kindergarten home is full—
Saturday night—with kin and compatriot:
My brothers playing Russian card-games; my   25
Mirroring sisters looking beautiful,
Humming the evening's imminent fox-trot;
My uncle Mayer, of blessed memory,
Still murmuring Maariv, counting holy words;
And the two strangers, come   30
Fiery from Volhynia's murderous hordes—
The cards and humming stop.
And I too swear revenge for that pogrom.

4
Occasions dear: the four-legged aleph named
And angel pennies dropping on my book;   35
The rabbi patting a coming scholar-head;
My mother, blessing candles, Sabbath-flamed,
Queenly in her Warsovian perruque;
My father pickabacking me to bed
To tell tall tales about the Baal Shem Tov,—   40
Letting me curl his beard.
O memory of unsurpassing love,
Love leading a brave child
Through childhood's ogred corridors, unfear'd!

5
The week in the country at my brother's—(May   45
He own fat cattle in the fields of heaven!)

Its picking of strawberries from grassy ditch,
Its odour of dogrose and of yellowing hay,—
Dusty, adventurous, sunny days, all seven!—
Still follow me, still warm me, still are rich   50
With the cow-tinkling peace of pastureland.
The meadow'd memory
Is sodded with its clover, and is spanned
By that same pillow'd sky
A boy on his back one day watched enviously.   55

6
And paved again the street: the shouting boys
Oblivious of mothers on the stoops
Playing the robust robbers and police,
The corn-cob battle,—all high-spirited noise
Competitive among the lot-drawn groups.   60
Another day, of shaken apple-trees
In the rich suburbs, and a furious dog,
And guilty boys in flight;
Hazelnut games, and games in the synagogue—
The burrs, the Haman rattle,   65
The Torah-dance on Simchas-Torah night.

7
Immortal days of the picture-calendar
Dear to me always with the virgin joy
Of the first flowering of senses five,
Discovering birds, or textures, or a star,   70
Or tastes sweet, sour, acid, those that cloy;
And perfumes. Never was I more alive.
All days thereafter are a dying-off,
A wandering away
From home and the familiar. The years doff   75
Their innocence.
No other day is ever like that day.

8
I am no old man fatuously intent
On memoirs, but in memory I seek
The strength and vividness of nonage days,   80
Not tranquil recollection of event.
It is a fabled city that I seek;

It stands in Space's vapours and Time's haze;
Thence comes my sadness in remembered joy
Constrictive of the throat;   85
Thence do I hear, as heard by a Jewboy
The Hebrew violins,
Delighting in the sobbed oriental note.

Doctor Drummond

It is to be wondered whether he ever really
saw them, whether he knew them more than type,
whether, in fact, his occupational fun—
the doctor hearty over his opened grip—
did not confuse him into deducing   5
his patients' health and Irish from his own.

Certainly from his gay case-histories
that now
for two-tongued get-togethers are elocutional,
one would never have recognized his clientele.   10

Consider this patrician patronizing the *patois*,
consider his *habitants*, the homespun of their minds and motives,
and you will see them as he saw them—as *white* natives,
characters out of comical Quebec,
of speech neither Briton nor Breton, a fable folk,   15
a second class of aborigines,
docile, domesticate, very good employees,
so meek that even their sadness
made dialect for a joke.

One can well imagine the doctor,   20
in club, in parlour, or in smoking car,
building out of his practice a reputation
as raconteur.
But the true pulsing of their blood
his beat ignores,   25
and of the temperature of their days, the chills
of their despairs, the fevers of their faith,
his mercury is silent.

Irving Layton 1912–2006

TIRGUL NEAMT, RUSSIA

'Because many poets have averted their eyes from this radical evil [the sight of a happy man], they strike me as insufferable blabbermouths. They did not retch enough; were too patient, courteous, civilized. A little brutality would have made them almost men,' said Irving Layton in the foreword to his volume of selected poetry, *A Red Carpet for the Sun* (1959), which won the Governor General's Award. What these poets lack is precisely what defines Layton as poet: an overbearing exuberance, an unabashed display of sexual bravado that he often identified with the Dionysian element, and a deep commitment to what he valued, which often translated into a cocksure attitude about things aesthetic and political. 'I am not at ease in the world (what poet ever is?),' he said; 'but neither am I fully at ease in the world of the imagination. I require some third realm, as yet undiscovered, in which to live. My dis-ease has spurred me on to bridge the two with the stilts of poetry, or to create inside me an ironic balance of tensions.'

One of the best but also one of the most controversial poets in Canada, Layton was born Israel Lazarovitch in Tirgul Neamt, a poor village in northern Romania, at a time of rising anti-Semitism. This, combined with his family's poverty, led to their immigration to Montreal a year after Layton's birth. He attributes his literary sensibility to his 'extraction'. 'My father was an ineffectual visionary,' he said; 'he saw God's footprint in a cloud and lived only for his books and meditations. A small bedroom in a slum tenement, which in the torrid days steamed and blistered and sweated, he converted into a tabernacle for the Lord of Israel. . . . Had my mother been as otherworldly as he was, we should have starved. Luckily for us, she was not; she was tougher than nails, shrewd and indomitable. With parents so poorly matched and dissimilar, small wonder my entelechy was given a terrible squint from the outset.' His family background certainly left its mark on young Layton, and he periodically dedicated himself to

reading about Jews, but, as poet Joe Rosenblatt once said, 'Layton's a fool. . . ; he's an ignorant man in terms of what Judaism is all about.'

An avid reader from his teenage years on, Layton went to Baron Byng High School, from which he was expelled and graduated only after A.M. Klein's intervention. He received a BSc in agriculture (1939) from MacDonald College, Ste Anne de Bellevue, Quebec, and an MA in political science and economics (1946) from McGill University, and in 1969 he moved to Toronto to teach at York University until his retirement in 1978. He often visited Europe, where he lived for short periods in Greece, France, and Spain.

In the 1940s, Layton was actively involved with the poetry movement in Montreal led by the literary magazines *First Statement* and *Northern Review*, and was one of the forces behind Contact Press that published some of the innovative poets at the time. Beginning with the publication of his first book, *Here and Now* (1945), Layton was heralded as one of the most important poets of the 1950s and 1960s. But his prolific, and often indiscriminate, output—'to sustain his image as a genius', for a long time he published a book a year—and his controversial ideas and attitudes have also established him, ironically, as a 'miserable clown', the image he himself attributed to poets who do not understand 'the joy and wonder that is poetry'. Writing out of a 'messianic' belief in exposing the 'disorder and glory of passion', '[t]he modern tragedy of the depersonalization of men and women', the 'hideously commercial civilization', Layton wrote powerful poetry, but also a poetry that was driven by disputable passions such as his misogyny: he saw 'Modern women . . . cast in the role of furies striving to castrate the male; their efforts aided by all the malignant forces of a technological civilization that has rendered the male's creative role of revelation superfluous.' This attitude, as well as the fact that his later publications often repeat his messages, has led reviewers and critics to view his last titles in disparaging ways.

Still, Layton remains one of the most anthologized and internationally known of Canadian poets. Translated into many languages, Layton was nominated for the Nobel Prize. His many titles include *In the Midst of My Fever* (1954), *The Cold Green Element* (1955), *The Improved Binoculars* (1956), the American edition of which was edited by William Carlos Williams, *The Swinging Flesh* (1961), *Droppings from Heaven* (1979), *The Gucci Bag* (1983), *Dance with Desire* (1986), and *Final Reckoning* (1987). *Fortunate Exile* (1987) is one of his many volumes of selected poems. His other books include *Engagements: The Prose of Irving Layton* (1972), *Taking Sides* (1977), prose, *An Unlikely Affair* (1980), letters, and *Waiting for the Messiah* (1985), a memoir. Suffering from Alzheimer's disease, he lived his final years in a Montreal medical facility. At his funeral service, Leonard Cohen, an old protégé and friend of Layton's, read from Layton's 'The Graveyard' from *The Shattered Plinths* (1968): 'There is no pain in the graveyard, for the voice whispering in the tombstone, rejoice, rejoice.'

Whom I Write For

When reading me, I want you to feel
   as if I had ripped your skin off;
Or gouged out your eyes with my fingers;
Or scalped you, and afterwards burnt your hair
   in the staring sockets; having first filled them   5
with fluid from your son's lighter.
I want you to feel as if I had slammed
   your child's head against a spike;
And cut off your member and stuck it in your
   wife's mouth to smoke like a cigar.   10

For I do not write to improve your soul;
   or to make you feel better, or more humane;
Nor do I write to give you any new emotions;
Or to make you proud to be able to experience them
   or to recognize them in others.   15
I leave that to the fraternity of lying poets
   —no prophets, but toadies and trained seals!

How much evil there is in the best of them
   as their envy and impotence flower into poems
And their anality into love of man, into virtue: 20
Especially when they tell you, sensitively,
   what it feels like to be a potato.

I write for the young man, demented,
   who dropped the bomb on Hiroshima;
I write for Nasser and Ben Gurion;   25

For Khrushchev and President Kennedy;
   for the Defense Secretary
voted forty-six billions for the extirpation
   of humans everywhere.
I write for the Polish officers machine-gunned   30
   in the Katyn forest;
I write for the gassed, burnt, tortured,
   and humiliated everywhere;
I write for Castro and Tse-tung, the only poets
   I ever learned anything from;   35
I write for Adolph Eichmann, compliant clerk
   to that madman, the human race;
For his devoted wife and loyal son.

Give me words fierce and jagged enough
   to tear your skin like shrapnel;   40
Hot and searing enough to fuse
   the flesh off your blackened skeleton;
Words with the sound of crunching bones or bursting eyeballs;
   or a nose being smashed with a gun butt;
Words with the soft plash of intestines   45
   falling out of your belly;
Or cruel and sad as the thought which tells you
   'This is the end'
And you feel Time oozing out of your veins
   and yourself becoming one with the weightless dark.   50

The Search

My father's name was Moses; his beard was black
and black the eyes that beheld God's light;
they never looked upon me but they saw
a crazy imp dropt somehow from the sky
and then I knew from his holy stare   5
I had disgraced the Prophets and the Law.

Nor was I my mother's prayer;
she who all day railed at a religious indolence
that kept her man warm under his prayershawl
while her reaching arm froze with each customer   10
who brought a needed penny to her store;
added to another it paid the food and rent.

An ill-matched pair they were. My father
thought he saw Jehovah everywhere,
entertaining his messengers every day   15
though visible to him alone in that room
where making his fastidious cheese
he dreamt of living in Zion at his ease.

My mother: unpoetical as a pot of clay,
with as much mysticism in her as a banker   20
or a steward; lamenting God's will for her
yet blessing it with each Friday's candles.
But O her sturdy mind has served me well
who see how humans forge with lies their lonely hell.

Alien and bitter the road my forebears knew: 25
fugitives forever eating unleavened bread
and hated pariahs because of that one Jew
who taught the tenderest Christian how to hate
and harry them to whatever holes they sped.
Times there were the living envied the dead.   30

Iconoclasts, dreamers, men who stood alone:
Freud and Marx, the great Maimonides
and Spinoza who defied even his own.
In my veins runs their rebellious blood.
I tread with them the selfsame antique road   35
and seek everywhere the faintest scent of God.

Eli Mandel 1922–1992

ESTEVAN, SASKATCHEWAN

One of the most important poets of his generation, and a writer–critic who shaped the traditions of Canadian criticism and poetry, Eli
Mandel was born to Russian Jewish parents in
Estevan, Saskatchewan, a place often revisited
in his work. Though he was not, strictly speaking, a regionalist poet, the sensibility as well as
the literary and intellectual traditions of the
Canadian prairies are strongly inscribed in his
writing. The 'landscape of Mandel's poems is a

collage in which . . . each picture evokes,
announces, its own violation; every violation
evokes its own parodic inversion back into (up
to) surface and the present (presence).'

After serving overseas with the Canadian
army, Mandel returned to Canada in 1946 and
began to study literature. He received a BA
(1949) and an MA (1950) from the University
of Saskatchewan and a PhD from the
University of Toronto (1957). Though his

dissertation was on Christopher Smart and his criticism was inflected by his far-reaching knowledge and the various influences—including those of psychoanalysis and structuralism—on his work, Mandel focused primarily on Canadian literature. Before joining the faculty of the Humanities department at York University, where he taught until his retirement (1967–86), he taught at the Universities of Alberta and Victoria. He was instrumental in introducing Canadian literature as a subject to be taught in its own right at a time when Canadian authors were still taught on an ad hoc basis, and often only in the contexts of American or British literatures.

Widely published, and a lecturer and guest professor at many universities in Canada, Europe, and India, Mandel broke new ground in many ways. He wrote one of the first essays on ethnic writing in Canada (1977), an essay in which he both identified the vibrant field ethnic literature was to become and anticipated the critical problems that were to plague this area of study. Acknowledging that the 'binary' paradigms and 'duplicitousness' he saw in ethnic writing 'look[ed] suspiciously like a form of structuralism', he announced the major issues at stake. 'As soon as the question of ethnicity is raised,' he wrote, 'the question of identity appears along with it.' But ethnic identity for Mandel—who was writing, we should remember, before the advent of official multiculturalism—was not essentialist; rather, it was the result of 'a restructured self, a fictional being'. Seeing 'ethnic writing as a self-reflexive form', as a 'literature existing at an interface of two cultures, a form concerned to define itself', Mandel recognized 'self-definition' as the principal concern in ethnic writing, a concern deriving as much from his sophisticated (at the time) notion of subject formation as from the social construction of otherness and the tensions between individual subjects and their ethnic communities.

Mandel was also instrumental in approaching the critical act in a manner that moved 'beyond paraphrase'. Arguing for the primacy of language, without losing sight of the cultural and social contexts that contribute to its materiality, Mandel was, again, one of the first critics to articulate the predicament of Canadian criticism in the early 1970s: 'Atwood's *Survival* stands at one end of a developing line of thematic and cultural criticism in Canada and in direct opposition to the kinds of literary sociology implied in the work of critics like George Woodcock, A.J.M. Smith, Desmond Pacey, or Ronald Sutherland.' His carefully nuanced criticism was matched by the self-reflexive poetics he practiced in his poetry. His many poetry books include *An Idiot Joy* (1967), which shared the Governor General's Award, *Stony Plain* (1973), *Out of Place* (1977), and *Life Sentence, Poems and Journals: 1976–1980* (1981). His critical essays have been collected in *Criticism: The Silent Speaking Words* (1966), *Another Time* (1977), *The Family Romance* (1986), and *A Passion for Identity: Introduction to Canadian Studies* (1987). A fellow of the Royal Society of Canada, Mandel also edited many anthologies, including the influential collection of essays, *Contexts of Canadian Criticism* (1971).

estevan, 1934:
    remembering the family we
    called breeds   the Roques
    their house smelling of urine
    my mother's prayers before
    the dried fish she cursed   5
    them for their dirtiness their
    women I remember too
            how

seldom they spoke and
they touched one another   10

even when the sun killed
cattle and rabbis
                    even
in poisoned slow air
like hunters   15
            like lizards
they touched   stone
they touched
            earth

the return:
            in the estevan poem, for example,
            how everyone can be seen eating
            or is it reading
                        but not everyone
            there is myself in the souris valley   5
            forty years later
                        Ann
            looking at wild flowers
            cactus   their thick colours

            I remember how I dreamt   10
            her
                  pale as a flower
                  in the white sun
            and in the dream
            she is taking pictures   15

            she photographs me
            walking away
            along a curving path
            the flowers coloured

                        and   20

            my father appears
            my mother appears
            saying no words
            troubled
                        and all   25

the ghostly jews
of estevan
            praying
in the synagogue
    of the valley   30
in the covenant
    of coal mines
in these pictures
    of estevan

signs:

and omens   windows
facing inward
            'an ideal
inserted into the plane
we call reality'   words   5
warning this is the place
you reach

to name
remember and recite

the Hebrew alphabet   10
Invictus the first three
lines of Genesis
the unremembered man who stole
children from an empty town and
Latin   heroes in the hills and   15
glyphs uncles cousins step-
grandfather's sons and sisters

whatever has been hidden here
remains of speech
                    the town lives   20
in its syntax we are ghosts

look   on the road beyond
mesas and moonscape
hoodoos   signs cut in rock
graffiti   gods   25
an indescribable border

Rienzi Crusz *b.* 1925

GALLE, SRI LANKA

Born in Galle, Sri Lanka (formerly Ceylon), Rienzi Crusz studied at the University of Ceylon, where he received an Honours BA. The recipient of a Colombo Plan Scholar fellowship in 1951, he studied at the School of Librarianship and Archives, University of London, England. After his arrival in Canada in 1965, he continued his studies in the library sciences, receiving a BLS from the University of Toronto. He holds an MA from the University of Waterloo where he was Senior Reference and Collections Development Librarian (1969–93).

Anthologized and widely published in Canadian literary magazines, Crusz's poetry is often about the immigrant experience. Although, as he writes in 'In the Idiom of the Sun', 'I must hold my black tongue', his poetry is permeated by ironic imagery that juxtaposes his native culture to that of his adopted land. Through strong rhythms and a caustic wit, Crusz attempts to construct an 'idiom of the Sun', a language that invests his 'black tongue' with layers of colonial history and traces of Canada's postindustrial society. As Arun

Mukherjee remarks, Crusz has constructed the 'mythic persona' of 'The Sun Man' that 'occurs in several poems': 'The persona allows Crusz to amalgamate the two segments of his life in a meaningful way while it works as a readily available device with which to build further.'

Crusz's collections of poetry include *Flesh and Thorn* (1974), *Elephant and Ice* (1980), *Singing Against the Wind* (1985), *A Time for Loving* (1986), *Still Close to the Raven* (1989), and *The Rain Doesn't Know Me Any More* (1992). The tension between nature and industrialized culture, the exploration of a self that is constantly changing, and a preoccupation with the act of writing are recurring elements in these books. While his poetry often contains lush imagery evoking his Sri Lankan past, Crusz never resorts to a comforting sense of nostalgia. His double perspective as an immigrant and a 'black man' compels him to keep in mind the complexity of cultural and racial differences. His most recent publications include *Beautidues of Ice* (1995) and *Insurgent Rain* (1997).

Civilization

Dollar-Daze, Days
at Zellers County Fair,
and the parking lot
like some African watering hole,
gathers in its animals.   5

The way they spill out
of their polished automobile skins,
drooling with Dollar-Daze,
ham on rye, the second cup free.

Supermarket vertigo,   10
and like everybody else
I roam the gleaming jungle,

now nowhere near the centre (of reason)
nothing but my head full

of cut prices, secret desires   15
to squeeze the CHARMIN,
jaws tight
on the raw meat of civilization.

Soon, I'm no more the hunter
but the hunted   20
as shelves beckon, seduce
like women of the evening,

and I surrender
to HEAVENLY HASH, pig tails,
cocktail wieners, almost anything   25
that bears a price slash on its face.

O God, I now feel
like the plastic bauble
at two-for-a-dollar,
the 50% discount coat   30
hanging limp and old

Interpreting the Clothesline

The fat lady sings
    as she steps into her backyard:
student guests
    sweat and swarm
over their smoking barbeque.   5

Over the fence,
    the coloured minutiae
of another civilization?
    The neighbour's clothesline
fluttering alien flags.   10
But where there's Molson, porkchops,
    sausages and the girls
from Village 1
    cultural anthropology, sociology of dress
have no place on the menu.   15

Not so for the fat lady.
    She's into social inquiry,
gossip. 'Getting to know
    your immigrant neighbour!'
So, what if she dares to catalogue,   20
    interpret those dancing items
that she's never seen
    or known before?

A dashiki simmers in gold and green;
    two sarongs stew   25
in their exotic dyes; black Gandhi jacket,
gold-laced saris, bedsheets
    with pink elephants walking all over them;
baby sleepers that parade sand crabs
    in a praying mode; an Arya-Singhala suit   30
taking in the afternoon sun.

Dashiki: a large loose-fitting buttonless shirt.
    Fat lady: 'Must be what hula-hula man wears!'
Sarong: a draped skirtlike garment
    worn by men and women in the Malayan Archipelago,   35
Sri Lanka and the Pacific Islands.
    Fat lady: 'What the hell is that?
Seamless piece of cloth like a tube with show flowers
    blooming all over it like crazy.'

Sari: outer garment, long piece of cloth   40
    wrapped around the body
with one end over the head.
    Fat lady: 'My! What soft material!
What do they use it for?
    To cover themselves,   45
or bury their dead?'

The fat lady shakes her head.
    Her beady eyes
still frozen on her neighbour's laundry line
    like an Irish setter's.   50
'Who are these people?' she asks herself,
    pinching her pink thighs
in utter frustration.

'Do elephants, sand crabs, strange flowers,
    gross and glaring colours   55
crowd their lives
    as do their clothes?
Must be some alien farmer type
    with no notion whatever
of fashion, style or decor!'   60

'Who knows. Could be even
    Asian gypsies or carnival circus folks!'

Roots

For Cleta Marcellina Nora Serpanchy

What the end usually demands
is something of the beginning,
and so
I conjure history from a cup
of warm Portuguese blood   5
from my forefathers,
black diamond eyes, charcoal hair
from my Sinhalese mothers;
the beached catamaran,
gravel voices of the fishermen,   10
the catch still beating like a heart
under the pelting sun;
how the pariah dogs looked urgent
with fish meal in their brains,
the children romped, sagged,   15
then melted into the sand.

A Portuguese captain holds
the soft brown hand of my Sinhala mother.
It's the year 1515 AD,
when two civilizations kissed and merged,   20
and I, burgher of that hot embrace,
write a poem of history
as if it were only the romance
of a lonely soldier on a crowded beach
in southern Ceylon.   25

Roy Kiyooka 1926–1994

MOOSE JAW, SASKATCHEWAN

'[W]hatever my true colours, I am to all intents and purposes, a white anglo-saxon protestant, with a cleft tongue,' said Roy Kenzie Kiyooka in the 1981 statement, which follows below, that he presented at the Japanese Canadian/Japanese American Symposium in Seattle. Born in Moose Jaw, Saskatchewan, Kiyooka was a *nisei*, a Canadian-born child of immigrant Japanese parents. His cleft tongue 'bears the pulse of an English'—'inglish', he called it—'which is not my mother tongue'. At five, Kiyooka had to put aside the Japanese he spoke at home, at once an act of 'survival' in an environment where the pressure was to assimilate and an act of recognition on his part of the need to 'hold my own', to 'come to an articulateness by which I could stand in this world of literate people'. Called a 'cultural autodidact', Kiyooka, who grew up in Calgary and never finished high school, was a 'multidisciplinary artist'. A painter and sculptor, with a national and international reputation already established by the late 1960s, but also—beginning in 1964 with the publication of his first book, *Kyoto Airs*—a poet, as well as photographer, collage-, music-, and film-maker, and an inspiring and dedicated art teacher, Kiyooka resisted the demands and conventions of the mainstream art world. Indeed, 'since the early 80s', he 'ventured willy-nilly into self-publishing under the logos of the "Blue Mule" a maverick photo gallery [he] kept for a few years on Power Street . . . all the . . . books have been printed, collated, and bound in my own good time in editions of 26 plus 10, with no thought for further editions. "the future of forethought is present-tense." i write the passages of time . . . i go on trying to hold, in my mind, an actual world of kinship/s.' As he also said, 'I think the most critical thing about my activity is the interface between myself as a painter and myself as a language artificer. But what has to be understood is how the two inform each other.'

Kiyooka, like Japanese Canadians of his generation, lived through the turmoil that followed the bombing of Pearl Harbor. 'Needless to say,' he wrote, 'it abruptly ended my education and our plain city life. I had the obscure feeling that something formless dark and stealthy had fallen upon me during my sleep but when I awoke nothing outward seemed to have changed, even though my childhood friends began to fall away from me. I might add that it's a loss I've never fully recovered from.' His father and older brother lost their hotel jobs, and the family left Calgary to settle in the small town of Opal, Alberta, where they found farm work. In 1942–6, Kiyooka worked there 'except for off-season work' that took him to the killing floor of the Swift Canadian plant in Edmonton and to the fishing plants of Great Slave Lake, where he 'was part of a motley crew of seasonal workers comprising West Coast Japanese fishermen Icelandic and Baltic fishermen and all the First Nation's People who were recruited by McInnes Products. . . . *all this and more for less than fifty cents an hour . . .*'.

In 1959, at the Emma Lake Artists' Workshop in Saskatchewan, Kiyooka encountered the American artist Barnett Newman, who influenced Kiyooka's shift from figurative to abstract painting. By the late 1960s he had exhibited in many galleries in Canada and overseas, had won the silver medal at the 1966 Sao Paulo Bienal, and had his painting represented in major galleries. Kiyooka taught art in many places across Canada, including the University of British Columbia. *transcanada letters* (1975, 2005), his first long book, gathers together many of his letters to family, friends, and peers during the years that he traversed Canada—'with a hostage of snapshots'. By its size and design alone, this book speaks of Kiyooka's desire to break through boundaries and to record the process of experience and language in all its minute shifts. Much of his writing begins in or deals with Japan, which he visited many times, journeys that he records, along with his thoughts about pedagogy, the nation, and cultural capital, in his posthumously published

Pacific Rim Letters (2005), edited by Smaro Kamboureli. Kiyooka's early publications include *Nevertheless These Eyes* (1967), *StoneDGloves* (1970), and *The Fontainebleau Dream Machine: 18 Frames From a Book of Rhetoric* (1977). Most of his poetry appeared in *Pacific Windows: Collected Poems by Roy K. Kiyooka* (1997), edited by Roy Miki. *Mother-talk: Life Stories by Mary Kiyoshi Kiyooka* (1997), also a posthumous publication, edited by Daphne Marlatt, documents—through transcribed and translated audio-recordings—his mother's immigrant experience. Kiyooka's writing directly engages—in form, content, and design—the visual. *Pear Tree Pomes* (1987), illustrated by David Bolduc, was nominated for the Governor General's Award, and was the last collection of poetry published before his death. In recognition of his cultural contribution, Kiyooka received the Order of Canada in 1977.

We Asian North Americanos: An unhistorical 'take' on growing up yellow in a white world

for Joy Kogawa & Tamio Wakayama
(read at The J.C/J.A. Symposium in Seattle, 2 May 1981)

Everytime I look at my face in a mirror I think of how it keeps on changing its features in English, tho English is not my mother tongue. Everytime I've been in an argument I've found the terms of my rationale in English pragmatism. Even my anger, not to mention my rage, has to all intents and purposes been shaped by all the gut-level obscenity I picked up away from my mother tongue. And everytime I have tried to express, it must be, affections, it comes out sounding halt. Which thot proposes that every unspecified emotion I've felt was enfolded in an unspoken Japanese dialect, one which my childhood ears alone remember. Furthermore, everytime I've broken into my own ofttimes unwelcome but salutory silences, I've been left with a tied tongue. All of which tells me that every time a word forms on the tip of my tongue, it bears the pulse of an English which is not my mother tongue. There's English 'English'. There's American 'English', paging Dr Hayakawa. Then, there's our kind of, callit, Canadian 'English', not to mention all the other English-speaking folks in the rest of the world, regardless of their race, colour, or creed. For good or bad, it's the nearest thing we have to a universal lingua franca. Unless the ubiquitous computer with its fearsome but cold-blooded logistical games has already usurpt its primacy. Having said all this, I would simply add that none of the above has anything to do with what I can say in my mother tongue.

I am reminded of these grave matters when I go home to visit my mother. She and she alone reminds me of my Japanese self by talking to me in the very language she taught me before I even had the thot of *learning* anything. If there's one thing I can say with a degree of certainty, it's that she did not, could not, teach me to speak English. Let alone, read and write it. After more than half a century in Canada her English is, to say the least, rudimentary. Not that that ever prevented her from speaking her mind. So it is that I find myself going home to keep in touch with my mother tongue and, it must be, the ghost of my father's silences.

Everytime I've been in Japan I've been acutely aware of the fact that my own brand of Japanese is previous to both the 2nd WW and television. That in fact it's contemporaneous with that original wireless talking machine, the radio. My more candid Japanese friends tell me that I sound, to their ears, a bit old-fashioned. Need I say that I didn't have enough of a handle on my mother tongue to tell them that all the Japanese I know had been distilled in me by the time I was six or seven. Keep in mind that my mother's Japanese was shaped towards the end of the Meiji era and the beginnings of the Taisho era and that's the Japanese she taught me. What has been grafted on down thru the years, is, like my mother's English, rudimentary. Right here and now I want to say that there's a part of me that is taken aback by the fact, the ironical fact, that I am telling you all this in English. Which proposes to me that, whatever my true colours, I am to all intents and purposes, a white anglo saxon protestant, with a cleft tongue.

Everytime I find myself talking, talking about anything under or even above and beyond the sun, I feel the very pulse of my thots in a North American/West Coast dialect of the English language with all its tenacious Indo-European roots. Now, concomitant with this recognition is the feeling that, when I am most bereft, it's the nameless Jap in me who sings an unsolicited haiku in voluntary confinement. I don't want to go on moanin' the old 'yellow peril' blues the rest of my days. Gawd save us all from that fate. For what it's worth I want to say that it's the N.A. Blackman's (African slave) Blues together with the Gaikaku with its grave intonations of an inexorable fate which holds me close to the earth. Talk about our 'aural' confabulations. Talk about the soul inherent in the heart-beat (the errant pulse) of a language. One day I want to tell you how music forms a linguistic bridge across the endless chasm of speech. One of these days I'll come by to play my dulcimer.

Everytime I look up at all of you I am astonished by how the very words we go on uttering all the days of our lives, together with all the different modes of silences we gather, like a harbinger, around ourselves, leave their myriad tracings upon your divers faces. I would go so far as to suggest that they have to all intents and purposes become an indivisible part of your very postures. I've been talking of how my mother gave me my first language, a language I began to acquire even as I suckled on her breast and what a motley mode of speaking it's all become in time. Need I say that she couldn't save me from that fate. But I have seen a look on her face that told me she understood (wordlessly . . .) the ardour of all such displacement. Thus it is that I always speak Japanese when I go home to visit her. More than that I can, for the time being, become almost Japanese. I realize that it's one of the deepest 'ties' I have in my whole life.

Here I want to say a few words about my father. He took pride in the fact that he had been able to shape a mask for the Asian in himself to speak thru by learning to read, write, and speak a no-nonsense English. He who kept a keen eye on the prairie politics of William Aberhart and the evangelical Social Credit party and spent the spare time he had left over from working his arse off in a garment factory reading. He who tended the flowers in my childhood gardens and prided himself in the fact that he never wore eye glasses thru-out his long life. Lately I've come to realize that I don't really know much about him or how he felt about the shape of his life. It was mostly an unspoken sense of the familial that tied us together. We spoke, when we had the occasion to, in cadences of silence, augmented by simple English or Japanese. I would remind you that the city of Vancouver wasn't much more than a forest clearing when he landed here in '04. Like the typical Asian immigrant of his day he had heard tall tales of a N.A. which was not much more than a mythical wilderness surmounted by a tall gold mountain and a handful of Indians, etc. You all know that hoary story. It's a part of our legacy as erstwhile North Americanos. Anyhow, I must have learned the efficaciousness of silences from him as he was, for the most part, a quiet, unsurly sort of man.

Now it's taken me all these years to understand the gravity of his silences and to abide the depth of my own and where it might take me. Let me add here that, where I'm coming from, silences are the measure of all that remains unconditioned in our lives. My father died of old age in his eighties. For what it's worth I want to say that we took a trip thru Honshu's Backcountry together in 1969. That brief memorable trip was the first and last time we travelled together since my youth. And I've spent a decade trying to see its shape. Write his/our silences. Like everything I've shaped in my life, it isn't what I intended, it isn't quite good enough. Such as it is, it's a homage to him who planted the tree-of-silences inside of me. Such as it is, it's the hard-won language of familial testament.

It's become a 'best seller' these days to say that everybody under the sun has roots, a trunk, and branches. That, therefore, everybody is rooted in the particulars of their own etymology. Preferences, hence all of our so-called references, tend, in the English I've learned, to take these things for granted. For instance, racism, as everybody can and does know it, has something to do with cultural dispositions and, despite all the rhetoric, it has its roots in the language of our fears and is, to all intents and purposes, wholly irrational. Hence our own vulnerableness in the face of it. Nonetheless, I am on the side of those who hold to the minority view that we have to attend to our own pulse and extend our own tenacities. Like they say, 'God helps those who help themselves.' It's right here that 'art' (in any tongue) can and does get into the act: like how do we cause the leaves on the topmost branches of the old family tree to burst into flower, sez it. Sounding all the old homilies (again), I want to insist that everybody is a bona fide member and an activist (each in their own way) in the ongoing histrionics of a given culture. Everybody's 'bearing' is, in that sense, equal and we N.A. Asians ought to act forthrightly on our own behalf. We shall have to remain vigilant if we are to insert ourselves in to the W.A.S.P. scheme of things, albeit their histories.

Thank you.

Nov. 21st '75 AD

Austin Clarke *b.* 1934

ST JAMES, BARBADOS

'This year I became eligible for Canadian citizenship,' said Clarke in 1963, 'but I do not intend to apply for it. Not because I undervalue this status which is so highly prized by so many immigrants from all over the world; rather, because I *do* value its privileges highly, but realize that I would be accepting in theory a status that Canada does not intend to give me in practice—because I am a black man.' Seventeen years later, and by then a Canadian citizen, Clarke won a nomination as a Progressive Conservative candidate for the provincial elections in Ontario. He was not elected, but his candidacy, together with the other political and cultural positions he later held, including Vice-Chairman of the Ontario Film Review Board (1983–5), suggests that, despite the fact that the 'system' still 'assault[s]' him, Clarke has found it possible to negotiate racial politics and art. As he says, 'There was a time when I revelled in the characterization of a black writer. . . . Now I am simply a writer and if someone knows me he knows I am black. I am not writing things simply of interest to blacks.' Not unlike some of the fictional characters in his first collection of short stories, *When He was Free and Young and He Used to Wear Silks* (1971), Clarke views the marginalized position of blacks in Canada as reflecting not only the bitter legacy of colonialism and the pervasiveness of racism, but also the inner and outer corruption and exploitation of communities forced to live under literal or psychological segregating conditions. His novel *The Prime Minister* (1977) and his memoir, *Growing Up Stupid under the Union Jack* (1980), a winner of the Cuban prize Casa de las Americas, directly address these issues.

Born in St James, Barbados, Clarke did not begin to write until after he arrived in Canada in 1955. A high school teacher on leave, he attended Trinity College, University of Toronto, where he studied Economics and Political Science. Instead of completing his degree, he began writing. After a number of odd jobs, Clarke worked as a freelance reporter and broadcaster for the CBC, for which he produced documentaries and literary programs that dealt, as Clarke writes, 'with the social and cultural problems of black people in the United States, Britain, Canada and the West Indies'. Following the success of his first novels, *The Survivors of the Crossing* (1964) and *Amongst Thistles and Thorns* (1965), he taught at various universities in the United States, including Yale, Brandeis, and Duke. He returned to Toronto in 1977, after serving as Adviser to the Prime Minister of Barbados (1973–6), as Cultural Attaché with the Embassy of Barbados in Washington, DC (1974–5), and as General Manager of the Caribbean Broadcasting Corporation (Barbados, 1975–6). The three novels *The Meeting Point* (1967), *Storm of Fortune* (1971), and *The Bigger Light* (1975), a trilogy about Toronto, established Clarke's reputation as the most prominent black writer in Canada. While serving on the Immigration and Refugee Board of Canada (1988–93), he wrote short fiction, gathered in the volumes *When Women Rule* (1985), *Nine Men Who Laughed* (1986), *In this City* (1992), and *There Are No Elders* (1993). Although most of these stories are set in Toronto, Clarke remains preoccupied with his place of birth and with the 'psycho-racial implications' of immigration and exile. Marked by different inflections of English—the colonial English of his schooling years, the Bajan dialect, Afro-American speech patterns, and colloquial Canadian English—his writing explores the vicissitudes of immigrant life as well as the legacy of colonialism and slavery. While the novels *The Origin of Waves* (1997), which was the first winner of the Rogers Communications Writers' Trust Fiction Prize, and *The Question* (1999), nominated for the Governor General's Award and winner of the W.O. Mitchell Prize, deal with the foibles and aspirations of educated characters living in Toronto, *The Polished Hoe* (2002) is set mostly in Birmshire (Barbados). The winner of the Giller, Trillium, and Commonwealth Writers' Prizes, it is a tour-de-force, a narrative (circa 1940s) in the voice of Mary-Mathilda, a daughter of slaves, who tries, through her storytelling-cum-confession, to appease the demons of her past that haunt her. 'I wanted to be able to do for Barbados what Chamoiseau did for Martinique and, one could say, what James Joyce did for Ireland,' said Clarke about *The Polished Hoe*, a novel that taught him 'how to write a novel for the first time'. Clarke, who has also written the memoirs *A Passage Back Home* (1994), about his friend- ship with Trinidadian writer Sam Selvon, and *Pigtails n' Breadfruit. The Rituals of Slave Food: A Barbadian Memoir* (2002), reissued as *Love and Sweet Food: A Culinary Memoir* (2004), an excerpt from which follows, holds Canada 'responsible for [his] ability to be patient, to be reflective, to be forgiving, and to be impul- sive. . . . Toronto has provided a means, with less frustration and exertion of energy and anxi- ety, than could have been the case had I returned to Barbados, . . . to do my writing.'

When He Was Free and Young and He Used To Wear Silks

In the lavishness of the soft lights, indications of detouring life that took out of his mind the concentration of things left to do still, as a man, before he could be an artist, lights that put into his mind instead a certain crawling intention which the fingers of his brain stretched towards one always single table embraced by a man and a wife who looked like his woman, her loyalty bending over the number of beers he poured against the side of her bottle he had forgotten to count, in those struggling days when the atmosphere was soft and silk and just as treacherous, in those days in the Pilot Tavern the spring and the summer and the fall were mixed into one chattering ambition of wanting to have meaning, a better object of meaning and of craving, better meaning than a beer bought on the credit of friendships and love by the tense young oppressed men and women who said they were oppressed and tense because they were artists and not because they were incapable, or burdened by the harsh sociology of no talent, seg- regated around smooth black square tables from the rest of the walking men and walk- ing women outside the light of our Pilot of the Snows; and had not opened nor shut their minds to the meaning of their other lives; legs of artless girls touching this man's in a hide-and-seek under the colourblind tables burdened by conversation and aspira- tions and promises of cheques and hopes and bedding and beer and bottles; in those days when he first saw her, and the only conversation she could invent was 'haii!' because she was put on a pedestal by husbandry, and would beg his pardon without disclosing her eyes of red and shots and blots and blood-shot liquor; the success of his mind and the woman's mind in his legs burnt like the parts of the chicken he ate, he was free and young and he was wearing the silks of indecision and near-failure. But he mustn't forget the curry: for the curry was invented by people and Blessings, Indians; or perhaps they were the intractable Chinese, the curry was the saviour of his mind and indigestion just as the woman guarded for no reason in the safe soft velvet of her unbe- lieving husband's love, guarding her in her turns as they sat opposite each other in the different callings of paint and metals and skin and negatives and thirst during all those dark days in the Pilot, the curry was the saviour of a madness which erupted in his mouth with the after-taste of the bought beer and the swirling bowels after the beer and after the curry; she was like the lavishness in the light except that the colour surrounding her in the darkened room hid everything, every thought in his mind just as the wholesome curry in the parts of chicken hid the unwholesome social class which it could not always distinguish from the bones any suitable dog in shaggy-haired and shaggy-sexed Rosedale would eat, and if the dog in Rosedale and the dog in him did eat them, the dog might make them, like this woman sitting with her drinking man, into an exotic meal packaged through some sense of beer and the sense of time and place, and looking at it in one imaginative sense, turn it into something called *soul food*: now, there are many commercial and irrelevant soul food kitchens these days in night-time Toronto, and any man could, if he had no soul and silks on the body of his thoughts, if his soul were occupied and imprisoned only with thoughts of *her* sitting there badly in the wrong light of skin, he could make a fortune of thoughts and sell them like dog meat and badly licensed food to all the becauseful people who wore jeans and heavy-weave expensive sweaters walking time into eternity in dirty clothes and rags because they were the 'beautiful people' as someone called their ugliness, like *her* of soon-time piloted to a tavern, married to a man who did not deserve the understanding of her; these the becauseful people, people who didn't have to do this because they didn't want to think about that, because they were people living in the brighter light of the soft darkness which they all liked because they were artists and people; the becauseful people like her, liked her and likened her to a white horse not because of the length of her legs nor the grey in her mind, but because in the lavishness of the wholesome light of the Pilot she looked as secure and was silent as the fingers of the tumbling *avoirdupois* of the man who made mud-pies in the piles of quarters and dollars mixmasterminding them in the cash register. It is so dark sometimes in the Pilot that if you wear dark glasses, which all the artists wore on their minds, you may stumble up the single step beside the fat man sitting on a humptydumpling stool and where she always sat on her pedestal of distance and protection chastised in pickled beer, and you may not know whether it is afternoon on Yonge Street outside, for time now has no boundaries, only the dimensions of her breasts which her husband keeps in the palm of his flickering eyeballs; it is so dark in the early afternoon that with your dark glasses on, you might be in Boston walking the climb in the street climbing like a hill to where the black and coloured people live; or you might be here in Toronto walking where the coloured people and the kneegrows say they 'live' but where they squat, here where E.P. Taylor says he does not live but where his influence strangles some resident life and breeds racehorses of the people, where Garfield Weston lives in a mad biscuit box crumbling in broken crackers; in the lavishness of the night thrown from your dark glasses, you might stumble upon a pair of legs and not know the colour of time, or what shape it is, or where you are, or who you are: he thinks he should haul his arse out of this bar of madness and mad dreams, drinking himself into an erection stiff to the touch of ghosts in her legs and the legs of the tables. He had seen her, 'this young tall thing', walking to the bar through winter in boots and rain in blue jeans and sandals, insisting without words in the fierce determination of her poverty and dedication to nothing she could prove or do that this was her personal calvary to the cross of being Canada's best poetic-photographer, unknown in the meaning of her life beyond the tavern, unknown like the word she would use, 'budgerigar', having years ago thrown out Layton, Cohen, Birney and Purdy in the dishwater of her weatherbeaten brow-beaten body and heavy sweaters; he could see her mostly among women stuck to their chairs by the chewing-gum beer, free women freed by their men for an afternoon while art imprisoned the men with beer, wallpaper along the talking walls like flowers, their own flower long faded into the dust of the artificial potato chips they all ate in the nitty of their gloom because it was like grit for their reality, their 'dinner' an unknown real-ity like her word, 'budgerigar', in the despised bourgeois vocabulary and apartment-lairs of their lives; and in this garden of grass growing in their beds he had hand-picked her out five years ago, this one wallflowering woman who wore large hats in the sum-merstreet, and cream sweaters in winter. She always sat beside the man who sat as if he was her husband; tall in her thighs with the walk of a man, this white horse woman with the body of a bull; and the eye of her disposition through the bottom of the beer bottle warned him that 'the gentlest touch of his desire might be fatal to the harmony' of the two ordered beers which they drank like Siamese twins in the double-bed of their marriage. He, the watchman-man, was harnessed by island upbringing and fear in the lavishness of the dim light, ravishing her ravishing beauty with his eyes they could not see, eyes they saw only once and spoke to once when they saw him entering or leaving; for five years. For five years of not knowing whether the sun would sink in the space between her breasts, or whether butter ever dried in the warmth of that melt-ing space, he watched her like a timekeeper. Once he saw her leaving her husband's side and he followed her spinster's canter all the way in his mind down the railing guard of parallel eyes honouring her backside sitting on the spinning stools where the working class reigned and into the bathroom, past two wash basins and the machine that saved pregnancies and populations with a quarter, on to the toilet bowl, under the dress she had plucked her hand and had pulled up her dress and did not soil her seat or sit on it because it was in the Pilot, and he smiled when she reappeared with fresh garlic on her lipstick mouth; and he looked at the edges of her powder, and he looked into the lascivious dimness and saw her and smiled and she smiled but the smile belonged to the mudpiling man at the cash register or to another table where they were talking about the Isaacs Gallery and the Artists Jazz Bann where Dennis Burton's garter belts were exhibited in stiff canvas and wore houndstooth suits and the thick heavy honey of colours and materials thicker than words. He had walked around her life in circles and bottle rings of desire and of lust and she was always there, the centre of dreams frizzled on a pillow soaked with the tears of drinking; he followed her like a detective in the wishes of his dreams, and from his inspection of a future together got a headache over them and over her, and over the meanings of these dreams. *Mickey* and *Cosmospilitane* and other dream books did not ease the riders of the head in his pain, and nothing could unhinge his desperation from the wishful slumber of those uncon-scious nights of double broken vision. And then, like a cherry falling under the tree because the sun had failed it, after long thoughts and wishes of waiting she fell into his path, and he almost crushed her. He remembered the long afternoons waiting for the indelible rings of the melting bottles to ripen, waiting for the departure of shoppers who lived above the Rosedale subway station to stop shopping in the Pickering Farms market so he could shop and not have to listen to the loud-talking friendly butcher in the fluorescent meat department, and whisper loud under the sun-tanned arms of the meaty housewives and commonlawwives, 'One pound of pigs feet, chicken necks and bones—for soup,' and hear the unfeeling bitch, 'Er-er! Who's next?' behind the counter dressed like a surgeon with blood on his chest, saying, 'You're really taking care of that dog, ain't you, sir?' Godblindyou, dog! godblindyou, butcher! this meat is for the dog in front of you; and he remembered her now, single, on this summerstreet under the large hat as she was five years ago under the drinking mural under the picture of hotdogs and fried eggs that some heartless hungry painter drew on the wall where she sat beneath when she was in the Pilot. He fell into the arms of her greeting like an apple to the core and he looked down into her dress and saw nothing not even one small justification for the long unbitten imprisonment of his mouth and his ambition, thinking of the nutseller selling his nuts next door. She was away now from the Pilot. And he did not even know her name: not for five years, he never was introduced to her name: 'Hurley or Weeks . . . Weeks or Hurley . . .' either one would do? 'they are both mine, and I use either one any time,' but Weeks is her maiden time; although she was no longer a maiden, though single and with no husband for weeks and months now. There was no large gold ring on the finger of her personal self-regard, which she said ended mutual on a visit of her once-accompanying husband warming radically, like forgotten beer, into her haphazard lover; there was no bitterness in the eyes of her separation because she missed only the cooking which he would do every evening, when she said she was too tired, or couldn't be bothered to cook, which was every evening, when he would do the cooking in her kitchen and leave her afterwards like the dishes, panting from thirst and a thorough cleaning, so her eyes said on this summer afternoon, hungry in the frying pan of their double-bed bedroom, where he kept the materials of his stockings, feet and trade, his love of meddling with medals and metals and sculpture, and where she kept a large overgrown blow-up of her brother's success in the cowboys and movies in the West, shooting the horses over the head of the never-setting bedpost, her brother with a gun in his hand, a gun loaded at the ready to be fired at the nearest rivalry of badmen and bad women, a gun which he gave her, a gun which remained nevertheless loaded, hung-up, cocked and frustrated and constipated from no practice or trigger-happiness; and this she talked about; she did not stay in one place, she said she was rambling, not along the streets because she did not like to walk, but that she was rambling and that she had to be alone in the constitutional of her thoughts, from one bar to the next bar; she admitted she might have a problem, but it was not this problem which changed her husband's heart into a dying lover drifting apart at the semen in the widening sea of her jammed ambition: 'I do not know what I want to do, I know what I don't want to do, and that is stay married, but I don't really know what I really want to do'; she bore her wandering in her hair, loose and landing on her broad shoulders like the rumps of two cowboy horses; and her dress was short, short enough for the eyes to roam about in and follow her over all her landscape at a canter—that's how she was put away; she was put away as if she could be put to pasture for work and for love and for bearing responsibility: 'I know I don't want to have a child. What am I going to *do* with a child? I know I can have children and I know I can have a child. I want a child, but not now, because a child *needs* love . . . and and and I I I haven't any left right now for . . .' He looked at her and wandered and wondered why she couldn't give a child a chance, a chance of love, with all the pasture in her body, all her body, with all her breasts, with all her milk bottled in brassieres that had no bones stitched in them, with all her thighs that spilled over her dress-hem, 'A-hem!', but perhaps she was really talking about another kind of love and another need for love, which was not the same as the need for love her lover-husband needed from her when she was a child in his arms late at night, and was crying with him in the doubleminded cradle of his sculptures. *Haii! Austin!* He looked into her eyes and made a wish that her body under his eye would not be completely bloodless as her hands sometimes seemed five years ago when she was fresh from the basement washroom, and the Snow on the women walking out of the cold corner of Yonge and Bloor in the arctic months; that her body would not reveal the theft he had in mind to put it through, the theft her husband had put it through; that she would not be like Desdemona and wax, but that she would be a queen from the entrails of Africa and Nefertiti, plucked out in olive blackness luscious to the core of her imagined seed, like the Marian from the alligator troughs of Georgia. He dreamed a long dream standing there on the street with summer before her, and he killed the colour of her body because it needed too much *Eno* before it could go down; and he wrapped her in a coffin stained in wood in blood, and made her again to look like Marian from way across the bad lands of enroped and ruptured Georgia. *Haii, Austin!*: he was back in those good old days, good because they had no responsibility for paying the good deeds artists incurred in debts and made them bad, bad debts and artists on the segregation of walls and memories, he was here and he was there in Georgia in the double ghost of a second, for artists were bad for debts and for business in those young days when he was free and the only silk was his ambition; he remembered her in those days, and on this summer afternoon already obliterated in the history of the past, nights in the crowded Pilot Tavern, searching the faces of the girls and women for one face that would have had a meaning like Marian's, and he could not find one head with truth written in its clenched curled black-peppers of hair, one mask with the intelligent face of Nefertiti the history of Africa from Africa, not from the store on Yonge Street, 'Africa Modern' selling blackness cheap to whites, written brazenly upon its ivory; a mask, a mask from that land not unlike Georgia, he had watched for one face like a timekeeper keeping a watch that had no end of time in it, and he had to paint the faces black, blacken them as he had blackened the red clay sculpture a woman did of him once, like an Indian in his blood, and had made it something approaching the man he wanted to be, something like the man Amiri Baraka talked about becoming in the later years of his new Muslim wisdom; he remembered the sweet-smelling Georgia woman in those soft nights when the bulbs were silk as moths among the books overhead like a heavy chastisement to be intelligent, like a too-self-conscious intention; with the sherry which she drank in proper southern quantities, like bourbon warm to the blood, and her fingers were long and pointed and expressive, impressing upon his back, once, her once beautiful intent, as they writhed in pain with glory and some victory, after she lay like a submarine in a watery pyre of soft soapy suds, white flowers of *Calgon* upon her black vegetation, going and coming, he remembered her in the shiny cheap stockings proclaiming her true colour of mind and pocket and spirit and background and intention: *a black student*; a black woman, black and shining in that velvet of time and black skin, a black woman, black and powerful down to her black marrow; there was something in the ring of her laughter, perhaps in the gurgle of her bourbon, in the *ding-ing* of her voice when she laughed in two accents, northern and southern, something that said she was true-and-through beautiful, and because she was black, and because she was beautiful, she was beautiful; she could withstand any ravages of history, of storms, of stories that wailed in the rope-knotted night of Georgia; she could stand on a pedestal under any tree which no village smithy in white Georgia would dare to stand up to: a man who had no burning conviction could not put his arms as high as her waist, for she had seen certain sheets of a whiteness which were wrapped around a black man's testicles in a bestial passion-play, and she had seen, in her mother's memories, this play as it showed the germ of someone's bed linen made into sheets that were worn as masks of superiority testing a presumption that some men would always walk on all-fours like a southern lizard; *Haii, Austin!* this woman standing on the summerstreet in the silk of time stopped without desire; and that woman lying in the rich water with her smell whom he remembered best holding down her head in love, in some shame, looking into a book of tears because his words were spoken harder than the text of any African philosophy. He remembered that woman and not this woman, well: Marian, his; ploughing the fields of poverty and a commitment in her barefoot days, dress tangled amongst the tango of weeds, sticking in the crease of her strength silken from perspiration, and her dreams cloggy as the soil, and in her after-days in the northern rich-poor city, her longfingered hands again dipping into the soil of soiled sociology Jewished out of some context, maintained backyards, maintained yardbird poverty, backward in instruction the smell of soil the soiled smell of the land in which she was born, the smell of poverty, a new kind of perfume to freshen her northern ideas, a new kind of perfume truer than the fragrance of an underarm of ploughing, more telling than the tale in the perspiration of her body, in the fields, in the sociology, in the kitchen, in the bed, in the summer subway sweaty and safe with policemen and black slum dwellers from Dorchester, in the heat, in the bus stations, in the bathtub in Boston; a perfume of sweet sweat that clothed her body with a blessing of pearls, like a birthwrap of wet velvet skin: 'Honnn-neee!' the word she always used; honey was the only taste to use; honey was the only word she used always; for it was a turbulence of love and time from the lowered eyelids from the vomiting guts up to the tip of the touch of her skin. She was a woman; she was a woman without woe; she was to be his woman, she should be here in the summerstreet; now in the summerstreet, he watches this alter-native of that woman, he understands that the transparency of this dress, tucked above her knees by the hand of fashion, is really nothing but the vagueness of this doll; he sees now that this transparency is the woman, like the negatives she meddled in, for five years' time, like the film on a pond's surface, like white powder, like a glass of water with *Eno* in it, like a glass of water in the sun, the water clear and unpolluted, the water the topsoil of the sediments at the sentimental bottom; he wanted to mix this water with that water in the bathtub in Boston, the water and the mud into some heart, into that thick between-the-toes soul of the

Georgia woman; he wanted to break the glass that contained that water for the *Calgon* bath and the sherry and the bathwater; break the vessel, spill and despoil, spill and expel this wateringdown of the drink of his long thirst; stir it up and mix the sentiments in the foundation with the upper crust of the water, shake it to the foundation of its scream and yell and turn it to the thickness of chocolate rich in the cup, thick and rich and hot and swimming with pools of fat, so he could drink, so he would have to put his hand into the black avalanche of feeling and emotion and sediment, deep and gurgling as the tenor in her laughter, down the tuningfork of her throat resounding with love and make her say a word, speak a thought, be some witness to the blood in her love. This was his Marian in the vision in the summerstreet. This was Marian. And the five-year stranger, estranged from her husband's love in a transparency, in the costume of a lover, this woman who used to sit upon the pin of his desires, now on this summerstreet where he thought he saw her, she is nothing more vivacious than a feather worn in her broad-grinned hat: not like the scarf *she* wore with conch-shells and liberty-scars and paisley marked into it with water; this negative of Marian passed like the cloud above the roof of the Park Plaza where one afternoon she sat drinking water, when he was playing he was playing golf in the new democratic diminutive green of the eighteenth floor bar; and a cloud passed overhead like the loss of lust of a now dead moment, with the woman; and when the sun was bright again, when the sun was like the sun in Georgia, fierce and full, when the sun was a purpose and passion, when the sun was as bright as the sweat it wrung from the barrels of a black woman's breasts, the laughing beautiful Marian was there, not in his mind only but larger, dispossessing the summerstreet in the buxom jeans of her hips, red accusing blouse belafonted down the ladylike tip of the gorge of sustenance between her breasts, and around her neck around her throat, a yellow handkerchief and a chain of a star and a moon in some quarter of her sensual religion. He saw her with passion and with greed, he saw her clearer than the truth-serum syrup of a dream, than the germ of love, true as the *Guinness* in the egg and the Marian was his stout, this woman. He remembered all this standing in the summerstreet: when before she climbed the steps to her hospital, she held his hands like a wife going in to die upon a cot, and drew him just a suggestion of new life closer to the relationship and her breasts, and with the sweet saliva of her lips she said in the touch of that kiss, 'Take care of yourself.' He was young and free again, to live or to travel imprisoned in a memory of freed love, chained to her body and her laughter by the spinal cord of anxious long distance, reminders said before and after, by the long engineering of a drive from Yale to Brandeis to Seaver Street to Brandeis dull in the winter Zion of brains, dull in the autumn three hours in miles hoping that the travel won't end like an underground railroad at the door of this nega-tive woman, but continue even through letters and quarrels and long miles down the short street up the long stairs in the marble of her memory, clenched in her absent embrace but rejoicing with his fingers in the velvet feeling of her silken black natural hair . . .

Rudy Wiebe *b.* 1934

FAIRHOLME, SASKATCHEWAN

'I've never really thought of writing as a way of achieving identity or national unity, or anything political. I've always felt that the only way a national literature—if such a thing exists—could develop is for everyone to write out of their own kind of experience, their own kind of imaginative world, and together you build,' said Rudy Wiebe in 1991. '[P]laces rather than regions' and the rewriting and revisioning of history have been the primary concerns of the many novels and short stories he has produced. His first two novels, *Peace Shall Destroy Many* (1962), written as his master's thesis (University of Alberta, 1960), and *First and Vital Candle* (1966) deal with the history as well as the religious and cultural beliefs of Mennonites who settled in western Canada, while *The Blue Mountains of China* (1970) traces, in the epic style that has come to characterize much of his more recent fiction, the experiences of diasporic Mennonite communities.

Wiebe was born in the Mennonite community of Speedwell-Jackpine, near Fairholme, Saskatchewan. He was the first Canadian-born child of Mennonite parents who had arrived on the prairies in 1930, having been dispossessed of their land in Russia. Until he began attending school—first in Fairholme and then in Coaldale, Alberta—he spoke only German. After he graduated from the University of Alberta with a BA in English (1956), he received a BTh degree from the Mennonite Brethren Bible College in Winnipeg and then went to Germany to study for a year at the University of Tübingen. Until his early retirement in 1990, Wiebe was a professor of Canadian literature and creative writing at the University of Alberta.

A writer who believes 'in *place*, not *race*', Wiebe has twice won a Governor General's Award for fiction, first for *The Temptations of Big Bear* (1973) and then for *A Discovery of Strangers* (1994). These novels, together with *The Scorched-wood People* (1977) and the short-fiction collections *Where Is the Voice Coming*

From? (1974) and *The Angel of the Tar Sands and Other Stories* (1982), display the imaginative control with which he sets out to question the hegemonic views of Canadian history, especially the history that deals with Canada's First Nations, Mennonite, Métis, and northern communities. Although he has often found himself involved in controversies surrounding the question of the 'appropriation of voice', Wiebe, having been brought up in a world where ' "The English" were always something very different from us,' does not share 'the imperial concept of history as it expressed itself in Canada': 'that imperial world, which is part of the expression of Canadian suppression of Native Indians and taking over their land, to me is just as strange and just as repulsive now as it is to a Native Indian.' His non-fiction book *Playing Dead: A Contemplation Concerning the Arctic* (1989) reflects his fascination with the North, specifically with Franklin's 1820 expedition and its impact on the Aboriginal people of the region, the history he fictionalized in *A Discovery for Strangers. Stolen Life: The Journey of a Cree Woman* (1998), which he co-authored with the great-great granddaughter of Big Bear, Yvonne Johnson, records her life of abuse and poverty, and her sentencing to life imprisonment for the death of a man accused of child abuse.

Wiebe's other novels include *The Mad Trapper* (1980) and *My Lovely Enemy* (1983), and *Sweeter Than All the World* (2002), an epic retelling of the Mennonites' expulsion from sixteenth-century Netherlands, their persecution in Russia, and their search for a new home in Paraguay and Canada. His fiction has been translated into nine languages, including French, Spanish, German, and Japanese. Whether they are set on the prairies or in the arctic territories, Wiebe's narratives demonstrate his belief that '[t]he here-and-now alone cannot give us the strength which a knowledge of our antecedents would provide: we can only be non-entities without the confidence our ancestral dead can give us.' His collection of essays *River of Stone: Fictions and Memories* (1995) and his memoir *Of This Earth* (2006) offer a powerful picture of the personal, spiritual, and intellectual contexts that inform his writing. Wiebe, who received an honorary degree from Wilfrid Laurier University (1991), is an Officer of the Order of Canada (2001).

A Night in Fort Pitt or (if you prefer) The Only Perfect Communists in the World

Late one November evening in the thirty-third year of the reign of Queen Victoria, a solitary horseman might have been seen riding along the hills that parallel the North Saskatchewan River. He had been riding west since before daybreak, but now long after sunset the giant sweep of the frozen river suddenly confronted him, forcing him south, or as near south as he could surmise from the stars that glittered occasionally, momentarily, between storm clouds. And the wind which had been threatening snow all day now roared, it seemed, with a malignant fury up the cliff down whose steep slope he could not risk his exhausted horse, though he knew that he must somewhere, somehow get across the valley if he was to find shelter at Fort Pitt, the only white settlement along three hundred miles of river between Fort Carlton and Victoria House.

The night before the rider and his small party had endured among bare poplars in the fold of a creek; when they emerged that morning onto the prairie before dawn to continue their journey, they discovered the entire sky brilliant with aurora, torn sheets of light gently glowing and leaping into blaze above them and smouldering away again. The man had stopped his horse, watched, stunned; felt himself shrink as it were into and then grow incandescent in that immense dome of brilliance until sunrise burned it into sheer light, and he became aware that his Indian guide and Métis companion had vanished into the apparently flat earth; leaving nothing but the line of their passing in the hoary grass. The quick winter afternoon was already darkening before he caught up with them in their relentless track. The radiance of aurora still informed him and he told them they had veered too far south; sunset perhaps verified his perception, for after the long day's ride they still had not encountered the river. He refused to accept another night in the open and swung onto this weary mount. His men had already unburdened theirs, preparing to weather the storm they insisted was driving up from the west in brushy hollow. So they watched him ride west alone, the prairie so open he could inevitably be found if lost, as impatient and as superior with all necessary knowledge as every white man they had ever met, riding into darkness following stars.

And now in stinging snow the stars were lost, though it did not matter since he had found the North Saskatchewan River. Well, it did matter, because he knew that every Hudson Bay settlement was on the north bank; he must cross over the river or he would miss Pitt, he could ride as far as he had already ridden in a month, another five hundred miles across prairie into the glacial mountains themselves and not encounter a white man. As if at the thought, his horse stopped. No urging could move it so he slid off, straightening his long legs against the ground with a groan. The horse turned its long, squarish head to him, nudged him, breaking the icicles off its nostrils against his buffalo coat and then finding the warmth of his armpit. Perhaps this hammer-headed bay from Fort Carlton could become as good a companion to him as Blackie had been—the storm shifted an instant and he realized they were on a point of cliff. Perhaps a tributary cut its way into the river here as steeply as the main river. Where was he? Even if he got down into the valley, if Fort Pitt was built half a mile back from the river in a bend like Fort Carlton, he would never find it. He sheltered his crusted eyes against the whistling snow that enclosed him: the air seemed as solid as any frozen prairie. He would walk on it easily as dreaming out into the sky. . . .

The cheekstrap of the bridle hit his frozen face when the horse moved. He felt that, his arm slid onto its neck.

> He knew he could not lose this one certain warm body also, his mittens clamped onto its stiff mane and so suddenly he was led forward and down, sideways and down, the incline almost vertical and shifting like relentless sand, but that one body was solidly with his, there, whenever they slipped they slid closer together, their six feet all one and always somehow set certainly into the side of what incline of what might be rock or frozen clay, deadly as ice, but so reliable, so trustworthy he would never let go of this horse, never leap aside even if river ice parted into water as it had when he leaped from Blackie sinking, scrambled to safety while seeing his horse sink into blackness and there was its beautiful head bursting up, its front legs, neck arched, and knees clawing ice with its deadly shod feet, trying to climb up into the bright air by sheer terror, nostrils flaring bloody and the ice smashing now again and again in ringing iron, and he turned away, sprinted for his rifle—he was an English soldier, soldiers can always offer the ultimate mercy of running for their bloody rifles—and he knelt there expert sharpshooter on the white, deceptive ice until the shots hammered back at him tripled from the cliffs and the long water ran flat again and implacably empty; on his knees, crying.

But his hammerhead bay led him so easily down . . . down five hundred feet or a thousand—instinctively he was counting steps, an officer must always carry some facts, even if they are estimated—and they scrambled out between broken boulders (or were they frozen buffalo?) and there was river ice again, certainly, hard as the cliff here and he was still clutching the horse. But with his arms and legs now, completely, and it moved with his frozen face in its mane, he could smell prairie slough hay, hear scrub oaks at Fort Garry scarlet as cardinals in October light, the chant of *Te Deum* prayed by monks in a roofless Irish ruin, and he became aware that the sting of snow had quietened: there was an upthrust, darkness moving beside him, a dense blackness and he loosened one hand, reached out: it was most certainly the usual twenty-foot spruce palisade. Never anything in stone like the permanent ruins of Ireland. And a gate in the wooden wall; hanging open. Perhaps the Indians here were all dead, the gates hanging so open.

The bay followed him through that hanging gate like any dog and the storm was so abruptly quiet he felt himself breathing. High peaked roofs, gabled, around a square, he could not distinguish a light or a sound. Perhaps smallpox had discovered them all, Indian and Métis and white alike, as in Fort Carlton. Winter would keep the bodies perfectly, death already blossomed over them like spring flowers. He limped across the open square to avoid what lay at the edge of every shadow, what might move, dreadfully: a door, darkness in the centre building. He seemed to have reached the heart of something, corpses were keening all around him, at the very hoared edges of his fur cap and he wheeled around, listening. But there was only his own small breathing, nothing but the horse snoring, bent low like grass behind him. So he turned back to the door and began to pound on it. Nothing. The plank door would not budge to his fists, its cracks blacker than its wood, and he tilted forward, hands, face clutching the frame, they were all dead, O open up, *o miserere mei* . . . he heard a sound. Inside. Against his face an opening, of light, the skin of a face, a young woman's face. Impossibly beautiful.

Such materializations are possible out of the driving blackness of a prairie blizzard, lantern-light and such sudden woman's beauty as perfect as it is unbelievable? He found himself bending forward slowly, past the worn planks of the doorframe, tilting slowly into her light, his frozen cheek, his still tactile tongue . . . and felt . . . nothing. Those eyes, the black brows and exquisite nose, was it white, that skin in the golden light? Was it believable though impossible?

It is possible that when Lieutenant General, the Right Honourable Sir William Francis Butler, Knight Grand Cross of the Order of the Bath and member of the Privy Council of Ireland died in his bed in Bansha Castle, County Tipperary, on June 7, 1910, died as his daughter then wrote, 'of a recent affection of the heart . . . that was brought to a crisis by a chill', it is possible that on his deathbed thirty-nine and a half years later Sir William could still not decide: was that face he instantly loved at Fort Pitt on the North Saskatchewan River in the North-Western Territories of Canada on November 18, 1870, loved as only the truest Victorian male who believed all his life that Jesus Christ and Napoleon Bonaparte were the greatest men in all of human history could love, a latter day romantic when romanticism was still acceptable in a male if he was also practical and above all heroic, dear god, was a man who championed the innocent and detested the brutalities of war all his life while becoming one of Victoria's most honoured and decorated soldiers, a member of Field Marshal Wolseley's brilliant Officers' Ring that fought for the Empire on four continents, and who dreamed for forty years of 'the Great Lone Land' as he called the Canadian prairie and never saw again and idealized every Indian person he lived near for those few months in 1870 and 1871 when they were either dying of smallpox or more or less starving despite their unselfish greedless tradition of sharing everything, which makes Indians, as he wrote then, 'the only perfect communists in the world, who, if they would only be as the Africans or the Asiatics it would be all right for them; if they would be our slaves they might live, but as they won't be that, won't toil and delve and hew for us, and will persist in hunting, fishing, roaming over the beautiful prairie land which the Great Spirit gave them: in a word, since they will be free—we will kill them'; this Butler who on the same journey contemplated the parklands of the Saskatchewan, observed their remarkable similarity to the English downs and found it 'mortifying to an Englishman' that they were, as he so concisely put it, 'totally undeveloped': this Butler was forced over an unseeable landscape by a November blizzard to be confronted by a woman's face, her thick black braids hanging to her hips; wearing a loose nightgown.

The nightgown was probably not thin. More likely it was heavy flannel since any Hudson Bay fort at the time (they were really nothing of forts but rather clusters of log buildings surrounded by log palisades, all of which could and did, as easily by accident as by design, burn to the ground) was badly heated by cavernous open hearth fireplaces, doubtless she wore that heavy flannel of solid red or delicate floral design which the Company traded with the Cree and which those people suspended as gift offerings to the Thunderbird on the Centre Tree of their thirst dance lodges in June. And here it would hang as gracefully, draping between braids, shoulders and arms and nipples and hips a slender revelation. And the very handsome, six-foot-two and always brave and presently very hoarfrosted Lieutenant Butler, late of her Majesty's 69th Regiment in India and the Fenian Raids in Quebec across the Canadian border from New York, and most recently renowned as Intelligence Officer of the Colonel Wolseley Red River Expedition against the Métis founder of Manitoba, Louis Riel: frozen or not, Butler must fall instantly in love.

As he stood there, erect and frozen, clamped to the handsawn plank of the doorframe, his faithful pony having discharged its final faithful duty of carrying him to safety and about to collapse in faithful exhaustion behind him, did Lieutenant Butler say, 'Madam, I very nearly gave up hope of ever reaching succour'?

And did she reply as stiffly, 'O sir, our rude abode is but little better than the storm, nevertheless . . .'?

And he, accepting her hesitation: 'Madam, if I may be so importunate . . .'?

And she, accepting his: 'O sir, of course, do come in sir, come in out of the storm'?

And did she turn to send the dark servant woman standing behind her scurrying to the kitchen to revive the fire that was no more than embers in the hearth?

Perhaps that was how Fort Pitt, named after the great Prime Minister but doomed never to be as famous as Pittsburgh, named after his father the Great Commoner, perhaps that was how Fort Pitt offered itself to him. Or did she exclaim out of the lamplight, 'O la sir, what a storm brings you here!' and he, bursting into laughter, reply, 'What you see is mere weather, my fine wench. There will yet be greater storms than this!' Staring so closely down into the luminous whiteness of breasts her nightgown made but small attempt to contain.

Her father, Hudson Bay Factor John Sinclair, had only a brutal litany of disease and starvation and death to offer him at Fort Pitt. He always kept the palisade gate locked—some damn Indian had tore it loose—every building locked, they were under siege and if thirty-two of sixty people at Fort Carlton were dead, including the factor, and half the McDougall missionary family at Victoria dead too, then Pitt had been saved because he wouldn't let one goddamn Indian into the place, trade or no trade, locked them all out, and he had been damn quick in summer when he first heard the smallpox spreading and he got some blood out of a Saulteaux Indian vaccinated at the mission in Prince Albert and used that to vaccinate everybody—well, damn near everybody—in Pitt and he had kept every Cree locked out, every bloody one of them:

Butler could barely restrain himself. Use them, use them any way you can, use their very blood . . . but he sat at the kitchen table devouring (with perfect Army manners, of course) the mound of buffalo steak and potatoes Mary (now properly dressed, of course) served him before the pine fire blazing on the hearth—where was the mother, the inevitable Indian, at best Métis, mother? The free traders, muttered Sinclair into his rum, had destroyed the hide and fur trade anyway, what did they care about Indians, just soak the buggers in whiskey, steal all they could from them today and to hell with tomorrow, so now even at Pitt, the very heart of buffalo country, the beasts were gone, not enough robes this summer to make three decent bundles and he'd have nothing at all to eat except potatoes if Big Bear, that ugly little bastard that never got sick, hadn't dragged in ten to trade and he'd risked taking them even though half of Big Bear's band was spitting blood, they caught it fighting the Peigans near the border who got it from the American Bloods, hell, they said it was the U.S. Army deliberately infecting the Indians down there to wipe them off the face of the earth because it was costing them damn near a million dollars each to shoot them! The smallpox was sure cheaper, about as cheap as wolfers throwing strychnine all over the prairie, and about as effective. There'd soon be nothing but corpses stinking up the whole goddamn stinking North-West.

Butler looked at him carefully: Sinclair was typical enough, a poor Scot forced to spend his whole life remembering home from the other side of the world, living who knows how in what overwhelming monotony of daily life and endless, endless miserable seasons repeating themselves, too old now for even the occasional Indian woman to rouse him, and suddenly a government official appears out of the night at whom he could momentarily blurt whatever he wanted, an official not on the summer boats but riding an assignment in the dead of a deadly boring winter on orders from the Lieutenant Governor of the Territories—there was one at long last—someone who had been within breathing distance of all those invisible Hudson Bay lords in London barely seven months before, who had often smelled the 'goddamn heather' and seen the Queen herself who had finally survived her grief for Albert and was now the emerging mother of a world empire: what poor lonely sot of a homesick Scot wouldn't seize such an opportunity to snore every pessimistic worry he had aloud into his grog?

To be starving in Pitt, Sinclair suddenly roared, is like freezing to death in Newcastle! This is buffalo country, one herd moved over these hills for seventeen days and nights in '62, over two million, there was no end of them summer or winter and he'd fed every fort from Rocky Mountain House to Vermilion and the Pas, every goddamn fur dragged out of this country and every bloody ounce of stuff dragged back into it in every bloody York boat—every fuckin' trader had Pitt pemmican in his gut and now Big Bear brings in ten jesus carcasses and he has to burn the hides and boil the fuckin' jesus christ out of the meat! But at least that old bugger knew what he was doing, telling his people to leave the fort and scatter in the bush and maybe the winter would be cold enough to kill the white man's disease, though what they would live on, even their dogs and miserable horses so far gone . . . .

Butler saw Mary Sinclair turn like a flame in front of the fire. After a month of half-fried bannock and pemmican—which had all the taste of boiled shoeleather—her baked potatoes were beyond any remembered cream and butter, dear god their very aroma—and she facing solitary winter darkness, a lifetime of that incredible skin drying up in cold and mosquito-and-blackfly heat, such a shape hammered slack by year after year pregnancies. At her bend by the hearth for another rack of buffalo rib he felt his body thaw and stretch completely, his powerful legs, toes flaring so fluidly, a kind of tensile vividness she awoke in his hands hard from cold and clenched reins all day, a touch of, somehow, flesh and resistance needed; despite heavy cotton the length of her leg, her curved thigh, her quick smile past her shoulder, her extraordinary face even when seen sideways or upside-down. Her father snored, fat arms flat on the table: every night such a lullaby and every night lying somewhere innocent, somewhere in this clumsy building, every night she was here naked against cotton and he rolled in his deerskin sack on the frozen prairie, sweetest jesus why is there no comfort in the world ever *together?*

The Métis servant came sluffing down the stairs. The bed for the gentleman was warming with hot stones between buffalo robes, would he go up? It was Mary who spoke, Mary who led him up the narrow stairs through her own shadow to the door, opening it without so much as a glance: she gave him the lantern and was gone, not a gesture of her lithe body even at his stumbled goodnight, and thank you again . . . the hall was empty before he grasped her going. Wind moaned in crevices. Well, doubtless to help the Métis woman hoist her father back into bed again. He stripped quickly, blew out the light. The stones were too hot, the robes total ice; he felt his body slowly shrinking into a huddle. Be I as chaste as ice, as pure as snow, I shall not . . . he sensed a footstep and sat up: she was there, he knew. But it was several seconds before the rustle she made told him she was lifting the heavy cotton nightgown over her head.

Could he say anything when she came in beside him, he the Irishman of endless easy words, when she laughed aloud so gently at all his sweaty underwear? And she peeled it off him, chuckling again at the memory of his goodnight, did he think Pitt was a hotel and she a chambermaid? Hot stones in bed were no better than campfires: you were always roasted on one side and freezing on the other. He may have had a small hesitation.

The bed . . . is too narrow.

Wide enough for one is wide enough for two.

And her skin fit completely around him, her head warm as opening lips in the hollow of his neck. If despite twelve years of Her Majesty's army his body still did not know what to do, she doubtless helped him to that too; and perhaps his own skin and various tongues in that black room taught him something of her invisible shape.

Perhaps this happened to William Francis Butler in Fort Pitt in the North-Western Territories of Canada on the night of November 18, 1870. Perhaps, if he was *really* lucky and Mary Sinclair was, thanks to her mother (certainly not her father), one of the world's perfect communists.

There is of course another story; the one Mary Sinclair told forty years later. Before the rebellion, she said, when I was only a young girl, an English officer came to Fort Pitt. He was tall and very good looking and he talked and talked and he could talk so well I thought perhaps I could love him. He told me about his home in Ireland, he came out of the snow and storm one night like someone from a different world and then when his men arrived after him he rode on to Fort Edmonton and I could only think about him. But he came back again, and he asked me to marry him. He asked me to go live with him in the Old Country. There I was, a child of the Saskatchewan, what would I do in another country? Perhaps I cried a little, but I sent him away. And after a while I did not think about him so often.

I sent him away. That is how Mary Sinclair later told it; but not Butler. He wrote a book, and he mentions her only in the same sentence as 'buffalo steaks and potatoes'. For these in Fort Pitt, he writes, 'I had the brightest eyed little lassie, half Cree, half Scotch, in the whole North-West to wait upon me,' and he mentions this 'lassie' not at all on his return journey from Fort Edmonton at the end of December, 1870, when bitter cold and a lack of sled dogs forced him, so he writes, to wait at Fort Pitt for seven days. Did she then also with steak and potatoes wait upon him? Serve him? Such a handsome Victorian soldier wrapped in tall furs on government assignment would perhaps not have remembered that she sent him away, especially not after he discovered in Ottawa a mere four months later that all the 'excellent colonial ministers', as he calls them, had large families and that 'an army officer who married a minister's daughter might perchance be a fit and proper person to introduce the benefits of civilization to the Cree and Blackfoot Indians on the western prairies, but if he elected to remain in single cussedness in Canada he was pretty certain to find himself a black sheep among the ministerial flock of aspirants for place.' Premier John A. Macdonald's only daughter Mary was handicapped beyond any possible marriage, and the most beautiful girl on the prairies could certainly not have helped Butler be an 'aspirant for place' in lumber Ottawa so, despite letters as excellent as excellent colonial ministers could make them for his excellent service, the tall officer returned to the heart of Empire still a lieutenant, still without a permanent government appointment, still without a steady war in which to achieve the fortune that could purchase his promotion; he could not know that soon the kingdoms of hot Africa would provide him with a quarter of a century of men he could, with his enormous organizational efficiency, help to kill. In Fort Pitt on the North Saskatchewan in November and December, 1870, during cold so severe no Englishman could imagine it, a beautiful young woman 'waited upon me', as he said; sent him away, as she said.

Or is a fourth story possible? Did they dream together, narrow bed or not? Did they see those enormous herds of buffalo that once flowed along the rivers there, such a streaming of life never again seen anywhere on the surface of the earth or even in the depths of the sea? And in the darkness did they see the long, hesitant parade of the Cree chiefs approaching Treaty Number Six that ordered them thereby to cede, release, surrender and yield up all that land forever, and behind them the one chief who would not, the chief Big Bear as the whites called him, but perhaps better translated 'Too Much' or 'More Than Enough Bear' who would ask them all how could one person give away forever what they had all forever had, who had more than enough of everything except the power to persuade his people of his defiant vision until Fort Pitt was burning, was becoming a great pillar of smoke bent over the river and the empty hills and all that flour and rancid treaty pork they had never wanted, had abhored as soon as ever they saw it, surrounded them, rained on them, dripped black and stinking out of the very air they were forced to breathe?

> She knows that darkness alone can offer what he longs to accept. Smell and touch and the tongue in the ear, yes, taste itself, yes, yes—but not sight. Eyes for him are impossible.

The fire locked inside each palisade log, the factor's house, the spruce walls close about their narrow bed springs into light, fire lifts Fort Pitt, transforms it into air and its place, here, on this earth, is lost to any memory, the valley and the hills changed as they are already eternally changed beyond the going of the animals and some day the Hutterite farmers will break through the bristly poplars, domesticate them into wheat fields and a plough furrow along the bank of the still relentless river one day reveals a shard of blue willow china; its delicate pastoral a century's confirmation of her waiting upon him, of her serving him?

> Behind the double darkness of his clenched eyes he sees again the length of his rifle barrel and the black hair whorled behind Blackie's straining ear: the blood explodes exactly there! They had to cross today, the daily plan is irrevocable, iron shoes or not on thin ice or no ice they must cross, and his groans, his endlessly contained and most irregular, totally unplanned, tears.

They may have dreamed something together. Possibly they dreamed the scarlet riders of the police he would recommend the Canadian government establish to force English law upon the western plains, the police whose thin implacable lines would weave the red shroud of the old Queen's authority over every child of the Saskatchewan until Inspector Francis Jeffrey Dickens, the great novelist's third son who aspired to his appointment by patronage, not by excellent merit of excellent colonial service, would at Fort Pitt become the most infamous officer in the history of the world-famous force. Force indeed.

Or they dreamed again the gaunt Cree dying, scraping their pustulated legs and arms and breasts and infants' faces along the gates, the doorframes, the windows of the locked fort to force the white man's disease back upon him, to somehow smear him and his own putrefaction. And perhaps they also dreamed Big Bear walking so emaciated among his people, his magnificent voice persuading them they must scatter to the woods and the animals, that only on the solitary land would they be given the strength to destroy this invisible, this incomprehensible evil that rotted them, his words and his great scarred face proof of his lifelong power over the white diseases, his name certain and forever More Than Enough Bear for everything except the white words on the white paper, words that would one day endlessly whisper to him behind the thick, sweating walls of Stony Mountain Penitentiary.

Was it Big Bear who helped her say to him then: go away.

Only she could dream that. It is impossible for Lieutenant William Francis Butler to dream such a hopeless dream; even in a narrow bed in Fort Pitt, even in Mary Sinclair's warm and beautiful arms.

Joy Kogawa *b.* 1935

VANCOUVER, BRITISH COLUMBIA

'We have within us the political person and at times I think that person is yanked out of silence to speak,' said Joy Kogawa in 1989. For her, it is not so much a matter of balancing the tension between political action and silence, but rather a matter of recognizing the source from which language stems. Following her first collection of lyric poems, *The Splintered Moon* (1967), Kogawa shifted her ground in both thematic and writerly ways. Her second poetry collection, *A Choice of Dreams* (1974), marked the beginning of her exploration of her ancestral origins: the poems are a powerful articulation of the sensibilities and sentiments she 'discovered' as a Canadian when she visited Japan. Her exploration of what this double legacy of origins entails was eloquently expressed in her first novel, *Obasan* (1981).

This novel, inspired in part by Muriel Kitagawa's letters, which Kogawa happened upon while doing research at the National Archives, is based on Kogawa's experiences as a child born in Vancouver and who lived there until the Second World War, when her family, like all other Japanese Canadians, was uprooted. Her characters follow the route that Kogawa's father, an Anglican minister, was forced to take. The family was sent to Slocan, one of the internment camps in the interior of British Columbia. They subsequently moved to Coaldale, Alberta, in 1945, where Kogawa finished school, and eventually to Toronto, where she studied music and theology. She moved back to Vancouver where she married, but returned to Toronto in the late 1970s after her separation.

As the excerpt from the novel included here illustrates, much of the impetus in *Obasan* revolves around the first-person narrator, Naomi, and her maternal aunt, Emily. The two women, although profoundly aware of what the labelling of their community as 'enemy aliens' means, have different ways of articulating their pain and revisiting their past. Naomi embraces the passive silence of her elderly aunt Obasan, who has become a surrogate mother to her, while Emily dedicates her entire life to unearthing all the documents necessary to demonstrate what is already apparent to all the Japanese Canadians, namely the racism directed against them. As Kogawa has said, Naomi 'doesn't say anything, she doesn't do anything. . . . Whereas Aunt Emily acts. I think that we have within us the Aunt Emily and the Naomi.' The novel has played a considerable role in alerting Canadians to past injustices committed against the Japanese Canadians, and contributed, along with Kogawa's own activism, to the redress sought by them from the Canadian government. Its sequel, *Itsuka* (1992), meaning 'someday', offers a fictionalized version of those events. *Obasan* received many awards, including the *Books in Canada* First Novel Award, the Canadian Authors Association Book of the Year Award, and the Before Columbus Foundation American Book Award. A third novel, *The Rain Ascends* (1995), about the sexual abuse of children by a Japanese Canadian Anglican minister, reveals more clearly the humanistic and Christian values that inform Kogawa's personal and political views. In the fall of 2005, after initial resistance from the Vancouver City Council, the Save the Kogawa House Committee—supported by a large number of associations and many individuals—was successful in delaying the demolition of the house (West 64th Avenue) where Kogawa lived before her family's internment and where part of *Obasan* takes place, in the hope that it will become a writer-in-residence centre.

Kogawa's other books include three poetry collections, *Jericho Road* (1977), *Woman in the Woods* (1985), and *A Song of Lilith* (2001), which includes artwork by Lilian Broca, as well as an adaptation of *Obasan* for children, *Naomi's Road* (1986). A translation of the latter has appeared in Japanese, and an expansion of it ('Obasan without Aunt Emily') has been adopted as a textbook for Japanese junior high schools. It has also been adapted (libretto by Ann Hodges) as an opera by Vancouver Opera (2005), composed by Ramona Leungen. Kogawa's accomplishments and contributions to Japanese Canadian culture in particular and Canadian culture in general have been acknowledged by many awards, including her induction into the Order of Canada (1986), the Urban Alliance Race Relations Award (1994), the National Association of Japanese Canadians National Award (2001), the Lifetime Achievement Award (Association of Asian American Studies, 2001), and honorary degrees from the University of Lethbridge (1991), University of Guelph (1992), Simon Fraser University (1993), the University of Toronto (1999), and the University of British Columbia (2001).

from *Obasan*

The ball I found under the cot that day was never lost again. Obasan keeps it in a box with Stephen's toy cars on the bottom shelf in the bathroom. The rubber is cracked and scored with a black lacy design, and the colours are dull, but it still bounces a little.

Sick Bay, I learned eventually, was not a beach at all. And the place they called the Pool was not a pool of water, but a prison at the exhibition grounds called Hastings Park in Vancouver. Men, women, and children outside Vancouver, from the 'protected area'—a hundred-mile strip along the coast—were herded into the grounds and kept there like animals until they were shipped off to road-work camps and concentration camps in the interior of the province. From our family, it was only Grandma and Grandpa Nakane who were imprisoned at the Pool.

Some families were able to leave on their own and found homes in British Columbia's interior and elsewhere in Canada. Ghost towns such as Slocan—those old mining settlements, sometimes abandoned, sometimes with a remnant community—were reopened, and row upon row of two-family wooden huts were erected. Eventually the whole coast was cleared and everyone of the Japanese race in Vancouver was sent away.

The tension everywhere was not clear to me then and is not much clearer today. Time has solved few mysteries. Wars and rumours of wars, racial hatreds and fears are with us still.

The reality of today is that Uncle is dead and Obasan is left alone. Weariness has invaded her and settled in her bones. Is it possible that her hearing could deteriorate so rapidly in just one month? The phone is ringing but she does not respond at all.

Aunt Emily is calling from the airport in Calgary where she's waiting for Stephen's flight from Montreal. They'll rent a car and drive down together this afternoon.

'Did you get my parcel?' she asks.

The airport sounds in the background are so loud she can hardly hear me. I shout into the receiver but it's obvious she doesn't know what I'm saying.

'Is Obasan all right? Did she sleep last night?' she asks.

It's such a relief to feel her sharing my concern.

Obasan has gone into the bathroom and is sweeping behind the toilet with a whisk made from a toy broom.

'Would you like to take a bath?' I ask.

She continues sweeping the imaginary dust.

'Ofuro?' I repeat. 'Bath?'

'Orai,' she replies at last, in a meek voice. 'All right.'

I run the water the way she prefers it, straight from the hot-water tap. It's been a while since we bathed together. After this, perhaps she'll rest. Piece by piece she removes her layers of underclothes, rags held together with safety pins. The new ones I've bought for her are left unused in boxes under the bed. She is small and naked and bent in the bathroom, the skin of her buttocks loose and drooping in a fold.

'Aah,' she exhales deeply in a half groan as she sinks into the hot water and closes her eyes.

I rub the washcloth over her legs and feet, the thin purple veins a scribbled maze, a skin map, her thick toenails, ancient rock formations. I am reminded of long-extinct volcanoes, the crust and rivulets of lava scars, criss-crossing down the bony hillside. Naked as prehistory, we lie together, the steam from the bath heavily misting the room.

'Any day now is all right,' she says. 'The work is finished.' She is falling asleep in the water.

'It will be good to lie down,' I shout, rousing her and draining the tub. I help her to stand and she moves to her room, her feet barely leaving the floor. Almost before I pull the covers over her, she is asleep.

I am feeling a bit dizzy from the heat myself.

Aunt Emily said she and Stephen would be here by four this afternoon. I should clear up the place as much as I can before they arrive. Find a safe place for all the papers.

This diary of Aunt Emily's is the largest I have ever seen. The hard cover is grey with a black border and 'Journal' is written in fancy script in the middle. What a crackling sound old paper makes.

It has no page numbers and most of the entries begin 'Dear Nesan'. It's a journal of letters to my mother. 'Merry Christmas, Dearest Nesan, 1941' is printed in a rectangular decorated box on the first page.

Should I be reading this? Why not? Why else would she send it here?

The handwriting in blue-black ink is firm and regular in the first few pages, but is a rapid scrawl later on. I feel like a burglar as I read, breaking into a private house only to discover it's my childhood house filled with corners and rooms I've never seen. Aunt Emily's Christmas 1941 is not the Christmas I remember.

The people she mentions would be my age, or younger than I am now: her good friends, Eiko and Fumi, the student nurses; Tom Shoyama, the editor of the *New Canadian*; Kunio Shimizu, the social worker; my father, Tadashi Mark; Father's good friend, Uncle Dan; and Father's older brother, Isamu, Sam for short, or Uncle as we called him. Obasan is fifty years old in 1941.

In the face of growing bewilderment and distress, Aunt Emily roamed the landscape like an aircraft in a fog, looking for a place to land—a safe and sane strip of justice and reason. Not seeing these, she did not crash into the oblivion of either bitterness or futility but remained airborne.

The first entry is dated December 25, 1941.

Dearest Nesan,

In all my 25 years, this is the first Christmas without you and Mother. I wonder what you are doing today in Japan. Is it cold where you are? Do your neighbours treat you as enemies? Is Obaa-chan still alive?

When you come back, Nesan, when I see you again, I will give you this journal. It will be my Christmas present to you. Isn't it a sturdy book? It's one of Dan's Christmas gifts to me.

I'm sitting in the library, writing at the desk which has the picture of you and me beside the ink bottle. There are so many things to tell you. How different the world is now! The whole continent is in shock about the Pearl Harbor bombing. Some Issei are feeling betrayed and ashamed.

It's too early yet to know how the war will affect us. On the whole, I'd say we're taking things in our stride. We're used to the prejudice by now after all these long years, though it's been intensified into hoodlumism. A torch was thrown into a rooming-house and some plate-glass windows were broken in the west end—things like that.

The blackouts frighten the children. Nomi had a crying bout a few nights ago. I don't tell you this to worry you, Nesan, but I know you will want to know. There was a big storm during the last blackout. Nomi woke up. That peach tree is too close to her window. When the wind blows, it sways and swings around like a giant octopus trying to break in. Aya had the spare bed in Nomi's room just as you arranged before you left, but since she's had to stay so much longer, she's moved in the main bedroom and Mark sleeps in the study downstairs. Aya slept through the whole storm but Mark woke up to find Nomi sitting on his pillow, hitting the Japanese doll you gave her. He tried to take the doll away from her and she started to cry and wouldn't stop. He said it's the first time she's ever really cried. She doesn't understand what's going on at all. Stephen does, of course. He went through a phase of being too good to be true but now he's being surly. He told Aya to 'talk properly'.

All three Japanese newspapers have been closed down. That's fine as far as I'm concerned. Never needed so many anyway. It's good for the *New Canadian* which is now our only source of information and can go ahead with all the responsibility. Our December 12 headline is 'Have Faith in Canada'. Thank God we live in a democracy and not under an officially racist regime. All of us Nisei are intent on keeping faith and standing by. We were turned down for the Home Defense training plan but we're doing Red Cross work, buying War Savings bonds, logging for the war industries and shipyards, benefit concerts—the regular stuff.

There have been the usual letters to the editor in the papers. Rank nonsense, some of them. The majority are decent however. The RCMP are on our side. More than anyone else, they know how blameless we are. When the City Fathers proposed cancelling all our business licences they said we did not rate such harsh treatment. Isn't that encouraging? But now the North Vancouver Board of Trade has gone on record to demand that all our autos be confiscated.

What would doctors like Dad and the businessmen do? If they take something that essential away from 23,000 people the rest of British Columbia will feel some of the bad side effects. Remember the boat that Sam and Mark finished last winter with all the hand carvings? It was seized along with all the fishing boats from up and down the coast, and the whole lot are tied up in New Westminster. Fishing licences were suspended a couple of weeks ago as well. The dog-salmon industry, I hear, is short-handed because the Japanese cannot fish any more. But the white fishermen are confident that they can make up the lack in the next season, if they can use the Japanese fishing boats.

There was one friendly letter in the *Province* protesting the taking away of the right to earn a living from 1,800 people. Said it wasn't democracy. But then there was another letter by a woman saying she didn't want her own precious daughter to have to go to school with the you-know-who's. Strange how these protesters are so much more vehement about Canadian-born Japanese than they are about German-born Germans. I guess it's because we look different. What it boils down to is an undemocratic racial antagonism—which is exactly what our democratic country is supposed to be fighting against. Oh well. The egg-man told me not to worry.

It's the small businesses that are most affected—the dressmakers, the corner store etc.—because the clientele are shy of patronising such places in public. Lots of people have been fired from their jobs. Business on Powell Street is up slightly since most of us who usually go to the big department stores like Woodwards don't any more.

A couple of Sundays ago the National President of the Imperial Order of Daughters of the Empire, who obviously doesn't know the first thing about us, made a deliberate attempt to create fear and ill-will among her dominion-wide members. Said we were all spies and saboteurs, and that in 1931 there were 55,000 of us and that number has doubled in the last ten years. A biological absurdity. Trouble is, lots of women would rather believe their president than actual RCMP records. It's illogical that women, who are the bearers and nurturers of the human race, should go all out for ill-will like this.

Are you interested in all this, Nesan?

I've knit Dad and Mark a couple of warm sweaters. Dad is back in full-time service in spite of his heart. When gas rationing starts he won't be able to use the car so much. It's so sleek it's an affront to everyone he passes. I wish he'd bought something more modest, but you know Dad.

He has to report every month to the RCMP just because he didn't take time to be naturalized, and didn't look far enough ahead to know how important it was. Politics doesn't seem to mean a thing to him. I feel so irritated at him.

But worse than my irritation there's this horrible feeling whenever I turn on the radio, or see a headline with the word 'Japs' screaming at us. So long as they designate the enemy by that term and not us, it doesn't matter. But over here, they say 'Once a Jap always a Jap', and that means us. We're the enemy. And what about you over there? Have they arrested you because you're a Canadian? If only you'd been able to get out before all this started. Oh, if there were some way of getting news.

The things that go on in wartime! Think of Hitler ship-loading people into Poland or Germany proper to work for nothing in fields and factories far from home and children—stealing food from conquered people—captive labour—shooting hundreds of people in reprisal for one. I'm glad to hear that the Russian army is taking some of the stuffing out of Hitler's troops. War breeds utter insanity. Here at home there's mass hatred of us simply because we're of Japanese origin. I hope fervently it will not affect the lives of the little ones like Stephen and Nomi. After all they are so thoroughly Canadian. Stephen and the Sugimoto boy are the only non-white kids in their classes. Mark says Nomi thinks she's the same as the neighbours, but Stephen knows the difference. Came crying home the other day because some kid on the block broke his violin. Children can be such savages.

There is a lapse of over a month until the next entry.

February 15, 1942.
Dearest Nesan,

I thought I would write to you every day but, as you see, I haven't managed that. I felt so sad thinking about what the children are having to experience I didn't want to keep writing. But today I must tell you what's happening.

Things are changing so fast. First, all the Japanese men—the ones who were born in Japan and haven't been able to get their citizenship yet—are being rounded up, one hundred or so at a time. A few days ago, Mark told me he felt sure Sam had been carted off. I took the interurban down as soon as I could. Isamu couldn't have been gone too long because not all the plants were parched though some of the delicate ones had turned to skeletons in the front window. I tried to find the dog but she's just nowhere. I looked and called all through the woods and behind the house.

Grandma and Grandpa Nakane will be so upset and confused when they find out he's gone. You know how dependent they are on him. They went to Saltspring Island a couple of weeks ago and haven't come back yet. I know they're with friends so they must be all right.

We know some people who have left Vancouver. Dad says we should look around and get out too, but we just don't know any other place. When we look at the map it's hard to think about all those unknown places. We were thinking of going to Kamloops, but that may be too close to the boundary of the 'protected area'.

It's becoming frightening here, with the agitation mounting higher. It isn't just a matter of fear of sabotage or military necessity any more, it's outright race persecution. Groups like the 'Sons of Canada' are petitioning Ottawa against us and the newspapers are printing outright lies. There was a picture of a young Nisei boy with a metal lunch box and it said he was a spy with a radio transmitter. When the reporting was protested the error was admitted in a tiny line in the classified section at the back where you couldn't see it unless you looked very hard.

March 2, 1942.

Everyone is distressed here, Nesan. Eiko and Fumi came over this morning, crying. All student nurses have been fired from the General.

Our beautiful radios are gone. We had to give them up or suffer the humiliation of having them taken forcibly by the RCMP. Our cameras—even Stephen's toy one that he brought out to show them when they came—all are confiscated. They can search our homes without warrant.

But the great shock is this: we are all being forced to leave. All of us. Not a single person of the Japanese race who lives in the 'protected area' will escape. There is something called a Civilian Labour Corps and Mark and Dan were going to join—you know how they do everything together—but now will not go near it as it smells of a demonic roundabout way of getting rid of us. There is a very suspicious clause 'within and *without*' Canada, that has all the fellows leery.

Who knows where we will be tomorrow, next week. It isn't as if we Nisei were aliens—technically or not. It breaks my heart to think of leaving this house and the little things that we've gathered through the years—all those irreplaceable mementoes—our books and paintings—the azalea plants, my white iris.

Oh Nesan, the Nisei are bitter. Too bitter for their own good or for Canada. How can cool heads like Tom's prevail, when the general feeling is to stand up and fight? He needs all his level-headedness and diplomacy, as editor of the *New Canadian*, since that's the only paper left to us now.

A curfew that applies only to us was started a few days ago. If we're caught out after sundown, we're thrown in jail. People who have been fired—and there's a scramble on to be the first to kick us out of jobs—sit at home without even being able to go out for a consoling cup of coffee. For many, home is just a bed. Kunio is working like mad with the Welfare society to look after the women and children who were left when the men were forced to 'volunteer' to go to the work camps. And where are those men? Sitting in unheated bunk-cars, no latrines, no water, snow fifteen feet deep, no work, little food if any. They were shunted off with such inhuman speed that they got there before any facilities were prepared. Now other men are afraid to go because they think they'll be going to certain disaster. If the snow is that deep, there is no work. If there is no work, there is no pay. If there is no pay, no one eats. Their families suffer. *The Daily Province* reports that work on frames with tent coverings is progressing to house the 2,000 expected. Tent coverings where the snow is so deep? You should see the faces here—all pinched, grey, uncertain. Signs have been posted on all highways—'Japs Keep Out'.

Mind you, you can't compare this sort of thing to anything that happens in Germany. That country is openly totalitarian. But Canada is supposed to be a democracy.

All Nisei are liable to imprisonment if we refuse to volunteer to leave. At least that is the likeliest interpretation of Ian Mackenzie's 'Volunteer or else' statement. He's the Minister of Pensions and National Health. Why do they consider us to be wartime prisoners? Can you wonder that there is a deep bitterness among the Nisei who believed in democracy?

And the horrors that some of the young girls are facing—outraged by men in uniform. You wouldn't believe it, Nesan. You have to be right here in the middle of it to really know. The men are afraid to go and leave their wives behind.

How can the Hakujin not feel ashamed for their treachery? My butcher told me he knew he could trust me more than he could most whites. But kind people like him are betrayed by the outright racists and opportunists like Alderman Wilson, God damn his soul. And there are others who, although they wouldn't persecute us, are ignorant and indifferent and believe we're being very well treated for the 'class' of people we are. One letter in the papers says that in order to preserve the 'British way of life', they should send us all away. We're a 'lower order of people'. In one breath we are damned for being 'inassimilable' and the next there's fear that we'll assimilate. One reporter points to those among us who are living in poverty and says 'No British subject would live in such conditions.' Then if we improve our lot, another says 'There is danger that they will enter our better neighbourhoods.' If we are educated the complaint is that we will cease being the 'ideal servant'. It makes me choke. The diseases, the crippling, the twisting of our souls is still to come.

March 12.

Honest Nesan, I'm just in a daze this morning. The last ruling forbids any of us—even Nisei—to go anywhere in this wide dominion without a permit from the Minister of Justice, St Laurent, through Austin C. Taylor of the Commission here. We go where they send us.

Nothing affects me much just now except rather detachedly. Everything is like a bad dream. I keep telling myself to wake up. There's no sadness when friends of long standing disappear overnight—either to Camp or somewhere in the Interior. No farewells—no promise at all of future meetings or correspondence—or anything. We just disperse. It's as if we never existed. We're hit so many ways at one time that if I wasn't past feeling I think I would crumble.

This curfew business is horrible. At sundown we scuttle into our holes like furtive creatures. We look in the papers for the time of next morning's sunrise when we may venture forth.

The government has requisitioned the Livestock Building at Hastings Park, and the Women's Building, to house 2,000 'Japs pending removal'.

White men are pictured in the newspaper filling ticks with bales of straw for mattresses, putting up makeshift partitions for toilets—etc. Here the lowly Jap will be bedded down like livestock in stalls—perhaps closed around under police guard—I don't know. The Nisei will be 'compelled' (news report) to volunteer in Labour Gangs. The worse the news from the Eastern Front, the more ghoulish the public becomes. We are the billygoats and nannygoats and kids—all the scapegoats to appease this blindness. Is this a Christian country? Do you know that Alderman Wilson, the man who says such damning things about us, has a father who is an Anglican clergyman?

I can't imagine how the government is going to clothe and educate our young when they can't even get started on feeding or housing 22,000 removees. Yet the deadline for clearing us out seems to be July 1st or 31st—I'm not sure which. Seems to me that either there are no fifth columnists or else the Secret Service men can't find them. If the FBI in the States have rounded up a lot of them you'd think the RCMP could too and let the innocent ones alone. I wish to goodness they'd catch them all. I don't feel safe if there are any on the loose. But I like to think there aren't any.

March 20.
Dearest Nesan,

Stephen has been developing a slight limp. Dad's not sure what's wrong with the leg. He suspects that the fall he had last year never healed properly and there's some new aggravation at the hip. Stephen spends a lot of time making up tunes on the new violin Dad got him. The old one, I told you, was broken. It's lucky our houses are so close as I can get to see the children fairly often, even with the miserable curfew.

Your friend Mina Sugimoto takes her boys to play with Stephen a fair amount but she's acting like a chicken flapping about with her head cut off since her husband left.

Last night over a hundred boys entrained for a road camp at Schreiber, Ontario. A hundred and fifty are going to another camp at Jasper. The Council (United Nisei) has been working like mad talking to the boys. The first batch of a hundred refused to go. They got arrested and imprisoned in that Immigration building. The next batch refused too and were arrested. Then on Saturday they were released on the promise that they would report back to the Pool. There was every indication they wouldn't but the Council persuaded them to keep their word. They went finally. That was a tough hurdle and the Commission cabled Ralston to come and do something.

On Thursday night, the confinees in the Hastings Park Pool came down with terrible stomach pains. Ptomaine, I gather. A wholesale company or some-thing is contracted to feed them and there's profiteering. There are no partitions of any kind whatsoever and the people are treated worse than livestock, which at least had their own pens and special food when they were there. No plumbing of any kind. They can't take a bath. They don't even take their clothes off. Two weeks now. Lord! Can you imagine a better breeding ground for typhus? They're cold (Vancouver has a fuel shortage), they're undernourished, they're unwashed. One of the men who came out to buy food said it was pitiful the way the kids scramble for food and the slow ones go empty. God damn those politicians who brought this tragedy on us.

Dan has to report tomorrow and will most likely be told when to go and where. A day's notice at most. When will we see him again? Until all this happened I didn't realize how close a member of the family he had become. He's just like a brother to me. Nesan, I don't know what to do.

The Youth Congress protested at the ill treatment but since then the daily papers are not printing a word about us. One baby was born at the Park. Premature, I think.

If all this sounds like a bird's eye view to you, Nesan, it's the reportage of a caged bird. I can't really see what's happening. We're like a bunch of rabbits being chased by hounds.

You remember Mr Morii, the man who was teaching judo to the RCMP? He receives orders from the Mounties to get 'a hundred to the station or else and here's a list of names'. Any who are rich enough, or who are desperate about not going immediately because of family concerns, pay Morii hundreds of dollars and get placed conveniently on a committee. There are nearly two hundred on that 'committee' now. Some people say he's distributing the money to needy families but who knows?

There's a three-way split in the community—three general camps: the Morii gang, us—the Council group—and all the rest, who don't know what to do. The Council group is just a handful. It's gruelling uphill work for us. Some people want to fight. Others say our only chance is to co-operate with the government. Whichever way we decide there's a terrible feeling of underlying treachery.

March 22, 1942.
Dear Diary,

I don't know if Nesan will ever see any of this. I don't know anything any more. Things are swiftly getting worse here. Vancouver—the water, the weather, the beauty, this paradise—is filled up and overflowing with hatred now. If we stick around too long we'll all be chucked into Hastings Park. Fumi and Eiko are helping the women there and they say the crowding, the noise, the confusion is chaos. Mothers are prostrate in nervous exhaustion—the babies crying endlessly—the fathers torn from them without farewell—everyone crammed into two buildings like so many pigs—children taken out of school with no provision for future education—more and more people pouring into the Park—forbidden to step outside the barbed wire gates and fence—the men can't even leave the building—police guards around them—some of them fight their way out to come to town to see what they can do about their families. Babies and motherless children totally stranded—their fathers taken to camp. It isn't as if this place had been bombed and *everyone* was suffering. *Then* our morale would be high because we'd be *together*.

Eiko says the women are going to be mental cases.

Rev. Kabayama and family got thrown in too. It's going to be an ugly fight to survive among us. They're making (they say) accommodation for 1,200–1,300 women and children in that little Park! Bureaucrats find it so simple on paper and it's translated willy-nilly into action—and the pure hell that results is kept 'hush hush' from the public, who are already kicking about the 'luxury' given to Japs.

I'm consulting with Dad and Mark and Aya about going to Toronto. We could all stay together if we could find someone in Toronto to sponsor us. People are stranded here and there all over the BC interior. I want to leave this poisoned province. But Aya wants to stay in BC to be closer to Sam. I'm going to write to a doctor in Toronto that Dad knows.

March 27.

Dan's been arrested. The boys refused to go to Ontario. Both trainloads. So they're all arrested. Dan had a road map friends drew for him so they suspected him of being a 'spy' and now he's in the Pool.

Nisei are called 'enemy aliens'. Minister of War, or Defense, or something flying here to take drastic steps.

April 2, 1942.
Dearest Nesan,

If only you and Mother could come home! Dad's sick in bed. The long months of steady work. Since the evacuation started he's had no let-up at all. Two nights ago, one of his patients was dying. He tried to arrange to have the daughter go to the old man's bedside but couldn't. Dad stayed up all night with the man, and now he's sick himself.

I'm afraid that those kept in the Hastings Park will be held as hostages or something. Perhaps to ensure the good behaviour of the men in the work camps. Dan was cleared of that idiotic spying charge and is helping at the Pool. The cop who arrested him was drunk and took a few jabs at him but Dan didn't retaliate, thank heavens. I'm applying for a pass so I can get to see him.

Dan has a lawyer working for him and his parents about their desire to stay together, especially since Dan's father is blind and his mother speaks no English at all. The lawyer went to the Security Commission's lawyers and reported back that he was told to let the matter drift because they were going to make sure the Japs suffered as much as possible. The Commission is responsible to the Federal Government through the Minister of Justice, St Laurent. It works in conjunction with the RCMP. The Commission has three members—Austin C. Taylor, to represent the Minister of Justice, Commissioner Mead of the RCMP, John Shirras of the Provincial Police.

Only Tommy and Kunio, as active members of the Council, know what's going on and they're too busy to talk to me. The *New Canadian* comes out so seldom we have no way of knowing much and I've been so busy helping Dad I can't get to Council meetings very often. There's so much veiling and soft pedalling because everything is censored by the RCMP. We can only get information verbally. The bulletins posted on Powell Street aren't available to most people. Besides, nobody can keep up with all the things that are happening. There's a terrible distrust of federal authorities and fear of the RCMP, but mostly there's a helpless panic. Not the hysterical kind, but the kind that churns round and round going nowhere.

My twenty-sixth birthday is coming up soon and I feel fifty. I've got lines under my eyes and my back is getting stooped, I noticed in a shop window today.

Mina Sugimoto heard from her husband. Why haven't we heard from Sam? Stephen asked me the other day 'Where's Uncle?' What could I say?

April 8, 1942.

Ye gods! The newspapers are saying that there are actually Japanese naval officers living on the coast. It must be a mistake. Maybe they're old retired men. I heard someone say it was just that they took courses when they were kids in school and that's the way schools are in Japan. I'd hate to think we couldn't tell a fisherman from a sailor. Maybe the articles are true. I wonder if there's a cover-up. Surely we'd know if there were any spies. But gosh—who can we trust? At times like this, all we have is our trust in one another. What happens when that breaks down?

A few days ago the newspaper reported Ian Mackenzie as saying 'The intention of the government is that every single Japanese—man, woman and child—shall be removed from Vancouver as speedily as possible.' He said we were all going to be out in three or four weeks and added it was his 'personal intention', as long as he was in public life, 'that these Japanese shall not come back here.'

It's all so frightening. Rumours are that we're going to be kept as prisoners and war hostages—but that's so ridiculous since we're Canadians. There was a headline in the paper yesterday that said half of our boats 'of many different kinds and sizes' have been released to the army, navy, air force, and to 'bona fide white fishermen'. I wonder who has Sam's beautiful little boat. It was such an ingenious design. They said they were hopeful about all the boats because one plywood boat passed all the tests. The reporter found someone he called a 'real fisherman', a man from Norway who had fished all his life and used to have a 110-foot steam fishing boat when he fished off Norway and Iceland 'close to home'. That's one man who's profiting by our misery. He's quoted as saying 'We can do without the Japanese', but he's not loath to take our boats. Obviously white Canadians feel more loyalty towards white foreigners than they do towards us Canadians.

All this worrying is very bad for Dad. He's feeling numbness on the left side. I'm trying to keep him still but he's a terrible patient. He's very worried about Stephen—the limp is not improving. Dad is so intense about that boy. He's also worried about Mark, says his coughing is a bad sign and he's losing weight too fast. A lot of his patients, especially the old ones, are in a state of collapse.

I hadn't been to meetings of the Council lately. Too occupied with the sick ones around me. But I'm trying to keep an eye on what's happening. The Nisei who were scheduled to leave last night balked. I don't know the details. We haven't heard whether they're in the jug or the Pool or on the train. It's horrible not being able to know.

April 9.

It seems that all the people who are conscientious enough to report when they have to, law-abiding enough not to kick about their treatment—these are the ones who go first. The ones on the loose, bucking the authorities, are single men, so the married ones have to go to fill the quota. Lots of the fellows are claiming they need more time to clear up family affairs for their parents who don't understand English well enough to cope with all the problems and regulations.

I had a talk with Tommy on the phone. He said they can't do much more than they're doing without injuring a lot more people. 'All we've got on our side,' he said, 'is time and the good faith of the Nisei.' At times I get fighting mad and think that the RCMP in using Morii are trusting the wrong man— the way he collects money for favours—but in the end, I can see how complaining would just work even more against us. What can we do? No witnesses will speak up against him any more. I'm told our letters aren't censored yet, but may be at any time.

April 11.
Dear Nesan,

Dad had a letter the other day from his friend Kawaguchi at Camp 406 in Princeton. It's cheered him up a lot. You remember Kawaguchi? His wife died a few years back. He left his kids with friends and he's asking us to see what we can do to keep Jack's education from being disrupted. He says 'I think we should always keep hope. Hope is life. Hopeless is lifeless. . . . '

This morning Dad got out of bed and went to the Pool bunkhouse for men (the former Women's Building). He was nauseated by the smell, the clouds of dust, the pitiful attempts at privacy. The Livestock Building (where the women and kids are) is worse. Plus manure smells. The straw ticks are damp and mouldy. There are no fresh fruits or vegetables. He ate there to see what it was like. Supper was two slices of bologna, bread and tea. That's all. Those who have extra money manage to get lettuce and tomatoes and fruit from outside. Nothing for babies. He's asking for improvement and so is the Council.

Dad saw Dan. He earns about two dollars a day at the Pool helping out—minus board of course. There are a handful of others working there as well, getting from ten to twenty-five cents an hour for running errands and handling passes, etc. Dad, being a doctor, has a pass to come and go freely. The fact that he retired a few years ago because of his heart means the Commission is not pressing him into service in the ghost towns.

We'll have to rent our houses furnished. Have to leave the chesterfield suite, stove, refrig, rugs, etc. We aren't allowed to sell our furniture. Hits the dealers somehow. I don't understand it, but so they say.

It's an awfully unwieldy business, this evacuation. There's a wanted list of over a hundred Nisei who refuse to entrain. They're being chased all over town.

April 20.

I have gone numb today. Is all this real? Where do I begin? First I got my pass and saw Dan at last. He's going to Schreiber in two days. I didn't feel a thing when he told me. It didn't register at all. Maybe I'm crazy. When I left, I didn't say good-bye either. Now that I'm home I still can't feel. He was working in the Baggage—old Horse Show Building. Showed me his pay cheque as something he couldn't believe—$11.75. He's been there an awfully long time.

After I saw Dan, and delivered some medicine for Dad, I saw Eiko and Fumi. Eiko is working as a steno in the Commission office there, typing all the routine forms. She sleeps in a partitioned stall—being on the staff so to speak. The stall was the former home of a pair of stallions and boy oh boy did they leave their odour behind! The whole place is impregnated with the smell of ancient manure. Every other day it's swept with chloride of lime or something but you can't disguise horse smells, cow, sheep, pig, rabbit, and goat smells. And is it dusty! The toilets are just a sheet-metal trough and up till now they didn't have partitions or seats. The women complained so they put in partitions and a terribly makeshift seat. Twelve-year-old boys stay with the women too. The auto show building, where the Indian exhibits were, houses the new dining room and kitchens. Seats 3,000. Looks awfully permanent. Brick stoves—eight of them—shiny new mugs—very very barracky. As for the bunks, they were the most tragic things I saw there. Steel and wooden frames at three-foot intervals with thin lumpy straw ticks, bolsters, and three army blankets of army quality—no sheets unless you brought your own. These are the 'homes' of the women I saw. They wouldn't let me or any 'Jap females' into the men's building. There are constables at the doors—'to prevent further propagation of the species', it said in the newspaper. The bunks were hung with sheets and blankets and clothes of every colour—a regular gypsy caravan—all in a pathetic attempt at privacy—here and there I saw a child's doll or teddy bear—I saw two babies lying beside a mother who was too weary to get up—she had just thrown herself across the bed. I felt my throat thicken. I couldn't bear to look on their faces daring me to be curious or superior because I still lived outside. They're stripped of all privacy.

Some of the women were making the best of things, housecleaning around their stalls. One was scrubbing and scrubbing trying to get rid of the smell, but that wasn't possible. And then, Nesan, and then, I found Grandma Nakane there sitting like a little troll in all that crowd, with her chin on her chest. At first I couldn't believe it. She didn't recognize me. She just stared and stared. Then when I knelt down in front of her, she broke down and clung to me and cried and cried and said she'd rather have died than have come to such a place. Aya and Mark were sick when I told them. We all thought they were safe with friends in Saltspring. She has no idea of what's going on and I think she may not survive. I presumed Grandpa Nakane was in the men's area, but then I learned he was in the Sick Bay. I brought Eiko to meet Grandma but Grandma wouldn't look up. You know how yasashi Grandma is. This is too great a shock for her. She whispered to me that I should leave right away before they caught me too—then she wouldn't say any more. Nesan, maybe it's better where you are, even if they think you're an enemy.

Eiko has taken the woes of the confinees on her thin shoulders and she takes so much punishment. Fumi is worried sick about her. The place has got them both down. There are ten showers for 1,500 women. Hot and cold water. The men looked so terribly at loose ends, wandering around the grounds—sticking their noses through the fence watching the golfers. I felt so heavy I almost couldn't keep going. They are going to move the Vancouver women now and shove them into the Pool before sending them to the camps in the ghost towns.

The other day at the Pool, a visitor dropped his key before a stall in the Livestock Building, and he fished for it with a wire and brought to light manure and maggots. He called the nurse and then they moved all the bunks from the stalls and pried up the wooden floors, and it was the most stomach-turning nauseating thing. So they got fumigators and hoses and tried to wash it all away and got most of it into the drains. But maggots are still breeding and turning up here and there, so one woman with more guts than the others told the nurse (white) about it and protested. She replied: 'Well, there are worms in the garden, aren't there?' This particular nurse was a Jap-hater of the most virulent sort. She called them 'filthy Japs' to their faces and Fumi gave her what for and had a terrible scrap with her, saying 'What do you think we are? Are we cattle? Are we pigs?' You know how Fumi gets.

The night the first bunch of Nisei refused to go to Schreiber the women and children at the Pool milled around in front of their cage, and one very handsome Mountie came with his truncheon and started to hit them and yelled at them to 'Get the hell back in there.' Eiko's blood boiled over. She strode over to him and shouted 'You put that stick down. What do you think you're doing? Do you think these women and children are cows, that you can beat them back?' Eiko was shaking. She's taken it on herself to fight and now she's on the blacklist and reputed to be a trouble-maker. It's people like us, Nesan—Eiko and Tommy and Dan and Fumi and the rest of us who have had faith in Canada, who have been more politically minded than the others—who are the most hurt. At one time, remember how I almost worshipped the Mounties? Remember the Curwood tales of the Northwest, and the Royal Canadian Mounted Police and how I'd go around saying their motto—*Maintiens le droit*—Maintain the right?

The other day there were a lot of people lined up on Heather Street to register at RCMP headquarters and so frightened by what was going on and afraid of the uniforms. You could feel their terror. I was going around telling them not to worry—the RCMP were our protectors and upholders of the law, etc. And there was this one officer tramping up and down that perfectly quiet line of people, holding his riding crop like a switch in his hand, smacking the palm of his other hand regularly—whack whack—as if he would just have loved to hit someone with it if they even so much as spoke or moved out of line. The glory of the Redcoats.

April 25.
Dearest Nesan,

Mark has gone.

The last night I spent with him and Aya and kids, he played the piano all night. He's terribly thin. Dad has been too ill to see him but he says Mark should not be going to the camps.

Is it true, Nesan, that you were pregnant just before you left? Mark said he wasn't sure. Oh, is there no way we can hear from you? I'm worried about the children. Nomi almost never talks or smiles. She is always carrying the doll you gave her and sleeps with it every night. I think, even though she doesn't talk, that she's quite bright. When I read to her from the picture books, I swear she's following the words with her eyes. Stephen spends his time reading war comics that he gets from the neighbourhood boys. All the Japs have mustard-coloured faces and buck teeth.

April 28.

We had our third letter from Sam—rather Aya did. All cards and letters are censored—even to the Nisei camps. Not a word from the camps makes the papers. Everything is hushed up. I haven't been to meetings for so long now that I don't know what's going on. Sam's camp is eight miles from the station, up in the hills. Men at the first camps all crowd down to the station every time a train passes with a new batch of men. They hang from the windows and ask about their families. Sam said he wept.

The men are luckier than the women. It's true they are forced to work on the roads, but at least they're fed, and they have no children to look after. Of course the fathers are worried but it's the women who are burdened with all the responsibility of keeping what's left of the family together.

Mina Sugimoto is so hysterical. She heard about a place in Revelstoke, got word to her husband and he came to see her on a two-day pass. She wanted them to go to Revelstoke together but of course that wasn't possible. He wasn't able to make it back to road camp in the time limit so now they're threatening to intern him. In the meantime, Mina has gone off to Revelstoke, bag, baggage, and boys. I'll try to find out what happens to them for you, Nesan.

Eiko has heard that the town of Greenwood is worse than the Pool. They're propping up old shacks near the mine shaft. On top of that local people are complaining and the United Church parson there says to 'Kick all the Japs out'.

Eiko, Fumi, and I have gotten to be so profane that Tom and the rest have given up being surprised. Eiko says 'What the hell', and Fumi is even worse.

What a mess everything is. Some Nisei are out to save their own skins, others won't fight for any rights at all. The RCMP are happy to let us argue among ourselves. Those of us who are really conscientious and loyal—how will we ever get a chance to prove ourselves to this country? All we are fighting for inch by inch just goes down the drain. There are over 140 Nisei loose and many Japanese nationals (citizens of Japan). The Commission thinks the nationals are cleared out of Vancouver but oh boy, there are a lot of them who have greased enough palms and are let alone.

April 30.

We got another extension and are trying to get a place here in BC some-where—somewhere on a farm with some fruit trees. We may have to go to some town in Alberta or Saskatchewan or Manitoba. I have to do some fast work, contacting all the people I think could help in some way. Dad doesn't want to leave BC. If we go too far, we may not be able to come back. With you in Japan and Mark in Camp, Dad feels we should stay with the kids—but everybody has the same worry about their kids.

Stephen's leg was put in a cast. Dad thinks that rest will heal it. He says Grandma Nakane's mind is failing fast. She didn't speak to him when he was there today. He thought she'd be all right if she could see Grandpa Nakane but he wasn't able to arrange it. Dad's worried about both of them. I'm trying to get them out of there but the red tape is so fierce.

May 1.

I have to work fast. The Commission put out a notice—everyone has to be ready for 24-hour notice. No more extensions. Everything piled on at once. We're trying to get into a farm or house around Salmon Arm or Chase or some other decent town in the Interior—anywhere that is livable and will still let us in. Need a place with a reasonable climate. Some place where we can have a garden to grow enough vegetables for a year. Somewhere there's a school if possible. If there's nothing in BC, I think we should go east and take our chances in Toronto. Fumi and Eiko and I want to stick together.

Monday, May 4.

Got to get out in the next couple of weeks. Dad's had a relapse. The numbness is spreading. He doesn't think it's his heart.

There's another prospect. McGillivray Falls, twenty miles from Lillooet. Going there would eat up our savings since that's all we'd have to live on but at least it's close to Vancouver and just a few hours to get back. There's no school. I'd have to teach the children.

It's because so many towns have barred their doors that we are having such a heck of a time. The Commission made it clear to us that they would not permit us to go anywhere the City Councils didn't want us. Individuals who offer to help have to write letters saying they undertake to see that we won't be a burden on the public. Who among us wants to be a burden on any-one? It'd be better if, instead of writing letters to help one or two of us, they'd try to persuade their City Councils to let us in. After all we're Canadians.

Eiko and her mother might go to a ghost town to be closer to her father. Also most likely she'll have to teach grade-school. The pay is two dollars a day out of which she'd have to feed and clothe the four younger kids and try to keep them in a semblance of health. Honest, Nesan, I wonder if the whites think we are a special kind of low animal able to live on next to nothing— able to survive without clothing, shoes, medicine, decent food.

Aya just phoned that there's no electricity at McGillivray. What does one do without electricity? There are so many complex angles in this business my head aches.

Another thing that's bothering Aya is the cost of transportation and freight. We can take only our clothes, bedding, pots and pans, and dishes. We've sold our dining-room suite and piano. Mark didn't sell anything. Aya's house was looted. I haven't told her. It's in such an out-of-the-way place. When I took the interurban on Friday to see if the dog might have shown up, I was shocked. Almost all the hand-carved furnishings were gone—all the ornaments—just the dead plants left and some broken china on the floor. I saw one of the soup bowls from the set I gave them. The looting was thor-ough. The collection of old instruments Mark talked about was gone too and the scrolls. No one will understand the value of these things. I don't have the heart to tell Aya.

We're all walking around in a daze. It's really too late do anything. If we go to the ghost towns, it's going to be one hell of a life. Waiting in line to wash, cook, bathe—

I've got to go to sleep. And I've got to pack. If we go to McGillivray, Fumi, Eiko, and family are coming with us. We have to go in a week or two. The Commission won't wait.

May 5.

Dearest Nesan,

We've heard from Mark. Crazy man. All he thinks about are Stephen's music lessons. He sent two pages of exercises and a melody which he thought up. He wrote about some flowers he found which he stuck on the end of his pick and says he thinks about you as he works. I read the letter three times to Dad. Dad says Stephen's health is more important than his music right now. Nomi is fine. She's so silent though. I've never seen such a serious child before.

I got a letter from Dan as well. His address is Mileage 101, Camp SW 5-3, Jackfish, Ontario.

We've had three different offers since yesterday. Mickey Maikawa wants us to go to his wife's brother's farm in Sicamous. We're considering it. Everything is confusion and bewilderment.

Eiko has heard awful things about the crowding and lack of sanitation in the ghost towns. People have been freezing in tents. She's dead set against them now. She and Fumi and I are still trying to stick together. But you never know when we'll have to go, or which way our luck's going to jump. Every day's a different story, from nowhere to go to several choices. I want to go east. Rent at McG. Falls was reduced to $80.00 per year.

May 14.

Dear Nesan,

Aya, kids, Dad, and I have decided to go to Slocan. We hear that's one of the best of the ghost towns. It used to have a silver mine, or maybe a gold mine—I'm not sure. There are just abandoned old hotels there now and a few stores. I don't know the size of the white population but it's not very large.

The family—or what's left of it—intends to stick together one way or another, and after days and nights of discussion, chasing this elusive hope or that, worrying, figuring, going bats with indecision, with one door after another closing then opening again—we finally realize the only thing to do is give in and stay together wherever we go, and moving to Slocan is the easiest.

Rev. Nakayama, who's already in Slocan, wrote and told me about a small house that Dad and I can have to ourselves, close to the mountains and away from the crowding. It makes all the difference. I'm so glad I thought to ask him for help. We'll be able to manage something for the kids—build an addition if we have to.

Now that the decision is taken, I don't want to be upset all over again. I don't want to go through all the hopes and the uncertainty of trying to find a loophole to escape from. I'm resigned to Slocan—and anyway, Rev. Nakayama says it's a nice place. It even has a soda fountain. So I'll settle for that until they say it's okay for us to join Mark and Sam and Dan again somewhere. Grandma and Grandpa Nakane have orders to go to New Denver.

We've tried everything, I've cried my cry, I've said good-bye to this home. All fluttering for escape has died down. Just wish us luck, Nesan. We'll wait until that happy day when we can all be together again.

Now I must get to serious packing and selling and giving away and the same thing at your house.

I asked too much of God.

May 15, Friday.

There's too much to do. Dad's unable to help though he tries. After we get to Slocan things should calm down. The furor will die down when there are none of us left on the Coast. Then we can discuss moving to Ontario. It's time that defeated us for the present but we won't give up yet. Not by a long shot.

Dan's new address—Dalton Mills, c/o Austin Lumber Co., Dalton, Ontario.

We got a letter today from the doctor in Toronto offering us the top floor of his house. That would be wonderful, but heck! how I'd hate to impose on anyone. Imagine being dependent like that. I think it was fated for me to taste the dregs of this humiliation that I might know just what it is that all the women and children are enduring through no fault of their own.

Once we're in Slocan, chances of going east are better than here. The officials are terribly harassed with the whole thing and exasperated with individual demands for attention. So, Slocan City, here we come.

Goodness, I think I'll keep my golf clubs.

May 18, 1942.
Dear Nesan,

It's flabbergasting. I can't believe any of it. Here's what happened.

I was all packed for Slocan and Dad was reasonably okay. In the middle of helping Aya, I thought—just as a last gesture and more for my own assurance than out of any hope—that I'd write to Grant MacNeil, secretary of the Commission. So I wrote asking for written assurance that I could continue negotiations from Slocan about going to Toronto. That's all. Just the word that there was hope for us all to get to Ontario. No further aspirations. I was too tired to start all over again anyway. Mailed the letter around noon from the main post office on Friday. A little after three o'clock, Mrs Booth who works there phoned to say that they'd got the letter and I was to come right away. I couldn't believe it. I dropped everything and ran. Mrs Booth, speaking for Mr MacNeil, said they were not giving any special permits but they'd make this one exception and told me to return next day with bank accounts, references, etc. I was so excited and happy, I assumed that included Dad and Aya and the kids. Next day, Mrs Booth said the permit was only for the Kato family. One family only. I told her Stephen and Nomi are my sister's kids but she said something about Commission rulings and their name is Nakane and then she asked about the Nakane family and I had to say they were nationals and I think that settled it. But she said she would look into the business of the kids. I was so frustrated not having Mark or Dad or Aya to confer with. It seemed to me at that point that I should opt for Toronto with Dad and then negotiate having everyone else come to join us.

Do you think I did the right thing, Nesan? Eiko says I did and that we should try to keep as many out of the ghost towns as possible. So I went back and told Dad and he didn't say anything one way or the other. Just kept nodding his head.

When I discussed it with Aya, she was adamant about the kids. She says you entrusted them to her and they're her kids now until you return and she won't part with them. It's true they're more used to her than to either me or Dad. And as for being so far away, Aya says ten miles or ten thousand miles makes no difference to a child.

The whole point of all our extensions was to find a way to keep together, but now at the last minute everything has exploded. Aya is being very calm and she doesn't want any discussion in front of the kids. All she's told them is that they're going for a train ride.

Fumi is resigned to not coming with us. Eiko's mother wants to go to Slocan, but I can tell Eiko wants out. I don't know what Fumi is going to do now. I think she's going to Kaslo with Rev. Shimizu's group.

I'm going to the Custodian tomorrow and then to the Commission again. Maybe the permit won't be given at the last minute. What if I transfer the Slocan papers to someone else and then don't get the Toronto permit? There could be trouble with all these forms and deferments.

Well, I'm going to go ahead, repack everything and hope. The mover, Crone, is sending our boxed goods, beds, and Japanese food supplies—shoyu, rice, canned mirinzuke, green tea. I'm taking the Japanese dishes, trays and bowls. Can't get any more miso now.

I'll just have to live on hope that Aya and kids will be all right till we can get them to Toronto. I tell myself that at least they'll have their own place till then.

What will it be like, I wonder, in the doctor's house? I'll wire them as soon as I get the permit and we'll head their way for the time being. Do we eat with the family? First thing I'll do when I get to Toronto is go out *at night*.

In Petawawa there are 130 Nisei interned for rioting and crying 'Banzai', shaving their heads and carrying 'hino-maru' flags. Damn fools.

May 21.
Dearest Nesan,

Aya and kids are leaving with others bound for Slocan tomorrow. RCMP came in person to order Kunio off to camp. Rev. Shimizu and Rev. Akagawa had to leave immediately.

Yesterday I worked so hard—tied, labelled, ran to Commission, ran to bank, to Crone movers, to CPR, washed and cooked and scrubbed. Dad is saying good-bye to the kids now. They're spending the night in the church hall at Kitsilano. I'm going over there too as soon as I pack this last item. Merry Christmas, Nesan.

This is the last word in the journal. The following day, May 22, 1942, Stephen, Aya Obasan and I are on a train for Slocan. It is twelve years before we see Aunt Emily again.

Claire Harris *b.* 1937

PORT OF SPAIN, TRINIDAD

'I have always known that I was a writer,' Claire Harris has said. She began writing in 1974 during a year-long leave of absence from her teaching in the Separate Schools in Calgary, Alberta. She spent that year in Lagos, Nigeria, studying at the University of Nigeria, where she received a Diploma in Mass Media and Communications. Her stay and studies there proved to be a crucial experience: Nigeria's 'entirely different culture forced me to pay attention', she says, and to realize that her 'task' as a writer is 'to return Africa to its place at the centre, the heart of Western Civilization'. Her recognition of what her subject matter is comes from her painful awareness that 'Africans in North America, and of course, Europe, have suffered a traumatic loss. The nations which inflicted and continue to inflict that loss have never acknowledged their crime. . . . There can, of course, be no healing while one group continues to see the other as inherently less than acceptable. There is no acceptance of our joint inheritance, no recognition of the scar tissue embroidering it.'

Harris, who was born in Port of Spain, Trinidad, emigrated to Calgary in 1966, after completing her studies at the University College, Dublin, Ireland, where she received a BA Honours (with a major in English and a minor in Spanish), and at the University of the West Indies, Jamaica, where she received a postgraduate diploma in Education. Retired from her teaching career, Harris has been active in promoting Canadian literature to Canadians, especially through *Poetry Goes Public*, a project

that involved the circulation of poetry posters by major poets in public spaces, including buses, and through her work as a member of the Writers' Guild of Alberta, as poetry editor of *Dandelion* (1981–9), and as founding editor and manager of *blue buffalo* (1984–7), an all-Alberta literary magazine.

Appearing in numerous literary magazines and anthologies, her poetry includes *Fables from the Women's Quarters* (1984), which won the Commonwealth Award, Americas Region, in 1985; *Translation into Fiction* (1984); *Travelling to Find a Remedy* (1986), winner of the Writers' Guild of Alberta Award for poetry in 1987 and the Alberta Culture Poetry Prize; *The Conception of Winter* (1989), which received an Alberta Special Award in 1990; and *Drawing Down a Daughter* (1992), which was short-listed for the Governor General's Award in 1993. 'I write/ for us all we must change/the fictions before the fictions/play us out,' she writes in *Dipped in Shadow* (1996). Selections of her poetry as well as her essay 'Why Do I Write?' are included in *Grammar of Dissent* (1994), edited by Carol Morrell, which gathers together Harris's work and that of Dionne Brand and Marlene Nourbese Philip. Harris is also the co-editor, with Edna Alford, of *Kitchen Talk* (1992), an anthology of women's writing.

Her poetry is written in a variety of styles—short lyrics, long sequences, haiku, prose narratives, texts that often claim all the space of a page—that reflect, as Harris says, 'the different ways of approaching things': 'To mirror the profound disharmony' of our world, 'collages would have to take form, languages would have to knock against each other, genres would have to dissolve.' Her formal and linguistic virtuosity is evident in *She* (2000), a long poem about a woman who has different personalities. Though she offers no easy answers, as the poems that follow illustrate, Harris is intent on re-examining how we are the products of our culture, how racialization and gender construction inform the ways in which we think we understand our culture as well as the cultures of others.

Black Sisyphus

To propitiate the dreaming god at his centre
for months my father drove down green uneven

roads to the capital where tar flowed under
noonday heat in daily manouevres around new obstacles

to take form again in cold pale morning   5
he drove those roads in mutters searching through

the crumpled pathways of his brain while his
voice rose and stumbled in the sibilant argument

he enjoyed with life he could not be
convinced that being human was not enough   10

that there was no bridge he could cross
he would not 'forget de man' nor 'leave

him to God' these were his sky/trees/
his streets to name was he not greeted

by all he passed naming from a wilderness   15
of loss his fathers created this island garden

he would not be cast out again he
rode his right to words pointed and named

the road from one way of life to another is hard
those who are ahead have a long way to go*   20

missionary zeal could not stomach such clarity
they damned him thundered fire brimstone the sin

---

* Transtromer, 'From an African Diary' (1963)

of pride thus my father and his letters
raced weekly to the centre the apology

won he stood nodded bowed strode in his own   25
echoing silence out of lowered eyes/bells/incense

the worn organ's cough out of village voices
wheeling in cracked Kyries

to stand on the church steps muttering:
it is enough to be a man today   30

his fingers kneading my six year old hands
as if they would refashion them

No God Waits on Incense

for Rosemary

while babies bleed this is not the poem i wanted
it is the poem i could   though it is not that insistent
worm   it will not burrow through deaf ears
lay its eggs in your brain   yet it is all
for change   5
and it is not that beautiful weapon
it will not explode in the gut
despite your need   this poem is not that gift
it brings you nothing   you who insist on drinking
let your buckets into green and ruined wells   haul   10
in darkness   village women will lead you smiling
step back polite in the face of skulls
this poem will not catch you as you fall
not a net   no   it is nothing this poem
not a key   not a charm   not chicken soup   15
and it is no use at all   at all
nothing at all
it won't beat a drum   it can't dance   it can't
even claim to be written in dust if this morning
the Bow sky-sheeted in light   the silver air is bright   20
with balloons   yet it talks from a dark bed
this poem   though no
woman can lie curled beneath its covers
can hide before boots

can hope to be taken for bundles of clothes   can hope   25
not to cry out when the knife probes
pray her blood not betray her   nor the tiny sigh
no   this poem   not even a place where anyone is safe
it can nothing   still nothing   still nothing at all
at all   in the night and disinterested air this poem   35
leaves no wound

Wayson Choy b. 1939

VANCOUVER, BRITISH COLUMBIA

Raised in Vancouver's Chinatown, where he was most likely born, the son of Toisanese-speaking restaurant owners, Choy discovered in the 1990s that he was adopted, and that his biological father was an actor in the Cantonese Opera. He writes of how he ended up being adopted, a story that is part and parcel of the complex history of Chinese immigrants in Vancouver in the 1940s, in his compelling narrative *Paper Shadows: A Chinatown Childhood* (1999), a memoir nominated for many awards.

Following his studies in English and Sociology at the University of British Columbia in the late 1950s, where he was mentored by such writers as Earle Birney, Choy began publishing short fiction. But despite his immediate success—his first short story was included in *Best American Short Stories* (1962)—he 'found writing very hard and isolating', and so he taught remedial English at Humber College in Toronto for many years before he returned to creative writing. A short story he was asked to write on a slip of pink paper for a creative writing class taught by Carol Shields eventually led to his highly successful novel, *The Jade Peony* (1996). The co-winner of the Trillium Award and the Vancouver City Book Award, it is written in the 'language memory' Choy has 'inherited from Chinatown', a memory of various Chinese dialects and patterns of thought that 'has somehow transmuted into the narrative voices' of the Chen family's children. Set in the 1930s and 1940s, it captures the tensions

between the old values of the first generation of Chinese immigrants and the conflicting experiences of the second generation. 'When I was a child,' Choy says, 'I first dreamed of becoming a sword-slashing warrior in a Chinese opera; soon after seeing my first cowboy movie I changed my mind. But both dreams became part of me.' It is also a novel that deals with the impact of the Depression on Chinatown, as well as with the inter-ethnic conflicts that marked the relations of the Chinese and Japanese Canadians in Vancouver in that period.

His second novel, *All That Matters* (2004), nominated for the Giller Prize, continues the saga of the Chen family, this time from the point of view of Kiam-Kim, the first-born son, whose life trajectory, like that of Choy's, is marked by his attempts to negotiate the demands of his Chinese heritage with his sense of belonging to contemporary North America. Trying to deal with racialization and racism—'children like myself,' Choy says, 'were often called "bananas"—we were yellow on the outside and white on the inside'—his protagonist has to 'choose', in Choy's words, 'between becoming a bridge that connects the differences or a wall'. Echoing a saying by Confucius, the title of this novel points to what matters for Choy, namely, that 'the living truth of any place—the moral truth—exists between memory and fiction.' This truth is the result of intense listening to the voices of his past; though he does not believe in ghosts, the spirits of the past, along with the 'signs' through which they reveal themselves to him, 'occupy [Choy's] mind' and his fiction.

Involved as a volunteer with many literacy projects and AIDS groups, the elected President of Cahoots Theatre in Toronto, and a member of the Order of Canada (2005), he is the subject of *Wayson Choy: Unfolding the Butterfly* (2000), a documentary film by Michael Glassbourg that was screened internationally. In the film, shot, in part, in China, Choy speaks of his 'process of writing, memory, racism and the importance of writing'. He was also the host of the documentary film, *Searching for Confucius* (2005), directed by Trevor Grant and premiered on VisionTV. While 'standing beside towering stone pillars carved with dragons', Choy says, 'I suddenly realized that they belonged to me, too. It was the oddest and most wonderful feeling . . . I suddenly thought proudly, paradoxically, of those exquisite Haida totem poles. I could only feel this way because I had been given the burden and gift of many cultures, and so, too, those gifts and burdens are given to my characters.'

from *Paper Shadows: A Chinatown Childhood*

'I saw your mother last week.'

The stranger's voice on the phone surprised me. She spoke firmly, clearly, with the accents of Vancouver's Old Chinatown: 'I saw your *mah-ma* on the streetcar.'

Not possible. This was 1995. Eighteen years earlier I had sat on a St Paul's Hospital bed beside Mother's skeletal frame while she lay gasping for breath: the result of decades of smoking. I stroked her forehead and, with my other hand, clasped her thin, motionless fingers. Around two in the morning, half-asleep and weary, I closed my eyes to catnap. Suddenly, the last striving for breath shook her. I snapped awake, conscious again of the smell of acetone, of death dissolving her body. The silence deepened; the room chilled. The mother I had known all my life was gone.

Eighteen years later, in response to a lively radio interview about my first novel, a woman left a mysterious message: URGENT WAYSON CHOY CALL THIS NUMBER.

Back at my hotel room, message in hand, I dialled the number and heard an older woman, her voice charged with nervous energy, insist she had seen my mother on the streetcar.

'You must be mistaken,' I said, confident that this woman would recognize her error and sign off.

'No, no, not your mother'—the voice persisted—'I mean your real mother.'

'My first crazy,' I remember thinking. *The Jade Peony* had been launched just two days earlier at the Vancouver Writers' Festival, and already I had a crazy. My agent had, half-whimsically, warned me to watch out for them. The crazies had declared open season upon another of her clients, a young woman who had written frankly of sexual matters. I was flattered, but did not really believe that my novel about Vancouver's Old Chinatown could provoke such perverse attention. Surely, my caller was simply mistaken.

'I saw your *real* mother.' The voice emphatically repeated the word 'real' as if it were an incantation.

My *real* mother? I looked down at the polished desk and absently studied the Hotel Vancouver room-service menu. My real mother was dead; I had witnessed her going. I had come home that same morning eighteen years ago and seen her flowered apron folded precisely and carefully draped over the kitchen chair, as it had been every day of my life. I remember quickly hiding the apron from my father's eyes as he, in his pyjamas and leaning on his cane, shuffled into the kitchen. Seeing that the apron was missing from the chair, he began, 'She's . . . ?' but could not finish the question. He stared at the back of the chair, then rested his frail eighty-plus years against me. Unable to speak, I led him back to his bed.

The voice on the hotel phone chattered on, spilling out details and relationships, talking of Pender *Gai*, Pender Street, and noting how my novel talked of the 'secrets of Chinatown.'

I suddenly caught my family name, pronounced distinctively and correctly: *Tuey*. Then my grandfather's, my mother's and my father's formal Chinese names, rarely heard, sang into my consciousness over the telephone.

'Those are your family names?' the voice went on.

'Yes, they are,' I answered, 'but who are you?'

'Call me Hazel,' she said.

She had an appointment to go to, but she gave me a number to call that evening. 'Right now, I can't tell you much more.'

'Oh,' I replied lamely, 'I understand.'

I did not understand. I meant it as a pause, a moment in which to gather my thoughts. I wanted to learn more. Provoked and confused, I said what came immediately into my head:

'Where should I begin?'

The line went dead. Hazel was gone.

That afternoon, in my fifty-seventh year, a phone call from a stranger pushed me towards a mystery. The past, as I knew it, began to shift.

When I think of my earliest memories, I do not worry about family history, nor do I think of the *five-times-as-hard* hard times my parents endured.

I think, instead, of first hauntings.

At the age of four, something vivid happened to me. I woke up, disturbed by the sound of a distant clanging, and lifted my head high above the flannelled embankment that was my mother's back to see if a ghost had entered the room. Mother rolled her head, mouth partially open, sound asleep. I rubbed the sleep from my eyes to survey the near-darkness. What I saw, reflected in the oval mirror above the dresser, was the buoyant gloom alive and winking with sparks. A cloud of fireflies.

The wonder of it jolted me fully awake.

The clanging began again. Then it ceased.

For a moment, I forgot about the noise. Mother's soft breathing pulled at the silence, stealing away a bit of my nameless fear. As I shook Mah-ma to wake her so she could see the fireflies, there was a rush of wind. I turned my head to look at the windows. A strong breeze lifted the lace curtains and fluttered one of the three opaque pull-down shades. Pinpoints of outside light sprayed across the room and spangled gems across the ceiling. I looked back at the wide, tilted mirror, at the reflected lights dancing within. I remembered how fireflies came together to rescue lost children in the caves of Old China. Mah-ma, her back to me, mumbled something, then receded into sleep.

I sank into the bed and leaned tightly against Mah-ma's great warmth. The clanging grew louder. A monster was approaching. My mind conjured a wild, hairy creature, eyes like fire, heaving itself, and the chains it was dragging, towards our bedroom cave. I turned to stone.

My child's wisdom said that Mah-ma and I had to lie perfectly still, or the monster would veer towards our bed, open its hideous wet mouth and devour us. Rigidly, I watched the pinpoints of light crazily dancing up the wall and across the ceiling.

Suddenly the wind died.

The blind hung still, inert.

I looked up. A ceiling of stars shimmered above me. The monster would be dazzled by the stars. It would be fooled. It would turn away from us. We were sky, not earth. I shut my eyes and whispered, 'Go away, monster! Go away!'

There was rattling and banging, a clinking, and then a crescendo of sharp, steady *clip-clop, clip-clop*s. . . . The monster, now frustrated by the lack of prey, shuddered— and turned into the milkman's old chestnut horse, its chains into *clink-clank*ing bottles.

When I told Grandfather the next day how Mah-ma and I had escaped the hairy monster, he laughed. He said I was very smart to lie very still and not wake Mah-ma, who had been working two shifts and was tired. When I told Fifth Aunty, who often took care of me, she smiled, pinched my cheeks and said, 'You lucky boy. Fireflies and stars always fortunate.'

This haunting, Grandfather and Father both assured me, was only a child's dream. Many years later, Fifth Aunty reminded me of the old horse, how one late morning, when the milkman came to her alleyway door to sell her a strip of milk tickets, she had lifted me up to the animal's large, snorting head, and I, squirming in her arms, trembling, let it snatch a carrot stump from my palm.

'Only an old mare.' She laughed.

Fifth Aunty told everyone how I had wiped the horse saliva on her face. I remembered none of it.

At five, I had my second haunting. This one, I recall clearly.

The distant clattering and clanging began again. I knew by now it was the sound of the approaching milkman. I lay still, listened for the comforting sound of the old horse, its hooves going *clip-clop, clip-clop* on the cobblestones, a rhythmic drumming that I can still hear today.

I sat up, not letting go of Mah-ma. She stirred and her breath deepened. My mother and I were utterly alone in the island kingdom of the double bed. Father was away again, on one of his frequent alternating three- and five-week stints as a cook on a Canadian Pacific steamship liner.

For my own amusement, I dared to imagine a slimy three-eyed monster somewhere in the dark outside, coming towards us, dragging its clanking chains.

I was lucky. I was brave. At will, I could render the great monster harmless and go back to sleep in the comfort of my own created magic. The chain's rattling had become as familiar as the sound of a chopstick hitting a milk bottle.

But that morning, for a reason I could not understand, I did not go back to sleep. From somewhere within me, a nameless fear slithered up my spine and gripped me by the nape of my neck. Then it began to pull me down. During the summer evening, the blanket and sheet had been pushed away. My pyjama top, rolled up, exposed my back. I could not reach the bedding wadded below my feet. I clung to Mah-ma, my cheek tight against her flannel nightgown. Her body heat and sweet salty smell anchored me.

As the morning sun began to bleach the darkness from the ceiling, the pinpoints of light faded. I needed to pee. But I did not get up and go down the hall, as I had been taught to do. An odd feeling fettered me, made me feel inadequate, like a helpless baby. And yet I knew that a big boy doesn't cry out for his *mah-ma*.

Carefully, I sat up.

A faint, distant clattering came through the open window: the milk wagon was lumbering down the street. I pushed myself off the big bed. The cold linoleum floor tickled my soles. I listened. The milk wagon halted. Except for Mother's breathing, and a scattering of birdsong, there was no sound. The world seemed to me to have suddenly altered, slipped into enchantment, like in a Grimm fairy tale.

In the near-dark, the scratched oak dressing table stood with squat authority. On its polished top lay a cluster of bottles filled with mysterious amber liquid, tortoiseshell combs, silver-topped jars, and fancy cylinders holding fragrant talc. I resolved to go there, pull out the seat, and climb up and play with the bottles. But then the single opened window dispatched a rapid tattoo of clopping hooves. The wind rose. The window shade lifted like a hand and beckoned me.

I was tall enough to lay my head on the window sill. Standing there, I then turned my head and stuck my tongue out to lick the rough, paint-flaked wood. It was real enough. I stared at the pull-cord ring swinging from the blind. When the wind faltered, the beige wooden ring *click-click*ed against the glass. Outside, the milkman's horse whinnied and shook its bells. The wagon stopped, started, stopped, started. My heart thumped against my chest. But I was not afraid of the milk wagon. It was something else I feared.

I turned my head and glimpsed, in the dresser mirror, my mother, a length of warm shadow stretched out along the far edge of the bed. From where I stood, I could not see the rise and fall of her back. Suddenly, I could not breathe: she seemed too still.

I swallowed hard and stared at her.

The milk wagon clattered on, the bump, bump, bump of the wheels on the cobblestones fading into nothingness. I did not cry out.

This is all I know of the second haunting.

To this day, the vision of that moment—me with my head on the window sill, breathless, watching my sleeping mother—has not left me. Whenever this image comes to me, unbidden, my heart pounds, my lungs constrict. I taste a second or two of panic, then, catching my breath, I tell myself I am being foolish.

Years after that moment, at the age of thirty-seven, I was at my mother's funeral, and Fifth Aunty was saying how pleased my mother must be that her last ride was in a Cadillac, and that Father had bought her such a fine oak casket.

'The lid good enough for a dining table, Sonny,' she said, using my English name. 'First class!'

Fifth Aunty leaned on my arm as we walked to my cousin's car. She looked up at the bright, cloudless sky and frowned. She had almost tempted the gods: if she made the funeral sound too perfect, the gods would humble us. She had to find something wrong. She stopped, casually curved her finger into her mouth and popped out her ill-fitting false teeth. They dropped into a Baggie. The handbag snapped shut. Fifth Aunty sighed; she was stalling, thinking how to tell me (as family should tell each other) what had gone wrong. She would have to be diplomatic, yet frank.

'Oh, but if you win the lottery, Sonny, you remember: I want a horse-drawn hearse. More fancy.' She stopped, cleared her throat carefully. 'Everything should take longer, Sonny. Cadillac so fast! Service too fast! Even your dear *mah-ma*, why so fast! Today everything too fast.'

I laughed—exactly what Aunty wanted me to do. She went on, cheeks flapping. 'If up to me, I order, you know, an *old* horse and a shining first-class wagon with lace curtains!'

Fifth Aunty touched my shoulder with her cane and giggled. Death never scared her. She had seen too much death in Old Chinatown. I told her that, if I won the big lottery, I would see her ride into the sunset in the grandest, and slowest, horse-drawn hearse.

'Remember that day you little boy and saw your very first one, Sonny?' she said. Aunty always went back to the old days.

'No, I don't,' I said. 'I remember big milk wagons.'

'Yes, yes, you remember,' she insisted. 'We stand on Hastings Street, I hold your hand, and your aunty finally tell you that black thing no fancy milk wagon.' Fifth Aunty broke into toothless laughter. 'Oh, you looked so surprised that people died, just like your goldfish.'

'What did I say?'

'You cry out, "*Mah-ma won't die!*" '

I think of that morning of the second haunting, when I was five years old—the haunting that has never left me. In my mind's eye, the looking-glass reflects half the bed where my mother lies; its cool surface mirrors the dappled wall where my shadow first ambled towards the morning light.

As Fifth Aunty gets into the car, I know now why I stood there at the window, unable to speak. My cousin's car drives away.

I listen.

There is birdsong.

There is silence.

That early memory, that haunting, sends me on a search for other remembered moments. Some come in dreams, mere fragments, weighted with a sense of mystery and meaning. At such times, a sadness pervades me. I close my eyes: older, long-ago faces, a few of them barely smiling, push into my consciousness. I hear voices, a variety of Chinatown dialects, their sing-song phrases warning me: 'You never forget you Chinese!'

Now I am a child stumbling against Mother in an alley barely wide enough for two people, my three-year-old legs scooting two or three steps ahead of her. I am jerked backwards. 'Walk properly,' Mother says. I jump a few steps more, her arm extends and she tugs me back. I look up at the wintry strip of sky. We are going to visit some-one who lives up the stairs at the back of the building.

'Remember what I told you to say,' Mother cautions.

I nod, laughing.

'No'—her tone is solemn—'*no laughing.*'

At the end of the narrow alley, Mother stops walking and kneels beside me. She wets her fingers and brushes down my cowlicks. Other people angle themselves to pass us. A damp wind whistles above us. Mother pulls me closer to her. A man wearing a black fedora pats my head and tells me I'm a good boy. Two women push by us. Each speaks a few words to Mother, and their long, dark coats brush against my face. Everyone is going in the same direction. Mother shakes me to get my attention.

'Whisper to me what you are going to say.'

I whisper. Every word. Clearly.

'Good,' Mother says, wetting her fingers to push back a lock of hair that has fallen over my eye. 'Remember. No laughing.'

We follow some people up the stairs to the second or third floor of the building. A long hallway holds cardboard boxes the size of me; the cartons are piled on top of each other against one wall. As Mother and I walk down the dim corridor, the two women in the dark coats, single-file ahead, look back at us, as if to make sure we are safely following them. I do not laugh. It does not feel like a place for laughing.

'She's in here,' one of the women murmurs to Mother, and the two women step aside to let us through. Mother holds my hand as we enter a tiny room that smells of incense and medicine. On one side, a big woman bends over someone on a bed and whispers, 'He's here.'

Mother lifts me up. I see a lady with damp black hair straining to raise her head and focus her eyes on me. The pillow is embroidered with flowers. Mother says, 'What do you have to say, Sonny?'

I gulp. I know what I have to say, but I can't understand why the lady does not ask me anything. I am not afraid, but what I was told to say sounds, to me, like an answer. And an answer needs a question. Finally, the lady on the bed smiles and nods at me. I am satisfied.

'I'm fine,' I say. 'My name is Choy Way Sun and I'm a good boy.'

The lady on the bed breathes heavily and closes her eyes. Mother puts me down. Whatever was to be done is done. We walk out of the room and down the two or three flights of stairs, pushing against people coming the opposite way.

'My, my,' a voice exclaims. There is whispering.

Mother says nothing, only pulls me along and back out onto Pender Street. I blink. The street is filled with a bluish light.

After that strange visit, Mother bought me an ice-cream cone and a paper snake with a wiggling clay head. At Ming Wo's hardware store, I sat on the oak counter in my new clothes, and Helena Wong popped a hard candy into my mouth. She distracted me with some nails she was weighing out for a customer. While my head was turned, another lady came and took Mother's place.

'Where's Mah-ma?' I ask.

Mother is not beside me, but I feel safe with Chulip Sim, one of Mother's best friends. She always smells of perfume and gives me squeezing hugs, and makes funny faces until I laugh aloud.

'Your mother will be right back,' Chulip Sim says, but she does not hug me or make any funny faces. She holds me, as we both stare at Mother climbing quickly up the mezzanine staircase. I remember that I did not lick the ice-cream cone or even notice the paper snake bobbing its head. I remember watching Mother wipe her eyes with a handkerchief.

'I'm fine,' I whisper. 'I'm Choy Way Sun and I'm a good boy.'

Chulip Sim gives me a big hug.

These are the documented facts that I have known all my life: I was born Choy Way Sun, on April 20, 1939, in Vancouver, in the province of British Columbia, to Nellie Hop Wah, age thirty-eight, and Yip Doy Choy, age forty-two, the *gai-gee meng*, the *false-paper names*, officially recorded in my parents' immigration documents. A midwife, listed as Mrs Eng Dick, attended the birth.

'We waited a long time for you,' Father used to say to me. Mother always pointed to my baby picture, that pudgy baby that was me, and shook her head.

'You were *soooo* big!' she would say. 'Weighed eight or nine pounds!'

'Why didn't you have more?' I'd ask.

'You were enough.' Then Mother would laugh. 'I was too old to try for another one!'

Father always joined in the laughter.

Years later, after I knew something about how babies arrived into the world, I asked Mother about my delivery. How did she manage with an eight- or nine-pound baby? The year was 1967 and I was twenty-eight; my friend Donna Alexander and I were talking about a mutual friend who had endured a difficult labour. Mother was cutting up the home-made upside-down cake Donna had brought us for tea. The fresh pink roses my friend had brought for the house perfumed our kitchen.

'Were there any problems?' I asked. 'Was it a difficult birth?'

'*Ho-naan wahtak teng,*' Mother continued in Toisanese. '*Not easy to say for certain.*' Mother handed me a slice of cake. '*Aiihyaah: too long ago!*'

I translated into English for Donna.

'Sonny, your mother has small, delicate hips,' she said, and gently laughed. 'You don't have to ask your poor mom if it was difficult.'

Mother never liked to discuss bodily matters of any kind, so I wasn't surprised she would rather not remember. She looked down, hesitated, then shifted the conversation.

'You remember how you got your name?'

'Think about your Chinese name,' Mother always said to me, tapping my head. 'Think what it means. Your grandfather came from Victoria to give you your name.'

Six weeks after my birth, Grandfather left Grandmother and his family in Victoria and took the overnight ferry to Vancouver, where he proudly pronounced the formal name he had selected for his first grandson:

'Choy Way Sun.'

A half-dozen jade and gold baby bracelets ringed my crib as he said my new name aloud three times to a gathering of friends and relatives.

The two Chinese characters Grandfather selected for my name form a political motto: '*Way Sun,*' that is, '*to rehabilitate*', was an epigram in Old China, a promise 'to reform old ways through peaceful means'.

When Grandfather informed my parents of the name he intended to give me, Mother mentioned to him, very gently, how it seemed too distinctive, too unlike the usual names for boys; Father as well politely hinted that the reform sentiments might prove to be more of a burden than a blessing for his First Son. Even Third Uncle came on his day off to suggest that 'Way Sun' was perhaps too idealistic for a *Gim San,* a *Gold Mountain,* child. The name 'Gold Mountain', what the Chinese, during the fabled gold-rush days, called North America, was a symbol for those who craved or dreamed of earning lucky fortunes. No one in our family had had any such luck.

Grandfather did not reply. With an air of authority, he picked up his brush and dipped it into the prepared ink stone. With exquisite strokes of black ink, Grandfather slipped onto the surface of the vermilion-coloured paper the two characters of my name. He held the lucky-coloured sheet up for all to witness. At once, everyone, even Third Uncle, joined in the chorus of approval:

'Yes, yes! Fine, very fine!'

Grandfather's generation believed that names were potent, significant. In Old China, the act of naming a First Son, a First Grandson, involved the advice of numerologists and astrologers, fortune-tellers divining appropriate meanings and symbols. The 'right' name assigned to the 'right' child is an invocation against bad fortune. Grandfather's naming me, following tradition, could not have been a shallow or pointless act. But I wonder if the old man had reflected upon his own failed dreams in naming me, or if he had just looked to his heart and simply knew: *this name and no other.*

On my desk, I have a family photograph from 1939, taken in Chinatown's Yucho Chow Photo Studio, shortly after the naming ceremony.

The chubby three-month-old baby propped cozily against his mother is Choy Way Sun, soon to be called by his English nickname, 'Sonny', because his parents had been fond of Al Jolson's rendition of 'Sonny Boy', and because, as a child, he had a sunny disposition.

Looking beautiful, Lilly Choy (also Nellie Hop Wah), her makeup fresh, is holding her son securely on her lap.

Toy Choy (also Yip Doy Choy), stands proudly behind his wife and his new son, their only child. In the tradition of Old China—for the child's long life and for his good fortune—a jade bracelet encircles the tiny wrist.

Fred Wah *b.* 1939

SWIFT CURRENT, SASKATCHEWAN

The author of many volumes and chapbooks of poetry, including *Lardeau* (1965), *Mountain* (1967), *Pictograms from the Interior of B.C.* (1975), *Breathin' My Name With a Sigh* (1981), *Music at the Heart of Thinking* (1987), and *Alley Alley Home Free* (1992), Fred Wah was one of the founding editors of the avant-garde poetry newsletter *Tish* while a student at the University of British Columbia in the 1960s. Since then he has been at the forefront of poetic innovation in Canada, a poet writing out of a profound sense of place and, under the influence of Charles Olson's projective verse theory, of breath and movement.

Born in Swift Current, Saskatchewan, Wah grew up in the West Kootenay region of British Columbia. Following his studies in music and English literature at UBC (BA, 1963) and a short period of study at the University of New Mexico, Albuquerque, where he edited *Sum* magazine, he received an MA (1967) from the State University of New York at Buffalo. It was there that he met and studied with Charles Olson, while also co-editing *The Niagara Frontier Review* and *The Magazine of Further Studies*. In the late 1960s he returned to the Kootenays, where he edited the literary magazine *Scree*. The founding coordinator of the writing program at David Thompson University Centre, he taught for a time at Selkirk College before moving in 1989 to the University of Calgary, where he taught creative writing and poetics until his retirement in 2003. He now lives in Vancouver, where, since 2004, he has been a member of the Kootenay School of Writing Collective.

'Much of the impetus of my writing', Wah says, 'comes from the hyphen in "half-bred" poetics—Half-bred poetics as a game of

reaction from within the egg-yolk of my own cultural ambivalence (white on the outside, yellow on the inside).' *Faking It: Poetics and Hybridity* (2000) is his Gabrielle Roy Prize-winning book of criticism cum meditation on what he calls 'ethno-poetics'. In it he examines the politics of racialization and multiculturalism in the context of radical poetics. The self-reflexiveness and the complex texture of Wah's writing make for demanding reading. As he remarks, 'I've tried to make language operate as a non-aligned and unpredictable material, not so much intentionally difficult as simply needing a little complication—A little complication for me has always been how to create enough camouflage so that the grand intentions of meaning don't get to name me before I do—Before I do any writing I always stop whatever I'm doing—Whatever I'm doing might make a difference—Make a difference.'

Waiting for Saskatchewan (1985) won the Governor General's Award in 1986, while *So Far* (1991) received the Stephan G. Stephanson Prize. His 'biotext', *Diamond Grill* (1996), which won the Howard O'Hagan prize for short fiction, is a prose narrative that traces, through many detours and elliptical movements, his Chinese and Swedish family background. Comprising family anecdotes and recipes, fiction and life-writing, theory and criticism, its generic hybridity exemplifies his mix-raced background. Wah, who has also collaborated with visual artists, has co-edited, with Roy Miki, *Colour. An Issue* (1994), on race and literature, and, with Frank Davey, *The Swift Current Anthology* (1986). He has given hundreds of readings and talks in North America, Australia, Asia, and Europe, and is the poetry editor of *The Literary Review of Canada*.

Waiting for Saskatchewan

Waiting for saskatchewan
and the origins grandparents countries places converged
europe asia railroads carpenters nailed grain elevators
Swift Current my grandmother in her house
he built on the street   5
and him his cafes namely the 'Elite' on Centre
looked straight ahead Saskatchewan points to it
Erickson Wah Trimble houses train station tracks
arrowed into downtown fine clay dirt prairies wind waiting
for Saskatchewan to appear for me again over the edge   10
horses led to the huge sky the weight and colour of it
over the mountains as if the mass owed me such appearance
against the hard edge of it sits on my forehead
as the most political place I know these places these strips
laid beyond horizon for eyesight the city so I won't have to go   15
near it as origin town flatness appears later in my stomach why
why on earth would they land in such a place
mass of pleistocene
sediment plate wedge
arrow sky beak horizon still waiting for that   20
I want it back, wait in this snowblown winter night
for that latitude of itself its own largeness
my body to get complete
it still owes me, it does

Father/Mother Haibun #4

Your pen wrote Chinese and your name in a smooth swoop
with flourish and style, I can hardly read my own tight
scrawl, could you write anything else, I know you could
read, nose in the air and lick your finger to turn the large
newspaper page pensively in the last seat of those half-   5
circle arborite counters in the Diamond Grill, your glass
case bulging your shirt pocket with that expensive pen,
always a favourite thing to handle the way you treated it
like jewellery, actually it was a matched pen and pencil set,
Shaeffer maybe (something to do with Calgary here), heavy,   10
silver, black, gold nib, the precision I wanted also in things,
that time I conned you into paying for a fountain pen I
had my eye on in Benwell's stationery store four dollars

and twenty cents Mom was mad but you understood such
desires in your cheeks relaxed when you worked signing   15
checks and doing the books in the back room of the cafe
late at night or how the pen worked perfectly with your
quick body as you'd flourish off a check during a busy
noon-hour rush the sun and noise of the town and the cafe
flashing.   20

**High muck-a-muck's gold-toothed clicks ink mark red green
on lottery blotting paper, 8-spot (click, click)**

from *Music at the Heart of Thinking*

2

PREACT THE MIND AHEAD OF THE WRITING BUT STOP TO
think notation of the mind ahead of the writing
pretell the 'hunt' message doesn't run like the
wind simile makes it the belief of the wild
imagination or trees or animals too to preface up   5
the head ahead but notice the body as a drum-
mer preacts the hands to do to do insistent so it
can come out tah dah at every point simply the
mind at work won't do or the body minding
itself thinking (which is why the drum's cedar)   10
get it right or get it wrong just strike from the
body falling back thoughts felt behind to the
notes sometimes gives it shape or thought as
body too my drum tah dum

10

NOW I GET TO HEAR THE LANGUAGE RATHER THAN
only see it in French over my head fingers want
to touch the sight of the letter oral tactile
fragment hunger in another language the wolf's
ear to make it up before it happens to hear it   5
somewhere inside my body before the lips
touch the mouthpiece or fingertip valves as soft
as silk intelligence like that gets carried in the
language by itself the cow simply eats the
whole field I have to practise to get it right and   10
blow away anyway

50

Going through the language of time.
Chronometrics. Horologicals. A book of years.

I like the water in it. And the footprints.
That movement. As you look for words
'sans intermission'.   5

Of course it's the heart. Pictograph—
                              pictogram.
Epigram—epigraph. Cardiogram. Histograph.
The paw again.

Cellular. Un instant. Je vais voir si je la trouve   10
dans ce livre.
It's that 'yelping pack of possibilities'
the hour as the order.

The predication, the pre-form of foot
in snow, log   15
on truck, finding out it never was lost,
                              fooling.

51

Everywhere I go here, here I go again.
But even if I worked it out ahead of time
I'd do it.

I know me. This train
crosses all the Chinese rivers in Canada.   5
Each one the same world water, the same
trestle, same deep gulley.

In Japan Mt Fuji no more
than a quiet, black Shinkansen tunnel,
out of sight, out of mind.   10

When Dorn said
the stranger in town
is the only one who knows
where he's been and where he's going
I could see Pocatello's tracks.   15

Your symbol as 'accent
to the basic drum of consciousness' lurks.
St Am stutters and stumbles.
These rails are only half continuous.

52

tongue mist lip boat brown gull hill town bed
stone shadow crow tooth rain boat flood hammer star gill shadow skin hammer mouth town
mist hill rock brown bed bird tongue snow creek
lip crow circle brown lip wave boat shadow city   5
light hill sky mouth talk snow gull hammer fog
moon wet grey stone boat bed mist skin gill
word flood crow tongue river mouth star brown
lip night flood sail wave sky tooth rock red bird
shadow stone snow city blue hammer bed hill   10
crow tongue

55

Map of streets stream of dreams
map of creeks street of cream, fragments
and imago imprint, geomance a glyph,
a place on earth, under, or from it.

Name's broken letters maybe   5
words your body made.
Idiot bridges to parts of our selfs still lost
in the palindrome.

A found chain on the coffeetable,
Some Scapes as a bookmark   10
to automobile between 3 and 6;
flex, flux, flooding, fl-

    (ә Creekscape: Looking Upstream)

Fred Was. Fred War. Fred Wan. Fred Way.
Fred Wash. Fred Wag. Fred Roy. Fred What.   15

Creek water hits rock with hollow sound.

David Arnason *b.* 1940

GIMLI, MANITOBA

'Because of the nature of our country and the way it came into being,' David Arnason says, 'a very real and heightened physical, spiritual, and cultural isolation has been and continues to be a fact of Canadian existence. This isolation, and the alienation that sometimes accompanies it, has meant that Canadian writers and artists, reflecting their own cultural situation, have turned again and again to isolation as the central focus of their work.' Arnason's writing registers this kind of isolation and alienation, but it does so with a wit and irony that reflect the author's postmodern sensibility. His writing plays with and against the limits of realism, self-consciously constructing narratives of great formal versatility.

Arnason has written often about the background of his great-grandparents who emigrated from Iceland, and much of his fiction is set in Gimli, on Lake Winnipeg—the main Icelandic settlement in Canada—where he was born. He received his BA (certificate in Education) and his MA (English) from the University of Manitoba, and his PhD (English) from the University of New Brunswick. A founder and editor of the *Journal of Canadian Fiction*, the General Editor of the Macmillan 'Themes in Canadian Literature' series, the co-founder and co-editor of Turnstone Press (Winnipeg), a Board Member of the Manitoba Arts Council, and a member on the advisory board of the House of Anansi, Arnason has long played an active role in the cultural indus-

tries in Canada. He is a professor of Canadian literature and Head of the Department of English at the University of Manitoba. His books include two poetry collections, *Marsh Burning* (1980) and *Skrag* (1987), the short fiction titles *Fifty Stories and a Piece of Advice* (1982), *The Circus Performers' Bar* (1984), *The Happiest Man in the World* (1989), *If Pigs Could Fly* (1995), and *The Demon Lover* (2002), nominated for the McNally Robinson Book of the Year, and the novels *The Pagan Wall* (1992) and *King Jerry* (2001), shortlisted for the Stephen Leacock Award. As a playwright, and radio and television scriptwriter, Arnason has had many of his plays produced on stage and CBC radio, including *The Lake* (NFB), and has adapted *The Tin Drum*, *Tom Jones*, and *Settlers of the Marsh* for CBC. The editor of Dorothy Livesay's *Right Hand, Left Hand* (1977) and *Raymond Knister: Poems, Stories and Essays* (1975), he has also authored history books, *The Icelanders* (1981), written with Michael Olito, and *The New Icelanders* (1994), co-authored with Vincent Arnason. He has lectured and read from his work in Europe, including Iceland.

'All writing is writing,' Arnason has said, 'but you can code it in a voice that sounds like it's a storytelling oral voice, and that's the voice I prefer.' This is indeed the case with the story that follows, a tale that belongs to the oral storytelling tradition but whose tight structure reflects Arnason's self-reflexiveness about the act of writing.

The Sunfish

Dawn was just spreading its red glow across Lake Winnipeg when Gusti Oddson reached for the buoy to pull in the first of his seven nets. And what was he thinking, that second cousin once removed of my great-grandmother, on a June morning in 1878? Perhaps he was thinking of the smallpox epidemic that had recently taken his wife and three children, or perhaps he was thinking about nets and why they sometimes caught fish and sometimes didn't. He wasn't thinking about talking fish, or at least the scattered diaries he left behind give no indication that he was thinking about talking fish, and why, after all, should he have been? That's why he was startled when the sunfish he had just pulled into his boat, the first sunfish of the day, spoke to him.

'Gusti,' the sunfish said, its silver scales bright in the first rays of the rising sun, 'listen to me. I have much to tell you.'

Gusti did not answer right away. He was a man of common sense, and he knew that fish do not speak. Still, in the past three years, his faith in common sense had been somewhat shaken. Common sense worked perfectly well in Iceland, but it seemed to be of less value in this new country. Common sense had told him that when water is covered with ice, you do not bother to fish. Here though, you fished underneath the ice, and when you pulled fish up through the ice, they gasped and froze solid in the winter air. Common sense told you that land which could grow trees fifty feet high could also grow potatoes, but that was apparently not necessarily so.

He had come to the Republic of New Iceland three years ago. The first year, he had nearly starved. The second year, his family had died in the smallpox epidemic. The third year, religious argument had split New Iceland into two warring camps. Seri Bjarni argued that the struggle between God and the devil was being fought out for the final time on the shores of Lake Winnipeg. Seri Jon argued that there was no devil, that Jesus was not the Son of God, but only a religious leader, and that God was a spirit that was in everything in the world, but was not a person.

So, when the sunfish spoke to him, Gusti asked it, 'Are you of the devil's party?'

'Don't talk nonsense,' replied the sunfish, 'there is no devil, or God either, for that matter.'

Gusti pondered for a moment, then asked, 'Are you then a Unitarian?'

'I am a sunfish,' said the sunfish, 'and I'm not here to give you any selfish wishes. Greed and lust,' he went on sadly, 'that's all you find nowadays.'

'Then you are one of the Huldafolk,' Gusti said, 'or maybe a Mori raised by enemies to bring me bad luck.'

'More nonsense,' the fish replied. 'Ignorant superstition. How could your luck be any worse than it is? Everybody you love is dead. You haven't got a penny to your name. You hardly catch enough fish to eat, much less to sell. Everybody in New Iceland calls you Gusti Foulfart because you live on dried beans and never wash your clothes. No woman will look at you.'

'There is no need,' Gusti told the fish, 'to be rude. Things have not gone well for me in the last while, it is true, but that is not to say that they will not soon improve.'

'Progress,' sneered the fish, if indeed his opening and closing his mouth could be counted a sneer, 'delusion, a snare and a trap, the vast enslaving device of the western world. Only peasants and fishermen and fools believe in progress. Things never get better, they only get different.'

'How is it that you speak Icelandic?' Gusti asked the fish, who seemed to be having some trouble with his breathing.

'A better question might be, "How is it that you come to speak Sunfish?"' the fish replied, flopping around on the bottom of the skiff, as if to get a better view of Gusti. 'Or indeed, it might be more to the point to ask, "What is the nature of language?"'

'There are plenty of preachers on land,' Gusti told the fish. 'Already the sun is well above the horizon, and I have seven nets to lift. In New Iceland they have taken to calling me Gusti Madman because my wife sometimes comes to me in dreams and I cry out for her. I have no time to argue religion with a fish.'

'Wait,' cried the fish, with what might have been real fear, 'I am speaking to you. Is this not remarkable? Do you not want to know what I have come to tell you?'

'I believe the evidence of my senses,' Gusti replied, 'when my senses give me evidence I can trust. I know that fish do not speak. Perhaps there is a voice-thrower on the shore, or perhaps I am still in my bed dreaming of fish. The least likely thing is that I am actually in my skiff talking with a fish. So, I am going to hit you on the head with my oar, and I will take you in and boil you and eat you with potatoes and butter. You are not a large fish, but you will do.'

'Wait,' the fish almost shouted, alarmed that Gusti had picked up an oar and seemed to mean business. Gusti had let go of the line and they were drifting away from the net toward the southeast. 'I'll give you a wish. Not three wishes, but just one, and try to be reasonable.'

Gusti put the oar down. 'I'll have my wife back.'

The fish groaned, or made a sound that was close to a groan. 'I asked you to be reasonable. Your wife has been dead two years. How could you explain her return? Bringing people back from the dead destroys the natural order of things. Besides, you fought like cats and dogs when she was alive. Let me give you a new boat instead.'

Gusti reached for the oar again.

'No, wait,' the fish continued. 'I can give you Valdi Thorson's wife, Vigdis Thorarinsdottir, instead. She's the most beautiful woman in New Iceland and you know you've lusted for her for years, even when your wife was alive.'

Gusti pondered for a moment then replied, 'No. She is a fine woman, but a man shall cleave to his wife. It is either my wife that you give me, or I eat you for supper this very night.'

'OK,' the fish grumbled, 'but it's not the way you think. She won't be there waiting for you when you get back. She'll arrive in two weeks as a young woman, the cousin of your wife. Her name will be Freya Gudmundsdottir and she'll claim kin and come to live with you. But you'll have to woo her. And you'll have to shape up or else she'll marry Ketil Hallgrimsson, and then you'll have neither wife nor supper.'

'Good,' said Gusti, 'that's fair. Now what have you come to tell me?'

The fish appeared to be sulking. 'It's ridiculous,' he complained. 'I appear at great personal risk to offer mankind wisdom, and I get petty arguments, greed and lust. It's always the same. And I don't suppose you'll pay any attention to what I tell you anyway. Do you think I like to breathe air? Do you think it's comfortable here on the bottom of this boat? I don't know why I do it.'

The sunfish fell silent. Gusti felt a little sorry for it and he asked gently, 'What is it I should know? I will listen carefully, and if things work out as you say and my wife returns, I will try to carry out your instructions.'

The fish seemed a little mollified at this. 'OK,' he said, 'listen carefully.'

Gusti leaned forward, attentive. 'It's over,' the fish told him. 'Done. Finished. Kaput. They're closing down the whole show. Moving on to bigger and better things. Cutting their losses.'

'What do you mean?' Gusti asked the fish, who by now was slowly opening and closing his mouth.

'All of it. Everything. Sun, moon, stars, trees, birds, animals, men, dogs, cats, the whole shooting works.'

'You are telling me then,' said Gusti, 'that the world is going to end.'

'You got it,' said the fish, 'go to the head of the class.' He flopped once and continued, 'And not a moment too soon. Nothing but greed, lust, dishonesty, and pride. And self-righteousness. If it weren't for self-righteousness, they might give it another go. If you knew how often I've flopped around the bottom of boats trying to explain things, talking to selfish louts with no more in their minds than their own little comforts, it'd make you sick.'

'And when is this to happen?' Gusti asked.

'I don't know. Maybe tomorrow, maybe a couple of millennia. They're busy, they've got things to do. Anyway, I've done my part. I've delivered the message. Now if you just heave me over the side, I'll be on my way.'

Gusti ignored the fish. 'This,' he said, 'is no great news. Everyone knows that the world will end some day. What matters is to live a proper life while you are here.'

'Makes no difference,' said the fish. 'Proper or improper. What one man does is of no concern. If the whole world changed then maybe they'd reconsider. But it's far too late now for that. Go ahead, rob, murder, steal, it isn't going to make any difference. And if you don't get me in the water soon, you're going to have my death on your conscience as well.'

The fish's eyes had started to cloud over. 'Just one last question,' Gusti went on. 'What day will my wife arrive?'

'You see,' said the fish, as if addressing someone not in the boat but in the blue sky overhead, 'you see what I have to put up with. I bring the most important message in the history of the universe and I have to answer foolish questions. Friday. Or Wednesday, or maybe Saturday. A week or a month. I've given you your wish. I'm not in charge of travel arrangements.'

The fish had ceased to gasp, and lay in the bottom of the boat like a dead fish. Gusti picked it up gently, and slipped it into the water. The fish lay on its side, drifting slowly away from the boat. Gusti watched it for a long time, until finally, with a flick of its tail, it disappeared under the shining surface of the lake.

The next morning Gusti did not go out to his nets. Instead, he hauled water from the lake and heated it over an open fire. He took every article out of his shack and washed it. Then he washed the entire shack, inside and out, including the roof. He rechinked every crack he could find with clay, and then he whitewashed the shack inside and out. The entire community came out to watch him with wonder. The children began by singing the song they always sang when he came near, 'Gusti Foulfart, Gusti Foulfart, smells like rotten meat. Stinky beans and stinky fish is all that he will eat.' Their parents hushed them and threatened to send them home unless they stopped.

Vigdis Thorarinsdottir was the only one brave enough to speak to him. She knew she was the most beautiful woman in New Iceland and she had seen Gusti look at her out of the corner of his eye.

'Gusti,' she asked, 'what happened? Are you expecting someone?'

'There has been a change,' he replied. 'The world will end soon and so a man cannot mourn forever. I will fish no longer. From now on I will be Gusti Carpenter. If you will make two blankets of the finest wool, I will repair the leaking roof on your shack which your husband will not repair because he prefers to sit on the dock repairing nets and telling stories. And, Alda Baldvinsdottir,' he went on, 'you have a cow. If you will give me a jug of milk each day for a year, I will put another room on your shack so that the twins will not have to sleep in the same bed with you and your husband, and you will not have to worry that he will roll over and smother them.'

In this way, Gusti conducted business with the entire community. Halli Valgardson exchanged a year's supply of firewood for a new boat. Inga Gislasdottir agreed to make him a new suit in exchange for a brick chimney. The fishermen agreed to provide him with all the fish he could eat if he kept the dock in good repair. When the sun went down that day, Gusti was the richest man in New Iceland, and everyone had forgotten to call him Gusti Foulfart or even Gusti Madman.

One month later, twenty new settlers arrived on Hannes Kristjanson's boat. They told frightening stories of the trip, how their ship had nearly foundered on the rocks on the coast of Scotland, and how a marvellous silver fish had appeared and led the boat to safety; how, coming up the St Lawrence, they would surely have crashed into another ship had not a marvellous silver fish come to the captain in a dream and warned him in time. Just that morning, coming down the Red River, they had run aground in the delta, but a school of silver fishes had bumped into the boat until it floated free.

Among the passengers was Freya Gudmundsdottir. She was eighteen years old, with blonde hair that hung down to her waist and eyes so blue that from that day on, no one in New Iceland called anything blue without explaining that it was not as blue as Freya's eyes. She looked like Gusti's wife had looked when she was young, but Gusti's wife had only looked pretty, and Freya was beautiful.

Ketil Hallgrimsson was the first to meet her when she got off the boat. He asked her to marry him then and there, and he vowed to devote his life to making her happy. Ketil was a handsome young man, only twenty-three years old, with hair that hung in curls and muscles that rippled when he moved. The smile with which Freya answered him made Gusti's blood freeze. Still, she said she had not come to marry the first man she met, and she asked for Gusti. She told him she was the orphaned cousin of his wife, and asked if she might live with him until she could support herself. Gusti's tongue was so tied in knots that he could barely stammer yes.

She gave him her trunk to carry and followed him down the street to his newly whitewashed shack. The first thing she said when she got into the shack was, 'I can see there hasn't been a woman's hand around here for a while.' Then she scrubbed the table that Gusti had scrubbed until the top was thin. She sniffed the blankets that Vigdis Thorarinsdottir had just made and which had never been used. She screwed up her nose and hung them out on a tree to air. Then she swept the cleanest floor in New Iceland, threw out the fish that had been caught that morning, saying they had gone bad, and she started to make bread. Gusti sighed and thought, 'Yes, this is my wife all right. The fish has delivered his part of the bargain.'

And that was pretty much the way things went until the following spring. Gusti found himself occupying a smaller and smaller part of the house. He left early in the morning to do the jobs he had promised the others, and he came back late at night to find the house getting cleaner and cleaner. Freya made him new clothes. She cut his hair and clipped his fingernails and toenails. He had almost no time to write in his diary, but what he wrote pretty well describes his life. 'Thursday, January 11. More snow, the weather very cold. Freya is cleaning again. Worked all day repairing Helgi's roof. I may no more chew tobacco.' Any entry reads like any other.

Then that spring, Freya was chosen to be protector of the god in the wagon. Gusti should have expected it. Each year the prettiest young woman in the community was chosen, and Freya was certainly the prettiest of the young women.

Things changed very quickly. One morning Gusti awoke to find that his breakfast had not been made and Freya was not in her bed. He thought, because it was spring, that she might have gone for a walk, but she was not on the beach, nor was she in the garden behind the house. He walked to the dock and asked the fishermen if she had gone by. They laughed and said it would be some time before he saw her. He asked the children on the road, but they only laughed and ran away. Finally, he knocked on the door of Vigdis Thorarinsdottir, and she told him not to be a fool. 'When the god in the wagon comes you will see her,' Vigdis said, 'now go away and act like a man.'

Gusti knew then that he was in trouble. The protector of the god must marry that spring, and Gusti had not begun his wooing. Though they had shared the house for eight months, they were no closer than the day she had arrived. Gusti had been silenced by her wonderful beauty and even more silenced by her terrible temper. Still, he had changed for her. He was clean, obedient, sober and hard-working, an ideal husband. Ketil Hallgrimsson, on the other hand, had given up all work, and did nothing but sulk on the dock and wait till Freya came by, when he would leap to his feet and do tricks of strength until she had passed.

It was time, Gusti thought, to consult the fish. He walked all the way out to the south point and around to the channel, where the water was deep and he knew that fish liked to sun themselves. He stopped near a large white rock and shouted to the gentle waves that lapped at the shore. 'Sunfish, come out of the water, I have to talk to you.' The only reply was the splash of a tern diving for minnows. He shouted again but still there was nothing but the quarrelling of gulls. He was about to leave, when he decided, 'No, I have walked all this way, I will try once more. Sunfish,' he cried, 'come out.' With a splash, the sunfish landed at his feet.

'If you would read something besides the newspaper,' the sunfish said, 'you would know that you have to call three times. Now what's wrong? Is the wife I brought you not good enough?'

'Oh, she's fine,' Gusti replied, 'even more beautiful than I remembered, though her temper is strong.'

'You just forget,' the fish said. 'She is exactly as she was. You were just younger and didn't pay as much attention to her.'

'Well,' said Gusti, 'she has now been chosen as protector of the god in the wagon, and so must marry this spring. What shall I do?'

'Marry her.'

'I am not so sure she will marry me.'

'Well, that's your problem, isn't it?' said the sunfish. 'I've fulfilled my part of the bargain. Face it, you're getting on, you're not a young man anymore. And besides, you've become incredibly dull. You've given up tobacco, you don't drink, you work hard all the time, you've even shaved off your beard. What woman would give you a second glance?'

'There is no need to be insulting,' said Gusti. 'I have only asked you politely for advice.'

'I'm busy,' said the fish. 'The world is coming to an end. I've got things to do. I have no time to give advice to the lovelorn.' With a flick of his tail, he flipped himself back into the lake. Then his head appeared, silver in the sunlight, and he added, 'Give her a philtre,' and disappeared.

'What kind of philtre?' Gusti shouted at the waves, but the sunfish was gone and the waves didn't answer.

For the rest of the week, Gusti stayed in his house, watching the dishes go dirty, the dust begin to gather on the table and the floor. He stopped shaving and began to chew tobacco, spitting the juice into a basin on the floor. Freya did not appear. She was gone wherever the women had taken her to prepare, and he knew there was no reason to expect her. Once, Ketil Hallgrimsson came over and they shared a bottle, but neither had anything to say. In the community, women were frantically baking, and the men were decorating the doors with willow boughs. The first green leaves were starting to sprout on the poplars and maples, and already in some yards, the poppies were starting to bloom, white and yellow and red.

On Friday at dawn, she arrived. The whole community, men, women and children, had gathered in the street to await her. She came down the road from the south, dressed in a flowing white robe, her long golden hair ruffling in a slight breeze, her blue eyes flashing. Gusti thought he had never seen anything so beautiful. She was leading Helgi Gudmundson's white ox. The ox had a garland of flowers around its neck and was pulling the wagon with the god. The god was the largest Gusti had ever seen. He towered above the wagon and swayed with every step of the ox. His heavy hands, palms upturned for rain, rested on the front of the wagon. His shirt was a brilliant patchwork of colour and his great painted face beamed at the whole community. The wagon was filled with flowers, and there were flowers and branches with green leaves sticking out of every crevice in the enormous body. Gusti noticed that one of the legs was draped in the blanket that Vigdis Thorarinsdottir had made for him. 'Where,' he wondered, 'where do the women find so many flowers, so early in the season?'

The ox stopped right at the foot of the dock, and Freya climbed into the wagon and seated herself in the lap of the god. She began the oration, and all the community sat down on the ground to listen. Gusti was so entranced by her beauty and her frailty, there in the lap of the god, that he hardly heard what she said. She spoke of rain. She spoke of sunlight and crops. She spoke of trees bursting out of the earth, of animals in the fields, of nets dripping with fish. She spoke of love and of little children. Her voice mingled with the voices of birds and the lapping of waves. And then she was gone.

Then the women brought out the steaming vats of coffee and plates full of pönnukökur. They brought out turkeys glazed with honey and chokecherries, chickens and pigeons and ducks. They brought out roasts of venison and roasts of beef, plates of boiled sunfish and fried pickerel and broiled whitefish. They brought out hangikjot and rullupylsa, lifrapylsa and slàtur. They carried out bowls of skyr and ram's heads pickled in buttermilk. They brought out vinarterta and kleinur and àstarbolur.

The men pulled corks out of bottles and threw away the corks. They said, 'It is never too early for good whiskey,' and they aimed the bottoms of the bottles at the sun. The children were into everything, laughing and crying and squealing, but no one paid any attention to them. Husbands and wives who had hardly spoken for months kissed like young lovers, so it is no surprise that no one noticed that Gusti had slipped away and returned to his house.

Freya was there. She had changed from her white robe into an old blue housedress. She was staring out the window and hardly noticed Gusti's arrival. She seemed not even to have noticed the mess in the house. 'You were wonderful,' Gusti began. 'Never has there been such a beautiful protector nor so clever an oration.'

Freya glanced at him, then looked out the window once more. 'I shall marry,' she said. 'In nine days, I shall marry.'

'And who shall you marry?' Gusti asked, his heart wrenching inside him.

'There are many I might marry,' Freya responded, though without enthusiasm. 'In the meanwhile, it is not seemly that I should live longer with you. I will go to stay with Vigdis Thorarinsdottir until my wedding day.' Then she packed her trunk, and Gusti carried it down the road to Vigdis's house.

The next day was quiet as the community rested from the celebration, but by Monday the town was buzzing with rumours. Who had Freya chosen? Would it be Ketil Hallgrimsson, or one of the other young men of the community? Or had she perhaps betrothed herself to an outsider who would arrive on the wedding day? There was even a rumour that the priest was angry because they had received the god in the wagon, and that he would refuse to perform the wedding ceremony. Ketil Hallgrimsson was dressed in his best clothes, and stood in the road before Vigdis Thorarinsdottir's house, doing feats of strength.

That week, Gusti had plenty of time to write in his diary. He pondered over what he might put in the philtre to gain Freya's love, and he wondered who might help him. He considered whether it was right to use a philtre at all. Could love that was gained by a trick be real? In the end, he decided that the philtre should contain pure water. What else, he thought, is so close to love? It may be taken cold or hot, it is clear and insubstantial, it refreshes, but when it is consumed it is gone. And most important, there is more of it in the world than anything else.

Here you must bear with me, because the diaries end, and so I have had to reconstruct what actually happened. My aunt Thora, whose mother was there, says that Gusti went to Vigdis Thorarinsdottir and told her of his trouble. She led him to a clearing in the bush where she comforted him in her own way and promised to slip the contents of the philtre into Freya's coffee on the morning of the wedding day. That morning, Freya chose Gusti and they were married and had thirteen children. Ketil Hallgrimsson was so sad that he drowned himself in the lake the same day.

My aunt Lara, Thora's sister, agrees with the story, but claims that Vigdis drank the water herself. That morning, Freya chose Ketil Hallgrimsson and he did not drown for twenty years. By that time, he had fathered all the children whose descendants now live in Arborg. Vigdis left her husband and went to live with Gusti and they had thirteen children, though they never married. All their descendants now live in Riverton.

The people from Arnes tell a story very much like the story of Gusti, but in their version, a marvellous stranger dressed all in silver appeared on a magnificent boat and claimed Freya for his bride. They moved to Wynyard and had thirteen children and all the Icelanders in Saskatchewan are descended from them.

My cousin Villi, who is only six years older than me, but who speaks better Icelandic, says that the family is trying to hide something. He has overheard whispers, and he believes that Freya chose both Gusti and Ketil, that the three of them raised thirteen children and no one ever knew who was the father. He says the whole thing about the fish is just made up so people will think it is only a fairy tale and not enquire any further. After all, our uncle is the mayor, and any scandal might go bad for him in the next election.

I have my own ideas. If I were making up this story, I would tell you that, yes, Gusti did go to see Vigdis and tell her his troubles, and yes, she did comfort him in her own way, telling him of the secret love she had always felt for him and begging him to forget Freya. If it were my story, I could tell you that Gusti was not a flexible man, that he had made the faithful Vigdis pour the water into Freya's coffee, that she had chosen Gusti and they had married. Then, because I would want a happy ending, I would show you how Freya's bad temper and wicked tongue drove Gusti away, so that he married the faithful Vigdis, while Freya chose the hapless Ketil, who, for all his feats of strength, could never get the better of her. I would say they each had thirteen children, and all the people of Gimli are descended from them.

But I would go even further, because a story needs a proper ending, and I would do something about the fish. I would let Gusti catch him once more in a net and when the fish began all that nonsense about the end of the world, I would have Gusti take him home to Vigdis, who would boil him and feed him to the thirteen children. So there you are.

Beth Brant *b.* 1941

TYENDINAGA MOHAWK TERRITORY, ONTARIO

'I started writing when I turned forty,' Beth Brant has said. 'It was a gift brought to me by Eagle. In these ten years I have been writing, I am always conscious that I am writing for my own People. That is my audience. That is who the stories are about and for. And if non-Natives pick up a book of mine and learn about the effects of racism and colonialism on Native Peoples and then take that within themselves to make change, that is a good thing.' Since 1981, the beginning of her writing career, Brant has edited *A Gathering of Spirit: Writing and Art by North American Indian Women* (1988), the first anthology of Native women writers, and published two collections of short fiction, *Mohawk Trail* (1990) and *Food and Spirits* (1991), which includes the story that follows. A frequent instructor, Brant has taught at the University of British Columbia (1989–90) and at the University of Toronto (1993), and has published widely in many literary magazines, including those focusing on lesbian and gay issues. One of the founders of Turtle Grandmothers, a group that both facilitates the editing and publishing of manuscripts by Native women and gathers archival information about North American Native women writers, she is the editor of *I'll Sing Til the Day I Die: Conversations with Tyendinaga Elders* (1995), a collection of interviews and stories that gives voice to the experiences of the elders in her community.

Beth Brant (Degonwadonti), a Bay of Quinte Mohawk from the Tyendinaga Mohawk Reserve in Deseronto, Ontario, was born in Melvidale, Michigan, where her grandparents had moved because her mother's Irish family did not approve initially of her marriage to a Mohawk man. Marriage and motherhood at age 17 led her to drop out of high school, but lacking the 'advantage' of formal education did not prevent her from becoming a major force of learning and unlearning in her community. When using 'the enemy's language to hold onto my strength as a Mohawk lesbian writer,' Brant has said, 'I use it as my own instrument of power in this long, long battle against racism.' Following the end of her abusive marriage, Brant met Denise Dorsz in 1976, her partner for many years. A resident of Detroit, Michigan, Brant writes about working-class Native families, urban Natives, lesbian relationships, and the gift of spiritual re-empowerment that traditional Native stories offer to Native people. Behind the confident voice of her writing, there lies, however, the painful process that leads to it. As she says in her preface to *Food and Spirits*, 'This pen feels like a knife in my hand. / The paper should bleed, like my peoples' bodies. . . . How do I show the blood of them? The ink of our own palette? / Medicine. / Who will heal the writer who uses her ink and blood to tell? / Telling. / Who hears?' *Writing As Witness: Essay and Talk* (1994) offers a record of Brant's writing process and her belief that writing can heal, but also of her concern with the appropriation of Native spirituality through such movements as 'new-age religion': 'I long,' she writes, 'for . . . a healthy respect for sovereignty and the culture that makes Nationhood. We do not object to non-Natives praying with us (if invited). We object to the theft of our prayers that have no psychic meaning to them.' In collaboration with Sandra Laronde (Teme-Augama Aishnaabe), a major force behind the Toronto Native Women in the Arts organization, Brant has edited the anthologies *In a Vast Dreaming* (1995) and *Sweet Grass Grows All Around Her* (1996). She has received, among other grants, a National Endowment Arts Award (1991).

This is History

for Donna Goodleaf

Long before there was an earth and long before there were people called human, there was a Sky World.

On Sky World there were Sky People who were like us and not like us. And of the Sky People there was Sky Woman. Sky Woman had a particular trait: she had curiosity. She bothered the others with her questions, with wanting to know what lay beneath the clouds that supported her world. Sometimes she pushed the clouds aside and looked down through her world to the large expanse of blue that shimmered below. The others were tired of her peculiar trait and called her an aberration, a queer woman who asked questions, a woman who wasn't satisfied with what she had.

Sky Woman spent much of her time dreaming—dreaming about the blue expanse underneath the clouds, dreaming about floating through the clouds, dreaming about the blue color and how it would feel to her touch. One day she pushed the clouds away from her and leaned out of the opening. She fell. The others tried to catch her hands and pull her back, but she struggled free and began to float downward. The Sky People watched her descent and agreed that they were glad to see her go. She was a nuisance with her questions, an aberration, a queer woman who was not like them—content to walk the clouds undisturbed.

Sky Woman floated. The currents of wind played through her hair. She put out her arms and felt the sensations of air between her fingers. She kicked her legs, did somersaults, and was curious about the free, delightful feelings of flying. Faster, faster, she floated toward the blue shimmer that beckoned her.

She heard a noise and turned to see a beautiful creature with black wings and a white head flying close to her. The creature spoke. 'I am Eagle. I have been sent to carry you to your new home.' Sky Woman laughed and held out her hands for Eagle to brush his wings against. He swooped under her, and she settled on his back. They flew. They circled, they glided, they flew, Sky Woman clutching the feathers of the great creature.

Sky Woman looked down at the blue color. Rising from the expanse was a turtle. Turtle looked up at the flying pair and nodded her head. She dove into the waters and came up again with a muskrat clinging to her back. In Muskrat's paw was a clump of dark brown dirt scooped from the bottom of the sea. She laid it on Turtle's back and jumped back into the water. Sky Woman watched the creature swim away, her long tail skimming the top of the waves, her whiskers shining. Sky Woman watched as the dark brown dirt began to spread. All across Turtle's back the dirt was spreading, spreading, and in this dirt green things were growing. Small green things, tall green things, and in the middle of Turtle's back, the tallest thing grew. It grew branches and needles, more and more branches, until it reached where Eagle and Sky Woman were hovering.

Turtle raised her head and beckoned to the pair. Eagle flew down to Turtle's back and gently lay Sky Woman on the soft dirt. Then he flew to the very top of the White Pine tree and said, 'I will be here, watching over everything that is to be. You will look to me as the harbinger of what is to happen. You will be kind to me and my people. In return, I will keep this place safe.' Eagle folded his wings and looked away.

Sky Woman felt the soft dirt with her fingers. She brought the dirt to her mouth and tasted the color of it. She looked around at the green things. Some were flowering with fantastic shapes. She stood on her feet and felt the solid back of Turtle beneath her. She marveled at this wonderful place and wondered what she would do here.

Turtle swiveled her head and looked at Sky Woman with ancient eyes. 'You will live here and make this a new place. You will be kind, and you will call me Mother. I will make all manner of creatures and growing things to guide you on this new place. You will watch them carefully, and from them you will learn how to live. You will take care to be respectful and honorable to me. I am your Mother.' Sky Woman touched Turtle's back and promised to honor and respect her. She lay down on Turtle's back and fell asleep.

As she slept, Turtle grew. Her back became wider and longer. She slapped her tail and cracks appeared in her back. From these cracks came mountains, canyons were formed, rivers and lakes were made from the spit of Turtle's mouth. She shook her body and prairies sprang up, deserts settled, marshes and wetlands pushed their way through the cracks of Turtle's shell. Turtle opened her mouth and called. Creatures came crawling out of her back. Some had wings, some had four legs, six legs, or eight. Some had no legs but slithered on the ground, some had no legs and swam with fins. These creatures crawled out of Turtle's back and some were covered with fur, some with feathers, some with scales, some with skins of beautiful colors. Turtle called again, and the creatures found their voice. Some sang, some barked, some growled and roared, some had no voice but a hiss, some had no voice and rubbed their legs together to speak. Turtle called again. The creatures began to make homes. Some gathered twigs and leaves, others spun webs, some found caves, others dug holes in the ground. Some made the waters their home, and some of these came up for air to breathe. Turtle shuddered, and the new place was made a continent, a world.

Turtle gave a last look to the sleeping Sky Woman. 'Inside you is growing a being who is like you and not like you. This being will be your companion. Together you will give names to the creatures and growing things. You will be kind to these things. This companion growing inside you will be called First Woman, for she will be the first of these beings on this earth. Together you will respect me and call me Mother. Listen to the voices of the creatures and communicate with them. This will be called prayer, for prayer is the language of all my creations. Remember me.' Turtle rested from her long labor.

Sky Woman woke and touched herself. Inside her body she felt the stirrings of another. She stood on her feet and walked the earth. She climbed mountains, she walked in the desert, she slept in trees, she listened to the voices of the creatures and living things, she swam in the waters, she smelled the growing things that came from the earth. As she wandered and discovered, her body grew from the being inside her. She ate leaves, she picked fruit. An animal showed her how to bring fire, then threw himself in the flames that she might eat of him. She prayed her thanks, remembering Turtle's words. Sky Woman watched the creatures, learning how they lived in community with each other, learning how they hunted, how they stored food, how they prayed. Her body grew larger, and she felt her companion move inside her, waiting to be born. She watched the living things, seeing how they fed their young, how they taught their young, how they protected their young. She watched and learned and saw how things should be. She waited for the day when First Woman would come and together they would be companions, lovers of the earth, namers of all things, planters and harvesters, creators.

On a day when Sky Woman was listening to the animals, she felt a sharp pain inside of her. First Woman wanted to be born. Sky Woman walked the earth, looking for soft things to lay her companion on when she was born. She gathered all day, finding feathers of the winged-creatures, skins of the fur-bearers. She gathered these things and made a deep nest. She gathered other special things for medicine and magic. She ate leaves from a plant that eased her pain. She clutched her magic things in her hands to give her help. She prayed to the creatures to strengthen her. She squatted over the deep nest and began to push. She pushed and held tight to the magic medicine. She pushed, and First Woman slipped out of her and onto the soft nest. First Woman gave a cry. Sky Woman touched her companion, then gave another great push as her placenta fell from her. She cut the long cord with her teeth as she had learned from the animals. She ate the placenta as she had learned from the animals. She brought First Woman to her breast as she had learned, and First Woman began to suckle, drawing nourishment and medicine from Sky Woman.

Sky Woman prayed, thanking the creatures for teaching her how to give birth. She touched the earth, thanking Mother for giving her this gift of a companion. Turtle shuddered, acknowledging the prayer. That day, Sky Woman began a new thing. She opened her mouth and sounds came forth. Sounds of song. She sang and began a new thing—singing prayers. She fashioned a thing out of animal skin and wood. She touched the thing and it resonated. She touched it again and called it drum. She sang with the rhythm of her touching. First Woman suckled as her companion sang the prayers.

First Woman began to grow. In the beginning she lay in her nest dreaming, then crying out as she wanted to suckle. Then she opened her eyes and saw her companion and smiled. Then she sat up and made sounds. Then she crawled and was curious about everything. She wanted to touch and feel and taste all that was around her. Sky Woman carried her on her back when she walked the earth, listening to the living things and talking with them. First Woman saw all the things that Sky Woman pointed out to her. She listened to Sky Woman touch the drum and make singing prayers. First Woman stood on her feet and felt the solid shell of Turtle against her feet. The two companions began walking together. First Woman made a drum for herself, and together the companions made magic by touching their drums and singing their prayers. First Woman grew, and as she grew Sky Woman showed her the green things, the animal things, the living things, and told her they needed to name them. Together they began the naming. Heron, bear, snake, dolphin, spider, maple, oak, thistle, cricket, wolf, hawk, trout, goldenrod, firefly. They named together and, in naming, the women became closer and truer companions. The living things that now had names moved closer to the women and taught them how to dance. Together, they all danced as the women touched their drums and made their singing prayers. Together they danced. Together. All together.

In time the women observed the changes that took place around them. They observed that sometimes the trees would shed their leaves and at other times would grow new ones. They observed that some creatures buried themselves in caves and burrows and slept for long times, reappearing when the trees began their new birth. They observed that some creatures flew away for long times, reappearing when the animals crawled from their caves and dens. Together, the companions decided they would sing special songs and different prayers when the earth was changing and the creatures were changing. They named these times seasons and made different drums, sewn with feathers and stones. The companions wore stones around their necks, feathers in their hair, and shells on their feet, and when they danced, the music was new and extraordinary. They prepared feasts at this time, asking the animals to accept their death. Some walked into their arrows, some ran away. The animals that gave their lives were thanked and their bones were buried in Turtle's back to feed her—the Mother of all things.

The women fashioned combs from animal teeth and claws. They spent long times combing and caressing each other's hair. They crushed berries and flowers and painted signs on their bodies to honor Mother and the living things who lived with them. They painted on rocks and stones to honor the creatures who taught them. They fixed food together, feeding each other herbs and roots and plants. They lit fires together and cooked the foods that gave them strength and medicine. They laughed together and made language between them. They touched each other and in the touching made a new word: love. They touched each other and made a language of touching: passion. They made medicine together. They made magic together.

And on a day when First Woman woke from her sleep, she bled from her body. Sky Woman marveled at this thing her companion could do because she was born on Turtle's back. Sky Woman built a special place for her companion to retreat at this time, for it was wondrous what her body could do. First Woman went to her bleeding-place and dreamed about her body and the magic it made. And at the end of this time, she emerged laughing and holding out her arms to Sky Woman.

Time went by, long times went by. Sky Woman felt her body changing. Her skin was wrinkling, her hands were not as strong. She could not hunt as she used to. Her eyes were becoming dim, her sight unclear. She walked the earth in this changed body and took longer to climb mountains and swim in the waters. She still enjoyed the touch of First Woman, the laughter and language they shared between them, the dancing, the singing prayers. But her body was changed. Sky Woman whispered to Mother, asking her what these changes meant. Mother whispered back that Sky Woman was aged and soon her body would stop living. Before this event happened, Sky Woman must give her companion instruction. Mother and Sky Woman whispered together as First Woman slept. They whispered together the long night through.

When First Woman woke from her sleep, Sky Woman told her of the event that was to happen. 'You must cut the heart from this body and bury it in the field by your bleeding-place. Then you must cut this body in small pieces and fling them into the sky. You will do this for me.'

And the day came that Sky Woman's body stopped living. First Woman touched her companion's face and promised to carry out her request. She carved the heart from Sky Woman's body and buried it in the open field near her bleeding-place. She put her ear to the ground and heard Sky Woman's voice, 'From this place will grow three plants. As long as they grow, you will never want for food or magic. Name these plants corn, beans, and squash. Call them the Three Sisters, for like us, they will never grow apart.'

First Woman watched as the green plant burst from the ground, growing stalks that bore ears of beautifully colored kernels. From beneath the corn rose another plant with small leaves, and it twined around the stalks carrying pods of green. Inside each pod were small, white beans. From under the beans came a sprawling vine with large leaves that tumbled and grew and shaded the beans' delicate roots. On this vine were large, green squash that grew and turned orange and yellow. Three Sisters, First Woman named them.

First Woman cut her companion's body in small pieces and flung them at the sky. The sky turned dark, and there, glittering and shining, were bright-colored stars and a round moon. The moon spoke. 'I will come to you every day when the sun is sleeping. You will make songs and prayers for me. Inside you are growing two beings. They are not like us. They are called Twin Sons. One of these is good and will honor us and our Mother. One of these is not good and will bring things that we have no names for. Teach these beings what we have learned together. Teach them that if the sons do not honor the women who made them, that will be the end of this earth. Keep well, my beloved First Woman. Eagle is watching out for you. Honor the living things. Be kind to them. Be strong. I am always with you. Remember our Mother. Be kind to her.'

First Woman touched her body, feeling the movements inside. She touched the back of Mother and waited for the beings who would change her world.

Andrew Suknaski *b.* 1942

WOOD MOUNTAIN, SASKATCHEWAN

Although Andrew Suknaski has not published a new book of poetry in twenty years, he remains one of the most important poets to have come out of Saskatchewan. Of Ukrainian and Polish ancestry, Suknaski was born in the farming community of Wood Mountain, Saskatchewan, whose history, both Native and immigrant, has had a profound impact on his writing. As he says, 'the first things connected with the far EAST are my UKRAINIAN father (once a european wanderer/labourer—a man who still has difficulty with twelve languages) and JIMMY HOY who came from HONG KONG to build a small cafe in the first hamlet of WOOD MTN near the old NWMP POST OF WOOD MOUNTAIN. . . . HOY built the first cafe/HOTEL where he began to hang his calendars from HONG KONG. my word/picture vision began there. . . . a few years before i left WOOD MTN, HOY went to HONG KONG (JIMMY was 80 then) and brought home a beautiful young bride. for me she compared to the picture of the VIRGIN i saw on my mother's POLISH calendars.' The writing style and imaginative associations here are typical of his many poetry collections. *Wood Mountain Poems* (1973; a revised and enlarged edition was edited by Al Purdy in 1976), like many of his other titles, celebrates the layers of Saskatchewan's past but also laments the bitter legacies of history, especially in relation to Native culture.

Suknaski began learning English only after he entered grade one, and did not finish high school until years later, having wandered in the meantime in Canada and around the world as an itinerant worker and aspiring artist. He studied at the University of Victoria (1964–5); the School of Fine Art and Design at the Montreal Museum of Fine Arts (1965); the Kootenay School of Art, where he received his only diploma (1967); the University of British Columbia (1967–8); and Simon Fraser University (1968–9).

During his stay in Vancouver in the 1960s he was introduced to the new poetry movement there, influenced by the Black Mountain school of poets, but Suknaski's art had already found forms of expression that went beyond the conventional venues of writing. Interested in found and concrete poetry, he constructed poetry books out of, among other things, brown paper bags and, as Douglas Barbour records, made 'poems to be dropped from an airplane, and one issue of [his underground *Elfin Plot*] magazine which was floated down the North Saskatchewan River in Al Purdy's empty cigar tubes'.

Writing on Stone: Poem Drawings 1966–76 (1976) shows how his concrete poetry has its roots in Jimmy Hoy's Chinese calendars and in his own desire to escape 'from a neurosis generated from a CHRISTIAN background'. These early influences, however, keep surfacing in many of his works, for example *Four Parts Sand* (1972) and *Old Mill* (1972). The formal and cultural hybridity of these books results from Suknaski's use of Chinese ideograms and Eastern Orthodox iconography. As a concrete poet, he was one of several artists to represent Canada at the Expo/International de Proposiciones a Realizar exhibition held in Buenos Aires in 1971.

Whether written in a romantic, humorous, or despairing voice, all of Suknaski's poetry reveals his deep concern with disenfranchised peoples and with displacement. *Octomi* (1976), whose title refers to the spider as trickster figure, gathers together Teton Sioux stories for children. *The Ghosts Call You Poor* (1978) casts the poet's preoccupation with Native and immigrant cultures within a wider range to embody material about the Métis, Chinese 'coolies', and Ukrainian immigrants in British Columbia. *East of Myloona* (1979) incorporates some of his best drawings. *In the Name of Narid: New Poems* (1981) reflects his growing despair about political suffering in places like the former Soviet Union, whereas *Montage for an Interstellar Cry* (1982) is a book written in a prophetic kind of voice that continues to explore the history of such troubled places as Chile, Hiroshima, and Dresden. In 1982, Stephen Scobie edited a selection by Suknaski, *The Land They Gave Away: New & Selected Poems*. The most recent book by Suknaski, who won the Canadian Authors Association prize for poetry in 1978, is *Silk Trail* (1985).

Philip Well

prairie spring
and i stand here before a tire crimper
two huge vices held by a single bolt
(men of the prairies were grateful to a skilled man
who could use it and fix wooden wheels
when the craft flourished)

5

i stand here
and think of philip well found in his musty woodshed
this morning
by dunc mcpherson on edge of wood mountain—   10
philip well lying silent by his rusty .22

and i ask my village: *who was this man?*
this man who left us

in 1914
well and my father walked south from moose jaw   15
to find their homesteads
they slept in haystacks along the way
and once nearly burned to death
waking in the belly of hell they were saved by mewling mice
and their song of agony—   20
a homesteader had struck a match and thought he
would teach them a lesson

well and father lived in a hillside and built fires
to heat stones each day in winter
they hunted and skinned animals to make fur blankets   25
threw redhot stones into their cellars
overlaid the stones with willows
and slept between hides

father once showed me a picture
nine black horses pulling a gang plough   30
philip well proudly riding behind (breaking
the homestead to make a home)

well quiet and softspoken
loved horses and trees and planted poplars around his shack
when the land began to drift away   35
in tough times well brought a tire crimper
and fixed wheels tanned hides and mended harnesses
for people

and later (having grown older and often not feeling well)
moved to wood mountain village   40
to be near people who could drive him to a doctor
if necessary

today in wood mountain
men's faces are altered by well's passing
while they drink coffee in jimmy hoy's cafe   45
no one remembers if well had a sweetheart
though someone remembers a school dance near
the montana border one christmas—
well drunk and sleeping on a bench in the corner
while the people danced   50
well lonelier than judas after the kiss
(the heart's sorrow like a wheel's iron ring
tightening around the brain till
the centre cannot hold and
the body breaks)   55

West to Tolstoi, Manitoba (circa 1900)

the story of the young ukrainian immigrant
imprisoned   in his language and ghetto
his name no longer remembered
but an aging woman in assiniboia
tells the rest about him   5
spending those lonely winters in montreal with nothing
but a friend's letters from tolstoi
ukrainian hamlet in rural manitoba
whitewashed   straw and mud shacks
with thatched roofs   10
the way it was done   in the homeland

others who relate the story   are not certain
how many times he left montreal on foot
each spring
with never more than a couple dollars change in his pocket 15
and how he always followed   the railway tracks west
stopping at some station   to check a map
to see where he was
occasionally helped   by some station agent
who offered food   and a bed   20
hassled by railway officials
who always failed to understand his talk
and sent him   back on an eastbound train
free

no one knows   how far he got each time   25
until one year   he met some ukrainian immigrants
at a station   in central ontario
where he embraced one of them   and told his story
'please   take me with you
i never   want to speak   30
to another englishman
for the rest of my life'

Vasylyna's Retreat

vasylyna
      retreating into wilderness
                       had it
    po vukha!
    'to the ears'   5
        with people
vasylyna
      perfectly able
          building herself
      adobe house   10
        with straw roof
vasylyna
      constructing
        a simple shelter
    of shakes   15
      and scrap lumber
               for a goat
      one milk cow
         and a few chickens
    arrive alone   20
       on the margins
           of vasylyna's
poplars
        and the ghostly
flatbreasted   25
      figure
        with a doublebarrel shotgun
delicately
    angled
      across the right shoulder   30
will call

KHTO TAM
'WHO GOES THERE'
and failing to answer
                    in vasylyna's language   35
                                        or going
        any further
                    can only end
        in feet
                e x p l o d i n g   40
                            beneath one

        though vasylyna's gun
                        has never been fired
                                    in fifty years
but go there   45
            with mykola
                        if you ever find him
        and vasylyna
                    will make tea
                                and reveal   50
        unspeakable things
                        in translation

        '. . . do you know
        the englishmen
        they are snakes!   55
        sometimes   i fry them
        in my frying pan! yes!

        . . . and the frenchmen
        they are   dogs! yes!
        i keep them tied   60
        in the poplar! yes!

        . . . do you know   last night
        there was a mist
        Jesus Christ   and i
        we flew high above vita!   65

        children   would you care
        for some more tea?

In the Beginning was The

after barry mckinnon's the inquiry

lady coyote
        in the beginning was *the*
                      whole *world*
    swelling
        a single cock   5
              inside
                  her mouth
    in the beginning was
             the sea
        around
            her small   10
                mountain
        his tongue
             like *the*
               fabled ark
          ploughing   15
              through damp
                      earth
lady coyote
        that was
             the ascent   20
  the cat from
             nazareth
                fled
stipple it in memory
             forever   25
                lady coyote
that
  was the beginning
             and millennia later
                     the word is   30
             doled out
                  like fucking
             sunday
                mints

Letter to Big Bear

World's Best Coffee
Broadway / W 158th Street
Uptown Manhattan
NYC
April 24, 1979

Big Bear
c/o *NeWest Review*
10123–112 Street
Edmonton, Alberta
Canada

Dear Big Bear,

Here at THE MUSEUM OF THE AMERICAN INDIAN your medicine bundle lies in some dusty drawer. And I must confess, I came here wanting to look into your sacred bundle; however, having arrived here now in Washington Heights on the edge of the Hudson River, it now seems more important not to do that. After all, Big Bear, some things are sacred. Your people kept talismans and sometimes certain remains of ancestors in such bundles. And they say before a long journey, or for many other reasons, you would carefully open your medicine bundle. And pray for strength.

I donno, Big Bear, it seems wiser to understand clearly what lured me here. It seems best to let these things be—part of those private things on earth. For the truth is, there were always only two places where the medicine bundle ever went: one being where the possessor, and all of us, must someday finally go; the other, remaining in the caring hands of one's lineage. This place is neither of those. Making it sad.

Best to you,
Mahzahkahzah

The Faceless Goodbyes

what little is
            remembered
                        the borgesian problem
        memory's
                betrayal   5

                   each image
        the nebulous
             vestige
                 witnessed
      in distortion   10
             of things serving
      as amazing
            mirrors

what little
      endures   15
           clear enough
suknatskyj
         traitor
            of spirit
acquiescing   20
        to cruelty
               never facing
   women
        when things
               got tough   25
        portents
           of unrequited
                 love

what little
      traces that   30
         faceless parting
   following the
       razed church
            suknatskyj's
        mother   35
          a profile
              mirrored
       by a window
             beneath
               an ikon   40
       where she
           feigned
      a fainthearted
         . . . goodbye

Daphne Marlatt *b.* 1942

MELBOURNE, AUSTRALIA

From *Frames of a Story* (1968), her first publication, to her now classic novel, *Ana Historic* (1988), Daphne Marlatt's work deals with the representation of otherness and with the desire to question, and write over and against, formal and social boundaries. Difference—in her own words, 'a high-intensity beam'—characterizes both her treatment of language and her subject matter.

Her continuous engagement with various aspects of displacement reflects her cultural background. Born in Melbourne, Australia, to British parents, she lived in Penang, Malaysia, until her family emigrated to Vancouver in 1951. She often writes out of the 'common wealth of memories' of her childhood years. 'In the Month of Hungry Ghosts' (1979), a text comprising letters, poems, and diary entries, records her first visit back to Malaysia. From her Canadian perspective, but also through memory that 'seems to operate . . . like a murmur in the flesh one suddenly hears years later', Marlatt responds to the complex impact of colonialism's legacy on class, race, gender, and sexual differences. In *Taken* (1996), her second novel, the protagonist Suzanne's narrative straddles at once her present, a time that coincides with the Gulf War and separation from her female lover, and her mother's past, which overlaps with the Second World War in Australia and Malaya. 'All my stories turn in this transition hour just before dawn when light begins to intimate the differences between things still rooted deep in earth's shadow,' Suzanne says.

Marlatt studied English and Creative Writing at the University of British Columbia (BA 1964), where she was a contributing editor to *Tish* (1963–5). Her attention to language as a living thing, as what constructs the world, and her experimentation with genre and form can be traced back to those days, as well as to the influence of the Black Mountain poets. After studying comparative literature at the University of Indiana (MA 1968), she returned to Vancouver in 1970, where, as an oral historian, she edited *Steveston Recollected: Japanese Canadian History* (1975), and co-edited *Opening Doors: Vancouver's East End* (1979). An active editor, she co-founded and co-edited *Periodics* (a magazine of innovative prose) and *Tessera* (a bilingual journal of feminist theory). The Programme Coordinator for the 'Women and Words/Les femmes et les mots' conference held at the University of British Columbia in 1983, and the Ruth Wynn Woodward Professor in the Women's Studies, Program at Simon Fraser University (1988–9), she has taught English, Women's Studies, and Creative Writing at the Universities of Victoria, Windsor, and British Columbia.

Her early poetry books—*leaf leaf/s* (1969), *Rings* (1971), and *Vancouver Poems* (1972)—demonstrate her attentiveness to images and speech patterns as the means of registering the pulse of a place, and point the way to her much anthologized long poem, *Steveston* (1974, 2001), with photographs by Robert Minden. In a later text that includes poetry and a novella, *Salvage* (1991), Marlatt revisits that same territory and works through her earlier 'blocked' perceptions in the light of her feminist consciousness. The autobiographical *What Matters: Writing 1968–1970* (1980) shows Marlatt's continuous exploration of the relationship between body and language, while *How Hug a Stone* (1983), a prose text of poems and journal entries, records her visit, with her son Kit, to England in an attempt to trace her mother's origins. It was *Zocalo* (1977), a prose narrative set in Mexico, often seen by critics as a novel, which announced Marlatt's ongoing interest in life-writing and established her as a writer who challenges the boundary line between prose and poetry, fiction and reality. These last two texts, along with 'In the Month of Hungry Ghosts', have been collected in *Ghost Works* (1993). As Marlatt says, 'remembering is a fiction . . . we have this funny thing . . . remembering is real, and inventing is purely imaginary or fictional. What interests me is where those two cross.'

Her concern with the cultural construction of motherhood—'the mother's so strong,' she says, 'and we all have this in common'—and its correlation with language is the driving force in much of her writing, including in her influential essay, 'Musing with Mothertongue' (1983), collected, along with her other essays in *Readings from the Labyrinth* (1998). Her representation of lesbian desire takes on both cultural mythologies about female desire and poststructuralist thinking, as is the case with *Touch to My Tongue* (1984), a prose poetry volume, included in *Two Women in a Birth* (1994), a book that gathers together her collaborations with poet Betsy Warland, her partner between 1981 and 1993.'Woman's body,' Marlatt says, 'is never present in its own desire, so if you start writing about it, you have to combat a kind of fear that you feel because you know you're breaking a taboo.'

Influenced by some of the feminist writers of Quebec, Marlatt has collaborated with Nicole Brossard in *Mauve* (1985) and *character / jeu de lettres* (1986). One of the editors of *Telling It: Women and Language Across Cultures* (1990),

and the editor of the posthumous publication *Mothertalk: Life Stories of Mary Kiyoshi Kiyooka* (1997) by Roy Kiyooka, her partner from 1974 to 1981, she is committed to exploring 'the ways in which we are connected to other forms of life, to other races, other classes' in order to 'work against the domination of one over all the others'. *This Tremor Love Is* (2001), love poems spanning a period of twenty-five years, and *Seven Glass Bowls* (2003), an excerpt from her novel-in-progress, are her most recent publications. The winner of the Brissenden Award and the Macmillan Award for Writing, Marlatt has received honorary degrees from the University of Western Ontario (1996) and Mount Saint Vincent University (2004), and has been inducted into the Order of Canada (2006). Her most recent work is a contemporary Canadian Noh play, 'The Gull', a bilingual Canada–Japan project, co-directed by Akira Matsui and Richard Emmert, with music by Emmert. The story of two Nisei brothers born in Steveston and returning to the coast to fish after the years of internment, it was produced in May 2006 by Pangaea Arts (Vancouver).

from *Month of Hungry Ghosts*

22nd July
Penang 11:30 PM

A cheecha running along the ceiling above makes a funny chirping noise—light brown almost pink legs, one beady eye upon me writing at this glasstopped desk. Waves of cricket & treefrog sounds continuously breaking outside around the house. Barking dogs in the distance. Hot. Dark.

Once out on the road by myself, walking down it—vague memories of walking down it as a child, knew where the golf course was where we used to pick mushrooms in the early morning—once out in that humming dark, the trees—one I did seem to know, spreading its great umbrella arms (sam-cha? the same?) writhing in the light (streetlamp), it's the *vivid*ness of everything here—I was afraid, had to force myself to walk—afraid of this life & what the night hides, bats? cobras? At the last house on the road (such huge gardens around each mansion) a tall frangipani tree dropping white blossoms on the grass (which isn't grass but a kind of low growing broadleafed plant). I came back to find Mr Y in his pyjamas & Dad outside looking for me. Locking up. Then a to-do about locking the ironwork gate in the upper hall that separates the bedrooms from the rest of the house ('we've had a spot of trouble') . . .

Mr Y moves like water in a conversation, either rushing forward with endless talk of company affairs or receding into not hearing much else. A habit of not directly answering questions, the servants do that too. Very kind. The old world courtesy, the constant talking about a thing to be done while doing it, the concern over little things like leaving a door open or closed—Yeat's lapis lazuli old man with a touch of the absurd. His passion is business, he's full of gossip about all the people whose lives have been involved with the company to any extent—& all the internal dissensions, inner politics—absorbing, the game business is, played with utter seriousness. He hints at many things yet overstates, 'it was cruel' etc., which makes for a curious style of conversation.

Eng Kim: recognized her as soon as I saw her, but curiously didn't want to show my recognition immediately. She's hardly changed at all—so amazingly similar in appearance after 25 years. Still that almost shy, perfectly naïve sweetness—how can she have lived these years so apparently untouched? She's 'worked for the bank' (i.e. looked after the bank manager & family) most of the time. The perfect servant, neat & unassuming, quiet as a shadow—yet I catch a glint of humour in her smile. Will it be possible to know her better? It's so strange to be, now 25 years later, someone she serves, instead of the child she chivvied along.

O the disparities—how can I ever relate the two parts of myself? This life would have killed me—purdah, a woman in—the restrictions on movement, the confined reality. I can't stand it. I feel imprisoned in my class—my? This is what I came out of. & how else can I be here?

July 28th

Dear Cille,

. . . It's not so much a holiday as a curious psychic re-dipping in the old font, & most of the time I'm kicking against it. Because it's so insidious, the English habits of speech & perception, English patterns of behaviour. (Suppose I got the longest conditioning anyhow, of the 3 of us kids.) But what's amazing is that it still exists, much as it has done, tho obviously it's the end of an era. It ain't *my* era, or Pam's, tho everyone we meet seems to want to suggest it is, implicate us in it. I've never before understood what a big move it was for them, to come to Canada.

Sometimes I panic—I want to rush home, as if I might get trapped here, this honey-eyed land. Mrs J. saying how she didn't want to leave Penang, 'it's such a beautiful place.' It is, & yet it all feels unreal to me—there's no authentic ground here for 'Europeans'. I want to rip out of myself all the colonialisms, the taint of colonial sets of mind. That's why as kids we hated everything 'English'—not because it was English but because we equated what was English with a colonialist attitude, that defensive set against what immediately surrounds as real on its own terms—because to take it on as real would mean to 'go native' & that was unthinkable to them.

July 29th

Dad speculates, as we peer over the bridge into the rushing darkness of the brook, cicadas trilling all around us, that in some previous life he must have been a rich

Chinese in Malacca with a fleet of junks trading spices to China. Says he always feels at home here, loves the smell of camphorwood chests, the songs of birds, the plants. I ask him has he never felt alien, never felt there were places he couldn't enter, wasn't welcome in? He says only recently, with the political situation the way it is, but that before, the only animosity he remembers encountering was in the Indian temple where he filmed the Typoosum rites & he could understand that. That leads to the further comment that he's never liked Indian temples anyhow.

What we make our own—or separate from us. The interests of the Chinese middle class here as commercial as the British, & the same sense of formality, & pragmatism.

Earlier, as we rode a trisha down to the Chartered Bank Chambers, Pam wondered how people on the street regard white women (she herself thinks English women look 'dumpy') & whether they found us sexual or not, commented on the looks various people gave us as we passed. We both felt separate & visible in our hired trisha pedalled by someone else (an incredibly skinny man)—uncomfortable parodies of the leisured class. Is this the only way to be a white woman here? Or is this the condition of being a member of an exploitive & foreign moneyed class?

& yet the sun shines on all of us alike—everywhere the flare of colour, glint of metallic thread running thru a sari, shining flesh, oil gleaming off black hair—we feel pale by comparison, & immaterial (living always in our heads?) It's the same feeling I had coming home from Mexico, that people walk the streets of Vancouver mostly as if they are invisible. Here people sleep on the sidewalks, piss in the gutters, women nurse their babies by the roadside, everyone selling food & eating it, or fingering goods, or eyeing each other (likewise tactile)—but not separate. The press in the streets is almost amniotic, it contains & carries everyone.

Today I've heard both an Indian (the cloth salesman in the market whose son is training to be a doctor in England) & a Chinese (Catholic convert, committed to both Christianity & the English language, living in a nation devoted to advancing Islam & teaching Malay) protest against the unfairness of the Malayanization policy of the govt (e.g. how 65% of all university entrants must be Malays, the other races compete for what's left). & yet this *is* Malaysia & the largely rural & labouring Malays have a lot to catch up on, fast. I can't believe the stereotype passed on to us that they're 'lazy', don't want to work, don't have a head for business, etc. & yet how long, how many generations these Chinese & Indian families have lived here, feel they belong, & then are separated off on the basis of race. All the separations.

Penang
July 23/76

Love,

Frangipani fading on the desk, Eng Kim just ran by in bare feet, so quiet in pajamas, it's 6 p.m., post-tea, post evening rain like a monsoon, mosquitoes out in the fading light (dark here by 7) & what i've tracked in the birdbook as the black-naped oriole (a yellow as brilliant as the saffron robes of the yellow men monks) trilling from the trees, flame of the forest just outside my window . . .

(dusky pink cheecha playing peekaboo behind a gilt frame, me not at all sure i want to feel those pale pink lizard feet suddenly land here, just shot up the wall to nab a midge then leap six inches onto a post & disappear to a ledge four feet above me) so much life here not even the walls are still . . .

It's strange being a princess again, the sheer luxury of this house, its spaciousness, its accoutrements (every bedroom has its own bathroom), everything kept spacious, uncluttered, unlittered & clean by servants who pick up after you, wash your clothes, cook your food, do your dishes, ad nauseum (a little work would make me feel at home). & Eng Kim herself, oh Roy that is the strangest. I recognized her as soon as she came down the steps to greet us (old baronial family style), she's hardly changed in 25 years, still climbs the stairs with all that girlish quickness & like any good servant, utterly silent. But more her smile—it's as if i'd never gone away i know that smile so completely & love it, yet it's the love that astonishes me. That face told me as much as my mother's, by its changing weather, how the world was with me, or against, what i, as any rebellious child, was up against. I must have spent hours of accumulated moments watching it. & yet her face is not maternal in any way, at age 45 or whatever it's still utterly girlish & in our smiles i catch a little of the old mischief we shared, playing our own peekaboo with all the rules.

& my god, the rules of the house & how it's been explained to Pam & me several times that we mustn't 'upset the routine', how difficult it is to finally 'get things done the way you want them' (breakfast at such & such an hour, for instance, & how the toast or coffee should be etc.),—how 'they' get confused if you alter things, so that the routine becomes itself a prison. As the women of the house, Pam & I are supposed to 'look after things', give the orders, make sure the system functions smoothly. Both of us dislike the role & like children, rebel by acting dumb. What we want is to break down the wall that separates us from Eng Kim in the very fact of our roles & yet we haven't quite figured out how.

Except that tonight we began by earlier expressing an interest in the terrible durian fruit whose stench has been much mythified since we were little (& the old durian tree in the garden where our dog was buried is gone, cut down). One of the Chinese men in the office said he'd be happy to bring some durians round for us to try tonight & kindly did so. Mr Y., when told, requested that they not be brought into the house (haven't i learned the dialect well?) so our benefactor & Pam & I regaled ourselves at an old wooden table on the walkway from kitchen to servants quarters, as he chopped them open with a cleaver (they look like wooden pineapple bombs) & split the meat to reveal the butterycovered seeds: an incredible flavour, not fruitlike, something like coffee & bitter spices compounded with onions, really strong. Eng Kim & Ah Yow (the cook) love them & when we brought Dad down to try some a little while later, they were perched on the table happily eating away & watched with amusement Dad's valiant but obviously ginger chewing & swallowing—Eng Kim's amusement in her eyes tho she'd never speak it to 'the tuan'.

I'm going to stop this, being haunted by echoes of earlier (age 12 etc) letters & journals, that so stilted proper English. 'To the manner born.' How completely i learned to talk Canadian (how badly i wanted to). & how fast it drops away here. Wonder how it sounds to you?

July 25th

Sunday & the frangipani blossoms on the desk have gone all brown. Hot today, hottest yet, tho it clouded over as usual (haven't seen a sunset, been mostly cool for here, & cloudy—waterfalls of rain the other morning, woke up to its wet descent all round the open verandahs of the house, the open windows—no glass on some, for breeze).

We drove up to Ayer Itam, the Buddhist hill shrine—driving is such a trip. I love winding thru throngs of brilliant sarong & sari dressed women, children, sellers of ramibitans & chinese noodles, cyclists of all sorts, young chinese youths zooming by on Honda bikes, cars trucks hundreds of buses all dodging the cyclists & the goats.

Went up to the reservoir above the temple & walked a path thru jungle, o the smell came back so vivid, that deep sandloam fern palm dank smell. Everybody drives on the left here so the whole car is reversed, i keep reaching for an invisible gear shift & frightening Dad & Pam by turning into oncoming traffic. But i think i'm the only one who enjoys driving. Unfortunately it's a fancy Ford Cortina the company owns so i can't just take off in it whenever i want to.

My (hardwon) independence as a Western woman is being eroded every day & of course i'm seduced by my senses into just giving in—to the heat as much as to everything else. Finally let myself have an afternoon nap today, but the swimming—every afternoon the sea takes me in, old mother sea, sand dusky (no clarity like the Caribbean), & warm.

Mostly it's a struggle, an old old resistance against the colonial empire of the mind. For all the years that Mr Y's been here he knows almost nothing about what surrounds him, what the trees or birds are, what the fruits are—he doesn't like native food, exists on a kind of dilute European diet that includes lots of canned food. Private hedges of the mind as complete as the locked & bolted doors, the iron schedule of the house. Living in armed defensiveness against even the earth (don't go barefoot, nevah, nevah, for fear of hookworm etc.) I remember it all from my childhood, the same. Everything tells me this is not where i belong (including the odd intense look from Malays, boomiputras, 'sons of the soil'): the tourist experience compounded with colonial history. Europeans don't live here: they camp out in a kind of defensive splendour that's corrosive to the soul.

Aug 1st

Amah, age 74, in her sarong & shirtwaist, light gauze scarf hung round her neck, hair grey underneath the black, Amah, with her deep voice, expressive ways, 'yah yah', enthusiastic confirmation when Pam turned into the right road, driving her home— home to the house she works in, still housekeeping. 'Daphne mari, Pamela mari,' exclaiming over & over on the fact that we'd come. A lovely resilience, living in the present, genuine affection for the 'tuan', being herself a complete person with physical grace, even at 74, & dignity, not heavily insistent on it, only sufficient to herself. Her grace has to do with accepting what life brings & marvelling at it, laughing much, a deepthroated chuckle, & laying claim to nothing.

Buddhism says it is want that chains us to the world, us 'hungry ghosts'. & I see (just as I stands for the dominant ego in the world when you is not capitalized), that i want too much, just as, a child, i wanted affection. Growing sense of myself as a Westerner wanting, wanting—experience mostly. Anxiety arises from the discrepancy between my wants & my actual condition. Why plans so chain me—wanting too much from the day, wanting too much from others who can never be more than they are. In want: in fear. The 'liberated' woman in me insisting on her freedom & in terror of its being taken away. Passive resistance a better stance. Say 'yes' to restraints & simply do what you need to: act in silence.

Roy Miki *b.* 1942

WINNIPEG, MANITOBA

'As a Japanese-Canadian school kid growing up in the 1950s, I can remember wondering about the absence of writers who told stories that mirrored my community's turbulent history in BC. The literature studied was always from "over there" in England and Europe. One exception was the prairie poem of the Depression years, Ann Marriott's "The Wind Our Enemy". Though it was supposed to be a representation of "our" local place, for me all the tension focussed on one line: "Japs Bomb China." Sure enough, on the day the class read it out loud, my turn came at that line, and I had no choice but to speak the word that was anathema in my home. I'm sure the other students weren't aware of my anguish—many simply chuckled at the match between the word and the "me" speaking.'

A *sansei*, or third-generation Japanese Canadian, Roy Miki was born in Winnipeg only months after his family relocated there in 1942 after having been forced to evacuate their home in Haney, British Columbia. His experiences as a child and the racist policies that affected the entire Japanese Canadian community in the 1940s have had a lasting effect on him. From the late 1960s to the present, Miki has undertaken personal and academic research into the uprooting and internment of Japanese Canadians. In the 1980s, together with his brother Art Miki, he rose to prominence as a leader and spokesperson for the Japanese Canadian redress movement. A community leader, researcher, strategist and negotiator, editor, and writer, Miki worked both locally, for the Greater Vancouver Japanese Canadian Citizens Association, and nationally, for the National Association of Japanese Canadians (NAJC). As a member of the NAJC Strategy Committee, he was one of the Japanese Canadians who negotiated the historic Redress settlement with the Canadian government in September 1988. Combining personal reminiscences, archival material, and analysis, his recent book *Redress: Inside the Japanese Canadian Call for Justice* (2005) offers a record of this movement's history. *Justice in Our Time: The Japanese Canadian Redress Settlement* (1991), which Miki co-authored with Cassandra Kobayashi, also documents that process. In recognition of his work, Miki received the Dr William Black Award from the Vancouver Multicultural Society (1985), The President's Award for outstanding contribution to Simon Fraser University and Canadian society (1989), and the Renata Shearer Human Rights Award from the United Nations Association and the BC Human Rights Coalition (1990).

Miki's reputation does not rest on his political activities alone. Since moving to Vancouver in 1964, after obtaining a BA in English from the University of Manitoba, he has been an important figure in the city's cultural and intellectual life. After earning his master's degree (English, 1969) at Simon Fraser University and his PhD at the University of British Columbia (1980), he became a professor of American literature and poetics and Canadian literature at Simon Fraser University. Since then, Miki, who has read and lectured widely in Japan, Australia, and Europe, has been an active editor, poet, and critic. He is the founder and editor of the literary journal *Line* (recently renamed *West Coast Line*) and the editor of *Pacific Windows: Collected Poems of Roy K. Kiyooka* (1997), which won the Association of Asian American Studies Award. Among his other edited works are *Meanwhile: The Critical Writings of bpNichol* (2002), *This Is My Own: Letters to Wes and Other Writings on Japanese Canadians, 1941–48* by Muriel Kitagawa (1985), and *Tracing the Paths: Reading & Writing The Martyrology* (1987), a collection of critical essays on Nichol. His book *A Record of Writing: An Annotated and Illustrated Bibliography of George Bowering* (1990) won the Gabrielle Roy Prize for Canadian Criticism (1991). Since the publication of *The Prepoetics of William Carlos Williams: Kora in Hell* (1983), most of Miki's critical work has focused on

Canadian literature, especially Asian Canadian writing. Widely published as poet and critic, his most recent critical study, *Broken Entries: Race, Subjectivity, Race* (1998), deals with racialized subjectivities, as well as with the critical and disciplinary practices that impact on the creation of literature.

As the chair of the Racial Minority Writers' Committee of the Writers' Union of Canada, Miki coordinated 'Writing Thru Race: A Conference for First Nations Writers and Writers of Colour' (Vancouver, 30 June–3 July 1994). The first conference of its kind in Canada, 'Writing Thru Race' was designed 'to provide a safe space for writers to talk about the impact of racism on their lives'. A month before the conference took place, under pressure from a Reform party member of Parliament who had attacked the conference as 'racist' because it was intended only for First Nations writers and writers of colour, the Department of Canadian Heritage withdrew its promised financial support, touching off a nationwide media controversy. Many artists and artist-run organizations, as well as cultural and labour organizations, 'rallied to save the conference'. 'Writing Thru Race' ended up being a resounding success. As Miki says, in his 1994 article 'From Exclusion to Inclusion', an account and analysis of the events that surrounded the conference, this event succeeded in creating a forum where 180 First Nations writers and writers of colour could come together 'to share histories, cultural contexts, issues and strategies, to build networks and coalitions, and to find ways of making contact, to intervent the otherwise in/visible lines of "race" that separate and isolate.'

A highly acclaimed poet, Miki has published four collections of poetry: *Saving Face: Poems Selected 1976–1988* (1991), *Market Rinse* (1993), *Random Access File* (1995), and *Surrender* (2001), which won the Governor General's Award. His poetry, with its precise attention to language and formal elements, addresses the need to reconceptualize space—including the formal space of a poem—and to question inherited notions of power, authority, and subjectivity.

make it new

i have altered my tactics to reflect the new era

already the magnolia broken by high winds
     heals itself

the truncated branches already
speak to me.   5

the hallucinated cartoons spread their wings
no less eagles than the amber destination
of wanton discourses—
                     discards

     say what you will   10
the mountain ranges
once so populated with fleeting images
       look more attractive

     histoires statistics documents
daily polls headlines make the blood rush   15

       the earth is not heavy
with the weight of centuries
                    nor do bodies
of multitudes tread muted on fleet denizens

in the declension of plumed echoes   20
     or is it contractual fumes
   the sunset clause expires

material recovery

lisbon

currents funnel in
and round the burgeoning
mound of boxes

       named archive
the abstraction summons all   5
to suspension in the shaft of
the escalators

        on the down side
of paper reside the muted tones
that travel alongside the routine   10

no markers on
the lathered stone

          a throw away

the house lay dormant
waiting for an organ donor   15

material recovery two

lisbon to coimbra

resin does not resonate
ricochet does not return
rebellion does not make an
easy truce with frenzy

arrested weights   5

where did that come from?

the science of crowd control
had not yet been invented

singular statue monumentalist
bargain walls corridor archway   10

i missed you in the past tense

        how dense of me
        i should have dipped
        the crust in olive oil
        before swallowing   15

the aqueduct stood still
for centuries

kiyooka

for fred wah

morning light laves
this futon couch

     dying
         died

           'dead   5

to the world'

•

river rush in
rushes played

blame
     at the doorstep   10

curled up
like a cat

•

'without reading

    there is

       no body'   15

•

dis   sem   blance
paternal sputter

let the utter &
outer skin
     to skin   20

•

'send me your sign
      asap
           by priority post
if necessary'

              'no freedom   25
      in this column
of print'

'but it seems
           to be talking
in the (air)   30
        currents'

'make it out here soon please'

•

size is   dis
pro   portion   ate

      e.g. the creeping vine   35

to mortgage your time
letter by letter
by litter

      aaaaaaaahhhhh
      hhhhhaaaaaaaa   40

one more
    chapbook
        for the road

•

pro   life   ration
    is only   45
      a word

          after all
      is sd
  & done

•

disguise   50
          discloses
                    funds in reserve

                    the gas tank
          too is deceptive
in the short run   55
          drive on empty

see where
          the freeway   takes
                              the body

•

at the stroke   60
of midnight
the beaker
over
flows
over   65

•

foreign
four eyes

school daze?

          yeah yeah
school daze   70

•

hidden reaches
bone lines
skin folds

          'i'm not
                    after that   75
                         stride

          oh no
no no'

fool's scold, 1.4.97

*to commemorate april 1, 1949, the day the last of the restrictions
on freedom of movement was lifted for japanese canadians*

for peggy m @ irvine, california

•

48 years since the last restriction lifted on jcs. the USA of it
all this year. set out with irvine english department secretary
pm to get a social security number to legitimate my sojourn
as a lowly canuck. a routine procedure, i'm told. few minutes
drive to pick up the card needed for my stay. get there, but   5
no, i need to be approved first by immigration and
naturalization. ok, ok, drive across town. a line up already
forming, and the sun is bright, the breeze just right, children
fidgeting. the opaque glass window speaks, then minutes pass
with her supervisor. no, can't do. require to be re-examined   10
by justice, section for aliens.

re-examined? when was i examined? that's the problem. the
voice said, i wasn't, at the vancouver border. new
regulations. since? today.

•

astride the fault lines   15
the enemy within stutters

'it was all an ordinary day'

warm california sun
        casting a glow
                on the landscape   20

sinecures planned in absentia
climb the wall to perch on parapets

'canadian? pass'

as limply as a hand falling off a cart
(strain the figure for the sake of time spent   25

the passage into empire made so glibly
on this auspicious day before the coastal dawn

    ie the moon rose on march 31

  •

on the freeway to LA. if we rush we can make it by noon.
pm knows the route, and before we finish exchanging lives,   30
we're turning off and circling justice looking for a place to
park. peripheral vision signals we're right next door to
nihonbashi or j-town.

  •

sinuous thread dialects about which nothing
has been written   35
                ecological damage on over
drive
    the slack alters the speech task

    ie the sun rose on april 1

'but why didn't you   40
            declare your intent
    on the way through?'

in tent? the nomadic armour had fallen away
leaving only the mask to fill the passage

now the LA freeway's intent has gripes on the wall   45
the mouse mandate to get the cursor on track

at the entrance to the halls of justice the burly
blue uniform before the security gate electrons

the weave of short fuses
                        the fiery hearts arc   50

•

7th floor, down the long deserted hallway, to the
interrogation room, and a hand behind glass posts a sign.
closed for lunch.

back at 1:30, the room has filled with restlessness as lawyers
and clients whisper inaudible words. my examination form is   55
5 pages with questions of identity, intent, motive,
declaration, and why i hadn't been examined. at the canlit
border? i mused for a second. i can't understand why, she
says, when i hand her back the form, my hand sore. i didn't
know. well, if you ever do this another time, you'll have to   60
leave.

•

set on demos magnetic no registration card needed
the US is not my telos no sir no sir no sir no sir i
won't tell sir no sir won't tell won't tell i promise
cross my jc heart but i won't hope to die no sir   65
no sir just passing no really i'm not looking for a
home yes this english is genuine the form is no problem
sure i can wait until after lunch no problem i love
grilled fish and rice i understand the problems you have
with so many trying to sneak through the nets no joking   70
i'm canadian and was sent here to speak on redress
for the internment of jc's at irvine university no i can't
stay longer but thanks for making such a fuss on
this fool's day memorial ok glad to be of service

•

new regulations, she continues, needed to deal with illegal   75
aliens here. are there legal aliens here? i don't ask but at this
interstice i imagine the border zone of 'enemy alien,'
thinking of the ja's expelled from the coast in 42.

this is all an allegory i assure pm who by this time is
incredulous. the plight of a lowly canuck, i tell her, april 1 is   80
always a trial day for jc's—a day the spectral 'enemy alien'
plays tricks on us.

sure enough i'm given permission. april fool, i thought she
would say through the glass, but she only smiled as she passed
me the coveted 'J' form.   85

•

                across the firmament
                            this marked marvel
                heads for the hills

            the blue candles lit
    the litter on the causeway   90

            the foils in the narrative

Thomas King *b.* 1943

OKLAHOMA

Although the question of 'what it means to be Indian' is not one that concerns Thomas King 'all that much personally', as he says in an interview, 'it is an important question in my fiction. Because it's a question that other people always ask. . . . [I]t's part of that demand for authenticity within the world in which we live. It's the question that Native people have to put up with. And it's a whip that we get beaten with— "Are you a good enough Indian to speak as an Indian?" '

King's treatment of these questions relies formally on both the Native oral storytelling and the Western narrative traditions, thus reflecting his life and personal heritage. The son of a Greek mother and a Cherokee father, he was born in Oklahoma but doesn't 'think of Oklahoma as home. If I think of any place as home, it's the Alberta prairies, where I spent ten years with the Blackfoot people.' Although he is both a Canadian and an American citizen, King 'think[s] of [him]self as a Canadian writer because that's all [he] write[s] about'. If anything, his double citizenship and mixed heritage—'With my looks', he admits, 'I could have gone either way'—have made him all the more aware of borders—between countries, between Native and non-Native people, between men and women, between urban Natives and Natives living on reserves. As he says, for 'Native people, identity comes from community, and it varies from community to community. I wouldn't define myself as an Indian in the same way that someone living on a reserve would. That whole idea of "Indian" becomes, in part, a construct. It's fluid. We make it up as we go along.'

King, who worked as a photojournalist in Australia and still practises photography, holds a PhD in English and American Studies from the University of Utah and a BA and MA from Chico State University, California. He was a professor of Native studies at the University of Lethbridge, Alberta, for ten years, where, with N. Scott Momaday as his model, he began writing fiction. In 1993, after being a professor and the chair of American Indian Studies at the University of Minnesota in Minneapolis, King moved to Toronto, where he worked as a story editor for *Four Directions*, a CBC-TV dramatic production about Native people, and wrote and directed *The Dead Dog Cafe* comedy series for CBC Radio. Since 1994 he has taught at the School of English and Theatre Studies at the University of Guelph.

King's poetry and fiction has been published in numerous literary magazines. His first book, the novel *Medicine River* (1990), was a finalist for the Commonwealth Writers' Prize and won the Alberta Writers' Guild Best Novel Award and the Josephine Miles Oakland PEN Award. The film adaptation, starring Graham Greene and Tom Jackson, won an award for best screenplay at the American Indian Film Festival and was nominated for a Gemini. King's first children's book, *A Coyote Columbus Story* (1992), earned him his first Governor General's Award nomination. His second nomination came with the publication of his second novel, *Green Grass, Running Water* (1993), which won the Canadian Authors Award for fiction. It is a highly complex but also heavily ironic and entertaining narrative that tackles head-on the impact of the political, social, and cultural legacy of colonization on Native people. From the fetishization of Indians by seemingly benevolent tourists and authors like James Fenimore Cooper to the recasting of such Western religious and literary icons as Ah-damn, Moby Dick, and Robinson Crusoe, from the aspirations and anxieties of urban Natives to the tenacity of the prudent and patient elder Norma, the range of the interrelated stories and references the novel encompasses is stunning, as too is King's masterful way of combining Native storytelling and western literary techniques. The interplay of the past and the present and the relentless re-appropriation of stereotypes in *Green Grass, Running Water* are also elements of King's short story collection *One Good Story, That One* (1993).

King's fiction, including the story that follows, illustrates that 'the range of "Indian" is not as narrow as many people try to make it.' Through Coyote, which King often uses as a 'sacred clown', through puns, which he has learned from '[t]alking to storytellers and to Native people', and through humour—'Comedy', he says, 'is simply my strategy'—King has proven himself to be one of the most innovative and popular Canadian Native writers. His recent titles include the children's book *Coyote Sings to the Moon* (1998), the novel *Truth and Bright Water* (1999), the short story collection *A Short History of Indians* (2005), and *Dreadful Water Shows Up* (2002), a humorous detective story about an ex-cop and Cherokee photographer written under the pseudonym Hartley Goodweather.

In addition to writing his own fiction, King has edited a number of collections of writing by and about Native people, including *The Native in Literature: Canadian and Comparative Perspectives* (1987), *All My Relations: An Anthology of Contemporary Canadian Native Writing* (1990), and *First Voices, First Words* (*Prairie Fire*, 2001). He was the first Native intellectual to be a Massey fellow at the University of Toronto (2002–3); his Massey lectures, gathered together in *The Truth About Stories* (2003), won the Trillium Award. King was recently inducted into the Order of Canada and received a lifetime achievement award from the Western American Literary Association.

The One About Coyote Going West

This one is about Coyote. She was going west. Visiting her relations. That's what she said. You got to watch that one. Tricky one. Full of bad business. No, no, no, no, that one says. I'm just visiting. Going to see Raven.

Boy, I says. That's another tricky one.

Coyote comes by my place. She wag her tail. Make them happy noises. Sit on my porch. Look around. With them teeth. With that smile. Coyote put her nose in my tea. My good tea.

Get that nose out of my tea, I says.

I'm going to see my friends, she says. Tell those stories. Fix this world. Straighten it up.

Oh boy, pretty scary that, Coyote fix the world, again.

Sit down, I says. Eat some food. Hard work that, fix up the world. Maybe you have a song. Maybe you have a good joke.

Sure, says Coyote. That one wink her ears. Lick her whiskers.

I tuck my feet under that chair. Got to hide my toes. Sometimes that tricky one leave her skin sit in that chair. Coyote skin. No Coyote. Sneak around. Bite them toes. Make you jump.

I been reading those books, she says.

You must be one smart Coyote, I says.

You bet, she says.

Maybe you got a good story for me, I says.

I been reading about that history, says Coyote. She sticks that nose back in my tea. All about who found us Indians.

Ho, I says. I like those old ones. Them ones are the best. You tell me your story, I says. Maybe some biscuits will visit us. Maybe some moose-meat stew come along, listen to your story.

Okay, she says and she sings her story song.

> Snow's on the ground the snakes are asleep.
> Snow's on the ground my voice is strong.
> Snow's on the ground the snakes are asleep.
> Snow's on the ground my voice is strong.

She sings like that. With that tail, wagging. With that smile. Sitting there.

Maybe I tell you the one about Eric the Lucky and the Vikings play hockey for the Oldtimers, find us Indians in Newfoundland, she says. Maybe I tell you the one about Christopher Cartier looking for something good to eat. Find us Indians in a restaurant in Montreal. Maybe I tell you the one about Jacques Columbus come along that river. Indians waiting for him. We all wave and say, here we are, here we are.

Everyone knows those stories, I says. Whiteman stories. Baby stories you got in your mouth.

No, no, no, no, says that Coyote. I read these ones in that old book.

Ho, I says. You are trying to bite my toes. Everyone knows who found us Indians. Eric the Lucky and that Christopher Cartier and that Jacques Columbus come along later. Those ones get lost. Float about. Walk around. Get mixed up. Ho, ho, ho, ho, those ones cry, we are lost. So we got to find them. Help them out. Feed them. Show them around. Boy, I says. Bad mistake that one.

You are very wise grandmother, says Coyote, bring her eyes down, like she is sleepy. Maybe you know who discovered Indians.

Sure, I says. Everyone knows that. It was Coyote. She was the one.

Oh, grandfather, that Coyote says. Tell me that story. I love those stories about that sneaky one. I don't think I know that story, she says.

All right, I says. Pay attention.

Coyote was heading west. That's how I always start this story. There was nothing else in this world. Just Coyote. She could see all the way, too. No mountains then. No rivers then. No forests then. Pretty flat then. So she starts to make things. So she starts to fix this world.

This is exciting, says Coyote, and she takes her nose out of my tea.

Yes, I says. Just the beginning, too. Coyote got a lot of things to make.

Tell me, grandmother, says Coyote. What does the clever one make first?

Well, I says. Maybe she makes that tree grows by the river. Maybe she makes that buffalo. Maybe she makes that mountain. Maybe she makes them clouds.

Maybe she makes that beautiful rainbow, says Coyote.

No, I says. She don't make that thing. Mink makes that.

Maybe she makes that beautiful moon, says Coyote.

No, I says. She don't do that either. Otter finds that moon in a pond later on.

Maybe she make the oceans with that blue water, says Coyote.

No, I says. Oceans are already here. She don't do any of that. The first thing Coyote makes, I tell Coyote, is a mistake.

Boy, Coyote sit up straight. Them eyes pop open. That tail stop wagging. That one swallow that smile.

Big one, too, I says. Coyote is going west thinking of things to make. That one is trying to think of everything to make at once. So she don't see that hole. So she falls in that hole. Then those thoughts bump around. They run into each other. Those ones fall out of Coyote's ears. In that hole.

Ho, that Coyote cries. I have fallen into a hole, I must have made a mistake. And she did.

So, there is that hole. And there is that Coyote in that hole. And there is that big mistake in that hole with Coyote. Ho, says that mistake. You must be Coyote.

That mistake is real big and that hole is small. Not much room. I don't want to tell you what that mistake looks like. First mistake in the world. Pretty scary. Boy, I can't look, I got to close my eyes. You better close your eyes, too, I tell Coyote.

Okay, I'll do that, she says, and she puts her hands over her eyes. But she don't fool me. I can see she's peeking.

Don't peek, I says.

Okay, she says. I won't do that.

Well, you know, that Coyote thinks about the hole. And she thinks about how she's going to get out of that hole. She thinks how she's going to get that big mistake back in her head.

Say, says that mistake. What is that you're thinking about?

I'm thinking of a song, says Coyote. I'm thinking of a song to make this hole bigger.

That's a good idea, says that mistake. Let me hear your hole song.

But that's not what Coyote sings. She sings a song to make the mistake smaller. But that mistake hears her. And that mistake grabs Coyote's nose. And that one pulls off her mouth so she can't sing. And that one jumps up and down on Coyote until she is flat. Then that one leaps out of that hole, wanders around looking for things to do.

Well, Coyote is feeling pretty bad, all flat her nice fur coat full of stomp holes. So she thinks hard, and she thinks about a healing song. And she tries to sing a healing song, but her mouth is in other places. So she thinks harder and tries to sing that song through her nose. But that nose don't make any sound, just drip a lot. She tries to sing that song out her ears, but those ears don't hear anything.

So, that silly one thinks real hard and tries to sing out her butt hole. Pssst! Pssst! That is what that butt hole says, and right away things don't smell so good in that hole. Pssst.

Boy, Coyote thinks. Something smells.

That Coyote lies there flat and practise and practise. Pretty soon, maybe two days, maybe one year, she teach that butt hole to sing. That song. That healing song. So that butt hole sings that song. And Coyote begins to feel better. And Coyote don't feel so flat anymore. Pssst! Pssst! Things smell pretty bad, but Coyote is okay.

That one look around in that hole. Find her mouth. Put that mouth back. So, she says to that butt hole. Okay, you can stop singing now. You can stop making them smells now. But, you know, that butt hole is liking all that singing, and so that butt hole keeps on singing.

Stop that, says Coyote. You are going to stink up the whole world. But it don't. So Coyote jumps out of that hole and runs across the prairies real fast. But that butt hole follows her. Pssst. Pssst. Coyote jumps into a lake, but that butt hole don't drown. It just keeps on singing.

Hey, who is doing all that singing, someone says.

Yes, and who is making that bad smell, says another voice.

It must be Coyote, says a third voice.

Yes, says a fourth voice. I believe it is Coyote.

That Coyote sit in my chair, put her nose in my tea, say, I know who that voice is. It is that big mistake playing a trick. Nothing else is made yet.

No, I says. That mistake is doing other things.

Then those voices are spirits, says Coyote.

No, I says. Them voices belong to them ducks.

Coyote stand up on my chair. Hey, she says, where did them ducks come from?

Calm down, I says. This story is going to be okay. This story is doing just fine. This story knows where it is going. Sit down. Keep your skin on.

So.

Coyote look around, and she see them four ducks. In that lake. Ho, she says. Where did you ducks come from? I didn't make you yet.

Yes, says them ducks. We were waiting around, but you didn't come. So we got tired of waiting. So we did it ourselves.

I was in a hole, says Coyote.

Pssst. Pssst.

What's that noise, says them ducks. What's that bad smell?

Never mind, says Coyote. Maybe you've seen something go by. Maybe you can help me find something I lost. Maybe you can help me get it back.

Those ducks swim around and talk to themselves. Was it something awful to look at?

Yes, says Coyote, it certainly was.

Was it something with ugly fur?

Yes, says Coyote. I think it had that, too.

Was it something that made a lot of noise, ask them ducks.

Yes, it was pretty noisy, says Coyote.

Did it smell bad, them ducks want to know.

Yes, says Coyote. I guess you ducks have seen my something.

Yes, says them ducks. It is right there behind you.

So that Coyote turn around, and there is nothing there.

It's still behind you, says those ducks.

So Coyote turn around again but she don't see anything.

Pssst! Pssst!

Boy, says those ducks. What a noise! What a smell! They say that, too. What an ugly thing with all that fur!

Never mind, says that Coyote again. That is not what I'm looking for. I'm looking for something else.

Maybe you're looking for Indians, says those ducks.

Well, that Coyote is real surprised because she hasn't created Indians, either. Boy, says that one, mischief is everywhere. This world is getting bent.

All right.

So Coyote and those ducks are talking, and pretty soon they hear a noise. And pretty soon there is something coming. And those ducks says, oh, oh, oh, oh. They say that like they see trouble, but it is not trouble. What comes along is a river.

Hello, says that river. Nice day. Maybe you want to take a swim. But Coyote don't want to swim, and she looks at that river and she looks at that river again. Something's not right here, she says. Where are those rocks? Where are those rapids? What did you do with them waterfalls? How come you're so straight?

And Coyote is right. That river is nice and straight and smooth without any bumps or twists. It runs both ways, too, not like a modern river.

We got to fix this, says Coyote, and she does. She puts some rocks in that river, and she fixes it so it only runs one way. She puts a couple of waterfalls in and makes a bunch of rapids where things get shallow fast.

Coyote is tired with all this work, and those ducks are tired just watching. So that Coyote sits down. So she closes her eyes. So she puts her nose in her tail. So those ducks shout, wake up, wake up! Something big is heading this way! And they are right.

Mountain come sliding along, whistling. Real happy mountain. Nice and round. This mountain is full of grapes and other good things to eat. Apples, peaches, cherries. Howdy-do, says that polite mountain, nice day for whistling.

Coyote looks at that mountain, and that one shakes her head. Oh, no, she says, this mountain is all wrong. How come you're so nice and round? Where are those craggy peaks? Where are all them cliffs? What happened to all that snow? Boy, we got to fix this thing, too. So she does.

Grandfather, grandfather, says that Coyote, sit in my chair, put her nose in my tea. Why is that Coyote changing all those good things?

That is a real sly one, ask me that question. I look at those eyes. Grab them ears. Squeeze that nose. Hey, let go my nose, that Coyote says.

Okay, I says. Coyote still in Coyote skin. I bet you know why Coyote change that happy river. Why she change that mountain sliding along whistling.

No, says that Coyote, look around my house, lick her lips, make them baby noises. Maybe it's because she is mean, I says.

Oh, no, says Coyote. That one is sweet and kind.

Maybe it's because that one is not too smart.

Oh, no, says Coyote. That Coyote is very wise.

Maybe it's because she made a mistake.

Oh, no, says Coyote. She made one of those already.

All right, I says. Then Coyote must be doing the right thing. She must be fixing up the world so it is perfect.

Yes, says Coyote. That must be it. What does that brilliant one do next?

Everyone knows what Coyote does next, I says. Little babies know what Coyote does next.

Oh no, says Coyote. I have never heard this story. You are a wonderful storyteller. You tell me your good Coyote story.

Boy, you got to watch that one all the time. Hide them toes.

Well, I says. Coyote thinks about that river. And she thinks about that mountain. And she thinks somebody is fooling around. So she goes looking around. She goes looking for that one who is messing up the world.

She goes to the north, and there is nothing. She goes to the south, and there is nothing there either. She goes to the east, and there is still nothing there. She goes to the west, and there is a pile of snow tires.

And there is some televisions. And there is some vacuum cleaners. And there is a bunch of pastel sheets. And there is an air humidifier. And there is a big mistake sitting on a portable gas barbecue reading a book. Big book. Department store catalogue.

Hello, says that mistake. Maybe you want a hydraulic jack.

No, says that Coyote. I don't want one of them. But she don't tell that mistake what she wants because she don't want to miss her mouth again. But when she thinks about being flat and full of stomp holes, that butt hole wakes up and begins to sing. Pssst. Pssst.

What's that noise? says that big mistake.

I'm looking for Indians, says that Coyote, real quick. Have you seen any?

What's that bad smell?

Never mind, says Coyote. Maybe you have some Indians around here.

I got some toaster ovens, says that mistake.

We don't need that stuff, says Coyote. You got to stop making all those things. You're going to fill up this world.

Maybe you want a computer with a colour monitor. That mistake keeps looking through that book and those things keep landing in piles all around Coyote.

Stop, stop, cries Coyote. Golf cart lands on her foot. Golf balls bounce off her head. You got to give me that book before the world gets lopsided.

These are good things, says that mistake. We need these things to make up the world. Indians are going to need this stuff.

We don't have any Indians, says Coyote.

And that mistake can see that that's right. Maybe we better make some Indians, says that mistake. So that one looks in that catalogue, but it don't have any Indians. And Coyote don't know how to do that either. She has already made four things.

I've made four things already, she says. I got to have help.

We can help, says some voices and it is those ducks come swimming along. We can help you make Indians, says the white duck. Yes, we can do that, says that green duck. We have been thinking about this, says that blue duck. We have a plan, says that red duck.

Well, that Coyote don't know what to do. So she tells them ducks to go ahead because this story is pretty long and it's getting late and everyone wants to go home.

You still awake, I says to Coyote. You still here?

Oh yes, grandmother, says Coyote. What do those clever ducks do?

So I tell Coyote that those ducks lay some eggs. Ducks do that, you know. That white duck lay an egg, and it is blue. That red duck lay an egg, and it is green. That blue duck lay an egg, and it is red. That green duck lay an egg, and it is white.

Come on, says those ducks. We got to sing a song. We got to do a dance. So they do. Coyote and that big mistake and those four ducks dance around the eggs. So they dance and sing for a long time, and pretty soon Coyote gets hungry.

I know this dance, she says, but you got to close your eyes when you do it or nothing will happen. You got to close your eyes tight. Okay, says those ducks. We can do that. And they do. And that big mistake closes its eyes, too.

But Coyote, she don't close her eyes, and all of them start dancing again, and Coyote dances up close to that white duck, and she grabs that white duck by her neck.

When Coyote grabs that duck, that duck flaps her wings, and that big mistake hears the noise and opens them eyes. Say, says that big mistake, that's not the way the dance goes.

By golly, you're right, says Coyote, and she lets that duck go. I am getting it mixed up with another dance.

So they start to dance again. And Coyote is very hungry, and she grabs that blue duck, and she grabs his wings, too. But Coyote's stomach starts to make hungry noises, and that mistake opens them eyes and sees Coyote with the blue duck. Hey, says that mistake, you got yourself mixed up again.

That's right, says Coyote, and she drops that duck and straightens out that neck. It sure is good you're around to help me with this dance.

They all start that dance again, and, this time, Coyote grabs the green duck real quick and tries to stuff it down that greedy throat, and there is nothing hanging out but them yellow duck feet. But those feet are flapping in Coyote's eyes, and she can't see where she is going, and she bumps into the big mistake and the big mistake turns around to see what has happened.

Ho, says that big mistake, you can't see where you're going with them yellow duck feet flapping in your eyes, and that mistake pulls that green duck out of Coyote's throat. You could hurt yourself dancing like that.

You are one good friend, look after me like that, says Coyote.

Those ducks start to dance again, and Coyote dances with them, but that red duck says, we better dance with one eye open, so we can help Coyote with this dance. So they dance some more, and, then, those eggs begin to move around, and those eggs crack open. And if you look hard, you can see something inside those eggs.

I know, I know, says that Coyote, jump up and down on my chair, shake up my good tea. Indians come out of those eggs. I remember this story, now. Inside those eggs are the Indians Coyote's been looking for.

No, I says. You are one crazy Coyote. What comes out of those duck eggs are baby ducks. You better sit down, I says. You may fall and hurt yourself. You may spill my tea. You may fall on top of this story and make it flat.

Where are the Indians? says that Coyote. This story was about how Coyote found the Indians. Maybe the Indians are in the eggs with the baby ducks.

No, I says, nothing in those eggs but little baby ducks. Indians will be along in a while. Don't lose your skin.

So.

When those ducks see what has come out of the eggs, they says, boy, we didn't get that quite right. We better try that again. So they do. They lay them eggs. They dance that dance. They sing that song. Those eggs crack open and out comes some more baby ducks. They do this seven times and each time, they get more ducks.

By golly, says those four ducks. We got more ducks than we need. I guess we got to be the Indians. And so they do that. Before Coyote or that big mistake can mess things up, those four ducks turn into Indians, two women and two men. Good-looking Indians, too. They don't look at all like ducks anymore.

But those duck-Indians aren't too happy. They look at each other and they begin to cry. This is pretty disgusting, they says. All this ugly skin. All these bumpy bones. All this awful black hair. Where are our nice soft feathers? Where are our beautiful feet? What happened to our wonderful wings? It's probably all that Coyote's fault because she didn't do the dance right, and those four duck-Indians come over and stomp all over Coyote until she is flat like before. Then they leave. That big mistake leave, too. And that Coyote, she starts to think about a healing song.

Pssst. Pssst.

That's it, I says. It is done.

But what happens to Coyote, says Coyote. That wonderful one is still flat.

Some of these stories are flat, I says. That's what happens when you try to fix this world. This world is pretty good all by itself. Best to leave it alone. Stop messing around with it.

I better get going, says Coyote. I will tell Raven your good story. We going to fix this world for sure. We know how to do it now. We know how to do it right.

So, Coyote drinks my tea and that one leave. And I can't talk anymore because I got to watch the sky. Got to watch out for falling things that land in piles. When that Coyote's wandering around looking to fix things, nobody in this world is safe.

Michael Ondaatje *b.* 1943

COLOMBO, SRI LANKA

Michael Ondaatje was nine years old when, in 1952, he left his birthplace of Colombo, Ceylon (now Sri Lanka), to attend Dulwich College in England. As he says, 'I was part of that colonial tradition of sending your kids off to school in England, and then you were supposed to go to Oxford or Cambridge and get a blue in tennis and return. But I never went to Oxford or Cambridge, I didn't get a blue, and I didn't return.' Instead, in 1962 Ondaatje moved to Canada to attend Bishop's University, and subsequently the University of Toronto, where he received his BA in English (1965). After receiving his MA (1967) from Queen's University, he taught in the English departments of the University of Western Ontario (1969–71) and Glendon College, York University (1971–83).

As a poet, novelist, critic, editor, scriptwriter, and documentary filmmaker, Ondaatje sees himself as belonging to the generation of writers that 'was the first of the real migrant tradition . . . of writers of our time—Rushdie, Ishiguro, Ben Okri, Rohinton Mistry—writers leaving and not going back, but taking their country with them to a new place.' Still, not until *Running in the Family* (1982)—a book about his parents that defies generic definition by combining elements of the novel, autobiography, poetry, and documentary—did Ondaatje's country find its way into his work in an extended form. His poetry books, which include *The Dainty Monsters* (1967), *Rat Jelly* (1973), *There's a Trick with a Knife I'm Learning to Do* (1979), winner of a Governor General's Award, and *Secular Love* (1984), are collections of lyrics. Through an intensely private, if somewhat exotic and violent, imagery they reflect, in his own words, 'my landscape here in Canada, my family here, certain rural landscapes here'.

In contrast, his other books seem to 'have begun with . . . the germ of document, with the rumour or incident that one reads about in the newspaper, or some paragraph in a biography.' His fascination with documents, and the way they tease the boundaries of truth and history,

began with his second poetry book, *the man with seven toes* (1969), a long poem in which Ondaatje reinvents a Mrs Fraser's historical encounter with a convict in Australia. It was, however, with the publication of his second long poem, *The Collected Works of Billy the Kid* (1970), which earned him his first Governor General's Award, that Ondaatje's characteristic mode of writing took flight. Its collage of poetry, prose, and illustrations and its imaginative and deliberate distortion of facts about the famous American outlaw announced Ondaatje's preoccupation with characters that occupy extreme positions, with the romantic possibilities of life-in-art, with the limits of literary forms. 'I am not really interested in inventing a form, as such,' says Ondaatje; 'I want my form to reflect as fully as possible how we think and imagine. And these keep changing, of course. With each book I try to do something I think I cant do.' Ondaatje's other books of poetry include *Elimination Dance* (1978), *Claude Glass* (1979), *Tin Roof* (1982), *The Cinnamon Peeler: Selected Poems* (1989), *Handwriting* (1988), and *The Story* (2006).

Coming Through Slaughter (1976), which won the Books in Canada First Novel Award, is about yet another legendary American figure, this time jazz musician Buddy Bolden, and is set in New Orleans. It resonates with jazz rhythms against 'a kind of mental landscape' that is, as Ondaatje says, 'believable, tactile', a poetic narrative in prose of a 'personal story' that 'wrestles against the documentary'. *In the Skin of a Lion* (1987), which Ondaatje has called his first novel, is indeed more direct in its treatment of setting and characters but still reflects Ondaatje's attention to language and his inclination to aestheticize experience. Set in the Toronto of the late 1920s and 1930s, the narrative casts its central character, Patrick Lewis, among immigrants, especially Macedonians. As the excerpt that follows demonstrates, the novel attempts to 'represent', as Ondaatje says, 'the unofficial story' of Toronto's history, in particular the events concerning the construction of the Bloor Street Viaduct and the water filtration plant by immigrants. '[R]eclaiming untold stories', Ondaatje remarks, 'is an essential role for the writer. Especially in this country, where one can no longer trust the media.' *The English Patient* (1992), a novel that catapulted Ondaatje into international prominence, takes place at the end of the Second World War, and is set mostly in Italy. It shared the Booker McConnell Prize in 1992, while its film adaptation (dir. Anthony Minghella) won nine Oscars. His most recent novel, *Anil's Ghost* (2000), winner of the Giller Prize and the Prix Medicis, is set in Sri Lanka, where Anil, a forensic anthropologist representing an NGO, goes on a human rights mission and attempts to come to terms with her family's past in Colombo as well as her own diasporic trajectory.

Ondaatje, who has also written essays and the study *Leonard Cohen* (1970), has edited many anthologies, including *The Long Poem Anthology* (1979), and was an editor with Coach House Press and *Brick*. A resident of Toronto, he has also produced and directed the films *Sons of Captain Poetry* (1970) on bpNichol and *The Clinton Special* (1972) on Theatre Passe Muraille's *The Farm Show*. His numerous awards include The Canada–Australia Prize (1980), two Trillium Book Awards (1987, 1992), the Chianti Ruffino-Antonio Fattore International Literary Prize (1994), the Premio Grinzane Cavour (1996), and the Irish Times International Literature Prize (2001).

from *In the Skin of a Lion*

A truck carries fire at five AM through central Toronto, along Dundas Street and up Parliament Street, moving north. Aboard the flatbed three men stare into passing darkness—their muscles relaxed in this last half-hour before work—as if they don't own the legs or the arms jostling against their bodies and the backboard of the Ford.

Written in yellow over the green door is DOMINION BRIDGE COMPANY. But for now all that is visible is the fire on the flatbed burning over the three-foot by three-foot metal dish, cooking the tar in a cauldron, leaving this odour on the streets for anyone who would step out into the early morning and swallow the air.

The truck rolls burly under the arching trees, pauses at certain intersections where more workers jump onto the flatbed, and soon there are eight men, the fire crackling, hot tar now and then spitting onto the back of a neck or an ear. Soon there are twenty, crowded and silent.

The light begins to come out of the earth. They see their hands, the textures on a coat, the trees they had known were there. At the top of Parliament Street the truck turns east, passes the Rosedale fill, and moves towards the half-built viaduct.

The men jump off. The unfinished road is full of ruts and the fire and the lights of the truck bounce, the suspension wheezing. The truck travels so slowly the men are walking faster, in the cold dawn air, even though it is summer.

Later they will remove coats and sweaters, then by eleven their shirts, bending over the black rivers of tar in just their trousers, boots, and caps. But now the thin layer of frost is everywhere, coating the machines and cables, brittle on the rain puddles they step through. The fast evaporation of darkness. As light emerges they see their breath, the clarity of the air being breathed out of them. The truck finally stops at the edge of the viaduct, and its lights are turned off.

The bridge goes up in a dream. It will link the east end with the centre of the city. It will carry traffic, water, and electricity across the Don Valley. It will carry trains that have not even been invented yet.

Night and day. Fall light. Snow light. They are always working—horses and wagons and men arriving for work on the Danforth side at the far end of the valley.

There are over 4,000 photographs from various angles of the bridge in its time-lapse evolution. The piers sink into bedrock fifty feet below the surface through clay and shale and quicksand—45,000 cubic yards of earth are excavated. The network of scaffolding stretches up.

Men in a maze of wooden planks climb deep into the shattered light of blond wood. A man is an extension of hammer, drill, flame. Drill smoke in his hair. A cap falls into the valley, gloves are buried in stone dust.

Then the new men arrive, the 'electricals', laying grids of wire across the five arches, carrying the exotic three-bowl lights, and on October 18, 1918 it is completed. Lounging in mid-air.

The bridge. The bridge. Christened 'Prince Edward'. The Bloor Street Viaduct.

During the political ceremonies a figure escaped by bicycle through the police barriers. The first member of the public. Not the expected show car containing officials, but this one anonymous and cycling like hell to the east end of the city. In the photographs he is a blur of intent. He wants the virginity of it, the luxury of such space. He circles twice, the string of onions that he carries on his shoulder splaying out, and continues.

But he was not the first. The previous midnight the workers had arrived and brushed away officials who guarded the bridge in preparation for the ceremonies the next day, moved with their own flickering lights—their candles for the bridge dead—like a wave of civilization, a net of summer insects over the valley.

And the cyclist too on his flight claimed the bridge in that blurred movement, alone and illegal. Thunderous applause greeted him at the far end.

On the west side of the bridge is Bloor Street, on the east side is Danforth Avenue. Originally cart roads, mud roads, planked in 1910, they are now being tarred. Bricks are banged into the earth and narrow creeks of sand are poured in between them. The tar is spread. *Bitumiers, bitumatori,* tarrers, get onto their knees and lean their weight over the wooden block irons, which arc and sweep. The smell of tar seeps through the porous body of their clothes. The black of it is permanent under the nails. They can feel the bricks under their kneecaps as they crawl backwards towards the bridge, their bodies almost horizontal over the viscous black river, their heads drunk within the fumes.

Hey, Caravaggio!

The young man gets up off his knees and looks back into the sun. He walks to the foreman, lets go of the two wooden blocks he is holding so they hang by the leather thongs from his belt, bouncing against his knees as he walks. Each man carries the necessities of his trade with him. When Caravaggio quits a year later he will cut the thongs with a fish knife and fling the blocks into the half-dry tar. Now he walks back in a temper and gets down on his knees again. Another fight with the foreman.

All day they lean over tar, over the twenty yards of black river that has been spread since morning. It glistens and eases in sunlight. Schoolkids grab bits of tar and chew them, first cooling the pieces in their hands then popping them into their mouths. It concentrates the saliva for spitting contests. The men plunk cans of beans into the blackness to heat them up for their lunch.

In winter, snow removes the scent of tar, the scent of pitched cut wood. The Don River floods below the unfinished bridge, ice banging at the feet of the recently built piers. On winter mornings men fan out nervous over the whiteness. Where does the earth end? There are flares along the edge of the bridge on winter nights—worst shift of all—where they hammer the nails in through snow. The bridge builders balance on a strut, the flares wavering behind them, aiming their hammers towards the noise of a nail they cannot see.

*   *   *

The last thing Rowland Harris, Commissioner of Public Works, would do in the evening during its construction was have himself driven to the edge of the viaduct, to sit for a while. At midnight the half-built bridge over the valley seemed deserted— just lanterns tracing its outlines. But there was always a night shift of thirty or forty men. After a while Harris removed himself from the car, lit a cigar, and walked onto the bridge. He loved this viaduct. It was his first child as head of Public Works, much of it planned before he took over but he had bullied it through. It was Harris who envisioned that it could carry not just cars but trains on a lower trestle. It could also transport water from the east-end plants to the centre of the city. Water was Harris' great passion. He wanted giant water mains travelling across the valley as part of the viaduct.

He slipped past the barrier and walked towards the working men. Few of them spoke English but they knew who he was. Sometimes he was accompanied by Pomphrey, an architect, the strange one from England who was later to design for Commissioner Harris one of the city's grandest buildings—the water filtration plant in the east end.

For Harris the night allowed scope. Night removed the limitations of detail and concentrated on form. Harris would bring Pomphrey with him, past the barrier, onto the first stage of the bridge that ended sixty yards out in the air. The wind moved like something ancient against them. All men on the bridge had to buckle on halter ropes. Harris spoke of his plans to this five-foot-tall Englishman, struggling his way into Pomphrey's brain. Before the real city could be seen it had to be imagined, the way rumours and tall tales were a kind of charting.

One night they had driven there at eleven o'clock, crossed the barrier, and attached themselves once again to the rope harnesses. This allowed them to stand near the edge to study the progress of the piers and the steel arches. There was a fire on the bridge where the night workers congregated, flinging logs and other remnants onto it every so often, warming themselves before they walked back and climbed over the edge of the bridge into the night.

They were working on a wood-facing for the next pier so the concrete could be poured in. As they sawed and hammered, wind shook the light from the flares attached to the side of the abutment. Above them, on the deck of the bridge, builders were carrying huge Ingersoll-Rand air compressors and cables.

An April night in 1917. Harris and Pomphrey were on the bridge, in the dark wind. Pomphrey had turned west and was suddenly stilled. His hand reached out to touch Harris on the shoulder, a gesture he had never made before.

—Look!

Walking on the bridge were five nuns.

Past the Dominion Steel castings wind attacked the body directly. The nuns were walking past the first group of workers at the fire. The bus, Harris thought, must have dropped them off near Castle Frank and the nuns had, with some confusion at that hour, walked the wrong way in the darkness.

They had passed the black car under the trees and talking cheerfully stepped past the barrier into a landscape they did not know existed—onto a tentative carpet over the piers, among the night labourers. They saw the fire and the men. A few tried to wave them back. There was a mule attached to a wagon. The hiss and jump of machines made the ground under them lurch. A smell of creosote. One man was washing his face in a barrel of water.

The nuns were moving towards a thirty-yard point on the bridge when the wind began to scatter them. They were thrown against the cement mixers and steam shovels, careering from side to side, in danger of going over the edge.

Some of the men grabbed and enclosed them, pulling leather straps over their shoulders, but two were still loose. Harris and Pomphrey at the far end looked on helplessly as one nun was lifted up and flung against the compressors. She stood up shakily and then the wind jerked her sideways, scraping her along the concrete and right off the edge of the bridge. She disappeared into the night by the third abutment, into the long depth of air which held nothing, only sometimes a rivet or a dropped hammer during the day.

Then there was no longer any fear on the bridge. The worst, the incredible, had happened. A nun had fallen off the Prince Edward Viaduct before it was even finished. The men covered in wood shavings or granite dust held the women against them. And Commissioner Harris at the far end stared along the mad pathway. This was his first child and it had already become a murderer.

The man in mid-air under the central arch saw the shape fall towards him, in that second knowing his rope would not hold them both. He reached to catch the figure while his other hand grabbed the metal pipe edge above him to lessen the sudden jerk on the rope. The new weight ripped the arm that held the pipe out of its socket and he screamed, so whoever might have heard him up there would have thought the scream was from the falling figure. The halter thulked, jerking his chest up to his throat. The right arm was all agony now—but his hand's timing had been immaculate, the grace of the habit, and he found himself a moment later holding the figure against him dearly.

He saw it was a black-garbed bird, a girl's white face. He saw this in the light that sprayed down inconstantly from a flare fifteen yards above them. They hung in the halter, pivoting over the valley, his broken arm loose on one side of him, holding the woman with the other. Her body was in shock, her huge eyes staring into the face of Nicholas Temelcoff.

Scream, please, Lady, he whispered, the pain terrible. He asked her to hold him by the shoulders, to take the weight off his one good arm. A sway in the wind. She could not speak though her eyes glared at him bright, just staring at him. *Scream, please*. But she could not.

During the night, the long chutes through which wet concrete slid were unused and hung loose so the open spouts wavered a few feet from the valley floor. The tops of these were about ten feet from him now. He knew this without seeing them, even though they fell outside the scope of light. If they attempted to slide the chute their weight would make it vertical and dangerous. They would have to go further—to reach the lower-deck level of the bridge where there were structures built for possible water mains.

We have to swing. She had her hands around his shoulders now, the wind assaulting them. The two strangers were in each other's arms, beginning to swing wilder, once more, past the lip of the chute which had tempted them, till they were almost at the lower level of the rafters. He had his one good arm free. Saving her now would be her responsibility.

She was in shock, her face bright when they reached the lower level, like a woman with a fever. She was in no shape to be witnessed, her veil loose, her cropped hair open to the long wind down the valley. Once they reached the catwalk she saved him from falling back into space. He was exhausted. She held and walked with him like a lover along the unlit lower parapet towards the west end of the bridge.

Above them the others stood around the one fire, talking agitatedly. The women were still tethered to the men and not looking towards the stone edge where she had gone over, falling in darkness. The one with that small scar against her nose . . . she was always falling into windows, against chairs. She was always unlucky.

The Commissioner's chauffeur slept in his car as Temelcoff and the nun walked past, back on real earth away from the bridge. Before they reached Parliament Street they cut south through the cemetery. He seemed about to faint and she held him against a gravestone. She forced him to hold his arm rigid, his fist clenched. She put her hands underneath it like a stirrup and jerked upwards so he screamed out again, her whole body pushing up with all of her strength, groaning as if about to lift him and then holding him, clutching him tight. She had seen the sweat jump out of his face. *Get me a shot. Get me. . . .* She removed her veil and wrapped the arm tight against his side. *Parliament and Dundas . . . few more blocks.* So she went down Parliament Street with him. Where she was going she didn't know. On Eastern Avenue she knocked at the door he pointed to. All these abrupt requests—scream, swing, knock, get me. Then a man opened the door and let them into the Ohrida Lake Restaurant. *Thank you, Kosta. Go back to bed, I'll lock it.* And the man, the friend, walked back upstairs.

She stood in the middle of the restaurant in darkness. The chairs and tables were pushed back to the edge of the room. Temelcoff brought out a bottle of brandy from under the counter and picked up two small glasses in the fingers of the same hand. He guided her to a small table, then walked back and, with a switch behind the zinc counter, turned on a light near her table. There were crests on the wall.

She still hadn't said a word. He remembered she had not even screamed when she fell. That had been him.

*   *   *

Nicholas Temelcoff is famous on the bridge, a daredevil. He is given all the difficult jobs and he takes them. He descends into the air with no fear. He is a solitary. He assembles ropes, brushes the tackle and pulley at his waist, and falls off the bridge like a diver over the edge of a boat. The rope roars alongside him, slowing with the pressure of his half-gloved hands. He is burly on the ground and then falls with terrific speed, grace, using the wind to push himself into corners of abutments so he can check driven rivets, sheering valves, the drying of the concrete under bearing plates and padstones. He stands in the air banging the crown pin into the upper cord and then shepherds the lower cord's slip-joint into position. Even in archive photographs it is difficult to find him. Again and again you see vista before you and the eye must search along the wall of sky to the speck of burned paper across the valley that is him, an exclamation mark, somewhere in the distance between bridge and river. He floats at the three hinges of the crescent-shaped steel arches. These knit the bridge together. The moment of cubism.

He is happiest at daily chores—ferrying tools from pier down to trestle, or lumber that he pushes in the air before him as if swimming in a river. He is a spinner. He links everyone. He meets them as they cling—braced by wind against the metal they are riveting or the wood sheeting they hammer into—but he has none of their fear. Always he carries his own tackle, hunched under his ropes and dragging the shining pitons behind him. He sits on a coiled seat of rope while he eats his lunch on the bridge. If he finishes early he cycles down Parliament Street to the Ohrida Lake Restaurant and sits in the darkness of the room as if he has had enough of light. Enough of space.

His work is so exceptional and time-saving he earns one dollar an hour while the other bridge workers receive forty cents. There is no jealousy towards him. No one dreams of doing half the things he does. For night work he is paid $1.25, swinging up into the rafters of a trestle holding a flare, free-falling like a dead star. He does not really need to see things, he has charted all that space, knows the pier footings, the width of the crosswalks in terms of seconds of movement—281 feet and 6 inches make up the central span of the bridge. Two flanking spans of 240 feet, two end spans of 158 feet.

He slips into openings on the lower deck, tackles himself up to bridge level. He knows the precise height he is over the river, how long his ropes are, how many seconds he can free-fall to the pulley. It does not matter if it is day or night, he could be blindfolded. Black space is time. After swinging for three seconds he puts his feet up to link with the concrete edge of the next pier. He knows his position in the air as if he is mercury slipping across a map.

Patrick Friesen *b.* 1946

STEINBACH, MANITOBA

'Writing to me is medicine,' Patrick Friesen has said. 'It's a life and death issue. . . . It's better yet than medicine, yes.' But Friesen, who spent the first nineteen years of his life in the Mennonite community of Steinbach, Manitoba, has also had to fight against the Mennonite notion that writing is 'immodest', a 'presumptuous act'. 'There was a time in my youth', he says, 'when preachers didn't preach sermons. All you were allowed to do was read the Bible. You couldn't comment on it. . . . that is the whole truth and that's the received truth and to do anything more is to be pretentious or unnecessary or maybe to admit failure of that book.'

Publishing, '[m]aking yourself go public', was for Friesen 'a wrenching act'—an act whose complex consequences and significance are apparent in the opening stanzas of his first poetry book, *the lands i am* (1976): 'I'll be staunch / subdue the rabble / and be aristocrat again / be king / for a moment.' Still, Friesen discovered that he 'couldn't reject the background which I was shying away from. . . . I realized that there was something to be redeemed and one of the main things was the language I grew up with . . . which was biblical, which was sermons and that kind of rhetoric. . . . So I began exploring that language, going back to it and saying, "Look, I can still like the language even though I don't like what was done with it. I can redeem it for myself, I can use it in different ways." '

Much of the rhythm and imagery of Friesen's poems go back to his roots, but the energy of his writing also comes from the ways in which his body registers the physical world around him. From the short lines characteristic of his first book and his second publication, *bluebottle* (1978), he moved to the undulating rhythms of longer lines in *Unearthly Horses* (1984) and *Flicker and Hawk* (1987). Obsession with death and with finding 'the intangible, finding god through the world' are two major themes running through his work. Friesen makes it clear, however, that the 'god' he seeks is not 'the "capital g" god. . . . That's a God that doesn't understand. Small g, I understand. Big g is a "daddy", something else. That's outside of me. Small g is inside.' His poetry book *You Don't Get to Be a Saint* (1992) was nominated for the McNally-Robinson Book of the Year and the winner of the Manitoba Book Design of the Year Award, while *A Broken Bowl* (1997) was a finalist for the Governor General's Award for poetry. His other poetry titles include *Blasphemer's Wheel: Selected and New Poems* (1994), which won the Manitoba Book of the Year Award; *St. Mary at Main* (1998), shortlisted for the Dorothy Livesay British Columbia Book of the Year; *carrying the shadow* (1999); *the breath you take from the lord* (2002); and the chapbook *Bordello Poems* (2004).

The Shunning (1980), a long documentary poem that consists of poetry, prose, and photographs, marks Friesen's shift from the lyricism of his early work to more dramatic tensions. Adapted for the stage in 1985, and later for CBC Radio (1990), it represents the start of Friesen's involvement with theatre and performance. His other stage work includes the plays *The Raft* (1992) and *Friday, 6:32 PM* (1993) and the multidisciplinary performances *Anna* (1987), with choreographer Stephanie Ballard and guest artist Margie Gillis, and *Handful of Rain* (1991), with choreographers Ruth Cansfield and Gaile Petursson-Hiley. Friesen has also produced and directed documentary films for the Manitoba Department of Education, including *Spy in the House: Esther Warkov* (1982), *The Spirit of Asessippi: Don Proch* (1983), and *Patrick Lane* (1994).

A resident of Winnipeg, a graduate of the University of Manitoba (BA, 1969), and the founding president of the Manitoba Writers' Guild (1981–3), Friesen is widely anthologized. In collaboration with Per Brask, he has translated *God's Blue Morris* (1993)—selected poems by Danish poet Niels Hav—and *Stealing Lines From A Dance, An Anthology of 21 Danish Poets*. *Calling the Dog Home* (2005) is a CD of Friesen's text and improvised music by Marilyn Lerner.

sunday afternoon

on sunday afternoons all the fathers in town slept
I think they dreamed of old days and death
sometimes you could hear them cry
the summer air was still at the window
flies on the screen and the radio playing softly in the kitchen   5

mother slid a fresh matrimonial cake onto potholders on the stove
picked up a book a true book of someone else's life
sunglasses a pitcher of lemonade and a straw hat
spread a blue blanket in the backyard near the lilac shrubs for shade
lay down one ear hearing children in the garden   10
she never escaped all the way nor did she want to not quite
this much on a sunday afternoon went a long way

downtown boys rode main street toward fiery crashes they imagined
twisted wrecks with radios playing
rock 'n' roll insulting the highway   15
townspeople gathered on the shoulder
standing as near as they could to the impossible moment between
     what's here and not

a girl's body sprawled in the ditch no one knew at first whose
     daughter she was
though someone pulled her skirt down for decency
the smell of alcohol and fuel everywhere   20
her lipstick so so red beneath the headlights
they couldn't take their eyes from her lips
what was she doing in a wild car like that? who was she?

at night I shivered in bed wondering how to get out of town
side-stepping wrecks they were everywhere on all the roads heading   25

out toward the lights and laughter
a dented hubcap an amazing shoe with its laces still done up
    made you wonder how someone could step right out of a shoe
    like that like the flesh was willing or surprised or not there to
    begin with

in nightmares angry lords walked through my room   30
it took my breath away how ferocious love could be
sometimes jesus hung on the wall or was it the shadow of an elm?
in the morning at the kitchen table green tomatoes on the window
    sill we held devotions with careful hands
father's eyes focused hard on me so he wouldn't remember but of   35
    course he did
listening often to mother's sunny childhood dreams
I thought I was free I was a child with a dancing mother
and my town was filled with children and my town had backstreets
    and sheds and black dogs and sugar trees but she disappeared
    and he died and I got out I'm getting out I'm getting out   40
what I left there the child gathering raspberries in an enamel bowl
he's not dead he went back to where you are before you're born again
waiting for the next time and another town

bible

the bible was a telephone book
of levites canaanites and reubenites
it was a television set
my favourite program being revelation
until someone told me what it meant   5

the bible whispered to itself at night
I thought I heard the song of solomon and lamentations
maybe job   and later second thessalonians
in the morning there were always new underlinings

it was a vacuum cleaner once   10
a week later it was a close shave

the bible was a cockroach
scuttling its dark way through the house

would it survive the holocaust?

it was a black dog behind the couch   15
I could see its muzzle from where I sat at the piano

the bible took me aside
and taught me how to squint
it grasped my hand
and showed me how to shake   20

once
I remember it was fall
the bible took me to a show
of time-lapse photography

evisceration

lord I'm coming apart this is the time of my evisceration this is
        when my singing ceases and something almost silent begins
I'm not safe in the night turning in my sleep I'm not safe throughout
        the day
in all weather in my walking or my talk in my room or when my
        heart is open there is no safety
I have danced and slipped I have fallen I have been cruel and I
        have lain in the arms of betrayal
everything has happened and I've gone nowhere I'm spinning   5
        you're not here you're not there
I'm bereft of love and sense I'm stupid in my collapse no one
        hears me I'm not saying the words that could make anyone
        see or know my descent
I'm bereft of words but not the need to find them

you may hear or not you may walk away still I will speak my fears
        I will admit the shoes and hats I wear
I'll be your fool take my foolishness and hold it up for me to know   10
I would drown for love because that's love it is hard and unrelenting
there is no return there is only the wall I walk toward

yesterday I threw my hat in the air today I wear it again gravity
        is not always a friend
I'm falling it's not this I fear it's falling forever

it's not love's refusal to forgive I fear I fear its absence   15
I fear my love will not reveal its true face I fear what I am in the
      night and what I conceal all day
lord I fear each breath I fear this paradise I do not fear death it will
      catch my fall

what do I ask where are you to hear there is emptiness everywhere
when I come to the end of myself when I stand at the basin and
      look through the window of the mirror what will I see?
give me ropes and water I will place them in my shrine   20
I will learn the love that tears me open
give me celestial burial my body spread-eagled and dispersed
      throughout the world
I will be your fool in the talons of an iron bird I will be free in the
      horrible sky

J.J. Steinfeld *b.* 1946

MUNICH, GERMANY

Although his imagination, as J.J. Steinfeld says, 'is attracted to many themes', it is 'the effect of the Holocaust on subsequent generations . . . that is most personal and dominant' in his work. *The Apostate's Tattoo* (1983), *Unmapped Dreams* (1989), *The Miraculous Hand and Other Stories* (1991), and *Dancing at the Club Holocaust* (1993), all collections of short stories, evolve out of Steinfeld's fictional dialogue with the past, and dramatize 'how the turmoil and struggle of existence stir some people to rage and action while paralyzing others.'

The son of Polish parents, Steinfeld was born in a displaced persons camp in Munich, Germany, and moved to Canada in 1972. Before arriving in Canada he had received a BA in English (1968) from Case Western Reserve University in Cleveland, Ohio, and had begun graduate studies at Ohio State University. He resumed his studies at Trent University, where he received an MA in History (1978). After two years in the doctoral program at the University of Ottawa, Steinfeld abandoned academic pursuits to become a

full-time fiction writer and playwright. 'Writing was the calling,' he says, 'the pull at the heart and spirit.' Since then he has been living in Charlottetown, Prince Edward Island: 'Displaced and misplaced, I have a place, sort of, and it's the Island.'

The inspiration Steinfeld has found in the work of Franz Kafka and Samuel Beckett is reflected in much of his writing, with 'captivity and escape' being one of the dominant themes in his fiction and plays, a theme that is especially obvious in the short story collection *Forms of Captivity and Escape* (1988). Nevertheless, while he feels driven by 'the need to confront the darkness' to write about how the spectre of the past haunts the present, creating 'a post-Holocaust sensibility', he is also interested in 'celebrat[ing] the wonder of the human spirit', and he does so with a great sense of irony, and often humour. His short stories, which have appeared in numerous literary magazines, have won him many awards, including the 1990 Creative Writing Award from the Toronto Jewish Congress Book Committee and the Award for

Distinguished Contribution to the Literary Arts on Prince Edward Island (2003). *Our Hero Is the Cradle of Confederation* (1987) was the winner of the Great Canadian Novella Competition in 1986. His other books of short fiction include *Should the Word Hell Be Capitalized?* (1999), *Anton Chekhov Was Never in Charlottetown* (2000), *Would You Hide Me?* (2003), and *Not A Second More, Not a Second Less* (2005). He has written two full-length plays, and five one-act plays that have all won the Theatre Prince Edward Island's Playwriting Competition.

Ida Solomon's Play

After a performance of my one-woman play, such as tonight, it takes me a long time to calm down, to escape the character I play. Sometimes I get frightened that I'll never become myself again, but I always do. I have my restorative ritual: several cups of strong tea, and then a long walk. Some nights I only need an hour or two, other nights all night, before I can go home to sleep, later awaking as myself. Lately, it's been all night.

On stage, performance after performance, I am Ida Solomon, born Radom, Poland, 1921, died Toronto, Ontario, Canada, 1977, through the eight stages of her life I selected as the most dramatically important to tell Ida's story. I go from sixteen in 1937 through age fifty-six in 1977, forty years of a woman's life, the transformation from the dancing, joyous teenager to the wailing, sad woman seeking a solitary death. My makeup and costumes create an incredible sense of realism; I have Sally and Heather to thank for that. I've learned to dissolve my own forty-one years and become sixteen or twenty-three or fifty-six, whatever I need to be.

This play means everything to me, but who would have ever thought that it would become a success, after the setbacks and bad luck associated with its production. Yet those very nerve-racking problems gave us what got the public interested in the play: priceless publicity, some of it more than a little concerned with the morbid. Fortunately, I'm not a superstitious person. My director Estelle is, but she has her good-luck charms and protective medallions. I wrote the play to keep from jumping off my balcony. Every time I stood too long on the balcony and that familiar dizziness started to take over, I went to my desk and wrote. Thank God for the play! For the years I knew my mother, I relied on memory; for the years before I was born, I talked to her two older sisters, the surviving ones.

The first time I left the theatre in costume I wasn't going to speak, just walk until I felt myself returning. I walked to a part of the city I ordinarily would never go near, and went into a bar that seemed to be out of a third-rate play about dead dreams and babbling drunks. I intended to sit in the bar silently, and drink myself into recovery. But I had to speak, in my mother's voice. Too much silence and I would have had to scream.

'I was in a concentration camp,' I heard myself tell the bartender. He was young, at least ten years younger than me. 'Too bad about that,' he said. Maybe if I had told him my house had burned down or I needed to have a tooth pulled, I would have received more of a reaction. The man sitting two stools away heard me. Through his drunkenness he said, 'Poor lady.'

'The Nazis raped me,' I told him when he moved to the stool next to mine. He groaned in sympathy and put his hands on my clenched fists. As he patted my fists, he kept repeating, 'Poor lady, poor lady. . . .' Then I gave him, word for word, my mother's speech to the unseen psychiatrist during the sixth scene, when she was forty-five and more than ever encased in her painful past. I saw that the man wanted to leave but I held him with my performance. Even that first night out in costume, I wasn't scared and didn't feel unnatural. My mother was an exceptional woman.

Another man who had been listening bought us both drinks. We moved to a table and talked about World War II and the old Nazis that he heard were living in the city, two around the corner from the very bar we were in. For a moment I suspected he was a Nazi in disguise. I drank until I was drunk, and started to cry. My tears are better on stage, but the barroom flow was convincing all the same. My mood changed for the better when I thought that I probably could get a lifetime of free drinks by going from bar to bar, city to city.

Before leaving I performed for the men the entire third scene, Ida twenty-three and in a concentration camp. When I awoke the next afternoon I wasn't certain if I had really done what I had remembered doing. My costume was folded neatly on a chair in the bedroom, but I didn't recall taking it off. The creative process exacts a large price, I told myself, both seriously and foolishly, the way I console myself whenever I do something troublesome or painful or excessive. The next performance was only a few hours away—had I slept *that* long, I remember thinking—and began to become my mother again. I need no less than an hour of mental preparation, even before setting foot in the theatre, to become my character.

I don't know how much longer the play will run or how much longer I want or need to play my mother. I'd like to see the play last as long as possible, but I don't know if I can trust another actress with the role. Perhaps as long as I have my outlets, the dismal bars and all-night eating places and dark streets, I can continue. I never considered myself much of an actress, but I knew Ida Solomon. Estelle thought that I was crazy even to attempt the role, but I won her over. I changed my walk and posture and voice; not knowing exactly how, but I transformed my entire being to resemble my mother. And on Sundays I would go to the cemetery and perform before my parents' graves. Then I would beg my parents for forgiveness. After a while, I no longer needed to be forgiven. I wanted to know their secrets, the ones I couldn't find out from relatives or books. What had they thought about during those days and hours and minutes of hell? How had they survived the concentration camps? I wanted to know if I could have survived. Every night on stage I tried to find out.

On occasion I consider going out as Ida at sixteen or thirty-five or forty-nine, but I never do; always in the costume I wear in the last scene, at fifty-six, when Ida releases her hold, allows the past to triumph. In a strange way, I feel safest at fifty-six, despite what happened to my mother and despite what sometimes happens to me in costume.

If not for the cut on my hand, I would have thought that it had been a dream. He seemed to be so sympathetic at first, a bright-eyed, sensitive night wanderer with a lovely face. He drank coffee, and I tea, strong tea like my mother drank. He told me that he had once lived with a Jewish woman, but she had left him two years ago. He pointed to his heart and said that he still had the scars. I told him about Ida's sexual experiences, the tender ones like the night I was conceived, and the horrid, damaging ones in concentration camp. I would never have gone back with the stranger to his apartment, but my mother did. Not to be alone another night, not after seven years of nights alone since her husband had died. I didn't know my mother as well as I had thought.

Almost from the first moment in his apartment my new acquaintance became aggressive. Pushing me about his living room, he said that he would make love to me the way a dirty old Jew deserved. I fought back, hitting the guard hard, and I couldn't believe the Nazis weren't going to kill me for resisting. He was surprised by my strength. That's when he picked up the knife. I smashed a flowerpot into his lovely face just as he cut me. After he fell, I ran from the apartment, from the concentration camp. So few were able to escape successfully. I think I got into a taxi. I never saw the man with the lovely face again, if he ever existed. The cut on my hand was real, but I could have gotten it anywhere that night.

After only two or three performances of the play about Ida Solomon, I became totally unaware of the audience, even when the play ended and applause filled the theatre. There was no audience when my mother died; her years in concentration camps were unscripted. Because of my need to prepare before the play, and calm down afterwards, the distinction between on stage and off stage grew vaguer and vaguer for me.

I don't know if I could have done this play if my mother were still alive. She died in 1977, when I was thirty, and it took me years to come to terms with her death. As long as I could remember, my father had his heart condition and that illness was real, graspable; his death, for me, was comprehensible. My mother appeared to be whole. Growing up, I thought that she was the strongest woman anywhere; her breakdown was not real for me, until I wrote the play. It frightens me knowing that what my mother had to endure is enabling me finally to make a living as a playwright and actress. When my mother was alive I went through the worst financial struggles and wrote the most abominable rubbish. I thought I was a writer in those days, but it was nothing but self-delusion and vanity. Now I am a writer, and an actress to boot.

None of the women who auditioned for the part could get it right. There were plenty of good actresses who wanted to play Ida Solomon but something was always missing. Maybe I was too critical, but it was my play . . . more than a play: a way to confront the past. The past is a tangible character in the play. The first actress Estelle and I decided on was adequate. At least she could handle the forty-year range. She was best as a sixteen-year-old; her fifty-six-year-old, however, was not an inspired performance. It made me somewhat uneasy that she wasn't Jewish; not that she needed to be a Jew—she was an actress, after all. The direction, makeup and costumes are superb; the women I have working with me on this play are dedicated and brilliant, especially Estelle, Sally, and Heather.

But for relaxation our first Ida liked to ski a little too fast and managed to break both a collarbone and a leg. That was our first setback, after three weeks of rehearsals.

The next actress to play Ida Solomon was also not Jewish. To her credit, she impressed me with her improvement as rehearsals progressed, becoming more 'Jewish' each day. She had been my fifth choice and Estelle's second, but I relied on my director's instincts. The second Ida neglected to tell us that she was undergoing chemotherapy for cancer. I assume in her mind she was determined to be the undaunted, show-must-go-on trouper, but she became weaker and weaker and finally backed out—doctor's orders—telling us that she wanted to spend the remainder of her life in London, England, going to plays.

The third actress's previous stage experience had been mainly in comedies and musicals, and I questioned her ability to handle the depth of emotion required for Ida Solomon's life. She did happen to be Jewish and that gave me hope if nothing else. But she was the mistake to end all mistakes. I should be thankful the little junkie didn't kill herself on stage. I think that was her intention. Estelle doesn't agree with me, but it's my theory that the third actress to play Ida got so disoriented she thought the dressing room was centre stage. She was dressed as the sixteen-year-old; it would have made more sense to me, of course, if she was the fifty-six-year-old; but then she would have been following the script and that I'm sure was no longer of interest to her. In the dead actress's dressing room, waiting for the police, is when I first thought that I might be able to play Ida Solomon—*had* to play her. The transition from tentative notion to fixed idea was swift, an explosive inner communication. No one knew the character better than I did. Estelle cried for the corpse, for the play she was directing; I thought about what my mother had endured in concentration camp.

'We'll put it on. I don't care how long it takes . . . I promise we'll do it,' I told Estelle, but she was convinced the play was both cursed and doomed.

'There won't be a sane actress in town who will touch the role now,' my director said.

'So, who needs to be sane,' I told her.

We barely needed two weeks of preparation before the play was ready to open again. The publicity we were getting was unbelievable. I refused to tell anyone that the play was about my mother, almost literally so. My standard reply became that my play was based on a composite of the mothers of two of my childhood friends. When a swastika was painted on the outside of the theatre, the publicity increased. We had a full house on opening night, and for most of the nights after that.

I can't remember exactly when I started to leave the theatre in costume, but it might have been the very first night. When I sat in the dressing room in front of the mirror, I swear I saw my mother. She needed some fresh air. I was going to take only a short walk, around the block at most. Soon I was unable not to take my after-show excursions.

As far as I know, I have been recognized only a few times on the street. I was startled the first time I was noticed by someone who had seen the play. I didn't understand right away what the person was saying to Ida. My mind was elsewhere, in Poland, worrying about getting through another dreadful, imprisoned day. The second time, an excited couple told me how wonderful my performance had been, and that they planned to see the play once more. I began to talk to them in Yiddish, and they walked away, smiling, as if I had been trying to entertain them. Usually it creates no great difficulty for a fifty-six-year-old Jewish woman to walk the streets; it is not an occasion for disbelief. Yet the streets I choose, the bars and dingy eating places I go to, and above all, my words, that is a different matter altogether.

There are so many people that Ida meets, but some stick in memory more than others. I'll never forget the guy who liked to rip up his money in the most wretched bar in the city. After I delivered the first part of Ida's pre-suicide soliloquy to my audience of one, the man began to tell me that this was going to be *his* last night on earth. He had had enough. I demanded justification: What was causing his suffering? What horrors had he seen? When had God betrayed him? The man told me that he failed at everything he had ever tried; he had no desire to try again. No purpose, no will, no sense, he babbled away. His desire to die seemed to be an offence against my mother's death, her need to die after surviving concentration camp and living with her European memories for thirty North American years. I belittled each reason for dying the man mentioned, perhaps attempting to bully him back to life, perhaps merely loathing him. I didn't know for certain.

'Have you ever tried acting on stage?' I asked the suicidal man. I'm sure he thought I was a lunatic. He took out money from his wallet and ripped up five ten-dollar bills, as if to confirm his resolution to die. 'I have money. Money is nothing, the Devil's toilet paper,' he shouted. I could hear protests from other parts of the bar against his sacrilege. I knew that his suffering was genuine, even if I couldn't accept it; what I didn't know was whether he was sincere in his desire to kill himself or just letting out a pitiful call for help. We sat in the bar together for what must have been an hour, debating the substance and validity and worth of his proposed act.

'You must go on living, no matter what the pain. No matter how great the adversity, there is always reason to live,' Ida told the man. I didn't believe in what Ida was telling him; I knew what *she* had been compelled to do. But Ida, for some reason, felt an obligation to attempt to keep this pathetic creature alive.

'What method are you going to use?' I asked. He smiled, or what looked like a smile brought on by a jolt of electricity. He left twenty-five dollars on the bar to cover his tab, and ripped two more tens before leaving. For a confused instant, I thought of following the man, of taking my costume off in front of him, of suggesting that making love was better than dying, but even the prospect of the pursuit sickened me. Several patrons in the bar came over to where I was sitting and gathered up the pieces of ripped money, and then went back to their tables for the attempt at restoration. I never returned to that bar or inquired if the man had followed through on his threat to kill himself. Maybe he had been acting too. I didn't care about him; Ida, bless her tormented heart, cared about that whimpering fool.

I want to write a new play—something about the old, lonely street women I have been observing on some of my walks—but I can't sustain anything new. Ida Solomon isn't interested in writing a play. She is sad because she was able to have only one child, and that child is grown and doesn't seem to need her.

Tonight another dismal bar and performing my play to another numbed soul. It's the numbed who draw me, seem to be the only adequate nighttime audience. I don't know why I want to inhabit their empty, deadening worlds. This man looked about Ida's age, perhaps five or six years older. He listened politely to Ida's recollections of Poland and her life during the war. Only his eyes indicated any interest. After I got good and drunk, I put two complimentary tickets to my play about Ida Solomon down on the bar. 'Good for thawing out your frozen soul,' I told the old man when he didn't touch the tickets. 'An evening at the theatre is better than this goddamn place.'

His expression remained fixed, indissoluble. 'So what do you think about the life I've lived?' I asked the old man, becoming annoyed that he wasn't saying anything. His eyes had a curious vitality to them, but I couldn't understand the messages they were sending. Improvising a new scene, I showed him my concentration camp number, the one Sally puts on for me with such care every night. The old man grabbed my left wrist and held it down against the wooden counter of the bar. He began to hurt me, but Ida could stand the pain, at least this kind of physical pain. The bartender came by and pulled the old man's hands away, slamming them down hard on the wooden counter. He kept slamming the old man's hands down again and again. 'Stop!' Ida screamed. With her own hands she forced the bartender to release his hold, told him to leave her and the old man alone.

Before I could deliver any more of Ida's lines, the old man had pushed up the left sleeves of his suit coat and shirt. His eyes closed as he showed me his concentration camp number. 'I'm so sorry,' I said; Ida had disappeared. I embraced the old man and searched for Ida.

I no longer want to be my mother in the play, to go through the eight stages of her life that I selected in some madly punishing and creative attempt to make sense of the past, to counteract my guilt, to justify remaining alive. I want the play to end, but I cannot under any circumstances allow my mother to die and remain lost to me, not again, never again.

Marlene NourbeSe Philip *b.* 1947

MORIAH, TOBAGO

'How does one write poetry from the twin realities of being Black and female in the last quarter of the twentieth century? How does one write poetry from a place such as Canada, whose reality for poets such as myself is, more often than not, structured by its absence? How does one write from the perspective of one who has "mastered" a foreign language, yet has never had a mother tongue[?] . . . How does the poet work a language engorged on her many silences? . . . Can she fashion a language that uses silences as a first principle?' These questions formed the opening paragraph of the letter Marlene NourbeSe Philip sent to publishers in 1987 accompanying her manuscripts for *She Tries Her Tongue, Her Silence Softly Breaks* and *Looking for Livingstone: An Odyssey of Silence*. They are also the questions at the core of all her writing. After twenty-five rejections, these manuscripts were published, in 1989 and 1991 respectively, establishing NourbeSe Philip as an evocative and polemical literary voice in Canadian writing.

An African Caribbean, NourbeSe Philip was born in Moriah, Tobago. NourbeSe, meaning 'wonderful child', is the Nigerian Benin name she adopted when she was eight years old. Upon completing a degree in economics at the University of West Indies (1968) she moved to Canada, where she received an MA (1970) in Political Science and a Law degree (1973) from the University of Western Ontario before practising immigration and family law (1973–82) in Toronto as a partner in Jemmott and Philip, the first black women's law firm in Canada.

For NourbeSe Philip writing is an integral part of culture 'as a site of contestation'. As a poet, novelist, and cultural critic, her task has always been to, on the one hand, examine language—not only as an instrument of writing, but also as the carrier of colonialist and racist attitudes—and, on the other, go beyond the fact that 'we Africans in the New World have been weaned forever on the milk of otherness.' A contributor to such journals as *Fuse Magazine*, her first books were the poetry collections *Thorns* (1980) and *Salmon Courage* (1983). Her youth novel *Harriet's Daughter* (1988) was originally published in England because it was rejected by Canadian publishers. When it subsequently appeared in Canada, it earned nominations for the Canadian Library Association Book of the Year Award for children's literature, The City of Toronto Book Award, and the Max and Greta Ebel Memorial Award; it was later adapted for the stage in Toronto. (A more recent title of hers, *Coups and Calypso* (2001), was produced in London, England, and Toronto in 1999.)

The selection that follows, 'Discourse on the Logic of Language', comes from *She Tries Her Tongue, Her Silence Softly Breaks*, which earned NourbeSe Philip the prestigious Casa de las Americas Prize, making her the first anglophone woman and just the second Canadian to win the prize. In 1990–1 she received a Guggenheim Award, which enabled her to move back to Tobago to finish *Looking for Livingstone: An Odyssey of Silence*. An experimental and ambitious text, spanning as it does 18 million years and the entire African continent, *An Odyssey of Silence* has been read both as a prose long poem and as a novel. Focusing on Dr David Livingstone 'as a concept' that presents the female traveller searching for him with 'an alternative view of history', she declares that 'history is not dead'. SILENCE, the word formed by the anagrams of the names of places she visits, emerges as a discursive place of possibilities. She is currently working on *Zong!*, a hybrid text consisting of 'fragmenting and mutilating' documents, and 'whiting and/or blacking out' words based on the 1781 legal decision to murder via 'natural death'—that is, by drowning or by thirst—470 African slaves on the ship *Zong*. Messrs Gregson, the ship's owners, had hoped to recover their losses over the annihilation of their human 'cargo', which was fully insured.

NourbeSe Philip's cultural statements and essays have been collected in *Frontiers: Essays and Writings on Racism and Culture* (1992); *Showing Grit: Showboating North of the 44th Parallel* (1993), a critical look at the cultural and political sources as well as conditions that have produced the musical play *Show Boat*; and *A Genealogy of Resistance and Other Essays* (1997)—essay writing, meditation, diaries—which includes her chapbook *Caribana: African Roots and Continuities: Race, Space and the Poetics of Moving* (1996). A resident fellow at the MacDowell Colony (1991), a writer-in-residence and guest scholar at such institutions as the Banff Centre for the Arts (1990), Queen's University (1993), and McMaster University (2003), and the winner of a Chalmers Fellowship in poetry (2002), NourbeSe Philip has also won recognition for her political and cultural contributions, including the Rebels for a Cause Award by the Elizabeth Fry Society and the YWCA Women of Distinction Award in the arts category (2001).

Discourse on the Logic of Language

WHEN IT WAS BORN, THE MOTHER HELD HER NEWBORN CHILD CLOSE: SHE BEGAN THEN TO
LICK IT ALL OVER. THE CHILD WHIMPERED A LITTLE, BUT AS THE MOTHER'S TONGUE
MOVED FASTER AND STRONGER OVER ITS BODY, IT GREW SILENT—THE MOTHER TURNING
IT THIS WAY AND THAT UNDER HER TONGUE, UNTIL SHE HAD TONGUED IT CLEAN OF
THE CREAMY WHITE SUBSTANCE COVERING ITS BODY.

English
is my mother tongue.
A mother tongue is not
not a foreign lan lan lang
language
l/anguish
 anguish
—a foreign anguish.

English is
my father tongue.
A father tongue is
a foreign language,
therefore English is
a foreign language
not a mother tongue.

What is my mother
tongue
my mammy tongue
my mummy tongue
my momsy tongue
my modder tongue
my ma tongue?

I have no mother
tongue
no mother to tongue
no tongue to mother
to mother
tongue
me

I must therefore be tongue
dumb
dumb-tongued
dub-tongued
damn dumb
tongue

EDICT I

*Every owner of slaves
shall, wherever possible,
ensure that his slaves
belong to as many ethno-
linguistic groups as
possible. If they can-
not speak to each other, they
cannot then foment
rebellion and revolution.*

Those parts of the brain chiefly responsible for speech are named after two learned nineteenth century doctors, the eponymous Doctors Wernicke and Broca respectively.

Dr Broca believed the size of the brain determined intelligence; he devoted much of his time to 'proving' that white males of the Caucasian race had larger brains than, and were therefore superior to, women, Blacks and other peoples of colour.

Understanding and recognition of the spoken word takes place in Wernicke's area—the left temporal lobe, situated next to the auditory cortex; from there relevant information passes to Broca's area—situated in the left frontal cortex—which then forms the response and passes it on to the motor cortex. The motor cortex controls the muscles of speech.

THE MOTHER THEN PUT HER FINGERS INTO HER CHILD'S MOUTH—GENTLY FORCING IT OPEN; SHE TOUCHES HER TONGUE TO THE CHILD'S TONGUE, AND HOLDING THE TINY MOUTH OPEN, SHE BLOWS INTO IT—HARD. SHE WAS BLOWING WORDS—HER WORDS, HER MOTHER'S WORDS, THOSE OF HER MOTHER'S MOTHER, AND ALL THEIR MOTHERS BEFORE—INTO HER DAUGHTER'S MOUTH.

but I have
a dumb tongue
tongue dumb
father tongue
and english is
my mother tongue
is
my father tongue
is a foreign lan lan lang
language/
l/anguish
  anguish
a foreign anguish
is english—
another tongue
my mother
    mammy
    mummy
    moder
    mater
    macer
    moder
tongue
mothertongue

tongue mother
tongue me
mothertongue me
mother me
touch me
with the tongue of your
lan lan lang
language
l/anguish
  anguish
english
is a foreign anguish

EDICT II

*Every slave caught
speaking his native
language shall be severely
punished. Where
necessary, removal of the
tongue is recommended.
The offending organ, when
removed, should be hung
on high in a central place,
so that all may see and tremble.*

A tapering, blunt-tipped, muscular, soft and fleshy organ describes
(a) the penis.
(b) the tongue.
(c) neither of the above.
(d) both of the above.

In man the tongue is
(a) the principal organ of taste.
(b) the principal organ of articulate speech.
(c) the principal organ of oppression and exploitation.
(d) all of the above.

The tongue
(a) is an interwoven bundle of striated muscle running in three planes.
(b) is fixed to the jawbone.
(c) has an outer covering of a mucous membrane covered with papillae.
(d) contains ten thousand taste buds, none of which is sensitive to the taste of foreign words.

Air is forced out of the lungs up the throat to the larynx where it causes the vocal cords to vibrate and create sound. The metamorphosis from sound to intelligible word requires
(a) the lip, tongue and jaw all working together.
(b) a mother tongue.
(c) the overseer's whip.
(d) all of the above or none.

Sadhu Binning *b.* 1947

CHIHERU, PUNJAB, INDIA

Born in Chiheru, Punjab, India, Binning moved to Canada in 1967. Settled in Vancouver, he has been teaching Punjabi at the University of British Columbia since 1988. As the Vice President of the Punjabi Language Education Association, Binning has been involved in many activities intended to increase the visibility, use, and status of his native language. Though spoken by thousands of Canadians, he says 'the reality is that Punjabi is still considered to be a foreign language in Canada.' He explains this as the result of the failure of multiculturalism to 'advance beyond a certain stage in the last thirty-four years. It is a well known and accepted fact that no culture can survive without its language'; 'language is the essential ingredient in the survival of a culture. Yet Canadian multicultural structure is steadfast against recognizing any language as Canadian other than its two official languages.'

A prolific author in Punjabi—he has published over fifteen books in India—Binning is a poet and novelist. His publications in English (most of them translations from his Punjabi publications by Binning himself) include *No More Watno Dur* (1995), a poetry collection dedicated to the passengers of the *Komagatu Maru*, a ship with 376 Indian immigrants which, upon arriving in Vancouver in 1914, was forced to turn back to Calcutta where many passengers, upon disembarkation, were shot by the British colonial police as they had been declared dangerous by its Canadian counterpart. A resident in Burnaby, BC, Binning was the editor of the literary monthly *Watno Dur* and co-edited the quarterly literary magazine *Watan*.

The Symptoms

it was clearly a question of roti
we jumped several oceans
as if they were puddles
formed by the monsoon rains
roti we did receive on this end   5
but from sunrise to sunset
we had to dance like a street juggler's bear
and often had to duck
from hoodlums' bricks

we intentionally forgot the history   10
before and after the *Komagata Maru*
we never payed any attention
to the plight of blacks and browns in America
why and how the Yankee farmers
use millions illegal Mexicans in their fields   15
and why the real owners of North America
prefer liquor as a method of suicide

we never concerned ourselves
with happenings in South Africa

not just that   20
we didn't even think about
why the vacant houses in our village back home
are being rented by the *Purbias*[1] only
and why *jathedar*[2] Tohra
denies *Purbias* the right to vote   25

now if you could just place
Mukadar Ka Sikandar[3] on pause
let us think and see
the all-night-long hymn-singing of the *Purbias*
our own building gurdwaras after gurdwaras   30
and keep on buying videos
native Indians keeping drunk around the clock
whether or not
are the symptoms of the same disease?

1 Easterns. Purbias is a derogatory term used for landless workers from Punjab's neighbouring province of Uttar Pradesh.
2 Leader.
3 A typical Hindi film.

To Mother Teresa

wrapped in a simple saree you resemble a goddess
to call you mother is really not a bad thing
granted you may have mountains of sympathy
oceans of love that can embrace the universe
and you may have unshakable belief in your Christ   5
but do love and belief alone ever satisfy a hungry body?
do they die due to lack of love and belief
those who slowly starve to death?

to feed a starving, suffering child
some would snatch food from the hoarding robbers   10
they are given death in reward
when by begging from the same robbers
you place a small bite in that child's mouth
you are given a Nobel prize

had these prizes been given   15
for loving and serving one's people
they would have chosen Mandela before Tutu
that somebody from Poland
probably would had to wait many more decades

the prizes are given for the service you provide   20
to the modern kings

these kings have always honoured you
you're a shield of magic in their hands
standing behind you they watch everything
yet themselves are rarely seen   25

using you as a commercial poster
they have handed out the bible
in all corners of the earth
people have bibles
but lost their homes and lands   30
and their right to be humans
regardless of all your noble intentions
you become a tool in the hands of these kings

a noble prize for you
simply means a sharper tool for them   35

the empires of these modern kings
do not run from one end of a country to the other
like that of great Ashok
instead they start from the thirtieth floor in New York
like electric current   40
pass through numerous countries
from their high-rises and electric windows
they rule their empires
and you dear mother Teresa
are their life insurance   45
as long as you keep on crying love, peace, belief
their reality will remain hidden
the starving will keep on starving
the rich will keep on getting rich

until these children learn   50
to become masters of their own fate
they can never defeat hunger

if you really want them to live
like dignified human beings
teach them to believe in   55
struggle for their rights
teach them about Bhagat Singh
about Che Guevera and Steve Biko
you will soon see
the effect of this lesson   60
you won't be given a Nobel prize
but a bullet triggered
from a New York window
and thrown in an unmarked grave
somewhere in El Salvador   65

H. Nigel Thomas *b.* 1947

DICKSON'S VILLAGE, ST VINCENT, WEST INDIES

Nigel H. Thomas was born in Dickson's Village, on the island of Saint Vincent, West Indies, and is a descendant of the colonial owner of that area, after whom the village is named. John Dickson, his maternal grandfather, taught him to read before he reached school age and 'was full of stories about his travels', stories that have inspired some of Thomas's fiction. His novel *Behind the Face of Winter* (2001) is dedicated to his grandfather as well as his grandmother, Hester Roban Dickson, a 'no-nonsense' but affectionate woman who also played a major role in Thomas's upbringing. Similar in structure to his first novel, *Spirits in the Dark* (1993), which was shortlisted for the QSPELL Hugh MacClennan Award, is the coming-of-age story of Pedro Moore, an embittered immigrant in Canada who recollects his past, and his devoted 'Grama', on the island of Isabella. The Caribbean setting of most of his fiction, Isabella Island 'is an invented island', an island 'obviously reflecting his St Vincent roots' but at the same time depicting what he calls a 'Pan-Caribbean reality'.

Before moving to Canada at the age of twenty-one, Thomas worked as an elementary and high school teacher and as a civil servant in St Vincent. Though he trained as a registered nursing assistant upon arriving in Montreal, he pursued an academic career. It was during this time that he became involved with the Montreal Free South Africa group. He holds a BA (1974) and an MA (1975) from Concordia University, and a Diploma in Secondary Education from McGill University (1976). During the twelve-year period in which he worked as a high school teacher of English and French as a second language, he pursued a PhD in American literature at the Université de Montréal (1985). He subsequently became a professor at Laval University (1988). *From Folklore to Fiction: A Study of Folk Heroes and Rituals in the Black American Novel* (1988) is based on his doctoral dissertation.

Thomas says that it was his experiences in Montreal's 'alien environment' that compelled him at once 'to probe my identity and to resist those who sought to restrict me'. This experience, along with his abiding interest in 'the mystery of the human psyche' and his 'awareness that survival is the fundamental instinct driving human behaviour', informs his writing. Seeing himself 'as belonging in the tradition of African artists, who, by tradition, have a sphere of responsibility to their audience', Thomas is interested in keeping his writing accessible, even when he writes from the perspective of Jerome Quashee, the intellectual protagonist of his first novel. While lengthy references to black intellectuals like Chinua Achebe and Richard Wright appear in the narrative, Caribbean folklore, humour, and the local idiom ensure that his writing remains approachable to a broad community of readers. Thomas has also published a collection of short fiction, *How Loud Can the Village Cock Crow and Other Stories* (1995), as well as a volume of poetry, *Moving Through Darkness* (1999), which, concerned with racialism and 'biomythography', reflects his interest in cultural myths and translates his own experiences into images and stories that mirror the human condition at large.

Thomas now resides in Montreal, having lived until recently in Quebec City, where he says he finds 'a tremendous amount of freedom . . . far more than is available in my native St Vincent. I could not live in peace in St Vincent and be gay. I couldn't express my thoughts as freely as I do here.' Still, what 'bothers' him 'are the stereotypes linked to blackness. In Montreal, people are more sophisticated when it comes to handling stereotypes. In Quebec City they are raw. Naked.'

The Village Ram

I entered the house and gazed at but did not recognize the obese figure sprawled in a morris chair at the far end of the living room. He was totally grey, and in that sweltering heat he wore a thick woollen, dark-blue blazer.

'Debo! How good it is to see you! My God, how long have you been away?'

'Fifteen years, mate.' He beckoned me to move closer.

A pair of crutches lay on the floor in front of him. He caught me staring at them. 'I been down with the arthritis.'

Silence began to grow between us, and to break it I said, 'But how you have changed! I still remember the day you told me you were leaving. My God, in fifteen years, so much change!'

'You never travelled to a cold country, but those seasons tell a man nothing ain't permanent.'

'I see you've become a philosopher. . . . And where's the missus?'

'Lucille!' he projected his voice in the direction of the room at the other end of the living room. 'Come and meet my closest friend, Victor.'

Lucille appeared. She was beautiful. She was about five-six, darkish-blonde, with electric blue eyes, and a finely sculpted body. She wore a yellow blouse and a pair of orange shorts. Her movement to where I stood was watery smooth. 'How do you do?' She extended her hand.

'I have been eager to meet you.' At this Debo flashed me a quick glance.

'Why, may I ask?' was her reaction.

'Oh, one is always eager to meet the wife of one's closest friends.'

'And are you married, Mr. . . . ?'

'Please, please call me Victor.'

'Marvellous! I like that. Formality is rather tiring. Don't you think so? Puts too much stiffness into things that ought to be quite flexible. You are married, I take it.'

'No, I'm not.'

'Wonderful! There are a few level-headed people left, I see. It makes things a lot easier, you know.'

We exchanged a few more banalities and I returned home.

My mind returned to the early years with Debo. His father lived in our village with another woman. He'd never claimed Debo as his son. From the look of things, his mother must have desperately tried to find a husband, but each man simply left her with another child. Debo was around twelve when child number nine came along and died and almost took Debo's mama with him. It was then that she'd had her tubes tied. We used to tease Debo: '*Debo's mama got her tubes tied, her tubes tied, her tubes tied; Debo's mama got her tubes tied—all the way to her backside.*' Once we asked Debo whether her tubes were tied outside or inside. And we all had visions of strings tied in a bow.

There was a bewitching quality about Debo that perhaps lay in the petalling curl his smiling lips took on, or his skin that was the closest shade to real blackness that I'd ever seen in a human being, or even in his black gums that contrasted strongly against his white teeth. A school friend swore that once he had seen Debo on a dark night and could discern only two moving spots which turned out to be Debo's eyes. He said he was on the verge of screaming, 'Jumbie!' when Debo said, 'How you doing, Percy?' After that we advised Debo that he should sing when walking alone on a dark night.

His habit of using words he did not fully understand delighted us constantly. Each day he studded his sentences with the new multisyllabic words we'd learned. He continued, sentence after sentence, no doubt encouraged by our torrents of laughter. 'Debo,' Charles once asked, 'Why you always wearing your drawers on your head?'

I was on my way home one December afternoon during my first year at Wesley High, when I met Debo at the bridge where our village began. He walked back with me. During the first few minutes he looked at me quickly and then back at the uninhabited, uncultivated stretch that bordered the road. Then solemnly, he asked, 'Victor, if you had a choice to be born again, you wouldn't want to be white?'

The question struck me like a stone on my forehead. I refused to reply. Instead my mind went back to what we had learned about slavery in our last year of elementary school. We walked on in silence until we got to the breadfruit tree that shaded his mother's house like a massive umbrella and whose numerous breadfruit, some of which they sometimes sold, kept Debo, his mother, and the others alive. The first signs of dusk and fireflies were already present. I had to be home to feed the chickens and secure the goats. Debo held my arm. 'Wait, let me show you something.' From his pocket he slowly removed a thin billfold and opened it. 'See this,' he pushed a photograph toward me, of a white woman, some nondescript film star. 'I want one just like her when I get married. Boy, a woman like that, I won't even let her go to the toilet!'

'No joking!'

He became suddenly pensive. 'Victor, you won't tell the other boys about this, now? eh? Promise me.'

I looked at him with curling lips and said through my teeth, 'Yes, I promise.'

That evening encounter weakened our friendship, though in the months that followed we pretended that nothing had changed. He dated a girl from our class (only three of us had gone on to high school), and they sometimes spent whole days together. I hoped he did not get her pregnant. I knew that because she wasn't white he would treat her as his father had treated his mother.

Two years later, one April—the Saturday after Good Friday, in fact—Debo told me that his aunt in England had sent for him. The moment of his announcing the news etched itself in my memory with a postcard clarity. The last rays of the setting sun bathed the canefields. The brown earth itself seemed dyed with it. Debo's back was turned to the sun; his face beamed with ebonic splendour, and his eyes danced. I felt joyful too. I was happy that Debo would be able to find a job in England and help to feed his brothers and sisters. His mother sometimes earned a trifle weeding people's gardens or doing the laundry for some sick person. My deepest fear was that, at a time when we were just beginning to take pride in our blackness, Debo would go to England, marry the first white woman willing to have him, and tell her how much he hated himself.

Two weeks after our conversation he left for England. He wrote me three letters. In the second letter he told me what a hit he was among the English girls. I did not comment on this when I replied.

The years passed. I graduated from high school and teachers college and I heard nothing more about Debo other than what Joanne Barnaby, who had been in elementary school with us, reported when she came home one August for her father's funeral. She'd heard that Debo married an English school teacher and no Blacks had been invited to the wedding. We both agreed that 'What sweet nanny goat does give her belly running.'

With the exception of Debo, all Miss Jones's children turned out to be quite bright. Five of them won scholarships to Expatriates Academy, and the other two had their tuition paid for by those who'd already graduated and were working. Their mother hadn't worked in anyone's garden for several years. Ruff, my oldest brother, was married to Debo's sister, and their son Geoff was already in grade one the night I was summoned to Miss Jones's house to discover that Debo had returned from England.

Our village population was then around 700. We didn't have a cinema then, no television either, so we relied on scandals for most of our entertainment; and sometimes we waited a long while before a truly delightful one came along.

The centre of life for the village's non-productive and less respectable males was the rumshop; not a just term, for it was here that most people, being without refrigerators, bought their groceries daily. By mid-afternoon the day after Lucille's arrival, she found the place. She lost no time introducing herself to the six or seven men in the shop swallowing rum and slamming dominoes. Following this, she bought a forty-ounce bottle of Old Oak. Within half an hour the shop was surrounded by men, women, and children in search of new drama.

The shop's counter was about three feet from the entrance. The drinkers sat in a tiny alcove where the counter ended. The shop was stacked with supplies all the way up to the ceiling. In some areas cobwebs dangled, and an odour of rum, rancid cooking oil, and tainted codfish was ever-present.

Lucille addressed her questions to Joe Burnbury. He was the burliest of the men.

The crowd around the shop continued to increase; but seeing no action, some of them were already leaving, when everyone heard, 'Joe, love, show me how you down this rum.' She held on to his biceps and squeezed them.

Joe looked at his drinking buddies with a wicked smile and a wink; he threw back his head and said, 'Miz Jones, yo' cock back yo' head like this and yo' pour it down yo' throat.'

Lucille picked up a tumbler, filled it to the brim with rum—as the bodies squeezed against one another to take in her action—threw back her head, and let the rum gurgle down her throat. The crowd guffawed, some clapped, some leaped in the air several times, others smiled scornfully.

Lucille turned scarlet. One hand clutched her throat, the other her stomach. Slowly her eyes filled and then it trickled down her face.

Mrs Jennings the shopkeeper motioned to Joe to give Lucille some ice water. This he did and gradually she recovered.

When she was able to speak, she looked around the entire crowd and exclaimed, 'Not bad for a beginning, eh? I'll outdo all of you before long.' And to prove she would, she promptly downed another half tumbler of rum, while Joe eagerly held the bottle of cold water, ready to pour. Women, unless they were prostitutes, never smoked or drank in public—and certainly not at a rumshop.

The crowd exchanged winks and looks of exasperation. Then, in the relative quiet Bertha Bowman's voice thundered, 'Pretty woman got dirty tricks. But look at the way she cock back she head and swaller that rum! The world is certainly turning upside down.'

Lucille responded: she tossed down another half tumbler of rum.

The first signs of unsteadiness began to show, so I pushed my way through the crowd in an attempt to rescue her from the ridicule; the villagers would not let me through. 'Lucille, get out of this place! This is not the sort of thing you do here!'

'Leave me alone. Oh, this is so much fun! Where is the music? I want to dance!'

'Lucille,' I shouted again. This time she peered among the bodies to see who was speaking.

'Kiss me first and tell me later.'

The crowd applauded.

'Why don't you let him through?'

A path was created instantly. As I stepped before her, her arms were around me, and she was tiptoeing to kiss me.

'Jesus Christ!' thundered Bertha. 'This one escape from Sodom and Gomorrah!'

There was a rustling sound and I saw the crowd parting to let Debo through. Next it was his voice, its English accent gone, 'Get out of my way, you corbeau!'

'You only find corbeau where you find carrion,' came Bertha's instant reply. 'Go bury that stinking carcass.'

There was scattered applause.

Debo hobbled into the shop on his crutches. He slapped Lucille on the left and again on the right before we restrained him.

'What did I do wrong?' she asked like a confused little girl, looking at the crowd and trying to rub away the sting.

'Time to go home, Miz Jones,' Joe told her. He took her hand and led her to her mother-in-law's gate. Debo hobbled along behind.

In the days that followed, everything else was pushed aside to discuss Lucille. Johnny Kemp, who on account of his partial paralysis had not witnessed the scene, remarked that many white women were cheap and could not find husbands of their own race, and there were always desperate Blacks eager to marry them. 'What we must do is don't talk to Debo, 'cause I'm sure he feel our race not good enough for him.'

Johnny's wife, who had witnessed the event, felt that Debo's mother should take him to see Bongo, the obeah man, to clean out of him what had twisted him up. Alice Tucker felt that a white rabbit should be killed at the shop, its blood sprinkled where Lucille stood, and the whole washed away with turpentine. 'Mark my words, she will bring a curse on this village.'

Lucille went to church the Sunday after her arrival and continued to go every Sunday after that. Around the time she started attending, there was no music in the church, for Mrs Brewster the organist was ill. One Sunday, Reverend Bushnell asked whether anyone could fill in for Mrs Brewster. Lucille volunteered. Her playing left the congregation hypnotized. We'd never before heard such a rendition of *A Mighty Fortress Is Our God.* We sat straight in our pews with held breaths. When the last note sounded our respect and awe enveloped her. Reverend Bushnell praised and thanked her profusely. When the service ended, many who'd consciously avoided her went over to embrace her and to compliment her for her fine playing. Someone remarked that had she offered her candidacy for the elections then taking place, she would have received every Methodist vote.

The Anglican priest must have resented her, for his evening worshippers, many of whom were spouses of the Methodists, deserted his evening services to hear Lucille play.

Not long after her musical debut, she informed the minister that for some time she had been thinking of organizing a charity for the region's poorest folk, of which there was plenty, Isabella Island's only major industry, the sugar industry, having closed, leaving thousands permanently unemployed. In England she had been a volunteer worker with the Salvation Army; she had connections with several aid agencies in Britain and they would supply her with useful items. All she needed was the use of the church hall as a distribution centre. Within two months four crates of food and clothing arrived and were promptly distributed.

Soon she was guest of honour in many of the wealthiest homes.

Her flame burned even brighter when the Camden Methodist Choir under her direction placed first in the island-wide Interdenominational Sacred Music Contest—a stunning achievement, considering that the choir had never participated during the fifty-three years of the contest's history. It was backwoods Camden that would be representing Isabella Island in the Caribbean Interdenominational Sacred Music

Contest to be held in Port-of-Spain in August of that year. So when a position became available at Hillsdale Elementary School, Lucille was Reverend Bushnell's obvious choice.

She soon established herself as a star teacher. She took seeds and insects and pieces of wood and articles of every shape and texture to teach biology and math and English and vocabulary and geography. Each day my nephew came home and talked about her as if she were a cult figure. The students told their parents about Buddha, Confucius, Shaka Zulu, Ashanti kings and queens, the Songhay Empire, the Incas, the Mayans. . . . Aside from the contempt we had absorbed from the colonial textbooks, we knew nothing about Africa; only British history was permitted in the schools and public libraries. She took tins of freshly-baked cookies to school, said that only those students who solved all their problems would get any, but ended up giving everyone.

The following year she was asked to teach the scholarship class, and decided that to do so well the students had to come to school on Saturdays and spend an extra hour on regular school days. When the results were announced, Hillsdale, one of the island's smallest elementary schools, took eight places; the runner-up, a school of ten times Hillsdale's population, took three; most schools took one; and several got none.

That August the education officer tried to persuade Lucille to join the Teachers College faculty. She refused. She loved the village too much to move to town; she loved the glow and inquisitiveness of youthful minds; she really could not accept the post.

But when September arrived and Lucille once more engaged her starry-eyed pupils, whispers about her were everywhere in the community, and gossip steadily diluted our affection for her. Many people came to her defence; some refused outright to hear her 'slandered'. In any case the subject became the topic of discussion at one of my aunt's tea parties. The women sipped tea and consumed cake and alighted on every subject before centring on that one.

'What's this rumour about Lucille?' Milly Barker asked.

'I couldn't tell you, my dear; somebody is trying to ruin her, somebody that's obviously jealous of her,' Bobsy Brown opined.

'Still, you know, you can't forget that show she put on the second day she got here,' my mother told them.

'Lizzy!' exclaimed my aunt, 'why do you have to dig that up? She was confused, that's all. Her coming from England for the first time, I'm sure the tropical heat made her drunk.'

'When I see that woman,' added Mensie Mayers, 'I see the light of God.'

'Why must you all think that every kind white person is holy? If we don't watch it around here, we're soon going to be offering sacrifices to statues of her.' Hilda Humphrey sucked her teeth and let them know she was not covering up. Hilda had been Hillsdale's most luminous teacher until Lucille eclipsed her and won away her scholarship class.

Encouraged no doubt by Hilda, Milly Barker, malice shining in her eyes, said, 'It's the fellows' groin—'

She did not finish, for my aunt's hand was over her mouth, and my mother was saying, 'You think we should encourage that kind of talk, Milly? She is the teacher of our children, you know. And if this thing grows she will have to leave. Where would we find another like her? Besides, look at the exposure she gave us! Did you ever think we could enter the music contest? win? and go on to place third in the Caribbean? Whoever paid attention to us before? Look at the charity work she's doing! Who's going to take it over when we drive her away? Let's not encourage these damn fools. As Christians, it's not our duty to condemn others. . . . Remember, "He that is without sin should cast the first stone."'

'Lizzy,' my aunt said, 'no one is throwing stones; we're only trying to establish whether these rumours are true. Anyway, let's drop the subject.' At this point she got up and took the teapot to the kitchen to refill it. My mother picked up the cake platter and began offering seconds.

There was less restraint in other circles. Whenever Bertha Bowman passed Debo's mother's gate (they were still living there), she would say in a sing-song, teasing way, 'Yo' like white meat but like yo' can't digest it'—and this with little regard for the fact that the dress she'd be wearing was from the crates that continued to arrive. On another occasion, she concluded one of her tirades with another of her Bowmanian expressions: 'Gawd, that woman common as spit!' After all, none of Bertha's six daughters had got married, though among them they had fourteen children, two of whom were already *fooling around*.

The Methodist minister was aware of the gossip. We never knew how he found out. One Sunday he devoted a part of his sermon to it. '. . . "Let him that is without sin among you cast the first stone." . . . My flock, I have of late been hearing distressing news concerning the absence of charity among you. As Methodists and Christians, our mission is to uplift, to hold firm those who sway, to return those who stray from the fold, and to stay the feet of those headed for the broader way. Charity, my brethren, is the first commandment of our creed. Its absence in our parent church motivated John Wesley to look another way, and that way became Methodism. Listening to, spreading and encouraging the spread of, rumours about your brethren is charity's enemy. There are among us those who have distinguished themselves in the service of the Lord. Of their time and their store they have given unstintingly. What, tell me brethren, is more heinous than ingratitude? Is it meet to reward kindness with slander and generosity with conniving meanness? . . .'

Right after church service, John Cudjoe, who was seeking the removal of Bushnell, began sounding out the group of which he was class leader. 'What you think Bushnell meant by his sermon?' he asked Jimmy Branch.

'Ain't got a clue,' Jimmy replied.

'Well,' continued John, 'if he thinks he and his ilk are going to turn us all into bulldogs and sluts, he's got another thing coming.'

John Cudjoe was ardently anti-British, loved a fight, especially one he couldn't win. He had been the SDP's candidate for four consecutive terms, and each time had received fewer votes. But we respected him, for he was wealthy, generous, unpretentious, articulate, and the only person for miles around who had gone away to university—only he had not stayed to graduate; for fear, it was said, that he'd destroy his record as a loser.

Because my mother was the church's society steward, it was customary for her to be the minister's hostess. On one such occasion, three weeks after Bushnell's sermon, she asked him whether he was aware of John Cudjoe's petition. He replied that he was. She went on to talk about Lucille.

At first Bushnell evinced hesitation, but perhaps on account of the strain he was under, relented and said, 'We must not judge her too harshly. Oh, Sister Fisher, we carry this treasure in earthen vessels. I'm sure she has no notion of the differences between moral values here and in England. You know, we English are so caught up in our superiority that we never think the natives in the colonies could resent our behaviour. I really think she should return to England. It would be quite a sacrifice, but if she stays here she's liable to go mad. Lucille would not understand why she's rejected. You see, she's one of those Whites with a guilty conscience for the wrongs we've committed against indigenous peoples worldwide. The British sugar companies close down when the profits decline; she thinks it's her duty to feed and clothe all those they leave unemployed. She wants to give her entire life to working with the poor in the colonies. Of course, I approve of this; nothing could be more radically Christian. Don't at all misunderstand me. She loves her husband—for the wrong reasons. She's turned white hatred for Blacks into her own peculiar form of love.

'Did you know that she organized Blacks in Nottingham to fight discrimination in housing and ended up losing her position with the Greater Nottingham Board of Education? Let me see, this was in . . . 1961? Yes, 1961. . . .'

He had hardly looked at us while he spoke. I asked, 'Why did you choose to work in the Caribbean, Reverend?'

He looked off into the distance, and his face became a painful mask. He took his handkerchief from his breast pocket, mopped his brow, and said, 'I truly do not know. I used to think it was some sort of missionary zeal; but six months after my arrival I knew it wasn't.'

'Are you happy among us, Reverend?' My mother asked.

'What is happiness, Sister Fisher?' He looked away, in deep reflection. 'Sometimes I think I am; other times I feel quite alone. I should have got married before coming here, but the church frowns on our getting married before we've served our probation. I wanted to come quite badly, so here I am. But I have been lonely.' He spoke slowly and made no attempt to hide the pain and bitterness he felt.

Before he left he begged us to invite Lucille over often, and my mother promised that she would.

The most memorable event that Christmas was the concert put on by the children of Hillsdale School. Lucille had used her influence with the Education Officer, himself an Englishman, to get a piano for the school. It arrived at the beginning of November, just when the children were preparing for the concert. The audience came from all the communities within a six mile radius, and was thrilled. Never before had we heard a so perfectly pitched and well-timed rendition of '*Once in*

Royal David's City': Percy Strides was divine. And when the choral group, twenty-five strong, pealed forth the baroque sounds of '*People Look East*', the audience jumped to its feet and clapped for joy. That night a sense of pride surged from the parents and fused in a tremendous euphoria that clung to the auditorium and later travelled to the village.

On Christmas day Lucille took a half dozen of these same choristers to the homes of three bedridden villagers and treated them to carols. People looked on in admiration too profound for words.

The houses of the village began on the eastern border of the stream that meandered along the valley floor. They rose with the gentle and finally the not so gentle gradient. The less steep western slope was the beginning of one of the canefields (now unharvested for two years) owned by the regional estate. It was there that pubescent boys and girls went to discover the pleasures and later the barbs of overpowering desire. And were the truth to be told, most of the unwed mothers made these fields beds of conception. One supposes that if there were acts of marital infidelity on the part of the women, they would have been committed there—in the utmost secrecy, for the community ostracized those women who cheapened the marriage vow. They were even harsher with men who copulated with married women. The phallic appearance of cane stalks must have been the attraction.

One Sunday afternoon in early February—it must have been around 4:30, for Sunday school had just finished and I had stayed behind to talk to another of the teachers—a shrill sound vibrated the air across the valley: 'EVERYBODY! COME QUICK! NISSA AND LUCILLE DOING IT IN THE CANEFIELD.'

Within seconds every man, woman, and child was running toward the canefield. A red-faced Lucille, her hair straggly, but otherwise composed, met us on the way; but Nissa hid for several days.

The drama was less intense than I had expected. People showed a great deal of restraint when talking about it. Even Bertha, having had the satisfaction of proving her point, lost interest in the subject.

Carnival was not far off. Then the acme of its celebration came on the two days before Lent. Among its three most important events was the Calypso Contest, first regional and later national. The most interesting of these calypsos treated scandalous episodes that went counter to the community's morals. Most communities had a good steelband and at least one good singer-showman, thus the calypsonian's wit was most important for winning the prize.

We did not know what the Hillsdale Steelband was working on. Contrary to past years, they chose to remain secretive. Each evening we heard the beating of the pans; but when we attempted to attend the rehearsals of the Mighty Whopper, our calypsonian, we were barred. A rumour began to circulate that the calypso was about Lucille. The village folk descended on Whopper and made him vow not to make her the subject of his song.

Whopper insisted that he too liked Lucille, was touched by the food and clothing she distributed to the community, 'all the scholarship and thing the children them done win. No, no (pendularly moving his right forefinger), I ain't going to expose she to no ridicule.'

The night of the contest arrived, and the sixteen regional steelbands and their calypsonians came all primed. There was a crowd of over twenty thousand. The festivity lasted well into the wee hours of the morning. Every hamlet emptied on such nights.

We from Hillsdale were uneasy. We held our breaths as Hillsdale's turn came round. A win wasn't terribly important.

The Whopper—he was really a whopper—hurled his two hundred and fifty pounds onto the scaffolding as the steel pans began slowly, then more assuredly, to set the pitch and tempo. He made a few erotic movements with his pelvis and told the crowd, 'Ladies and gentlemen, we is about to hear the niftiest calypso ever written. Some people ain't going like it, but in me gut, I feel this is the road march. Okay boys, Let's roolll!'

With this the volume of the band's playing increased to the deft pounding of the player's sticks.

Whopper's voice thundered:

> *If yo' blade is rusting,*
> *Yo' wife gon start fussing*
> *and you will lose yo' pussin.*

The spectators were hysterical with laughter, their guffaws imitating the wax-wane tempo with which the Whopper poured forth his song. When the laughter died down he resumed:

> *I know you don' believe me.*
> *Nissa the man is he,*
> *Village ram fo' the English dam'—*
> *She run with she bloomers in she hand.*

Explosive laughter. Foot-thudding.

> *The boy want milk in his coffee,*
> *The boy like white yam,*
> *The boy want to change the colour he born—*
> *He shouldda keep he rod o' correction warm.*

> *Ain't' nutten wrong with sharing.*
> *Some call it socializin'.*
> *Some say it Christianizin'.*
> *Lucy call it funnin'.*

> *Keep the fire burnin'.*
> *Keep the rod a-warmin' . . .*

The song continued for a while yet with a rearrangement of the lyrics, its last stanza sung with a seaward roll, and striking the audience with something of the impact of the nearby billowing, detonating Atlantic waves.

The volume of the steelband lowered and the calypso ended. There was applause for a full five minutes. We knew Whopper had won the contest. He would be in the national contest, which would be broadcast island-wide. The calypso won the regional contest and went on to become the national road march. It trilled the air waves throughout the carnival season. Whopper was interviewed on radio. He was vague about the origins of the calypso.

Shortly after the results of the national calypso competition were announced Lucille disappeared from the streets. Around 5 AM Ash Wednesday, Reverend Bushnell's car stopped at her mother-in-law's gate and drove away shortly afterwards. That was the last we saw of her—a pity. Thereafter she would have been left alone; she'd already been catalogued. Debo's arthritis worsened; he did not return to England. The Whopper too changed residence: he moved to the capital.

Jeannette Armstrong *b.* 1948

PENTICTON INDIAN RESERVE, BRITISH COLUMBIA

'It took a long time for me,' says Jeannette Armstrong, 'to realize the value of having a grandmother who could speak to me in the total purity of our language, the total purity of the words which have been handed down through thousands of years . . . I was given an understanding of how a culture is determined . . . It *is* through words, it *is* through the ability to communicate to another person, to communicate to your children the thinking of your people in the past, their history, that you *are* a people.' Armstrong comes from the Okanagan people of the Penticton Indian Reserve where she was born 'into a traditional family . . . with a long history' that it has passed down 'to other people in the Okanagan'. Armstrong considers herself 'one of the lucky people' on her reserve for coming from such a family, but also for having grown up speaking her mother tongue. Her family learned English from her older sister, when she began attending school at twelve. Armstrong was almost bilingual by the time she started grade one.

Her first education followed the traditional ways of Okanagan elders. She credits her love for storytelling and language partly to her mother's aunt, Hum-Ishu-Ma (Mourning Dove), an Okanagan living on the American side of the border and one of the first published Native authors in the United States; her stories about Coyote were read to Armstrong as a child. After receiving a Diploma in Fine Arts from Okanagan College (1975), Armstrong moved to Victoria, British Columbia, where she received a BFA (1978) from the University of Victoria. She returned to Penticton, to work as an educator, writer, researcher, and cultural and political activist for En'owkin Centre, a cultural and educational association directed by six bands of the Okanagan Nation.

Armstrong's first books, *Enwhisteetkwa* (*'Walk in Water'*) (1982) and *Neekna and Chemai* (1984), were told from the point of view of young girls and were written for children. Her novel *Slash* (1985), one of the best-known novels by a Canadian Native writer, follows the life of Tommy Kelasket ('Slash'), both on his reserve and in Vancouver, to retell the history of Native people in British Columbia and their participation in the American Indian Movement (AIM) in the 1960s and 1970s. Although Armstrong has said that 'I do write for my people. I do at all times speak to my people when I'm writing,' this novel, blending traditional oral storytelling and novelistic conventions, has played an important role in educating white readers as well. Widely anthologized, Armstrong has also produced video scripts and 'Rattle-Bag', a storytelling mini-series televised in 1989. She is one of the founders, and, since 1989, Director of the En'owkin International School of Writing in Penticton, the first credit-giving school established by and for Native writers. As she says in her introduction to *Looking at the Words of our People: First Nations Analysis of Literature* (1993), which she edited, 'First Nations cultures, in their various contemporary forms', be they 'urban-modern, pan-Indian', or 'tribal specific', 'have unique sensibilities which shape the voices coming forward into written English Literature'. Hence the need to see First Nations literature 'defined by First Nations Writers, readers, academics and critics'.

Armstrong's books include *The Native Creative Process: A Collaborative Discourse Between Douglas Cardinal and Jeannette Armstrong* (1991), with Métis architect Douglas Cardinal, and *Breath Tracks* (1991), which contains the poems that follow. Her roles as artist, educator, and activist come together in her desire to leave a legacy for her people, and others, about the history and losses, as well as what she calls the 'period . . . [of] rebirth' or 'renewal'. This accounts for her fiction's polemic

and 'didactic' character, as is evident in her second adult novel, *Whispering in Shadows* (2000). Filtered through the visual art, poetry, and diaries of Penny, its protagonist, it offers a record of her activism that is remarkably close to Armstrong's own work with regards to racism, ecology, and globalization. It is 'appalling', she says, 'that nobody thinks it is racism when a native person stands up and speaks his or her language and no one understands a single word'. On the Canadian Commission for UNESCO, and a consultant to such organizations as the World Institute for Humanities at Salado, the Esalem Institute, and the Omega Institute, she has published a large number of articles on globalization and ecoliteracy, especially as they pertain to First Nations peoples. She has also initiated a number of projects, such as EcoAction, intended to 'restore a black cottonwood riparian ecosystem that is home to many endangered species'. Her contributions to these causes have been acknowledged by the Mungo Martin Award (1974), the Helen Pitt Memorial Award (1978), and, more recently, the Buffett Award for Indigenous Leadership (2003). She also received an honorary degree from St Thomas University (2000).

History Lesson

Out of the belly of Christopher's ship
a mob bursts
Running in all directions
Pulling furs off animals
Shooting buffalo   5
Shooting each other
left and right

Father mean well
waves his makeshift wand
forgives saucer-eyed Indians   10

Red coated knights
gallop across the prairie

to get their men
and to build a new world

Pioneers and traders 15
bring gifts
Smallpox, Seagrams
and rice krispies

Civilization has reached
the promised land 20

Between the snap crackle pop
of smoke stacks
and multicolored rivers
swelling with flower powered zee
and farmers sowing skulls and bones 25
and miners
pulling from gaping holes
green paper faces
of a smiling English lady

The colossi 30
in which they trust
while burying
breathing forests and fields
beneath concrete and steel
stand shaking fists 35
waiting to mutilate
whole civilizations
ten generations at a blow

Somewhere among the remains
of skinless animals 40
is the termination
to a long journey
and unholy search
for the power
glimpsed in a garden 45
forever closed
forever lost

Indian Woman

I am a squaw
a heathen
a savage
basically a mammal

I am female 5
only in the ability
to breed
and bear papooses
to be carried
quaintly 10
on a board
or lost
to welfare

I have no feelings

The sinuous planes 15
of my brown body
carries no hint
of the need
to be caressed
desired 20
loved
Its only use
to be raped
beaten and bludgeoned
in some 25
B-grade western

I have no beauty

The lines
cut deep
into my aged face   30
are not from bitterness
or despair
at seeing my clan destroyed
one by one
they are here   35
to be painted or photographed
sold
and hung on lawyers walls

I have no emotions

The husky laughter   40
a brush of wings
behind eyes
soft and searching
lightly touching others
is not from caring   45
but from the ravaged
beat of black wings
rattling against the bars
of an insanity
that tells me   50
something is wrong here.

Some one is lying.

I am an Indian Woman

Where I walk
beauty surrounds me   55
grasses bend and blossom
over valleys and hills
vast and multicolored
in starquilt glory

I am the keeper   60
of generations

I caress the lover gently
croon as I wrap the baby
with quietness I talk
to the old ones   65
and carefully lay to rest
loved ones

I am the strength
of nations

I sing to the whispering   70
autumn winds
in the snow
I dance
slowly
filling my body   75
with power
feeling it
knowing it

I am the giver of life
to whole tribes   80

I carry the seeds
carefully   through   dangerous
wastelands
give them life
scattered   85
among cold and towering
concrete
watch them grow
battered and crippled
under all the lies   90
I teach them the songs
I help them to hear
I give them truth

I am a sacred trust
I am Indian woman.   95

Kristjana Gunnars *b.* 1948

REYKJAVIK, ICELAND

As her first books of poetry, *Settlement Poems, I and II* (1980–1), suggest, Kristjana Gunnars was as a child 'sandpapered with Nordic mythology', with Icelandic history, and with folklore. Her interest in her Icelandic origins continues to permeate her work, and she lives periodically in Iceland. Yet, as she says, 'I have tried to move away from the "ethnic" stuff. I didn't like always having to pose as an Icelander, rather than just as a writer. And I didn't like the marginalization of my work, so I tried just to participate in some sort of international setting. It's a hard skin to shed, because once people identify you as a member of a certain ethnic group, they won't drop it. They just won't let it go.' Influenced by such writers as Sheila Watson, Colette, and Marguerite Duras, and loving literary theory while avoiding incorporating its 'dogmas' into what she calls 'the frail openness of a work of poetry or fiction', Gunnars writes in a way that deliberately resists easy labels. This is especially the case with *The Rose Garden: Reading Marcel Proust* (1996), which combines fictional, essayistic, and memoir elements; *Zero Hour* (1991), a memoir of her father's death, which was nominated for the Governor General's Award; and *Night Train to Nykobing* (1998), an autobiographical meditation on silence.

Born in Reykjavik, Iceland, of an Icelandic father and a Danish mother, she immigrated with her family to Oregon in 1964 where, already fluent in four languages, she began learning English. Gunnars studied at Oregon State University where she received a BA in English (1974), at the University of Regina where she earned an MA in English (1977), and at the University of Manitoba where she pursued doctoral studies. Though she spends considerable time in Europe, Canada became her permanent home in 1969 and has lived in many Canadian cities, including Vancouver, Regina, Winnipeg, and Edmonton, where she was a professor of Creative Writing at the University of Alberta. The official translator of Stephan G. Stephanson's selected poetry, Gunnars is also the editor of *Unexpected Fictions: New Icelandic Canadian Writing* (1989), and *Crossing the River: Essays in Honour of Margaret Laurence* (1988). Her collections of poetry include *One-Eyed Moon Maps* (1981), *Wake-Pick Poems* (1982), *The Night Workers of Ragnarok* (1985), *Carnival of Longing* (1989), *Exiles Among You* (1996)—elegies about her mother's death—and *Silence of the Country* (2002). Widely anthologized, Gunnars has published two collections of short fiction, *The Axe's Edge* (1983) and *The Guest House* (1992). With the publication of *The Prowler* (1989), which won the McNally Robinson Award for Manitoba Book of the Year and was a finalist for the W.H. Smith Books in Canada First Novel Award, she moved into a self-reflexive writing mode that goes beyond the conventional boundaries of literary forms. Composed of numbered sections that do not follow a specific chronological order or story line, this book is as much about its writing process as it is about the experiences of a young girl growing up in Iceland during the Second World War. Her second novel is *The Substance of Forgetting* (1992).

Mass and a Dance

The ground crackled when she walked. It was frozen snow, not ice. Minus thirty-three. Smoke from all the chimneys filled the town of St Norbert. The air was white. The sky was white. The sun was white. She had learned to like this place from constant use. The cornerstore, the little post office, the crude statue of Mother Mary across from the

Catholic church. All the dedications in this tiny French Manitoba village to the battles of the Métis. History invaded by Winnipeg suburban developments: brand new single-storey homes erected in droves over the summer. When the wind blew, whole walls of the unfinished constructions collapsed. It was not a pretty village but it had that edge of ruined history about it. An old village cradled by the bend in the Red River that insinuated: you may have lost but you're still here.

That's the whole point right there, she thought to herself as she walked along the suburban street on her way home. To be *still here*. The thought stung her. She was placid enough yet maddened by a sense of inescapable grief: a grief that was like the atmosphere of the earth. Something so fundamental you know you cannot come out of it. A grief that comes to people when they know something that had life in it is irretrievably lost. It was not a person: it was a history. Is this how Native Indians feel, she asked herself, when they have lost territories to encroaching modernity? Or people who have lived in tiny railroad hamlets out on the prairies, when the railroad cuts service to them and the hamlet dies for lack of use? Do they feel like this?

She came to Canada because it was somehow no longer feasible to live in the town she came from. It was territory now laid waste. Since she could not stay there, she decided to quit the country altogether, refusing the daily reminders of loss: the cold rain, the northern wind, the midnight sun. She grew up in the Vestfirdir of Iceland, a desolate region far in the northwest of a desolate island in the North Atlantic. Life was never easy there, but when modernity invaded the island, new urban centers sucked people out of little hard-won villages and emptied them. She thought of modern civilization as a great sewer: a trashcan into which everything gets thrown.

What is still called Sléttuhreppur—'Plains District'—was once the northernmost inhabited region of the Vestfirdings. In nineteen-forty nearly five hundred people lived there. Ten years later it was a ghost fjord. The sun rose over Hornbjarg, illuminating the water in the bay, and no one saw. The church in Stadur was a ghost church. Small, wooden, white, four windows on each side and a tiny bell tower facing the sea. No one rang the bell. The Vestfirdings were gone.

She looked around her in the St. Norbert winter. It was so silent, she seemed to have lost her hearing. All she could see were bi-level houses squarely facing the sun. The crunchy sound of her footsteps seemed to come from inside a tunnel. A bird screeched. When she looked, there were only barren branches and the bird was gone.

She still did not know why all the Vestfirdings deserted Sléttuhreppur. Most of them went to the capital city in the south. Some went abroad: Greece, America, Spain. When they were gone, thinking they had improved their lot in life, they discovered they missed their northern Arctic environment. Services were cut so there was little hope of reestablishing a community. Instead they staged a *reunion*. The previous summer. She had come along with all the others. There would be a mass in the church and a dance in the schoolhouse. There was a chartered coach to Stadur in Adalvík and on the way they picked up Jakob, the priest from Ísafjördur, to bless them at the end of the weekend.

The last time she had been in the little church was at her confirmation. They were several very young angels draped in white from neck to toe. They made a holy procession down the isle, their black Psalters clutched to their chests. They knelt before the altar, hands folded, looking up. The priest placed his hand on her head. Her elaborate hairdo went down. She forgot about the blessing: her only thought was that the priest did not understand the matter of hairdos.

On Advent Sunday they always lit the candles and then they were angels holding candles. Hákon the composer brought a choir to sing for them. They sang a choral work he had composed: *The Gravestone Suite*. Hákon had gone to the graveyard and written chants of the inscriptions on all the tombstones. When he conducted this choir, he stood on a table so they could all see him. After Advent mass there was coffee in the community room. Hákon again got up on the table. He stood among the coffee cups and the choir sang a chant for the food.

For the reunion mass in Stadur, all the old relics were brought back and put in their former places. There must have been eighty people. No one could bring the organ on the coach, so Reynir the organist played the accordion instead. In the evening, Reynir the organist played his accordion for the dance.

At the dance many women wore the national costume. Black skirts, black vests, white aprons and black caps with long tassels. By midnight they were all tipsy. By two in the morning these black swans all had to be taken to the coach. They were smiling obliviously. She had left the dance at seven next morning. Dawn had long passed. The coach driver was waiting. Passengers were impatient. Some were draped over their seats, others curled into balls. An elderly Sléttuhreppur farmer had imprisoned her in conversation in the community kitchen, on the topic of education. Everyone thought they were doing something else. When she came out and realized the communal mistake, she was too embarrassed to correct it.

She crawled into her coach seat and went to sleep. The elderly farmer's son, whom she had a crush on as a teenager, had disappeared. He had long, dark blond locks and an athletic body. She used to frequent soccer matches just to look at his body. She went to men's swimming competitions for the same reason. He had not shown up for the reunion: they said he was somewhere in South Africa. After gymnasium in the city he went to college in America where he met an education student from South Africa, married her and went into the South African bush while she did research on the education of native tribes.

Meanwhile she found herself in the dead of winter in the Canadian prairie. Manitoba. Stalled cars with their hoods up littered the highway in this cold. They stood abandoned, collecting a coating of ice. Schoolchildren rolled like balls out of the yellow schoolbus and trundled home, packed in snowsuits, scarves and moon boots. They had trouble walking straight bundled up as they were.

She wondered whether her *bitterness*, that must be the word, over the *dissolution* of her birth community had something to do with the young farmer's son who had seemed to her the ideal of northern beauty. That they were *forced* to part company: forced to be the captives of *distance*?

There were moments when she appreciated the scattered clouds as they conspired with the frost to block out the sun. Every cloud over the prairie had a southeastern lining, in gold. On days like this, all seemed to her discontinuity. No single train of thought remained steady. Stories were broken into flakes: of memory, of history, of ice. Sometimes it snowed. She had never been able to relate a story from beginning to end in this place. Not even to herself. Yet life seemed to fall into patterns: obvious patterns, sometimes so startling she wondered who designed them.

The place she now lived in seemed to her a place without beginning. Without end. Without rise and fall. It was something else. She did not understand the ground she walked on, the air she breathed. Was this what they meant by the word *alien*? Alien: a person who does not understand the place she is in. Snow was falling on the St Norbert streets. Snow is a story that breaks off from heaven and falls down at random, she thought. Snow longs to be whole again. It longs for its origins and cannot remember when it was together. It has fallen on an unknown country. If there is a little wind, the snowflakes dance during their descent.

She recalled walking home from school, across the mountain. She was fifteen. There was a blizzard. Thick snowflakes filled the entire air, rushing from one mountain to another. She could not see. The road was no longer visible. She did not know whether she was walking into the desert tundra, forever to perish, or home. There was fear. Wanderers had been lost in these mountains since time immemorial. Their bones had been found in the spring, lying among the sheep. Suddenly headlights appeared behind her out of the snow. A car door opened and she was pulled in. Saved. She looked to see who her rescuer was: it was Fleming, the Danish fellow. Once again, bad luck.

The church in Stadur was cold the afternoon mass was again sung in Adalvík, after twenty years of standing empty. The day everyone arrived together in a coach for a reunion. People wore skin-lined jackets in the pews because there was no heat. A small kerosene camp heater stood on the floor in front of the altar. Jakob the priest prayed from behind the small communion railing. On the walls, the oil lamps tried to compete with the summer sun that never sets in the Arctic.

The wooden walls of the church had become attuned to silence. They echoed the silence of desertion. People could tell there were ghosts: and had the curious sensation that *they themselves were the ghosts come to haunt the place where they once lived.* Reynir sat in the first pew, against the wall by the window. He had his accordion in his lap. People sang from little black hymnals with woollen sweaters draped around their shoulders. On the lectern a frayed guestbook lay open and blank. No names were written in the pages for twenty years. The stairs up to the choir loft creaked.

She sat in the second pew on the eastern side. Next to her sat a man who had become her lover when they met in Greece: the writer who had settled in Athens. Hákon the choir director looked back over his shoulder. He was a friend of the writer's other lover, the violinist who had moved to Austria. There would be talk of triangles and quadrangles. She played dumb, for lack of a better idea. Halldór the red-cheeked school teacher sat behind them. He had taught them geometry when they were children.

She liked the way the snow fell in Canada. It did not come straight down, but meandered in the air for a long time before settling. She watched one snowflake float in spirals, then up a bit, to the left, up again, down. This could go on for ten minutes before the flake joined the others on the white bundle below. At night streetscrapers in St Norbert amused themselves by scraping the streets. They scraped down to the pavement and left mountains of packed snow cakes in front of the houses for the inhabitants to dig aside in the morning with useless tin shovels that folded under the impact of hard ice.

At the Adalvík reunion, after the mass people hung about outside the church. Wild angelica flowers reached up to their knees. A number of people were standing looking at the water in the bay. One by one the ripples gently licked the stones on the shore. Around the church, old gravestones leaned with the weather into the mountains.

The first time a rumor came that she would go to America occurred when she was eight. She told her friend Sjöfn. They had a game of exchanging all their clothes, including underwear and socks. Sjöfn pulled her into the street and pushed her in front of all passers-by crying out: *she's going to America*. Sjöfn pushed her into Jöi's grocery store and announced: *she's going to America*. The customers turned and looked at her. She was standing in her white jacket, embarrassed, playing imbecile for lack of a better idea. Many years later she got a letter from Sjöfn, posted in Ohio. She looked for a return address but found none. Evidently Sjöfn herself had gone to America.

It was said that Reynir the organist was a lucky piece of driftwood on the beach of the Vestfirdings. He was handy with several musical instruments and could, at one go, play for both the mass and the dance. The dance that night was held in the schoolhouse at Saebólsgrundir. Reynir pumped the accordion without pause all night. Like the midnight sun, he would not set.

They got their dance partners by matching halves of verses. The man who had the last two lines to go with her first two lines turned out to be Halldór the schoolteacher. Once again, bad luck. He was fond of the polka and they danced the polka for an hour. Then she sat down in the hall among the smiling black swans: the elderly women in their national costumes, seldom worn any more. She felt out of place in her white dress, purchased in Toronto.

She went outside during a lull in the dancing. A number of Adalvíkings had gathered on the grass tufts where the mountains began to rise a short distance away. It was the middle of the night, but still bright as day. A feeling of dusk pervaded the silent air. Reynir had taken his accordion out and Baldur, the priest's grandson, had brought a guitar. They were singing. Their mismatched voices sounded clearly in the stillness and echoed across the valley below.

It was a little chilly. She made her way across the tufts slowly, savoring the fresh air. Adalvík: where she liked to be alone among the singing of the ghosts. They did not see her. Many were busy covering up the left ear, the one facing the wind.

Those were the tufts of grass she ran across one day when she was twelve, very fast. She had the sudden notion that she wanted to be on the next Olympic swimming team and started training the same day. She ran the four miles from home to the sulphuric swimming pool, swam for two hours without stopping, racing from one end to the other. Then she ran the four miles back. She did not get as far as the Olympic team: she got sick instead and lay in bed all next day.

How the snow in St Norbert was floundering, undecided whether to go back up or come down for good. The flakes blew in swirls and patterns in the gentle gusts of wind. Oblivious to the cold, they swam about in the air.

The streetscrapers came and broke the peaceful quiet of this French-Canadian town. Clamorous machines lumbered up and down the road with scathing noise. Those monsters left mountains of brown snow cakes behind them. Children in moon boots who came out of yellow schoolbuses could barely climb over the ice mountains to get home. They wiggled up on their tummies, thick arms and legs clinging to protruding ice shelves. She stood on the other side watching. In case one of these little balls missed its footing. But they all made it over, like diligent winter ants.

As she stood, the singing of the Adalvíkings swirled in her head. It was still the middle of the night and the Adalvíkings were singing under the open sky. The sun, that had been sleeping on top of Hornbjarg mountain for a while, began to rise. Suddenly the eastern sky, the sea, the stones, the hair of the singers, became drenched in gold. It was for this moment everyone had come back, she thought. *For this moment when the sun begins to ascend and the earth becomes a stone garden drenched in gold.*

The Adalvíkings were singing fatherland songs. They started up on something from Hákon's *Gravestone Suite*:

> Sun sinks in the sea
> Showers the mountain peaks with gold
> Swans fly full of song
> South towards the warm wind
> Blossoms gently sway
> Smile in tender oblivion
> When this evening peace descends
> The most beautiful of all is Adalvík

That was from the tombstone of Einar the poet.

Mary Di Michele *b.* 1949

LANCIANO, ITALY

'My status as an ethnic writer is conferred, right?' was Mary di Michele's ironic response to an interviewer questioning her feelings about her 'status as an ethnic writer'. She finds ethnic labelling and the hyphens that come along with it limiting and discriminatory. 'That hyphen', she says, 'is the rift in us all, perhaps. One which is typographically evident in the language. . . . You run into me in Italian-Canadian writers' conferences because I know how important it was to me as a writer to find

in literature an imaginative construct that contained and reflected some of my own kinds of experience.' This involvement, together with the encouragement she received from novelist Joyce Carol Oates, facilitated her shift from 'the negative aspect of [her] academic training . . . [that] concentrate[d] primarily on intellectual information' to her own experiences and background. Born in Lanciano, Italy, she received her BA in English from the University of Toronto (1972) and her MA in

English and Creative Writing from the University of Windsor (1974). She has been a writer-in-residence in many places, including the universities of Toronto (1985–6), Rome (1991), and Bologna (2003), and since 1990 has taught in the English department of Concordia University.

Di Michele has published many collections of poetry, including *Tree of August* (1978), *Bread and Chocolate* (1980), *Mimosa and Other Poems* (1981), and *Necessary Sugar* (1984). 'All my poetry', she says, 'is meant to be heard as well as read. The voice, the music and rhythm of the human voice, is the animator, is the anima, of the poem.' Much of her earlier work addresses, in her own words, 'a sort of Houdini-like wrestling with' the values of her traditional immigrant background, with 'bonds which are sometimes restrictive, sometimes repressive . . . but which are also bonds of love, like family ties and sexual relations'. In her more recent poetry,

di Michele writes out of a strong sense that 'gender is the stronger factor in identity for me over ethnicity. The body', she says, 'is the more powerful sign.' The poems in *Immune to Gravity* (1986), as well as those in *Luminous Emergencies* (1990), which was shortlisted for the Trillium Prize, reflect 'how our bodies write our lives. . . . This is central to me,' she says, 'a desire always to incorporate, to make part of the whole body, not to amputate, but to find, through a process which is not either-or, but more like yes-and-no.'

Di Michele is the editor of *Anything is Possible: A Collection of Eleven Women Poets* (1984). Her other titles include the novels *Under My Skin* (1994), which deals with the representation of violence in the media, and *Tenor of Love* (2005), a story based on the life of opera singer Enrico Caruso, and the poetry books *Debriefing the Rose* (1998) and *Stranger in You: Selected Poems and New* (1995).

Life is Theatre

or

O to Be an Italian in Toronto
Drinking Cappuccino on Bloor Street
at Bersani & Carlevale's

Back then you couldn't have imagined yourself
openly savouring a cappuccino,
you were too ashamed that your dinners
were in a language you couldn't share
with your friends: their pot roasts,   5
their turnips, their recipes for Kraft
dinners you glimpsed in TV commercials—
the mysteries of macaroni with marshmallows.
You needed an illustrated dictionary
to translate your meals,   10
looking to the glossy pages of vegetables
melanzane became eggplant,
African, with the dark sensuality of liver.
But for them even eggplants were exotic or unknown,
their purple skins from outer space.   15

Through the glass oven door
you would watch it bubbling in pyrex,
layered with tomato sauce and cheese,
melanzane alla parmigiana,
the other-worldliness viewed as if   20
through a microscope
like photosynthesis in a leaf.

                    *

Educated in a largely Jewish highschool
you were Catholic.
Among doctors' daughters,   25
the child of a fruit vendor.
You became known as Miraculous Mary,
announced with jokes about virgin mothers.

You were as popular as pork on Passover.

You discovered insomnia, migraine headaches,   30
menstruation, that betrayal of the self
to the species. You discovered despair.
Only children and the middle aged are consolable.
You were afraid of that millionth part difference
in yourself which might just be character.   35
What you had was rare
and seemed to weigh you down
as if it were made of plutonium.
What you wanted was to be like everybody else.
What you wanted was to be liked.   40
You were in love with that Polish boy
with yellow hair everybody thought
looked like Paul Newman.
All the girls wanted to marry him.
There was not much hope   45
for a fat girl with good grades.

                    *

But tonight you are sitting in an Italian café
with a man you dated a few times,
fucked, then passed into the less doubtful
relationship of coffee and conversation.   50

He insists he remembers you as vividly
as Joan Crawford upstaging Garbo in *Grand Hotel.*
You're so melodramatic, he said.
Marriage to you would be like
living in an Italian opera!   55

Being in love with someone who doesn't love you
is like being nominated for an Oscar and losing,
a truly great performance gone to waste.
Still you balanced your espresso expertly
throughout a heated speech,   60
and then left without drinking it.
For you Italians, after all, he shouted after you,
life is theatre.

Afterword: Trading in on the American Dream

Listen, whatever I write here, what you read, is safe. It's between us. In North America writers don't disappear. They are not tortured. They are ignored. People are not arrested. They are illiterate.

Entertainment has become an industry, hybrid of boardroom and circus. How can we be touched by what the video screen dissolves into snow? It's a cold country.

Sitting on the floor, writing in my notebook, I can see under the table the network of spiderwebs holding up my printer. Displacement

is vision. How can we be touched? Two NASA planes from Punta Arenas, Chile, measure the damage to the ozone over Antarctica. There is a growing rent in the sky. The blue we will view as through O'Keeffe skulls. But not bovine, our own. Our skin and our children's will burn and fester. On the network the voice-over, with the gravity of an anchorman, urges the nation on. 'To survive is not success!' it proclaims. Images of executives, Wall Street grey suits, Rolex watches, leather portfolios, men scrambling to work: 'So America has been made GREAT!'

Over the planet the ozone is thinning, over the earth where to succeed is not to survive.

Lee Maracle *b.* 1950

NORTH VANCOUVER, BRITISH COLUMBIA

'Raven, why aren't you sleeping? You are dis-
rupting some important business with your
pitiful "broken wing again" dance. . . . It's a
bad joke Raven . . . to remind me that these
white men re-stirred dreams of you in me
when I was so young. Go to sleep, while I
wrestle with truth and conscience.' Wrestling
with truth and conscience is precisely what
characterizes Lee Maracle's work. And she does
so from within her Native tradition and
through a constant dialogue between history
and the present, as is evident in these opening
words of a 1989 essay.

Born in North Vancouver to a Métis
mother and a Salish father, a grandchild of the
late Chief Dan George and a member of the
Stoh:lo Nation, Maracle did not finish high
school. 'The difficulty for myself', she says, 'has
been mastering a language different from my
own, without having my own. Most of us
learned English from parents who spoke
English in translation. Many of our parents had
been to residential school and thus did not
speak the old language any better than the aver-
age five-year-old speaks English.' An avid reader
from a young age, Maracle has read widely in
history—especially that of her own people—
politics, and social issues, and studied creative
writing and sociology at Simon Fraser
University in 1987. Education, be it an instrument of control (as it was used in Canadian residential schools) or a form of empowerment
and self-knowledge, is one of the central themes
in her writing. It is also the goal of the large
number of lectures and oratories she has delivered to Native and non-Native audiences.

Beginning with *I Am Woman: A Native
Perspective on Sociology and Feminism* (1988),
published by Write-on Press in North
Vancouver, which was run by her husband at
the time, Maracle established her writing style
as that of 'oratory'. 'That's my political discursive style,' she says in *Oratory: Coming to Theory*
(1990): 'As orators, we are not short on vocabulary. . . . Our best orators, in English or their

own language, are those who have struggled
with the language unencumbered by the
tedious commas and colons of the English language.' Written as a collage of autobiographical
and testimonial statements, poetry, and illustrations, *I Am Woman* offers an anatomy of colonialism examined through Maracle's own
experiences as a First Nations person, woman,
writer, mother, and lover. Similar themes are
explored in *Bobbi Lee: Indian Rebel* (1990).
Initially presented orally in the 1970s, this book
is a first-person narrative account of Bobbi, a
Métis woman writer. Bobbi's writing journey
and activism offer a record of the systemic
racism, land appropriation, and government
policies that have had a devastating impact on
Aboriginal communities. As Maracle says, 'Part
of our colonial condition is that we are still too
busy struggling in the whirl of it, paddling
through the rapids of it, to be able to enter the
dreamspace at the edge of it. Few of us have had
the time to study our remembered story. Some
have no memories to ponder. But those of us
who have pondered our memorized stories
know we have a criteria for story.'

Maracle's fiction, as well as her many
essays that will be gathered together in a volume to appear in The Writer as Critic series
(NeWest), reflects her desire 'to integrate two
mediums: oratory and European story'. Her
stories, whose creative process she sharply contrasts to the European intellectual traditions,
'don't have orthodox "conclusions"'; instead,
they attempt 'to draw the reader into' their centres 'in just the same way the listener of our oral
stories is drawn in'. *Sundogs* (1992), a novel, is
about the lives of a Vancouver Native family in
1990, the year the Native Manitoba MLA Elijah
Harper blocked the Meech Lake Accord and
the summer of the Oka crisis. Her second
novel, *Ravensong* (1993), set in the early 1950s,
revolves around the lives of two sisters who, in
their different ways, try to keep their Native
community together during a flu epidemic.
Raven, as the trickster figure that she is,

inspires, admonishes, and teases the characters all at the same time. The younger sister, Celia, a seer, is the protagonist of *Celia's Song*, Maracle's forthcoming novel. Her recent novel *Daughters Are Forever* (2002), a narrative that elegantly integrates Native storytelling and Western narrative style, is about a troubled mother's neglect of her daughter but also about the disease and social problems that have affected the Turtle Island People.

Maracle has also published a volume of short stories, *Sojourner's Truth and Other Stories* (1990); a young adult novel, *Will's Garden* (2002); and a poetry book, *Bent Box* (2000). One of the earliest published and most important Native authors in Canada, she has been widely anthologized, has co-edited *Telling It: Women and Language Across Cultures* (1990), and has contributed to the Renga poetry project,

Linked Lives (1991), as well as to *First Fish, First People*, which won the American Book Award from the Before Columbus Foundation. An actor, scriptwriter, and more recently film director, she has been the Anne Decker Guest Professor at Southern Oregon University, the 2001 Stanley Knowles Visiting Professor in Canadian Studies at the University of Waterloo, the Distinguished Professor of Canadian Culture at Western Washington University, a Visiting Professor of Women's Studies at the University of Toronto, and a senior lecturer at the University of Toronto's Transitional Year Program. The co-founder of the En'owkin International School of Writing in Penticton, she has been the cultural director of the Centre for Indigenous Theatre in Toronto, and is the winner of the J.T. Stewart Voices of Change Award (2000).

Bertha

The accumulation of four days of rain reflected against the street lamps and the eternal night-time neon signs, bathing the pavement in a rainbow of crystal splashes. In places on the road it pooled itself into thin sheets of blue-black glass from which little rivulets slipped away, gutter bound. From eaves and awnings the rain fell in a steady flow; even the signposts and telephone poles chattered out the sounds of the rain before the drops split themselves on the concrete sidewalks. Everywhere the city resounded with the heavy rhythm of pelting rain. It cut through the distorted bulk of the staggering woman.

The woman did not notice the rain. Instead, the bulk that was Bertha summoned all her strength, repeatedly trying to correctly determine the distance between herself and the undulating terra beneath her feet to prevent falling. Too late. She fell again. She crawled the rest of the way to the row of shacks. Cannery row, where the very fortunate employees of the very harassed and worried businessmen reside, is not what one might call imaginatively designed. The row consists of one hundred shacks, identical in structure, sitting attached by common walls in a single row. The row begins on dry land and ends over the inlet. Each shack is one storey high and about eighteen by twenty feet in floor space.

They are not insulated. The company had more important sources of squander for its profits: new machines had to be bought, larger executive salaries had to be paid—all of which severely limited the company's ability to extend luxuries to the producers of its canned fish. The unadorned planks which make up the common walls at the back and front of each shack and at the end of each row are all that separate people from nature. A gable roof begins about seven feet from the floor and comes to a peak some eight feet later. Each roof by this time enjoyed the same number of unrepaired holes as its neighbour, enabling even the gentlest of drizzles in. The holes, not being part of the company's construction plan, are more a fringe benefit or a curse of natural unrepaired wear, depending on your humour.

None of the buildings are situated on the ground. All were built of only the sturdiest wood and were well creosoted at the base to fend off rot for at least two decades. Immersed in salt water and raw sewage as they have been this past half century, they are beginning to show a little wear. In fact, once during the usual Saturday night rough-housing which takes place on a pay night, X pitched his brother over the side. They had been arguing about whether the foreman was a pig or a dog. X maintained dogs did not stink and, what is more, could be put to work, while his brother held he would not eat a dog, and food being a much higher use-value, the foreman was a dog. He then let go with a string of curses at X, which brought X to grievous violence. On the way to the salt chuck X's brother knocked out one of the pilings. It was never replaced. The hut remains precariously perched on three stilts and is none the worse for that. Unfortunately, the water that filled X's brother's lungs settled the argument forever. The accused foreman has since been known as a pig.

Not to discredit the company. In the days before modern machinery, when the company had to employ a larger number of workers to process less fish, it used cheaper paint—whitewash to be honest. One day all the workers who had congregated in the town at the season's opening beheld a fine sight at the end of Main Street: exterior house paint of the most durable quality. These stains come in a variety of colours but the company, not wishing to spoil its workers with excessive finery, stuck with the colour which by then had achieved historical value.

The paint did not really impress anyone save the foreman. So delighted was he with the new paint that he mentioned it time and again, casually. The best response he got was one low grunt from one of the older, more polite workers. Most simply stared at their superior with a profoundly empty look. *Thankless ingrates,* he told himself, though he dared not utter any such thing aloud.

Although the opinion of the foreman about his workers had stood the test of time over the decade that had lapsed, the paint job had not been so lucky. The weather had been cruel to the virgin stain, ripping the white in ugly gashes from the row's simple walls. The rigorous climate of the North West Coast destroyed the paint in a most consistent way, exactly with the run of the wood grain. Where the grain grooved, the stain remained; where the grain ridged, the salt sea wind and icy rain tore the stain off.

At the front of the dwellings some of the doors are missing. Not a lot of them, mind you, certainly not the majority have gone astray. The plank boardwalk in front of cannery row completes the picture of the outside. Over the years, at uncannily even intervals, each sixth board has disappeared, some by very bizarre happenstances.

Inside, the huts are furnished with tasteless simplicity. A sturdy, four-legged cedar table of no design occupies the middle of the room. Four wooden, high-backed chairs built with unsteamed two-by-twos and a square piece of good-one-side plywood surround the table. The floors are shiplap planks. Squatted in the centre of the back wall is a pot-bellied cast-iron stove, though those workers who still cook use a Coleman. Shelving above the pot-bellied stove keeps the kitchenware and food supplies immodestly in view. Two bunks to the right and two to the left complete the furnishings. It was not the sort of place in which any of the workers felt inspired to add a touch of their personal self. No photos, no knick-knacks. What the company did not provide, the workers did not have.

The residence, taken as a whole, was not so bad but for one occasional nuisance. At high-tide each dwelling, except the few nearest shore, was partially submerged in water. It wasn't really such a great bother. After all, the workers spent most of their waking time at the cannery—upwards of ten hours a day, sometimes this included Sunday, but not always—and the bunks were sufficiently far from the floor such that sleeping, etc., carried on unencumbered. A good pair of Kingcome slippers[1] was all that was needed to prevent any discomfort the tide caused. The women who used to complain violently to the company that their cooking was made impossible by such intrusions have long since stopped. After the strike of '53 cooking was rendered redundant as the higher wage afforded the women restaurant fare at the local town's greasy spoon. Besides which, the sort of tides that crept into the residence occurred but twice or thrice a season. Indeed, the nuisance created was trifling.

Bertha is on the 'sidewalk' crawling. The trek across Main Street to the boardwalk had taken everything out of Bertha.

'F.ck.ng btstsh' dribbles from her numb lips.

She glances furtively from side to side. The indignity of her position does not escape her. Being older than most of her co-workers, she is much more vulnerable to the elements. Bertha donned all the sweaters she brought to cannery row and her coat to keep warm. She spent the whole night drinking in the rain on the hill behind the city and now all of her winter gear is water-logged. The fifteen extra pounds make it impossible for her to move. She curses and prays no one sees her.

Her short pudgy fingers clutch at the side of residence No. 13 in an effort to rise above her circumstances. She is gaining the upper hand when a mocking giggle slaps her about the head and ears.

'F.ck.ng btstsh.'

Trapped. Emiserated. Resigned. What the hell? She is no different from anyone else. Her memory reproaches her with the treasure of a different childhood. A childhood filled with the richness of every season, when not a snowflake fell unnoticed. Her memory retreats to another time.

*   *   *

The early autumn sunlight danced across lush green hillsides. Diamond dew drops glistened from each leaf. Crisp air and still warm sun excited the youth. Chatter and bantering laughter filled the air. Bertha in her glory punched out one-liners and smiled at the approval of the old ladies who chuckled behind their aging hands. Things were

1 Hip waders.

different then. Each girl was born in the comfort of knowing how she would grow, bear children and age with dignity to become a respected matriarch.

On the hills, basket on her back, Bertha was not called Bertha. She wanted to hear her name again, but something inside her fought against its articulation. In her new state of shame she could not whisper, even to herself, the name she had taken as woman. Old Melly staggered into view, eyes twinkling. Bertha didn't really want to see her now.

'Hey Bertie,' the giggle hollered out her nickname, unmindful of the woman's age and her own youth. 'I got some wine.'

'Khyeh, hyeh, yeh,' and the circle of memory that crept out at her from the fog dimmed, but refused to recede. You had another upbringing before all this, the memory chided her. The efforts of the village women to nurture her as keeper of her clan, mother of all youth, had gone to naught. Tears swole from behind her eyes. 'Damn wine,' she muttered to herself. In the autumn hills of her youth the dream of motherhood had already begun to fade. Motherhood, the re-creation of ancient stories that would instruct the young in the laws of her people and encourage good citizenship from even the babies, had eluded her.

In the moment of her self-recrimination, Bertie contemplated going home. Home? Home was a young girl rushing through a meadow, a cedar basket swishing lightly against dew-laden leaves, her nimble fingers plucking ripe fat berries from their branches, the wind playfully teasing and tangling the loose, waist-length black hair that glistened in the autumnal dawn while her mind enjoyed the prospect of becoming . . . becoming, and the words in English would not come. She remembered the girl, the endless stories told to her, the meanings behind each story, the careful coaching in the truth that lay behind each one, the reasons for their telling, but she could not, after fifty years of speaking crippled English, define where it was all supposed to lead. Now all that remained was the happiness of her childhood memories against the stark emptiness of the years that stretched behind them.

Her education had been cut short when her great-grandfather took a christian name. She remembered a ripple of bewildered tension for which her language had no words to describe or understand what had gone through the village. The stories changed and so did the language. No one explained the intimacies of the new feeling in either language. Confusion, a splitting within her, grew alongside the murmur that beset the village. Uncertainty closed over the children. Now, even the stories she had kept tucked away in her memory escaped her. She stared hard down the narrow boardwalk trying to mark the moment when her memories had changed.

The priest had christened the most important man in the village. Slowly, christians appeared in their ranks. The priest left no stone unturned. Stories, empowering ceremonies, became pagan rituals, pagan rituals full of horrific shame. Even the way in which grooms were chosen changed. The old women lost their counsel seats at the fires of their men. Bighouses were left to die and tiny homes isolated from the great families were constructed. Little houses that separated each sister from the other, harbouring loneliness and isolation. Laughter died within the walls of these little homes. No one connected the stripping of woman-power and its transfer to the priest as the basis for the sudden uselessness all the people felt. Disempowered, the old ladies ceased to tell stories and lived out their lives without taking the children to the hills again.

For a short time, life was easier for everyone. No more shaking cedar, collecting goat hair or carefully raising dogs to spin the wool for their clothing. Trade—cash and the securing of furs by the village men—replaced the work of women. Bertha could not see that the feelings of anxiety among the youth were rooted in the futureless existence that this transfer of power created. A wild and painful need for a brief escape from their new life drove youth to the arms of whiskey traders.

An endless stream of accommodating traders paddled upriver to fleece the hapless converts. Those who lacked trap lines began disappearing each spring to the canneries where cash could be gotten. Young women followed on their heels. The police, too, gained from this new state of affairs. As the number of converts increased so did the number of drinkers. Interdiction caught up with those unfortunates not skilled at dodging the police. Short stays as guests in the queen's hotel[2] became the basis for a new run of stories, empty of old meaning. The rupture of the old and the rift created was swift and unrelenting. Things could be bought with money, and wages purchased the things of life much more swiftly and in greater quantities than did their pagan practices. Only great-grandmother, much ridiculed for her stubbornness, remained sober and pagan to her death. Her face lingered in the fog while Bertha wondered why the old woman had stopped talking to her. The process was complete before Bertha was out of her teens. Then she, too, joined the flow of youth to cannery row.

Bertha had come to cannery row full of plans. Blankets could be purchased with the cash she earned. How could she have known the blankets they sold were riddled with sickness? She paid the trader who delivered the blankets, as had some of the other youth. She experienced the same wild abandon that life outside the watchful eye of grannies and mothers gave rise to. They learned to party away the days of closure when there were not enough fish to work a whole shift. At season's end they all got into their boats and headed home. A lone canoe bobbed in the water just feet from the shore of their village; a solitary old man paddled out to greet them.

'Go back, death haunts the village, go back.' Confused, they went back. The story of the blankets did not catch up to them until years later. In their zeal to gift their loved ones they had become their killers. In their confusion and great guilt, wine consoled them.

*   *   *

Bertha stared blankly at her swollen hands. With blurred vision she peered unsteadily towards hut number nine. It wasn't home. She had no home. Home was fifty years ago and gone. Home was her education forever cut short by christian well-meaning. Home was the impossibility of her ever becoming the intellectual she should have been; it was the silence of not knowing how it all came to pass. Slowly her face found the young girl leaning out of the doorway.

2 Jail.

'Ssr.'

She lumbered reluctantly to where the giggle sat, her mouth gaping in a wide grin exposing prematurely rotten teeth. Bertha could hardly look at her. No one as young as this girl should have rotten teeth. It marred her flawlessly even features. The large, thickly-lashed black eyes only sharpened the vileness of bad teeth. What a cruel twist of fate that this girl, whose frame had not yet acquired the bulk that bearing children and rearing them on a steady diet of winter rice and summer wine creates, should be burdened with a toothless grin before her youth was over.

The consumption of wine was still rational in the girl's maiden state, though not for long. Already the regularity of her trips to the bootlegger was beginning to spoil her eyes with occasional shadows. Her delicately shaped face sometimes hinted of a telling puffiness. On days like that it was hard for the girl to pose as a carefree and reckless youth. Today was not such a day.

Bertha hesitated before sitting, staring hard at the jug on the table. Unable to leave, but not quite up to sitting down, she remained rooted to the spot. She struggled with how it came to be that this girl from her village was so foreign to her. The moment threatened the comfort of shallow oblivion the girl needed. A momentary softness came over her face as she beckoned Bertha to sit. 'Relax, Bertha, have a drink.' Bertha sighed and sat down. The girl shucked the tenderness and resumed her gala self.

By day's end the jug was wasted and so were the women. There had been conversations and moments of silence, sentimental tears had been shed, laughter, even rage and indignation at the liberties white-male-bottom-pinchers took with Native women had been expressed. In all, the drunk had been relatively ordinary, except for a feeling that kept sinking into the room. It seemed to the girl to come from the ceiling and hang over their heads. The feeling was not identifiable and its presence was inexplicable. Nothing in particular brought it on. Only the wine chased the feeling from the windowless room. For the giggle, these moments were sobering, but Bertha seemed unruffled by it. If she was bothered, she betrayed no sign. At such moments, the giggle snatched the bottle and furiously poured the liquid into her throat. The wine instantly returned the young girl's world to its swaying, bleary, much more bearable state.

Bertha rarely left anything started unfinished, even as concerns a jug of wine. But the more she drank the more she realized she did not know this woman, this daughter who was not nurtured by her village grandmothers, but who had left as a small child and never returned to her home. She was so like all the youth who joined the march to cannery row of late. Foreign and mis-educated. Callous? Was that what made them so hard to understand? The brutal realization that she, Bertha, once destined to have been this young woman's teacher, had nothing to give but stories—dim, only half-remembered and barely understood—brought her up short. Guilt drove her from her chair before the bottle was empty. The feeling again sank from the ceiling, shrouding the girl in terror. Foreboding feelings raced through her body, but her addled consciousness could not catch any one of them and hold them long enough for her mind to contemplate their meaning.

Bertha stopped at the door, turned and stumbled back to the shaking girl. She touched her so gently on the cheek that the girl would hardly have been sure it happened except the touch made her eye twitch and the muscles in her face burn. The realization that the gulf between them was too great, their difference entrenched by Bertha's own lack of knowledge, saddened Bertha. Bertha wanted to tell her about her own unspoiled youth, her hills, the berries, the old women, the stories and a host of things she could not find the words for in the English she inherited. It was all so paralyzing and mean. Instead Bertha whispered her sorrow in the gentle words of their ancestors. They were foreign to the girl. The touch, the words, inspired only fear in her. The girl tried to relieve herself by screaming—no sound found its way out of her throat. She couldn't move. The queerly gentle and wistful look on Bertha's face imprinted itself permanently on the memory of the girl. Then Bertha left.

Bertha's departure broke the chains that locked the girl's body to the chair. Her throat broke its silence and a rush of sobs filled her ears. 'Damn wine, damn Bertie. Damn,' and she grabbed the jug. As the warm liquid jerked to her stomach the feeling floated passively to the ceiling and disappeared. Not convinced that Bertha's departure was final, she flopped the length of her body onto the bunk and prayed for the ill-lit, rat-filled cannery come morning to be upon her soon. Her body grew heavy and her mind dulled. Sleep was near. Before she passed out, her mind caught hold of the notion that she ought to have said goodbye to Bertha. Still, she slept.

*   *   *

Bertie's absence at the cannery went unnoticed by all but the foreman. The young girl had blocked the memory of the disturbing evening from her mind. They had been drunk. Probably Bertie's still drunk, ran her reasoning. The foreman, however, being a prudent and loyal company man, thought of nothing else but Bertie's absence. By day's end, he decided by the following reasoning to let her go: Now, one can withstand the not infrequent absences of the younger, swifter and defter of the Native workers. But Bertie is getting old, past her prime, so much so that even her half century of experience compensates little for the disruption of operational smoothness and lost time that her absence gives rise to. Smoothness is essential to any enterprise wishing to realize a profit, and time is money.

This decision was not easily arrived at. He was not totally insensitive to human suffering. He had been kept up all night weighing the blow to Bertie and the reaction of the other workers that firing her might cause, against the company's interest in profits, before finally resolving to fire her. Firing her could produce no results other than her continuing to be a souse. As for the workers, they would be angry but he was sure they wouldn't do anything. In any case, he was the foreman and if he didn't put his foot down these Natives were sure to walk all over him. Her absence again this morning convinced him that he had made the right decision. Still, he could not bring himself to say anything until the end of the day, in case the others decided to walk off the job. No sense screwing up the whole day over one old woman.

In a very loud voice, the foreman informed Bertie's nephew that his auntie Bertie was fired and could he tell her to kindly collect her pay and remove herself by week's end to whence she came.

'Can't be done.'

'I beg your pardon and why not? I have every authority to fire every one of you here.'

His voice rose and all became quiet but for the hum of machinery. The blood of the workers boiled with shame at the tone of this white man. No one raised their eyes from their fixed position on their work and no one moved.

'Can't be done is all,' the nephew flatly replied without looking at the foreman. His hands resumed work, carefully removing the fins from the fish.

'I asked you why not, boy.' Angry as he was, he couldn't fire Bertie's nephew. Had he been a shirker, he would have, but Bertie's nephew was one of the more reliable and able of his workers, so he could not fire him. All he could do was sneer 'boy' at him and hope that this, the soberest and most regular worker, did not storm out in defiance of the foreman's humiliating remark.

'She's dead.'

An agonized scream split the silence and the knife that so deftly beheaded the fish slipped and deprived the lovely young girl of her left thumb and giggle forever.

Gerry Shikatani *b.* 1950

TORONTO, ONTARIO

'I approach writing as a practice of attention, the possibilities of my openness to the quotidian particulars,' says Gerry (Osamu) Shikatani. 'It's . . . attending to that place where one can be stopped by presence and enables a return.' This 'practice of attention'—a 'practice of process', he also calls it—is rooted in Shikatani's upbringing. 'My parents had little material wealth,' he says, 'but attended to their work and children in an extraordinary generosity. It's this nurturing wealth, an unquestioned devotion and honouring which instructs me to writing as a devotion. Their names—Masajiro and Mitsuko (Mukai) Shikatani. Language offers the wondrous act of gently holding the luminous, the lasting shimmer of parents, in the process of descendance.'

Shikatani's poetry, be it traditional, visual, minimalist, or otherwise experimental, reflects his meticulous attention to craft, his careful listening to the cadences of language, and, above all, his intention to construct, through writing,

what he calls the 'tenuous thread in "ecological being" '. He perceives space as a palimpsest of ecological, social, and cultural scripts, and his concern with the various configurations of space—be it a formal garden, a cityscape, or the countryside—is reflected both in his major collection, *Aqueduct: Poems and Texts from Europe, 1979–1987* (1996) and in *First Book, 3 Gardens of Andalucía*, a book-length special issue of *The Capilano Review* (Winter/Spring 2003) featuring his work.

An inveterate traveller who has lived in Toronto, Montreal, and Paris, Shikatani is a Nisei, or second-generation Japanese Canadian, born in Toronto. His parents were evacuated from Port Essington, a small fishing community in northern British Columbia, and relocated to a camp in Slocan during the Second World War. 'The sounds, the silences I first felt and heard,' he says, 'were of their [his parents'] Japanese, and this first language . . . remains the starting point.' As he points out, 'the mothertongue with its dialects, its accents is for us all a place of art-making.' These early experiences account for the critical and formal approach he has taken in his poetry: 'because of my own broken, Canadian's Japanese,' he remarks, 'I ended up among writers who've pushed at and from margins,' writers like bpNichol and Roy Kiyooka.

Shikatani has long been active in Toronto's poetry scene and has published many chapbooks, including *The Book of Tree: A Cottage Journal* (1987), *Our Nights in Perugia* (1984), *Ship Sands Island* (1978), and *Barking of Dog* (1973). His first poetry books were *A Sparrow's Food* (1984) and *1988: Poems 1973–1988* (1989). His work has also been included in many English-Canadian, Quebecois, and French anthologies. The co-editor of *Paper Doors: An Anthology of Japanese-Canadian Poetry* (1981), Shikatani has also published a collection of stories, *Lake & Other Stories* (1996).

In addition to teaching creative writing at Concordia University, Sheridan College, and York University, Shikatani has worked as a creative and media writing instructor, as a research consultant specializing in gastronomy, as a restaurant critic (notably for the *Toronto Star*), and as a freelance food, travel, and sports columnist for CBC Radio. He is also an accomplished text-sound artist. His work in this area is represented by his collaboration with filmmaker Jesse Nishihata on *Kodo: heartbeat drummers of Japan* (1997), a film, shot on Sado Island, Japan, that documents his exploration into language and writing through his personal history. He also collaborated with Phillip Hoffman on *Kokoro is for Heart* (1999) and the multimedia piece *Parabolic Senses: A Presentation of Moving Pictures, Sounds and Images*.

from 'The Generalife Gardens, Alhambra, Granada, 1991'

*

A narrow aqueduct bordered by luxuriant flowers, trimmed myrtle hedges, orange trees and cypresses leads down the center of the patio; the slender jets arching over it are of relatively recent date. (Lehrman)

Now, once again this garden, again seated there.
She says . . .

'Not today. Not today when I am waiting' 'I am' is the 'in the pattern of' is too, 'in the mosaic' which look at action verb before noun regard at maybe a mouth a gesture is is blue diverts to angle this to that a reference dyslexia say to catch the point not today tidy answer in pattern   the cut hedge to fountain, angle to angle a verb most prominent after hue, concept blueness and greenness what is caught my idea, my, my, my, before speech spit the action of eye not . . . of the storm, a cloud approached, I read, ah, the ceramic   blue the ness confers.
Skip back. Look from a distant point ness, mouth gesture is that its hot is hot and cold the tile washed by rainwater, the eye fixed it is there the not today, today is just,   will try another, other ways to a maze today skip.

My, my, my, my, my. Possession. A possession, position. A tract between pronouns. Colon. Dialogue which aches in the forgetting and error. A dialogue which accedes to the intimate and singular you. Tread the garden path. Trench the soil. Convince a path, topsoil trail. The traffic below, the circular annunciation as debris, honking and motored exhaust swirl at the Arch of Triunfo.

May 19

Begin again once again: a death, a bus, petrol, the feed of parked
cars, bread crumbs cooked with hot oil, garlic, some water—this browning
the *migas*—the peasant's morning *desayuno*, begin
this way to a top landing,   then, Death—'Death, I jump at You from
here, jump, jump!'

And then Death says, 'Oh come on you rat, give me a break. A bit of
coffee, a little nice night music please. Time, time's what I want!
Time's in—time's out. Light music. My words are no longer my words, my
house no longer my own for you've brought in another one girl to tidy she's
pretty but too young, don't you remember how we've been sweethearts just
the two of us, I know what you mean your life's no couch, jump on my back,
we'll go for a spin. Come on down!'

Born again, begin again. Youpii!!
And so began the interruption by Death from a spiralling stair, just a short hop
skip anna jump,   spin, spin

                              Behind a dark fan.

Lumine.

And now my way has come clear the daisies in their hundreds bloom
toe-hold to the red bleeding hearts a longing, the bells of other reds climb their
particular fire,   necessity war, molests

                              the infant

And now my way has come clear
Broken crockery, nothing more than such Michelin

a tangle to feet, I'm tanglefragment foot-mister. Trying to
                    negotiate the terms . . .
                         physiology, stunned stupid

*

Try to look assiduously, fortuitously, precipitously,
gratuitously, interrogatively all, at the weeds, at the ivy, at the cedar and chestnut, try to
look at the golden daisies bloom, beneath a cypress cut as a column all this and still
nothing solved a meaning reservoir still a drinking fountain come upon, the worn way
to quench thirst for one then another, other and another my skin's cool is cool I think
of the corpse of a young blown Iraqi boy, I think of the young Iranian man serves coffee
at a donut shop in Toronto, his faith pressure cooker whistles sadness and trepidations
lose one in a spiritless land where flights are to melancholic fancy, spicy sauced chicken
wings a pitcher of beer, loses one and yet in this the surrendering interrogative, assidu-
ous, fortuitous, gratuitous adjectives leave a tremor of despair felt in the neck, pooom!
secret unrevealed, that vertebral blood-column kneeling, bowing down, coffee, the
currency exchange. Crummy knowledge, the child is being covered in a fatal
muddied cloth, a video cassette, a voice-over, the last burning light on a television the
button so pushed, power fading pin-light on a target screen, taken aim, the grid of
signature in such alphabet set, then nostalgia still the voice sets in, we begin crying,
finger still, feeling the pulse. Looky, looky! President George Bush is now on the video
screen, wide, wide, and the cigarette smoke haze hangs over lampshade cheer. Depleted
uranium's spoil carried by birds to Kosovo, Austria, to Sudan and on—Financial
planning, good, you've taken out life insurance at your age.

And now my way has come clear
And now my way has come clear
And now my way has come so clear
And now my way has come clear
And now my way has come so clear

Something 'cross the path, stops.
Raised paw.

A poem:
What? Quench? Clear.

*

Mother is Mitsuko, Father now dead since 1974, January 22 Masajiro,
Kimurasan still around over 90, Stan or Masato, Norma or Masako, Junko is
June but really it's just Junko, Miyako that same though she's now as much that
Margaret, and Alan or Noboru, I'm Gerry or Osamu, 'Hi!'

There, I've done it, named my family here on a page, passing thought of such
elemental minutes, the *saucissons*, the *salchichon*, salt of hanging ode to in th' air and

it and now my way has come clear
Cullar de Baza, in Granada province,
a here/there now sentimental on the dotted line
if you will.

(Horticulture Lesson:

Nothing to grow.
Nothing to learn.)

    *

Booked.

Each visitor has paid her due.
Reserve and a discount.
There is a stand of confections.
Trowel. a study of intentive notions.
A turnstile is a yup,
a turnstile.
Each visitor is everything in a garden. seeds,
cuttings,   Each visitor
in this history: formed in a pattern seen from afar, the seems
a point of view (attack? Salvo shy's hesitations);
moment of assault.
The ways are defined. Maybe. water at this point,   brink
Each visitor walks along
the lines, the
angles, the perimeters, stopping
perhaps for water   drink
at this point, stopping to rest,
snap a photo.   arcs, light,
This   not (horticulture.
That which that   this moon.)

M.G. Vassanji *b.* 1950

NAIROBI, KENYA

Moyez G. Vassanji sees his generation of writers as being '[u]niquely placed because we're just between independence and colonialism, and between cultures, and between religions, and between countries. And even in the West, many of us move from one country to another.' Vassanji finds the mobility of his diasporic generation to be 'exhilarating': 'I like that rawness; it's very exciting to have so many different experiences in one life.' An 'Afro-Asian', Vassanji was born in Nairobi, Kenya, and raised in Dar es Salaam, Tanzania, the son of parents who were second- and third-generation Indians in Africa. Vassanji explains that 'although we were Africans, we were also Indians. We were brought up as Indians. We grew up speaking two Indian languages—Cutchi and Gujarati—and we also understood Hindi from the movies we watched. And then we were also brought up speaking Swahili and English. We had all of this within us.' Vassanji made 'this Indianness . . . transformed by the Africanness' the central focus of his first novel, *The Gunny Sack* (1989), which won the Commonwealth Writers' Prize for the Caribbean–Canada Best First Book.

With the assistance of a scholarship, Vassanji moved to the United States in 1970 to study physics at the Massachusetts Institute of Technology (BSc, 1974). After obtaining his PhD in Nuclear Physics (1978) from the University of Pennsylvania, he moved to Canada to teach at the University of Toronto. After ten years and thirty published papers in his field, Vassanji, who had begun writing seriously in 1986, became a full-time writer.

Following *The Gunny Sack*, Vassanji produced a second novel, *No New Land* (1991), which reflects his move to Canada. Set in the Toronto suburb of Don Mills, it deals with what the author has called 'the predicament of "in-between" societies—in this case East and West',

dramatized by characters who have to reconcile their past with their Canadian reality, or, as Vassanji puts it, 'acknowledge the past and . . . move forward'. But if his characters' hard adaptation experiences represent the acculturation process of most immigrants, it is a process that, according to Vassanji, parallels the changes the dominant culture must undergo: 'Anything that is already old and is established needs new infusions; otherwise, it dies. So the mainstream society has no choice but to accept us. However,' he adds, 'if I felt completely oppressed, then I wouldn't live here.' And it is 'here'—Toronto—where Vassanji 'feel[s] most at home'.

In *Uhuru Street* (1992), a collection of short fiction that includes the story that follows, Vassanji returns to his African roots, but he continues to write about characters who are marked by their diasporic movements. Indeed, most of Vassanji's novels straddle the 'there' and the 'here' of his characters' diasporic lives, as is the case with *Amriika* (1999) and *The In-Between Life of Vikram Lall* (2003), his most recent novel, which earned him his second Giller Prize, the Commonwealth Writers Prize, a Libris Award, and the Trillium Book Award. The action, narrated by the protagonist after his flight to Canada, is set in Kenya at the time of major political upheavals and corruption that were part of its decolonization process.

Vassanji's other works include *The Book of Secrets* (1994), which won the first Giller Prize and the F.G. Bressani Prize, and *A Meeting of Streams: South Asian Canadian Literature* (1985), an edited critical collection. He is the co-founder, with his wife Nurjehan Aziz, and editor of *The Toronto South Asian Review* (1982), now called *The Toronto Review of Contemporary Writing Abroad*, and is the publisher of TSAR. He became a Member of the Order of Canada in 2005.

The London-Returned

We still went back for our holidays then and we formed a rambunctious group whose presence was hard to miss about town. We were the London-returned. For two or three joyously carefree months the city became a stage for us and we would strut up and down its dusty pavements parading overseas fashions, our newly acquired ways. Bare feet and Beatle-style haircuts were in then, drawing conservative wrath and doomsday prophecies. We sported flashy bell-bottoms, Oxford shirts and bright summer dresses. And fat pinkish-brown thighs below the colourful mini-skirts of our female companions teased the famished adolescent eyes of our hometown. Come Saturday morning, we would gather at a prearranged rendezvous and conscious of every eye upon us, set off in one large and rowdy group towards Independence Avenue. There to stroll along its pavements a few times over, amidst fun and laughter, exchanging jokes and relating incidences in clipped, finished accents.

The acacia-lined avenue cut a thin margin at the edge of town. It looked out at the ocean a short block away, black and rust red steamers just visible plying in and out of the harbour. Behind it was crammed the old town, a maze of short dirty sidestreets feeding into the long and busy Uhuru Street, which then opened like a funnel back into the avenue. From here Uhuru Street went down, past downtown and the Mnazi Moja grounds into the interior: the hinterland of squat African settlements, the main-road Indian stores, the Arab corner stores—in which direction we contemptuously sniffed, suppressing a vague knowledge of our recent roots there.

On Saturday morning you came to Independence Avenue to watch and to be seen. You showed off your friends, your breeding, your money. It was here that imported goods were displayed in all their glory and European-looking mannequins threw temptation from store windows. And yes, hearts too were on sale on these pavements. Eyes could meet and the memory of a fleeting instant live to fuel one's wildest dreams . . .

We walked among tourists and expatriate shoppers, civil servants and messengers in khaki. And we passed other fugitive groups like ours, senior boys and girls (always separate) from the high schools, who somehow had managed to walk away this Saturday. Our former classmates, many of these. With some I had managed to keep up a brief correspondence. Now some exchanged short greetings, others pretended not to see, and a few turned up their noses with the moral superiority of the uncontaminated. Yet they stoked our merriment no end—these innocents—by their sidelong glances at our mini-skirted companions, or their self-conscious attempts at English accents and foreign manners while sipping iced cappuccinos in the European surroundings of Benson's.

It was at Benson's where it began.

She was sitting with a group of friends sipping iced cappuccino. They were all in uniform, of course. How can I forget, the green and white, the skirt and blouse? For a brief instant, between two intervening sandy-haired tourist heads, our eyes met. And lowered. And then again a fleeting, fugitive appointment. She had me then.

I think of her as she was then. A small figure, not too thin, with a heart-shaped face: a small pointed chin, high cheekbones, a large forehead. Her hair was tightly combed back and tied into a plain pony tail. She sat sipping through a straw, stirring the frothy contents in the tall frosted glass to turn them more liquid. I hadn't heard her voice and I didn't know her. Yet I sat there a few tables away, flustered, self-conscious, saying silly things, laughing uncertainly.

At her table an animated conversation was underway. They talked in Cutchi, not too loudly nor timidly. How self-contained they looked, how comfortable with each other! I felt a little envious, looking in from outside. My subject never looked up again although she must have known I was watching. Presently they waved at the uniformed waiter and went out through the frosted glass door.

We had a word for the kind of state I was in in the few days that followed. Pani-pani: liquid. It means, perhaps, melted. With stylish and refined company—at least as I saw it then—beside me, what made me turn pani-pani at the sight of so plain a figure? The mating instinct, I tell myself a little cynically many years later; how surely it singles out and binds! Kismet, our elders called it. You could walk to the end of the world and not find the right partner, they told you, until your kismet opened up for you. And when it did, as surely and beautifully as a flower, no amount of reason could dissuade you from your choice. In our case it sought to bridge our two worlds. And where else should it strike but on Independence Avenue where these two worlds met.

*   *   *

She lived in what I called the hinterland; not in a squat mud and limestone dwelling but a modern two-storey affair that had replaced it. They were newly rich and moving up; they owned the building and ran the bustling store on the street floor. It had a perpetual sale on, announced by huge signs painted on the walls, pillars, and display windows. And periodically leaflets would be distributed in the area, announcing 'Sale! Sale! Sale!' This much I knew as soon as I came home and gave her description to my sister; it was common knowledge. I learned that she was the daughter of Amina Store. Four times a day an elegant blue hydraulic-suspensioned Citroën sailed smoothly over the potholes and gravel of our backroads, carrying the daughter of the house and her neighbourhood friends to school and back.

*   *   *

On Saturday nights, after a rest from our frolics of the day, we partied. We met on the rooftop of a modern residential building called Noor-e-Salaam in our new suburb of Upanga well away from the bustle of the downtown shops and streets. The latest from the London hit parade wafted down from here. We swung to the rhythms of the Mersey beat while our former friends still drooled over the lyrics of Elvis and Jim Reeves. And to friendly locals we dispensed some of the trendier scraps from our new lifestyles. We talked about nights out in London and trips to the Continent. We introduced new words and naughty drinks.

The Saturday night following my first sight of her I managed to get Amina invited, and also her gang just to keep talk from spreading that I had been stricken. Yet how long can one hide the truth where even the slightest conjecture or suspicion could become truth merely by the force of suggestion? The blue Citroën dutifully unloaded its passengers outside the garden of Noor-e-Salaam and sailed away. They had all come. But I paid attention only to her and what pleased me was that she let me. I had come prepared for the kill, to sweep her off her feet before anyone else realized that she was available. With these unspoilt maidens who haven't left home, I told myself, you can't go wrong with books. And so on the dance floor under a modestly bright series of coloured lightbulbs, while the Rolling Stones sang 'Satisfaction', while we sipped Coke and looked down over the sidewall at the rustling trees and the few people walking on the dark street below, we talked in soft tones about nothing but books. Books!

But it was by her books that my sister swore, a few days later, when she came back from school. Two years younger, she knew I was stricken and had me on the rack, torturing me with bits of information about Amina.

'Look! I swear by holy knowledge!' Brown-papered exercise books held up solemnly as if they meant that much to her.

'Don't lie, or I'll . . .'

'Okay, then.' A mock sullenness. The books are thrown on the sofa. She sits with a long face and draws her knees up close, looks from the corners of her eyes.

'So? What was she asking?'

'But you said I was lying! So I was lying.'

'Come on now, *what?*'

'What will you give me if I tell you?'

'You'll get a slap if you don't!'

'She was asking about you. They are teasing her about you, you know. The news has got around!'

'They are stupid.'

'Well, what do you expect? You danced with no one else. And to talk of studies all the time!' She chuckles.

'I don't know her, silly! What if she is the pious type?'

It didn't hurt, being laughed at like that in the Girls' School. To be studious was still a virtue in those days. No small matter. It was the way out. And it tickled my vanity no end to learn that I had been talked about in a conversation among girls. But perhaps she had found out about me only to reject me?

Because she never came to those parties again. That was the last time, for the entire group. It indicated a certain rejection on her part: of my lifestyle and my friends. She's chosen against me I thought. Perhaps she thinks I'm a loafer. Doesn't she know I go to school, I don't go around London cutting people's hair? I go to school. To have come this close to victory—and to lose out without explanation. Maybe she was teasing, testing me; to show how vulnerable even we could be, the sophisticates who seemed to have the world in the palms of our hands.

What agonizing days I spent, keeping a lookout for her up and down Independence Avenue, entering Benson's on impulse and coming out pretending to have forgotten something, a ridiculous figure altogether. There was no way of contacting her; you needed an excuse for that. I could not think of any that would not have seemed a direct proposition. But she could, and she did.

*   *   *

I stand on our balcony looking down on the street. It's five-thirty in the evening or thereabouts. There's not a moving car on the road but some pedestrians are about. Except around noon this sidestreet is shielded from the sun by buildings and it always feels like five-thirty in the evening. A gloomy street. The sun always shines on Uhuru Street a block away. There the heat roasts you and you seek the shelter of the shadier streets.

Below me two boys play marbles on the pavement. Some distance away a figure walks towards them. A circle with a diameter is drawn in charcoal, two marbles placed on the straight line. A game of 'pyu' beginning. I look away to the figure that is closer now and I see it's a girl. Below me a marble gets projected by a forefinger pulled back, lands on the ground, rolls for a while, then takes a sudden turn and sweeps away towards the road—Oh God, it's her! as she walks around them—'Aaaaaaah!' Rage and disappointment, fists clenched. What did he expect, on such a surface? It's the other one's turn now. My heart leaps: she's entered the doorway of our building. I picture her walking through the courtyard past the boys playing cricket against the wall and taking the stairs. I keep looking down at the road, chest pounding away, face flushed to a fever. Who could she be visiting?—four possibilities . . . no, three . . .

A knock on the door.

'Yes,' says my sister behind me in a voice obviously spilling over with glee, 'he's right here!' I turn away from the balcony and greet her.

She is in a hurry. 'Can I borrow Tranter's book from you? I need it for my revision.'

I bring the book, careful to avoid the mischief in my sister's eyes.

'You can keep it as long as you want—I'll tell you when I want it back.'

'Only for a few days. I have to rush now. Our driver's waiting. Thanks!'

So it was Tranter's *Pure Mathematics* to begin with. She kept it for two months. Meanwhile I borrowed Cooke's *Organic Chemistry* from her, and so it went on. Other books, other excuses, the books untouched. Anything for a chance to meet and talk under plausible cover. Education was not to be tampered with. I would on occasion miss my stroll on Independence Avenue and walk two miles down Uhuru Street with a book in my hand, past the barren grounds, the small dingy shops packed close together, to the flat above Amina Store where she lived. How delicious, luxurious, the anxieties of those days; how joyful the illusion of their pain! They consumed my existence. Her mother fed me hot bhajias when she was there, inviting me in with: 'Come on in, babu, don't stand there in the doorway!' The servant would bring in the delights. At other times her young brother would sit at the dining table doing sums in an old exercise book while we sat on the sofa. I tried sending him downstairs to buy a Coke or something, but he wouldn't budge. And the two of us would smile, embarrassed.

People noticed—and they talked, made up their minds. But for us nothing was decided—it could not be—the future was open. This was a chance to be together, to explore the bounds of possibility; and if it lasted long enough, it would lead to an eventuality that was acceptable. But of course, meanwhile, I had to leave. At the end of the holidays, when it was time for me to go back, I asked her: 'Can I write to you?' 'You may, if you want to,' she said. And so we corresponded.

*   *   *

All this is eighteen years ago, and dead: but surely, the dead deserve their due? Or, as our elders said, they come to haunt your dreams.

I sit here in the cosy embrace of a north Scarborough living room in winter, looking out through glass doors, mulling over the last years of our marriage. An intimacy that turned insipid, dried up. Not for us the dregs of relationships, the last days of alternating care and hatred. 'I need a life of my own,' she said. 'I can change; we both can change. You can quit work and go back to college. Is that it?' 'Alone,' she said, 'we've moved apart.' 'And she?—I'll want to keep her.' 'You may, if you want to.'

The open field before me stretches northwards—a vast desert of snow. There are towns out there, I tell myself, cities full of people. Yet I see only endless stretches, a bleak landscape with a few brambles blown by a light wind. And way beyond, beyond which I cannot see a thing, there is a point marked by a pennant strangely still on a short pole. The North Pole as I've always imagined it. In that landscape I see a figure from the past, a former hero . . . Captain Scott from my Standard Six reader, cowering from biting winds . . . Why Captain Scott, out of the blue, as it were and at the wrong Pole? I cannot say for sure . . .

I tell myself I walked too far, too north, and left too much behind. We inhabited a thin and marginal world in Toronto, the two of us. Barely within a community whose approval we craved, by whose standards we judged ourselves the élite; the chic and educated. Our friends we counted on our fingers—and we proudly numbered Europeans, Asians, North Americans. Friends to talk about, not to bring together; points on our social achievement score. Not for us the dull weekend nights of nothing to do. We loved to entertain. And we clamoured for invitations; when we missed one we would pretend not to care and treat ourselves to an expensive dinner instead. We had things to do.

This marginal life she roundly rejected now—just as she did once many years ago. But then she sought me out in spite of it. She came to borrow Tranter's blue and red book though I don't believe she ever needed it . . . and now? She's back in the bosom of Uhuru Street. Or rather the companionship that's moved up Uhuru Street and into the suburban developments of Toronto. Her friends gradually came, one by one, and set themselves up with their families long after we ourselves had moved from London. And it bloomed once more, that old comradeship of Uhuru Street with Amina at the centre—first helping them to settle and then being with them just like old times. Slowly, Toronto, their Toronto became like Dar, and I was out of it.

She came to London exactly a year after the summer in which we had exchanged books and shy but satiated looks in her sitting room, while her little brother pretended to do sums in his warped exercise book on the dining table. This was a time of political change in our country: Asian students from all backgrounds were now desperately trying to go abroad. Her arrival was therefore a surprise; a cousin went to pick her up. A week later, on a Sunday morning, she telephoned me and with heart beating wildly I went to see her. It had been a long wait, a year in which we exchanged letters which delicately hinted at increasing affection. At least I did, and she did not object. I told her I missed her, she reminded me of a funny thing I'd said. I graduated from signing 'Sincerely' to 'Affectionately' and finally 'With love'. She stuck to 'Affectionately'.

She had put up in a hostel on Gloucester Road not far from High Street Kensington run by a Mr Toto, our townsman and reputedly a former valet to an oriental prince. It was a dismal place, this hostel, and I had been through it too. It was your first stop in London when you hardly knew a soul there. It picked you up and prepared you, sometimes for the worst.

Here you could see what might become of you in a week, a month, a year. Previously it had been more pleasant, a hangout for rich kids, when Mr Toto let you have parties on Saturdays. Now, in the sixties, the faces were more desperate, lonely and white from the cold since they all flew in in September and October. Boys who left early in the morning in home-made Teteron suits carrying attaché cases full of certificates, returning late, hopeless, to a night of exchanging notes on the old, sunken mattresses Mr Toto provided for his iron bedsteads. English pop songs mingled with tear-drenched Hindi film songs, the atmosphere was darkly nostalgic supported by a hollow boisterousness in the corridors. I knew the place so well, its mildew-smelling interior, the migrant Spanish maids in black, landings full of clutter to be picked up, bathrooms stained, taps leaking. I had come here many times, to meet relatives, pick up parcels from home, give advice. Over the years how many must have wept on those soiled, striped mattresses of Mr Toto, prayed on them or indulged themselves in the cold, lonely nights of London!

I entered through the black door with the brass knocker that opened directly onto the street and went straight up to the first floor and knocked on Number One as instructed. There was a shuffle of feet behind the door, which was then opened by a girl in a faded pink home-style nightie with a laced neckline. Behind her, sitting on a bed already made, was my Amina, writing letters. On Sunday you write home I said to myself.

It was still breakfast time and we went down three flights of creaky stairs into the basement. There a narrow pathway through junk and clutter led into a medium-sized brightly lit room laid with blue linoleum, long tables and some benches. There was a steady trickle of traffic in and out of this room and up and down the stairs. Here you could get onion omelettes, cornflakes, and black tea and milk ('English style') from waiters with strangely familiar faces who added advice and humour to the morning's fare.

Later we went out sightseeing. She made her pilgrimage to Trafalgar Square and with her Instamatic I took a picture of her feeding the pigeons to send back home. Then Buckingham Palace and finally Parliament with Big Ben, which for ages had chimed out the nine o'clock hour to us over the radio. 'Eighteen hours, Greenwich Mean Time,' she echoed with amusement in a mock BBC accent.

That night we had dinner at my flat. Rice and curry from a take-away Indian store in Earls Court. After dinner we sat side by side on the sofa to watch television. From the floor below came the sounds of female laughter and hilarity. I knew them well, a group of Asian girls from back home who in their inimitable way mothered the boys they knew. I often stopped at their place and had dinner there. Later I was to introduce Amina to them, but meanwhile I hoped they wouldn't come up to fetch me this night. They didn't and we sat quietly holding hands. Then we went to bed. I slept on my box spring and she on my mattress on the floor. She would not have it otherwise. 'I have to learn to be tough,' she said. For a while we talked in the dark, holding hands. We caressed, touched, our hands trembling, groping for each other in the space between us. Finally the tension reached a breaking point and I looked down in the darkness at the figure below me. 'Can I come down?' I asked, my voice straining. 'Yes,' she said.

How frail our defences, how easily cast aside when the time comes. Nothing could have been more natural. Yet nothing could have shocked more, caused greater pain, in a different setting. How easy it was to judge and condemn from there. Yet no sooner were you here than a layer of righteousness peeled down from your being.

*   *   *

Last night we took a drive down Yonge Street, my daughter Zahra and I. We drove among the Saturday night traffic, among the Camarros and Thunderbirds swooping down south for the evening, or just a zoom past downtown, as we'd done before. This time we parked the car and started walking with the crowd, caught by the summer-like festive mood. People waited outside restaurants and cinemas; vendors of popcorn and nuts called out; cars hooted; stores were open and display windows lighted. At Bloor Street we exchanged salaams with a Sikh vendor, then stopped and I bought the little lady some flowers from him. We walked along Bloor Street for some time, arm in arm, talking about our joint future. Fortunately loneliness is not a word in her vocabulary yet. We reached the end of a queue outside an ice cream shop and joined it. We were happy, the two of us. We kept walking on Bloor Street. Somewhere nearby was her mother's apartment; she knew where, but I didn't ask. We reached a repertory cinema where another crowd was queueing and I picked up a schedule. Then, at a whim, I turned on her and asked, 'How would you like to see *Wuthering Heights?*'

Tugging my arm playfully she pulled me along. 'How about seeing *Star Wars*? Finally?'

Tomson Highway *b.* 1951

BROCHET, MANITOBA

In a public talk Tomson Highway gave a few years ago at the University of Victoria he spoke of smelling a stench the first time he landed in Europe, the stench of the 'blood' shed in the European colonies and on the continent over its long history. Despite this sentiment, and his criticism of colonialism's other legacies, such as his experience at the residential school he attended, he thinks Canada is 'funky'. This may be so, especially when thinking in comparative terms, as he does in the essay that follows, but the Canada that is represented in his two plays, *Dry Lips Oughta Move to Kapuskasing* (1988) and *The Rez Sisters* (1999), which have made people in the field call him 'Native theatre in this country', and his novel, *Kiss of the Fur Queen* (1998), reflect the profound complexity of his vision. It is the ambivalence that emerges from Highway's work, an ambivalence that prevents him from expressing solely a life of victimization, that has compelled artistic producer Martin Bragg to say that 'Tomson is not only a role model and inspiration for the Native community, he is a Canadian who has inspired us all to challenge ourselves both as artists and human beings.'

The eleventh child of a caribou hunter on the Cree reserve of Brochet in Northern Manitoba, Highway was born in a tent on his father's trap line. Of the twelve children in the family, only six are alive today. He lived the nomadic life of his family until age six, when he was forced to attend the Guy Indian Residential School in The Pas, Manitoba. During his years in this Roman Catholic boarding school, where he experienced and witnessed oppression and abuse, he saw his family for only two months in the summer. After completing grade nine, he was sent to attend the Churchhill High School in Winnipeg, where he lived with a number of white foster families until he graduated in 1970. It was during his years of residential schooling that he discovered he had a talent for the piano—'There were no grand pianos in Northern Manitoba,' he said once. He studied the piano at the Faculty of Music at the University of Manitoba, as well as under the supervision of William Aide in London, England, for a year. Subsequently, he pursued a degree in music at the University of Western Ontario (BMus, 1975), from where he also received a BA (English, 1976). Nevertheless, rather than pursue a career as a concert pianist, he opted to work for a number of Native and AIDS support organizations. It was in the 1980s that, in his own words, he 'started writing plays, where I combined my knowledge of Indian reality with classical structure and artistic language. It amounted to applying sonata form to the spiritual and mental condition of a street drunk.' A co-founder of Native Earth Performing Arts in Toronto, the first aboriginal-run theatre company in Canada, he was its Artistic Director for six years (1986–92).

Highway's plays, translated into many languages and staged internationally, won many prestigious awards, including the Floyd S. Chalmers Canadian Play Award, the Dora Mavor Moore Award, and the Governor General's Award for Drama. *Kiss of the Fur Queen* was similarly successful. Though the lives of the two brothers who are the novel's central characters follow the broad outlines of Highway's and his brother René's life, and the cover photograph of the first edition is of René—a renowned dancer who died from AIDS in 1990—it is not an autobiography. Through the interventions of the Fur Queen, who takes on the role of the Cree trickster Weesageechak, the two brothers in the novel rely on their art and Cree spirituality to rise above the dislocation and despair they experience, perhaps a manifestation of the vision of transformation Highway inherited from his father. As Highway tells it, someone had asked his father, ' "Do you think your people will find their way out of their current despair?" and he said "Yes". . . . So whatever I do, whatever my family does, it's for my dad's vision, to fulfill it.'

Highway's other plays include *A Ridiculous Spectacle in One Act* (1985), *Aria* (1987), *Annie and the Old One* (1989), *The Sage, The Dancer and the Fool* (1989), and *Rose* (2003), the third installment of the 'Rez' cycle that completed the trilogy begun by his first two plays. He has also written two children's books, *Cariboo Song* (2001) and *Dragonfly Kites* (2002). The first Native writer to be inducted into the Order of Canada (1994), Highway, who is trilingual, speaking Cree, English and French, lives part time in Paris, France.

My Canada

Three summers back, a friend and I were being hurtled by bus through the heart of Australia, the desert flashing pink and red before our disbelieving eyes. It never seemed to end, this desert, so flat, so dry. For days, we saw kangaroos hopping off into the distance across the parched earth. The landscape was very unlike ours—scrub growth with some exotic species of cactuses, no lakes, no rivers, just sand and rock and sand and rock for ever. Beautiful in its own special way, haunting even—what the surface of the moon must look like, I thought to myself as I sat there in the dusk in that almost empty bus.

I turned my head to look out of the front of the bus and was suddenly taken completely by surprise. Screaming out at me in great black lettering were the words 'Canada Number One Country in the World'. My eyes lit up, my heart gave a heave, and I felt a pang of homesickness so acute I actually almost hurt. I was so excited that it was all I could do to keep myself from leaping out of my seat and grabbing the newspaper from its owner.

As I learned within minutes (I did indeed beg to borrow the paper from the Dutchman who was reading it), this pronouncement was based on information collected by the United Nations from studies comparing standards of living for every nation in the world. Some people may have doubted the finding (what about Switzerland, Denmark, Sweden, and even Australia or New Zealand?), but I didn't, not for an instant.

Where else in the world can you travel by bus, automobile, or train (and the odd ferry) for 10, 12, or 14 days straight and see a landscape that changes so dramatically, so spectacularly. The Newfoundland coast with its white foam and roar; the red sand beaches of Prince Edward Island; the graceful curves and slopes of Cape Breton's Cabot Trail; the rolling dairy land of south shore Quebec; the peerless, uncountable maple-bordered lakes of Ontario; the haunting north shore of Lake Superior; the wheat fields of Manitoba and Saskatchewan; the ranch land of Alberta; the mountain ranges, valleys and lush rainforests of the West Coast. The list could go on for 10 pages, and still only cover the southern section of the country, a sliver of land compared with the North, whose immensity is almost unimaginable.

Have you ever seen the barrens of Nunavut? Have you ever laid eyes on northern bodies of freshwater vaster than some inland seas, titans like Great Bear and Great Slave Lakes? Have you ever seen the icebergs and whales of Hudson Bay, the gold sand eskers of northern Saskatchewan, northern Manitoba's rivers, rapids, waterfalls, and 10,000 lakes, all with water so clean you can dip your hand over the side of your canoe and drink it? Have you ever had the privilege of getting off a plane on a January day at a remote settlement in the Yukon and having the air hit your lungs with a wallop so sharp you gasp quite audibly—air so clean, so crisp you swear you see it sparkle pastel pink, purple, and blue in the midmorning light?

It has been six years in a row now that the United Nations has designated Canada the number one country in which to live. We are so fortunate. We are water wealthy and forest rich. Minerals, fertile land, wild animals, plant life, the rhythm of four distinct, undeniable seasons, the North—we have it all.

Of course Canada has its problems. We'd like to lower our crime rate, but it is under relative control, and, the fact is, we live in a safe country. We struggle with our health-care system, trying to find a balance between universality and affordability. But no person in this country is denied medical care for lack of money, no child need go without a vaccination. Oh yes, we have our concerns, but in the global scheme of things we are so well off. Have you ever stopped to look at the oranges and apples piled high as mountains in supermarkets from Sicamous, BC, to Twillingate, NL? Have you paused to think about the choice of meat, fish, vegetables, cheese, bread, cereals, cookies, chips, dips, and pop we have? Or even about the number of banks, clothing stores, and restaurants?

And think of our history. For the greater part, the pain and violence, tragedy, horror, and evil that have scarred for ever the history of too many countries are largely absent from our past. There's no denying we've had our trials and times of shame, but dark though they may have been, they pale by comparison with events that have shaped many other nations.

Our cities, too, are gems. Take Toronto, where I have chosen to live. My adopted city never fails to thrill me with its racial, linguistic, cultural—not to mention lifestyle—diversity. On any ordinary day on the city's streets and subway, in stores and restaurants, I can hear the muted ebb and flow—the sweet chorus—of 20 different tongues. At any time of day, I can feast on food from six different continents, from Greek souvlakia to Thai mango salad, from Italian prosciutto to French bouillabaisse, from Ecuadorian empanada to Jamaican jerk chicken, from Indian lamb curry to Chinese lobster in ginger and green onion (with a side order of greens in oyster sauce). Indeed, one could probably eat in restaurants every week for a year and never have to eat of the same cuisine twice.

And do all these people get along? Well, they all live in a situation of relative harmony, cooperation, and peace. They certainly aren't terrorizing, torturing, and massacring one another. They're not igniting pubs, cars, and schools with explosives that blind, cripple, and maim. And they're not killing children with machetes, cleavers, and axes. Dislike—rancour—may exist in pockets here and there, but not, I believe, hatred on the scale of such blistering intensity that we see elsewhere. Is Canada a successful experiment in racial harmony and peaceful coexistence? Yes, I would say so, proudly.

Much as I often love and admire the countries I visit and their people, I can't help but notice when I go abroad that most people in France look French, most in Italy, Italian. In Sweden they look Swedish and in Japan they look Japanese. Beautiful, absolutely beautiful. But where's the variety? I ask myself. Where's the mix, the spice, the funk?

Well, it's here, right here in Canada—my Canada. When I, as an aboriginal citizen of this country, find myself thinking about all the people we've received into this homeland of mine, this beautiful country, when I think of the millions of people we've given safe haven to, following agony, terror, hunger, and great sadness in their own home countries, well, my little Cree heart just puffs up with pride. And I walk the streets of Toronto, the streets of Canada, the streets of my home, feeling tall as a maple.

Alootook Ipellie *b.* 1951

NUVUQQUQ, BAFFIN ISLAND, NUNAVUT

Though he has lived in Ottawa for many years, Ipellie Alootook has never lost his 'spiritual connection' with the land of the Inuit people—'It pulls you,' he says; 'I've never lost that pull to the land.' This pull is perhaps the single most important influence on both Alootook's life and work. A writer, cartoonist, graphic artist, screen writer, and photographer, he translates the 'mixture of the two cultures' that shapes his experiences into stories and images that evoke the tensions between them, as well as the impossibility of keeping them apart. His collection of twenty stories and ink drawings, *Arctic Dreams and Nightmares* (1993), the first such single collection by an Inuit author, dramatizes the dialogue and dichotomy between the two cultures in highly nuanced, and often disturbing, ways. In his own words, these interlinked stories about 'an Inuk who has been dead for a thousand years, and who then recalls the events of his former life through the eyes of his living soul', are filtered through the 'streetsmart' consciousness of 'a powerful shaman who learned his shamanic trade as an ordinary Inuk'. Coming from a family that has a long history of 'shamans' over generations', Alootook feels compelled to write about his 'community in Iqaluit' and its passion for stories about shamanism. But the shaman in these stories inhabits a world that has been irrevocably hybridized. From Sedna, an Inuit sea goddess, to Brigitte Bardot, from Big Ben and Shakespeare to the Lenigrad Ballet School and Nureyev, the figures and situations that appear in these stories speak at once of the loss and tenacity that characterize Inuit culture today.

The son of a semi-nomadic family, Alootook was born in the small hunting camp of Nuvuqquq on Baffin Island. He went to school at Iqaluit in Frobisher Bay at a time when 'there were no Inuit teachers whatsoever, and everything we learned was about the South and the Qallunaat [white] culture, nothing else.' But, following his move to Ottawa, the summers he spent with an uncle and his family, as well as his continuous involvement with his community through his work as editor with local publications, have helped him maintain his bond with his cultural and spiritual origins. In the 1970s Alootook worked as a translator and reporter for *Inuit Monthly* (now called *Inuit Today*), and eventually became its editor (1979–82). The often-caustic humour of his 'Ice Box' cartoons at that time made them very popular in the Inuit community. As with the 'Ice Box', the ironic humour of his present comic strip, 'Nuna & Vut', which appears regularly in *Nunatsiaq News*, is directed as much at the South as at the cultural politics and life in the North. A mentor with the Baffin Writers' Project, and a role model for the younger people in his community, Alootook is working on a novel whose title, *Akavik, the Manchurian David Bowie*, reflects his penchant for marrying old traditions with postmodern reality.

Love Triangle

In small, isolated camps, relationships between my fellow Inuit were sometimes precarious. For the most part, all of us tolerated our life-long relationships because it was the only way we could survive. And only out of necessity, did we go to extremes to solve disagreements and rifts between certain members of our camp.

For me as a shaman, one of my functions was to help sworn enemies reach reconciliation. Some of these conflicts sometimes reached crisis proportions which, unfortunately, I could not do anything about before fatalities occurred. But most times, I was successful in healing bruised egos and initiating the rebirth of cordiality between hearts and minds.

One summer, the weather was unusually hot, made hotter by an ongoing feud between two men from our camp. One, named Ossuk, was a handsome young man who had recently moved in from another camp with his family. The other, Nalikkaaq, was an older man married to a beautiful woman, Aqaqa. Unbeknownst to Nalikkaaq, Ossuk had been having an affair with Aqaqa. It was by pure coincidence that Nalikkaaq found out about their amorous relationship.

One day, when Nalikkaaq was out on the sea on his qayaq hunting for seal, a snow bunting landed on the bow of his qayaq and started bantering on about Ossuk and Aqaqa. Nalikkaaq couldn't believe what he was hearing from the snow bunting.

Although the weather was perfect for seal hunting that day, Nalikkaaq could no more concentrate on the task at hand and kept missing seal after seal even at close range. Ossuk's face kept getting in the way of his number one priority and that was to bring back the much-needed seal to his family. He eventually lost all patience and headed back to camp determined to get at the throat of Ossuk.

When he arrived at the camp, he went straight to his tent to confront his wife. Madness had taken hold of him and, in his rage, he only grunted and mumbled unrecognizable words. Aqaqa could only shrug and continue her sewing.

'What is it you want to say?' Aqaqa asked Nalikkaaq. 'Did you bring me seal?'

Nalikkaaq opened his mouth and tried once again but failed. He had to sit on the platform bed beside Aqaqa to calm down.

After a time, Nalikkaaq was calm enough to say the first words of inquiry into the alleged affair.

'Ossuk . . .' Nalikkaaq hesitated. 'Ossuk . . . I hear, has been visiting your private parts. Is this true? Aqaqa, enlighten me, please!"

'Ossuk? Who is Ossuk? I have never heard of Ossuk. Who do you mean to speak of? Who is Ossuk?'

'I was out in the middle of the sea and this little snow bunting landed on my qayaq and told me the whole story about you and Ossuk. Don't try to deny anything with me, Aqaqa. I have heard it all . . . that you two have been entertaining each other for many days while I was out doing my husbandly chores to bring food to your side. Come on, Aqaqa, admit that you have betrayed me. Admit!'

'Nalikkaaq, Nalikkaaq . . . please give me the privilege of denying anything to do with Ossuk. Ossuk is a stranger in my life. I have never heard of Ossuk. I have never seen anyone by the name of Ossuk. Nalikkaaq, I plead with you to believe me when I say I have never had the privilege of being entertained by or to entertain a fictional man named Ossuk.'

'But the snow bunting . . . is a messenger I have trusted for a lifetime. It knows what it speaks of. It spoke of amorous liaisons between the two of you. Don't deny this now, Aqaqa. Don't deny. Don't deny!'

'Nalikkaaq, I deny, I deny. And that is it.'

Nalikkaaq decided to drop the inquiry for the moment. He had better things to do than to be stonewalled by his own wife about the rumour of her amorous interludes with Ossuk. He got up and went out of the tent. He looked down to the water's edge and spotted Ossuk preparing his qayaq to paddle out on a hunt. Nalikkaaq ran down to meet Ossuk. His curiosity was getting the better of him. He just had to get to the bottom of the wild rumour brought about by the snow bunting.

'Ossuk, are you about to go seal hunting?'

'Yes, Nalikkaaq. That is the purpose of my preparation.'

'You mind if I join you? You see, I was out hunting earlier and did not bring back any seal for my wife and children. Maybe I will have better luck hunting with you.'

'Fine. Suits me. One never knows when we might run into beluga whales. We must always be prepared for that.'

In due time, Nalikkaaq and Ossuk paddled out together into the open sea. The wind was so calm, the sun bright with energy. A perfect day for hunting wild game.

They paddled for a long time until their camp was out of sight. Nalikkaaq raged secretly in his mind and heart. Somehow he kept everything to himself. But he knew he could explode any moment. The thought of Ossuk entering the private parts of his wife Aqaqa drove him on the brink of striking Ossuk in the back with the beluga whale harpoon. He was in a perfect position to do so, paddling slightly behind. He could do it at any moment, if he wanted to. However, he hesitated several times, knowing full well that one strike in the back would not guarantee a fatal blow. He was afraid that Ossuk would end up retaliating, and then he, Nalikkaaq, would be the one killed instead of Ossuk. The safer plan would be to wait until they went ashore somewhere. He would then be more certain of killing Ossuk.

Nalikkaaq decided to concentrate on finding and hunting seals that were so urgently needed in camp. Killing a human could wait. It wasn't long before a seal popped up from under the surface of the water to breathe. Nalikkaaq and Ossuk paddled towards it, harpoons ready. In time, the seal popped up once again very close to their qayaqs. Nalikkaaq and Ossuk hurled their harpoons, both stabbing the seal at the same time. There was a minor dispute as to which of them had hit it first. In a situation like this, it was custom to give the older man credit for the kill. Nalikkaaq smiled ear to ear. The seal was on its way to his wife and family. He was a happy man.

It wasn't long before another seal popped up and Nalikkaaq had thoughts of picking up the beluga whale harpoon instead of the seal harpoon. He was again imagining Ossuk embracing his beautiful wife Aqaqa and, God forbid in his own tent! The two of them paddled in the direction of the seal. Nalikkaaq had decided this was the moment he would make Ossuk pay for his dire deeds. He readied the beluga whale harpoon to be fatally plunged into the flesh of Ossuk. However, Ossuk was a very perceptive young man. He noticed Nalikkaaq holding the beluga whale harpoon.

'Nalikkaaq, why are you using the beluga whale harpoon when there aren't any belugas around?'

'Ossuk, I just wanted to make sure the little seal died instantly with this larger harpoon. I have had experiences with seals escaping my seal harpoon because it wasn't powerful enough. This is the reason why.'

'You know, as well as I, Nalikkaaq, that it is a bad omen to use a beluga whale harpoon on a seal. It will only bring you bad luck. You must respect the seal, and using the beluga whale harpoon means you do not respect it.'

'You are so bloody right, Ossuk. I forgot. I wasn't thinking.'

Nalikkaaq had no choice but to put away the beluga whale harpoon. He felt a little embarrassed by the young man since he was considered the elder and should, in the eyes of Ossuk, have known better. Nalikkaaq quickly reverted back to his seal harpoon and paddled on. He felt incensed by Ossuk's very presence. He was boiling inside.

The seal popped up again to the right of Ossuk. Nalikkaaq could hardly see it. He went for it anyway as Ossuk easily plunged his harpoon into the hapless seal. Nalikkaaq's harpoon had misfired and strayed into Ossuk's qayaq, puncturing it. The hole was far enough from the water surface that it didn't spring a leak. Nalikkaaq's embarrassment turned into a feeling of humiliation. As he paddled close to Ossuk's qayaq to retrieve his harpoon, Nalikkaaq came up with an idea. The plan was to hit Ossuk's qayaq again, this time under the water surface so it would leak and drown this despicable adulterer.

'Please, Ossuk, forgive me for hitting your qayaq. The rope got tangled in my fingers as I released it. It was entirely accidental. I apologize.'

'Accidents do happen, Nalikkaaq. Accidents do happen.'

Ossuk pulled the seal onto his qayaq and prepared to paddle to the shore to butcher the seal. He was so hungry for it.

'Nalikkaaq, will you join me for a little feast on the shore?'

'I cannot refuse such an offer. I am famished for seal meat and blubber. And especially for warm blood.'

Nalikkaaq was salivating as he paddled toward the land. The sinking and drowning of Ossuk would have to wait. Warm blood was all that was on his mind. Warm blood, not just of the seal, but also the warm blood flowing out of Ossuk's body.

It wasn't long before they landed on shore. Ossuk hauled his seal on top of a smooth rock. He began cutting the seal from just under its chin and down to its flippers as if he was unzipping it. The carcass steamed. Its blood was indeed still quite warm. Nalikkaaq crouched over the seal, cupped his palms and sunk them into the warm blood and sucked the blood with fervour.

'Such a heavenly drink!' Nalikkaaq celebrated, his lips coloured in crimson. 'Nothing quite like it compares! Let me at its liver!'

Nalikkaaq retrieved his knife and cut out the liver. Then he cut off some blubber and ate it with the liver, mouthfuls at a time.

Nalikkaaq looked up toward the sky and put his arms up to acknowledge the Creator and said, 'This is food for the gods. Thank you. Thank you. Thank you.'

Ossuk wasn't saying much. He went about the business of filling himself. His appetite was fierce.

'What a blessed land we live in!' Nalikkaaq bellowed out. His voice echoed against the side of a mountain across the fiord. 'It is at these moments we rejoice the bounty of this great land!'

'Indeed Nalikkaaq, indeed,' smiled Ossuk, gobbling seal flesh down his throat.

Nalikkaaq had forgotten about the rumour of Ossuk and Aqaqa's sexual trysts until the knife in his hand began reminding him of its uses other than cutting up seal meat. His vengeful self re-emerged from the depth of his mind. 'I can end it all now,' he thought as he looked at Ossuk's busy throat.

Soon the little feast was over. Ossuk put holes alongside where he had slit the seal and closed the carcass by looping the holes with rope and put the seal back on his qayaq. Nalikkaaq cleaned his knife in the salt water and imagined it slicing up Ossuk. 'An adulterer deserves no dignity while alive,' he thought.

'Ossuk, did I tell you about the story of a bloody feud between two powerful shamans over the wife of one of the shamans?'

'No,' Ossuk nodded.

'As the story was related to me some time ago, one of the shamans had committed adultery with the other shaman's wife and a bloody feud ensued for many hours in a camp. The camp members were given the most frightening show of their lives. It turned out that the two of them bared their chests and fought the wrestling match of their lives. The bloody feud ended when one of the shamans took hold of the adulterer's penis and swung him around in midair four or five times and, the poor man, his penis and testicles were ripped right off his crotch! The penisless shaman managed to survive the ordeal but he was never to penetrate the private parts of a woman again, least of all the winning shaman's wife. It was a horrendous spectacle, made more so when the shaman looked at the severed penis and testicles in his hand and then flung them violently out to sea. They floated off to kingdom come.'

'Ouch,' Ossuk cringed his face. 'That's one of the most disgusting stories I've ever heard. Are you making it up?'

'Of course not. I think the adulterer got exactly what he deserved. Don't you think so?'

'According to the winning shaman, I suppose. What a way to be castrated. It hurts in the crotch just thinking about it. Would you have done that yourself if you found out that another man had been having an affair with your wife?'

'To give you an honest opinion, under the circumstances, I would probably do it.'

'Gruesome . . .'

'Ossuk, can I ask you a personal question?'

'Yes, as long as it's within the bounds of decency, I will try to answer it.'

'Have you ever committed adultery?'

'Never.'

'Ossuk, that's a lie. Earlier today, I was visited by a little snow bunting who spilled out you and Aqaqa's best-kept secret. The snow bunting revealed to me that you two had been having secret liaisons. Isn't that right?'

'A little snow bunting?' Ossuk gave out a nervous laugh. 'What a likely story. A pack of lies. Are you out of your mind, Nalikkaaq? It's a pack of incredible lies!'

'Don't deny, Ossuk. Don't you deny!'

'Pack of lies! Pack of lies! Pack of lies!' Ossuk yelled at Nalikkaaq and started to push his qayaq into the water. He jumped into it and was soon racing toward the camp. He was determined to get away from his accuser as quickly as possible.

Nalikkaaq jumped into his qayaq and paddled after Ossuk. 'So, Ossuk is paddling away from the truth!' He soon caught up to Ossuk. There they were, paddling side by side, one mouthing off vindictives, the other vehemently denying his accuser's words. The two men seemed like they were in an Olympic qayaq race as they skimmed at great speed through the calm sea.

'You'll pay for this!' Nalikkaaq yelled at Ossuk. They were nearing their camp. The people in camp heard and saw what was happening and watched the two qayaqers coming to land on the shore. They went down to find out what the commotion was all about.

Ossuk and Nalikkaaq simultaneously jumped out of their qayaqs. Nalikkaaq immediately went over to confront Ossuk. 'You are a dirty little adulterer!' Nalikkaaq yelled pointing an index finger at Ossuk. 'Let everyone know this dirty little truth! Ossuk, you cannot deny it any more!'

The people were a little shocked that something like this was taking place right in front of their faces. They looked at each other in utter amazement. Nalikkaaq was pushing Ossuk's chest and shoulders. 'Dirt!' he yelled. 'Dirt!'

I walked over to the two feuding men and told them to calm down. 'You are men who are capable of reasoning with each other and a fight like this will not solve any of your troubles. So, I suggest a wrestling match between the two of you. Right here and now.'

'Fair enough,' Nalikkaaq immediately agreed.

However, Ossuk was hesitant. 'I am an innocent man facing a false accusation of committing adultery with Aqaqa! I will not submit to such false pressure! Nalikkaaq, take your unfounded accusations and anger elsewhere!'

'Wait! Wait! Wait!' Aqaqa came running down to the shore from her tent. Everyone looked around to see a frantic Aqaqa with her sewing still in hand. 'I have a confession to make!' Aqaqa stopped and caught up with her breath. 'Nalikkaaq, the amorous rendezvous between me and Ossuk did happen. I have fallen in love with the man of my dreams.' Aqaqa turned to her lover. 'Ossuk, do not deny it any more. Let the truth be known. Confess! Confess! Confess!'

Ossuk was in a state of shock, mouth agape. 'What are you saying, Aqaqa? What are you saying?'

'Let the truth be known, and I have said it.'

Ossuk wasn't going to admit to anything, but everyone now knew the truth. Nalikkaaq could hardly contain his anger. 'Enough!' he yelled and lunged at Ossuk.

'Nooo!' I yelled at Nalikkaaq and went between the two men. 'Reason shall prevail. A wrestling match is in order. It is our ancient method of solving disputes and depressurizing a raging mind. Nalikkaaq and Ossuk, bare your chests.'

'So be it,' Ossuk succumbed to the pressure. At any rate, he would not back down from a challenge. He had the advantage of being younger and stronger than Nalikkaaq. He would rely on those qualities, if he could, to defeat Nalikkaaq.

The Arctic Wrestling Federation Championship Match was on. The women cried out of fear. The children held onto their mothers and shuffled their feet on the ground. The men yelled in excitement.

Nalikkaaq and Ossuk were almost a perfect match at the beginning. They would take turns lifting and slamming each other on the ground, to thunderous applause mostly from the men, cries of fear from the women, to wondrous curiosity from the children.

At one point, Nalikkaaq went after Ossuk's throat and almost choked him to death until Ossuk was able to knee Nalikkaaq in the crotch and release his hands just in time. There was a short pause in the struggle as Nalikkaaq clutched his crotch with both hands and Ossuk coughed out the effects of his near-choking.

'Come on, you wretched men!' A man yelled out from the crowd. 'We're not here to watch a bore-off! Get on with it!'

Aqaqa was unusually calm about what was happening in front of her. Perhaps it had something to do with her confidence in Ossuk, her lover, that his youth and strength would eventually prevail over the aging body of her husband, Nalikkaaq.

Aqaqa underestimated one thing, her husband's experience and maturity. Nalikkaaq was deft at checks and balances, leverages and angles that one acquired only with experience. He had practised wrestling holds for years and was exceptionally good at deception. He had plenty of moves that mesmerized the lesser-experienced Ossuk.

'No! No! No!' Aqaqa yelled as Nalikkaaq suddenly got hold of Ossuk's penis and began swinging him around in mid-air. 'No! No! No!' she yelled again.

'Aaaahhhh!' cried Ossuk as Nalikkaaq threw him to the ground, minus his penis and testicles! Then Nalikkaaq looked at the severed parts and threw them out to sea, bellowing out obscenities.

Aqaqa became hysterical, crying on her knees looking over Ossuk.

What Nalikkaaq hadn't told Ossuk earlier was that he was the shaman who had ripped off the penis of the other shaman! Now he had done it again, this time to the hapless Ossuk.

In Nalikkaaq's world, three's a crowd.

Janice Kulyk Keefer b. 1952

TORONTO, ONTARIO

'No writer, no matter how passionately she identifies with a particular community, ethnic or otherwise, can transparently and comprehensively project the views and voices of that community in her writing. . . . It is the task of the writer to situate herself off-centre from her own community in order to be able to critique as well as communicate what she knows of it,' says Janice Kulyk Keefer. And this is the position from which she writes, a position of ambivalence and, partly, the result of her upbringing 'as a hyphenated Canadian, the child of immigrants'. Born in Toronto, she 'grew up with the fact that [her] mother's experience as an immigrant', whose family had emigrated from a village in Poland that is now part of Ukraine, 'was a very painful one, for psychological as well as economic reasons'. As a young woman, Kulyk Keefer was 'convinced that only people with names like Smith or MacPherson could be published and read in this country—a belief that led me,' as she says, 'to think and write, for the most part, in what I understood to be the manner of a Smith or MacPherson.' The webs of 'otherness' within which she moved as a child continue to 'haunt' her. She has attributed part of the reason she wanted to study and live outside of Canada to her ambivalent feelings of being seen as 'ethnic'. Following her BA in English from the University of Toronto (1974), and with a Commonwealth Scholarship, she studied the University of Sussex where she earned an MA and a PhD in English. Her determination to become a writer made her aware of the kind of 'foreigner' she had become to her own literary tradition: 'I was discouraged at the university [in Canada] from reading Canadian writing, and encouraged to read American or British. And so I was really quite patronizing in my attitude toward my own culture.'

Kulyk Keefer launched her career as writer with the publication of a collection of poetry, *White of the Lesser Angels* (1986), and a collection of short stories, *The Paris-Napoli Express* (1986), having already won the CBC Radio Literary Competition First Prize (1985, 1986). Her stories about expatriate Canadians in Europe and Europeans living in Canada reflect the critical distance she believes a writer ought to keep from her background. Conversely, *Transfigurations* (1987), a collection of short fiction, and *Constellations* (1988), a novel, are both set in Nova Scotia, where Kulyk Keefer taught English for ten years at the Université Sainte-Anne (1980–90). Like her fictive imagination, her critical sensibility, too, focuses on figures and issues of ambivalence as is evident in *Under Eastern Eyes: A Critical Reading of Canadian Maritime Fiction* (1987), nominated for the Governor General's Award for non-fiction, and *Reading Mavis Gallant* (1989). A Professor of English and creative writing at the University of Guelph since 1990, Kulyk Keefer's writing displays her concern with indeterminacy, a condition that characterizes many of her journeying characters in the short story collection, *Travelling Ladies* (1990). Her memoir, *Honey and Ashes: A Story of Family* (1998), tracks her family's journey from Ukraine to Canada, while *Dark Ghost in the Corner: Imagining Ukrainian-Canadian Identity* (2005) offers a historical and critical perspective of Ukrainian immigration.

Despite her resistance to the marginalizing effect of the label of ethnicity, or perhaps because of it, Kulyk Keefer participated in the debates about multiculturalism in the early 1990s. Lamenting the use of the term multicultural in 'speak[ing] of a group of people, or of a writer', she argues for the need to employ a new term 'to denote those literary works in which a writer's ancestral country or culture seems as important as the country in which he or she actually resides'. The term she proposes, one also preferred by such writers as Ven Begamudré, is transculturalism, a concept that 'brings out the dynamic potential of cultural diversity, the possibility of exchange and change among and with different ethnocultural groups'. Winner of The Malahat Long Poem Prize, and of two National Magazine Award

First Prizes (1990, 1994), she published another poetry volume, *Marrying the Sea* (1998), which won the Canadian Authors Association Award (1999), as well as a juvenile fiction book, *Anna's Goat* (2000). The recipient of the Marian Engel Award, Kulyk Keefer has so far published four novels, *Constellations* (1988), *Rest Harrow* (1992), *The Green Library* (1996), a finalist for the Governor General's Award, and *Thieves* (2004), a lyrical and elegant narrative of the New Zealand short story writer Katherine Mansfield.

Nach Unten

I am on the Bloor Street bus with Annie—she is taking me home with her to the bungalow she and her husband bought after they sold the huge brick house downtown. We have long since exhausted her store of questions about the health of my parents and my sister and my brother, and so we ride side by side in silence. This is not just a matter of my being young enough to be Annie's granddaughter, and yet knowing no more about her than that I've always known her. Perhaps the truest reason for our silence is that the only language we have between us is still foreign ground to Annie, though she's lived in Canada for over half her life. Sometimes I hear English people saying things like, 'Fifty years since they got off the boat and they still can't speak a proper sentence—can't pronounce even the simplest words.' English people, you understand, are not necessarily from Britain: they are simply those who are born with the language like a silver spoon inside their mouths, who say Winnipeg instead of Veenipeg, Thunder and not Toonder Bay. They are the ones who have never been anywhere but home; who are disobliged when people who have lost everything but their lives go on carrying the one thing that will never abandon them.

The silence between Annie and myself is camouflaged by the fact that so many other people are talking. Across from us is an old, old woman with a face that could have been made out of flour, water, and a rake. What is left of her hair has been dyed the colour of the liver spots on her hands. The woman is talking in a high, precise voice to a man with a cast on his leg. They are speaking of their parents, of aunts and uncles a long time dead. 'Epsom salts,' she is saying. 'Every morning they drank a mixture of Epsom salts and lemon juice, and they never knew a day's sickness. No arthritis, and not a wrinkle on their faces.'

I smile at Annie but there's no response—she is staring at a child sitting further down the aisle. The girl is no older than five or six—her red socks and bright black shoes stick out over the edge of the seat, where an adult's knees would be. In her long, straight hair are barrettes shaped like flowers; her hair has the sheen of snow, and perhaps it's this that makes her eyes so blue, like blocks of azure or cerulean in a brand new paint box. Annie is smiling at the child, who has been warned, no doubt, never to speak to strangers, never to let them speak to her, even this silent kind of speech in which all the bones of Annie's face seem to lift and tilt. For a moment it's as if everything this woman has been burdened with—the years and years of labour in a foreign land and foreign tongue—slides off the shelf of her bones and is gone, leaving her as light as something still unborn.

The child folds her hands and begins to sing, first under her breath, then loud enough that I catch a few words: *nach unten geh'n, nach unten, nach unten*. It is a refrain of some kind, perhaps to a nursery rhyme or folk song. The child's mother looks at us uncertainly—that is not, she feels, correct behaviour for the bus. She whispers something to the child, who stops singing and stares into the windows of her bright, black shoes. Annie tugs my sleeve: this is our stop. She doesn't look after the bus as it pulls away, but points to her house, three doors down. It seems to be a point of pride with her that the stop is so close to her house, as though the Toronto Transit Commission had arranged this for her private convenience. Perhaps she feels this makes up for the noise and rush of the street; for the small brick box in which she has to spend her days.

It looks, in fact, no bigger than a gingerbread house. As we walk inside I keep thinking of the other house, the one Mike and Annie bought for a song when people like my parents were moving from old, dark, three-storey houses downtown into suburban split-levels with picture windows and prodigious lawns. Annie always kept as lush a garden as she could: summer after summer her narrow city yard would bear bushels of rhubarb and runner beans, onion and garlic, strawberries and cherries. '*Berih*'; she'd say to my mother: '*Yeest*. There's just the two of us—you have a family to feed.' And so we'd take and eat the food from Annie's garden, until even strawberries lost their savour, and there was no room on our cellar shelves for all her jars of pickles and preserves.

Mike is watching television; Annie simply turns down the volume, letting the colours blare instead of the voices: sports or soap opera or an endless succession of commercials, I can't tell which. The set is as diminutive as the house itself—everything is miniature and yet there is hardly room to move: I seem to have entered an overstocked ark, bearing icons instead of animals. Cross-stitched antimacassars, that same reproduction of Khmelnitsky's *Triumphant Entrance into Kiev* which my parents have exiled to the garage, egg-sized busts of the great patriotic poets: Shevchenko, Ukrainka, Franko; brandy snifters crammed with painted easter eggs.

Mike gets up to greet me: he shakes my hand and won't let go until Annie gently disengages us, asking Mike to go to the kitchen and bring us something to drink. I have made it clear that I cannot stay for very long—I've only a week before I leave, there are still a hundred things to pack, and, besides, my parents are expecting me for dinner. But the gift I've brought stays locked in my purse, for it is ginger ale, not whiskey Mike is offering. I'd forgotten that he doesn't drink any more; the chocolates I chose are shaped like small casks filled with cognac and Cointreau and Courvoisier. And so I sit, hands clasped around my glass, my purse tucked well behind my feet, smiling and saying nothing as Mike and Annie, equally silent, smile back at me.

Mike and Annie. Their English names seem as familiar to them now as the shape of their hands or the shoes on their feet. But were I to call out *Miháhsh, Hányu*, who would answer me? I want us to talk to one another, I want to hear their stories, but we sit in a silence loud as any shouting. If only they could speak to me in their own language and not in an English that breaks in their mouths, falling in awkward pieces that I gather stealthily, so as not to embarrass them. If only I could feel at home in their language, if to speak it were not to feel a stump instead of a tongue in my mouth. And

I feel before them the shame I knew as a child who could not understand more than a smattering of what my Ukrainian school teachers, who in Kiev and Lvov had been doctors and professors and who, in Toronto, were janitors and factory workers, called *móva réedna*, my true and native tongue.

As my mother says, I am going away for a long time, and who knows what may happen before I return. I have grown up under the eyes of these people. I have been told that they have had a hard life, and I, with my easy one, feel that edge of guilt which presses into everything that has to do with who and how I am. I am sitting here in Mike and Annie's living room because of a voyage made on a lucky hunch some forty years ago. Had my grandmother put off leaving Poland in 1936, and she stayed in the house where my mother was born, on land bought with the money my grandfather sent each month from Canada, then everything I am would be nothing. For my grandmother's house has disappeared, along with her village; the land she never sold belongs to a different country now, her only proof of ownership an envelope of brittle papers inscribed in a forbidden language: *moyèh pòleh*—my fields.

Mike and Annie have been lucky in a different sort of way. I know that they came to Canada after the war; that, like my Ukrainian school teachers, they were what we children called Dee-Pees, not knowing the grander terms on which they were with history: Displaced Persons. They survived the war, they made a new life for themselves— witness this house and all the belongings which make it look like a passport stamped on every page, with hardly a free space showing. Canada has been good to us, their silence seems to say—how can you leave, why are you going away? It's the same rebuke I seem to hear everywhere these days, and I counter it by talking too much and too fast. I don't know how much of what I say they understand—that I'm going by ship, that we dock first at Le Havre and then Tilbury, and that the boat goes onto Bremerhaven, Leningrad. I am studying English literature, I need to work with people in England, English is my mother tongue: English, not Ukrainian—.

There is silence then. I am reaching for my purse, signalling that it is time for me to go, when Mike begins to speak. He tells me that he and Annie went to England after the war.

'We be living in Leeds'—he pronounces it 'Lyeedz'. 'Five year. Annie, me, two both working in cloth factory. Five year until we coming to Toronto.' He is cradling the glass of ginger ale in his large, rough hands, but he does not drink.

'I be go to store one day. Five year I live in Lyeedz, and I be go to store, for buying'—he stops for a moment— *'bèelyee pahpèer.* "Paper white," I say, and shopkeeper, he look at me like I be dog or rat'—*rrrat,* he rolls his r's—*'Bèelyee pahpèer* behind him, on shelf, I point and he be shake his head, "I no know what you want, go on, get out, *gerrrroutta heeerrrr".'*

Annie gets up from her chair and, touching Mike's hand, takes the glass away from him. Then she asks if I would like to see round the house. I nod my head too brightly, too quickly, as if to say, 'Yes, please, show me everything.' And so we go in procession, Annie letting her husband explain about the cupboards he has made for the kitchen, the new doors he has put onto the bedroom closet, the shower installed from a kit he picked up at the hardware. And that is the house: sitting room, kitchen, bathroom, bedroom. Doll-sized, and looking curiously exposed, the way in a doll's house the rooms are always missing a wall, so that you can look in and rearrange the furniture.

This is all there is of the house, but Annie says there's a surprise I must see. She takes my hand as if I were a child who must be protected from my own excitement; she opens a wooden door and leads me into a glassed-in porch filled with potted plants, their small green hands pressed against the windows, beseeching whatever light can fall through the narrow glass. Between the leaves I make out something blue, impossibly blue, like a billboard image of tropical seas. But as Annie pushes open the last door it is clear that what I took to be a mirage is really there: a swimming pool that takes up the whole of the cemented-over yard.

Were Annie and Mike to get into the pool together they would scarcely have room to turn. But I know without asking that no one swims here, any more than angels float suspended in the blue above us. A leaf from the neighbour's poplar drifts into the water: it floats, a golden coin, a small, eye-shaped fish, until Annie gets down on her knees and leans over the edge to pluck it out. As she folds the leaf into her pocket I realize that it is not the leaf but the pool's blue absolute that she is rescuing. I remember the child singing on the Bloor Street bus, her eyes the blue of ice melting, of streams running under snow: I remember Annie looking, longing. And for no reason, and because it seems, suddenly, needful, I find some words to say. I repeat what I remember of the child's song: *nach unten, nach unten.*

'*Nach unten geh'n.*'

It is Annie speaking now, not me. She pulls herself up from her knees: I can hear her bones speak: hoarse, straining for breath. *Nach unten geh'n*—that was how, she says, they asked permission of the guards to go down to use the latrines. 'In the camp,' she explains. 'Work camp, labour camp.' And that is all she says, either because she has run out of words, or because the words themselves have run out of any meaning they could give.

Mike has come to join us: Annie unfolds the leaf from her pocket and shows it to him; he nods his head. They do not touch one another, yet they seem joined in a way I had never recognized. Perhaps it is the narrowness of the cement strip on which they stand, or a trick of the light, like the illusion of blue with which the pool's painted floor infuses the water.

When I tell them it is late, now, that if I do not hurry I will miss my bus, they step apart. Annie asks Mike to walk me to the bus stop; I insist that it isn't necessary. Annie leads the way inside and then the two of them stand at the window, waving goodbye to me as I walk away from their house. I walk past the first and then the second stop; finally I flag down a cab and ride all the way downtown.

That night I phone my mother—for I have not gone home to dinner, I have met with friends and spent the evening taking leave. When I phone it is nearly midnight, but my mother goes to bed late, and always needs to talk, she says, before she can fall asleep. I say I have seen Annie and Mike in their new house. It is she who mentions the swimming pool, saying how crazy it is for them to have taken on a burden like that; how, with their love of gardening, they ought to have bought a house with a bit of land attached. My mother points out how dangerous it is for two people who have never learned to swim to have a pool in their backyard. Supposing a small child hopped the fence and fell in and needed rescuing? They could be sued, stripped of everything they own. And then she says something that shocks me, though of course I might have expected it. 'Annie's my age, you know.'

After I hang up I think of everything I didn't tell her: that I have been told a story about a shopkeeper in Leeds, and have discovered the one phrase in German that Annie can, or will remember. And I think of that curious expression on Annie's face, half longing, half delight, when she smiled at the child singing in the Bloor Street bus, and knelt to look into the clear and perfect eyes of the water.

I am far away now, from Annie's and my parents' houses; from the country in which I was born and the country I have known only through other people's memories and stories. Living so far away, I have gone to books and films and photographs to find out things that I could never ask of anyone at home, that no one could ever have told me, no matter how much they knew.

In one of the books which I have read since leaving home, I learned of how, after the Nazi occupation of Ukraine, many of the country's people were shipped to Germany: slave labour for camps and arms and factories. It often happened, the book said, that doctors would round up the young women before they were boarded onto the trains and, as if they were so many sturdy glass beakers, would sterilize them, to ensure the right kind of productive capacity and, more importantly, the purity of their future owner's race. I believe that this is what happened to Annie—I believe this because, of course, I could never ask her, and because I saw her once on the Bloor Street bus, looking longingly at a small German child as she may have looked through barbed-wire fences at the children who lived in the town beside the labour camp: as beings not so much apart as immune. Immune just as angels, with all the buoyancy of their beauty, are immune from dirt and suffering and death.

My mother has stopped mentioning Mike and Annie in her letters, and I have never inquired after them, as if the act of asking, directly, whether they are still alive, would make their deaths a certainty. But now and again, on that blurred, shifting border between sleep and waking, I have caught a glimpse of Annie. She is not, as I have so often seen her, bent over the earth of her garden. She no longer feels the need to grow flowers and fruit, to fill glass jars with beets and cucumbers and peaches. Instead, she is walking down into the blue, painted waters of her swimming pool, stretching out and gently floating, her face tilted up to the night. There are lights like fallen stars, shining from the bottom of the water: they show the body of a young girl, bathed clean of all stains and wounds, of all loss and longing. She is singing to herself, though I can't make out the words; in the cool, blue water she is singing.

Di Brandt *b.* 1952

REINLAND, MANITOBA

'i came to writing as a powerfully transgressive act,' says Di Brandt. 'there was so much silence in me, so much that had been silenced over the years, by my strict religious Mennonite farm upbringing, my experience as *other* at the university, as immigrant from a separatist culture & as a woman (i tried so hard to learn how to think like Modern WASP Man at the university), trying to be a hippie, becoming a mother.' These contradictions, reflecting her background and gender consciousness, are at the heart of Brandt's poetry.

She was born in Reinland, a separatist Mennonite farming community in southern Manitoba. 'In contrast to a lot of other ethnic groups who are trying to become assimilated into Canadian culture, the Mennonite community worked very hard to stay separate from a Canadian identity and define itself against the rest of the world around it . . . in that sense they wanted to be treated with discrimination and in fact they have been.' Trying to write from within and against that background has involved coming to terms with 'three different languages, which referred to different codes of behaviour as well as consciousness. We used Low German at home for everyday life . . . High German was the public language we used in church. That was God's language. And then there was English, the worldly language we used in school that referred to the rest of the world.' Along with that, Brandt had to overcome feeling 'mute' as a woman, in that 'there was no language for' women.

Although she left her community at 17, it has taken 'the rest of my life to begin to make sense of the huge cultural differences that exist between that community and modern Winnipeg'. After receiving a BTh (1972) at the Canadian Mennonite Bible College, Brandt studied at the University of Manitoba, where she received a BA in Honours English (1975), at the University of Toronto, where she received an MA in English (1976), and then again at the University of Manitoba, where she received her PhD (1993). Nominated for the McNally Robinson Award for Manitoba Book of the Year, her revised dissertation, *Wild Mother Dancing* (1993), is a critical study dealing with one of the pervasive themes in her work, the role of mothers. Brandt, who was a professor of English and creative writing at the University of Winnipeg and University of Windsor, has been actively involved as poetry editor with various magazines, including *Prairie Fire* and *Contemporary Verse 2*.

Her first poetry book, *questions i asked my mother* (1987), won the Gerald Lampert Award, and was nominated for the Governor General's Award and the Commonwealth Poetry Prize. Although its publication caused a scandal in her community, it found an 'intense and warm' response in many Mennonite women who are 'scared to say' aloud what Brandt articulates in her poetry. A dialogue of many voices, it challenges the authority structures of her heritage in her attempt to invent a separate identity for herself. *Agnes in the sky* (1990), winner of the McNally Robinson Award for Manitoba Book of the Year, is, as Brandt says, 'about what do you do after you've exploded your family story'. About 'specific abuses' in her culture, it is written in the rhythm and language that characterize all of Brandt's poetry. In fact, as Brandt says, 'what turns me on in writing most of all is rhythm, trying to capture "orality" in writing, making the text disappear by lifting the sound off the page, running words together to subvert proper syntax and punctuation, playing with breath and spacing, making the body present on the page.' *mother, not mother* (1992), nominated for the Pat Lowther Award, is written in similar style.

Though her writing continues to echo her Mennonite background, Brandt's poetic vision increasingly reflects her unflinching interest in injustices beyond her immediate world. *Jerusalem, Beloved* (1995), shortlisted for the Governor General's Award and the recipient of the Canadian Authors' Association National Poetry Award, bears witness to the Intifada of occupied Palestine, visited by Brandt in 1991, as well as to a city that is at once real and mythical, a palimpsest constructed by different, albeit conflicting, cultural and religious histories. *Now You Care* (2004), a finalist for the Griffin Poetry Prize, the Pat Lowther Award, and the Trillium Prize for Best Book, reflects her unremitting attention to the nuances of language and form, this time a language that serves as a bold indictment against the complacency toward environmental degradation. Her unflinching interest in social and cultural issues also informs *Dancing Naked: Narrative Strategies for Writing Across Centuries* (1996) and her forthcoming collection of essays, *This Land that I love, This Wide Wide Prairie*. These concerns, propelled by her belief that poetry has the ability to transform our consciousness, form the basis of her ecopoetic creative and scholarly project she is presently pursuing as Canada Research Chair at Brandon University.

foreword

learning to speak *in public*   to write love poems
for all the world to read   meant betraying once &
for all the good Mennonite daughter i tried so
unsuccessfully to become   acknowledging in myself
the rebel traitor thief   the one who asked too   5
many questions   who argued with the father & with
God   who always took things always went too far
who questioned every thing   the one who talked too
often too loud   the questionable one   shouting
from rooftops what should only be thought guiltily   10
in secret   squandering stealing the family words
the one out of line   recognizing finding myself
in exile   where i had always been   trying as
always to be true   whispering in pain the old
words   trying to speak the truth as it was given   15
listening in so many languages & hearing in this one
translating   remembering   claiming my past
living my inheritance on this black earth   among
strangers   prodigally   making love in a foreign
country   writing coming home   20

Zone: < le Détroit >

after Stan Douglas

I

Breathing yellow air
here, at the heart of the dream
of the new world,

the bones of old horses and dead Indians
and lush virgin land, dripping with fruit   5
and the promise of wheat,
overlaid with glass and steel
and the dream of speed:
all these our bodies
crushed to appease the 400 & 1 gods   10
of the Superhighway,
NAFTA, we worship you,
hallowed be your name,
here, where we are scattered
like dust or rain in ditches,   15
the ghosts of passenger pigeons
clouding the silver towered sky,
the future clogged in the arteries
of the potholed city,
Tecumseh, come back to us   20
from your green grave,
sing us your song of bravery
on the lit bridge over the black river,
splayed with grief over the loss
of its ancient rainbow coloured   25
fish swollen joy.
Who shall be fisher king
over this poisoned country,
whose borders have become
a mockery,   30
blowing the world to bits
with cars and cars and trucks and electricity and cars,
who will cover our splintered
bones with earth and blood,
who will sing us back into—   35

2

See how there's no one going to Windsor,
only everyone coming from?
Maybe they've been evacuated,
maybe there's nuclear war,
maybe when we get there we'll be the only ones.   40
See all those trucks coming toward us,
why else would there be rush hour on the 401
on a Thursday at nine o'clock in the evening?
I counted 200 trucks and 300 cars

and that's just since London.   45
See that strange light in the sky over Detroit,
see how dark it is over Windsor?
You know how people keep disappearing,
you know all those babies born with deformities,
you know how organ thieves follow tourists   50
on the highway and grab them at night
on the motel turnoffs,
you know they're staging those big highway accidents
to increase the number of organ donors?
My brother knew one of the guys paid to do it,   55
$100,000 for twenty bodies
but only if the livers are good.
See that car that's been following us for the last hour,
see the pink glow of its headlights in the mirror?
That's how you know.   60
Maybe we should turn around,
maybe we should duck so they can't see us,
maybe it's too late,
maybe we're already dead,
maybe the war is over,   65
maybe we're the only ones alive.

3

So there I am, sniffing around
the railroad tracks
in my usual quest for a bit of wildness,
weeds, something untinkered with,   70
goldenrod, purple aster, burdocks,
defiant against creosote,
my prairie blood surging
in recognition and fellow feeling,
and o god, missing my dog,   75
and hey, what do you know,
there's treasure here
among these forgotten weeds,
so this is where they hang out,
all those women's breasts   80
cut off to keep our lawns green
and dandelion free,
here they are, dancing
their breastly ghost dance,
stirring up a slight wind in fact   85

and behaving for all the world
like dandelions in seed,
their featherwinged purple nipples
oozing sticky milk,
so what am I supposed to do,   90
pretend I haven't seen them,
or like I don't care
about all these missing breasts,
how they just vanish
from our aching chests   95
and no one says a word,
and we just strap on fake ones
and the dandelions keep dying,
and the grass on our lawns
gets greener and greener   100
and greener

4

This gold and red autumn heat,
this glorious tree splendour,
splayed out for sheer pleasure
over asphalt and concrete,   105
ribbons of dark desire
driving us madly toward death,
perverse, presiding over
five o'clock traffic
like the queens on Church Street   110
grand in their carstopping
high heels and blond wigs
and blue makeup, darling,
so nice to see you, and what,
dear one, exactly was the rush?   115
Or oceans, vast beyond ridicule
or question, and who cares if it's
much too hot for November,
isn't it gorgeous, darling,
and even here, in this   120
most polluted spit of land
in Canada, with its heart
attack and cancer rates,
the trees can still knock
you out with their loveliness   125
so you just wanna drop

everything and weep, or laugh,
or gather up the gorgeous
leaves, falling, and throw yourself
into them like a dead man,   130
or a kid, or a dog,

5

O the brave deeds of men
M*E*N, that is, they with phalli
dangling from their thighs,
how they dazzle me with   135
their daring exploits
every time I cross the Detroit River
from down under, I mean,
who else could have given
themselves so grandly,   140
obediently, to this water god,
this fierce charlatan,
this glutton for sailors and young boys,
risking limbs and lives, wordlessly
wrestling primordial mud,   145
so that we, mothers and maids,
could go shopping across the border
and save ourselves twenty minutes
coming and going, chatting about
this and that, our feet never   150
leaving the car, never mind
the mouth of the tunnel
is haunted by bits and fragments
of shattered bone and looking
every time like Diana's bridge   155
in Paris, this is really grand, isn't it,
riding our cars under the river
and coming out the other side
illegal aliens, needing passports,
and feeling like we accomplished   160
something, snatched from
our busy lives, just being there

SKY Lee *b.* 1952

PORT ALBERNI, BRITISH COLUMBIA

'I want all our community art and writing to become part of mainstream culture,' says SKY (short for Sharon Kwan Ying) Lee. 'But we shouldn't have to *goy* (change). Canadian attitudes should change. . . . "Canadian" is not just hockey and apple pie. It means all kinds of things—anything from any immigrant, new or old—because we're all immigrants here. None of us have been in Canada long enough to set cultural standards for other people. . . . We've all been sucked in by these colonial in-group versus out-group values.' Lee's sense of Chinese Canadian identity is synonymous with her political consciousness as an artist.

She was born in Port Alberni, a mill town on Vancouver Island, British Columbia, to parents who did not participate in the community's life, in part because of their poverty but also because of the racism that surrounded them. Lee's father, born and raised in Victoria, married her mother in 1936 on one of his trips back to China. It was not, however, until 1951 that his wife and their three children arrived in Canada. Born about a year after her mother's immigration, Lee says that her parents' 'stubborn refusal to accept Canadian culture ironically boosted [her] identity'. As one of the few Chinese Canadian children in town, she 'learned basic survival techniques' and had her 'own tough neighborhood group': 'We were the clique of poor ethnics—Italians, Japanese, East Indians. There were enough of us from the wrong side of the tracks that I didn't suffer too much from not being invited to parties.' She began developing a different sense of identity in 1967, when her family moved to Vancouver. There she discovered not only that her Hong Kong friends did not speak Toisanese (the Taishan dialect of Chinese), but that they were also 'prejudiced against Canadian-born'. It was after her trip to China in 1972 that she saw her 'identity as definitely Canadian' and realized that the 'only *real* Chinese left in this world are the Chinese in China'.

In Vancouver, Lee became a member of the Asian Canadian Writers Workshop, founded by Jim Wong Chu, a writer who was instrumental in encouraging Lee to publish. While studying toward her BFA at the University of British Columbia, discouraged by the lack of support she encountered as a woman of colour, Lee joined the Makara Women's Art Collective (1976–7). Her visual work has appeared, among other places, in the children's book *Teach Me How to Fly, Skyfighter* (by Paul Yee) and in *Makara* magazine. Lee, who also holds a nursing diploma from Douglas College, works as a registered nurse to support herself and her son, Nathan Wong.

Lee's novel *Disappearing Moon Cafe* (1990), which was nominated for a Governor General's Award and was the winner of the City of Vancouver Book Award, chronicles the lives of four generations of Chinese Canadians. A family saga told from the point of view of Kae, it is, in effect, the novel she sets out to write by way of understanding the secrets of her family and her own needs as a woman who has just become a mother. Lee's second book, *Bellydancer* (1994), is a collection of stories. Written in a voice that she says is 'far more self-conscious' than that of her novel, these stories feature characters who, whether they be bag ladies, bellydancers, or lesbians, move in and out of situations that challenge the cultural barriers that have constructed the conventional notions of race, gender, and sexuality. 'I'm politicized enough', Lee says, 'to know that I want to look into cultural alternatives, and one of the most wonderful things about the '90s is that so many people are doing it. . . . Everybody's coming out with fantastic, inspiring ideas. So that kind of leaves me free as an artist to just fly off on my own tangent. I don't have to worry about being a representative of the community or whatever any more, I'm just like an artist on my own.'

from *Disappearing Moon Cafe*

Prologue

Search for Bones

WONG GWEI CHANG
1892

He remembered that by then he was worn out from fighting the wind. He had to stop and rest in a shaded spot, so he found a smooth, flat stone to sit on, beside a stream that meandered off around a sharp bend. He was bone-tired from all this walking, watching the land dry out and the trees thin out. He wasn't thirsty; he was hungry, the last of his provisions gone days ago. So very hungry, so very tired of quenching his thirst on cold mountain water, sweet as it was.

He wanted to complain out loud, 'Why send men out to starve to death?' But the wind snatched the words out of his mouth, and even he couldn't tell if he had spoken them or not. He looked up at the unsettled sky and realized that if a freak storm should happen, he would be finished. He slapped his knees and shook his head. Ill-equipped, ill-informed, he was doomed from the start.

Ha! he thought. A bone-searching expedition! We'll find bones all right, gleaming white, powdery in the hot sun, except they'll be our own. His feet ached relentlessly, throbbing cold from wading through ditches and icy creeks. Already, holes in the thinned soles of his borrowed boots.

'I suppose I should be damned grateful I am still alive to feel the ache!' he cursed out loud. Then there was the loneliness. He didn't want to think about the loneliness; it was the most dangerous struggle.

He didn't know why he'd been chosen. Perhaps because he was young and big, and had muscular shoulders. Maybe because his hair was thick and smooth, and not just black but blue-black. He had two whorls on the crown of his head—the sign of a non-conformist. He also had very big hands. Most likely the old men had liked his face and its look of kind innocence.

They said, 'This youth has a tender face, but he has the look of an old soul.'

'An old soul?' he asked when they leaned close, looking for promises.

'Yes,' they replied, 'you have been reincarnated many times. You have lived many lives fruitfully and have a deeper understanding of many things.' They told him that he must believe.

'Believe what!' he demanded.

'In your mission.'

'My mission is to search out the bones of those who have died on the iron road, so they can be sent back home . . . by you, the Benevolent Associations.'

'No!' the old eyes commanded brilliantly. 'It is more than that. To believe is to make it live! You must make your mission live, or else you will not succeed.'

Thus, they sent him into a trance. Around him, the mountain barricaded with trees reaching into the eternal mist, and the rain pressed down from the heavens. He felt totally hemmed in. His eyes untrained to see beyond the wall of wilderness, his heart unsuited to this deep, penetrating solitude. Hunger had already made him hallucinate, afraid of the rustling leaves and whistling animals.

So he thought she had to be a spirit when he met her. In this dreamlike state, he thought maybe he had died and she was another spirit here to guide him over to the other side.

'Look, a chinaman!' She crept up behind him and spoke in his language. He whirled around and his knees buckled under, the last of his strength not enough to contain his furious trembling. Meanwhile, she darted back into the safety of the under-brush and hid. He couldn't see her, but he could hear her laughing at him; the sounds gurgled like an infant's blown back and forth by the wind. The whole landscape wink-ing and flashing at him.

'You mock me, yet you don't dare show yourself to me,' he challenged, peering into a shimmering sea of leaves. 'Come out now!' he barked with bravado.

'Ah, so he speaks chinese,' the voice observed. Finally, a brown face peeped out of the stems and brambles. She was an indian girl, dressed in coarse brown clothing that made her invisible in the forest. Her mouth did not smile, but her eyes were friendly— a deer's soft gaze. He was astonished when she stepped out onto the tall grass.

'You speak chinese,' he said, indignant, unwilling to believe what he saw before him.

'My father is a chinaman, like you. His eyes are slits like yours. He speaks like you.' She spoke deliberately and demonstrated by pulling back the skin beside her dark, round eyes. He saw that she was wearing a crude cape made of a worn animal skin. A long blanket served as a skirt and covered her bare feet. A small basket hung across her chest and made her look stooped over. Yet she moved gracefully, swaying from side to side, small intense movements like a little brown bird. He stared like a crazy man, because he thought she would disappear if he didn't concentrate on her being.

'But you're a wild injun.' He spilled out the insults in front of her, but they were meaningless to her. In chinese, the words mocked, slanglike, 'yin-chin'.

'You look hungry, chinaman.' She tipped her head to one side as she looked him up and down. From her clothing, she drew out coiled strips of some kind of substance and held these out to him. 'My father tells me chinamen are always hungry.'

'I am not hungry,' he shot back. He could tell she was teasing him, and he was offended that she knew more than he did. She could tell he was hungry, that he had no more power*left, that in this wilderness he was lost.

'Ahh, he has no manners,' she exclaimed. He could only blink, astonished by this elegant rebuke from a 'siwashee', a girl, younger than he. It made him feel uncivilized, uncouth; the very qualities he had assigned so thoughtlessly to her, he realized, she was watching for in him.

It was then he recognized familiar features on her dark face. A melon-seed face, most admired in a beautiful woman. Her hairline high, inkstrokes by an artist's brush down both sides of her face. Cheeks caressed.

Ah, he thought, why be afraid of her! What was she but another human being? Why should she mean him harm? He stepped up to take whatever it was from her hand, but as he reached out, she sprang back, dropping the strange food behind her like one of those shy creatures who sense no great danger but move prudently out of range just in case. Again, he was surprised to see that she was wary of him. It emphasized the distance between them, as if she was not a human being as he was, or . . . as if he was not a human being as she was.

The food was seaweed, both crunchy and rubbery soft. As he chewed hungrily, she watched him and he watched her. After a while, she hoisted a heavily laden basket of freshly dug-up roots and bulbs up onto her back. She secured it with a wide band across her forehead. Her hand carried a slim stick, one end of which was dirtied, perhaps from digging the roots, and the other end of which was carved, perhaps bone. This she waved at him and called out, 'Come and sit!' nonchalantly as if the invitation was for any time, as if in a day or two he would not be dead of exposure. 'My father enjoys the company of his own kind. And he will be glad to help you find your way.'

'Yes,' he answered, his mouth full of gracefulness, 'perhaps I should have a word with your father.'

Then, as if the barren wasteland around him had magically opened and allowed him admittance, he followed her through dense thickets, up hills and down through ravines, a respectable distance between them. He marvelled at her bare feet, which padded softly along the forest floor without injury. Many times he sank to his knees, soaked in sweat, so tired he could hardly hold up his head. He was fearful that she would abandon him, but she paced her steps according to his strength and smiled encouragingly.

They followed the big river until they finally arrived at her home, which stood high up on the cliff side of a mountain overlooking the water. By then darkness had fallen and the wind was blowing fiercer than ever, the first raindrops of a storm about to descend.

He knew it was on a cliff because he could see the wide expanse of stars beyond the immediate trees, and he could hear rushing water far below them. She ran into the little cabin first, then a man and a woman came out and stood beside the door. They peered excitedly into the night, looking for their visitor.

'Come in!' said the man.

It was so dark, he couldn't see their faces. He just got the idea that they were older by their voices and the placid way they both moved.

'My name is Chen Gwok Fai. Come in and rest, sir! What is your precious surname, sir?'

'Wong,' he said, 'Wong Gwei Chang.'

Chen put his hands on Gwei Chang's shoulders and led him into the tiny cabin. Beside a small fire in the fireplace, Gwei Chang saw the girl kneeling, her hands in front of her, reaching for warmth. He noted the intelligence in her face, ignited by the firelight; hers was a beautiful face full of vision. He didn't remember anything else, because he fell unconscious right on the spot, and he slept for a long, long time. By the time he awakened, he had stayed for three years.

GWEI CHANG

1939

He was an old man now. And he played with his memories all day long. Or they played with him. He felt he must tell of a most peculiar dream he'd had around that period of his life when he went looking for the bones of dead chinamen strewn along the Canadian Pacific Railway, their ghosts sitting on the ties, some standing with one foot on the gleaming metal ribbon, waiting, grumbling. They were still waiting as much as half a century after the ribbon-cutting ceremony by the whites at the end of the line, forgotten as chinamen generally are.

In his dream, he was strolling down a street in a wealthy residential area of Victoria. He knew it was a street where rich people lived, because it was lined by fine old trees at neat intervals in front of each sprawling lawn. And he was troubled because he was about to turn down a job as a servant in one of these grand houses in order to go on a dangerous, almost senseless expedition. Not only was it going to be gruelling hard work, but the pay was a bad joke. Of course he knew that the rewards for the performance of such work would come later, but his family in China needed to eat now.

As he walked, he noticed some crested myna birds flitting back and forth, looking for nesting sites in the trees. They had a shrill, rasplike cry, which got on his nerves. In order to make himself feel better, he began to search the ground, hoping to spot a glimmer of gold in the dirt, convinced that the Gold Mountains weren't a myth at all. He got so crazed by this idea that he couldn't stop gawking at the sidewalk; then in a mad rush, he got down on his hands and knees, his hands groping and sifting the ground. He didn't care that he demeaned himself nosing through the dirt like a dog. Worse still, he panicked and started rummaging through the garbage cans. Whenever he glanced back, he noticed that the mynas were following him and were getting bigger, their black plumage and crests more and more distinct. But he was so intent on what he needed to do that he took little heed of them.

Suddenly, a huge shadow fell over him, and he heard the flapping of giant wings directly over his head. Unable to fight off his instincts, he crouched and his hands flew up to ward off attack, but he was too late. A bloodcurdling scream shattered his ears, and a windstorm caught him about the head and beat him to his knees. The rest was a blur, but he did manage a glimpse of the menace; huge wings of a black raven swooping down upon him. When its talons ripped into his flesh, he felt neither pain nor fear, just the sensation of being lifted into a flying dream.

KELORA CHEN

1892

Gwei Chang remembered being half-unconscious, with Old Man Chen telling him that it was the isolation that tore out a man's good senses. Then Chen told him that he had been delirious for days. 'The white men have a name for it. Cabin fever,' Chen laughed, 'cabin fever, he, he, he!' and made a grand gesture towards his surroundings. He was without a doubt a most peculiar man.

'I got this cabin from a white man,' Chen grinned foolishly. 'I climbed up here and found a white man dying of a festering gunshot wound, with his head in an indian woman's lap right here,' he pointed to the bed Gwei Chang was lying on. 'So, as he died, I just stayed and took over where he left off, you see. I took care of his woman like a wife and his cabin like a home. She had a daughter. Kelora—indian name. I taught her to speak Chinese. She's old enough to have a husband now,' Chen smiled down at Gwei Chang.

Gwei Chang didn't know whether he could believe Chen. Chen told him lots of strange, elusive stories, but who knows which ones were true and which ones were fragments of his own fantasy? As far as Gwei Chang could make out, Chen had worked on the railroad. He also seemed to have participated in the gold rush over thirty years ago. He also might have come because of the tong wars in San Francisco. For sure, life was hard for a chinaman, and Chen would have had to give up something in order to survive.

Nevertheless, he obviously had led a very enchanted life by the time Gwei Chang happened along. Even though Old Man Chen wasn't a very good provider for himself, he survived very well, because Kelora was more than a good provider—she was also a healer and a retriever of lost souls. Her family on her mother's side was very wealthy, old and well-respected, so their people always made sure that little Kelora was given any little extra that they could spare, as well as her father, of course. They called him 'Father of Little Kelora.'

So, when Kelora went to her aunties and uncles and told them that her father had chosen a young man for her to marry, they must have known it was just a formality. Still, they all found excuses to drop by her home to take a look at the man 'whom Kelora's father had chosen for her'. Summertime was a busy time of year, but for Kelora's family of the Shi'atko clan in 'the village at the mouth of the two rivers', finding a husband for their sister's daughter was important too. Kelora always had been a bit of a worry for them because, although well loved, she had no rank. But, on the other hand, they knew a girl with Kelora's abilities really chose her own husband. Nothing wrong with that! Not everybody was sure about another chinaman, but Kelora seemed to prefer it, and that was enough for them.

Of course, Gwei Chang was quite unaware of all this. At the time, he thought that Kelora's relatives and people normally dropped by often and visited a lot. For instance, the old woman he had seen the first night was not her mother, who had died over seven years ago, but an old aunt who was visiting.

Another time Gwei Chang awoke, he asked for hot water. Kelora brought him a crude swamp tea which cooled him too fast and started him sweating profusely. Her numerous aunts and female cousins stood about, watching without really looking, as if they were trying to get a sense of him. But after a long sleep, waking was difficult and confusing, made even more abstract by a beautiful woman. Turning his back on all of them, he was about to settle into some more sleep when Kelora suggested he go and bathe in the river. Exposing his already weakened body to such inclement elements was a foreign and foolhardy idea, he thought, but there was a challenge in her voice that quickly restored him.

Along the rock face of the cliff was a natural ridge that led down to the riverside. It was not a difficult descent, but the terrain was unfamiliar and Gwei Chang was still wobbly. He felt slow and awkward beside the children and old women who ran ahead of him.

However, he impulsively plunged into the roiling waters, as there was no other way to do it. Energy such as he had never experienced vaulted through his body, and a cold, raw reward of strength filled every muscle. He flung out his arms and churned through the muddied green water for as long as his lungs could hold out. The river's forces, tortuous with fast-flowing currents, pulled him in all directions at once, but he had no sense of danger and did not struggle.

When he bounced back up to the surface, Kelora was kneeling by the river's edge. She was naked except for her long hair draped wet against her. Naturally, Gwei Chang was curious, so he swam a little closer to the shore. Her old aunts, perched on soapstone boulders around her, seemed to approve of what she was doing; shading their faces against the glare of water and sun, they peered at him as if there was a connection between what she was doing and him. She picked up a small snake and dropped it in front of her. It fell onto the fleshiness of her thighs, twisted itself into the water, and slithered off.

Gwei Chang was shy of Kelora at first, clumsily dodging her stares whenever he could. There was something very untamed about her. Her casual nakedness used to devour him. When she realized this, she toyed with him for her own amusement. The summer got very hot. His first instinct was to run, but always with a backwards glance that grew longer and longer until it made him swell; his fear of her made him wince with love.

Chen's cabin was situated on a very strategic spot. The same ridge which served as a convenient ramp up to his house spooned out into a sizable terrace on which his little log abode stood. It made a cozy sight—his little home and vegetable garden snuggled into the edge of a pine forest that crept in from the windward side of the mountain. And it made a welcome respite for the indians who travelled up and down this busy avenue of commerce—'grease trail' they called it, naming it after the much sought-after fish oil they ate. When they came by they always left a little token for their stay, because they recognized Kelora and her father to be the keepers of this picnic site. The exchange was fluid though, flowed both ways, depending on the seasons of nature. Often enough Kelora and her father would share their food with a boatload of impoverished guests. Either way, it made a good life for them.

One day, Gwei Chang stood on the very edge of the bluff to admire the far-reaching beauty of this tiny spot on earth. The view was breathtaking, like a windy crevice against heaven. It made him dizzy with joy, his toes curled over rock as he pressed his body up against the wind. As the chinese say, 'mountain and water': the delirious heights and bottomless depths flung him out into the clarity of the sky.

'A view like a soaring eagle's.' Kelora had followed him, and Gwei Chang could feel her soothing powers reach out for him. He looked at her as she stepped up to the ridge, and she looked at him, and they both smiled down at the world, because they knew then and there that they would fly together.

THE BONES

Gwei Chang remembered that, one evening, after a meal of rice, fresh salmon, and unfamiliar mushrooms, Old Chen said, 'I've been waiting for someone like you to come along for many years—so many years that I even forgot I was waiting.' He always looked at Gwei Chang as though he was going to burst into laughter at any time. He said that he knew of many burial sites and had heard of many people who knew of many more, though the bones must be dust by now.

'But the Benevolent Associations have already sent many on the same mission,' Gwei Chang replied.

'Yes, but they have not thought to come up here to ask chinaman Chen, have they?'

'Well, it is a little out of the way!' Gwei Chang felt obliged to say, glancing at Kelora whose eyes looked remote and made him want to follow. Already, he was forgetting that there was a whole other world with its own determined way of life out there, some-where, and that he was from there.

'What are your plans, boy?' There was no edge to Chen's question, merely a sense of duty that had to be recalled.

Gwei Chang turned to face him squarely. 'I'm not sure, Uncle.' He shrugged his shoulders. Of course, he thought he was just being modest. He had maps, with sec-tions of the railroad numbered. He pointed out the gravesites, haphazardly described at the end of each section. He'd been told that there would be markers, or cairns, or something. How hard could it be . . .

'Hah! You're a dunce!' Chen's expletive clipped him on the chin. 'Come with me! Bring your so-called maps!'

'Now? It's black out there.'

'Light, dark, what difference does it make,' Chen's voice boomed, 'when we've got brothers to send home.' Since Kelora didn't even blink an eye, Gwei Chang could only imagine that this kind of gesture was not at all out of the ordinary, so he followed Chen out into the moonlit forest.

After a two-hour trek, mostly along the train tracks made silver now and then by an isolated moonbeam, Chen led Gwei Chang to the first of many leftover work camp gangs. This one, an independent group of gold dredgers, dour and suspicious, was camped out on the edge of a clearing beside a stream. That late at night, there were no words wasted. The only remark was from a watchman, that Old Man Chen had come. Gwei Chang was thrown a rag to sleep under, and he wandered about until he found some rotten barrels that would support a plank of sorts, and a sluice box. That was his bed for several nights.

In the morning, Gwei Chang shared their cold rice while they scrutinized his maps and criticized his information. Then he was given a shovel. They talked while they worked. That's how Gwei Chang found out a few things. He found out that old overseas chinese never wasted anything—not their time, not their leisure. They worked unceasingly, as if they would fall apart if they ever stopped. They also sat up all night, gossiping and swearing and laughing. They were strange men, maybe because of the shadow of loneliness and isolation that hovered over them. In their midst, Chen seemed less peculiar to Gwei Chang. In fact, Chen was well liked and a regular visitor. Because Gwei Chang came with Chen, he was immediately a friend. When Chen told them what Gwei Chang was doing, he was taken seriously at once.

News of Gwei Chang and his work went ahead of him. Eventually, he could stroll into any bull gang or small Chinatown, onto any farm or campsite, and they would have been expecting him, ready to share food and whatever else he needed. Over and over again, he watched groups shed their surliness at his approach and spread in front of him all that they had from their pitiful little hovels.

At first, he didn't value their reverence for him. Thinking back, he knew how unthinking he had been then, grabbing opportunities for fun—sitting up all night, gossiping, selfishly filling his pockets with goods and information to make his work easier. He saw the loneliness in the brothers, toiling, poor—left behind to rot because the CPR had reneged on its contract to pay the chinese railway workers' passage home. But he felt only a little disdain for them. He was fresh off the boat from China. When they hankered for news from their villages, he thought he was doing them a real big favour by telling them stories. He was too young, and he didn't understand.

Not until he touched the bones. When he finally did, he was awed by them. At first, he actually dreaded the macabre work. What were a few dried bones to him, except disgusting? But the spirits in the mountains were strong and persuasive. The bones gathered themselves into the human shapes of young men, each dashing and bold. They followed him about wherever he roamed, whispered to him, until he knew each one to be a hero, with yearnings from the same secret places in his own heart.

How could he not be touched by the spirit of these wilderness uncles who had trekked on an incredible journey and pitted their lives against mountain rocks and human cruelty? In the perfect silence of a hot afternoon, he used to stop here and there to run his hands along the sheer rock face of a mountain, the surface still biting hot from a dynamite blast. He imagined the mountain shuddering, roaring out in pain, demanding human sacrifice for this profanity. And the real culprits held out blood-splattered chinamen in front of them like a protective talisman.

By then, he understood. By then, in the utter peace of the forests, he had met them all—uncles who had climbed mountain heights then fallen from them, uncles who had drowned in deep surging waters, uncles who had clawed to their deaths in the dirt of caved-in mines. By then, he wasn't afraid and they weren't alien any more. Like them, he would piece himself together again from scattered, shattered bone and then endure.

The next time Gwei Chang walked into a work camp, he was ready to share with them instead of taking from them. He took on their surliness and learned to talk tough and blunt, a chiselled edge to his words to express the backbreaking task of survival that all of them shared day after day. They talked like comrades-in-arms after the battle, still grateful to feel the ache of so many work-worn years, to fill their lungs with mountain mist, to see their shadows walk ahead of them, homesick.

When Kelora took him into the forests of 'the hidden place', another world opened up. She had a way of murmuring as they walked. Gwei Chang remembered chinese women doing the very same.

'We go into the forest,' she might say. 'It's old. Look at how big the trees are.' He watched her as she smiled up at the canopy of wind-swept boughs against a glorious sky. Her braids fell away from her ears, exposing an earlobe that looked inviting, as if it would taste sweet.

'It is hot outside, but in here, it is always cool and wet,' she said. When he tore his eyes away from her, he looked up, and wished she could have shot him like an arrow, straight up into the endless blue.

'Look, a yellow cedar tree! If I need to gather cedar, then I have to say a few words to the tree, to thank the tree for giving part of itself up to me. I take only a small part too, but not today. Look, the path is worn and smooth. Many women have come here to gather what they need. When we walk in the forest, we say "we walk with our grand-mothers".' She wore a cotton shift, faded gingham against her deep brown skin. Her baskets, mats and hat hung by a thong behind her left shoulder.

'Look at that swampy place!' Kelora tugged on his arm, and Gwei Chang beamed down on her. 'See there! We call those rushes "the geese eat it" plant. The women say to boil it for medicine when some old men can't urinate.' This reduced them to gig-gles. She gave him a playful push that landed him in a garden of ferns. And he lunged at her, but she took off like a little bird.

Kelora and Gwei Chang wandered high and low in the summers, like deer forag-ing through new pastures, like children. Summertime gathering was women's work, and Kelora would have to go and gather her berries, dawn until dusk sometimes. And Gwei Chang would have to go and find his bones. Yet they found many ways to flow together, like wind brushing against leaves. Like lake and lakeshore, a slow meander-ing dance of lovers.

He would help her pound her berries, and she would help him scrape bones and carefully stack them into neat bundles. She wasn't afraid and seemed to understand the rituals that had to be performed around them. More amazing, she had a peculiar intui-tion for locating gravesites whose markers had long ago deteriorated. More than once, she wandered ahead of him; by the time Gwei Chang caught up, she would be point-ing at the site where he was to dig. These occasions made his skin crawl. She laughed at him, tittering behind a cupped hand.

When he asked her how she knew, she said, 'Chinaman, first listen to yourself sing! Every soul has its own voice.'

Chinamen are a superstitious bunch. Gwei Chang got to wondering what she heard. Before he became a human being himself, he mistook her meaning. Kelora was a strange one, with her own private language—neither chinese nor indian, but from deep within the wildness of her soul. Fascinated, he began to press his ear against the ground too. He followed her everywhere, even as she went about her woman's work. She taught him to love the same mother earth and to see her sloping curves in the mountains. He forgot that he had once thought of them as barriers. He learned how to cling onto her against a raging river, or bury into her away from the pelting rain. Or he could be somewhere, anywhere, cold and bone-tired, but he would stare at the consummate beauty of a bare branch trembling in the breeze. He would watch red buds bloom into freshly peeled blossoms. Clouds tinted pink-gold, slanting over the mirror of an alpine lake; this beautiful mother filled his heart and soul.

Old Chen came at Gwei Chang with two questions at the same time. He asked, 'How are you going to transport those bones down to the coast?'

He also asked, 'Do you have anything you can give me as a gift? If you don't have anything, then I'll give you something to give back to me.'

Gwei Chang played dumb. 'Huh?'

'It's the custom,' Chen said, 'to give a gift when you take a wife. Even nowadays.' Kelora's maternal aunt shuffled in and out of the cabin, excitedly shouting at the young boys who had followed her up the bluff, carrying fifty-pound bags of flour in their arms.

'I have a gold watch,' Gwei Chang replied without hesitation, 'and a bowie knife I bought off a drunk demon in Spuzzum. Oh yes, those farmers gave me six Hudson's Bay Company blankets in exchange for a few days' work—used but not worn out.'

Chen looked relieved. Gwei Chang didn't let on that he had been preparing all along. By then, he was well aware of what caught Kelora's eyes and what didn't.

'Not bad,' Chen said, 'not bad at all for a boy who was starving, eating "chinook" wind just a while back! Go with Kelora and give them all to her people. Politely! You and me, of course, we can forego the usual ceremony. They're just to keep the women happy anyway.'

The other question was not so easily answered. Gwei Chang knew it would provoke some controversy because he had already tried it on some elders in the Chinatown at North Bend. He figured Chen must have surely heard about his idea by now. He could well imagine the indignant sputters Chen would have had to face.

'You know what that crazy Wong boy was thinking about? Him and that hothead, Lee Chong. Did they get that stupid idea from you? People have been saying that that crazy old Chen had a hand in it. Who else!'

Gwei Chang had a wonderful idea! Lee Chong thought it was a good idea too. Kelora said it was worth a try. When you're young and stupidly proud, everything is worth a try. Lee Chong was a small, wiry fellow—face like a rat in those days. He had quit his laundry job in a huff, and when Gwei Chang met up with him, he was on his way back to Victoria. Lee Chong came up to Gwei Chang and asked if he would give him a job.

'Yeah,' Gwei Chang said, 'I need someone to take the bones all the way back down to Victoria.' Lee Chong looked enthusiastic, which was a relief to him. It wasn't easy trying to find someone who didn't mind hauling a load of skeletons back down the old Cariboo Road, through hostile territory ridden with whites, and camping out alone with ghosts in the mountains, in the dark.

Gwei Chang asked if Lee Chong had a horse and wagon. 'Nope,' he said, 'don't you?'

Lee Chong and Gwei Chang hit it off right away. It was the height of summer then, and Lee Chong didn't have much trouble finding odd jobs here and there, picking fruit, hand to mouth, so to speak, while he waited around for Gwei Chang to make up his mind. Lee Chong wasn't in any hurry. By then, Gwei Chang had been very successful at his bone-searching expedition and thought much of himself.

The Benevolent Associations hadn't given Gwei Chang any specific instructions on how to get the bones to Victoria. The assumption had been that the first bone searchers would find their own way, with the minimum of expense and manpower. All the monies for their transport had been donated, and there were so many bones left still. This was in 1892, the beginning of the retrieval of bones, which lasted well into the 1930s.

Gwei Chang had travelled up and down the Fraser Canyon and watched many an indian canoe skimming down the white rapids, the travellers whooping and hollering, their hair plastered straight back behind their heads. He thought it an exhilarating way to travel! Those raging waters mesmerized him. They didn't seem like dangerous obstacles. Then, one day, he saw white men, on axe-hewn rafts, come dancing around the bend, men and boxes securely tied down with a strong network of ropes. That decided him. What could be easier?

'Look,' he said to Lee Chong, 'I don't have a wagon, but I've got something better, faster. More challenging.'

Lee Chong and Gwei Chang started to build their craft. They asked around to find out how. They traded with indians for handwoven cedar ropes, and the indians told them which trees were the most buoyant; the hardwood for sternposts; tough flexibility for poles and hand-hewn rudders.

The other chinamen fumed, 'If you capsize and spill your cracked brains, that's OK by us, but if you lose any bones, you're condemning human spirits to ten thousand years of aimless wandering.'

Lee Chong and Gwei Chang saw things differently. They told each other, 'Old women, every one of them! Got no gall! We just want to give the spirits of those mountain heroes one last thrilling ride.' Lee Chong and Gwei Chang figured the spirits would laugh at peril. After all, they had died for adventure and daring. Why should they object now?

When they finished lashing their craft together, Lee Chong and Gwei Chang figured it could fall down hundreds of feet of a waterfall without splintering. They were ready to bet their lives on it, but were the dead ones prepared to risk their souls on another long shot?

Well, in order to avoid the wrong people answering that question, early at dawn the next morning, with cedar boxes full of bones lashed down in the centre of the raft, Lee Chong and Gwei Chang pushed off. Once out of Chen's protective cul-de-sac, the eddies of the big river grabbed the craft and threw them along the most dizzying, joyful ride of their lives.

The sun shone through the fine mist spray which lifted out of the river and doused them with fancy. They just let the river take them. Sometimes the river was calm and giving; sometimes it knocked their senses askew. The world encircling them was raw and beautiful. The life that blew into them was inspiring and intoxicating. They careened along, hemmed in by the steep rise of gorges and canyon cliffs. Sometimes the river was fretful, contorting back on itself, treacherous. Other times, the river sprawled and meandered through pastures and rich flatlands; they glided along its shimmering reflections. The pair felt like they had ridden the river dragon, and it had lifted their souls skyward. At the end of their journey, they walked away transformed, feeling a little closer to immortality.

Gwei Chang parted ways with the bones at the bone-house in Victoria and with Lee Chong on Tang People's Street, and began his trek back home to Kelora.

Rohinton Mistry *b.* 1952

BOMBAY, INDIA

'One must write for the sake of writing, to create good literature,' says Rohinton Mistry. 'The other things follow in a very natural way. I grew up in Bombay. Now I am here [Canada]. I'm a writer. I am determined to write good literature. . . . But to write well, I must write about what I know best. In that way, I automatically speak for my "tribe".' Mistry's 'tribe' is the Parsi community in Mumbai, India, where he was born. The Parsi characters in his fiction, and 'their dreams, ambitions, and fears, are as accessible to the Western reader as the Indian reader. The universalities of the story are sufficient.' Mistry believes that many of the themes taken to be the recurring motifs in immigrant literature are not just that: 'I don't think this looking forward and yearning backward is restricted to an immigrant. It's a universal phenomenon.' Though this may be true, the universalism characterizing his fiction, along with the many allusions to Western literary texts and paradigms, reveals Mistry's indebtedness to the West, perhaps one of the reasons the Parsi community in Mumbai has not always responded favourably to Mistry's representation of it. Ironically, while someone like Germaine Greer dismisses his accounts of life in India because he writes in Canada, John Metcalfe questions his Canadianness because he writes mostly about India.

Mistry received a BSc in mathematics and economics from the University of Bombay (1974) before immigrating to Toronto in 1975. He worked for ten years in a bank while studying English literature and philosophy part-time at the University of Toronto (BA, 1984). He began writing full-time in 1983 after winning the university-sponsored Hart House Prize for each of his first two short stories. Describing himself as 'a traditional writer. I am not trying to break new ground or pioneer new techniques,' Mistry published his first book to high acclaim. *Tales from Firozsha Baag* (1987), which was shortlisted for a Governor General's Award, is a collection of interlinked stories about Kensi, a young man and an aspiring writer, his childhood years in Mumbai and his later life in Canada. 'Swimming Lessons', the story included here, in which Kensi sends his first manuscript of stories to his parents back home, is the final story in the collection.

Mistry's first novel, *Such a Long Journey* (1991), received the Governor General's Award, the Commonwealth Writers Prize, and the W.H. Smith–Books in Canada First Novel Award; it was also a finalist for the Booker Prize. Set in Mumbai in 1971, the action takes place, as Mistry says, 'more than a thousand miles away' from the war between India and Pakistan that resulted in the creation of what is now Bangladesh. His third novel, *A Fine Balance* (1995), won the Giller Prize and the Irish Times International Fiction Prize. Set in both urban and rural India, it spans the years between 1975 and 1984 in the lives of an uncle and his nephew, two tanners, both of them 'untouchable' in the Hindu caste system, whose destinies converge with those of numerous other characters. *Family Matters* (2002), also nominated for the Booker Prize, deals with the tensions between Parsis and 'others', while focusing on a Parsi widower and his daughter's and stepchildren's response to his advanced age and ailing body. Treated as an 'other' himself while on tour to promote this novel in the US at the height of its anti-terrorist security meas-ures, Mistry interrupted his journey to return to Canada.

Mistry, who lives in Brampton, Ontario, does not try to write by way of moulding himself as a writer to what he says are the expectations 'in the establishment': 'I think they feel that when a person arrives here from a different culture, if that person is a writer, he must have some profound observations about the meeting of the two cultures. And he must write about racism. He must write about multiculturalism. He has an area of expertise foisted on him that he may not necessarily want, or which may not really interest him. He may not want to be an expert in race relations.' Mistry's impetus as a writer lies in his desire to be a storyteller.

Swimming Lessons

The old man's wheelchair is audible today as he creaks by in the hallway: on some days it's just a smooth whirr. Maybe the way he slumps in it, or the way his weight rests has something to do with it. Down to the lobby he goes, and sits there most of the time, talking to people on their way out or in. That's where he first spoke to me a few days ago. I was waiting for the elevator, back from Eaton's with my new pair of swimming-trunks.

'Hullo,' he said. I nodded, smiled.

'Beautiful summer day we've got.'

'Yes,' I said, 'it's lovely outside.'

He shifted the wheelchair to face me squarely. 'How old do you think I am?'

I looked at him blankly, and he said, 'Go on, take a guess.'

I understood the game; he seemed about seventy-five although the hair was still black, so I said, 'Sixty-five?' He made a sound between a chuckle and a wheeze: 'I'll be seventy-seven next month.' Close enough.

I've heard him ask that question several times since, and everyone plays by the rules. Their faked guesses range from sixty to seventy. They pick a lower number when he's more depressed than usual. He reminds me of Grandpa as he sits on the sofa in the lobby, staring out vacantly at the parking lot. Only difference is, he sits with the stillness of stroke victims, while Grandpa's Parkinson's disease would bounce his thighs and legs and arms all over the place. When he could no longer hold the *Bombay Samachar* steady enough to read, Grandpa took to sitting on the veranda and staring emptily at the traffic passing outside Firozsha Baag. Or waving to anyone who went by in the compound: Rustomji, Nariman Hansotia in his 1932 Mercedes-Benz, the fat ayah Jaakaylee with her shopping-bag, the *kuchrawalli* with her basket and long bamboo broom.

The Portuguese woman across the hall has told me a little about the old man. She is the communicator for the apartment building. To gather and disseminate information, she takes the liberty of unabashedly throwing open her door when newsworthy events transpire. Not for Portuguese Woman the furtive peerings from thin cracks or spyholes. She reminds me of a character in a movie, *Barefoot In The Park* I think it was, who left empty beer cans by the landing for anyone passing to stumble and give her the signal. But PW does not need beer cans. The gutang-khutang of the elevator opening and closing is enough.

The old man's daughter looks after him. He was living alone till his stroke, which coincided with his youngest daughter's divorce in Vancouver. She returned to him and they moved into this low-rise in Don Mills. PW says the daughter talks to no one in the building but takes good care of her father.

Mummy used to take good care of Grandpa, too, till things became complicated and he was moved to the Parsi General Hospital. Parkinsonism and osteoporosis laid him low. The doctor explained that Grandpa's hip did not break because he fell, but he fell because the hip, gradually growing brittle, snapped on that fatal day. That's what osteoporosis does, hollows out the bones and turns effect into cause. It has an unusually high incidence in the Parsi community, he said, but did not say why. Just one of those mysterious things. We are the chosen people where osteoporosis is concerned. And divorce. The Parsi community has the highest divorce rate in India. It also claims to be the most westernized community in India. Which is the result of the other? Confusion again, of cause and effect.

The hip was put in traction. Single-handed, Mummy struggled valiantly with bedpans and dressings for bedsores which soon appeared like grim spectres on his back. *Mamaiji*, bent double with her weak back, could give no assistance. My help would be enlisted to roll him over on his side while Mummy changed the dressing. But after three months, the doctor pronounced a patch upon Grandpa's lungs, and the male ward of Parsi General swallowed him up. There was no money for a private nursing home. I went to see him once, at Mummy's insistence. She used to say that the blessings of an old person were the most valuable and potent of all, they would last my whole life long. The ward had rows and rows of beds; the din was enormous, the smells nauseating, and it was just as well that Grandpa passed most of his time in a less than conscious state.

But I should have gone to see him more often. Whenever Grandpa went out, while he still could in the days before parkinsonism, he would bring back pink and white sugar-coated almonds for Percy and me. Every time I remember Grandpa, I remember that; and then I think: I should have gone to see him more often. That's what I also thought when our telephone-owning neighbour, esteemed by all for that reason, sent his son to tell us the hospital had phoned that Grandpa died an hour ago.

The postman rang the doorbell the way he always did, long and continuous; Mother went to open it, wanting to give him a piece of her mind but thought better of it, she did not want to risk the vengeance of postmen, it was so easy for them to destroy letters; workers nowadays thought no end of themselves, strutting around like peacocks, ever since all this

Shiv Sena agitation about Maharashtra or Maharashtrians, threatening strikes and Bombay bundh all the time, with no respect for the public; bus drivers and conductors were the worst, behaving as if they owned the buses and were doing favours to commuters, pulling the bell before you were in the bus, the driver purposely braking and moving with big jerks to make the standees lose their balance, the conductor so rude if you did not have the right change.

But when she saw the airmail envelope with a Canadian stamp her face lit up, she said wait to the postman, and went in for a fifty paisa piece, a little baksheesh for you, she told him, then shut the door and kissed the envelope, went in running, saying my son has written, my son has sent a letter, and Father looked up from the newspaper and said, don't get too excited, first read it, you know what kind of letters he writes, a few lines of empty words, I'm fine, hope you are all right, your loving son—that kind of writing I don't call letter-writing.

Then Mother opened the envelope and took out one small page and began to read silently, and the joy brought to her face by the letter's arrival began to ebb; Father saw it happening and knew he was right, he said read aloud, let me also hear what our son is writing this time, so Mother read: My dear Mummy and Daddy, Last winter was terrible, we had record-breaking low temperatures all through February and March, and the first official day of spring was colder than the first official day of winter had been, but it's getting warmer now. Looks like it will be a nice warm summer. You asked about my new apartment. It's small, but not bad at all. This is just a quick note to let you know I'm fine, so you won't worry about me. Hope everything is okay at home.

After Mother put it back in the envelope, Father said everything about his life is locked in silence and secrecy, I still don't understand why he bothered to visit us last year if he had nothing to say; every letter of his has been a quick note so we won't worry—what does he think we worry about, his health, in that country everyone eats well whether they work or not, he should be worrying about us with all the black market and rationing, has he forgotten already how he used to go to the ration-shop and wait in line every week; and what kind of apartment description is that, not bad at all; and if it is a Canadian weather report I need from him, I can go with Nariman Hansotia from A Block to the Cawasji Framji Memorial Library and read all about it, there they get newspapers from all over the world.

The sun is hot today. Two women are sunbathing on the stretch of patchy lawn at the periphery of the parking lot. I can see them clearly from my kitchen. They're wearing bikinis and I'd love to take a closer look. But I have no binoculars. Nor do I have a car to saunter out to and pretend to look under the hood. They're both luscious and gleaming. From time to time they smear lotion over their skin, on the bellies, on the inside of the thighs, on the shoulders. Then one of them gets the other to undo the string of her top and spread some there. She lies on her stomach with the straps undone. I wait. I pray that the heat and haze make her forget, when it's time to turn over, that the straps are undone.

But the sun is not hot enough to work this magic for me. When it's time to come in, she flips over, deftly holding up the cups, and reties the top. They arise, pick up towels, lotions and magazines, and return to the building.

This is my chance to see them closer. I race down the stairs to the lobby. The old man says hullo. 'Down again?'

'My mailbox,' I mumble.

'It's Saturday,' he chortles. For some reason he finds it extremely funny. My eye is on the door leading in from the parking lot.

Through the glass panel I see them approaching. I hurry to the elevator and wait. In the dimly lit lobby I can see their eyes are having trouble adjusting after the bright sun. They don't seem as attractive as they did from the kitchen window. The elevator arrives and I hold it open, inviting them in with what I think is a gallant flourish. Under the fluorescent glare in the elevator I see their wrinkled skin, aging hands, sagging bottoms, varicose veins. The lustrous trick of sun and lotion and distance has ended.

I step out and they continue to the third floor. I have Monday night to look forward to, my first swimming lesson. The high school behind the apartment building is offering, among its usual assortment of macramé and ceramics and pottery classes, a class for non-swimming adults.

The woman at the registration desk is quite friendly. She even gives me the opening to satisfy the compulsion I have about explaining my non-swimming status.

'Are you from India?' she asks. I nod. 'I hope you don't mind my asking, but I was curious because an Indian couple, husband and wife, also registered a few minutes ago. Is swimming not encouraged in India?'

'On the contrary,' I say. 'Most Indians swim like fish. I'm an exception to the rule. My house was five minutes walking distance from Chaupatty beach in Bombay. It's one of the most beautiful beaches in Bombay, or was, before the filth took over. Anyway, even though we lived so close to it, I never learned to swim. It's just one of those things.'

'Well,' says the woman, 'that happens sometimes. Take me, for instance. I never learned to ride a bicycle. It was the mounting that used to scare me, I was afraid of falling.' People have lined up behind me. 'It's been very nice talking to you,' she says, 'hope you enjoy the course.'

The art of swimming had been trapped between the devil and the deep blue sea. The devil was money, always scarce, and kept the private swimming clubs out of reach; the deep blue sea of Chaupatty beach was grey and murky with garbage, too filthy to swim in. Every so often we would muster our courage and Mummy would take me there to try and teach me. But a few minutes of paddling was all we could endure. Sooner or later something would float up against our legs or thighs or waists, depending on how deep we'd gone in, and we'd be revulsed and stride out to the sand.

Water imagery in my life is recurring. Chaupatty beach, now the high-school swimming pool. The universal symbol of life and regeneration did nothing but frustrate me. Perhaps the swimming pool will overturn that failure.

When images and symbols abound in this manner, sprawling or rolling across the page without guile or artifice, one is prone to say, how obvious, how skilless; symbols, after all, should be still and gentle as dewdrops, tiny, yet shining with a world of meaning. But what happens when, on the page of life itself, one encounters the ever-moving, all-engirdling sprawl of the filthy sea? Dewdrops and oceans both have their rightful places; Nariman Hansotia certainly knew that when he told his stories to the boys of Firozsha Baag.

The sea of Chaupatty was fated to endure the finales of life's everyday functions. It seemed that the dirtier it became, the more crowds it attracted: street urchins and beggars and beachcombers, looking through the junk that washed up. (Or was it the crowds that made it dirtier?—another instance of cause and effect blurring and evading identification.)

Too many religious festivals also used the sea as repository for their finales. Its use should have been rationed, like rice and kerosene. On Ganesh Chaturthi, clay idols of the god Ganesh, adorned with garlands and all manner of finery, were carried in processions to the accompaniment of drums and a variety of wind instruments. The music got more frenzied the closer the procession got to Chaupatty and to the moment of immersion.

Then there was Coconut Day, which was never as popular as Ganesh Chaturthi. From a bystander's viewpoint, coconuts chucked into the sea do not provide as much of a spectacle. We used the sea, too, to deposit the leftovers from Parsi religious ceremonies, things such as flowers, or the ashes of the sacred sandalwood fire, which just could not be dumped with the regular garbage but had to be entrusted to the care of Avan Yazad, the guardian of the sea. And things which were of no use but which no one had the heart to destroy were also given to Avan Yazad. Such as old photographs.

After Grandpa died, some of his things were flung out to sea. It was high tide; we always checked the newspaper when going to perform these disposals; an ebb would mean a long walk in squelchy sand before finding water. Most of the things were probably washed up on shore. But we tried to throw them as far out as possible, then waited a few minutes; if they did not float back right away we would pretend they were in the permanent safekeeping of Avan Yazad, which was a comforting thought. I can't remember everything we sent out to sea, but his brush and comb were in the parcel, his *kusti*, and some Kemadrin pills, which he used to take to keep the parkinsonism under control.

Our paddling session stopped for lack of enthusiasm on my part. Mummy wasn't too keen either, because of the filth. But my main concern was the little guttersnipes, like naked fish with little buoyant penises, taunting me with their skills, swimming underwater and emerging unexpectedly all around me, or pretending to masturbate— I think they were too young to achieve ejaculation. It was embarrassing. When I look back, I'm surprised that Mummy and I kept going as long we did.

I examine the swimming-trunks I bought last week. Surf King, says the label, Made in Canada–Fabriqué Au Canada. I've been learning bits and pieces of French from bilingual labels at the supermarket too. These trunks are extremely sleek and streamlined hipsters, the distance from waistband to pouch tip the barest minimum. I wonder how everything will stay in place, not that I'm boastful about my endowments. I try them on, and feel that the tip of my member lingers perilously close to the exit. Too close, in fact, to conceal the exigencies of my swimming lesson fantasy: a gorgeous woman in the class for non-swimmers, at whose sight I will be instantly aroused, and she, spying the shape of my desire, will look me straight in the eye with her intentions;

she will come home with me, to taste the pleasures of my delectable Asian brown body whose strangeness has intrigued her and unleashed uncontrollable surges of passion inside her throughout the duration of the swimming lesson.

I drop the Eaton's bag and wrapper in the garbage can. The swimming-trunks cost fifteen dollars, same as the fee for the ten weekly lessons. The garbage bag is almost full. I tie it up and take it outside. There is a medicinal smell in the hallway; the old man must have just returned to his apartment.

PW opens her door and says, 'Two ladies from the third floor were lying in the sun this morning. In bikinis.'

'That's nice,' I say, and walk to the incinerator chute. She reminds me of Najamai in Firozsha Baag, except that Najamai employed a bit more subtlety while going about her life's chosen work.

PW withdraws and shuts her door.

Mother had to reply because Father said he did not want to write to his son till his son had something sensible to write to him, his questions had been ignored long enough, and if he wanted to keep his life a secret, fine, he would get no letters from his father.

But after Mother started the letter he went and looked over her shoulder, telling her what to ask him, because if they kept on writing the same questions, maybe he would understand how interested they were in knowing about things over there; Father said go on, ask him what his work is at the insurance company, tell him to take some courses at night school, that's how everyone moves ahead over there, tell him not to be discouraged if his job is just clerical right now, hard work will get him ahead, remind him he is a Zoroastrian: manashni, gavashni, kunashni, better write the translation also: good thoughts, good words, good deeds—he must have forgotten what it means, and tell him to say prayers and do kusti *at least twice a day.*

Writing it all down sadly, Mother did not believe he wore his sudra *and* kusti *any more, she would be very surprised if he remembered any of the prayers; when she had asked him if he needed new* sudras *he said not to take any trouble because the Zoroastrian Society of Ontario imported them from Bombay for their members, and this sounded like a story he was making up, but she was leaving it in the hands of God, ten thousand miles away there was nothing she could do but write a letter and hope for the best.*

Then she sealed it, and Father wrote the address on it as usual because his writing was much neater than hers, handwriting was important in the address and she did not want the postman in Canada to make any mistake; she took it to the post office herself, it was impossible to trust anyone to mail it ever since the postage rates went up because people just tore off the stamps for their own use and threw away the letter, the only safe way was to hand it over the counter and make the clerk cancel the stamps before your own eyes.

Berthe, the building superintendent, is yelling at her son in the parking lot. He tinkers away with his van. This happens every fine-weathered Sunday. It must be the van that Berthe dislikes because I've seen mother and son together in other quite amicable situations.

Berthe is a big Yugoslavian with high cheekbones. Her nationality was disclosed to me by PW. Berthe speaks a very rough-hewn English, I've overheard her in the lobby scolding tenants for late rents and leaving dirty lint screens in the dryers. It's exciting to listen to her, her words fall like rocks and boulders, and one can never tell where or how the next few will drop. But her Slavic yells at her son are a different matter, the words fly swift and true, well-aimed missiles that never miss. Finally, the son slams down the hood in disgust, wipes his hands on a rag, accompanies mother Berthe inside.

Berthe's husband has a job in a factory. But he loses several days of work every month when he succumbs to the booze, a word Berthe uses often in her Slavic tirades on those days, the only one I can understand, as it clunks down heavily out of the tight-flying formation of Yugoslavian sentences. He lolls around in the lobby, submitting passively to his wife's tongue-lashings. The bags under his bloodshot eyes, his stringy moustache, stubbled chin, dirty hair are so vulnerable to the poison-laden barbs (poison works the same way in any language) emanating from deep within the powerful watermelon bosom. No one's presence can embarrass or dignify her into silence.

No one except the old man who arrives now. 'Good morning,' he says, and Berthe turns, stops yelling, and smiles. Her husband rises, positions the wheelchair at the favourite angle. The lobby will be peaceful as long as the old man is there.

It was hopeless. My first swimming lesson. The water terrified me. When did that happen, I wonder, I used to love splashing at Chaupatty, carried about by the waves. And this was only a swimming pool. Where did all that terror come from? I'm trying to remember.

Armed with my Surf King I enter the high school and go to the pool area. A sheet with instructions for the new class is pinned to the bulletin board. All students must shower and then assemble at eight by the shallow end. As I enter the showers three young boys, probably from a previous class, emerge. One of them holds his nose. The second begins to hum, under his breath: Paki Paki, smell like curry. The third says to the first two: pretty soon all the water's going to taste of curry. They leave.

It's a mixed class, but the gorgeous woman of my fantasy is missing. I have to settle for another, in a pink one-piece suit, with brown hair and a bit of a stomach. She must be about thirty-five. Plain-looking.

The instructor is called Ron. He gives us a pep talk, sensing some nervousness in the group. We're finally all in the water, in the shallow end. He demonstrates floating on the back, then asks for a volunteer. The pink one-piece suit wades forward. He supports her, tells her to lean back and let her head drop in the water.

She does very well. And as we all regard her floating body, I see what was not visible outside the pool: her bush, curly bits of it, straying out at the pink Spandex V. Tongues of water lapping against her delta, as if caressing it teasingly, make the brown hair come alive in a most tantalizing manner. The crests and troughs of little waves, set off by the movement of our bodies in a circle around her, dutifully irrigate her; the curls alternately wave free inside the crest, then adhere to her wet thighs, beached by the inevitable trough. I could watch this forever, and I wish the floating demonstration would never end.

Next we are shown how to grasp the rail and paddle, face down in the water. Between practising floating and paddling, the hour is almost gone. I have been trying to observe the pink one-piece suit, getting glimpses of her straying pubic hair from various angles. Finally, Ron wants a volunteer for the last demonstration, and I go forward. To my horror he leads the class to the deep end. Fifteen feet of water. It is so blue, and I can see the bottom. He picks up a metal hoop attached to a long wooden stick. He wants me to grasp the hoop, jump in the water, and paddle, while he guides me by the stick. Perfectly safe, he tells me. A demonstration of how paddling propels the body.

It's too late to back out; besides, I'm so terrified I couldn't find the words to do so even if I wanted to. Everything he says I do as if in a trance. I don't remember the moment of jumping. The next thing I know is, I'm swallowing water and floundering, hanging on to the hoop for dear life. Ron draws me to the rails and helps me out. The class applauds.

We disperse and one thought is on my mind: what if I'd lost my grip? Fifteen feet of water under me. I shudder and take deep breaths. This is it. I'm not coming next week. This instructor is an irresponsible person. Or he does not value the lives of non-white immigrants. I remember the three teenagers. Maybe the swimming pool is the hangout of some racist group, bent on eliminating all non-white swimmers, to keep their waters pure and their white sisters unogled.

The elevator takes me upstairs. Then gutang-khutang. PW opens her door as I turn the corridor of medicinal smells. 'Berthe was screaming loudly at her husband tonight,' she tells me.

'Good for her,' I say, and she frowns indignantly at me.

The old man is in the lobby. He's wearing thick wool gloves. He wants to know how the swimming was, must have seen me leaving with my towel yesterday. Not bad, I say.

'I used to swim a lot. Very good for the circulation.' He wheezes. 'My feet are cold all the time. Cold as ice. Hands too.'

Summer is winding down, so I say stupidly, 'Yes, it's not so warm any more.'

The thought of the next swimming lesson sickens me. But as I comb through the memories of that terrifying Monday, I come upon the straying curls of brown pubic hair. Inexorably drawn by them, I decide to go.

It's a mistake, of course. This time I'm scared even to venture in the shallow end. When everyone has entered the water and I'm the only one outside, I feel a little foolish and slide in.

Instructor Ron says we should start by reviewing the floating technique. I'm in no hurry. I watch the pink one-piece pull the swim-suit down around her cheeks and flip back to achieve perfect flotation. And then reap disappointment. The pink Spandex triangle is perfectly streamlined today, nothing strays, not a trace of fuzz, not one filament, not even a sign of post-depilation irritation. Like the airbrushed parts of glamour magazine models. The barrenness of her impeccably packaged apex is a betrayal. Now she is shorn like the other women in the class. Why did she have to do it?

The weight of this disappointment makes the water less manageable, more lung-penetrating. With trepidation, I float and paddle my way through the remainder of the hour, jerking my head out every two seconds and breathing deeply, to continually shore up a supply of precious, precious air without, at the same time, seeming too anxious and losing my dignity.

I don't attend the remaining classes. After I've missed three, Ron the instructor telephones. I tell him I've had the flu and am still feeling poorly, but I'll try to be there the following week.

He does not call again. My Surf King is relegated to an unused drawer. Total losses: one fantasy plus thirty dollars. And no watery rebirth. The swimming pool, like Chaupatty beach, has produced a stillbirth. But there is a difference. Water means regeneration only if it is pure and cleansing. Chaupatty was filthy, the pool was not. Failure to swim through filth must mean something other than failure of rebirth—failure of symbolic death? Does that equal success of symbolic life? death of a symbolic failure? death of a symbol? What is the equation?

The postman did not bring a letter but a parcel, he was smiling because he knew that every time something came from Canada his baksheesh *was guaranteed, and this time because it was a parcel Mother gave him a whole rupee, she was quite excited, there were so many stickers on it besides the stamps, one for Small Parcel, another Printed Papers, a red sticker saying Insured; she showed it to Father, and opened it, then put both hands on her cheeks, not able to speak because the surprise and happiness was so great, tears came to her eyes and she could not stop smiling, till Father became impatient to know and finally got up and came to the table.*

When he saw it he was surprised and happy too, he began to grin, then hugged Mother saying our son is a writer, and we didn't even know it, he never told us a thing, here we are thinking he is still clerking away at the insurance company, and he has written a book of stories, all these years in school and college he kept his talent hidden, making us think he was just like one of the boys in the Baag, shouting and playing the fool in the compound, and now what a surprise; then Father opened the book and began reading it, heading back to the easy chair, and Mother so excited, still holding his arm, walked with him, saying it was not fair him reading it first, she wanted to read it too, and they agreed that he would read the first story, then give it to her so she could also read it, and they would take turns in that manner.

Mother removed the staples from the padded envelope in which he had mailed the book, and threw them away, then straightened the folded edges of the envelope and put it away safely with the other envelopes and letters she had collected since he left.

The leaves are beginning to fall. The only ones I can identify are maple. The days are dwindling like the leaves. I've started a habit of taking long walks every evening. The old man is in the lobby when I leave, he waves as I go by. By the time I'm back, the lobby is usually empty.

Today I was woken up by a grating sound outside that made my flesh crawl. I went to the window and saw Berthe raking the leaves in the parking lot. Not in the expanse of patchy lawn on the periphery, but in the parking lot proper. She was raking the black tarred surface. I went back to bed and dragged a pillow over my head, not releasing it till noon.

When I return from my walk in the evening, PW, summoned by the elevator's gutang-khutang, says, 'Berthe filled six big black garbage bags with leaves today.'

'Six bags!' I say. 'Wow!'

Since the weather turned cold, Berthe's son does not tinker with his van on Sundays under my window. I'm able to sleep late.

Around eleven, there's a commotion outside. I reach out and switch on the clock radio. It's a sunny day, the window curtains are bright. I get up, curious, and see a black Olds Ninety-Eight in the parking lot, by the entrance to the building. The old man is in his wheelchair, bundled up, with a scarf wound several times round his neck as though to immobilize it, like a surgical collar. His daughter and another man, the car-owner, are helping him from the wheelchair into the front seat, encouraging him with words like: that's it, easy does it, attaboy. From the open door of the lobby, Berthe is shouting encouragement too, but hers is confined to one word: yah, repeated at different levels of pitch and volume, with variations on vowel-length. The stranger could be the old man's son, he has the same jet black hair and piercing eyes.

Maybe the old man is not well, it's an emergency. But I quickly scrap that thought—this isn't Bombay, an ambulance would have arrived. They're probably taking him out for a ride. If he is his son, where has he been all this time, I wonder.

The old man finally settles in the front seat, the wheelchair goes in the trunk, and they're off. The one I think is the son looks up and catches me at the window before I can move away, so I wave, and he waves back.

In the afternoon I take down a load of clothes to the laundry room. Both machines have completed their cycles, the clothes inside are waiting to be transferred to dryers. Should I remove them and place them on top of a dryer, or wait? I decide to wait. After a few minutes, two women arrive, they are in bathrobes, and smoking. It takes me a while to realize that these are the two disappointments who were sunbathing in bikinis last summer.

'You didn't have to wait, you could have removed the clothes and carried on, dear,' says one. She has a Scottish accent. It's one of the few I've learned to identify. Like maple leaves.

'Well,' I say, 'some people might not like strangers touching their clothes.'

'You're not a stranger, dear,' she says, 'you live in this building, we've seen you before.'

'Besides, your hands are clean,' the other one pipes in. 'You can touch my things any time you like.'

Horny old cow. I wonder what they've got on under their bathrobes. Not much, I find, as they bend over to place their clothes in the dryers.

'See you soon,' they say, and exit, leaving me behind in an erotic wake of smoke and perfume and deep images of cleavages. I start the washers and depart, and when I come back later, the dryers are empty.

PW tells me, 'The old man's son took him out for a drive today. He has a big beautiful black car.'

I see my chance, and shoot back: 'Olds Ninety-Eight.'

'What?'

'The car,' I explain, 'it's an Oldsmobile Ninety-Eight.'

She does not like this at all, my giving her information. She is visibly nettled, and retreats with a sour face.

Mother and Father read the first five stories, and she was very sad after reading some of them, she said he must be so unhappy there, all his stories are about Bombay, he remembers every little thing about his childhood, he is thinking about it all the time even though he is ten thousand miles away, my poor son, I think he misses his home and us and everything he left behind, because if he likes it over there why would he not write stories about that, there must be so many new ideas that his new life could give him.

But Father did not agree with this, he said it did not mean that he was unhappy, all writers worked in the same way, they used their memories and experiences and made stories out of them, changing some things, adding some, imagining some, all writers were very good at remembering details of their lives.

Mother said, how can you be sure that he is remembering because he is a writer, or whether he started to write because he is unhappy and thinks of his past, and wants to save it all by making stories of it; and Father said that is not a sensible question, anyway, it is now my turn to read the next story.

The first snow has fallen, and the air is crisp. It's not very deep, about two inches, just right to go for a walk in. I've been told that immigrants from hot countries always enjoy the snow the first year, maybe for a couple of years more, then inevitably the dread sets in, and the approach of winter gets them fretting and moping. On the other hand, if it hadn't been for my conversation with the woman at the swimming registration desk, they might now be saying that India is a nation of non-swimmers.

Berthe is outside, shovelling the snow off the walkway in the parking lot. She has a heavy, wide pusher which she wields expertly.

The old radiators in the apartment alarm me incessantly. They continue to broadcast a series of variations on death throes, and go from hot to cold and cold to hot at will, there's no controlling their temperature. I speak to Berthe about it in the lobby. The old man is there too, his chin seems to have sunk deeper into his chest, and his face is a yellowish grey.

'Nothing, not to worry about anything,' says Berthe, dropping rough-hewn chunks of language around me. 'Radiator no work, you tell me. You feel cold, you come to me, I keep you warm,' and she opens her arms wide, laughing. I step back, and she advances, her breasts preceding her like the gallant prows of two ice-breakers. She looks at the old man to see if he is appreciating the act: 'You no feel scared, I keep you safe and warm.'

But the old man is staring outside, at the flakes of falling snow. What thoughts is he thinking as he watches them? Of childhood days, perhaps, and snowmen with hats and pipes, and snowball fights, and white Christmases, and Christmas trees? What will I think of, old in this country, when I sit and watch the snow come down? For me, it is already too late for snowmen and snowball fights, and all I will have is thoughts about childhood thoughts and dreams, built around snowscapes and winter-wonderlands on the Christmas cards so popular in Bombay; my snowmen and snowball fights and Christmas trees are in the pages of Enid Blyton's books, dispersed amidst the adventures of the Famous Five, and the Five Find-Outers, and the Secret Seven. My snowflakes are even less forgettable than the old man's, for they never melt.

It finally happened. The heat went. Not the usual intermittent coming and going, but out completely. Stone cold. The radiators are like ice. And so is everything else. There's no hot water. Naturally. It's the hot water that goes through the rads and heats them. Or is it the other way around? Is there no hot water because the rads have stopped circulating it? I don't care, I'm too cold to sort out the cause and effect relationship. Maybe there is no connection at all.

I dress quickly, put on my winter jacket, and go down to the lobby. The elevator is not working because the power is out, so I take the stairs. Several people are gathered, and Berthe has announced that she has telephoned the office, they are sending a man. I go back up the stairs. It's only one floor, the elevator is just a bad habit. Back in Firozsha Baag they were broken most of the time. The stairway enters the corridor outside the old man's apartment, and I think of his cold feet and hands. Poor man, it must be horrible for him without heat.

As I walk down the long hallway, I feel there's something different but can't pin it down. I look at the carpet, the ceiling, the wallpaper: it all seems the same. Maybe it's the freezing cold that imparts a feeling of difference.

PW opens her door: 'The old man had another stroke yesterday. They took him to the hospital.'

The medicinal smell. That's it. It's not in the hallway any more.

In the stories that he'd read so far Father said that all the Parsi families were poor or middle-class, but that was okay; nor did he mind that the seeds for the stories were picked from the sufferings of their own lives; but there should also have been something positive about Parsis, there was so much to be proud of: the great Tatas and their contribution to the steel industry, or Sir Dinshaw Petit in the textile industry who made Bombay the Manchester of the East, or Dadabhai Naoroji in the freedom movement, where he was the first to use the word swaraj, *and the first to be elected to the British Parliament where he carried on his campaign; he should have found some way to bring some of these wonderful facts into his stories, what would people reading these stories think, those who did not know about Parsis—that the whole community was full of cranky, bigoted people; and in reality it was the richest, most advanced and philanthropic community in India, and he did not need to tell his own son that Parsis had a reputation for being generous and family-oriented. And he could have written something also about the historic background, how Parsis came to India from Persia because of Islamic persecution in the seventh century, and were the descendants of Cyrus the Great and the magnificent Persian Empire. He could have made a story of all this, couldn't he?*

Mother said what she liked best was his remembering everything so well, how beautifully he wrote about it all, even the sad things, and though he changed some of it, and used his imagination, there was truth in it.

My hope is, Father said, that there will be some story based on his Canadian experience, that way we will know something about our son's life there, if not through his letters then in his stories; so far they are all about Parsis and Bombay, and the one with a little bit about Toronto, where a man perches on top of the toilet, is shameful and disgusting, although it is funny at times and did make me laugh, I have to admit, but where does he get such an imagination from, what is the point of such a fantasy; and Mother said that she would also enjoy some stories about Toronto and the people there; it puzzles me, she said, why he writes nothing about it, especially since you say that writers use their own experience to make stories out of.

Then Father said this is true, but he is probably not using his Toronto experience because it is too early; what do you mean, too early, asked Mother and Father explained it takes a writer about ten years time after an experience before he is able to use it in his writing, it takes that long to be absorbed internally and understood, thought out and thought about, over and over again, he haunts it and it haunts him if it is valuable enough, till the writer is comfortable with it to be able to use it as he wants; but this is only one theory I read somewhere, it may or may not be true.

That means, said Mother that his childhood in Bombay and our home here is the most valuable thing in his life just now, because he is able to remember it all to write about it, and you were so bitterly saying he is forgetting where he came from; and that may be true, said Father, but that is not what the theory means, according to the theory he is writing of these things because they are far enough in the past for him to deal with objectively, he is able to achieve what critics call artistic distance, without emotions interfering; and what do you mean emotions, said Mother, you are saying he does not feel anything for his characters, how can he write so beautifully about so many sad things without any feelings in his heart?

But before Father could explain more, about beauty and emotion and inspiration and imagination, Mother took the book and said it was her turn now and too much theory she did not want to listen to, it was confusing and did not make as much sense as reading the stories, she would read them her way and Father could read them his.

My books on the windowsill have been damaged. Ice has been forming on the inside ledge, which I did not notice, and melting when the sun shines in. I spread them in a corner of the living-room to dry out.

The winter drags on. Berthe wields her snow pusher as expertly as ever, but there are signs of weariness in her performance. Neither husband nor son is ever seen outside with a shovel. Or anywhere else, for that matter. It occurs to me that the son's van is missing, too.

The medicinal smell is in the hall again, I sniff happily and look forward to seeing the old man in the lobby. I go downstairs and peer into the mailbox, see the blue and magenta of an Indian aerogramme with Don Mills, Ontario, Canada in Father's flawless hand through the slot.

I pocket the letter and enter the main lobby. The old man is there, but not in his usual place. He is not looking out through the glass door. His wheelchair is facing a bare wall where the wallpaper is torn in places. As though he is not interested in the outside world any more, having finished with all that, and now it's time to see inside. What does he see inside, I wonder? I go up to him and say hullo. He says hullo without raising his sunken chin. After a few seconds his grey countenance faces me. 'How old do you think I am?' His eyes are dull and glazed; he is looking even further inside than I first presumed.

'Well, let's see, you're probably close to sixty-four.'

'I'll be seventy-eight next August.' But he does not chuckle or wheeze. Instead, he continues softly, 'I wish my feet did not feel so cold all the time. And my hands.' He lets his chin fall again.

In the elevator I start opening the aerogramme, a tricky business because a crooked tear means lost words. Absorbed in this while emerging, I don't notice PW occupying the centre of the hallway, arms folded across her chest: 'They had a big fight. Both of them have left.'

I don't immediately understand her agitation. 'What . . . who?'

'Berthe. Husband and son both left her. Now she is all alone.'

Her tone and stance suggest that we should not be standing here talking but do something to bring Berthe's family back. 'That's very sad,' I say, and go on. I picture father and son in the van, driving away, driving across the snow-covered country, in the dead of winter, away from wife and mother; away to where? how far will they go? Not son's van nor father's booze can take them far enough. And the further they go, the more they'll remember, they can take it from me.

All the stories were read by Father and Mother, and they were sorry when the book was finished, they felt they had come to know their son better now, yet there was much more to know, they wished there were many more stories; and this is what they mean, said Father, when they say that the whole story can never be told, the whole truth can never be known; what do you mean, they say, asked Mother, who they, and Father said writers, poets, philosophers. I don't care what they say, said Mother, my son will write as much or as little as he wants to, and if I can read it I will be happy.

The last story they liked the best of all because it had the most in it about Canada, and now they felt they knew at least a little bit, even if it was a very little bit, about his day-to-day life in his apartment; and Father said if he continues to write about such things he will become popular because I am sure they are interested there in reading about life through the eyes of an immigrant, it provides a different viewpoint; the only danger is if he changes and becomes so much like them that he will write like one of them and lose the important difference.

The bathroom needs cleaning. I open a new can of Ajax and scour the tub. Sloshing with mug from bucket was standard bathing procedure in the bathrooms of Firozsha Baag, so my preference now is always for a shower. I've never used the tub as yet; besides, it would be too much like Chaupatty or the swimming pool, wallowing in my own dirt. Still, it must be cleaned.

When I've finished, I prepare for a shower. But the clean gleaming tub and the nearness of the vernal equinox give me the urge to do something different today. I find the drain plug in the bathroom cabinet, and run the bath.

I've spoken so often to the old man, but I don't know his name. I should have asked him the last time I saw him, when his wheelchair was facing the bare wall because he had seen all there was to see outside and it was time to see what was inside. Well, tomorrow. Or better yet, I can look it up in the directory in the lobby. Why didn't I think of that before? It will only have an initial and a last name, but then I can surprise him with: hullo Mr Wilson, or whatever it is.

The bath is full. Water imagery is recurring in my life: Chaupatty beach, swimming pool, bathtub. I step in and immerse myself up to the neck. It feels good. The hot water loses its opacity when the chlorine, or whatever it is, has cleared. My hair is still dry. I close my eyes, hold my breath, and dunk my head. Fighting the panic, I stay under and count to thirty. I come out, clear my lungs and breathe deeply.

I do it again. This time I open my eyes under water, and stare blindly without seeing, it takes all my will to keep the lids from closing. Then I am slowly able to discern the underwater objects. The drain plug looks different, slightly distorted; there is a hair trapped between the hole and the plug, it waves and dances with the movement of the water. I come up, refresh my lungs, examine quickly the overwater world of the washroom, and go in again. I do it several times, over and over. The world outside the water I have seen a lot of, it is now time to see what is inside.

The spring session for adult non-swimmers will begin in a few days at the high school. I must not forget the registration date.

The dwindled days of winter are now all but forgotten; they have grown and attained a respectable span. I resume my evening walks, it's spring, and a vigorous thaw is on. The snowbanks are melting, the sound of water on its gushing, gurgling journey to the drains is beautiful. I plan to buy a book of trees, so I can identify more than the maple as they begin to bloom.

When I return to the building, I wipe my feet energetically on the mat because some people are entering behind me, and I want to set a good example. Then I go to the board with its little plastic letters and numbers. The old man's apartment is the one on the corner by the stairway, that makes it number 201. I run down the list, come to 201, but there are no little white plastic letters beside it. Just the empty black rectangle with holes where the letters would be squeezed in. That's strange. Well, I can introduce myself to him, then ask his name.

However, the lobby is empty. I take the elevator, exit at the second floor, wait for the gutang-khutang. It does not come: the door closes noiselessly, smoothly. Berthe has been at work, or has made sure someone else has. PW's cue has been lubricated out of existence.

But she must have the ears of a cockroach. She is waiting for me. I whistle my way down the corridor. She fixes me with an accusing look. She waits till I stop whistling, then says: 'You know the old man died last night.'

I cease groping for my key. She turns to go and I take a step towards her, my hand still in my trouser pocket. 'Did you know his name?' I ask, but she leaves without answering.

Dionne Brand *b.* 1953

GUAYGUAYARE, TRINIDAD

'Every word turns on itself, every word falls after it is said,' writes Dionne Brand. 'None of the answers that I've given over the years is the truth. Those answers have all been given like a guerrilla with her face in a handkerchief, her eyes still. She is still, poised for quick movement, but still. . . . And I've answered like the captive giving answers in an interrogation, telling just enough to appease the interrogator and just enough to trace the story so she could repeat it without giving anything away and without contradiction the next time she has to tell it.' Brand's self-portrait as writer reveals the energy and tensions in her writing, but also the cultural and political conditions informing her work as a black lesbian writer.

Born in Guayguayare, Trinidad, Brand moved to Toronto in 1970, after graduating from a private school. 'I really didn't think of myself as an immigrant *per se*,' she says. 'I could escape being an immigrant, but along with the black people who have lived in this country for three centuries, I would not escape my race at any point.' She studied at the University of Toronto, where she received a BA in English and Philosophy (1975), and at the Ontario Institute for Studies in Education, where she received an MA in History and Philosophy (1989). In the 1970s and 80s, she worked with such community organizations as the Black Education Project, the Immigrant Women's Centre, the Caribbean Peoples' Development Agency, and the Agency for Rural Transformation in Grenada. Her collaborative books, *Rivers Have Sources, Trees Have Roots: Speaking of Racism* (1986), which records people's experiences with racism, and *No Burden to Carry: Narratives of Black Working Women in Ontario 1920s to 1950s* (1991), which contains the life narratives of 16 black women, demonstrate Brand's ongoing commitment to combatting racism: 'I don't see Marxism and feminism as theories I need to graft onto people. I see them as living things.' This kind of 'living', rigorous creative analysis, characterizes *Bread Out of Stone:*

recollections sex recognitions race dreaming politics (1994), her impassioned and eloquent essays about her life as an artist, intellectual, and activist, and *A Map to the Door of No Return* (2001), her unyielding look at the lingering effects of the Middle Passage as they survive in the memory and bodies of her family and black community at large. 'We're now battered by multicultural bureaucracy,' she says, 'co-opted by mainstream party politics, morassed in everyday boring racism.' Only by addressing '[r]eal power—which is economic power and political power'—can we begin to deal with racism. What multiculturalism 'does essentially is to compartmentalize us into little cultural groups who have dances and different foods and Caribana. But it doesn't address real power.'

A contributing editor of such journals as *Spear* and *Fuse Magazine*, Brand has also produced documentaries. She worked with the National Film Board, Studio D, to produce *Older, Stronger, Wiser* (1989), *Sisters in the Struggle* (1991), and *Long Time Comin'* (1993), documenting the art and politics of various black women in Canada, as well as *Listening for Something: Adrienne Rich and Dionne Brand in Conversation* (1996). Brand's writing, beginning with her first books of poetry, *'Fore Day Morning* (1978), *Earth Magic* (1979), for children, *Primitive Offensive* (1982), and *Winter Epigrams: Epigrams to Ernesto Cardenal in Defense of Claudia* (1983), is directly engaged in questioning power and the traditional constructs of femininity. The elegiac and militant *Chronicles of the Hostile Sun* (1984) that documents her ten-month sojourn in Grenada after the US invasion, the lyrical and documentary *No Language is Neutral* (1990), nominated for the Governor General's Award, as well as *Land to Light On* (1997) that won that Award, and *thirsty* (2003), a finalist for the Griffin Prize—all reflect the elegance and tenacity of her poetic language, the 'language that I grew up in', and her unwavering attention to social issues. Poetry, as she says, can 'offer an alternative to the unrelenting idiocy of corporate culture'. Her fiction, too—*Sans Souci and Other Stories* (1994) and her novels, *In Another Place, Not Here* (1996), winner of the Trillium Book Award, and *At the Full and Change of the Moon* (1999)—is written in a language that 'creates its own sensory space', that tells stories through 'poetic gestures'. Whether she writes about Elizete and Verlia's intense contemporary relationship in the former or the descendents of the defiant slave, Marie Ursule, being haunted by the spectres of the 1824 mass suicide she plotted in the latter, Brand's politics, be it about gender issues or about racialization and racism, is never moraliz-ing, but a 'lived thing' often endowed with 'grace'. 'I never begin from what might be universal,' she says. 'Wary of appeals to universality', her 'writing is directed against stereotypes'. Her most recent novel, *What We All Long For* (2005), set in Toronto in early 2000 and in a Thai refugee camp, offers an undaunted view of global politics, interracial relationships, and misplaced longings. *Inventory* (2006) is her most recent poetry book.

Brand, who has taught in a number of universities, is University Research Chair in the School of English and Theatre Studies at the University of Guelph. She lives in Toronto.

from *No Language Is Neutral*

No language is neutral. I used to haunt the beach at
Guaya, two rivers sentinel the country sand, not
backra white but nigger brown sand, one river dead
and teeming from waste and alligators, the other
rumbling to the ocean in a tumult, the swift undertow   5
blocking the crossing of little girls except on the tied
up dress hips of big women, then, the taste of leaving
was already on my tongue and cut deep into my
skinny pigeon toed way, language here was strict
description and teeth edging truth. Here was beauty   10
and here was nowhere. The smell of hurrying passed
my nostrils with the smell of sea water and fresh fish
wind, there was history which had taught my eyes to
look for escape even beneath the almond leaves fat
as women, the conch shell tiny as sand, the rock   15
stone old like water. I learned to read this from a
woman whose hand trembled at the past, then even
being born to her was temporary, wet and thrown half
dressed among the dozens of brown legs itching to
run. It was as if a signal burning like a fer de lance's   20
sting turned my eyes against the water even as love
for this nigger beach became resolute.

There it was anyway, some damn memory half-eaten
and half hungry. To hate this, they must have been
dragged through the Manzinilla spitting out the last   25
spun syllables for cruelty, new sound forming,

pushing toward lips made to bubble blood. This road
could match that. Hard-bitten on mangrove and wild
bush, the sea wind heaving any remnants of
consonant curses into choking aspirate. No   30
language is neutral seared in the spine's unravelling.
Here is history too. A backbone bending and
unbending without a word, heat, bellowing these
lungs spongy, exhaled in humming, the ocean, a
way out and not anything of beauty, tipping turquoise   35
and scandalous. The malicious horizon made us the
essential thinkers of technology. How to fly gravity,
how to balance basket and prose reaching for
murder. Silence done curse god and beauty here,
people does hear things in this heliconia peace   40
a morphology of rolling chain and copper gong
now shape this twang, falsettos of whip and air
rudiment this grammar. Take what I tell you. When
these barracks held slaves between their stone
halters, talking was left for night and hush was idiom   45
and hot core.

*   *   *

Leaving this standing, heart and eyes fixed to a
skyscraper and a concrete eternity not knowing then
only running away from something that breaks the
heart open and nowhere to live. Five hundred dollars   50
and a passport full of sand and winking water, is how
I reach here, a girl's face shimmering from a little
photograph, her hair between hot comb and afro, feet
posing in high heel shoes, never to pass her eyes on
the red-green threads of a humming bird's twitching   55
back, the blood warm quickened water colours of a
sea bed, not the rain forest tangled in smoke-wet,
well there it was. I did read a book once about a
prairie in Alberta since my waving canefield wasn't
enough, too much cutlass and too much cut foot, but   60
romance only happen in romance novel, the concrete
building just overpower me, block my eyesight and
send the sky back, back where it more redolent.

Is steady trembling I trembling when they ask me my
name and say I too black for it. Is steady hurt I feeling   65
when old talk bleed, the sea don't have branch you

know darling. Nothing is a joke no more and I right
there with them, running for the train until I get to find
out my big sister just like to run and nobody wouldn't
vex if you miss the train, calling Spadina *Spadeena*   70
until I listen good for what white people call it, saying I
coming just to holiday to the immigration officer when
me and the son-of-a-bitch know I have labourer mark
all over my face. It don't have nothing call beauty
here but this is a place, a gasp of water from a   75
hundred lakes, fierce bright windows screaming with
goods, a constant drizzle of brown brick cutting
dolorous prisons into every green uprising of bush.
No wilderness self, is shards, shards, shards,
shards of raw glass, a debris of people you pick your way   80
through returning to your worse self, you the thin
mixture of just come and don't exist.

*   *   *

from *Land to Light On*

IV i

Arani, I meet my old friend at Arani. Arani is a piece of what
someone carried all the way here from Kerala and set down on
Spadina, all he might cull of where he came from is commerce
now, is laid out in trays hurriedly set on fire. So Arani, I sit with
my old friend at Arani, my old friend. Between us there's a boy,   5
his son he hasn't seen, a friendship I'm holding for ransom until
he does. Who loves a Black boy? I ask him. It's not hard to
abandon him, whole cities have. So this between us, I meet my
old friend at Arani, his whole head soaked in that teardrop off
the chin of India, or is this the way we've learned to look at it,   10
the teardrop, the pearl dangling on the imperial necklace. We sit
at Arani, I know about necklaces, archipelagos, and in some
lurching talk he jumps over the Indian Ocean, back and forth,
the north full of armed Tigers, tea workers, the south, treachery,
prime ministers and generals, and here the telephone calls of   15
more fracture and more of the same, wife beatings in St James
Town, men I'm certain cook with too much pepper because at
home they never cooked and now only remember pepper.
I could be wrong I admit but still, and yes the boy who could do

with or without him, his head boiled in all we should have   20
been on those islands failing us because who ever had a chance
to say how it might be and our own particular vanity and
smallness, hatreds thinning our mouths and yellowing our
fingers. This we suspect. On any given day, he says,

there are seven hundred Asian maids in their embassies in   25
Kuwait, right now there are three hundred Sri Lankan maids
hiding in the Sri Lankan embassy in Kuwait, that bulwark of
American democracy, he says, a British ornithologist pursued a
rare owl for years following it to a village in the south of India,
there the ornithologist wept, distraught as villagers captured the   30
bird, cooked and ate it, there were lots of these birds around they
said, lots, the ornithologist wept, look, he says, I know you say
they're all in it but Chandrika is caught between the generals,
and the boy, I say, what about him adding my own disagreements,
he gets local prices in Tobago, he goes to bars at night there and   35
dances, they think he is a local, you know it doesn't matter this
Chandrika, the generals, her mother, Bandaranaike before,
they're all in the same class, they have tea together, all you can
count on is their benevolence, how they got up this morning,
and that's no revolution, anyway we will never win now. I   40
hardly know why I'm fighting any more, 'we', my we, taking
most of the world in my mouth, we, between my lips, the
mouth of the world is open, the boy's mother told me her
mother called menstruation. The mouth of the world is open
she'd say. Anyway I was driving here and you can't believe this   45
city, man, it is filthy and look at you, year in year out hoping
about someplace else, you ever wonder why don't we live here
ay, why don't we live here, by the way the Sri Lankans cannot
hope to beat the West Indies at cricket, don't make yourself
think about it you'll only be disappointed;   50

they're all the same, why are you hoping, I say, all the same class
and the Americans have them, you think anything will pass
now, peaceful solution, negotiating, look someone whispered
something to the Tigers and they got up from the table, a mistake,
a mistake, he wags, man, they want them dead, this class has only   55
disdain, man, you should read Balzac, he skips, Balzac was
saying these things, it's incredible, riffing conspiratorially at
Arani as if he's talking about arms caches, Balzac is incredible,
there is going to be another massive offensive, they're going to
kill everyone. The pope wants to beatify Queen Isabella, I tell   60
him, and has made thirty-three saints and seven hundred

blesseds, do you realise just how absurd we are here sitting at
Arani, and the boy, JFK's rocking chair sold for 450,000 dollars
and European neo-fascists are glamour boys in the *New York
Times*, do we realise they are more afraid of communists   65
than fascists, that is not good news for us. I sit here and listen
to radios, I hear their plots, and stagger, and the boy, well all
there is is the boy, just like any ordinary person, we are not
revolutionaries, we were never drawn into wars, we never
slept on our dirty fingers and pissed in our clothes, why, why   70
didn't we do that, but here, here we grind our teeth on our stone
hearts and foretell and mistake, and jump around the world in
our brains. Whether we are right is unimportant now, Leningrad
is St Petersburg and God is back in vogue, this is the future. I've
forgotten how to dance with him, something heavy is all in my   75
mouth, I get exhausted at Arani, my eyes reach for something
domestic, the mop in the Kerala man's hand, well, the boy is still
between us, and all the wars we've pried open and run our
tongues over like dangerous tin cans.

IV x

here is the history of the body;
water perhaps darkness perhaps stars
bone then scales then wings then legs then arms
then belly then bone then nerves then feathers then scales,
then wings then liquid then pores then bone   5
then blood pouring, then eyes, then distance, only this,
all that has happened since is too painful,
too unimaginable

'I never saw Managua when miniskirts were in,' Ortega
wrote in prison and newsprint bleeds with weeping   10
the walls of this room weep, a Saturday weeps,
what do we make of it, a miniskirt measuring
time, senses missed, dates, a life and people walking
in streets and thoughts as you walk along that are taken
for granted and forgotten at the end of a journey,   15
Ortega sitting in his cell could not have these
but had we given another shape to bodies
as well as theory and poems and speeches
what would we have missed and wept for and forgotten

Remembering Miranda's campaigns as if he were there   20
and Bolivar as if fighting for his own life and Jose Marti

like a son grown from a pebble tossed in the Caribbean basin
a comrade in his last speech and his last hope
ignites the hall in Montreal,
he is the one left alive and left here   25
he is a stranger in another millennium, in another room
with his passion and his shimmering ancestry,
a question from the back of the hall about armed struggle,
he has been waiting,
he sticks his grapple in its rock face and there's   30
a ruthlessness in him, a touch of the old sexy revolutionary,
and he stumbles on now, then his hand touches a greying chin
and it is as if he is startled and ashamed
and unable to land in now, all left undone.
There is a sign that he must make us,   35
the shape of the one thing that he has never written, ever

we stumble on the romance of origins,
some stories we all love like sleep, poured in our mouths like
milk. How far we've travelled now, still we stoop at a welcome
fire and hum, to a stick stringed with hair, our miscalculations,   40
we return to the misology in heat and loneliness, the smell of
meat and hunger

here again the history of the body
men romance the shape they're in
the mythologies they attach to it   45
their misunderstandings
and this is what James should have said to Trotsky
as they drank in Mexico City,
what might have happened if one had said to the other,
comrade, this is the time you betray the body   50

nearly late, we are in a hall waiting for a gesture,
Ortega out of prison if his prison is not the whole
of South America now, Jose Marti's son if the hall in Montreal
is not his coffin,
we are waiting for some language to walk into   55
like a large house
with no rooms and no quarter
all waiting for his signal
we happen on what was wrong in the first place,
how the intangible took over,   60
the things left in a language with carelessness or purpose,

men's arms and legs and belly, their discreet assignments
and regulations
the things kept secret with a hand pressed to the mouth
by priests, judges, mullahs   65
this way they resist what they must become
full knowing that we must throw our life away
and all impressions of ourselves.
Comrades, perhaps this is what you might whisper
on the telephone to the young men who adore you still,   70
'Goodbye, then. And well . . . betray your body.'

Antonio D'Alfonso *b.* 1953

MONTREAL, QUEBEC

'1977 was an important year for me,' says Antonio D'Alfonso. 'It was the year I became an Italian. One is not born an Italian; one becomes an Italian. Especially when you come from the *campagna*, the country; especially when you are not born in Italy.' D'Alfonso was born in Montreal, three years after his parents' emigration from Italy to Quebec. He grew up trilingual, and studied at Loyola College where he received his BA in Communication Arts (1975), and at the Université de Montréal, where he received his MSc in Communication Studies, specializing in semiology. The year he 'became' an Italian was also the year he discovered the poetry of Pier Giorgio di Cicco and other Italian Canadian writers. It was at this point that he began not only questioning what it means being Italian in Canada—'To be a Wop, a worker without a permit, a poet without a language of his own, without a tradition to work in, or to fight against?'—but also constructing his own identity as writer and becoming a major force in creating the very tradition he felt he lacked as an Italian poet in Canada. A prolific author, he writes in both English and French.

In 1978 he founded Guernica Editions and has since published numerous books of literature and criticism by authors from Canada and around the world, many of them focusing on issues of hyphenated identities. D'Alfonso moved his press to Toronto in 1991, where he continues to be an active publisher, editor, translator, and writer. He is also the co-founder of the Montreal magazine *Vice Versa* (1982). Some of his essays on writing, publishing, and cultural politics have appeared in *In Italics: In Defense of Ethnicity* (1996), *Gambling with Failure* (2005)—'failure as the only way to cultural survival'—and *Duologue: On Culture and Identity* (1998), with Pasquale Verdiccio.

'Being an Italian,' writes D'Alfonso, 'is nothing to be frightened of or arrogant about. It is a fact of life, and one must live with it, like one's gender . . . . In many ways, coming to terms with one's *Italianity* is very much like coming out of the closet. Nevertheless you cannot shed overnight the layers of skin you have wrapped yourself in . . . . The transformation is slow and often painful. You have to *become* yourself. And this is what interests me most: the process of becoming. Struggle is the force behind the process of identity which manifests itself in different ways. Not all struggle, however, need be expressed in stammers or with violence.' D'Alfonso's poetics and politics, the transformation and struggle he talks about, are clearly reflected in his writing. Beginning with his early books of poetry, *La chanson du shaman* à *Sedna* (1973), *Queror* (1979), and *Black Tongue* (1983), D'Alfonso explores, through sensuous and often surreal imagery, the layers of identity while inhabiting a space of discordances— 'Dissimilar we coalesce. / We are hybrid.' With his later titles, D'Alfonso begins to 're-invent' himself in forms that allow his lyrical voice to speak from a position of both innocence and experience. *The Other Shore* (1986), translated into French as *L'autre rivage* (1987), *Panick Love* (1988), also available in French as *L'Amour panique* (1992), and *Julia* (1992) show D'Alfonso to be the kind of 'essential poet' that he sees emerging from the Italian Canadian literary tradition: 'an *essential* poet is one who not only finds a point of intersection, no matter how durable or ephemeral, for all the contradictory forces working within and without him, but also a new language or a new way of using the language he chooses. A poet who finds himself in such a *situation* cannot be expected to vacuously adhere to the norms prescribed by the tradition imposed by the language he chooses.' Similar preoccupations characterize his fiction as well, as is the case with his early novel, *Avril ou L'anti-passion* (1990); *Fabrizio's Passion* (2000), winner of the Bressani Award; and *Un vendredi du mois d'août* (2005), winner of the Trillium Prize in the French language, about a filmmaker who, upon returning to his home town, reminisces about his past life. His most recent poetry book in English is *Getting on with Politics* (2002). A filmmaker himself, he has produced three 16 mm black-and-white films, *L'Ampoule brûlée* (1973), *La Coupe de Circé* (1974), and *Pour t'aimer* (1982–7), and the 90 mm *My Trip to Oaxaca* (2005), and has collaborated either as scriptwriter, cameraperson, or as editor on other films.

Im Sachsenhausen

> *La mia lingua / mi isolava /*
> *l'ho abbandonata / con la tua /*
> *imputridiscono / in me / i sensi.*
> —Gino Chiellino

The language of one country in another country. Listen to the music coming in from the other room. Workers speak about the land in which they planted seeds of children and wives. Who knows what *father* and *mother* mean to them?

Not a question of nativeland. Our nativeland, a plane bringing us from point A to point B. Place, country: what do these mean to you, my love? Foreigner in a foreign land . . .

What do we desire from the soil of our bodies? Country without borders, country of our love. The language we speak is the language of our bodies, divided, united, poetry, poetry, why do you make love like this? Always telling me what I am not. Why do you come to me this way? Unexpectedly.

The Loss of a Culture

Not the trip to a land where words are pronounced as you were taught to pronounce them. Not the adage your grandmother serves you at dinner. The language you speak as a child, flushed down the toilet bowl. Your mother-tongue sounds as foreign to you as any language you do not understand. Forgotten as the life-style you once had. Latin engraved on darkened school desks. What do you tell yourself when you find yourself alone at night? The uneaten bread becomes stale. The avoided meeting of a one-night stand, dreadful. Squashed tomato on the floor sinks into the tiles of your perfection. You forget the past but the past will not forget you. You sit on broken chairs and get cramps when you are about to say something intelligent. If you collapse and smash your head on the floor, it will not be from lack of proper diet, it will be your ancestors who will shoot you from behind.

The Family

Images one does not want to see. Images of sterility, images of life. Miraculous progenity. Unrolling, a homemovie, a scroll. Every father a daughter, every mother a son. A family rejuvenating itself without hardening into a fossil. Bones prove that death does not sign with an X: the only son with only a son and no son. 'I want to be modern. Drink down those images and forget them.' Images one refuses to look at, images one has been taught are vulgar, stilted, trite. O miraculous progenity. O imaginative life. Who gives you power to put marble on quicksand, build cities on water? What stubbornness of creation. You give birth, enhance the chances of change. Inventor of possibilities.

On Being a Wop

Per Patrizia Di Pardo

Who can say what national pride means? The feel for people living here, though they need not necessarily care? Not to come back to this place. What is my excuse if not the fear of what this country would do to me? Born abroad, this is how the world wants it. But national pride? This place, this city, this territory: almost twenty-seven centuries old. O Italia, nation beyond nation, where will we take you now? You are not nervous when you walk among your citizens in Rome, Montreal, or Frankfurt. You drink a few beers and are beyond the grasp of people who wish to talk to you. *Foro Romano.* You, fired for having demonstrated on Via Nazionale. Protesting against the Mafia and the Heroin Plague. You want this march to be more than just a testimony, you want to express your people's desire to change. People without boundaries, people with homes in every country. The meaning of being Italian? The meaning of being European? American? To reconcile yourself to the world you belong to. What reconciliation is possible in what makes up the contradictions of being? To be one thing, to be another: what choice have you today? (Cold Frascati wine against your teeth . . .) What does struggle stand for, if not the people who gave you birth? Peasants without lands who have voices not for singing but rumours blowing in the wind. The cultures of being what being can never again be. Here or there: cultureless identity. The Italian culture: what does it mean to be Italian today if you live outside Italy? 'If you don't live in Italy, you're not Italian.' What does such a phrase mean? What does it stand for? To be anywhere just as long as you live your culture. To keep your batteries in full charge in order to become what you essentially are.

Roma, 30 ottobre 1984

Aritha van Herk *b.* 1954

WETASKIWIN, ALBERTA

'The writer is a mute in disguise,' says Aritha van Herk, 'knowing the deceptions of shaping words with mouth or on the page. Words are themselves trickery, only too often mockery, and their sounding, the displacement of tongue and lips to effect oral language, gestures a double danger. Once spoken, once written, words are not easily recalled/renounced/disavowed/rescinded/recovered: they hover over our lives in ghostly shapes and suggestions meddling with a mythology better left unstated/inart/iculate.' These words from the title text in her book *A Frozen Tongue* (1992) are an instance of what van Herk calls 'ficto-criticism', writing as reading, a self-reflexive act that also characterizes her second collection of essays, *In Visible Ink: crypto-frictions* (1991).

Born in Wetaskiwin, Alberta, the first Canadian child of Dutch parents who arrived in Canada in 1949, van Herk grew up on her family's farm. She studied at the University of Alberta, where she received a BA Honours (1976) and an MA (1978) in English. A professor of Creative Writing and English at the University of Calgary since 1983, van Herk has read and lectured widely, both in Canada and overseas, and is the editor of many anthologies

of western Canadian fiction, including *Alberta Re/Bound* (1990) and *Boundless Alberta* (1993).

Her novel, *Judith* (1978), was the first recipient of the Seal First Novel Award. It deals with the only woman farmer in a community set in the region where van Herk grew up. '[F]estive and mournful,' in van Herk's words, it reveals her 'injunction to write the familiar and [her] fascination with the rural grotesque'. It also announces her preoccupation with female characters who rise above the normative behaviour expected of them. Ja-el, the central character of her second novel, *The Tent Peg* (1981), disguises herself as a man in order to get a job in the Yukon, while Arachne, the picara protagonist in her novel, *No Fixed Address: an Amorous Journey* (1986), has an adventurous and promiscuous spirit that both challenges gender stereotypes and leads to her disappearance in the Canadian North. This novel won the Howard O'Hagan Prize for Best Novel in Alberta and was nominated for the Governor General's Award. Her fiction, as van Herk says, is 'concerned with the unexplored geographies of landscape and person and with the recovery of mythical voice and identification in contemporary time and place'. The indeterminacy, irony, playfulness, and deconstruction of inherited paradigms that characterize the postmodernism of van Herk's fiction are elements that are also evident in *Places Far From Ellesmere: Explorations on Site* (1990), a book she calls 'geografictione', a coming together of geography and fiction. Echoing, yet again, her obsession with the Canadian North and re-imagining the life of Tolstoy's Anna Karenina in ways that may release her from the inevitability of suicide, it reflects van Herk's relentless testing of the boundaries of fiction and criticism, her inclination to locate herself in places where there is friction between the real and the imaginary, the objective and the subjective, the present and the past. If her critical imagination puts a woman's suicide under erasure in that work, in her more recent novel, *Restlessness* (1998), the female protagonist relies on her story-telling about her life both to delay her impending death and explain her reasons for it to the man she has hired to kill her—an enthralling, yet disquieting, narrative.

'Resistant to and yet complicit with my invented ethnicity', van Herk seeks 'to read and write through the palimpsest of class, gender, and multiple personality'. At once a regional writer and a writer who keeps redefining the borders of regions, van Herk approaches the question of origins by spelling out the hyphen that marks ethnicity—'I am a Dutch hyphen Canadian,' she says—by rereading what Canadian means. 'Canadian: a global immigrant dreaming the future, not conqueror but supplicant, outcast, exile, artist; creator of both past and point of arrival. The *act* of immigration has been omitted, deliberately excluded as an embarrassing part of our lack of definition. After all, it is journey, travel, movement, no *place* to it, maybe no purpose either, only longing and a continuous coming. The ethnic fixation, because it is an easy one, ignores immigration, would rather that decisive and displacing act had never occurred. Pretends it was only a temporary condition, a movement rather than a state of mind.'

Van Herk's novels have been translated into many languages. The 1986 recipient of the 45 Below Award as one of the ten best young Canadian fiction writers, she is also the author of *Mavericks: An Incorrible History of Alberta* (2001), a history that twists the genre of history around, which won the Grant MacEwan Author's Award for Alberta Writing.

Of Dykes and Boers and Drowning

And oh, the mouth so full of words that never say themselves, bundled up in a backwash of that other language, forbidden, choking, the one that everyone laughs at: Dutch, Dutch, Dutch, as ugly as its sound and the throaty gutturals of its pronunciation. Full of connotations of lowness, levelity; Netherlandish the bottom, like the bottom of a throat where words fathomage, clogged, choking, thick with *drakestijn* and drunkenness, their derogatory dungeons clanking in chains around the duplicities of Dutch concerts and Dutch courage, Dutch treats and Dutch cousins, Dutch collars and Dutch flight. Such yawning language is a sham, a cover-up, the language itself insists, compared to English and the derogation of the seventeenth-century Anglo-Dutch wars. Ah, to be a Dutchman; I'm a Dutchman if I do. Synonymous with all despicabilities, and as a term of refusal, the strongest possible term of refusal. And Dutch nightingales may be frogs, yes, lovely in their deep swamps, and yes, in Dutch is prison, terrible trouble, and this reputed fondness for heavy drinking as a substitute for courage, not to mention the constant mention of meanness, going Dutch going Dutch going Dutch going going gone, no generosity, and where shall we find such courage if not in *jenever* (yes, gin) with the *Engels* (yes, English) pursuingly there on the high seas. And in an endlessly Anglo alloy, where can another metal be discerned or alchemized, why not merely take issue with issue and be damned to this Dutchness, this thick-tongued accusation of the floundering sea against dykes and dykes and dykes. And although the claim may be that dyke is a twentieth-century slang word, a neutral ground from which to name against heterosexist declension, or Rita May Brown's, 'Are you really a dyke, Harriet?' 'I rather thought of myself as the Hoover damn' (*Sudden Death*, 1983). Those famous little boys and their famous fingers in the famous story of the famous dyke are really the plug of language grown thick in the back of the throat, grown mossy and sticky with twigs, holding back a flood of sea/she, the articulate water, a breach.

Tied to this tongue is a cartage of humiliation, enumerated and cavilled uncivilization, the *gauwigheid* (yes, quickness, immediacy, a jump to the gun) of affiliation with all that Dutch not, or nothing, or absence. A Dutch uncle isn't there, Dutch courage is cowardice shored by alcohol, and Dutchness, oh the sheer thickheaded, cleanser-coated blue serge milkcowedness of it, so boorish, it is better to be not.

Boer.

Another accent, classness classified on top of Dutchness, and yes, there to be defined as well: 'A Dutch colonist or person of Dutch descent in South Africa; of or pertaining to the Boers.' And of course, all their fault, *apartheid* is Dutch, its segregation not only Afrikaans but certainly inscribed by that Dutch origin, its heavy glottal speaking of decision and division. But the division goes deeper, into every corner of a languaged judgment, from *boer* to *boor*, an awkward and always ill-mannered person, a clownish rustic, he's the guy who doesn't know enough to wipe his wooden shoes, let alone take them off at the door, and he is always a peasant, irreversibly a Dutch peasant. Carrying with him his own associations of servitude and boorishness, not to mention rascality and baseness, rusticity, uncouthness, and yes, certainly, simple simple-mindedness. Always, of course from the Dutch *boer*. Strictly, a farmer.

A Dutch farmer, mind you, a farmer who will toil in muck and swamp to recover an inch of land from the north sea, and then will insist on grassing it and ferrying his cows across a canal and leaving them stranded on those soggy islands with nothing to do but eat that grass, in order to produce thick holstein milk from which will be churned butter, and renneted cheese, and both will be spread on renneted *roggebrood* (yes, tough brown bread) and stuffed between the teeth of the same *boer* who doesn't know enough to chew with his mouth shut. The *boer's* circle, endless, unforgiving, inarticulate, indefensible in all that churlish, loutish, clownish uncouthedness, from his blue serge coat with its row of horny buttons to his clodhopping feet.

And the *boerin* (yes, recognizably the feminine form) is no better, with her ersatz apron riding over a hefty chest beside a set of upper arm muscles like hams, she will give birth in the upper bedroom of her farmhouse at seven in the morning and be up to milk those same heavy holsteins that evening, maybe even slapping their flanks just as energetically, while the barely day-old baby in the *kram* (yes, the crib, the baby basket) is already learning to squall without answer, will certainly learn to wait her turn.

Ah yes, *boer*, tied to jacks and knaves and their belches, the way they turn the cards the other way, like the Dutch and their auctions, every possible order reversed to a contrary of what everyone else knows is good sense. And where's the melody in any Dutch concert, its uproar, its quarrelsome speechifying? While the *Boer* enjoys himself and the *boerin* shugs her shoulders, willing to tussle or lunge. And the *boerderij* (the farm, of course) continues on its merry and impossibly productive way, the animals bearing and breathing and switching their tails over great splats of cowshit, and the hens pecking the eyes out of the garden.

It is clear they have no sense of place or location, culture be damned, *de boer opgaan* (yes, it's the road) there they go, peddling round the countryside, selling whatever they can, and stopping often for flagons of beer, so that they can (albeit happily) *een boer laten*, let go a boer, or belch. And yes, there's a strange acceptance of adversity, *lachen als een boer die kiespijn heft*, laughing like a boer who has toothache, oh yes, laughing on the wrong side of one's face, out of the wrong side of one's face, bittersweet, *zuurzoet*, contrary again, and who cares if the teeth are rotten, or the boer can't bear the snotty dentist with his eternally clean and manicured hands, that has nothing to do with anything, at least not with making a living or putting up with the tribulations that persist.

And neither *boer* nor *boerin* minds their cousinal *boerenbedrieger* (yes, the one who takes the money and runs), trickster incarnate, pissing behind the *bomen* (yes, trees, ordinary trees), and even the trees have more culture and nature, more history than that ugly lot, celebrating its eternal country wedding, *boerenbruiloft*, with noisy noise, amplified glee and yodelling. For the *boerendochter* (yes, the farmer's daughter), that country girl, doesn't know the difference, does she, that you don't lick the jam from your knife, or scratch your inner thigh without thinking too hard about the itch or its need. And even the *boerenjongens*, who might be her brothers, or the country lads, their ruddy faces and their ill-cut thatched hair, enjoy slurping up their namesakes, *boerenjongens* (yes, raisins in brandy), the cheap stuff of course, strong enough to make the eyes water and the palms tingle. The more elegant, effete, the more christmassy and fussed over *boerenmeisjes*, and the *je* diminutive is a given for those peasant daughters (yes, peasant girls), love to fish finger them out of the crockery crocks with their nails never quite clean, *boerinmeisjes*, (yes, apricots in gin). Such excess calls for a celebration, doesn't it, loud and unruly? *Boerinkermis* (yes, a country fair), and every one of those clodhoppers can roam from kiosk to kiosk with their mouths open, jocular noise filling their over-large ears, *boerenkool* (yes, curly kale), but cabbages are delicate and refined next to those great handles, jug ears.

Ah, easy to want to believe that this rusticity is overdone, overstated, there must be a redemptive strain under such a language act, such judgment in the usage. No, there's more. The (yes, the stupid ones) *boerenkinkels* and *boerenkaffirs*—and of course, *kaffir* (yes, the Afrikaner designation for black, or useless, depending on the occasion) has been shifted onto the shoulders of the other, again South African parlance, but the *boer* still hears, carries, and weighs. Dull, beneath contempt. The knowledge of being and the essence of *boer*. Quite simply, calmly, without mitigation, stupid, in manners, in habit, in knowledge. Accepted parlance, and in an English-speaking enclave of superiority, my students can make fun of boors—the mannerless—in every pejorative way, and never even conceive of the hurt they inflict. The quick flash of pain in my father's eyes, he who has always been a *boer*, a genuine, quiet, and simple man who believed and still believes in working hard with his hands, who believes that raising food is a good thing to do for other people, for the world, and although he has never gotten rich, and although he is not a sophisticated thinker, he knows that *boer* is a word that degrades him, although his actions have never come out of a desire to degrade others. And as for the farmer's daughter, with the cumulative associations of both boorishness and déclassé availability, she who will sleep with every trickster in every hayloft, whose foreground is ignorance, how then to translate that 'delevated' role to the one I am trapped in now, where language is a high-strung, well-bred instrument that my clumsy hands and manners are supposed to manage well? If oblivion is no excuse for racism, does it pass for classism?

Boer.

And why not *agrariër*, the wider more politic arm of agrarian, agriculturalist; or *iemand die een agrarisch bedriff leidt* (yes, someone who runs an agricultural business)? No fun there, the appropriations of manners and mores get effaced in such technicalities and *wat een boer!* (yes, what a boor!) is of no use if it doesn't attribute superiority. *iemand zonder manieren, lomperd, kinkel;* someone without manners, a clodhopper, a yokel; *boerenpummel*, a lout. And annexed to those attributions, the parking garage of staticity, refusal to change, such loutishness implies the luddite too, unable to adjust, accept progress. *Wat de boer niet kent, dat eet hij niet*, if the food is unfamiliar, the farmer won't eat it, meat and potatoes better be what they pretend to be. *Ter aanduiding van een conservatieve houding*; the mark of a resistant conservative, and all its baggage, conservatism. Easy to rest that attribution on the shoulders of a *boer*, those shoulders are broad, drafthorses to pull the heavy load of cultural distinctions and intolerances.

And the permissions of paternalism, the generous condescension of those who know better, who can afford to practise the cultural superiority of imitation. *De boer opgaan* (going out), said with a lilt, a note of humour, indulgence; *naar buiten gaan om te wandelen*, a leisured attendance of the outdoors for a stroll, imagining that leafy country lanes and glorious ponds are the life-realm of farmers, those lucky folks who never have to endure the heft of the silver fish knife, the lozenge of *neetjes voorgebeeld* (yes, nicely turned out, polite). And this imperial gesture will go so far as to bestow a patrician nod of recognition—*soms* (only sometimes, mind)—*als aanduiding van zuivere kwaliteit*, an indication of genuine quality! What a pinnacle to achieve, but the subtext here too, the class beyond and above using the mark of *boer* to anoint authenticity.

Examining these connotative figurations now, under the glass of *Inglish*, I begin to see and to understand why, in the powerfully Anglo world that my parents (Dutch *boers*) chose to emigrate to, displacing themselves from the comfort and safety of their known context, Dutch as place and language, I have tried and remarkably succeeded in effacing as much as possible of both my Dutch and my *boer*.

Passing, bell hooks calls it, and her analysis of passing as a cultural camouflage is one that I understand more clearly recognizing my own abrogation of both Dutch and *boer*. And it might seem easy enough, given my skin, visibility invisible, my only marker my name and sometimes a tinge of pronunciative oddness left over from the language I first spoke, before I so assiduously attached myself to English, determined to pass. Although there are certainly those who will smilingly and patronizingly insist there's an indelible mark of the boer in my vernacular enthusiasms, my often *common* language. So be it. I must, I suppose *Inglish* them too.

Back to the ubiquitous Dutch fable of the famous little boy with his famous finger in the famous *dyke*, the imploded metaphor of holding back a flood, an inundation, a wash of sea/she. More than anyone and with good cause, for a people who wrested land, inch by inch, from the sea, the Dutch fear of drowning, the landperson's (yes, *boer*) dread.

It was with a shock of recognition, my own terror of water, having once almost drowned because I stepped into a sudden and ear-filling hole in Buffalo Lake, Alberta, that I read in Simon Schama's *The Embarrassment of Riches: An Interpretation of Dutch Culture in the Golden Age*, his research on the Amsterdam *Tugthuis*, or house of correction (yes, jail), where one of the sentences or ' "correctives" . . . was the drowning cell or "water house" ' (Schama, 22). Jan de Parival refers to it in 1662:

> If they do not want to work [the incorrigibly idle] they are tethered like asses
> and are put in a cellar that is filled with water so that they must partly empty
> it by pumping if they do not wish to drown. (Schama, 22)

Tourists went to watch. And many accounts there apparently are, describing this punishment cell as a cistern where delinquents or lawbreakers were set to work, 'placing only a pump by them for relief whereby they are forced to labour for their lives' (Schama, 22). One observant observer bothered to note that it took only a quarter of an hour for the cell to fill, were the pump not energetically employed. This drowning, a submersion. But most important, a punishment especially reserved for the incorrigibly idle, those unwilling to work with their hands, to use the *boer's* instrument.

Each time I hear the word *boer* I imagine myself in such a cell, *vochtig* (yes, damp) and tight. There is a pump in there with me, the old-fashioned kind with a long handle and a gushing mouth, the kind we actually had in our farm kitchen when I was a child. Crazily, it is the wrong kind of pump, the kind that pours water into a space rather than pumping it out. But that is the uncontrollable nature of the imagination when it is coupled with our meagre experience.

For there is water, rising, full of voices, upper class, condescending. I am not sure if the pump is Dutch and the water is English; or if the water is Dutch and the pump is English. Or if the pump is what I pass for and the water is my inevitably lower class background. All I know is that I must work the handle (with my solidly Dutch peasant body), because the water is rising and I cannot swim. Right now, it is inching past my knees.

Makeda Silvera *b.* 1955

KINGSTON, JAMAICA

'Fascinated' with 'process'—the process of writing, of fighting for a space for herself and for other women writers of colour, of becoming an active participant in the making and unmaking of history about black women's lives—Makeda Silvera has striven energetically in the tradition of black women writers in Canada since the early 1980s. Born in Kingston, Jamaica, and brought up in a household of 'strong' and 'loving' women, she moved to Canada with her parents when she was thirteen. She began writing in the early 1970s as a reporter and freelance journalist, and later as an editorial assistant for the Toronto newspaper *Share.* Her journalism and community activism made her aware of, among other things, the problems facing Caribbean-born domestic workers in Canada. The result was Silvera's first book, *Silenced* (1983), a narrative documenting the lives of these women in their own first-person voices, not through the voices of 'academics who presumed to speak for them'. *Growing up Black* (1989), a resource guide for black youth, further reflects Silvera's involvement with her community.

A co-founder and publisher of Sister Vision Press, a Toronto press that publishes women of colour, Silvera has been instrumental not only in publishing books by women of colour, which were for a long time systematically rejected by mainstream publishers, but also in fostering younger women writers. The editor of *Piece of My Heart: A Lesbian of Colour Anthology* (1991), a groundbreaking collection in that it is 'the first such liaison of North American lesbians of colour', Silvera's own contribution to the volume is a piece called 'Man Royals and Sodomites: Some Thoughts on the Invisibility of Afro-Caribbean Lesbians'. This essay/memoir, perhaps the first attempt in writing to explore Caribbean lesbian sexuality within a historical and social context, has played a key role in reestablishing Silvera's links with her heritage. 'It was important for me', she says, 'to summon memory. . . . Again, I had to fall back on oral narratives to make sense of pieces of conversation from my mother, grandmother and women of their generation.' This essay/memoir, which 'was not written as a personal confession but as a family/community coming out', became, as Silvera notes, 'the basis for many of my stories. It became an opportunity to exercise that memory.' She is also the editor of *The Other Woman: Women of Colour in Contemporary Canadian Literature* (1995), a collection of essays and interviews that documents the writing lives of over twenty women of colour, and the co-editor of *Pearls of Passion: A Treasury of Lesbian Erotica* (1995) and of *Ma-Ka Diasporic Juks: Contemporary Writing by Queers of African Descent* (1997).

Silvera has published two collections of short fiction, *Remembering G* (1991) and *Her Head a Village* (1994). The former includes stories that come out of the 'ordinariness' of her roots—'I wrote about the things I knew as a child. I wrote about eating cornmeal pudding. . . . I could make magic and laughter out of the ordinariness.' The latter, written in the rhythms of Jamaican language, still remains rooted in past memories, but also includes stories that deal with the present conditions of the African Caribbean communities in Canada. Her first novel, *The Heart Does not Bend* (2003), praised for its sensuous evocations of landscape and food, was shortlisted for the Toronto Book Award. Set in both Jamaica and Canada, it is a story as much about a family whose destiny is in the hands of a courageous, yet overbearing, matriarch as about the tensions in loving and being loved.

Her Head a Village

(for Nan)

Her head was a noisy village, one filled with people, active and full of life, with many concerns and opinions. Children, including her own, ran about. Cousins twice removed bickered. A distant aunt, Maddie, decked out in two printed cotton dresses, a patched-up pair of pants and an old fuzzy sweater marched up and down the right side of her forehead. Soon she would have a migraine. On the other side, a pack of idlers lounged around a heated domino game, slapping the pieces hard against her left forehead. Close to her neck sat the gossiping crew, passing around bad news and samples of malicious and scandalous tales. The top of her head was quiet. Come evening this would change, with the arrival of schoolchildren; when the workers left their factories and offices, the pots, banging dishes and televisions blaring would add to the noisy village.

The Black woman writer had been trying all month to write an essay for presentation at an international forum for Third World women. She was to address the topic 'Writing as a Dangerous Profession'. This was proving to be more difficult as the weeks passed. She pleaded for quiet, but could silence only the children.

The villagers did not like her style of writing, her focus and the new name she called herself—feminist. They did not like her choice of lovers, her spending too many hours behind her desk or propped up in her bed with paper and pen or book. The workers complained that she should be in the factories and offices with them; the idlers said she didn't spend much time playing with them and the gossiping crew told so many tales that the woman writer had trouble keeping her essay separate from their stories. Some of the villagers kept quiet, going about their business, but they were too few to shut out the noise. Maddie did not often side with the writer, but neither did she poke at her. She listened and sometimes smiled at the various expressions that surfaced on the woman writer's face. Maddie stood six feet tall with a long, stern face and eyes like well-used marbles. The villagers said Maddie was a woman of the spirits, a mystic woman who carried a sharpened pencil behind her ear. She walked about the village all day, sometimes marching loudly, and other times quietly. Some days she was seen talking to herself.

'When I first come to this country, I use to wear one dress at a time. But times too hard, now you don't know if you coming or going, so I wear all my clothes. You can't be too sure of anything but yourself. So I sure of me, and I wear all my clothes on my back. And I talk to meself, for you have to know yourself in this time.'

The villagers didn't know what to make of her. Some feared her, others respected her. The gossipers jeered behind her back.

Plugging her ears against spirit-woman Maddie, the Black woman writer sat in the different places she thought would be good to her. She first sat behind her desk, but no words came. It was not so much that there were no words to write down—there were many—but the villagers were talking all at once and in so many tongues that it was hard for her to hold onto their words. Each group wanted her to feature it in the essay.

Early in the morning, after her own children left for school, she tried to write in her bed. It was large queen-size pine bed with five pillows in a small room on the second floor. The room was a pale green and the ceilings a darker shade of green—her favourite colour. She was comfortable there and had produced many essays and poems from that bed. Its double mattress almost reached the ceiling. She felt at peace under the patchwork blanket. It took her back to her grandparents' wooden house a mile from the sea, in another village, the tropical one where she was born. Easter lilies, powder-puff trees, dandelions and other wild flowers circled the house. She saw a red-billed Streamertail, then a yellow-crowned night heron and a white bellied Caribbean dove. Their familiar voices filled her head: 'Quaart, Tleeoo-ee, cruuuuuuuuuuu,' and other short repeated calls.

She wrote only lists of 'To do's.'
washing
cleaning
cooking
laundry
telephone calls
appointments.
At the edge of the paper birds took flight.

Nothing to do with writing, she thought. On days like these, convinced that she would get no writing done, she left the village and lunched with friends. She did not tell her friends about the village in her head. They would think her crazy, like Maddie. When she was alone, after lunch, scores of questions flooded her head.

What conditions are necessary for one to write?

What role do children play in a writer's creativity?

Is seclusion a necessary ingredient?

Questions she had no answers for.

Sometimes, she holed up in the garden shed at the edge of the backyard. She had cleared out a space and brought in a kerosene heater. The shed faced south. Old dirty windows ran the length of it and the ceiling's cracked blue paint threatened to fall. There she worked on an oversize ill-kept antique desk, a gift from a former lover. She had furnished the space with two chairs, a wooden crate stacked with a dictionary and a few books, a big armchair dragged from the neighbour's garbage, postcards pasted on the walls to remind her of Africa. There were a few things from her village: coconut husks, ackee seeds, photographs of birds, flowers and her grandparents' house near the sea.

One afternoon, however, the villagers discovered the shed and moved in. The idlers set up their gambling table. Gossip-mongers sat in a large area and Maddie walked around quietly and read everything written on every piece of paper. Soon they all wanted to read her essay. The idlers made fun of her words. The gossip-mongers said they had known all along what she would write. Offices and factories closed early, as the others hurried into the shed to hear what all the shouting was about.

They were all talking at once, with varying opinions.

'Writing is not a dangerous profession, writing is a luxury!' shouted one of the workers.

'Many of us would like to write but can't. We have to work, find food to support our families. Put that in your essay.'

'Look here, read here, something about woman as a lover and the danger of writing about that.'

The Black woman writer's head tore in half as the villagers snatched at the paper. She shouted as loud as she could that there was more to the paper than that.

'See for yourselves—here, read it, I am also writing about the economics of writing, problems of women writers who have families.' Almost out of breath, she continued, 'See I also wrote about cultural biases.'

'Cultural biases,' snarled a cold, grating voice. 'Why not just plain old racism? What's wrong with that word?' Before she could answer, another villager who was jumping up and down silenced the rest of them. 'This woman thing can't go into the paper. It wouldn't look right to talk about that at a Third World conference.' They all shouted in agreement.

She felt dizzy. Her ears ached. Her mouth and tongue were heavy. But she would not give in. She tried to block them out by calling up faces of the women she had loved. But she saw only the faces of the villagers and heard only the sounds of their loud chatter.

'No one will write about women lovers. These are not national concerns in Third World countries. These issues are not relevant. These,' they shouted, 'are white bourgeois concerns!'

Exhausted, the Black woman writer tried again. 'All I want to do is to write something about being a Black lesbian in a North American city. One where white racism is cloaked in liberalism and where Black homophobia . . .' They were not listening. They bombarded her with more questions.

'What about the danger of your writing being the definitive word for all Black women? What about the danger of writing in a liberal white bourgeois society and of selling out? Why don't you write about these things?'

She screamed at them to shut up and give her a voice, but they ignored her and talked even louder.

'Make it clear that you, as a Black woman writer, are privileged to be speaking on a panel like this.'

'And what about the danger of singular achievement?' asked a worker.

'Woman lover,' sniggered another. 'What about the danger of writing about racism? Police harassment? Murders of our villagers?'

Many times during the month the Black woman writer would scream at them to shut up. And when she succeeded in muting their voices she was tired because they refused to speak one at a time.

On days like these the Black woman writer escaped from the garden shed to play songs by her favourite blues singer, drink bottles of warm beer and curl up in her queen-size pine bed. She held onto the faces of her lovers and tried to forget the great difficulty in writing the essay.

The writer spent many days and nights staring at the blank white paper in front of her. The villagers did not ease up. They criticized the blank white paper. It was only a few days before the conference. 'You have to start writing,' they pressured her. 'Who is going to represent us?'

Words swarmed around her head like wasps. There was so much she wanted to say about 'Writing as a Dangerous Profession', about dangers to her as a Black woman, writer, lesbian. At times she felt that writing the paper was hopeless. Once she broke down and cried in front of the villagers. On this particular day, as the hour grew close, she felt desperate—suicidal, in fact. The villagers had no sympathy for her.

'Suicide? You madder than Maddie!' they jeered. 'Give Maddie the paper and let her use her pencil,' they heckled.

'I'm not mad,' she protested with anger. 'Get out of my head. Here'—she threw the blank paper on the ground—'write, write, you all write.'

'But you are the writer,' they pestered her. They were becoming hostile and vicious. The woman writer felt as if her head would burst.

She thought of Virginia Woolf's *A Room of One's Own*. She wondered if Woolf had had a village in her head.

She took to spending more time in bed with a crate of warm beer at the side. Her eyes were red from worry, not enough sleep and too much drink. She studied her face in a small hand-mirror, examining the lines on her forehead. They were deep and pronounced, lines she had not earned, even with the raising of children, writing several essays and poetry books, cleaning, cooking and caring for lovers. She gazed at all the books around her and became even more depressed.

Interrupted by the angry voices of the villagers, overwhelmed by the force of their voices, she surrendered her thoughts to them.

'Well, what are you going to write? We have ideas to give you.' The Black woman writer knew their ideas. They were not new, but she listened.

'Write about women in houses without electricity.'

'Write about the dangers of living in a police state.'

'Write about Third World issues.'

'Write about . . . about . . .'

'Stick to the real issues that face Black women writers.'

'Your sexuality is your personal business. We don't want to hear about it, and the forum doesn't want to know.'

They accused her of enjoying the luxury of being a lesbian in a decaying society, of forgetting about their problems.

She tried to negotiate with them. 'Listen, all I want is a clear head. I promise to write about your concerns.' But they disagreed. 'We gave you more than enough time, and you've produced nothing.' They insisted that they all write the paper. She was disturbed by their criticism. She would never complete the paper with so many demands. The Black woman writer was full of despair; she wanted to explain to the villagers, once again, that what made writing dangerous for her was who she was—Black/woman/lesbian/mother/worker. . . . But they would not let her continue. In angry, harsh voices they pounded her head. 'You want to talk about sexuality as a political issue? Villagers are murdered every time they go out, our young people jailed and thrown out of schools.' Without success, she explained that she wanted to talk about all the dangers of writing. 'Have you ever heard of, read about lesbians in the Third World? They don't have the luxury of sitting down at an international forum and discussing this issue, so why should you?'

Her head blazed; her tiny, tight braids were like coals on fire. The villagers stayed in her head, shouting and laughing. She tried closing her eyes and massaging her forehead. With her eyes still closed, she eased her body onto the couch. Familiar footsteps sounded at the side of her head. Maddie appeared. 'All this shouting and hollering won't solve anything—it will only make us tired and enemies. We all have to live together in this village.' Not one villager joked about her two dresses, pants, and sweater. Not one villager had anything to say about the pencil stuck in her hair, a pencil she never used. Maddie spoke for a long time, putting the villagers to sleep.

The Black woman writer slept late, dreaming first of her grandparents' village and then of her lovers. Now Maddie's face came. She took Maddie's hand and they set out down the village streets, through the fields of wild flowers, dandelions, Easter lilies. Maddie took the pencil from her head and began to write. With Maddie beside her, she awoke in a bed of wild flowers, refreshed.

Neil Bissoondath *b.* 1955

TRINIDAD, WEST INDIES

'The only label that I am happy with,' says Neil Bissoondath, 'is that of "Canadian writer" . . . because it means everything and it means nothing, because it includes Rohinton Mistry, Margaret Atwood, Robertson Davies, Timothy Findley, Neil Bissoondath and M.G. Vassanji. It is such an open concept. There is no label, there is no stereotype to be attached to it any more. . . . And that makes that label comfortable.' Bissoondath's acceptance of the label 'Canadian' serves as the point of departure of his controversial book *Selling Illusions: The Cult of Multiculturalism in Canada* (1994), an excerpt from which appears below. A 'book of a somewhat pugnacious kind', as he says in an interview, it begins by declaring Bissoondath's 'complete independence of all political parties', or, as he puts it elsewhere, that he is 'an enemy of ideology of any kind, political, racial,

religious. All ideology depends on stereotypes, and human life is not so simple.' He acknowledges, and traces, his origins—'I was born a Trinidadian . . . But that was a long time ago. I am no longer Trinidadian. . . I do not share the hopes, fears, joys and views of Trinidadians'— but, at the same time, he privileges his present: 'Nowhere [in Canada] have I felt myself a stranger. Alienation, expatriation, exile: they are just words to me now, not personal issues; they are intellectual concepts that fascinate me precisely because they are so distant.' Presenting his book as one that 'does not claim to be an objective examination of multiculturalism', Bissoondath attacks the Canadian federal policy and its various forms of implementation because they 'manipulate the ethnic communities'. As he says, 'multiculturalism constantly throws your ethnicity at you, thereby putting you at arm's length from society at large.' Multiculturalism and such cultural events as the 'Writing Thru Race' conference, he argues, do not help eliminate discrimination. It is 'through effort, through work, through education' that 'Italians, or the Jews, or the Irish, or the Japanese . . . [who] suffered through a period of discrimination, sometimes very serious discrimination . . . made their way into the mainstream'. His vision of Canadian society, as he says in an interview, is one 'that from the beginning makes an attempt to be colour-blind'.

The descendent of indentured labourers from India, Bisoondath was born in Arima, Trinidad, and grew up in Sangre Grande before arriving in Toronto in 1973 to study at York University. After he graduated with a BA in French (1977), Bisoondath taught French and English as second languages while pursuing his writing. With the assistance of a Banff School of Fine Arts scholarship, he completed his first book, *Digging Up the Mountains* (1986), a collection of short fiction about immigrant characters from various ethnic backgrounds. *A Casual Brutality* (1988), Bisoondath's highly acclaimed novel, was the winner of the W.H. Smith-Books in Canada First Novel Award and a finalist for the Trillium Award. Its protagonist, Raj, an East Indian who arrives in Toronto as a foreign student but ends up taking residency, narrates his life story while he is on a return flight from his Caribbean island to Canada. Having lost a Canadian wife and their son to the racial violence that has torn his Caribbean

island apart, Raj shares Bisoondath's resistance to ethnicity and avoids any identification, including glances of recognition, with other Caribbeans in Toronto. This novel was followed by another collection of short fiction, *On the Eve of Uncertain Tomorrows* (1990), also about various immigrants who lean for support on each other in their encounters with the Canadian system.

Bisoondath believes that 'writers have no social function. Writers have one function, and that is to tell a good story.' Yet his fiction revolves around many of the social problems that afflict immigrants. His second novel, *The Innocence of Age* (1992), shifts its focus from immigrants, who now appear only as secondary characters, to deal with the relationship between a father and a son. Written after his father's death, it is, as Bisoondath has described it, about 'people very different from myself, who have appropriated white, wasp faces'. Nevertheless, while his most recent novel, *Doing the Heart Good* (2002), which won the Hugh MacLennan Prize for Fiction, focuses on the reminiscences of Alistair MacKenzie—a lover of Dickens and sherry—the female protagonist in an earlier novel, *The Worlds Within Her* (1998), flies from Toronto to Trinidad to scatter her mother's ashes. Like other writers, Bisoondath does not want to be pigeonholed. Bisoondath, who lives in Quebec City, was the writer and host of a documentary about fathers and sons broadcast on CBC television.

from *Selling Illusions: The Cult of Multiculturalism in Canada*
The Uses of Ethnicity

> The cult of ethnicity exaggerates differences, intensifies resentments and antagonisms, drives ever deeper the awful wedges between races and nationalities. The endgame is self-pity and self-ghettoization.
> —Arthur M. Schlesinger Jr, *The Disuniting of America*

Some years ago, a book-promotion tour took me to Washington, DC, and to a radio studio where I was to be the guest on a phone-in show. The host and I chatted for a few minutes about my background, my novel, *A Casual Brutality*, and its themes of colonialism, immigration, and displacement. I fielded a few calls, answered a few questions—and then I heard through the headphones a soft-spoken young woman calling in to set the historical record straight on the origins of people like myself, people historically and ethnically of India. Of herself she said only one thing, that she was black, and she went on to explain that Indians were a fairly recent invention, the result of a British plot to exterminate the black race not through genocide but through a kind of genetic breeding.

The land called India, she said, had not long ago been populated by Africans. Then one day the English arrived. They took a dislike to the Africans they found and instituted a policy of enforced copulation between Englishmen and black women, the goal being the overwhelming of the black genes by the white genes and, so, the eventual extermination of blacks. The black genes had proven resistant, though, and the rapes instead had produced the people we now call Indians. It was, she explained, the reason that Indians had dark skin with straight, black hair and facial features that appeared a blend of European and African.

I was speechless for a moment and then admitted my ignorance of this version of history—at which point the host's hand gestured a question at me and at my own gestured response, pressed a button for the next call.

Ethnicity is the classification of human beings by race, religion, language, cultural traditions and other traits held in common. Notions of ethnicity allow academics and social engineers to order, and so more easily study, the vicissitudes of the human race. They can, to a point, be useful.

Ethnicity, it must be noted, is not restricted to race alone. Just as 'whites' are not ethnics (but Danes, all of whom are white, are), so 'blacks' are not ethnics (but Jamaicans, most of whom are black, are). Nor can the black communities of Nova Scotia, people who have lived in this country for as long as the oldest white families, justifiably be considered 'ethnic' communities in the popular way—or can they? Moreover, 'ethnic' as a synonym for 'foreign' or 'exotic' or 'visible'—as in the term 'ethnic food'—is essentially meaningless. I think always with delight of a good acquaintance who, with his traditionally 'Canadian' demeanour, likes to complain tongue-in-cheek that he too should be considered an ethnic in view of his Danish heritage—but in the Canadian concept of ethnicity no one is willing to recognize him as such; he's too invisible, he fades into the landscape.

Such categorizations are not without their controversies. They allow the less stable among us to order the human race into ethnic hierarchies (with Jews and blacks usually competing for last place in the ranking of some; with whites in the cellar in the ranking of others). They lend a veneer of respectability to studies such as the one conducted by Professor Philippe Rushton some years ago on the supposed link between penis length and intelligence—a study that suggested that more is not necessarily better. (Guess which ethnic group turned out to be the best endowed and, thus, the least intelligent. Hint: the 'results' could be used to explain away the woes of much of the African continent.)

Further controversy arises when it comes to the ethnic/racial breakdown of crime statistics. In 1990, Metropolitan Toronto Police Sergeant Ben Eng broke force policy by collating race and crime data to conclude that the vast majority of crime in the Oriental community was being committed by 'phoney refugees' from mainland China and Vietnam.[1] Sergeant Eng's approach was less than scientific—he simply drew conclusions from the names entered in arrest forms and daily occurrence sheets—and so his conclusions attracted a fair amount of outrage (although, tellingly, '30 groups in the Chinese community sprang to his defence'[2]).

Two problems in particular are troubling to opponents of this approach to crime statistics. The first is the question of the actual collection of data. As the head of the Metro Police Services Board, Susan Eng (no relation to the sergeant), asked how far such studies should pursue the racial breakdown: 'Are you a Jamaican black, an African black? Are you a Danish white? A Scottish white?'[3] The second problem concerns the use that would be made of the statistics: would they simply be made the basis for official discrimination? As Judge David Cole, chair of the Commission on Systemic Racism in the Ontario Criminal Justice System, so succinctly stated it, 'People are torn between "The truth shall make you free" and "The numbers will be abused." '[4]

Perhaps most importantly, though, few opponents subscribe to the belief that firm evidence of a racial/ethnic component in crime and similar bias in the justice system would ever lead to the institution of concrete and positive measures, the only goal that could firmly justify the pursuit of such statistics. Antoni Shelton, executive director of the Urban Alliance on Race Relations, made what seems a remarkable statement in this regard: 'Statistics have an academic, not real-life, value and they have political impact on people's lives. . . . Stats won't dispel the myth that blacks are predisposed to crime. And proving in a lab with numbers that injustice exists won't create the will to do anything about it.'[5]

The statement is remarkable for this reason: if statistics of race and ethnicity carefully collected and collated can be used to ensure employment equity, why can they not be used to combat crime? Without the full picture, such policies and programs will always be inadequate—and we deny ourselves the full picture, it seems to me, by denying ourselves certain knowledge because of the fear of misuse.

And, even with the most complete data, even with the most careful and considered application of the results, there would undoubtedly be misuse. Statistics, we all know, are a tool of the devil, easily bent to serve any purpose. A finding of a high percentage of, say, Vietnamese or South Asians involved in criminal activity would surely be used by racists to justify calls for an active and official discrimination. Some abuse is inevitable—but while statistics cannot guarantee the political will necessary to bring about change, neither has fear of inevitable abuse ever prevented the statistical study of social problems and the institution of remedial programs as a result of the knowledge gained.

In the end, though, the larger context provides an uncomfortable perspective: refusing to collect such data is to be untrue to the selves that we claim. It is to allow

1 Lynda Hurst, 'Colouring crime stats by race', *Toronto Star*, 27 November 1993.
2 Ibid.
3 Ibid.
4 Ibid.
5 Ibid.

ethnic communities to have it both ways: to exist as officially protected, promoted, and enhanced entities and yet to remain in an important way untouchable, and so subject to abuse from both within and without. Could this explain the decision by at least thirty groups in the Chinese community to defend Sergeant Eng?

Ethnicity can be like a futon mattress; it can cushion and comfort, it can provide a safe and warm place—but the stuffing sometimes shifts, becomes lumpy and irksome, and the lumps must either be accepted or pounded out. Accepting the lumps makes for uneasy sleep. Too often, ethnic communities accept the uneasy sleep. Or, as novelist Joy Kogawa more elegantly put it: 'In an age when loneliness, malaise and an overwhelming bigness assail us, our ethnic communities are sometimes no more than bits of driftwood to which a few people cling in the midst of a typhoon. What we need are lifeboats. What we need is Noah's ark.'[6]

At the heart of multiculturalism bob these 'bits of driftwood': communities shaped by notions of ethnicity; more particularly, by a heightened sense of ethnicity; most particularly, by a heightened sense of their own ethnicity. They are, many of them, what the poet and professor Roy Miki, a Canadian of Japanese descent and a man with a powerful sense of historical grievance, has termed 'racialized'.

To be 'racialized' is to have acquired a racial vision of life, to have learnt to see oneself, one's past, present, and future, through the colour of one's own skin. It is not new—*Mein Kampf* hinges on a racial vision; apartheid could not have existed without a racial vision—but it is, in certain circles, acquiring a new respectability as old enemies grow to resemble each other. Nor is this as simple or as agreeable a proposition as it may appear. Ethnicity, race, and their permutations are peculiarly conducive to the spinning of fantasy, so that Christopher Columbus becomes merely the evil European who enslaves and massacres noble natives by conquering Paradise; so that the Toronto writer and social activist June Callwood is transformed into a racist; and so that the ethnic genesis of Indians is cast as yet one more nefarious colonial machination.

A sense of one's racial and cultural background, like a sense of one's personal likes and dislikes, is essential to an individual sense of self. Confusion over one's ethnicity, the desperate search for a personal centre and a meaning to one's life, leads to the kind of despair evident in the words of that young woman in Washington. It was clear that her view of history, as peculiar and as misinformed as it was, not only placed her in what was to her a satisfactory historical context, but it also offered the calming notion of herself as a victim of that history. It solidified the nebulous; it soothed the pain of drift. To see oneself in history rather than outside it, to see oneself as a victim of history rather than as one of its victimizers, is to confer on oneself a delicious sweet-and-sour confirmation of one's own existence: deliciously sweet because you cannot be denied; deliciously sour because you have been brutalized. This life you lead is not your fault.

But neither history nor race nor culture is destiny: human beings are saved from that by intelligence and the gift of irony. And it is the ironic eye, questioning, judging, that ultimately refuses to simplify.

6 Joy Kogawa, in *Cultures and Writers: A Cultural Dialogue of Ethnic Writers*, ed. Yvonne Grabowski, in *The Dictionary of Canadian Quotations*, ed. John Robert Colombo (Toronto: Stoddart, 1991).

Nor does ethnicity guarantee anything in a complex world. Samuel Selvon,[7] Bharati Mukherjee,[8] Rohinton Mistry,[9] Hanif Kureishi,[10] and I are all writers, all of the same 'ethnicity' to a certain extent, all ethnically 'South Asians', all 'Indians'. Yet I suspect that, as a group, we are at least as dissimilar as similar. Selvon and I were both born in Trinidad, but of different generations and with lives that have followed very different paths to different cities in the same country. Mukherjee, born in Calcutta, found Canada an unhappy place and has built a more satisfying life in the United States. Mistry and I both moved to Toronto from elsewhere and share the experience (with many others) of living and writing in that city. Kureishi, born in England of Indian parents, lives in London: we met once, shook hands, found we had little to say to each other.

Each of these people and I can claim a certain similarity, but we must also acknowledge vastly different contexts, contexts that have shaped personalities sufficiently dissimilar to render the ethnic category, beyond certain superficialities, essentially useless. Selvon remained a Trinidadian all his life. A few years ago, when he was in his mid-sixties and had long been considered a cornerstone of West Indian literature, he said to me, 'People keep asking me when I'm going to write my Canadian novel. Man, I'm still dealing with things that happened in my childhood.' Kureishi, in manner and imagination, is nothing if not British. Mukherjee has embraced the exuberance of America, while I prefer the quieter pleasures of Canada.

When we meet, it is not as fellow ethnics sharing unspoken similarities. There is no gravitation around an ethnic bonfire. These are writers whose work I cherish—just as I cherish the work of Kazuo Ishiguro or Ian McEwan or John Irving. I feel a greater affinity for the work of Timothy Mo—a British novelist born of an English mother and a Chinese father—than I do for that of Salman Rushdie, with whom I share an ethnicity. Like those of Gabriel Garcia Marquez, Rushdie's fictions are alien to me. Ethnically, Mo and I share nothing, but imaginatively we share much. In Mo's fictional worlds, as in those of the Peruvian novelist Mario Vargas Llosa, I recognize aspects of myself. As Salman Rushdie once wrote of a similar 'community' elsewhere: 'England's Indian writers are by no means all the same type of animal. Some of us, for instance, are Pakistani. Others Bangladeshi. Others West, or East, or even South African. And V.S. Naipaul, by now, is something else entirely. This word "Indian" is getting to be a pretty scattered concept.'[11] Scattered, I would venture, to the point of near meaninglessness.

This diversity within the same 'ethnic group' is a growing reality in Vancouver, where the 'Chinese community' numbers 250,000. It can easily appear monolithic, and yet there are tensions brewing both within the community itself and between the

7 Trinidad-born novelist (*A Brighter Sun, The Lonely Londoners*); lived for many years in London before moving to Calgary. He died suddenly in April 1994, while on a visit to Trinidad. He was 71.
8 Novelist (*The Tiger's Daughter, Wife, Jasmine*) and short-story writer (*Darkness, The Middleman and Other Stories*, which won the 1988 [US] National Book Critics Circle Award).
9 Short-story writer (*Tales from Firozsha Baag*) and novelist (*Such a Long Journey*, which won numerous prizes including the Governor General's Award).
10 Screenwriter (*My Beautiful Laundrette, Sammy and Rosie Get Laid*) and novelist (*The Buddha of Suburbia*).
11 Salman Rushdie, 'Imaginary Homelands', in *Imaginary Homelands*, Granta Books in association with Penguin Books, 1991, 16–17.

community and others. Raymond Chan, an MP from Richmond, BC, and secretary of state for Asian-Pacific Affairs, has pointed out the diversity within the community. 'Don't look at them as a block,'[12] he has cautioned.

And a block they are not. A clear illustration of this is provided by Shue Tuck Wong, a geography professor at Simon Fraser University.[13] One day, his daughter, a grade nine student, called him a 'banana'. She explained that other Chinese students, recent arrivals from Hong Kong, Taiwan, and China, had called her a banana—yellow on the outside, white on the inside—'because I cannot speak or write Chinese'.

A banana: not, then, a real Chinese. It is evidence of arrogance, of a vision informed by notions of racial and ethnic purity. And it was within this context that Professor Wong advised his daughter to respond: 'Tell them back that you are a Canadian. If there is anyone who calls you a banana, he must be a racist. It's important you should be recognized on the basis of who you are, rather than what language you speak.'

Jim Kwong, a police-community liaison officer who moved from Hong Kong in 1991, offers the 'general impression . . . that many Chinese Canadians who were born here and speak only English prefer to mix with the Canadian mainstream rather than the Chinese community.'[14] But language choices are not the only source of division. Business competition is stiff and political disagreements profound. Raymond Chan has alienated many in the Chinese community by organizing protests against the human-rights record of the Beijing government.

Professor Wong is a pragmatic man, a man not blinded by sentimentality: 'Learning Chinese is very useful if you are going to make your living in an area that speaks Chinese,' he said. 'But if you are living in a non-Chinese environment, it's more important to have a good command of the language where you live.'[15] It is evidence that Professor Wong has a firm grasp not only on who he is but also on where he is. It is evidence of great personal integrity.

Mr Chan, who was born in Hong Kong and emigrated to Canada at the age of seventeen, claims no ethnic political base for himself, explaining that part of his motivation in running for office was 'to show that even without the support of the [Chinese] establishment, I have the support of the people. I am a Canadian.'[16] In the world of multiculturalism, it is a courageous admission.

My point is simple, but it is one usually ignored by multiculturalism and its purveyors—for to recognize the complexity of ethnicity, to acknowledge the wild variance within ethnic groups, would be to render multiculturalism and its aims absurd. The individuals who form a group, the 'ethnics' who create a community, are frequently people of vastly varying composition. Shared ethnicity does not entail unanimity of vision. If the individual is not to be betrayed, a larger humanity must prevail over the narrowness of ethnicity.

12 Robert Matas, 'Minister loathes ethnic politics', *The Globe and Mail*, 8 January 1994.
13 Robert Matas, 'A "banana" split in Vancouver', *The Globe and Mail*, 25 February 1994.
14 Ibid.
15 Ibid.
16 Ibid.

To preserve, enhance and promote the 'multicultural heritage' of Canada, multiculturalism must work against forces more insistent than any government policy. If a larger humanity does not at first prevail, time and circumstance will inevitably ensure that it ultimately does.

When I was in my early teens and already interested in a writing career, I ran into a problem not unfamiliar to every would-be writer: What was I to write about? I soon decided that I, a Trinidadian of East Indian descent (or extraction, as we used to say, making it sound appropriately wrenching), was destined, maybe doomed, to write pastoral stories of dhotied, cow-owning, cane-cutting Hindu peasants in dusty central Trinidad villages.

This was a tall order and the cause of some despair, since I neither knew nor had ever seen any Hindu peasants in dusty Trinidad villages. Having grown up in a modern suburb of Port of Spain to the sounds of Motown, I didn't know whether they even existed. And yet, it seemed to me, I had to tell the story—even if it meant creating it from pure imagination—of an entire community, my community, ethnically inherited, of turbans and woodfires and huts of packed mud and thatch.

This belief, limiting and quickly jettisoned, came from the earnestness of ambition swathed in an idea of race and religion, an idea, finally, of belonging.

Community and belonging: they are at the heart of every immigrant dilemma. In the contentious introduction to her 1985 short story collection *Darkness*, Bharati Mukherjee writes: 'In my fiction, and in my Canadian experience, "immigrants" were lost souls, put upon and pathetic. Expatriates, on the other hand, knew all too well who and what they were, and what foul fate had befallen them.'[17] Ms Mukherjee saw herself as an expatriate, and she began to write of characters equally self-aware, engaging an irony she describes, unflinchingly, as 'mordant and self-protective': 'Irony promised both detachment from and superiority over, those well-bred post-colonials much like myself, adrift in the new world, wondering if they would ever belong.'[18] And then she adds a paragraph that neatly delineates one of the great themes of so-called 'immigrant' literature: 'If you have to wonder [whether you will ever belong], if you keep looking for signs, if you wait—surrendering little bits of a reluctant self every year, clutching the souvenirs of an ever-retreating past—you'll never belong, anywhere.'[19]

Mukherjee looked forward (and not backward) to an idea of immigrant perfection, since found in the United States. It is an idea so alien to the Canadian approach that this country, 'hostile to its citizens who had been born in hot, moist continents like Asia',[20] could not help but seem darker than it probably was at the time.

This wondering, this looking for signs, this failure to belong takes many forms. It is sometimes sad and enervating, sometimes exuberant and colourful. It is always unsettling.

17 Bharati Mukherjee, *Darkness* (Toronto: Penguin, 1985), 1–2.
18 Ibid., 2.
19 Ibid.
20 Mukherjee, *Darkness*, 2.

In his novel *No New Land*,[21] M.G. Vassanji explores this theme—a particularly tragic aspect of the immigrant experience—through the story of a man named Nurdin Lalani, his friends, family, and community of Muslim Indians exiled to Toronto by the racial politics of Africa.

Vassanji offers a remarkable portrait of the teeming and almost self-sufficient community that has established itself in a large apartment building in the Don Mills section of Toronto. He captures its past and its present, its ambitions and its intrigues, the sounds of its conversations and the smells of its foods: a little society hectic with activity behind tightly closed doors.

Its members make perilous sorties out into the wider society only when they must, usually for work. And who can blame them? For it seems that Toronto offers little beyond humiliation and danger, corruptive peep-shows and physical violence lurking around every corner. When the well-meaning but hapless Nurdin tries to lend a helping hand to a woman in distress, he ends up being charged with indecent assault—merely a pretext for blackmail, it turns out, since the complainant is easily bought off. Even the immigrant haven of Kensington Market holds unholy temptations for Nurdin when he comes close to having an affair with a widowed childhood friend he happens to run into. As a character in another novel by another writer—Nazruddin in V.S. Naipaul's *A Bend in the River*—says about ethnic attitudes in Canada: 'The thing about some of those ethnic groups over there is that they don't like moving around too much. They just want to go home as fast as they can and stay there.'[22]

The Canadians encountered—all whites, in fact, including a German *fräulein* in Tanganyika who slaps Nurdin's father when his admiring glances grow too frank—reveal a distinct lack of goodwill: any warmth they may display is merely camouflage for their attempts to fleece the newcomers. Only a Montreal immigration officer is friendly, but then his genial 'Welcome to Canada' costs him nothing.

These people are, it is clear, Mukherjee's immigrants, put-upon and pathetic. Bitter-sweet descriptions of Dar es Salaam offer a nostalgic vision of the past and make the present seem even darker than it really is, emphasizing the central point that there are, as the title states, no new lands, only new circumstances.

No New Land is a novel, and the community it examines is fictional. But it is fiction based on reality. Such buildings and neighbourhoods are to be found in most major cities of Canada, pockets of ethnicity we choose to honour, as Toronto has done, by erecting street signs in the ethnic language most prevalent. It makes for the appearance of tolerance and, like the park signs asking visitors to PLEASE WALK ON THE GRASS, good tourist photographs. But Vassanji's description of this community of exiles—so tight, so self-contained, so alienated from the mainstream—is that of an almost classic ghetto. It is not an extreme of multiculturalism but its ideal: a way of life transported whole, a little outpost of exoticism preserved and protected.

And yet one can detect vital changes in the younger generation. Nurdin's teenaged children, for instance, speak a language different from that of their parents, their

21 Toronto: McClelland & Stewart Ltd, 1992.
22 V.S. Naipaul, *A Bend in the River* (New York: Alfred A. Knopf, 1979), 236.

attitudes—when compared to the young Nurdin in Dar es Salaam—are more independent. The inevitable change, both generational and experiential, is a challenge to the
parents—Nurdin interprets his daughter's impatience as a growing hatred of her origins—but the children, it is clear, are leaving behind the ghetto of the mind, their hori-
zons different; Canada for them, unlike for their parents, is indeed a new land. Yasmin,
a secondary character, has already found this freedom in the United States, displaying
what Mukherjee characterizes as 'a movement away from the aloofness of expatriation,
to the exuberance of immigration'.

If the undeniable ghettoization is bad news for the purveyors of multiculturalism,
so too is this uneasy but equally undeniable distancing of the next generation. These
children, and their children after them, will in all likelihood shrug off the restraints of
ethnicity. They will acquire friends of various backgrounds who share their experience,
some of them will intermarry, and most if not all will blend into the mainstream of the
society around them, itself already irrevocably changed. They will, in a word, integrate.

Despite the attraction of the past, the changes wrought by immigration and radically different circumstances must be recognized, assimilated and accepted. It is the only
way to get on with one's life, the only way to take full advantage of the new possibilities. It is a reality multiculturalism, with its obsessively backward gaze, fails to recognize.
Immigration is essentially about renewal. It is unjust, to individuals and to the communities from which they emerge, to require it to be about stasis. To do so is to legit-
imize marginalization; it is to turn ethnic communities into museums or exoticism.

Marilyn Dumont *b.* 1955

OLDS, ALBERTA

Of Cree and Métis origins, Marilyn Dumont has been writing since 1985. Widely anthologized, she won the Gerald Lampert Memorial Award for her first collection of poetry, *A Really Good Brown Girl* (1996), and both the Stephan G. Stephansson Award in Alberta and the Alberta Book Award for Poetry for her second collection, *green girl dreams Mountains* (2001). Her poetry, in her own words, is 'certainly writing back to the history that [she] learned, but it is also a way of creating a new history too'. This 'new history' derives in part from her 'own urban experience', an experience often sidelined by the 'traditional' accounts of Native life many readers expect Aboriginal writing to reflect. While Dumont is not 'arguing that native culture is dying and that [traditional] symbols do not exist

within the full integrity of the living culture', she is interested in capturing the 'continuum of exposure to traditional experience in native culture', a continuum that includes 'the experience of the urban native': 'The urban native who participates in all the trappings of a wage economy as best he/she is able to. The urban native who is increasingly becoming the majority.' As many of her poems illustrate, 'the urban native experience' reveals that 'internalized colonialism is alive and well,' on the one hand, and 'that there is a connection between domination and representation', on the other. A 'misconception' she is interested in dispelling concerns the assumption that she may be 'deficient in [her] Nativeness' because she 'didn't grow up with an actual story'. 'This is really screwed up,' she says, 'because . . .

if it's an oral tradition, I'm not going to come away with stories that I can narrate as if I had read them in a library.'

Born in Olds, in northeastern Alberta, Dumont—a descendent of Métis leader Gabriel Dumont—studied at the University of Alberta, earning a diploma in Social Work and a BA in English, and at the University of British Columbia, where she obtained an MFA. In addition to her work as a radio and television broadcaster, and her video production work with the National Film Board, she has taught creative writing at Simon Fraser University, Kwantlin College, and the University of Alberta.

Letter To Sir John A. MacDonald

Dear John: I'm still here and halfbreed,
after all these years
you're dead, funny thing,
that railway you wanted so badly,
there was talk a year ago 5
of shutting it down
and part of it was shut down,
the dayliner at least,
'from sea to shining sea,'
and you know, John, 10
after all that shuffling us around to suit the settlers,
we're still here and Metis.

We're still here
after Meech Lake and
one no-good-for-nothin-Indian 15
holdin-up-the-train,
stalling the 'Cabin syllables /Nouns of settlement,
/. . . steel syntax [and] /The long sentence of its exploitation'[1]
and John, that goddamned railroad never made this a great nation,
cause the railway shut down 20
and this country is still quarreling over unity,
and Riel is dead
but he just keeps coming back
in all the Bill Wilsons yet to speak out of turn or favour
because you know as well as I 25
that we were railroaded
by some steel tracks that didn't last
and some settlers who wouldn't settle
and it's funny we're still here and callin ourselves halfbreed.

1 F.R. Scott, 'Laurentian Shield'.

Still Unsaved Soul

If I hear one more word
about your Christian God
I'm gonna howl
I'm gonna crawl outta my 'heathen'
skin and trick you   5
into believing I am the Virgin
Mary and take you to bed.

If I hear one more line
about your white church
I'm gonna start singing and dancing   10
with all my 'false gods'
in a giveaway dance and honour
you with all the 'unclean' sheets from my bed.

If I hear one more blessed thought
or witness one more holy act   15
I'm gonna throw-up
35 years of communion hosts
from this *still unsaved soul.*

The Devil's Language

1. I have since reconsidered Eliot
   and the Great White way of writing English
   standard that is
   the great white way
   has measured, judged and assessed me   all my life   5
   by its
   lily white words
   its picket fence sentences
   and manicured paragraphs
   one wrong sound and you're shelved in the Native Literature section   10
   resistance writing
   a mad Indian
   unpredictable
   on the war path
   native ethnic protest   15
   the Great White way could silence us all
   if we let it

its had its hand over my mouth since my first day of school
since Dick and Jane, ABC's and fingernail checks
syntactic laws: use the wrong order or   20
register and you're a dumb Indian
dumb, drunk or violent
my father doesn't read or write
the King's English says he's
dumb but he speaks Cree   25
how many of you speak Cree?
correct Cree not correct English
grammatically correct Cree
is there one?

2. is there a Received Pronunciation of Cree, is there   30
a Modern Cree Usage?
the Chief's Cree not the King's English

as if violating God the Father and standard English
is like talking back(wards)

as if speaking the devil's language is   35
talking back
back(words)
back to your mother's sound, your mother's tongue, your mother's
back to that clearing in the bush
in the tall black spruce   40

3. near the sound of horses and wind
where you sat on her knee in a canvas tent
and she fed you bannock and tea
and syllables
that echo in your mind now, now   45
that you can't make the sound
of that voice that rocks you and sings you to sleep
in the devil's language.

Armand Garnet Ruffo *b.* 1955

CHAPLEAU, ONTARIO

'Native literature,' Armand Garnet Ruffo writes, 'while grounded in a traditional, spiritually based worldview, is no less a call for liberation, survival, and beyond to affirmation.' This view has shaped the second anthology of critical essays by and about Canadian Aboriginal authors that Ruffo has edited, *(Ad)Dressing Our Words: Aboriginal Perspectives on Aboriginal Literatures* (2001), but it is also inscribed in his own criticism, as well as his poetry.

His first poetry collection, *Opening in the Sky* (1994), shows that the disaffection and loss Native people have suffered under the impact of European colonialism has reached a point of 'such magnitude that', in Ruffo's own words, 'it has moved beyond an individual response and into the realm of the collective psyche of a people.' In *At Geronimo's Grave* (2001), the winner of the 2002 Archibald Lampman Award for poetry, Ruffo focuses on the historic figure of Geronimo (1829–1909) both to tell the story of one of the most well-known Native warrior figures and to deconstruct the 'Whiteman's Indian', the 'imaginings that have been projected and readily imposed upon' Geronimo. Goyathlay ('One Who Yawns'), renamed Geronimo by Mexican soldiers, was a fearless Bedonkohe Apache, born in a territory that was then part of Mexico, now part of the state of New Mexico. A medicine man, he resisted the encroachment of white settlers and the relocation forced upon his people. Following the killing of his family by Spanish soldiers in 1858, and his retaliation attempts, he went into hiding, but was forced to join his people at the San Carlos reservation. He led the small group of Natives that were among the last to surrender to the United States in 1886, and was one of the 450 Apache people imprisoned at Fort Pickens, Florida. Following his release in 1894, he relocated to a farming community in Oklahoma. In the final years of his life, he took advantage of his celebrity status by selling photographs of himself. Ruffo retells the story, again through poetry, of another famous 'Native' man, the impostor Grey Owl, in his creative biography *Grey Owl: The Mystery of Archie Belaney* (1997). Ruffo's familiarity with the Grey Owl myth derives in part from stories he heard from his grandmother, Jane McKee (Espaniel), who had met the famous impostor.

Ruffo was born in Chapleau, Northern Ontario, and is a member of the Biscotasing group of the Sagamok First Nation. He holds a BA in English from York University, an Honours BA from the University of Ottawa, and an MA in English and Creative Writing from the University of Windsor. A noted critic, he is a professor of Aboriginal culture and literature and Canadian literature in the Department of English at Carleton University, where he was the director of Centre for Aboriginal Education, Research, and Culture. He has also taught at the En'owkin International School of Writing in Penticton, British Columbia, and at the Banff Centre for the Arts. Ruffo has written the plays *A Windogo Tale*, which won the 2001 CBC Arts Performance Showcase Competition for Drama, *Portrait of the Artist as an Indian*, and an adaptation of his book on Grey Owl. His most recent book is *Norval Morrisseau: Man Changing Into Thunderbird* (2006).

Poem For Duncan Campbell Scott

(Canadian poet who 'had a long and distinguished career
in the Department of Indian Affairs, retiring in 1932.'
The Penguin Book of Canadian Verse)

Who is this black coat and tie?
Christian severity etched in the lines
he draws from his mouth. Clearly a noble man
who believes in work and mission. See
how he rises from the red velvet chair,   5
rises out of the boat with the two Union Jacks
fluttering like birds of prey
and makes his way towards our tents.
This man looks as if he could walk on water
and for our benefit probably would,   10
if he could.

He says he comes from Ottawa way, Odawa country,
comes to talk treaty and annuity and destiny,
to make the inevitable less painful,
bearing gifts that must be had.   15
Notice how he speaks aloud and forthright:
        This or Nothing.
        Beware! Without title to the land
        under the Crown you have no legal right
        to be here.   20
Speaks as though what has been long decided wasn't.
As though he wasn't merely carrying out his duty
to God and King. But sincerely felt.

Some whisper this man lives in a house of many rooms,
has a cook and a maid and even a gardener   25
to cut his grass and water his flowers.
Some don't care, they don't like the look of him.
They say he asks many questions but
doesn't wait to listen. Asks
much about yesterday, little about today   30
and acts as if he knows tomorrow.
Others don't like the way he's always busy writing
stuff in the notebook he carries. Him,
he calls it poetry
and says it will make us who are doomed   35
live forever.

Power

From where does the Power
come? The old ones see it
in a moment of desert twilight,
in a basket of slithering snakes,
lumbering in a white-tipped bear,   5
flying in a crow that speaks,
see it in you.

Beware. Do not pray
for what you might receive.
This beast, this stallion   10
is not for the weak willed
who bloat like frog
for personal gain
and turn themselves
to dust.   15

From where does the Power
come? In the voice
that calls four times your name
when wife and children
are murdered. Tells you   25
no bullet will harm you
(as none ever does)
as it breathes
into you.

At Geronimo's Grave

Fierce, tenacious, master of guerrilla warfare.

It's what the history books say. Though
at his grave, out of an unyielding sun,
and into a sanctuary of leafy shade, I move
through all that is said and not said   5
and touch the flowers left for him,
which make me wonder if it is possible for anyone
to have the last word. And I am reminded
that it took five thousand troops to track down
what was left of his Apache, thirty-five   10

men, women and children. Caught,
they say herded from New Mexico to Florida to Alabama
and finally all the way here to Oklahoma, to so-called
Indian territory (as if the rest of the country wasn't).

They say more.   15

That by the time he died at eighty he had embraced Christianity
and even taken part in a Presidential inauguration.
Part of the parade I suspect, the evidence committed
to memory: last year in England, at the Brighton Museum
(of all places), I bought a postcard of him lost   20
behind the wheel of a Model T Ford,
looking like he had just fallen out of the sky and
onto the driver's seat. Portrait of an old Chief in a top hat.
(It was my only purchase.) From there to here in one fatal swoop
as though giant talons have dropped me unexpectedly   25
onto this site. If I could I would ask him
if he too got plucked up by something larger than himself.

Last of the holdouts, they call him.

This morning at Fort Sill I saw the windowless cellar
they held him in (not open to the public)   30
and the other building they transferred him to,
the one turned into a museum and whitewashed.
A notice said he really spent little time in his cell
since he had the run of the place,
like a bed and breakfast, I am led to believe.   35
Yet, with wilted petals between my fingers soft as grace,
soft as old sorrow, and an even older sun overhead
guiding me beyond this arbour and back onto the highway,
I am left wondering about who he really was.
Oilfields and prairie flowers, barbed wire and distant mesas   40
red as a people locked behind aging vision
telling me it is the land that will have the last word.

For him whom they also call Prisoner of War.

Detour

Once upon a time I rode shotgun for a trickster kind of guy who thought we lived in a western, and it would always stay that way. The Lone Ranger and Tonto riding into the sunset. Both of us wanting to be the Lone Ranger. That's us in the picture he carried around in his head, six years old, leather holsters and cowboy hats. Fringed shirts and moccasins from my auntie. The two of us, into the world at the same time, the same neighbourhood, and before long crawling into cars through windows, wrecks with doors wired shut, locked in as we had been from birth. Roaring down the road in one gear. Full speed come what may.

I wonder
where you are these days
last time
you were working in a distillery
and bought an empty barrel
you soaked
and let sit
later
we drank the whisky water
and got piss drunk
for old times' sake
talk about a hangover

How many times did we make it into town and finish up at the Sportsman's Hotel on some Friday evening. Meeting the folks from up and down the line who would come in and get loosened up. Until we too got bent out of shape and then back into the car and back into the bush. Thought we could live like that forever. Though I remember looking around at all the boozed-up old-timers and swearing their end wouldn't be mine. Some weren't even old. Like Terry. When the doctors opened him up to stop the hemorrhaging, they took one look and closed him back up again. His stomach looked like a tire blown to hell from all the Aqua Velva and cleaning fluid.

Last time we rode together
you ended up with a woman
you picked up
hitchhiking
you always
had a way with women
about the time
I decided
enough was enough
it was time

to move on
about the time
you lost your son.

Remember? We weren't much older than him when we got stuck between those two fence posts. We'd been raiding gardens for strawberries, your own mother's, which always seemed so absurd because she gave us all we wanted, but I guess you preferred to eat them at night with the earth still clinging. Or was it sitting in front of her with a blank face when she complained about the little devils. We were heading down the lane when a car appeared, and we dashed for a gateway and got jammed together. Like so much that came later, we had to wiggle our way out of that one. Like the time you ran away from home because you had fallen in lust with a girl up the line and were bound to get to her. And me walking the tracks behind you wishing I were fishing. Why I tagged along I still don't know. Though I suppose for the ride. Always the ride, and a wild one it was, riding high in trickster style.

Ven Begamudré *b.* 1956

BANGALORE, INDIA

'I try to be as authentic as a fiction writer can be in my writing, which means using my memories, using photographs,' says Ven (Venkatesh) Begamudré. Besides achieving verisimilitude, this kind of authenticity also relates to what Begamudré defines as the process of 'transculturalism', a process reflecting the various steps Canadian writers born in or coming from another country have to go through in order to approach their material. 'Because I am not really a part of the Indian community and I don't want to deal with the Indian community where I live simply for material,' he says, 'I write about what I know, what I don't know I research, and what I can't research, I make up. As a result of that, sometimes a scene which I will make up can seem more real than the actual place.' Constructing a fictional world that relies partly on memories and dreams and partly on the imaginative loops of story telling is characteristic of Begamudré's writing process.

Born in Bangalore, India, he was a year old when his parents left him with his grandmother on the island of Mauritius while they pursued their graduate studies in North America. His mother returned to take him back to Bangalore when he was three, and the two of them moved to Canada in 1962 to reunite with his father in Vancouver. The plot of his first novel, *Van de Graaff Days* (1993), although not autobiographical, deals with a family 'that doesn't know how to be a family' because of separations that resemble those in Begamudré's early years. Set in both India and Canada, the novel depicts a couple that must reshape the power dynamics of their roles as husband and wife when they reunite in Canada; it also explores the impact of the Indian caste system on relationships. '[T]hose conflicts,' he says, referring to his novel, 'are much more insidious than the conflicts that occur in Canada based on race. It's not that I try to play down issues of racism or prejudice, but they have to be looked at in the context of the people involved.' This context, Begamudré stresses, is a matter of class background.

Coming from a Brahmin family where women had at least one university degree, Begamudré is very conscious of class differences and how they can shape one's experiences in Canada, as is the case with the central character in the story that follows. 'There's a lot of agonizing going on about the role of the minority writer in this country,' he says. 'But you have to look at what kind of minority the writer is from, and what class they belong to. The kind of person who comes here from a Third World country and has to write when he's not mopping somebody else's floor is in a completely different position from someone whose parents were allowed into the country because Canada needed doctors or scientists.' His concern with racialization and its impact is also the focus of a personal essay he published in *The Globe and Mail*, 'Racial Bigotry in Aisle 66' (16 June 2005), referring to a disturbing encounter he had in a Canadian Tire store with three young white men.

Begamudré, who studied International Administration and French at Schiller College, Paris, holds a BA (1977) in Public Administration from Carleton University, and worked as a civil servant in Saskatchewan for a number of years before becoming a full-time writer. He began writing during his student years in Ottawa—'three huge novels for mass-market publication' that were never published—but his writing took a different turn after his first visit back to India, to which his father had returned, and after he won a scholarship to the Saskatchewan School of the Arts where he studied creative writing and discovered Canadian literature. He also holds an MFA in Creative Writing from Warren Wilson College, Ashville, NC (1999). His first publication was *Sacrifices* (1986), a novella.

He is the editor of two anthologies, *Lodestone: Stories by Regina Writers* (1993) and, with Judith Krause, *Out of Place: Stories and Poems*

(1991), the latter described by Begamudré as an anthology of prairie literature 'on transcultural and other forms of dislocations'. His short fiction has been published in many literary magazines and anthologies, including *The Journey Prize Anthology* (1989). His collection of short stories, *A Planet of Eccentrics* (1990), which includes the story that follows, was the recipient of the F.G. Bressani Literary Prize for prose and the winner of the Saskatchewan Book of the Year Award, as well as the City of Regina Book Award. The collection is about characters that occupy off-centre positions, whose understanding of who they are—as immigrants, as women, as old people—depends a lot on how they see themselves mirrored in their immediate world or the world of their memories. Begamudré's immigrant characters, however, be they from India or the Czech Republic, as is the case with the protagonist in the opening story included in *Laterna Magika* (1997), never occupy a position that is inherently marginal. A finalist for this collection of stories for the Canada–Caribbean region for the Commonwealth Writers Prize, Begamudré was the writer-in-residence at the University of Calgary Markin-Flanagan Distinguished Writers Program (1994–5), at the University of Alberta (1996–7), and in Edinburgh's Canada–Scotland Exchange Writer-in-Residence Program (1996). An occasional poet, and an essayist, Begamudré has also published a memoir, *Extended Families* (1997), as well as fiction for children, including the novel *The Phantom Queen* (2002), nominated for the Snow Willow Award, and the historical biography *Isaac Brock: Larger Than Life* (2000) about the adventures and distinguished military career of British-born Brock (1769–1812). Begamudré lives in Regina.

Mosaic

(I) ELLEN WHITMORE

Who? Oh, you mean Mr Ramesh. Of course I remember him. He was the sweetest little man. If he'd been taller, he would have been quite the ladies' man, too. I don't see what that particular incident had to do with anything, but, yes, I saw it all. He walked in just after twelve, not the best time on a payday. Especially not before Labour Day weekend. He took one look at the line-up and turned to leave. Then he changed his mind and started making out his deposit slips. What did he call them now? Chits. He did the same thing every month. He deposited half his cheque and bought a rupee draft with the rest.

I don't know if I should say, but he cleared about fifteen hundred a month. He sent the draft home, to India, for about five thousand rupees depending on the exchange rate. I teased him once about having a wife hidden away back home, and he came right back with, 'A Muslim can have as any wives as he pleases. I send the money to a different one each month.' I thought he was serious until I remembered his telling me once he was an orthodox Hindu. When I asked if he ate meat. That's why I liked serving him. I learned something every time.

He was concentrating so hard, he didn't even hear the man. They made such a strange pair: the man with his pot belly hanging out over his cowboy belt buckle, and Mr Ramesh in his charcoal grey suit. That's one thing I could never get over. He had such fine clothes, but he never had that extra bit of sense about how to dress. He always wore cufflinks and a tie clip, though they went out of style years ago. At any rate, he didn't even hear the man say, 'Buddy, can you help me out?' Those were his exact words. The second time, the man spoke louder: 'I said, can you help me out here?' This time Mr Ramesh looked up and did something so totally out of character I thought, 'This can't be the sweet little man I know.' He picked up his things and turned his back on the man. Normally he was so polite he even held doors open for other men. It was all a misunderstanding. Still, there was no reason for the man to shout what he did.

Something like . . . no, I can't repeat what he said. It makes you wonder when you hear language like that in public. Half the people in line turned to look, and some of them had the gall to smirk. Now, it's one thing to laugh at ethnic jokes. I like Irish ones myself, my maiden name being O'Reilly. But racist slurs are a different matter. Mr Ramesh pretended he hadn't heard, but he had. He was facing me, and I saw his mouth go hard, and the tips of his ears turned red. It's strange, isn't it? You'd never think coloured people blush, but they do. You just have to know where to look. Let me tell you something about observing people. We take the train every Christmas to see our grandchildren in Vancouver, and I always insist on sitting near the washroom. Everyone has to go to the washroom, so that way I see everyone in the car at least once. I get to know a lot of people by the end of the trip. Elwood, my husband, says I'm just a snoop, but that's not snooping. That's taking an interest in your fellow man.

Anyway, I felt so sorry for Mr Ramesh, I called him over. Some of the people in line grumbled, but if anyone deserved a good deed just then, it was him. The slip was made out exactly the same as every month, but this time he wanted a hundred dollars in cash. Almost immediately, he said, 'Imagine that fellow begging in a bank! No one begs indoors in India, and certainly not in a bank.' He had such a cute accent, it always made me want to laugh, as if he were imitating Peter Sellers imitating an Indian. 'Oh, Mr Ramesh,' I said, ' "help me out" doesn't mean "give me money." It means exactly what it says. Look, that lady is showing the gentleman how to make out his slip. He must be new with us.' Mr Ramesh's face fell after he looked, so I simply had to reassure him. 'I think you did the right thing, though,' I said. I handed him his cash and his passbook and started making out his draft. 'We have people like that in India,' he said. 'They are called scheduled castes. They used to be called outcastes, but one cannot call them that any more.' He raised his eyebrows, like this, only they joined in the middle. 'It would be discrimination,' he said. 'So now the government discriminates against good students by lowering pass marks in college so these people will get degrees. It results in mediocrity only, not equality.' I asked him did he mean they still have castes in India. 'What caste are you then?' I asked. 'Is it not obvious?' he said, almost proudly. 'We are brahmins. We are lighter skinned than most South Indians because, centuries ago, our ancestors intermarried with the Aryans, who came into India over the Hindu Kush. That fellow had no business calling me a black man!'

No, those weren't the man's exact words, but they were close enough. 'Don't you worry about him,' I said. 'He couldn't know a thing about East Indians. But just a second now. I thought brahmins were priests. I read that somewhere.' I simply had to keep him talking, he was so interesting. 'We used to be priests and teachers only,' he said. 'That is why most modern brahmins are well-educated. But now anyone can become a teacher. There is no future in India for brahmin boys, so I came away here.' I said, 'Well, you certainly are making a fine contribution to Canadian society.' I meant it. 'All your people do,' I said. He laughed then and said something I still don't understand: 'That is because the government lets only well-educated Indians into Canada.' Do you think he meant we keep the uneducated ones out? 'Well,' he said, putting his draft away, 'I must be getting back to my office. I am expecting good news this afternoon.' I asked him oh, what's that, but he simply grinned and waved as he walked away.

(II) KAREL LUCHINSKI

Gimme a break. I don't ask people their names. Ya can't reserve a table 'cause there aren't any, not for sittin', an' there's lotsa guys in suits come in. Used to be lot more 'fore that Corn-hole Centre open' up.

Oh him. I read papers too. You sure you're not a reporter, Sweetheart?

Okay, he came in three, maybe four times a week. Always bought a veggie sub. Come to think of it, he does stick out in my mind. First time he came in must've been, Christ, I don't know. Asked for ground chilli peppers on his sub. I told him, 'You want ground chillies, go find a pizza joint.' Yeah, he was in that day all right. I remember those two girls were in here. Do you believe it? Twelve-thirty on a Friday and I could swing a cat in here. Hey, know how to make a cat go woof? Use a bit of starter fluid, light a match and it goes, 'Whhooof!'

The girls that were in here same time as him. Came in just before and ate in. Didn't ask their names either. Made a real mess and didn't throw their garbage in the can. But they were whores, I know that much. You can smell them a mile away. This neighbourhood always smelled of whores and it's getting worse. Used to be they hung out at the hotel other side of Broad. Then people around there got all pious. Cops shut it down, made it respectable. So where do they hang out now? Half a block that way, past the bank. Maybe not such a bad idea. Deposits, withdrawals.

It's coming back to me now. What they looked like, I mean. I only noticed because the guy kept staring at them. One of them was about your, ah, his height. Couldn't've been more than fourteen. I don't care if it was hot that day, I'd blister my daughter's ass if she dressed like that. Problem is, she does. Now this first whore, she was dressed like she was open for business. Haw, haw! Get it? Used to be the government's motto. Had a yellow halter top on. Hell, her old man could've strained Sterno through it, that top was so skimpy. Plus she was wearing these shiny blue gym shorts and sandals. I've seen more cotton on a Barbie Doll. No wonder the little guy's eyes were popping out of his head. He pretended he was trying to make his mind up what to order. As if he ordered anything but a veggie and a milk, day in, day out. Now the other girl, she was older. More sensible, too. Didn't have a sign saying, 'Rape me,' across her chest. Wore a red tube top and real tight jeans. Bet nothing got between her and her Calvin Kleins! Only she wasn't the Brooke Shields type. Sort of dumpy, with boobs like sacks of flour. Bit on the dog side. Hey, know how to make a dog go meow? You freeze it, lay it on a table saw and it goes, 'Nnneeow!'

Funny thing but she was white, so I thought maybe she wasn't a whore after all till she starts coming on to him. Right here, in front of the cash. Smiles real nice and says, 'Hi, want to go somewhere?' That pisses me right off. I yell, 'Hey, I'm selling subs in here, I ain't selling ass!' She just shrugs and goes back to her friend, but the guy actually takes a step over. 'Go somewhere for what purpose?' he asks. Is he kidding or what? Thinks they're tour guides or something? The younger one, the native Barbie Doll looks him straight in the eye and says, 'To fuck.' They start laughing and so do I. Who wouldn't've? The guy had it coming. He was practically slobbering over Miss August there, checking her navel for staples maybe. But when he turned around, he didn't look pissed off at all. Sort of squared his shoulders and said, 'One vegetarian submarine and a white milk, please.' In that Poonjab voice of his. I had everything ready so I handed it over. He must've been pissed off, though, because he paid with a five and walked out before I could make change. Maybe he was just embarrassed. Just the type who would be, all clean hands and genteel. Don't get me wrong. I keep these hands clean because they handle food, but these nails have seen their share of dirt.

No, I didn't go after him. Gimme a break. Christ, he must've had money to burn. Me, I have to work for a living, on my feet. Look, you want a coffee or what? It's on the house, but you don't have to drink it on the roof. Haw, haw! Get it?

(III) JONI LEWVAN

You know what gets me? Ramesh was the only guy I ever worked with who never made a pass at me. When he talked to me, he looked at my face, not my body. He had class. I'm not crying the blues about how tough it is to have looks, but the way some guys look at you sometimes, it's like you're a banana they're itching to peel. I can see if it happened to a guy like Joe Tschepurny (he's one of the other consultants), but why a nice guy like Ramesh? Getting fired, I mean, not. . . . You know what Joe does if I'm wearing a low-cut dress? He makes sure he's got a handful of paper clips, and when he walks past the word processor, he tries to toss one in here—two points if it slips down.

Honestly. Ramesh told him off once, just after starting here, so Joe stopped. I was so proud of him. Ramesh, I mean.

That's when we had the going-away lunch for Mel Smith, at the Chelton. He's our old business manager. Ramesh said he couldn't make it on account of having a doctor's appointment, but I knew he was just making excuses. He came to a barbecue we had on Willow Island in June a couple of months after he started. A meet-the-clients do. You get good at saying, 'Now, now!' when they get you alone and hum, 'You Light Up My Life.' He was so tongue-tied, he just stared at the lake all afternoon. He was the only one who showed up without a date. Poor guy. He just didn't fit in. After four months he still called Mel, Melvin, and Joe, Joseph. Al and Yvan he always called Mr McKendrick and Mr Larouche. They're the ones the outfit's named after? McKendrick-Larouche Consulting. Mel said once Ramesh was too. . . .

Not just distant. Aloof. But that's what I liked about him. It's like being introduced to a guy at a cabaret, and every time he catches your eye, he sort of bows. You know if you even dance with him, you'll end up not liking him as much. That's what being married is like, I guess. If I had to do it all over again, I'd still marry Steve—it's just that before we got married I never thought I'd be hiding his hockey equipment. So he wouldn't sneak out of the house for a game with the boys. Honestly. I put my foot down last winter when he broke his nose again.

I left the lunch a couple of minutes early to drop by the hardware store and get Steve's cheque. Ramesh was in his office when I got in, just after one I guess. He was kind of down, but after I told him Al and Yvan asked about him at lunch, he brightened up for a sec. He'd been waiting to hear about this survey he was designing for one of our clients. Then he went sort of dull-eyed, so I figured I'd sit right down and try and cheer him up. When I asked what the matter was, he said, 'Oh, it is nothing.' He always talked like that—like he learned his English from a book coming over on the boat. Then he told me how he'd made a fool of himself at the bank. 'Oh Ramesh,' I said, 'that guy probably didn't even need the help. I remember this Indian pulled the same stunt at the credit union last week. Expected everyone to help him and tried to butt in ahead of me. The main problem with guys like that—I meant the guy at the bank, not the Indian; everyone knows they've got it rough—is they don't have enough pride.' Ramesh thought about that for a while and said, 'It is probably true what you say about pride. I suppose that is why I am still angry at the fellow. Why could he not have tried to fill a chit and taken it to a teller? She would have helped him.' Then he bursts out with, 'No one helps landed immigrants here! We have to work harder than white men, because we have no constitutional right to be mediocre!' I laughed at that part. 'Oh Ramesh,' I said, 'you don't have to work harder. You're smarter than us. All the Indians I've heard of are doctors or lawyers or big-shot professors.' That's true, you know. The doctor who operated on my mom's spine is East Indian. You won't find many of them running grocery stores like the Chinese people do. Though I hear there's one just opened up near the General. Ramesh used to buy pickles and stuff there. Not dill pickles, mango and lime. He liked his food hot, and I don't mean temperature-wise. He kept a jar of ground chillies in his filing cabinet to eat with his subs. He always had subs for lunch, or cheese sandwiches. That's where he kept those newspapers he read during lunch, flimsy ones that came rolled up in brown paper. First time I opened one, I thought it was an Indian skin mag or something. I wouldn't blame him for reading them, though. I don't know how anyone could live alone like that, but then he has this girl waiting for him back home. I still don't see why he didn't just bring her over here.

He told me once, but I'm lousy with long names. Can you imagine having some-one arrange a marriage for you? No way for me, boy. Ramesh said when he finished his degree, he wrote home to his mom and asked her to find him a wife. She sent back a list of six girls with—would you believe it—their pictures. He picked out the three he liked best and went back to India to meet them. He got along really well with one of them, and they decided to get married after he saved up some from working here. Isn't that the craziest thing you ever heard? I wouldn't kiss a guy my mom picked for me, never mind . . . let him touch me. Ramesh never talked about her much, but he said once her name was really poetic and she could play the violin. Not that I know anything about classical music. I could listen to Waylon and Willie till kingdom come. Plus Anne Murray. It really gets me when they talk about that farmer who's always chasing her. They always say he's from Saskatchewan. They drag out 'Sas-katch-e-wan' like it's the boonies. Honestly.

The only thing you could call unusual was after Ramesh went into Al's office. After I got back to the word processor. The door was closed but you could hear them yelling. I even heard Al call Ramesh a wimp. Ramesh opened the door and said some-thing foreign-sounding to Al. Then he slammed the door and walked into his office. He didn't look mad. He just looked . . . defeated if you know what I mean. Didn't even look at me when I asked, 'You okay?' Ten minutes later he left with a cardboard box. I went in his office and saw his degree wasn't on the wall, and the garbage can was full of those flimsy newspapers. He—Oh, shoot, there I go again. I'm sorry. I can't help it. It's just so unfair. I mean, why him of all people?

(IV) AL MCKENDRICK

Sorry about the mess. These are just temporary quarters till we move to the new loca-tion. Business is booming. So, let's kick this thing off. Now there's one thing I want to set straight from the start, so there's no misunderstanding. I didn't put Ramesh on waivers because he was Indian. Or because he was short or had an accent. The people we play ball with don't care about such things. They want results. Of course I knew what a blow losing the job would be to him, but it's happened to all of us. Ramesh was out of his league, and he fumbled it. We had good defence in the form of Joe Tschepurny, though. He's the one who suggested, when I first handed Ramesh the ball, we send a draft of the model to our client. To see if it was what they wanted. The answer came back pretty damn quick: n-o. Like a rebound. By the way, are you inter-ested in sports?

Rowing, eh? I took one look at you when you walked in here and thought, 'Now there's a young woman who knows how to look after herself.'

Basically the contract was to study the fiscal health of volunteer organizations. Ramesh had to design a model to survey them and analyze the results. It wasn't a huge job, so I thought he could go it alone. Besides, he'd been treasurer of the international students' club at York. He had an MBA from there and a BSc in math from some Indian university. His qualifications in the statistical area were first class, and he did two years as a stat clerk in Queen's Park before coming to us. He wanted a private-sector challenge, he said, so we gave him one. Unfortunately, he knew as much about our provincial scene as I do about . . . gourmet cooking. I'm a meat and potatoes man myself. Are you hungry? There's a new steak house around the corner.

That's all right, and it's Al, remember? I won't pull any punches, even at myself. I used to shadow box until my knuckles got too bruised. Hah! Certainly I overestimated his ability to learn about the province, but there was more to it than that. We were up to our eyeballs in alligators. Joe never had time to go over Ramesh's model in detail before we sent it off.

I don't concern myself with details. Now Joe's in extra innings revising the model. Something about nominal variables being used instead of ordinal ones, and too many open-ended questions on the survey. You likely know more about those things than I do. I'll be the first to admit I wasn't easy on Ramesh, but he didn't exactly make it easy on me. If he'd been at Mel's lunch it might have been a different ballgame, but damn it all, he wasn't a team player. Never went for a drink with us after work. Didn't even enter Corporate Challenge. Yvan—Mr Larouche, my partner—wanted me to fire him to set an example, but I convinced him to let the rookie opt for free-agent status. It was the decent thing to do. After lunch, I went to his office, the one next to the word processing station. Great girl, that Joni. You should talk to her too. Ramesh was reading his *India-Canada Times,* as usual, waiting for Joe to assign him more work. He'd always drag out a copy at coffee break and lecture us about why the Tamils were massacred in Assam or the Moslems were massacred in Sri Lanka. Sorry, it's the other way around. Last Friday, I remember he was circling an article about Sikhs rioting over that Golden Temple business, something about Mrs Gandhi getting herself in too deep. He grinned and said, 'Good afternoon,' as he showed the paper to me. 'These Sikhs are such violent people, you know. They would make good ice hockey players.' I wasn't too amused, but I wasn't about to break the news with Joni listening. I asked him to step in here and close the door. When he saw me take the letter from our client out, he leaned forward and said, 'So, how do they like our model?' He grinned, he was so excited. 'They don't like your model,' I said calmly. I never raise my voice. The grin stayed on his face, but a twitch started pulling at his right eye. 'That's not possible,' he said. 'You are making a joke.' I told him to see for himself and held the letter up for him to read. Then we had an exchange about how everyone had approved the model before it went out. 'You've embarrassed both Yvan and myself,' I said. 'It practically says in here McKendrick-Larouche doesn't know anything about the volunteer sector. If I hadn't smoothed things over, we'd be out a twenty-thousand-dollar contract. I was late for lunch, but you wouldn't have noticed. How did your appointment go by the way?' He fumbled for an answer, and we both knew why. If he hadn't been so big on playing games, if he'd only admitted he wasn't God's gift to mankind—Womankind? Personkind. Under different circumstances, I might have gone to bat for him more. He said, 'Sir, there is no need for all this worry. I will revise the model.' You had to give him credit, he was cool. Even picked a piece of lint off his suit and put it in this ash-tray. Nice, eh? It was a going-away present when I left Manitoba. Know what *Nil Illegitimi Carborundum* means? 'Don't let the bastards grind you down.'

Cute? I suppose so. At any rate, I told him, 'You won't revise anything except your CV. You don't know a thing about this province. We knew that when we hired you, but you're obviously not too quick on the uptake. I'm sorry but you'll have to submit your resignation.' I told him to make it effective the end of September, but not to bother coming in next month. Meaning this month. No one can say I'm not generous, but he read my signals all wrong and said something that riled me; 'You simply want to replace me with a Canadian. I shall report you to the Human Rights Commission. I shall even take you to the Supreme Court!' I didn't know whether to laugh or pick him up by the scruff of the neck and throw him out. If there's one thing I hate, it's minorities trading on their so-called disadvantages. It's all the rage now. Of course, it's different with women. 'You don't have a hope in Hades,' I told him. Then I remembered the day I received my notice in Winnipeg, after the last election, and put myself in his shoes. First comes the disbelief, then the shock, then the anger. You need someone to show you the bright side of things. 'Look,' I said, 'can't you see I'm trying to do you a favour? I convinced Yvan to let you resign even though UIC will penalize you for quitting. It'll look better on your CV.' He stood up with his fists clenched and his eyes simply wild. I didn't know what to expect. He looked as if he'd either throw a punch or break down in tears. Punches I can handle. Tears, no. Except from women. 'My people do not collect unemployment insurance,' he said. That's a laugh and a half. Then he opened the door without looking behind him and said, '*Nil Illegitimi Carborundum*, Mr McKendrick. At least I'm not being fired for being a well-known party hack as you were.'

If he hadn't slammed the door I would have gone for him right there, even with Joni in the outer office. So help me, I was furious. That was truly a low blow. I was a political appointee in Winnipeg, not a hack. I'll tell you the difference. A political appointee is competent. A hack isn't. I guess that would make Ramesh a hack, eh?

I do say so. And what happened to him after he left had nothing to do with our letting him go.

(V) MYSORE, 18TH AUGUST, 1984

My Dear Son,

I received your aerogramme dated the fourth this instant. I am glad to note your duties are proceeding satisfactorily and you expect a good reception of your study. Do not work too hard. You will strain your health, especially during the coming winter, which I have heard can be very cold in the west of Canada.

Your Putu Uncle says he does not know where we have failed. Instead of coming home directly when you became bored with your duties in Toronto, why then did you move to such a Godforsaken place as Saskatchewan? He is still concerned you should secure an appointment here well before your marriage, and he has finally found one for you as purchasing officer at the ISRO factory in Bangalore. It does satellite research and assembly, and your appointment could begin 1st January. He thinks you will be very happy there, and you will be very close to Mysore, so you can visit us often.

I know your late father would be extremely proud of you. The factory is not at all like his foundry. You will have a clerk to take dictation and another to type your letters. I very much hope you will give this opportunity serious consideration.

Shakuntala's parents are anxious you should accept this appointment and be married on an auspicious day convenient to the both of you. She is very dark, it is true, but she is very good-natured, and she has taken a first class in her MSc. Also your horoscopes match perfectly. Please do not think I am insisting. I simply want to see you happily settled before I move to the ashram at Pondicherry. There I can renounce the world, but I can do so more happily if I am assured you also are happy.

Your loving Amma

Postscript. I hesitate to write this, but I feel you are postponing your return to India without intimating the reason. Do you not remember how Shakuntala's namesake, the heroine of Kalidasa's play, pleaded with her husband after he returned to court and forgot her? I realize you are not King Dushyant and this Shakuntala is not a heroine living in a forest, but please consider these words for your future peace of mind. No matter how much you earn there, you will always be a stranger in Canada.

(VI) PRAKASH DAVID

You copied the letter?

You're welcome. Nothing but the odd bill since. His mother phoned again last night. I still don't see what good flying all the way here will do. She can't even leave for another week, what with all the red tape over there. Still, I suppose she could do some good. They became really close after his father died. Now that was bizarre.

It doesn't really have anything to do with what you're after. Not directly, anyway. Ramesh's father worked his way up to foreman in a foundry. Seems one day the overhead crane got stuck, and his father decided to climb up to the catwalk to take a look. A mechanic could have done it, but Ramesh said he thought his father was trying to prove something—maybe that he hadn't gone soft as foreman. He must have, though, because he had a stroke up on that catwalk. Not that they could prove anything afterwards. He clutched his right arm and doubled over. Fell right off the catwalk, but instead of landing on the ground and breaking his back, he fell into a vat of molten lead.

You can say that again. What really hurt Ramesh was there wasn't even a body left to cremate, never mind ashes to immerse. I didn't find out about this till after he moved here. We were at an Indian film night at a prof's house in March. He was showing a classic, *Three Daughters* by Satyajit Ray. Ramesh came right up to us and introduced himself I didn't care for him at first—he shook hands like overdone broccoli—but he knew a lot about Satyajit Ray films. Told us things like why the fellow in the beginning had to be a postmaster and not, say, a teacher. It turned out Ramesh was in town for his interview with McKendrick-Larouche, so we gave him a standing invitation to stay here till he found a place. If he got the job. Turned out he did, and a month or so later he was back for good. That's when I regretted the invitation.

It's hard to explain without going into the story of my life. He had this habit of crying, 'Rama! Rama!' if he spilled something or the baby started crying when he made a funny face. My sister used to do that when she got depressed, and I still can't stand people like that, who call on God for every little thing. It's as though, well, as though I'll be contaminated by their weakness. Huh, I'm no saint. I'm no crusader, either. I'd be the last one to say that attack was racially motivated, the way they're claiming in the news. Neither was his being fired. Sure, he was brilliant, but he was out of it even after four years in Canada, and it wasn't his being an immigrant either. Guys like Ramesh would be meek and mild even if they were white. But they survive. That's what I liked about him. Like, I should say. We finally found him the place near the tracks. I'd never live in a place like that—not now, anyway—but I've lived in worse during my BFA days.

I guess he'd gone home to check the mail first, when he showed up last Friday. This was his second home. He even listed us as next of kin. That's why the police called here. He showed up around three. I remember I'd just put the baby down and plugged in the kettle. I could tell something was wrong, he looked so dejected. I unplugged the kettle and got him a beer. He could have used a good stiff Scotch, but he never drank, so a beer was a lot for him. I sat here, and he sat where you are. He liked that chair because he could see the Fafard better. Melissa's parents gave it to us last Christmas. We both think boxing is stupid, but he's sort of grown on us. We call him 'George' because he was apparently modelled on George Chuvalo.

Sure, I'm good at giving advice even if I'm not asked. 'The Good Doctor,' Melissa calls me, after the Chekhov play I think. I told him to accept the new job. It was a gift from heaven. His mother couldn't have timed the letter better, but after we talked for an hour or so, he dug in his heels. I don't know if it was the beer—he was on his third by then and proud he could hold it—or if it was staring at 'George,' or if it was pride. A bit of each, I'll bet. 'Prakash,' he said slowly, 'I cannot go back. People would laugh if they knew why.' I asked so who would know. 'Is that what you would do?' he asked, and I said we weren't talking about me. He let his feet fall off the coffee table. I remember the thump. It must have hurt, but he didn't seem to notice. 'Oh,' he said, 'you are somehow better than me? You would not be in this predicament?' He was talking slowly, compensating for the alcohol. I poured some more Scotch and said, 'I'm not better, just different.' He snorted at that and I got annoyed. 'I came over when I was five,' I told him. 'I grew up here but you, you grew up in India. You belong there with your family. Besides, do you think I could have got a marriage arranged like you? What would I do? Bring the woman over halfway around the world from her folks? You know damn well she'd want to go back for a visit every couple of years. What would I say? "Sorry, Sweetie, but I'm just another struggling photographer, so find yourself a doctor"? I never thought I'd meet someone like Melissa.' Then, right out of the blue, he said, 'Do you recall that fellow from Guyana? Sammy someone-or-other?'

Nobody we knew. Sammy Narayan, I think. Ramesh was talking about an incident he'd told me about once. I think it happened the year he started at York. 'Strange,' he said. 'All the bad things happen in Toronto. Those goondas pushed Sammy down on the subway train tracks, and he broke both his legs. He came to Canada to succeed and he ended up being a cripple only. Why were all those liberal-minded people so shocked when he hanged himself? Everything was in his note: "I cannot go back like this." ' I asked if that was him talking or you, Sammy or Ramesh. 'What is the difference?' he said. 'For one thing, you're a professional,' I reminded him. 'You told me he was a worker. You'll be better off in India than he could ever have been in Guyana. Besides, you were going to go back and marry Shakuntala after you saved some money. You've been working for more than two years.' Then it occurred to me. I can be a bit slow at times. 'You don't want to go back, do you?' I said. 'As long as you stay here, you're a big shot to the folks back home. And what about that poor girl?' That's when he lost his temper. 'Go home and leave Canada to people like you?' he said. 'People who turn their backs on their ancestry? I will not go home!' I was sure he'd wake the baby. 'Look at your boxer,' he said. 'Sometimes I think he is wondering, "What am I doing here?" but sometimes I think he is wondering, "I will show them!" That is what he is thinking now, and I will show them also. If I go back, people will ask me how much I am making as a foreign-returned officer. You know how they talk. They are crazy for coming to Canada or the US, any place to get away from the corruption. But I will know I did not return to earn a higher salary than my classmates. I will know I fled this place. That is exactly what people like Mr McKendrick and you expect me to do. Such people think I am a coward. I will remain in Canada. I will remain in Saskatchewan. I will remain in Regina. But I will never walk on the same pavement as goondas like Joseph Tschepurny. He is at fault for losing my position!' Ramesh was just livid, but the baby started crying, so I got up. He started following me upstairs. When I reached the landing, I heard a thump. He'd passed out at the foot of the stairs and spilled his beer. I checked to see if he was all right. After I brought the baby downstairs, I carried Ramesh in here and laid him on the sofa. He was still sleeping when Melissa got home from work. The three of us ate out so we wouldn't wake him up. And, I guess, so he wouldn't feel embarrassed at waking up with Melissa around. He had his rules about what men did or didn't do around women. I left him a note saying he could stay the night if he wanted, but by the time we got back—after seven—he was gone.

Not so much uncomfortable around women as . . . Too chivalrous would be a better way to describe it.

There's no contradiction. A man doesn't always go to a hooker because he's, um, desperate for sex. Sometimes all you really want is companionship. He didn't know any women except Melissa. As far as he's concerned, we're married, and some Indians won't even talk to a married woman unless her husband's in the room. I remember once the three of us went to see *Gandhi* when it came back. After we found our seats, I went to get popcorn. The minute I turned to go, he got up and offered to help, because he couldn't even stay one seat over from Melissa without fidgeting. The only other woman he knew was his secretary, Joni Lewvan. He couldn't very well visit her, so he sat through two showings of some movie and had a drink—a Scotch, he told me—before he went looking for *Irma la Douce*. Fifty dollars isn't much, you know. You can spend more than that on an evening out. I don't think losing his virginity had anything to do with it either, though he probably was one. The farthest he'd got was kissing a girl once—in

Toronto, after they'd gone out for coffee or something—and he thought that was daring. He was like a kid when it came to women. He'd tell me about the great articles he read in *Playboy* or *Penthouse* and say, 'Of course, I only buy them for the articles.'

Look, let's leave the magazines out of it. I shouldn't have mentioned it. As for the hooker, you're confusing exploitation with the real issue. Besides, a man who goes to a hooker isn't necessarily exploiting her any more than she's exploiting him. Companionship, that's the issue. Just being able to touch someone. For a guy like Ramesh, fifty dollars is a small price to pay if he can actually hold a woman in his arms for fifteen minutes. It would be the high point of his life. Something he could romanticize till the day he died. Obviously it didn't turn out to be such a bargain.

Tell me what you find out from her if the cops do let you in. Oh, there's one other thing I liked about Ramesh besides his knack for survival. Even if his idea of survival was keeping a low profile. He had a real sense of humour. One day he brought over a song he wrote, or at least the beginning of one. How did it go? He had a thing about Sikhs. Thought they gave Indians a bad name. In India they tell Sikh jokes the same way we tell Ukrainian jokes here. The verse he wrote went something like, um:

Most Sikhs you see have turbans and masculine physiques.

Carry knives and bangles, don't shave for weeks and weeks.

But don't forget this simple rule or they can get quite piqued:

Every Sikh's a Singh, but not all Singhs are Sikhs!

That last line is sort of a litany in India. You know how we remember how many days in a month, 'Thirty days hath September'? The song had a lot of potential. Has, I should say. I don't know why I think about him in the past tense. Knowing him, though, he'll wish he were. He's the sort of person who could die of shame. Promise me something.

Don't try to see him after he gets better. He couldn't tell you anything. He wouldn't. He won't need crutches, not like Sammy Narayan did, but he'll need whatever is left of his pride.

(VII) CHARMAINE DES RIVIÈRES

I never laid a hand on th' guy. You b'lieve me, don'tcha? I tol' the cops an' the jerk from Legal Aid an' they keep hasslin' me, 'fess up! 'fess up! like broken records, an' that son-'f-a-bitch Wayne's got somethin' comin' if he thinks I'm takin' a rap for excess'ry. Th' little oinkers're talkin' outa their assholes if they think they can keep me here till they find him, an' when I get out I'll find him first an' break his arms, th' son-'f-a-bitch!

Talk about a weird scene. This guy you're so keen on showed up around midnight, walking real slow with his hands in his pockets and his shoulders all hunched up like a tough guy. I'm just leaning against a sign, minding my own business, and he sort of slows down as he goes past. I know the type. Too scared to ask you out, but they keep licking their lips like you're a double fudge hold the cherry. So I ask him instead, 'Want to go out?' He sort of looks me over real slow, like he's checking out the ingredients. Instead of saying okay, he says, 'Why not?' in this prissy voice and I think, 'Shit, another refugee.' Place is crawling with them. Only he isn't dressed like one. Has this white shirt on, nice pants, and shoes with silver buckles. Fancy watch, too. So I tell him to follow me around back, then I'll go in, open the door for him. Ask what his name is, and he doesn't answer, so I ask him again, and he says, 'Um, Prakash. What's your name?' Real polite, so I laugh and tell him to call me anything he wants. Except smoked meat; I'm not. He says, 'Very well,' like he's teaching school, 'I will call you Joni.'

You heard me right: Joni, like in Mitchell. I stop and look at him then because, I don't know, the way he says it makes me feel cold all of a sudden, like he's playing games. Turns out he was, too. Wayne's in the bar and I get my key from him, and you know what? The guy's still waiting in the alley near the big red garbage can, still licking his lips. I was sure he'd chicken out. He's moving his hands in his pockets like he's checking it's still there or something, but he just stands there staring at my tits and I think, 'Shit, he needs an invitation.' Next thing I know, he comes running up the stairs like he's afraid he'll lose whatever he's got. Turns out he must have. After we get in the room, I go to the can and when I come out he's staring at the bed like he's never seen a double before. I sit down and say, 'Sixty dollars,' and he says, 'Of course,' so I shrug and undo my jeans. Pull everything down to the floor, but he's still staring at my tits. Gives me the creeps, the way he stares at everything. Then he says, 'You have such lovely breasts,' and I think, 'Shit, this guy's a loser or what?' You want to see tits, you go to Victoria Park and look at the office girls at lunch time. Suntan in those bikinis they wear under their working clothes like they're not really for sale, just us. I should have told him that, but he's looking real spaced and says, 'Your breasts are like those of the ap-sa-ras.' Something like that. 'They are the daughters of pleasure carved from the unyielding stone of temples.' That's when I get scared for real and think, 'Shit, the guy's a psycho. Gets off just looking.' But he puts his hand on my shoulder and it's real soft, kind of nice, so I let him move it down. But when he slides it under my top—I'm wearing my new red tube top—I tell him, 'The money first. Then you can touch.' He just squeezes my tit, and I look up to see him staring at me like I've hit him in the balls. He practically whines, 'It is so soft. It should be firm.' So I tell him, 'You want melons, there's a Safeway other side of Broad,' but he doesn't crack a smile. Yanks his hand out and takes a step back. Bangs into the dresser and doesn't even feel it. Says, 'This is all so wrong, so unfeeling. No, never mind. I have shamed you enough.' Talk about straight or what? I just sit there and think, 'Shit, the guy's a fucking social worker.' That's when I recognize him. He was in the Mr Submarine at lunch when I went with Pearl and she scared him off.

What do you mean so I'm the one? I never did anything to him. Not there, not later on.

What happens is, he looks like he's going to have a fit, foaming at the mouth or something, but he turns around and walks out with his head high like he doesn't like the smell. I do just what Wayne told me long time ago. I holler for one of the girls to get him, and before I've got my jeans done up, I hear Wayne flying down the hall and out the back. I tell him the guy grabbed my tit and didn't pay, and he says to the guy, 'You trying to get a freebie? Fucking Pakis make more than us and try to get freebies!' The guy looks real insulted and says, 'I am not a Pakistani.' Looks down for a sec and says, 'It was a mistake. I changed my mind.' Wayne just laughs and says, 'After wasting her time like that? Sixty bucks, asshole. Let's see your wallet!' The guy looks around, but Wayne's got him backed up against the wall real good, so he takes his wallet out, and Wayne grabs it. There's a bunch of bills, so he takes them all and hands it back to the guy. It's all real civilized up till now, but Wayne says, 'Eighty-five bucks?' The guy starts to say, 'It is for a new battery for my car,' as if we care and Wayne says, 'A lousy eighty-five bucks for all our time you're wasting? You're going to pay. Take that watch off.' But the guy says, 'I cannot. My mother exchanged a thousand rupees for hard currency, and I bought this very wristwatch in the duty-free shop at Heathrow Airport.' Then it all happens so fast. I should have known something was up because the guy's flattening himself against the wall like he's going to climb it. I don't know who he thinks he is, Spiderman maybe. Wayne goes for the watch. The guy screams and kicks him in the balls. Wayne doubles over, starts swearing, but before the guy can make his break, he gets one in the stomach. Not hard, but he probably never took a punch in his life. Talk about soft. Starts whimpering like a kid, something about, 'Ra-ma, Ra-ma,' and Wayne gets a couple in to the face. That's when the guy goes down. I just stand there, but when Wayne starts kicking the guy, I try to pull him back. I tried. You believe me, don't you? I yell, 'Let it go!' and the whimpering stops. He must be out cold now, but Wayne just keeps kicking, kicking, and the guy's jerking like he's being shot. The way they do on TV? When some guy puts a couple extra shots in to make sure. In the end Wayne's so tired out he lets up, and we go back in. That's when I freak out. What would you do, huh? For all I know, the guy's dead. Wayne brings me down with some real good stuff, what he saves for when one of the freshies wants out. They always fall for it. Next thing I know, somebody's waking me up and the place is crawling with cops. They get the cuffs on before I can even get my jeans up and march me out the front with all these people staring. Saturday shoppers. The pigs throw a blanket on top and we're off, sirens going and the whole bit, like it was some celebrity Wayne dumped in that big red garbage can out back. The jerk from Legal Aid says he's going to get those motherfuck-ers for police brutality and some other stuff I can't remember.

Rights? Girls like us don't have rights. Only the customer's right. Say, do you know if the guy's okay? He won't die or anything?

Naw, nobody told me shit about him. Just his name. Nar-ay-an-dra Ku-mar Ramesh. I can even spell it now, paper's having a field day. Poor Pakis come over here looking for a better life and see what they get. What about us? If they've got it so rough here, why don't they just go back where they're from!

Yasmin Ladha *b.* 1956

MWANZA, TANZANIA

'I am a word-shaper, creating and shaping words that are very strange and, at the same time, natural,' says Yasmin Ladha. 'The purpose of crafting words newly is to spur, ignite something hidden, in both the reader and myself. In writing then, I want to evoke *rasa*: juice, dance, music, magic, startle, both for my reader and myself.' Ladha embraces the word *rasa*, a Hindi word, not only because of its fluid meanings, but also because 'its English counterpart, "essence", [has] become blunt with over-use,' and because 'it is an elitist word, used by clergy and scholars.' In its rhythms, styles, and idiosyncratic use of words, Ladha's fiction demonstrates the delight with which she subverts literary conventions and the fondness with which she addresses her reader. Her writing, as she says, 'occurs in the proximity of an evoker, the reader, whom I call Reader*ji*.' Speaking to the reader directly is a deliberate strategy: 'One of the "tools" I implement in order to do away with a consumptive reader is to address my reader, personally. Her name is Reader*ji*. In Hindi and Urdu,' she explains, 'the suffix "*ji*" added to a name is a polite form of address. I also use "*ji*" as an endearment: "My Reader*ji*," "Ooi Reader*ji*," "Come back, Reader*ji*." In other words, I seek a connection with my Reader*ji*.' This desire to address her reader makes the borderline between fiction and reality a fluid one, and also creates what Ladha calls 'a process of disclosure to myself'.

Born in Mwanza, Tanzania, two years before the independence of Tanzania, Ladha grew up knowing 'very, very early that Africa is for the Africans'. Arriving in Canada, with her mother and brother, when she was eighteen, she considers the word home to be 'a dictionary word. A hard word'. Thinking of herself as a 'nomad', she strives to create out of what she calls 'an inward geography'. Ladha studied at the University of Calgary, where she received an MA in Creative Writing (1993). She has been a facilitator of creative writing workshops and a teacher of English as a second language. The guest editor of *Rungh*'s special issue on food, she taught English in Chonbuk, South Korea, and is now an English instructor at the Alberta College of Art and Design in Calgary.

Her collection of short fiction, *Lion's Granddaughter and Other Stories* (1992), which includes the story that follows, clearly reflects the multiple positions from which she writes. 'Being woman, Muslim, immigrant, first-born, thirty-five, beloved, plaiting the prairie in my craft, sprouting multiple goddess arms in the grasslands, occupying feminist theory, abandoning theory, Hindu-ing Allah out of my Gujarati Hindu heritage, writing out of the landscapes of Janpath–Delhi and Kensington–Calgary, incorporating Urdu calligraphy in English, whamming imperial English in a racist policeman's face'—all this forms the core of her writing. She has also published a chapbook, *Bridal Hands on the Maple* (1992) and *Women Dancing on Rooftops: Bring Your Belly Close* (1997).

Beena

Readerji, you have never wanted me forever
But this time
Won't you come a little farther?

I shan't call you reader. One who reads, hah! That's so undeclared. Blank as a daft blue form: 'Resident of?' 'In the Dominion of?' 'Port of Embarkation/Disembarkation?' 'Destitute-Festitute?' Blue muscle of power. Generic.

Between you and me, there is no glint of a badge. Badges are razor sharp. Between you and me, the ink quivers. Beena exists declared (fetch the trumpet, fetch the *dholak: dha dhin dhinaka*) because of you and me.

'A reader,' you say? You correcting me? My Allah! You have joined the critic's English! May he forever be buried in the Sahara. *Readerji,* I command you, banish the critic from your eye, this instant, *fatafat* ! Look at his beauty nose, wide as a camel's nostrils!

My *yaar-Readerji,* sometimes with my own, I forget this definite and not so definite article stuff. Allah! You are turning grey because I call you my own! *Readerji,* by bending, yes-Masta, yes-Masta, you follow the colonizer-critic to his bed!

You and me: Our relationship is declared and you are off to the Camel-*wallah*'s bed. *La*! I am breaking my bangles, because of you, *you Readerji.* You have made me a widow. Wait, I will even wipe off my red-*bindi,* this moon-dot between my eyebrows, my *shakti*-power. And the vermilion from my hair parting. *Readerji,* you are turning a nastier grey. You frighten me. Oh, I frighten you? No need to be so vehement with your nod. This *maha* critic's sun never sets, not even a wheezy sound of setting. You, breaker of my bangles, salaaming with yes-Masta, yes-Masta deference. *Readerji,* I ask you, will the critic's privilege, his Brahmin privilege, will it never cease? You are content to drink the incantations from his *soma* drink? He works on formulas while I, my precious reader, create. Without you *Readerji,* my *shakti*-power is swollen but my text is a widow, *gumsum*/quiet-quiet/sawdust. So. So. So. Fill my arms with green, green bangles, *Readerji.* From you, my hefty fertility. And the critic/Brahmin/camel/colonizer is out, out of text! *Readerji,* Beena *soma*-wine, yours-mine, *salut*! That needly bone in my kabob is the critic. So I have the camel-nostril-wallah mincemeated in a yellow plastic bowl. Do you know *Readerji,* I make lovely kababs, full of garlic and wet coriander? You would lick your fingers dry. Now this is religion. Only the critic's nostrils put me off.

Come *Readerji,* sit on my bed where I write. Make cool circles on the sheet with the heel of your foot. I dream of a study with pipe smoke and wooden floor (so briskly polished you want to wear your hair up). No colonizing table with loopy gold handles and filched Koh-i-Noors. Just rosewood mailboxes one finds in old fashioned hotels. But *Readerji,* dreams aside, I write here, on this bed. Have some carrot *achar* on *chapatti.* No my precious Reader, these are not green chilies, just peppers. Beena loves carrot *achar.* Your eyes have grown large. Why can't you accept you are declared in Beena? Don't smell my ink in the critic's nostril. I have a heart beat too.

Such a hoard of treasure I lay before you, yet you read like a *fakir.* A critic's *fakir.* Living off his scraps. Hey, don't leave me to my new-found independence! What do you mean I am scaring the shit out of you? Even I am unaccustomed to popping in and out of pages with *achar* and *chai.*

Careful, the *chai* is hot. Sugar? Only half a teaspoon? No wonder you are so disciplined. I take one, two, and finally three teaspoons of sugar. I like syrup in my throat. *Readerji,* trust me. No, I should not say this. At least, not when I am with Satya.

How do you know that *satya* means truth? Oh, the Gandhi film. Well, my dear friend's lies would send firecrackers up Gandhiji's ass, may his soul rest in peace.

One day on the C-Train, this friendly man comes up to us, Satya and me. Asks if we are sisters? Satya tells him, 'We have the same mother but different fathers.' And when the friendly man, now red, turns to me, Satya adds, 'Oh, she's the bastard.'

Readerji, this frown of yours is breaking Satya's magic. Her tongue is lightning. Satya in Beena's story? Faintly, I guess. *Readerji*, hood your glaring eye. There is never only *a* story. That's why a story's collar bones are chubby (always) because she carries layers and layers of stories.

Satya is my *sakhi*, my dearest friend. We hang rainbow saris on rooftops and fetch water from the well. *Ooi Readerji*, will you now forget the C-Train? Stand clear of the doors. And imagine a century where women wear pleated *lenga* skirts with tiny *bindi*-shaped mirrors around the hem. The skirts blast with colour, violent pink on orange, and green on pollen yellow. Each doorway arch painted with tendril leaves and parrots and water pitchers. The outside walls stamped with the orange benevolent elephant God. At doorsteps, coloured rice powder in sprawling circular patterns.

From the discreet *jharoka*, two *sakhis* stare out into the town square. One is a writer, the *Pen-walli*. The other is Satya, the *zenana* law-breaker.

'In this slumbering afternoon, not even a crow in sight,' says *Pen-walli*.

'I want *paan*.'

'Satya, *Amma* will eat us raw.'

'Only if she finds out. Don't know how a timid rabbit like you is a writer. Ring for *Maharaj* of the Kitchen.'

'The *Maharaj*, here! In the *zenana*! But all the women are sleeping and he will look in on each one of them!'

'That's why *pronto, fatafat*, he will rush to the female quarters. *Maha* opportunity for *Maharaj* to let his eyes slip on slumbering beauties.'

Knock. Knock.

'*Bibijis*, you remembered me.'

'*Nahi Maharaj*, it is we who remembered you.'

'*Salaam*, Satyaji, friend of our *Pen-bibiji*!'

'*Maharaj*, there is not a just word for this afternoon's yogurt lamb sauce and your *halva* full of blanched almonds, *hai* Allah, all my words have lost elasticity.'

'Lady Satyaji, and my bow grows insufficient in light of such praise. Bestow a command, my way.'

'But I have not finished, *Maharaj*. I swear in the presence of my writer *sakhi*, if you are lifted one fine day and find your auspicious self in the humble kitchen of our *haveli*, you must relieve me of any blame. You are a Koh-i-Noor meant to be stolen.'

'Satyaji, your *haveli* is the Grand Palace of our city.'

'Then, dear *Maharaj*, I hope you will not refuse the request of the dweller of the Grand Palace.'

'Your wish is my command, daughter of the Grand Palace.'

'*Maharaj*, you are forwarding us your precious tongue.'

'Indeed, my treasured organ on which spices punch and dance.'

'Then *Maharaj*, the secret mariner of sauces, maintainer of heirloom secrets, I bid you to fetch us *paan*, and an attached favour, spittoons from the male quarters.'

Readerji, now our *Maharaj* is Shinto calm. Not a crack in his eye. He has given his word. But he is a professional tongue shaker in more than just the Bengali fish *pilaff* way:

'Hot or sweet, O *cleverest* daughter of the Grand Palace?'

'*Maharaj* of the Kitchen, if I were a lamb, my throat would be at your disposal—awaiting on your stone slab. But today, the *zenana* rules, made possible of course, by your lavish promise. *Sweet-ta paan* with fragrant red paste for my writer *sakhi*. In mine, a hefty pinch of tobacco. And I must reiterate I have the honour of your tongue.'

'O Grand Palace one, I have been groomed by *haveli* nobility. To consume an ocean of secrets without a burp is my *dharma*.'

'*Cookji*, and if you would indulge us further—a small *taklif*-imposition on our behalf. . . .'

'Clever one, my pound of flesh at your service.'

'Dear *Cookji*, then if you would *purdah* your eyes on your way out, how can I say? As an extension of your *dharma*-duty, if you please.'

Satya and *Pen-walli* sit on the balcony on this slumbering afternoon. They rest their henna-painted feet on ice-wrapped cushions, their spittoons close by. Actually, of the two, the writer is the smart spitter. From her lightly bulged cheeks, the betel juice forms a red-rusty arc and lands unsplit in the silver receiver engraved with a cheetah chasing a deer. (*Readerji*, engraved on a courtesan's spittoon is an arched woman holding a mirror.)

Readerji, now what's the matter? Even you should know that courtesans never do things plainly. Anyway, the most important event in the history of story-telling is about to occur. Out with the *dholak: dhum dhum dhaa aha, dhum dhum dhaa*. (Forget the dictionary tom-tom—drums of India and West Indies, hah! Then I can only think of Tom of peep holes who peep-peeping so fast becomes Tom-Tom.) Twirling fingers swift on the drum, and the palm-beat, *dhumaka dhumaka dhaa*. LISTEN ONE AND ALL: *Readerji* IS ABOUT TO ENTER THE STORY.

Ooi Readerji, where are you off to? If you run away, how will I continue with the story? You will come to no harm, I swear on the story. You don't trust the story. How can I coax you to step in? You want no knotted embrace with the courtesan? Agreed. *Readerji*, tell me, what if I plan her *haveli* by a lake? Not possible, you say? You figure that her brothel is most likely behind the *paan-wallah*'s shop. Of course, *Readerji*! One lucrative trade massages another. You co-create very logically, *Readerji*, but this is no city planning course. I like the idea of a languorous boat ride. Okay, okay, I won't put you on a boat ride with her. Why do you get so worked up? But *ooi* my friend, in the story, you have such style.

Satya sees you first.

'What a walk! Allah, thank you for releasing him, our way!'

The *Pen-walli* is content spittoon spitting. Now she ogles at you. *Readerji*, this time, she forgets to let out the proper cheek pressure and the juice lands on her bodice.

As you are about to pass under their balcony, Satya and *Pen-walli* bend over.

Only Satya clutches her heart. '*Hai hai*, what a city walk! What a cut in this lurch of a walk!'

My proper *Readerji*, rub away that hairpin frown of yours, for you *would* look up, I swear. Because Satya has ropy power. It pulls you. Look up, look back, heck, look anywhere you please. In this story, you won't turn to stone. Ah! You too are drawn to her voice. I know, I know, there lies a pressed thickness in it. Ah yes, you do look up, definitely.

(*Readerji*, shshsh! Just between you and me, you have that certain walk. It is a walk that finishes one like Emma Bovary's eyes.)

Readerji, do you want to see your picture in words? Sleek silk pantaloons. Not those billowy village pyjamas. Pantaloons and the embroidered belt, just above the hips, have a language of their own. They slice forward with a hint of a buck, while your hair jolts back, like wings at a terrific speed.

Ooi, now I see that I have lost my reputation with you. *Nahi Readerji*, I have never observed your walk this minutely. Don't pull your collar any higher, for I am not a courtesan. My microscopic eye is words.

Readerji, for a change, let me ask you a question? Why *Beena* from all the other books choked with dust (but oh so patient) on the tenth floor of the Library Tower?

The name pulled you. I told you, I create magic, my precious. Certainly, Beena is not of the common Safeway variety. Do you know there was once a filmstar in the fifties and her name was Beena? No, no, our Beena doesn't become an actress. But you asked! I have not given away anything! Then what is a Safeway and a filmstar doing in an Indian village where women wash their clothes by the river? Hey *Readerji*, where did you get these details? Imagination! Good for you. (May the critic forever remain in a yellow plastic bowl.) But did I mention a river? Yes, I know I mention a boat which you don't want to share with a courtesan. Ah! this reminds you of *Kama Sutra*. Oh no, don't turn shy, *Readerji*, please go on. You say that *Kama Sutra* brings forth positions which you allow yourself to conjure only with the condition that a chiropractor's office is in visible proximity. And figs and a river, of course. *Readerji*, co-create Beena with me but don't be disappointed. You see, there is no *Kama Sutran* gymnast in this story. No, no, I am not patronizing you. I want to set the story straight, on my part at least. Oh this mad hairpin frown of yours. I know what it means. Don't bang the book shut, you will chop off my nose, I swear.

Readerji, may I speak the truth? *Nahi* what I told you before is also the truth, but now truth at the balcony level. What nonsense! What do you mean I am doing transcendental hocus pocus on you? No, I am not transmitting you to the Himalayas. Of course, I know you are not a California reader. Reader, my Reader, slow-slow. Tell me, what does an image of a balcony convey to you?

Ooi Readerji, how could you? I see Him, The Only Mr Pen, Mr *Vilayat*—Great UK, Mr #1 name in the Canon, top-top English, zoomed on your forehead. He is in his famous tutu pantaloons laden with oval-nosed conceit. This famous Mr *Penwallah's* balcony hogs other balconies in literature. Rub Him off! *Pronto*! *Fatafat*! Away with the Romeo and Juliet blinkers. Give this lovers' balcony a deserved break, au revoir, heart-bye, foot-bye, bye-bye, for ever! *Yaar*, there are other balconies too and other love stories, like Heer and Ranjha. In the desert, Heer shrieked for her lost Ranjha. There are some shrieks which can't be described. Heer's was such a shriek that God in heaven shook and descended instead. And Heer said to the Almighty Bufferer, 'But you are not my Ranjha!'

Yaar-Reader, balconies remind me of the *balcony level truth*. It is difficult to explain. When it happens, you don't know if it happened or not because it is a scratch, an instant recognition, clutching, and then a black out. Finished. Balcony level truth 'pings'. It hits you privately, in the eye or stomach. (Yes, yes I acknowledge you are not a California reader.) Okay *Readerji*, let me explain. On television, I see a veiled woman hurrying down the street. For the first time, she is voting for a woman leader. At the ballot box, the woman extends her wrist, uncovering rose bangles. The 'ping' for me isn't her vote for Benezir Bhutto as much as her rose bangles excited, out of black *purdah* shroud, out of prison. This 'ping' and I write 'Muslim Woman Pictures'.

> My friend paints women
> rib-eyed
> excavation stiff.
> She strokes them patiently
> hardening black paint
> head to heel.
> Nostrils flicked shut.
> On top of their hood skulls
> she fastens
> wingy birds.

Readerji, you and me on the balcony. Eye-lash, heart-beat, itch-scratch, Be-eena. I am because you are. No, *Readerji*, no need to giddy up to the parasitic critic. There is no hidden hyphenated meaning in Be-eena, though I am sure the critic will suck the book dry and author-interpret Beena. Yes, yes, I have my reasons for choosing the name. Have patience. Your eyes crackle like hers. You have eyes like her, my Guruji, Green, and slashing like a machete. 'If you bring a gun into the story, in the end, it must go off,' she says. That's when I get mad at you, *Readerji*. I am no large-lapped goddess, churning out word after word, which you devour, chug, chug, left, right, until the book finishes. Can't you pull the trigger sometimes? And let me warn you there is no guru in the story either. I see, you want to co-create by including a police station in the story. How odd you want police in the story. Ah, because you don't trust my dis-order. *Abra Kadabra Jadhu Manter Phoosh*, kiss a toad! And a one and two and a three sugars in my tea! Presto! There *is* an RCMP in this story but Indian *ishtyle*.

What do you mean, also a Petro-Canada gas station? *Readerji*, in a bullock village? Ah, you are only kidding! Ha! Ha! Ha! Finally, *Readerji* my *yaar*, you are de-starching but don't lose all your solemnity, what will happen to Beena?

I am not allowing you to read? I am chaotic, an interrupter, untrustworthy, fibber. Whoa! Whoa! I will tell you two things, and then I will disappear, in a flick second.

Beena's village has a *panchayat*. *Panch* means five. Five fingers. Five wise men of the village who handle disputes and maintain law and order. Oh yes, *Readerji*, Beena's father, Pindi, is one of the *panchayat-wallahs*. Hey, you know Pindi! So, your critic thinks Pindi is a scholar? *Readerji*, forget the critic with the small 'c.' Come with me a little farther. There are many hearts in Beena, yes, Pindi's included.

And now finally, *Readerji*. Turn around, it is time. Your hand. This is the edge of Beena's village. No, I still cannot abandon you. First, pour some water in the bathing bucket. Beena's mother is fanatic about cleanliness. Once you are through, rub the bucket well with sand and rinse it thoroughly. It should gleam like Mr Sunlight's bulge. Yes, yes, I know this is in poor taste. But not the time to argue, my pet. It is hot *Readerji*, so why don't you bathe under the *pipal* tree?

. . . Tepid water. The water splashing on the baked sands sprouts peppery smells. There is a sudden gust of wind and the air is hued with the smell of mangoes. And then, thud, a mango falls.

'*Amma*, let me go, a mango's fallen.'

'It won't run away, let me finish your hair.'

'*Amma*, gently!' Beena's slender form is caught between her mother's strong legs.

Beena's mother grunts an acknowledgement. Under her rough fingers, the saucer of coconut oil clatters.

'Don't hunch child, how can I do your scalp properly?'

Beena has a heavy wave like a squirrel's tail and in sunlight, her black hair glints purple. When her mother is lost in thought, her fingers turn violent in her hair.

When Beena is a child, her mother makes a bony basin with her thin legs and sinks her into it. Hoarsely, she sings:

> Sleep child sleep!
> Harass not your mother
> who has
> yet to boil the *dal*
> and grind spices.
> Lie soft
> so I can fetch water.
> The floor is unswept
> and Baba's trousers unpatched.
> Child,
> I have forgotten about firewood
> yet yet yet
> Oh scuttle off to sleep!

Beena also remembers her mother's ringed finger. She no longer wears the ring. She asks her about the ring but her mother's eyes only fill up. Beena cannot bear when her mother cries. She can't remember the ring except for the rhythmic thick sounds it made on her forehead, when she lay in her mother's lap, as a child. Each time her mother's hand came down on her forehead, her face must have screwed up like now, two wiry slits with thorny lashes. A dreadful grey creeps over her crunched face.

'Beena!, why so you always jump like that? You make my heart fall out! Up! Your hair is done.'

I am Beena's mother. As a young bride, when I stand in the doorway of my husband's home, everyone gasps, even the village priest, who is supposed to be above such matters, for my colouring is that of limpid gold. Even now, with Beena shot up, the priest says it outright to our shopkeeper, '*Lalaji*, how can you say this dotty honey is pure? In this village we know that the clearest honey must measure up to Pindi's wife's colouring.' The market crowd laughs. *Lalaji* does not let the *pandit* get away. '*Panditji*, don't stick me with a wandering bowl in my prime. How can I explain to your milk-lined stomach that dirty juice oils commerce?'

I have left my ring in *Lalaji*'s care. Until Beena's wedding. It is a powerful ring with three rubies and two sapphires. Will hold merit amidst her shoddy dowry. There is also a silver water pot. Beena's father—I cannot leave anything to him. My shoulders are heavy. So heavy.

Yes, I am Pindi's wife.

I fell in love with my husband's walk. Tight gait of hips and hair flying back. There is a song in my village, 'whenever the city-boy walks like this, the virgin's heart is fish out of water.' Even now he startles me. The blue sky falls back as he strides forward, diminishing the mango tree and the thatched huts. His bent hip swerves, just, just so. It rushes his beauty and my green bangles turn dark.

That hot sleepy afternoon by the well. Shabnam and I are eating raw mangoes. Our skirts hitched up for any breeze. Now I am called Beena's mother. Pindi's wife. But my name is Dhano.

'Dhano, look, a city goat released our way. *Ooi*, he is wearing gold eye glasses, like white *dipti afficer*.'

'Shabnam, pull down your skirt! His vision with four eyes must be sharp.'

'*Ooi Babuji*, you with four eyes, in our village, the well is woman-space. You walk over here informally. Why? Is my friend Dhano getting married to you?'

'*Babuji*, my friend is cocky. Are you lost?'

'Perhaps I am. *Bibiji*, you with the edged tongue, tell your friend that her colour is intoxicating as a dimple.'

'*Babuji*, so this is how city-men praise women, with a saki-wine tongue?'

'Forgive my indelicate comparison. Your Dhanoji's colouring is warm like butter and honey.'

'Easy city-*Babuji*, you may slip on your oily-tongue, and this would be a pity, because your city strut has knocked us senseless. But really *Babuji*, our Dhano isn't a Maharani of some bakery. Butter and honey, hah!'

'Don't you offer a visitor water, friend of Dhano?'

'In our village, to feed you water, stranger-*Babu* is half the ritual.'

'The other half?'

'Marriage *dholaks*, city-*Babu*.'

'*Babuji*, I apologise for Shabnam's insolence.'

'Dhanoji! Thank you for intervening. Your friend's tongue is nothing like shabnam-dew. It's lightning sharp. Will you pour water for me? I may receive some sweetness from your bounty.'

'*Ooi Babuji* with four eyes, careful you don't get cramps in your tongue.'

'Shabnamji, tell your friend I will seal the vacant half of the ritual with *dholaks* and feed her a tumbler of almond milk.'

He kneels by me and holds out cupped palms. I lift my silver water-pot in one big arc and pour out a waterfall. He catches my eyes in an eye-lock.

'My name is Pindi,' he says.

Readerji, Beena's father, Pindi. Yes, I am back. Pindi is a scholar. Actor. Actually, neither. His speech is slightly chilled at the top. Scholars and actors cultivate the brisk tone. Never fails to harness an audience. (Even your critic.) Pindi the village hero.

I can't resist to deviate, *Readerji*. 'Hero' is a 'ping' word for me. Oh no, in Beena's story, there are no heroes. But for a while, pretend there is a young widow. (Really, I can't resist this deviation.) It's like a *pucca*-ripe film script.

Story (and *Ooi Readerji*, see this through a lens): There is a young widow. Her husband is butchered on the train. It is 1947. Partition of India. The husband and wife have left everything and are fleeing to India on a ghost train from Lahore. But her husband is butchered on the train. The hero of our story is a *Teacherji*. The refugee widow makes her new home in his village, the village where the train drops off all the refugees from Pakistan. This *Teacherji* is a radical. He wants change after independence. With the British ousted, it is now the turn of the Brahmin rule-setters. Away with the practice of wife burning on her husband's pyre. Away with widow exile and her food without garlic. Shake life into her mummy existence. Let the red marriage vermilion seep into her bloodless hair parting. Let her wear passionate green bangles.

Of course not *Readerji*, this is not a teacher-student romance, leave that to the Harlequin caste. But it is a teacher and widow romance. *Yaar*, we are talking progress. Feminism.

(Action): The radical *Teacherji* blocks her path. She is returning from the river. He asks her for water from a widow's pot! In her confusion, the white-clad widow, with loose blowing hair tilts her pot and fills his cupped palms. *Fatafat* the Panchayat gathers under the banyan tree.

O the commotion, *Readerji*!

Heaved dust, hooves, children thrown up their mothers' waists, clanking of padlocks on shops, men's voices thrown right across, only to be drowned by temple bells, and picnic food.

Oh yes, *Readerji*, picnic food is a must when stripping takes place. Who wrote that story, you know, after witnessing a violent beating, the heroine says she could eat a horse? This is no theft or shopkeeper fight-commotion. *Yaar*, a widow has stepped out of bounds. Hero-*Teacherji* will get a beating. But it is the widow's end. She should have known better.

Deftly, the hawkers form an unending line, with baskets full of roasted peanuts, spiced peas, fried cassava dipped in paprika, coconut cubes, and sweet creamy *burfi* spotted with purple flies, but no one cares. The widow has already created a juicy hunger. Food and picnic. Blaring loudspeaker churns out fast-fast songs.

Readerji, ping! I tell you, I can see this all on the screen. The middle part: their eye love story and how it all began (*Ooi* I've yet to work out the details). But right now, I want to run to the end. The Brahmin-Khomenis wait with *lathis* and stones to hurl at our avant-garde hero. His forehead gleams and the cool green veins mapping his temples burst with power. He turns toward the widow, his last look, deep as a tongue in the desert (rub that frown of yours! I think the image conjures urgency/passion. So what if it doesn't make sense. Don't be such a tight accountant). His last look is really a tongue kiss (you cannot kiss on the Indian screen but all professional cinema goers know that deep-deep look is *really a kiss*). The hero is about to open the door, ready to be kicked in the face and belly.

But the widow hurls him round (their first touch and in the background the *dholak* goes wild! *dha-dhin dhin dhin*). She picks a blade which he uses for sharpening pencils from his desk and makes a gash in his thumb. Clutching his bloody thumb, she paints her hair parting. Now she is married to him. Her hair parting a pumping red. She pushes him behind her and opens the door. She steps out. He follows. (Cut.)

> I am Pindi, the tailor. Never wanted to be a tailor but somehow I have become one. I live for my newspaper from the United Kingdom. It is greatly revered by the villagers because it is from *Vilayat*, the land of my British sahibs, my mother and father. The villagers insist that all sahibs live in *Vilayat*, London country. I tell them about America but they are not interested. The postmaster treats the paper reverently. Before my house he stops at Shiva's temple. The *Vilayat* paper under his arm. No one will steal it from his government khaki letter carrier, but it is out of respect for the newspaper. That's why my paper arrives tied with marigolds, and a yellow speckle of food at the top. The Postman's offerings at the temple returned after being blessed by the priest. Yes, the villagers never tire of feeling the newspaper. When the postmaster arrives, Beena's mother brings my tea, never in a tumbler but a proper cup and saucer. I like to frown and let my chin sink into my chest as I scan the headlines. The postmaster withdraws silently. I have never been to *Vilayat*. I know I never will. I label all garments sewn by me: 'By Pindi of Jamuna Village, London Returned.'

Readerji, in the evenings, everyone gathers around the Banyan tree to listen to Pindi. He adjusts his gold glasses and relates to the villagers the real news. 'Real news is from *Vilayat*,' he tells them. His fringed shawl never slips off this shoulder. ' "One step for

Man and a giant step for Mankind" says Neil Armstrong, the first man to set foot on the moon.'

A village boy asks, 'Pindi *Baba*, the *Vilayat*-London sahibs have even reached up there! They are God's special chosen, no?'

'Child, how many times must I tell you that *Neil-Babuji* is from America.'

'But *Baba*, even Amrika is in London country, no?'

The village Granny who is a medicine mother and the keeper of stories pushes Pindi's shawled shoulder, '*Ooi* Pindi child, what fairy wonder have your white *Babus* done now?'

Pindi laughs. 'Granny of the village, first of all, they will give your story of *Mamaji* who lives on the moon an eternal holiday! *Grannyji*, such stories you make of a wife's brother living on the moon. And when the moon looks scratched, it means *Mamaji* is carrying sticks on his back, and when the moon is low and swift between puffy dark clouds, *Mamaji* is playing "shut your eyes" with the children.'

'O villagers, and when children want to hear stories, don't send them to me but to Pindi, the favourite child of sahib *Babus*. Hah, as if the children will be content with stories of stiff machines on *Mamaji*'s moon!'

Everyone giggles but they look at Pindi widely. He knows so much. *Readerji*, Pindi even swayed your intelligent critic.

> At one time Beena's mother had soft eyes. Now I could stitch up her taunting eyes and chop off Beena's curving hair. Shabnam's lightning would have matched my passion. But I fell in love with my wife's colouring. Like honey, like bread gathering gold in warmth.

Beena catches her mother's sharp glare at her father as soon as he steps into the courtyard. Beena rushes to her father to deviate his attention. 'Come *Baba*, wash your hands, I will set out the food.'

Beena's mother storms into the kitchen to join her daughter.

'Why is he home for lunch today? Is he unwell?'

'He had to go to post office to fill out a money order to send to the landlord. The landlord will remain in the city for another month.'

'Is he planning to open shop this afternoon? Or is he going to spend the afternoon with his *Vilayat* papers. Those papers are my husband's other wife, and my wretched enemy.'

'*Amma*, let *Baba* eat in peace.'

'Let him have peace. That's his male-tribe right. Worrying about my daughter's dowry is all my headache. What's it to this village if the *Vilayat* country catches fire? Can't your father stick his nose in his own kitchen for once?' She grabs the straw hand fan, sprinkles water on it, and goes into the courtyard. She fans her husband while he eats.

'When I prepared the tiffin for you this morning, you never mentioned that you were coming home in the peak of the afternoon.'

'To visit the Post Office was not an item in my plans. My good friend Mirza Rashid and I entered into a discussion, and in the midst of our discourse, the matter of rent occurred to me and so I repaired to the Post Office.'

Yes husband. Revel in philosophies. Sit with your cronies, you empty spoon of the white sahibs. You would even praise the white sahibs' drawstrings! Let Beena age unbrided. Even in this frightening burden, I cannot ask your shoulder.

'I made my way to Ram Lal, the book seller next door,' continues Pindi, 'and gave him the food. His wife, as you well know, is away at her parents.'

Why husband, why? In the tiffin, I had packed a large coconut biscuit, an offering from the temple. No, not for *you*! My Beena loves these biscuits. I packed it out of wifely duty. Always, husband first. My true *dharma*. Damn!

'Beena, take this fan and sprinkle more water on it so your *Baba* can eat in cool peace. And Beena's father, won't you have more carrot *achar*, your daughter's favourite.'

Nothing pleases my mother more than the arrival of the milk seller. She squats beside him in the courtyard, feet newly washed. She won't cook anything in milk. Fresh from the cow, a tumbler of milk is poured for my father and myself. She sings to me then:

> One day
> He will come
> The king of grooms
> Saffron turbaned, kohled eyes
> And lift my Beena
> Bathed in milk
> She will rise from his navel
> And encircle his shoulder
> under the hood of
> the unhurt Goddess
> My Goddess of Protection

'*Hai* Beena, this silver-pot is your dowry piece! How dare you open the trunk!'
'*Amma*, I had nothing to do. It is such a heavy afternoon, not even a crow on the roof.'
'Then come daughter, let me oil your scalp.'
'And tell me the story of the silver water-pot.'
'Once upon a time, by the well one day, on a hot, slumbering afternoon, two girls with hitched skirts laugh and eat raw mangoes. One of the girls has a honey-yellow skin, like the flesh of a chickpea. Her friend is bold, her tongue lightning. She sees the groom-prince first. I remember his stylish pyjamas and his brocade hip belt. His walk slicing the sluggish afternoon. . . .'
Beena gently removes her mother's fist from her hair. The greased fist heavy on Beena's shoulder.
'When he asked for water, he knelt by me and held out cupped hands. I lifted my silver pot in one big arc and poured out a waterfall. He said, "My name is Pindi."'

Beena is washing her hair. She takes a bunch of hair and throws it over, not caring when the wet strands smack her shoulder. Her back has flushed, spindly marks. She feels the clutch of coconut oil which sticks her hair together.

> *Amma*, drink from this waterfall pot. Throw back your head and let the water cool your ashed liver. Mother mine, you are a bride. Your thick ring glitters. You stand in the hushed doorway. And *Panditji* keeps staring at you. When you meet your husband's eye, he hues you pink, In his gaze, you stand under a pomegranate shower. Open your mouth wider, mother. I am your unhurt Goddess. Your Goddess of Protection.

No, not yet, she decides, and grabs more hair soap. She has her father's dreamy throat in her fingers. Her digging fingers tear into her scalp, and where the scratching is violent, the soap burns.

Beena's mouth waters.

Readerji, don't shout. All these stories knotted together are also giving me a headache. What? No *Readerji*, no one can be at our door. Listen, Beena is yours-mine. This is *our zenana*. Textbook stories of this equals that are a critic's formula. *Yaar-Readerji*, life isn't organized linearly because it is constantly piling. When I go to heat the milk or clean the fridge, other small things happen along the way: I pick up my mother's sock from the couch (which really needs to be cleaned), close the bathroom door, slam down the receiver when I realize it is a salesman, and finally, finally, I come to the milk. God, I hope the saucepan is clean. Similarly, a story is never linear. A story's collar bones are full of meat—by her very nature, she is massing constantly.

Indeed, what happens to Pindi? Both you and your critic are partial to him. *Yaar*, the satisfaction from this kind of fiction is you cannot compel a single intention or conclusion.

You are getting edgy *Readerji*, are you about to chop off my nose? Okay, let's talk about Pindi. Why are you staring at the door? What do you mean, Beena is outside?

Readerji, don't spook me. No, I don't hear her scraping her scalp. She does not exist outside the door. Of course I'm sure—I'm writing her! Because . . . enough! Look, I don't like your game. Come back! *Readerji*, NO!

Lawrence Hill *b.* 1957

The son of a black American father, raised by an African Episcopal minister, and a white American mother, a civil rights activist of Protestant Republican background, Lawrence Hill was born in Toronto where his parents immigrated in 1953. His 'allegiances are multitudinous and they cross all sorts of boundaries and nationalities and racial groups', but it is race, especially the question, 'Who, exactly, is defined as black?' that emerges as a major force in Hill's writing. 'Race' may be 'nothing more than an invention of human beings', he says, but 'having one black and one white parent, myself, and having interviewed more than 30 other Canadians of mixed race about identity issues, I have come across many people who love and respect their white parents, but who definitely have come to see themselves as black. Why? Because that's how the world sees us.' His non-fiction book, *Black Berry, Sweet Juice: On Being Black and White in Canada* (2001), focuses on the ambivalence that characterizes this issue, beginning with his parents' story and including 36 interviews with interracial couples and their children. The irony and humour through which this narrative is filtered also punctuate his first novel, *Some Great Thing* (1992), which was translated into French, and was dramatized over 15 episodes on CBC Radio's 'Between the Covers' (2001).

Hill, who has studied Economics at the University of British Columbia and at Laval University (BA, 1980), has worked as a reporter focusing on economic issues for the *Globe and Mail* (1982) and the *Winnipeg Free Press* (1982–5) and holds an MA in Writing from John Hopkins University (1992), where he taught for a year. One of the Ontario Black History Society's interviewers for its history projects, he is also the author of *Trials and Triumphs: The Story of African Canadians* (1993), a children's history book, and *Women of Vision: The Story of the Canadian Negro Women's Association* (1996). Trilingual, speaking English, French, and Spanish, Hill has worked in Spain, France, and West Africa, as well as working as senior writer for various Ontario government ministerial branches. Though not autobiographical, part of his travelling and his journalistic and speech-writing experiences, in fictionalized form, inform some of the characters in his acclaimed novel, *Any Known Blood* (1997). Driven by its protagonist's need to research and write about his black father's fugitive slave origins, Langston V, who has spent most of his adult life passing as neither black nor white, but taking on the racial and cultural heritage of minority groups in Canada, eventually comes to identify himself as black. A first-person narrative, which incorporates fictional letters and archival material, it reflects the influence on Hill of such writers as Frederick Douglass and Langston Hughes. Langston's desire to tell the story of his father's black heritage, a heritage that is part of the Underground Railway and the history of blacks in Oakville, Ontario, turns him into a novelist; the novel he writes is the novel we read.

Hill's most recent novel is *The Book of Negroes* (2005), the fictionalized first-person narrative of Anne-Marie Peters, a black former slave in Nova Scotia who joins the exodus to Sierra Leone.

from *Any Known Blood*

I was not looking forward to Mill's dinner party. There would be women in church hats. There would be more fried chicken. It was the only thing Mill knew how to make, apart from potato salad. But I wanted to keep looking at Mill's box of information on my grandfather, Langston the Third, and figured I could sneak a peek—or perhaps even borrow some materials—if I attended. So I drove over, like the dutiful nephew, and brought along Yoyo.

Annette Morton opened Mill's door. She was young. Too young. Twenty-seven, tops.

'Hi. Come on in. How are you, Langston?'

'Annette, how're you doing? This is my friend, Yoyo.'

She nodded and shook his hand, watched Yoyo get ushered inside by Mill, turned back to me, and took my hand. Her hand was warm, as if it had been in a pocket, and it held mine long enough to be more than a formality. I felt a quick stirring in my groin and tried to check it by telling myself that it would be just my luck to mistake the signals of a born-again Christian. Still, I couldn't help looking at her again. Her eyes were burnt hazel, her lips on the edge of a grin. She smelled of strawberries.

'Are you two gonna eye each other all night or are you gonna join the party?' Mill broke in. 'There's people for you to meet, Langston. Annette, check the corn bread, will you?'

I was reintroduced to Eleanor and Maggie, the two women I'd met when first walking to the A.M.E. church. I met Ishmael, who had watched over my car, twice, while I was in church. Ishmael was a high school senior. He had brought along his older brother, Derek, who wanted to talk. Derek wanted to talk awfully bad. It appeared that he'd been wanting to talk for five years, and that I was the first person willing to listen. After several minutes, Annette came up behind me. I turned to acknowledge her, but was dragged back into Derek's rant.

'It's rough here, rough in Baltimore,' he said. 'How you find it here? I mean, being a black man and all. Well, partially black, I guess you qualify, especially if you identify, if your thoughts, your mind, your culture are one with ours. I mean, man, I've got to assume that, since you've been at Bethel and up on Pennsylvania. I'll assume you've accepted the burden of blackness. So how do you find it here, compared to Canada?'

'It's an interesting city. It's—'

'Interesting is a white word, man. Interesting isn't a word for people of colour. It's a word for politicians, man. But I'll cut you some slack, coming from Canada and all. Black people use that word up there?'

'Well,' I said, 'where I'm from, I haven't run into masses of black people fleeing the word *interesting*. It's not generally seen as a betrayal of one's racial identity.'

'Aha! I detect a capacity for irony. A sign of higher intelligence, no doubt. Racial identity, that's a happening concept. I —'

Annette took my arm. 'Cool it, Derek. The man hasn't even had something to drink yet, and you want to get into the only thing you know how to talk about.'

'Drink, drink. Be my guest. Make off with the lovely Annette, but return, my friend. Place some interesting ice cubes in an interesting mug of Canada Dry ginger ale and come back for some more interesting and elucidating rap.'

'Right,' I said. Annette had her arm through mine. It felt lovely. She released me in the kitchen. 'I had to get you out of there. You have to steer around Derek. If you get drawn into a conversation, you'll never get away.'

I considered asking how I should talk so that she wouldn't get away from me, but ditched the idea. Instead, I poured her a soft drink, gallant gent that I am, and poured myself one, and stood by her silently. We watched Derek work on Yoyo.

'Man, I hear you're an African. That must feel deep, Yoyo. You must have a real sense of racial resonance.'

Yoyo laughed loudly and pleasantly. 'I don't know much about resonance, my friend. I'm tone deaf.'

'But you're black, man. Indisputably undiluted.'

'Yes, and I have ten toes and ten fingers, too, but I don't spend much time thinking about how perfect they are.'

'What did it feel like, to be in a country where everybody is black, I mean, all the people in power are black, and you know who you are, and what your rights are, and where you're headed as a people?'

'Not toward civil war, I hope. We've got 250 ethnic groups in Cameroon. And as for what it feels like to be in a country where everybody is black, I don't think of it that way. First of all, not everybody is black. There are a few whites. There are some in-betweens. There are some Asians. We, the black Cameroonians, feel very united. Many people who are young and educated spend their time figuring out how to leave.'

'Leave?'

'Travel. Visit America. Visit Canada. See the world. You want to see what's out there. You feel you haven't lived a full life unless you get out and see the world.'

'But man, what is there to see out here? Racism and ruination. Crippled cities, crippled people. The only—'

Mill stopped Derek this time. She put a drumstick in his hand. 'Put that mouth of yours to use on some chicken. If you keep talking about racism and ruination, just as sure as Moses came down from the mount, my kitchen broom is gonna come down on your head.'

Derek took a bite and asked Yoyo what he did.

'I clean houses, lately. You know anybody who needs housecleaning?'

'That's bourgeois.'

'I'm not bourgeois yet,' Yoyo said. 'But I'm working on it. Maybe I'll be bourgeois after I've cleaned another two hundred houses.'

Mill ordered everybody to sit at the table. Yoyo helped her to carry out the plates. I sat next to Mill. Annette slipped in beside me. She put her hand on my arm, touched my foot with hers. We smiled.

On display were honey ham, baked corn biscuits, fried chicken, potato salad, baked acorn squash with honey and butter, Coke and ginger ale and white wine, potato chips, taco chips, and salted cashews. There was also lemonade. The eight of us sat around the table. Mill said grace.

'For what we are about to receive, all these good things, all these good people, for people like Langston here, who sticks up for little ones on Pennsylvania Avenue, for people like Yoyo, who has nothing and doesn't yap about it and works his backside off and never runs his mouth except to ask for more money, which I won't give him, for people like Maggie and Eleanor and Ishmael and me, who give so much time to the church, for people like Annette for their beauty and their brains, but not in that order, for people like Derek, who have their heart in the right place even if they say the wrong thing, but mostly for life and for love between people, may the Lord make us truly thankful, Amen. You can dig in now.'

The table fell silent for a few seconds, except for the clinking of knives and forks and spoons and the dropping of bread and squash onto plates. We all started eating. Annette's foot pressed against mine. I turned to look at her. Mill nudged me with her elbow. 'Cute, isn't she?'

I pretended I hadn't heard. Thankfully, we were interrupted by three sharp raps on the door. I knew those raps. Instantly. Not too many people think enough of themselves to announce their arrival that way. He used to do it when I was a child, in my room, and he had something to say to me. *Rap Rap Rap. Son. May I have a word with you?* If I didn't answer him pronto, he would open the door anyway.

Mill, too, recognized the sound.

'You know who that is, don't you?' she said, looking at me. 'I never did like people come visiting without announcing themselves.'

Mill got up, wiped an ant-sized trace of squash from the corner of her mouth, and walked to the door, mumbling. She slid the bolts free. Removed the chain. Turned the knob.

'You're just in time for dinner, come on in.' Mill returned to the table. As she sat down, she called over her shoulder, 'Turn those bolts back in place, fix the chain, and pull up a chair.'

'What kind of way is that to welcome your brother after forty-odd years?' My father took off his coat, slid open the closet door. 'I can't believe this, Mill. There's actually a place to hang a coat. There are actually guests sitting at your table. Have you changed? Some sort of profound organizational metamorphosis?'

'You should have left all them extra syllables up in Canada,' Mill said. 'No. I ain't changed. It was cleaned up by Yoyo, that's all.'

'Cleaned up by Yoyo,' my father mimicked. 'I won't even hazard a guess as to the meaning of that. A form of Zen meditation, perhaps.'

'Yoyo is my name, Dr Cane,' Yoyo said, standing up. 'It's a pleasure to meet you. I am a friend of your sister's, and of your son's.'

My father allowed his hand to be shaken. He peered at Yoyo's face. 'Pleasure to meet you, too. Pleasure to meet somebody sufficiently civilized to stand up and shake a stranger's hand.'

'Civilized!' Mill mumbled. 'Is dropping in unannounced civilized?'

Eleanor and Maggie gushed over my father, and said how proud the congregation was of me. Mill prevailed upon him to join us at the table.

My father's gaze fell swiftly on my face. My right eye and cheekbone were still swollen and discolored from the rubbing I had taken.

'I can see that he handled himself adroitly on Pennsylvania Avenue,' my father said. 'I'm not even going to ask what a son of mine was doing on Pennsylvania Avenue in this day and age.'

'Handling himself more honorably than his tomcatting father used to do on the same street half a century ago,' said Mill, who passed him a plate of ham and potatoes.

'How in the world did you hear about it?' I asked.

'From Aberdeen,' my father said.

I looked at Mill.

'All I did was tell Aberdeen what happened,' Mill said. 'If you don't want me talking about you, then don't go getting yourself half killed on Pennsylvania Avenue.'

Derek Wedburner, the man of monologues, the master of diatribes, inserted himself in the conversation.

'I can see, Dr Cane, that you're a man of some distinction. Of a refined vocabulary, undoubtedly the product of a sound education. That must be something of a shock for whites in Canada—to see such an educated African man in their midst.'

My father cut him off. 'I'm not an African. Yoyo, from the sound of his accent, is likely an African. I'm not an African, any more than you.'

'But I am an African,' Derek said.

'If you are an African,' Yoyo said, 'tell me the capital city of Burkina Faso.'

'I don't know, but—'

'It's Ouagadougou,' Yoyo said, 'and if you were African, you would know it.'

'This is not a matter of geography,' Derek said. 'It's a matter of the diaspora. We people of color—'

'*People of color*,' my father snorted. 'For all its pretension, it sounds to me just the same as *colored people*.'

'It's not the same,' Derek said. 'Not the same at all, if I may beg to differ. *Colored people* comes straight out of our American heritage of slavery and segregation. *People of color* evokes a diaspora, a scattering, a collectivity of people of all races—'

'Except whites,' I said. 'Except maybe Latin Americans. And Sicilians in the summer. Or perhaps you should have a new category for them: people nearly of color.'

Mill clapped her hands. 'I guess that's about what you'd be, Langston,' she said. 'Let me introduce you all to my nephew of near color.'

Derek said, 'People of color have some things in common, and should move collectively to—'

'I've never known Indians and blacks and Asians to get together with each other any more than they get together with whites,' my father said, 'and I don't see how the term *people of color* is going to make them all start loving each other.'

I asked Yoyo what he thought. He said he wanted to think about it. Perhaps he would write an opinion piece on the subject for the op-ed page of the *Toronto Times*. He could use the money, anyway.

'So you're a journalist, are you?' Derek asked.

'Well, I was in Cameroon. But I know somebody at the *Toronto Times*. She could help me get it published there, I bet.'

'And why did you leave your country? Why have you contributed to the brain drain from Africa?'

'Brain drain,' Yoyo said. 'That's very funny. My brain would probably have been draining, thanks to a blow from a shovel or a bullet, had I returned to Cameroon. I was a political columnist in a newspaper run by the government. And while I was over here on an assignment, the government was overthrown.'

'Forget that political stuff, nobody cares about it anyway,' Mill said. 'Clean homes. Set yourself up a little company. Keep your prices low. If you keep working as well as you did for me, I could find you ten new customers next week. You could make yourself a pot of money.'

'Son,' my father said, 'I'd like to have a word with you.'

'You haven't come all this way to taste my chicken?' Mill said. 'Why don't you leave that boy alone? He ain't botherin' no one. If he wants to look through old boxes and write us all up in his story, what's the problem?'

My father stood up and walked over to the window. He pulled back a blind, stared out into the night, and turned back. 'I'd rather not discuss this in a community forum.'

'These are my dinner guests, Langston. These are the first dinner guests I believe I've had since you abandoned the U.S.A. And I'm not asking them to leave. So why don't you just eat some chicken like ordinary folks do?'

My father surprised me by joining us again at the table and eating most of what Mill gave him.

When we had all finished eating, Mill looked at my father and asked, 'You're not mixed up in that kidnapping, are you?'

'No.'

'You should stick to doctoring.'

'Thanks for your opinion.'

'You've grown older, Langston. You've put on weight. Where'd all your hair go?'

'That's unkind, Mill, but I won't reciprocate.'

'You always liked to use big words when you were uneasy, Langston. So what do you want with us, then? Why have you come all this way?'

My father looked at me. 'I want you to come home, son. I don't want you mugged again on the streets of Baltimore. I want you to stop poking around in things that are best left alone. I'll tell you all you need to know.'

'Thanks, but no thanks,' I said. 'I've got a few things to do down here yet. But I'll let you know when I'm ready to come back.'

'Son,' my father said, 'It's been a long day and I'm tired. I'm staying at the Lincoln Hotel on St Paul Street, which isn't far, I believe, from where you are. Come have breakfast with me tomorrow morning. I have some things to talk about with you.'

'Okay,' I told him.

'You don't have to stay at no hotel,' Mill said. 'I got an extra bedroom here. It's clean. Yoyo fixed it up.'

'Thanks, Mill, but I've made a hotel reservation.' I noticed Annette again, who looked at me, too. My father stayed for an hour, absorbing mild barbs from Mill without reacting, and helping himself to peach pie and ice cream. He left after a decent interval. So did Maggie and Eleanor. I offered to give Annette, Derek, Ishmael, and Yoyo rides home, and managed to drop off the men first.

Making love to someone within a day of meeting her has not happened to me before, and I doubt it will happen again. Annette's front teeth were small and white and had the narrowest of spaces between them and seemed all the more delicious as I ran my tongue over them. But I had been moving quickly all day and I felt embarrassed about smelling bad. Those of us who haven't had sex or had any chance of it for a month or a year or a decade tend to let a few items of intimate hygiene slip. I was in need of a shower and I told her so, and I stayed in there for five or ten minutes, shampooing, cream-rinsing, sudsing until I felt a swoosh of the shower curtain and a nudge—no, two soft nudges against my back—and there was Annette pressing herself against me under the falling water. I had finished washing myself, so I washed her. I started with a bar of soap and a blue facecloth, and I moved it around her forehead, which was broad, and her lips, which were round, and her neck, which was smooth and cool, and everywhere the washcloth and soap had been, my mouth followed. It followed down her neck, along her arms, across her breasts, which sloped down and lifted out and up, perkily, and over her nipples, which were dark, very dark, and standing in salutation. I found her navel, and parts lower, and got to my knees. While she tugged my ears and played with my hair, I washed her and rinsed her and nibbled and sucked. She slid onto all fours and raised her lovely labia at me from behind and I entered her while reaching around to stroke her swollen clitoris and hanging breasts and she turned her mouth to the side and took mine in hers between gasps. That did not go on long, I will admit. Not nearly long enough. I lost my charge within minutes, but she seemed patient, seemed ready to wait. We separated and got out of the bathtub and toweled each other. She stretched me out on her bed and told me to close my eyes. That was the first thing she said. It was one of the only things she said that night. I had nothing to say at all. Wanted to say not a word. She began oiling and massaging and stroking my feet, and ankles, and calves, and—well, I am still amazed to think how many times and in how many ways we loved each other that night.

I found a parking ticket appended to my windshield wiper at four that morning. I didn't care. I unlocked the door. Had I really done those things? Home, Langston. Go home, I told myself. Get yourself three and a half hours of sleep. We know it will be deep. Get yourself up, shower, and get on over to meet your father.

I met my father in his hotel restaurant. 'What exactly are you doing down here, son, and how long do you plan to stay?'

My father sat well back in his chair, legs folded, in contrast to the directness of his question. He had already eaten, so I just ordered tea with cream. I have always liked cream in tea. I thought of Annette. *You want anything? Tea? Coffee?* she had asked as I was leaving.

No, I've had everything I could need or want. But a phone number. How about a phone number?

Why don't we just see when and where we meet again? You told me your address. And you know mine. Let's just leave this as simple as it has been.

'If this is to be an interrogation, I don't think I'll take part,' I told my father.

'Fair enough,' he said. I could see him thinking. You can build homes, build your life, build your career. You can even fertilize the egg that grows into a human being. You can fertilize five or ten of them, and nurture them. But you can't force an infant to eat something he won't eat. You can't force an infant to sleep when he won't sleep. And you can't force a son to grow up in a father's mold.

I stirred my tea. I put sugar in it. I never put sugar in tea, but it occupied my hands. My father was aging. His hair had faded gray, almost white. He had deep grooves under his eyes. He was a brown-skinned man of the indisputable variety. Your unthreatening black professional type.

'How's Mom?' I said.

'Wonderful. As usual. I love that woman, Langston. She's worried about me. This kidnapping stuff has not been easy on us. For the first two days of the kidnapping, reporters camped outside our house. Every time I came in or went out, they wanted a statement. It has affected her sleep. She's been up a lot at night.'

'But she's okay?'

'Yes. And doing better. Things seem to be settling down. No more press around all the time. They really run you ragged.' My father cracked his knuckles one by one.

'Mill is quite the woman,' I said. 'I'm sorry I missed out on her, all those years.'

'Well, we've been through a few things. I'm sure you'll find out about them. When you do, be generous, son. Be generous to your elders. You can't possibly know everything, even when you think you do.'

'I think I like you more when we're not at home together. In Oakville. At the house, I mean.'

'I catch your drift,' Dad said.

'Catch my drift? Don't tell me you're going to start talking like Derek.'

'You mean the people-of-color guy over at Mill's? No danger of that.'

'So what's this kidnapping all about, Dad?'

'I don't know. You've seen the papers. Norville Watson was out walking and never came home. Some group that calls itself Africa First is tabling ridiculous demands. It sent a video of Watson to a news station yesterday. I saw it on TV last night. Watson was shown sitting quietly, apparently unharmed, on a chair in an unmarked room. I'm sure the cops are viewing it carefully. He looked at the camera and said he hadn't been harmed, and seemed about to say that he would not cooperate when the tape was killed. He's one tough monkey.'

'You remember the time he sewed me up?'

'He phoned me in Stockholm to tell me about it. His secretary tracked me down and put Watson on the line, and he told me what had happened and that you were fine. He was very professional. I was grateful for that.'

'So what kind of hoax do you think is being pulled?'

'I don't think it's a black group that's got him.'

'That's a striking thing to say.'

'Because if a black group had taken him, they wouldn't be using inflammatory rhetoric. They'd be bending over to make sure everyone knew they were pros, and in control, and wouldn't act rashly. They wouldn't have asked for a measly hundred thousand dollars, because they would have known it would mark them as amateurs. And, being black, they sure as hell would have known that the government would never release black prisoners. So I think somebody else has Watson, and is trying to use the black community as a decoy. And it's working. In the last four days, police have brought in more than fifty blacks for questioning.'

'So what do you think this other group wants? Who do you think they are?'

'I haven't a clue.'

I finally gave in to my hunger and ordered a croissant and two poached eggs and a tall glass of orange juice.

'Good to see you're eating well, son.' My father grinned. 'When Aberdeen told me about your little accident, I wanted to come right down and see you.'

'Really?'

'Yup. Heard from Ellen lately, by the way?'

'Just a note the other day, basically telling me to get lost. Why?'

'Just wondering. Take care of yourself, son. You could have been hurt on Pennsylvania Avenue. It's worse than when I used to hang out there.'

'You knew it well, did you?'

'There was barely a bar I didn't know, or a bed I didn't share.' He smiled. 'But that was before I met your mother.' He stood up. He said his plane was leaving in two hours.

'Mill will be sorry you didn't attend church with her.'

'Well, I'm not waiting until next Sunday. Anyway, I couldn't stand it. They would make me stand up. They would treat me like a long lost son, instead of the miserable atheist that I am. They would invoke the wondrous names and accomplishments of my father and grandfather. And they would make me eat chicken. Which I detest. I can't face all that stuff. I'll leave it to you.'

'Thanks for dropping the interrogation, Dad.'

'It wouldn't have worked, anyway. See you soon, son. I hope.' He shook my hand and left the restaurant.

A week or so later, while I was with Annette again, and most of the rest of Baltimore was sleeping, Yoyo sat at his kitchen table and brought his pen to paper. I know, because he told me about it. Diversify, diversify, he kept telling himself. He had to keep all sorts of activities going. He had been selling barbecued meat, but had to let that go. He had sold croissants at the Saturday market, but now he had to let that go. He was getting more cleaning work now—at the dinner party, Maggie and Eleanor had both asked him to come over next week to clean their homes, and Yoyo had agreed, but wouldn't give a fixed price until he had seen their houses. But that was the only thing he had going now. What if that fell through?

Cleaning was not a sure thing. Yoyo had to diversify. He would write. Langston Cane was up writing every night and every morning in his kitchen, and he wasn't even a writer. He even admitted it. Had never published anything. Had never been paid for his writing, except for a few thousand speeches that an educated twelve-year-old could have written. Yet, nevertheless, he said he was writing. Didn't expect to make any money from it, didn't know if he'd finish it, didn't even know if it was worthy of being called a novel, but he was at it, writing every day. So would Yoyo. But Yoyo had to be focused. He couldn't afford to waste time on hand-wringing, anxiety-laden memoirs that might never be finished or published. No. He had to do something marketable. Something that he could finish in a day, and something that he could sell.

He would write an opinion piece. He had seen them frequently in North America. When he had worked during a year-long journalism apprenticeship a decade ago in St Boniface, Manitoba, he had noticed them appearing daily in the *Winnipeg Herald.* Yoyo would fire a few off to the *Toronto Times.* Two of his old friends from Winnipeg, Hélène Savoie and Mahatma Grafton, were working there. Hélène could help him publish his piece. He wanted to get in touch with her anyway. He wanted to see that woman again. She could help him negotiate a good fee at the paper. Three hundred dollars would be nice. It was more than one month's rent. It was exhilarating to think that he could make three hundred dollars just by sitting at a table and writing. Yes, Yoyo would start to write. He would take on the major issues of the day. He would sign them *Hassane Moustafa 'Yoyo' Ali, Underground in America.* The first one popped out in two hours.

Dear Reader,

I wish to propose an alternative to the terms used to describe people of African heritage.

I will start by focusing my attentions on a linguistic phenomenon— namely, the term *people of color.*

It is impossible to evaluate the term *people of color* without considering its predecessor, *colored people. Colored people* used to be a term sympathetic to people of Any Known Blood, but no longer. It is now reviled.

Some people today prefer the term *people of color.* This choice baffles me. You have a noun, a preposition, and another noun. Normally, such a construction would suggest belonging, such as People of France, or Jesuits of Italy, or Knights of Columbus. But it's an awkward construction. The preposition weighs down the term. Do we say People of Left Hands? It seems to me that *of* is the operative word. What is the difference, for example, between intelligent people and people of intelligence? The difference is in the attitude of the speaker. The user of the latter term wishes to emphasize the value of intelligence. The word suggests that the next word to follow is positive. That's why people say *The Duke of York* instead of *The York Duke.*

If one sets aside historical nuance, little remains to distinguish between *colored people* and *people of color.* The difference resides in the attitude of the speaker. If you use *colored people,* you convey that you don't care that the word offends black people today. If you use *people of color,* you wish to celebrate color. But to this writer, *people of color* rings with self-importance. It is one thing to celebrate one's heritage. But it is quite another to see oneself as the navel of the universe.

I propose that we entirely abandon the words color and colored.

May I submit the term *people of pigment*?

True, the weighty *of* remains. But the tone of self-importance is neutralized by alliteration. Matching the first letters of adjacent words is common in children's literature, and in cartoons. In English, even more than in French, alliteration has the effect of adding a touch of levity. Porky Pig. Mister McGoo. People of pigment. Follow me through, dear readers. To express this idea in terms of an arithmetic equation, *pomp + levity = equanimity*.

Let's examine other arguments in support of *people of pigment*. For one thing, the new term constitutes a clear departure from the word *color*. It is unlikely that any reasonable person will suggest replacing this expression with *pigmented people*, which, unlike *colored people*, has no tradition in our lexicon. For another, *pigment* is a compact and pithy little word. It is merely two syllables, and easy to pronounce. In the term people of pigment, both nouns start with the bilabial explosive *p*, a highly enjoyable consonant for the mouth to deliver—one that gives a person the sensation of power, or at least control of one's destiny. Finally, by retaining the word *of*—perhaps the most underrated preposition in the English language—we ensure that people enjoy the desirable connotations of pride and respect. People of pigment, unite under this new term.

Yoyo mailed the story to Hélène Savoie, who, as I heard later, fed the story to the op-ed editor—a man named Brian Coolidge. He tossed it down on his desk on top of a pile of unsolicited pieces. He said he didn't read handwritten copy. Hélène took it back, typed it on her computer, printed it, and gave it back to Brian.

'You're the most persistent—'

'Just read it,' Hélène said. 'This guy has a quirky take on things. You might like it.'

Brian pushed his reading glasses up the bridge of his long nose. He chuckled in the second sentence. He laughed midway through the fourth. He roared with laughter three more times and, at the end, declared the piece the best satire he'd seen in a year.

'He didn't intend it as satire,' Hélène told Brian.

'Do you think it's funny?' he asked her.

'Yes.'

'So do I. So will half the city. I'm using it on Friday.'

By Wednesday of the next week, the *Times* had received eighteen letters to the editor praising Yoyo's piece. One letter-writer complained that Yoyo's piece was a vitriolic attack on the sensitivities of people of color. But that writer drew fire from four other scribes in the following days. Brian asked Hélène to send Yoyo a note with the cheque. Could she please ask if he had any more articles kicking around?

Shani Mootoo *b.* 1957

DUBLIN, IRELAND

An accomplished multimedia and experimental video artist before she took up writing, Dublin-born Shani Mootoo grew up in Trinidad in a family of mixed Indian and Nepalese origins. Having been told by her grandmother not to repeat that an uncle had abused her sexually, Mootoo adopted the visual mode of expression early in her life as the primary means of articulating her innermost thoughts: 'I found it safer not to use words and started making pictures.' Her visual work—videos, photographs, and paintings—has been exhibited and screened nationally as well as internationally, including a show at the Museum of Modern Art in New York City. It includes the works *Father, Her Sweetness Lingers,* and *A Paddle and a Compass.* After coming to Canada in 1977, Mootoo studied at the University of Western Ontario, where she received a BFA (1980).

Beginning with her first book, the collection of short fiction *Out on Main Street* (1993), Mootoo established herself as a writer of sensuous prose that nevertheless deals with the complex processes of authenticating identity and such difficult issues as sexual abuse and displacement. *Cereus Blooms at Night* (1996), her first novel and a finalist for the Giller and Booker prizes, is a compelling narrative that takes a longer and more complex approach to sexual abuse, sexual desire, and family politics. As she says, her writing is 'very much about try-ing to find out what the purpose of life is, won-dering why certain things that happened to me as a child could be permitted to happen, and why the universe would allow such a child to survive. . . . it's about what to do with suffer-ing.' Her concern with the palimpsestic nature of subjectivity, as well as memory, also charac-terizes her poetry collection *The Predicament of Or* (2000).

Mootoo is a contributor to CBC Radio's 'This Morning' and has been a writer-in-resi-dence at a number of universities, including the University of Alberta. 'Delighted to be called a "Canadian" writer'—'the last thing she wants is to be known as is an Indo-Trinidadian-Irish-Canadian-lesbian writer'—Mootoo has lived in Vancouver, New York, and, occasionally, Ireland, but at present makes her home in Edmonton. As she says, 'The moment I feel set-tled about anything, I want to undercut it. I don't want to be told by anyone, including myself, what I am.' *He Drown She in the Sea* (2005), her second novel, written in the lyrical yet exact language that has become her trade-mark, is set in both Vancouver and the fictional Caribbean island of Guanagaspar. A story that begins during the Second World War in the Caribbean but moves toward its tentative reso-lution in Vancouver, it is about racial and class differences, the haunting legacy of colonialism, and longing.

For Naan

The alarm clock radio blurts out: CBC-Vancouver,
Fluorescent red glow pries me awake
To hear a letter from two flight attendants from New West

   On Holiday!

Pawing the foothills of the Nepalese Himalayas
Enamored of the primitive lives

5

Of beautiful smiles, white teeth
Of brass bells tinkling tinkling
On beasts of burden as they trek over
This pass, that summit—   10
How they wished to remain as long as they could
Before returning
To civilization;
If you're planning a trip,
Keep in mind it costs only ten rupees,   15
Or thirty cents, per night for a bed. What a deal!

They brought back trophies of authentic Kulu Valley topi.
Images I have hoarded jealously
From *National Geographic*
Span panoramic across my mind.   20
But how it irks me to know the color of the hills
Before the snow blues everything,
To know of pebbly faces creased like the hills,
To know of Naan's girlhood clothing swirling
Dusty red, dandelion, saffron   25
With sequins iridescent and beads of glass,
To know of yaks, yak butter, remote mountain culture,
To know of all these,
From travelogues, adventure journals and PBS-TV.

How it berserks me   25
That I have exoticized
My great-grandmother's land,
That someone else relentlessly
Tames conquers colonizes gazes objectifies leaves pawmarks
Where I can only dream of an embrace   30

If I were to do the White thing and pilgrimage there
Would my cousins, I wonder, gladly see Naan in me?
And I, Naan in them?
Do *I* dare wear a topi?
It's been so long that I, with my mineable traces   35
Of authentic Nepalese,
Surely *I* appropriate if *I* dare to wear
A topi from the Kulu Valley.

Let me suggest something:
When my presence in this land irks you   40
When your eyes curse me

Brown as I am
Other as I am
Ancestor of the pebbly face,
Remember how you love to climb all over   45
My great-grandmother's mountains, this pass, that summit
Primitive lives beautiful smiles white teeth
Brass bells tinkling tinkling, beasts of burden trek

Remember how you are charmed by my Naan's quaint ways
(as long as she stays in her place)   50
And remember how you love to photograph all of this
In another land.

Denudation

This sometime-urbanite's fiction is in the realisation of escape through dreaming
of—of dreaming as escape to—my other. . . the other that complements me, that
completes me. When safety has always been a stranger, courting strangeness becomes
habit. More content there than here, inspired by thereness rather than hereness, is
my security.

new york city subway trains:

Veins, arteries of busyness, motion,
danger, pace, aloneness, people pumped
like a million moles through darkness,
unseen, illusion of anonymity

layout plans of new york city,
new york city building interiors,
acupuncture charts
gray's anatomy:

mapping, mapping, mapping.
urban smarts. in the city, the body, like
the city, is the mind's commodity
necessarily objectified and scrutinised.

sky mapped.
(photographed through plane
window at fifteen minute
intervals):

literal and emblematic vehicle of
dreaming, desire, transportation, escape.
(getting there is as good as being there)

girlfriend:

same but not same, the other.
me, watching girlfriend picture the
other in a Oaxacan mountainscape

brother:

mountains, hot springs, lakes,
swimming pools, family, lover,
native home and old friends:

me:

same but not same. the other. me,
watching brother picture the other in a
Rocky Mountain-scape

the urbanites' abandon. respite. fiction

sometime-urbanite, by proxy fictioning,
desiring, picturing. . . courting distance,
when suddenly, there becomes *here*

*Q: when in my work I do not overtly sexualize, gender or race myself or rant or cry am I
truly capable of being an 'artist'? Can/will the vViewer and the cCurator and the
wWriter still be interested in my work? When the fad of identities and oppressions is over
and guilts have been stroked, placated, assuaged, and I choose not to exhibit my Achilles
heels (confirming the reassuring existence of scarred entry points) will there then be
room at the gGallery for me? Will I continue to be of any use if I appear to be happy and
without pain? Do I dare?*

Nice Rodriguez *b.* 1958

NAGA CITY, CAMARINES SUR, THE PHILIPPINES

'The longer I stayed in Canada, the more I felt I was being turned inside out into a different person,' says Nice (Maria Nicia) Rodriguez. Born in Naga City, Camarines Sur, the Philippines, Rodriguez came to Canada in 1988. Although she says that 'a Filipino never grieved for another who managed to escape the political turmoil in our country,' hers was neither an easy departure nor an easy arrival, as her memoir pieces published in anthologies indicate.

Rodriguez studied painting at the University of the Philippines, where she also received a BSc in Commerce and Accounting. Before immigrating, she was an established professional writer, providing trade and stock market reports for Manila's most prestigious business newspapers. As Assistant Entertainment and Lifestyle Editor for the *Philippine Daily Globe* and the *Philippine Tribune*, she wrote many feature articles. Following the assassination of Benigno Aquino, Rodriguez created and drew the daily comic strip, *Marcial*, published in *Malaya* (meaning 'freedom') and, later, in *The Tribune*. She also worked as a photojournalist for business and alternative newspapers and magazines during the People Power Revolution against Ferdinand Marcos. A resident of Toronto, Rodriguez is a production artist for *Now* magazine.

Since moving to Canada, her writing reflects her desire to record the range of feelings and changes she has experienced as a consequence of her immigration. 'It became important for me to document, even in fiction form, my experiences as a lesbian in the Philippines and a Filipino lesbian immigrant in Canada before I forgot who I was,' she says. Although 'aware that someone from a different culture would find [her] stories [about butch Filipino lesbians] sexist or absurd', that did not stop her from writing. Her collection of short fiction, *Throw It To The River* (1993), which opens with the story that follows, records that world without sentimentality. 'This is basically a butch book,' she says. 'When I was back home, people would tell me, "go away, it's more liberal out there.". . . I'm comfortable with myself now.' Humorous and ironic, Rodriguez's stories are written in a variety of forms, ranging from realism to fairy tales to parodies.

Big Nipple of the North

Once upon a time in the tropical village of Muñoz, there lived a girl who didn't like dresses. Folks said that even as baby, the girl had refused to wear any style of female clothing.

Once, when her mom dolled her up in a red polka dot dress, the baby cried all day and night. The infant ran no fever, but her swollen eyes expressed an untold agony and her voice was hoarse from days of ceaseless crying. Her parents felt helpless and finally took her to the village chiropractor.

The doctor quickly put the exhausted infant on the bamboo floor and undressed her for examination. The baby sighed with relief as though he had plucked a thorn from her heart, but as soon as he clothed her in the red dress, she resumed her wailing.

The chiropractor read the baby's pulse and aligned her supple spine. He tossed her front to back and checked her genitals for, indeed, she had female genitals. He found nothing wrong and certified her good health. The baby was wet so the doctor changed her diaper with his son's Pampers for boys. She giggled with delight and an aide rushed her out of the clinic wearing only a blue padded diaper.

The baby's face brightened as she recognized her parents, but when her mom appeared with the red polka dot dress, her hair stood on ends and her eyes widened with terror. She began to weep again as if begging for some intuitive understanding. She could only speak through tears.

Her parents showed her another dress, a yellow tube blouse, but the baby howled two decibels louder than before. Next, they tried to put the native dress on, a white *saya* adorned with stiff U-shaped sleeves. Not only did she scream, but she also threw her arms and legs about.

Then from out of a bag, her daddy took a blue athletic shirt and the baby stopped trembling.

'Goo, goo, goo, goo,' she babbled her first words. Her eyes twinkled with approval. The puzzled doctor watched all this unfold and prescribed boys' clothes and shoes for her. He said they were good for her spine, but as soon as the family left, he scribbled some notes and filed the case under Ghosts and Other Strange Phenomena.

Word about the sick child spread throughout the village. One breezy afternoon the elders met under the tamarind tree, concerned that the western settlers had brought the virus which caused the ailment. A hunter said he had seen similar deviations among adults in far-flung and unconquered tribal towns. He added that the baby was merely a young freak and that it was not an epidemic. Nevertheless, they put her on a watch list.

The child performed well in the arts and garnered honours from her school. She was bright and well-mannered, and got into fits of melancholia only when required to wear a dress during formal occasions. Nevertheless, people still saw her as a freak for now she was growing breasts, but looked and acted like a boy.

Every Wednesday, the girl offered a peso to the saint of despair and attended a novena, praying that the village god would make her breasts stop their growth. At last, they stopped swelling but she realized no prayer could flatten her chest again.

As she had with the pimples on her face, the girl learned to live with this pubescent burden. It seemed that her heart had swollen too for one night in the cold month of December, she disappeared with her female math teacher.

The whole village talked about the incident for weeks. The school administration, although shocked, said they broke no rule. They probably just went away to work on a statistical project. The teacher, known about town for her frigidity, arrived in town with an exotic aura of fulfilment. The girl, imbued with more confidence in life and algebra, headed on to a brighter path.

She attended the university. Yet when she graduated, she couldn't find any work. She passed all written tests but, because she did not wear a dress nor a bra, flunked all her job interviews. She found odd jobs in journalism where there were other freaks slaving like her. She also settled down with a nice city girl.

When she walked the alleys of Muñoz with her wife, men jeered at them. They scornfully asked what they did in bed for their own bored wives wondered why the two women looked radiant.

She grew tired of the villagers' meddling looks but had learned to ignore them. Her own small world sustained her, but she could not plan her future. She gained weight and grew depressed each day. One night in her sleep, a voice told her to go to the Big Nipple of the North.

At first she thought it was another wild dream again about her busty ex-lover from Ilocos. The village seer said no, for that Big Nipple of the North was a place called Canada. A land with rich resources, it was like a nipple that had nursed many settlers to lives of unimaginable prosperity. The people in Canada had survived the land's extreme winters.

'But beware,' the seer warned, 'many have perished in that cold land, for it is cursed with big taxes. Go find your destiny and be as resilient as the bamboo that thrives on the outskirts of Muñoz.'

Before she left, she asked the seer, 'If breasts come in pairs, where is the other nipple?' The seer said the Other Big Nipple of the North was a place called the United States.

'But don't go there,' he stressed, 'for it is infected with a malignant tumour which, if left unchecked, could quietly spread to the Canadian nipple.'

Thus enlightened, she went to the Canadian embassy and applied for immigration. On the day of her interview, she wore a tailored suit but she looked like a man and knew she did not stand a chance.

They did not want masculine women in that underpopulated land. They needed baby makers, for as much as Canadians loved to fuck they were not making enough babies. Her wife got a mascara and lipstick, and made her look like a baby maker.

During her interview with the consul officer, she looked ovulating and fertile, so she passed it.

Canada had strict immigration laws, but even bugs could sift through a fine mosquito net. Some of her village's most notorious people were now refugees in Canada. Like the mayor's killer and the textile magnate who ran away with millions of debts, causing the fragile economy of Muñoz to crumble. Also, the witch who enslaved her own children became a nanny there.

When the freak girl of Muñoz arrived in Mississauga, she had fear in her heart, but a vision overcame her when she saw the bi-coloured Canadian flag at the airport.

As the bright and blinding northern sun shone its rays through the flag, the red bars and the maple leaf gradually merged with the white. The banner's colour changed to pink—the rallying colour of radical freaks! She smiled with relief, for she knew she had found a home. She sang and danced towards Church Street, Toronto's gay capital. And lived happily on welfare.

Nino Ricci *b.* 1959

LEAMINGTON, ONTARIO

'[T]he artist', says Nino Ricci, 'is someone who stands outside the community and therefore sees it in starker, perhaps more realistic terms than those who are inside it and don't question its rules.' This kind of isolation informs the lives of Ricci's characters, as well as his own early life. 'In my life,' he says, 'it started out as a sense of being marginalized. I perceived it as being marked out for my ethnicity or for being an immigrant, but it quickly expanded into other areas: very soon I was marked out for many other reasons!' Similarly, the 'outside status' of his characters, be they Italians living in Italy or immigrants in Canada, is often the impetus behind their actions, as is the case in his first novel, *Lives of the Saints* (1990).

Reflecting the fact that Ricci 'came to writing from a desire to tell stories rather than from a concern with style and technique', *Lives of the Saints* is a realistic portrayal of the childhood of Vittorio, its child narrator. It is set in a village that resembles the Italian birthplace of Ricci's mother because he 'wanted . . . to give readers a sense of people within a community where they are not marginalized as ethnic.'

Ricci, who was born in Leamington, Ontario, visited his mother's village for the first time when he was twelve. His initial dislike of it—'it seemed backward and barbaric'—changed over the course of subsequent visits, when he developed 'a much stronger sense of what it meant to be Italian.' His appreciation for what it means to be Italian was also deepened by interviews of about a hundred and fifty Italian immigrants that he conducted in preparation for the novel.

The first of a trilogy of novels, *Lives of the Saints* received many awards, including the Governor General's Award, the W.H. Smith–Books in Canada First Novel Award, and, in England, the Winifred Holtby Prize of the Royal Society of Literature for best regional novel. It was followed by *In a Glass House* (1993), which centres on Vittorio's upbringing in Canada and his relationship with his father. Its focus on ethnicity reflects Ricci's intention to convey to his readers 'the strangeness of that label—ethnic—for someone who is living it from the inside' and to examine the 'mythology attached to the experience of immigration'.

Seeing this novel—as well as the last one of the trilogy, *Where She Has Gone* (1997), the winner of the Trillium Book Award—as forming a continuum with 'the whole history of Western mythology', Nicci is interested in exploring what constitutes what he calls the 'myth of the "other place".' His fiction illustrates that '[t]hat other world that appears to a lot of immigrants before they leave as "paradise" often becomes, upon arriving in that other place, "hell". . . . And over time the paradise they imagined they were coming to was replaced by the paradise they imagine they left behind.' These tensions between the mother country and the host country, between the past and the present, are dramatized in the story that follows. 'Going to the Moon' also reflects Ricci's upbringing close to Detroit: 'We . . . rooted for the Detroit Tigers, and watched American television. We only watched our one Canadian station for the American sitcoms. . . . So there was a palpable sense of the great empire to the south.' Still, as he stresses, 'one of the things I was trying to do in "Going to the Moon" was also to deal with the disillusionment with "America".'

Ricci, a resident of Toronto, studied at York University, where he graduated with an honours BA in English (1981), and at Concordia University, where he received a master's degree (1987). He has taught English in Nigeria and creative writing at Concordia. His novels, including his most recent one, *Testament* (2003), which attempts to re-imagine the life of Christ from different perspectives, have been translated into many languages.

Going To The Moon

Windsor seemed a kind of purgatory to me, a temporary stop between whatever hell my parents had left behind in Italy and the vague promise of the skyline that opened up beyond the Detroit River. In winter that skyline's tall buildings stood unnaturally still and crisp in the cold air, on the verge, it seemed, of singing; in summer they shimmered and burned in the heat and smog. But always they had a strange, unreal quality, at once both toy-like and profound, as if my eyes could not believe their own power to hold so much in a glance.

My great-uncle Bert had come over before the war, smuggling himself into Canada after he'd been turned away at New York and then working his way on road crews up the St Lawrence and along the Great Lakes till he'd arrived finally in Windsor. 'I stopped here because it was so close to the border,' he said. 'In those days there were people who would take you across the river at night, in little boats. But by the time I had enough money to pay them, well, I got lazy.'

Uncle Bert had shown me a picture once of the tiny room at the back of his old shoe-repair shop on Erie Street where he'd lived alone for twenty years, a room as grey and bare and gloomy as a prison cell. It seemed astonishing to me that he'd done that, that in all his years in Windsor he'd never so much as set foot in America, though its image had loomed over him daily, close enough to throw a stone at; and astonishing that we had all ended up in Windsor on account of him, family after family, aunts and uncles and cousins, stuck there in our narrow brown brick houses out of sheer inertia, like Dorothy falling asleep on the road to Emerald City. When my parents told stories about Italy they always talked about *miseria*, a word that meant 'poverty' but that conjured up in my anglicized mind images of vague tortures and chastisements; though according to my mother we were poor in Canada as well, owed thousands of dollars to the bank for our house, which was why she and my father both worked their long odd hours, my father at the Chrysler plant or in his basement workshop, building cabinets and tables he sold for extra money, his face always puckered as he worked as if he had just swallowed something sour, and my mother at different places, sometimes at a butcher's shop and sometimes cleaning houses and sometimes picking beans or tobacco on the farms outside Windsor.

My father had built a second kitchen in our basement, our upstairs kitchen too small to eat in comfortably and our dining room, with its heavy polished wood table, reserved for when we had special company, a non-Italian or someone from out of town. Whenever my uncle Mike came in from Ohio my mother made it seem as if eating in the upstairs dining room was something we did every day, putting on a new, strange, friendly personality then, talking to Uncle Mike and his American wife in English and letting their kids call her Aunt Tony instead of Zia Antonia; but normally she guarded the dining room like an avenging angel, keeping the doors that led into it perpetually closed and forever warning my brother Joe and me never to set foot in it while she was away at work. A tall china cabinet stood in one corner, housing small arrangements of silverware and copper pots that emerged from behind their glass doors only for their monthly cleaning; and on the cabinet's top, underneath a clear glass dome, sat a golden pendulum clock which my mother wound every Sunday after church with a special key, bringing an old chair in from the kitchen to reach it and setting aside its dome with a tenderness that seemed oddly out of keeping with the work-swollen ruddiness of her hands, with the hard set of her shoulders and chin. Two copper mementos, of John Kennedy and Pope John XXIII, hung on the far wall, and velour curtains covered the window; but the room's gloomy elegance made it seem sad somehow, as if it knew that it didn't belong to the rest of the house, its only purpose to remind us of the things that were forbidden to us.

Joe and I attended school at Assumption Separate. Before I started there I had looked up to Joe, because he was six years older and had his own paper route; but at school he seemed diminished, some of the older English boys calling him Mustasho because of the dark hairs that had begun to sprout on his upper lip. When the boys began to pick on me as well, Joe muttered insults at them; but I saw from the dark look that crossed his face then, and from the unthinking grimace he made when he found me waiting for him at the school entranceway at the end of the day, that it humiliated him to have a younger brother, to be made more conspicuous by my presence beside him, and I had the sense that we were both of us merely interlopers at school, moving uncertainly through a world that refused to admit us, that we had to hide ourselves within like animals changing the colour of their fur to fit into a landscape.

But each morning when my class filed into the grade one classroom and I saw again the varnished desktops, the polished floors, the multicoloured alphabet that ran across the tops of the blackboards, I felt the small bright hope that my life could be different, that the things that marked me out could be erased, a hope made urgent, desperate, by the love that I felt for our teacher Miss Johnson. Miss Johnson was one of the few lay teachers at Assumption, and she stood out from the stiff formality of the priests and nuns like a burst of colour in a grey landscape, coming to school in lipstick and high heels, in dress suits with trim vests and jackets, in blouses of shimmering silk, and leaving behind a fragrance of herself when she passed our desks that lingered like a spirit; and we were all in love with her, proudly, self-importantly, all vied with barely masked vehemence to sit beside her during our reading circles, all hoped to be chosen by her to wipe the blackboards or fetch chalk from the storeroom. I felt protected in that common love, in the importance I gained in sharing it, as if I'd been included in a game that could have no losers, no chance for ridicule or shame. Once near the beginning of the year Miss Johnson picked me out to stay in at recess to help her with a bulletin board, and while she stood shoeless on the seat of a desk, reaching down a braceleted arm for the pictures and pins I was to hand to her, she began to hum some song softly to herself as if she had forgotten that I was standing there beneath her; and it made me feel oddly relieved to be taken for granted like that, to have been drawn unthinkingly into the small private sphere of Miss Johnson's aloneness as if there were nothing strange or remarkable about me.

During first term Miss Johnson taught us about stars and planets. Every day she set some new vision before us like a brightly wrapped gift, brought in pictures and models of our solar system, read us stories about space travel and distant life. When we had learned to write she had us each compose in our careful inch-high letters a question to the astronauts at NASA, stuffing all of them afterwards into a large brown envelope; and a few weeks later, as if we had sent out like Noah a messenger who returned now with proof of a world that existed outside our own, a large packet arrived for us from NASA filled with brochures and posters and satellite photographs, so that while all the other classes in the school were doing up bulletin boards about Advent or All Saints' Day or the next year's Centennial, our own boards were filled with images of space, our prized centrepieces a foldout of an Apollo rocket and a poster-sized photo of the moon's Sea of Tranquillity.

One afternoon for art Miss Johnson had us push all our desks to the sides of the classroom and then covered the floor with two adjoining lengths of newsprint, shimmying along them in stockinged feet to join them together with long strips of masking tape. We spent the rest of that afternoon on hands and knees, paint trays and brushes and jars full of tinted water spread out on the floor around us as each of us, assigned to our own little squares of terrain on the newsprint, painted out our private versions of a lunar landscape. We ended up with a great hodgepodge of strange forms, green mountains vying with eerie yellow cities, four-armed monsters perched over ocean-filled craters, and in one corner Miss Johnson's own contribution, two bubble-headed astronauts looking out over the whole scene with expressions of alarm. When the paint had dried we folded our landscape at the seams, rolled it up, and deposited it at the back of our cloakroom; but thereafter, whenever rain kept us inside for recess or we had been especially well behaved, Miss Johnson would ask us again to move our desks into tight little rows at the sides of the classroom, and we would know that we were going to the moon.

To get to the moon we had to strap ourselves firmly into our seats and close our eyes. Miss Johnson would start the countdown, and on zero our spaceship would lift off and begin to climb; and as the earth receded and our ship veered off into space, Miss Johnson, to hide the crinkling of paper as she laid out our landscape, would lead us in our moon song:

> Zoom zoom, zoom,
> We're going to the moon.
> Zoom, zoom, zoom,
> We're going very soon.
> If you want to take a trip,
> Step into my rocket-ship.
> Zoom, zoom, zoom,
> We're going to the moon.

Now stray comets and satellites were flashing past our windshield as the moon balanced in the vastness of space, grew larger and larger, until with a bump and a lurch we touched down and opened our eyes to see its surface unfurled beside us; and when we had removed our safety straps and taken off our shoes and packed ourselves carefully into our spacesuits, we stepped out into space, our bodies moving weirdly because of the lack of gravity, and set off like tiny gods across the watercolour strangeness of the moon.

In the new year, Miss Johnson pinned to the centre of our largest bulletin board autographed photos of the three astronauts who would be flying *Apollo I* in February, the caption 'Bon Voyage' stapled beneath them in black cut-out letters. She promised us she'd bring a television into the classroom the day of the launch so that we could watch the liftoff together; and in a lower corner of the blackboard we kept a running countdown of the days remaining, all of us competing every day to change the number, anxious to show our excitement over an event that Miss Johnson had deemed worthy of our attention. But the liftoff never took place: with twenty-five days still left on our blackboard counter, the astronauts whose faces had become so familiar to our class were burnt to death when a fire broke out in their cockpit during a preflight test. I saw pictures of the fire at home on the television news, of the billowing smoke, of the burnt-out rocket, the charged solemnity of the reports stirring in me a vague memory of when John Kennedy had died; and it was strangely thrilling to see so much attention being paid to a thing that I had thought of as merely personal, as belonging only to Miss Johnson and our grade one class, as if suddenly something that had been a kind of fiction, a story that Miss Johnson had made up to indulge us, following its fixed course, had become pressingly, dangerously real, unpredictable, unknown.

At school the pictures came down, the blackboard counter was erased, Miss Johnson wheeling the school television into our classroom finally to watch not a liftoff but a long funeral procession; and for a few days we wore our sorrow for the astronauts as self-importantly as we had worn our love for Miss Johnson, wanting to be true to the grown-up sense of tragedy, of loss, which Miss Johnson tried to impart to us. But afterwards, when our bulletin boards were done up with Centennial themes like the boards in other classrooms, our lunar landscape forgotten now under the bench at the back of the cloakroom, and when the songs we sang were Centennial songs, as devoid of meaning as the hymns we sang in church, I felt cheated somehow, felt that I had touched for a moment some larger world that had receded again, that had remained as elusive finally as the promise of the tall buildings across the river or of the golden pendulum clock that sat in my mother's dining room.

All my life, it seemed suddenly, was merely waiting for the fulfilment of that promise, for a redemption from the narrowness and meanness of the world I came from; but it seemed possible finally that nothing would change, that I was stranded in my own small world as on some barren planet, with no way to bridge the gap between the promise and the hundred small humiliations that kept me from it, that refused simply to fall away from me like an old skin. When the chrome zipper on my winter coat split and my mother, instead of buying me a new coat as I hoped she would, as I thought other mothers would, merely sewed buttons down the coat's front and cut crude holes for them along the track of the broken zipper, I was certain that the kids at school, that Miss Johnson, would see in those makeshift repairs my mother's swollen hands, our poverty, our strangeness; and the next morning I left the house in only my sweater, my parents already at work and Joe merely shaking his head at my stubbornness as if he couldn't be bothered to fight with me, to pretend that he didn't understand. But at school one of the teachers saw me shivering outside the entranceway and sent me inside before the first bell had rung, and by then I had understood already how hopeless my situation was, how my humiliation was not something that other people did to me but something I carried inside me like a sin, that was there even if other people did not see it. I had begun to cry by the time I got to my classroom, and knowing that Miss Johnson would be there, making her silent mysterious preparations for the day, I slipped into the cloakroom and huddled onto the bench at the back, not wanting her to see me like that; but she must have heard the sound of my crying, for suddenly she was standing over me, with her silk blouse and her limpid eyes and her perfume smell, and she was so beautiful and soft and gently rounded, and her quick sad concern for me so misdirected, so much the promise of all the things I would not have, that I only cried harder, only thought, we'll never go to the moon again, we'll never go to the moon.

That summer Uncle Mike's son Benny was killed in the war in Vietnam. They had been to visit us at Easter, Benny in his uniform, seeming much older than I remembered him, and afterwards my mother and father had had an argument.

'He's an idiot,' my father had said. 'He thinks the war is a game.'

'He has to go, he doesn't have a choice.'

'He doesn't have to go, he volunteered, your brother told me himself.'

But when the news came that Benny had been killed there were no arguments, only an awkward, oppressive silence that seemed to carry some unexplained burden of guilt. My father could not get time off work for the funeral but my mother went down on the bus, dressed strangely in a dark dress and hat and in nylons and high heels. I thought that going to the States would change her in some way, or that she would return with some unexpected gift, something exciting and strange, that could not be found in the Woolco mall; but she came back a few days later empty-handed, changed only in that she was more short-tempered and curt than usual. I thought she was angry about the time she had missed from work; but one evening before bed I caught a glimpse of her through the kitchen doorway sitting at the table with her head in her hands as if she were crying, and I understood then that she had been carrying the shame of Benny's death inside her the whole time, that his death was not a special thing like the deaths of the Apollo astronauts but was merely private and grim, a blemish or failure that needed to be hidden away and forgotten like any other.

That was the summer, too, of the riots in Detroit, and for days the news was filled with images of fires and gunfights and broken windows. My mother forbade Joe and me to leave our neighbourhood while the riots were still going on, but when the two of us stole down to the riverfront one evening with two of our cousins we found that Windsor outside our own neighbourhood was still much what it had always been, people talking on street corners as if nothing had happened, traffic flowing unabated on the main streets, the river wrapped in its usual twilight gloom. But across the river, the streets, cloaked in the shadows of dusk, seemed almost deserted; it was only when I stared hard that I began to make out some movement along the riverfront, the dim outlines of Jeeps and cars, a few shadowy figures. Higher up, though, where the afterglow of sunset still held the sky in unearthly blue, great clouds of dark smoke had formed, and were leaning against the taller buildings as if to topple them into the river; and for a long time we sat at the water's edge staring silently at the skyline as if we were watching a movie, were waiting for it to draw to some inevitable conclusion. But then night settled in around us, leaving us stranded there at the river's edge as on an island; and finally we rose up together and began to make our way home.

George Elliott Clarke *b.* 1960

WINDSOR, NOVA SCOTIA

'I seek to bear witness to the beauty, history, and life of my too-often neglected, my too-often vilified community,' says George Elliott Clarke. 'I want to give voice to what it means, feels, to be Black Nova Scotian or, to use my neologism, Africadian. I plan to centralize my marginal homeland, to observe and decipher Canada, North America, and the world from the vantage point of my East Coast asylum, to apply African Baptist philosophy to literature, politics, and religion. I wish to recast the world in Africadian terms, to use the imperial against itself. I pledge to sing in a black, blues-scoured, saltspray-and-rum-tinctured voice.' The rhythm and 'orature' style of this statement, its emphasis on community, and its fusion of political and apocalyptic gestures mirror the major elements in Clarke's work as well as the ways in which he has defined the cultural and literal tradition to which he belongs. In *Fire on the Water: An Anthology of Black Nova Scotia Writing* (1991, 1992), the two-volume anthology he edited, his neologism Africadian defines that tradition: 'a word I have minted from "Africa" and "Acadia" (the old name for Nova Scotia and New Brunswick), to denote the Black populations of the Maritimes and especially of Nova Scotia.' Its origins go back to the black Loyalists and refugees who arrived in Nova Scotia in 1783 and 1815. This tradition, which includes oral literature, 'becomes a secular bible'; it speaks of a community that is simultaneously 'spiritual *and* political', it uses biblical imagery and rhetoric in abundance, and it focuses on the liberation or destruction of identity. Clarke has mined his family and community's memories and archives for forgotten stories, neglected authors, and unsung heroes and anti-heroes that have become the foundation of his poetry, criticism, and, more recently, librettos and fiction, but also a major part of the growing body of works about black Canadian writing.

Clarke's first collection of poetry, *Saltwater Spirituals and Deeper Blues* (1983), was a finalist for the Bliss Carman Award. Through a lyrical 'i', Clarke revisits the history and the ancestors of his community, as he does when he writes about 'Lydia Jackson, / slave Madonna', a woman indentured to the household of a Dr Bulman who beat and raped her. *Whylah Falls* (1990), which won the Archibald Lampman Award, is similarly indebted to that tradition, but here, as in his verse-novel, *Lush Dreams, Blue Exile: Fugitive Poems 1978–1993* (1994), Clarke makes use of formal elements that reflect the influence of such writers as Michael Ondaatje and Irving Layton. Often a combination of various kinds of lyrics, prose, and photographs, and inflected with the humour, irony, spirituality, and ribald passions of his personae and characters, his poetry—which includes the recent *Gold Indigoes* (2000), *Blue* (2001), and *Illuminated Verse* (2005)—is written in ' "blackened" English', a fusion of his Africadian tradition, 'the playground vernacular', and the 'Anglophiled speech he learned in school'.

A seventh-generation Canadian of African American and Mi'kmaq origins (on his maternal side), Clarke was born in Windsor, Nova Scotia, but grew up in North End Halifax. Culturally and politically active, he contributed to the establishment of the now-defunct Black Youth Organization of Nova Scotia, and was the organizer of the Weymouth Falls Justice Committee that protested racism in the Nova Scotian justice system in 1985. After receiving an Honours BA (1984) from the University of Waterloo, he became a social worker in the Annapolis Valley of Nova Scotia (1985–6). He received his MA in English (1989) (on Michael Ondaatje) from Dalhousie University, and his PhD (1993) from Queen's University (a comparative study of the Africadian and the English Canadian poetry traditions). A professor of English and Canadian Studies at Duke University, Durham, NC (1994–9), he is now the E.J. Pratt Professor of Canadian Literature at the University of Toronto where he has taught since 1999. Clarke, who has lectured widely around the world, has also written two librettos: *Beatrice Chancy: A Libretto in Four Acts* (1998, 2004), music composed by James Rolfe, which, inspired by Shelley's drama *The Cenci*, and based on the same historical material as that in his poetry book of the same title (1999), deals with slavery in 1800s Nova Scotia; the short, but ambitious and eclectic, *Québecité: A Jazz Fantasia in Three Cantos* (2003), music by D.D. Jackson, is a romantic story that touches on such issues as multiculturalism and Quebec politics. His novel, *George and Rue* (2005), based on the same material as his Governor General award-winning poetry book, *Execution Poems* (2001), is about George and Rufus Hamilton, distant cousins of Clarke's on his maternal side, hanged in 1949 for the brutal murder of a taxi driver in Fredericton. Clarke is also the editor of *Eyeing the North Star: Perspectives of African-Canadian Literature* (1997), and the author of numerous essays on black Canadian writing, many of which, along with his bibliography on black Canadian writing, have been collected in *Odysseys Home: Mapping African-Canadian Literature* (2002). His many awards include the Outstanding Writer in Film and Television Award (2000), the Portia White Prize for Artistic Achievement (1998), the Martin Luther King Jr Achievement Award (2004), and the Pierre Elliott Trudeau Fellows Prize (2005).

Look Homeward, Exile

I can still see that soil crimsoned by butchered
Hog and imbrued with rye, lye, and homely
Spirituals everybody must know,
Still dream of folks who broke or cracked like shale:
Pushkin, who twisted his hands in boxing,   5
Marrocco, who ran girls like dogs and got stabbed,
Lavinia, her teeth decayed to black stumps,
Her lovemaking still in demand, spitting
Black phlegm—her pension after twenty towns,
And Toof, suckled on anger that no Baptist   10
Church could contain, who let wrinkled Eely
Seed her moist womb when she was just thirteen.
    And the tyrant sun that reared from barbed-wire
Spewed flame that charred the idiot crops
To Depression, and hurt my granddaddy   15
To bottle after bottle of sweet death,
His dreams beaten to one, tremendous pulp,
Until his heart seized, choked; his love gave out.
    But Beauty survived, secreted
In freight trains snorting in their pens, in babes   20
Whose faces were coal-black mirrors, in strange
Strummers who plucked Ghanaian banjos, hummed
Blind blues—precise, ornate, rich needlepoint,
In sermons scorched with sulphur and brimstone,
And in my love's dark, orient skin that smelled   25
Like orange peels and tasted like rum, good God!
    I remember my Creator in the old ways:
I sit in taverns and stare at my fists;
I knead earth into bread, spell water into wine,
Still, nothing warms my wintry exile—neither   30
Prayers nor fine love, neither votes nor hard drink:
For nothing heals those saints felled in green beds,
Whose loves are smashed by just one word or glance
Or pain—a screw jammed in thick, straining wood.

The Symposium

Don't gimme nothin' to jaw about, Missy, and I won't have nothin' to holler for!
Just sit back, relax, and be black. I'm gonna learn you 'bout the mens so you can 'scape
the bitter foolishness I've suffered. A little thoughtful can save you trouble.

Missy, you gotta lie to get a good man. And after you gets him, you gotta be set to hurt him to hold him, so help my Chucky! 'Cos if you don't or won't or can't, you're gonna be stepped on, pushed 'round, walked out on, beat up on, cheated on, worked like a black fool, and cast out your own house.

Don't suck your teeth and cut your eyes at me! I be finished in a hot second. But you'll hear this gospel truth so long you, my oldest, eat and sleep in my house. Best cut your sass!

Pack a spare suitcase, one for him. If he proves devilish, it be easier to toss him out that way. Put one change of clothes into it so he can't beg and bug you for nothin'!

If he be too quiet, he'll ruminate and feel that bottle more than he will you. Rum'll be his milk and meat for months. It'll spoil him for anything. Won't be fit to drive his nail. So when he's sleepy drunk, smack the long-ass son of a gun in the head, tell him to wake his black-ass body up, and drive him out. If the fair fool don't come back sober, he don't come back. Am I lyin'?

And if he be sweet-lookin', a heavy-natured man, always pullin' on women, and he takes up with some spinny woman all daddlied up from the cash he's vowed to bring you, just tell him right up and down that you ain't his monkey in a dress, and raise particular devil. Don't give him no shakes. And if that don't work, don't waste another black word, grab yourself a second man.

Watch out for two-faced chroniclers. These women will grin in you face, lookin' for news 'bout you and your man. And just when you trust their acid chat and make your man groan and grump and get all upset these gold-dust whores creep behind your back, crawl right in your bed, and thief him away. That's how they act. I know: I've been gypped so bloody much. And they don't care if it's a used love, a second-hand love, a stolen love, 'cos it's love all the same. And if it's good to you, they'll try to trick some too. So don't put no business on the streets that's conducted 'tween your sheets. But if some big-mouth humbugs you, tell the black bitch not to mess 'cos she's terrible lookin' anyway; a knife gash 'cross her face would just be improvement.

Missy! Gimme some of that bottle! Preachin' parches the throat. Besides, my eyes feel kinda zigzaggy today.

If some woman is grinnin' at your man, tell her straight: 'If it was shit that I had, you'd want some of that too.' Make her skedaddle. If her fresh fool follows, take everything he got and don't give a single, black penny back!

Missy, life's nothin' but guts, muscle, nerve. All you gotta do is stay black and die.

Nalo Hopkinson *b.* 1960

KINGSTON, JAMAICA

The daughter of a poet, actor, and English and Latin teacher father (Slade Hopkinson) and a library cataloguer mother, Nalo Hopkinson was born in Kingston, Jamaica, but lived in other parts of the Caribbean before moving with her family to Canada in 1977. Growing up in a family and social environment that supported and practiced the arts, she has had many 'aunties' and 'uncles', supportive mentors that have encouraged her to pursue her own writing. An 'avid reader', she started writing to produce a portfolio to get admission into a course at Ryerson; the course was cancelled, but she continued writing. She encountered success with her first attempts at writing fiction. While still in manuscript form, her first novel, *Brown Girl in the Ring* (1998), won the Warner Aspect First Novel Award (1997), a contest that included its publication, and was nominated for the Tiptree Junior and the Philip K. Dick Awards. Set in futuristic Toronto, at a time when the marginalized poor are segregated in the inner city while the rich people and governing authorities have moved outside the urban centre, it is the story of Ti-Jeanne (named after Derek Walcott's *Ti-Jean and His Brothers*), who comes to value her Jamaican's grandmother's healing powers and acts according to her powerful visions. Its language, fantasy elements, setting, and the cultural particularities of its characters announce Hopkinson's preoccupations as a writer. 'I write about urban environments a lot,' she says, and she does so through the genre of speculative fiction, which she defines as 'fiction in which impossible things happen', a fiction that 'includes magic realism, fantasy, science fiction and horror'. The 'hybrid space' of this kind of writing 'reflects her hybrid reality', a reality she often represents through 'code-switching': 'Sometimes I code-switch, sometimes I don't. It depends on what the story needs.'

Hopkinson holds an Honors BA in Russian and French from York University (1982), a diploma in Recreation Management from Seneca College in Toronto, and an MA in Writing Popular Fiction from Seton Hill College, Greensburg, Pennsylvania (2002). A visiting creative writing teacher, writer-in-residence, and reader and lecturer in many colleges and universities across North America, including being the 'Guest of Honour' at Wisconsin, Madison, at the annual gathering of the 'feminist SF community,' Hopkinson has published her short stories in many anthologies and literary magazines, and collected them in *Skin Folk* (2001), winner of the World Fantasy Award. The editor of *Whispers From the Cotton Tree Root* (2000) and *Mojo: Conjure Stories* (2003), collections of Caribbean fabulist fiction, she has also published two other novels, *Midnight Robber* (2000), shortlisted for the Sunburst, Hugo and Tiptree Awards and winner of the Locus Award, and *The Salt Roads* (2003). 'Speculative fiction,' she says, 'is a great place to warp the mirror, and thus impel the reader[s] to view differently things that they've taken for granted.'

A Habit of Waste

These are the latitudes of the ex-colonised,
of degradation still unmollified,
imported managers, styles in art,
second-hand subsistence of the spirit,
the habit of waste,
mayhem committed on the personality,

and everywhere the wrecked or scuttled mind.
Scholars, more brilliant than I could hope to be,
advised that if I valued poetry,
I should eschew all sociology.
                    —Slade Hopkinson, from
            'The Madwoman of Papine: Two cartoons with captions'

I was nodding off on the streetcar home from work when I saw the woman getting on. She was wearing the body I used to have! The shock woke me right up: it was my original; the body I had replaced two years before; same full, tarty-looking lips; same fat thighs, rubbing together with every step; same outsize ass; same narrow torso that seemed grafted onto a lower body a good three sizes bigger, as though God had glued left-over parts together.

On my pay, I'd had to save for five years before I could afford the switch. When I ordered the catalogue from MediPerfiction, I pored over it for a month, drooling at the different options: arrow-slim 'Cindies' had long, long legs ('supermodel quality'); 'Indiras' came with creamy brown skin, falls of straight, dark hair and curvaceous bodies ('exotic grace'). I finally chose one of the 'Dianas' with their lithe muscles and small, firm breasts ('boyish beauty'). They downloaded me into her as soon as I could get the time off work. I was back on the job in four days, although my fine muscle control was still a little shaky.

And now, here was someone wearing my old cast-off. She must have been in a bad accident: too bad for the body to be salvaged. If she couldn't afford cloning, the doctors would have just downloaded her brain into any donated discard. Mine, for instance. *Poor thing*, I thought. *I wonder how she's handling that chafing problem. It used to drive me mad in the summer.*

I watched her put her ticket in the box. The driver gave her a melting smile. What did he see to grin at?

I studied my former body carefully as it made its way down the centre of the streetcar. I hated what she'd done to the hair—let it go *natural*, for Christ's sake, sectioned it off, and coiled black thread tightly around each section, with a puff of hair on the end of every stalk. Man, I hated that back-to-Africa nostalgia shit. She looked like a Doctor Seuss character. There's no excuse for that nappy-headed nonsense. She had a lot of nerve, too, wrapping that behind in a flower print sarong mini-skirt. Sort of like making your ass into a billboard. When it was my body, I always covered its butt in long skirts or loose pants. *Her* skirt was so short that I could see the edges of the bike shorts peeking out below it. Well, it's one way to deal with the chafing. Strange, though; on her, the little peek of black shorts looked stylish and sexy all at once. Far from looking graceless, her high, round bottom twitched confidently with each step, giving her a proud sexiness that I had never had. Her upper body was sheathed in a white sleeveless t-shirt. White! Such a plain colour. To tell the truth, though, the clingy material emphasized her tiny waist, and the white looked really good against her dark skin. Had my old skin always had that glow to it? Such firm, strong arms . . . .

All the seats on the streetcar were taken. Good. I let the bitch stand. I hoped my fallen arches were giving her hell.

Home at last, I stripped off and headed straight for the mirror. The boyish body was still slim, thighs still thin, tiny-perfect apple breasts still perky. I presented my behind to the mirror. A little flabby, perhaps? I wasn't sure. I turned around again, got up close to the mirror so that I could inspect my face. Did my skin have that glow that my old body's had? And weren't those the beginning of crow's feet around my eyes? Shit. White people aged so quickly.

I spent the evening sprawled on the sofa, watching reruns and eating pork and beans straight from the can.

That Friday afternoon at work, Old Man Morris came in for the usual. I stacked his order on the counter between us and keyed the contents into the computer. It bleeped at me: 'This selection does not meet the customer's dietary requirements.' As if I didn't know that. I tried to talk him into beefing up the carbs and beta-carotene. 'Alright, then,' I said heartily, 'what else will you have today? Some of that creamed corn? We just got a big batch of tins in. I bet you'd like some of that, eh?' I always sounded so artificial, but I couldn't help it. The food bank customers made me uncomfortable, Not Eleanor, though. She was so at ease in the job, cheerful, dispensing cans of tuna with an easy goodwill. She always chattered away to the clients, knew them all by name.

'No thanks, dear,' Mr Morris replied with his polite smile. 'I never could stomach the tinned vegetables. When I can, I eat them fresh, you know?'

'Yeah, Cynthia,' Eleanor teased, 'you know that Mr Morris hates canned veggies. Too much like baby food, eh, Mr Morris?'

Always the same cute banter between those two. He'd flattened out his Caribbean accent for the benefit of us two white girls. I couldn't place which island he was from. I sighed and overrode the computer's objections. Eleanor and old man Morris grinned at each other while I packed up his weekend ration. Fresh; right. When could a poor old man ever afford the fresh stuff? I couldn't imagine what his diet was like. He always asked us for the same things: soup mix, powdered milk, and cans of beans. We tried to give him his nutritional quota, but he politely refused offers of creamed corn or canned tuna. I was sure he was always constipated. His problem, though.

I bet my parents could tell me where in the Caribbean he was from. Give them any inkling that someone's from 'back home', and they'd be on him like a dirty shirt, badgering him with questions: *Which island you from? How long you been here in Canada? You have family here? When last you go back home?*

Old Man Morris signed for his order and left. One of the volunteers would deliver it later that evening. I watched him walk away. He looked to be in his sixties, but he was probably younger; hard life wears a person down. Tallish, with a brown, wrinkled face and tightly curled salt-and-pepper hair, he had a strong, upright walk for someone in his circumstances. Even in summer, I had never seen him without that old tweed jacket, its pockets stuffed to bursting with God knew what type of scavenge; cigarette butts, I supposed, and pop cans he would return for the deposit money. At least he was clean.

I went down to shipping to check on a big donation of food we'd received from a nearby supermarket. Someone was sure to have made a mistake sorting the cans. Someone always did.

My parents had been beside themselves when they found out I'd switched bodies. I guess it wasn't very diplomatic of me, showing up without warning on their suburban doorstep, this white woman with her flippy blond hair, claiming to be their daughter. I'd made sure my new body would have the same vocal range as the old one, so when Mom and Dad heard my voice coming out of a stranger's body, they flipped. Didn't even want to let me in the door, at first. Made me pass my new ID and the doctor's certificate through the letter slot.

'Mom, give me a break,' I yelled. 'I told you last year that I was thinking about doing this!'

'But Cyn-Cyn, that ain't even look like you!' My mother's voice was close to a shriek. Her next words were for my dad: 'What the child want to go and do this kind of stupidness for? Nothing ain't wrong with the way she look!'

A giggled response from my father, 'True, she behind had a way to remain in a room long after she leave, but she get that from you, sweetheart, and you know how much I love that behind!'

I'd had enough. 'So, are the two of you going to let me in, or what?' I hated it when they carried on like that. And I really wished they'd drop the Banana Boat accents. They'd come to Canada five years before I was even born, for Christ's sake, and I was now 28.

They did finally open the door, and after that they just had to get used to the new me.

I wondered if I should start saving for another switch. It's a rich people's thing. I couldn't afford to keep doing it. Shit.

'What's the matter with you?' Eleanor asked after I'd chewed out one of the volunteers for some little mistake. 'You've been cranky for days now.'

'Sorry. I know I've been bitchy. I've been really down, you know? No real reason. I just don't feel like myself.'

'Yeah. Well.' Eleanor was used to my moodiness. 'I guess it is Thanksgiving week-end. People always get a little edgy around the holidays. Maybe you need a change. Tell you what; why don't you deliver Old Man Morris's ration, make sure he's okay for the weekend?'

'Morris? You want me to go to where he lives?' I couldn't imagine anything less appealing. 'Where is that, anyway? In a park, or something?'

Eleanor frowned at that. 'So, even if he does, so what? I wish you'd take more interest in the people who come here. Some of them do have homes, all right? You know what it's like, trying to live on a government pension nowadays.'

She strode over to the terminal at her desk, punched in Mr Morris's name, handed me the printout. 'Just go over to this address, and take him his ration. Chat with him a little bit. This might be a lonely weekend for him. And keep the car till Tuesday. We won't be needing it.'

Mr Morris lived on the creepy side of Sherbourne. I had to slow the car down to dodge the first wave of drunken suits lurching out of the strip club, on their boozy way home after the usual Friday afternoon three-hour liquid lunch. I stared at the story-high poster that covered one outside wall of the strip club. I hoped to God they'd used a fisheye lens on that babe's boobs. Those couldn't be natural. Shit. Shouldn't have slowed down. One of the prostitutes on the corner began to twitch her way over to the car, bending low so she could see inside, giving me a flash of her tits into the bargain: 'Hey, darlin', you wanna go out? I can swing lezzie.' I floored it out of there.

Searching for the street helped to keep my mind off some of the more theatrical sights of Cabbagetown West on a Friday evening. I didn't know that the police could conduct a full strip search over the hood of a car, right out in the open.

The next street was Old Man Morris's. Tenement row houses slumped along one side of the short street, marked by sagging roofs and knocked-out steps. There were rotting piles of garbage piled in front of many of the houses. I thought I could hear the flies buzzing from where I was. The smell was like clotted carrion. A few people hung out on dilapidated porches, just staring. Two guys hunched into denim jackets stopped talking as I drove by. A dirty, greasy-haired kid was riding a bicycle up and down the sidewalk, dodging the garbage. The bike was too small for him and it had no seat.

Mr Morris lived in an ancient apartment building on the other side of the street. I had to double park in front. I hauled the dolly out of the trunk, and loaded Mr Morris's boxes onto it. I activated the car's screamer alarm, and headed into the building, praying that no weirdness would go down on the street before I could make it inside.

Thank God, he answered the buzzer right away. 'Mr Morris? It's Cynthia; from the food bank?' The party that was going on in the lobby was only a few gropes away from becoming an orgy. The threesome writhing on the couch ignored me. Two women, one man. I hoped that he was on some *very* special drugs tonight. I stepped over a pungent yellow liquid that was beetling its way down one leg of the bench, creeping through the cracks in the tile floor. I hoped it was just booze. I took the elevator up to the sixth floor.

The dingy, musty corridor walls were dark grey, peeling in places to reveal a bilious pink underneath. It was probably a blessing there was so much dirt ground into the balding carpet. What I could glimpse of the original design made me queasy. Someone was frying Spam for dinner ('canned horse's cock', my Dad called it). I found Mr Morris's door and knocked. Inside, I could hear the sound of locks turning, and the curt 'quack' of an alarm being deactivated. Mr Morris opened the door to let me in.

'Come in quick, child,' he said, wiping his hands on a kitchen towel. 'I can't let the pot boil over. Siddown on the *settee* and rest yourself. Why you come today? Don't Jake does deliver my goods?'

Standing in the entranceway, I took a quick glance around the little apartment. It was dark in there. The only light was from the kitchen, and from four candles stuck in pop bottles on the living room windowsill. The living room held one small, rump-sprung couch, two aluminum chairs, and a tiny card table. The gaudy flowerprint cloth that barely covered the table was faded from years of being ironed. I was surprised; the place was spotless, if a little shabby.

'Eleanor sent Jake home early today, Mr Morris. Holiday treat.' I wheeled the dolly into the living room and perched on the edge of the love seat.

He chuckled. 'That young lady is so thoughtful, *oui*? It ain't have plenty people like her any more.'

Settee. Oui. In his own home, he spoke in a more natural accent. 'You from Trinidad, Mr Morris?'

His face crinkled into an astonished grin. 'Yes, *doux-doux*. How you know that?'

'That's where my parents are from. They talk just like you.'

'You is from Trinidad?' he asked delightedly. 'I know that Trini people come in all colours, but with that accent, I did take you for a Canadian, born and bred.'

I hated explaining this, but I guess I'd asked for it, letting him know something about my life. 'I was born here, but my parents are Black. So was I, but I've had a body switch.'

A bemused expression came over his face. 'For true? I hear about people doin' this thing, but I don't think I ever meet anybody who make the switch. You mean to tell me, you change from a Black woman body into this one? Lord, the things you young people does do for fashion, eh?'

I stood up and plastered a smile on my face. 'Well, you've got your weekend ration, Mr Morris; just wanted to be sure you wouldn't go hungry on Thanksgiving, okay?'

He looked pensively at the freeze-dried turkey dinner and the cans of creamed corn (I'd made sure to put them in his ration this time). 'Thanks, *doux-doux*. True I ain't go be hungry, but I don't like to eat alone. My wife pass away ten years now, but you know, I does still miss she sometimes. You goin' by you Mummy and Daddy for Thanksgiving?'

The question caught me off guard. 'Yes, I'm going to see them on Sunday.'

'But you not doing anything tonight? You want to have a early Thanksgiving with a ol' man from back home? I making a nice, nice dinner,' he pleaded.

'*I'm not from "back home",*' I almost said, but the hope on his face was more than I could stand. Eleanor would stay and keep the old man company, if it were her. I sat back down.

Mr Morris's grin was incandescent. 'You going to stay? All right, *doux-doux*. Dinner almost finish, you hear? Just pile up the ration out of the way for me.' He bustled back into the kitchen. I could hear humming, pots and pans clattering, water running.

I packed the food up against one wall, a running argument playing in my head the whole time. Why was I doing this? I'd driven our jacker-bait excuse for a company car through the most dangerous part of town, just begging for a baseball bat through the window, and all to have dinner with an old bum. What would he serve anyway? Peanut butter and crackers? I knew the shit that man ate—I'd given it to him myself, every Friday at the food bank! And what if he pulled some kind of sleazy, toothless come-on? The police would say I asked for it!

A wonderful smell began to waft from the kitchen. Some kind of roasting meat, with spices. Whatever Mr Morris was cooking, he couldn't have done it on food bank rations.

'You need a hand, Mr Morris?'

'Not in here, darling. Just sit yourself down at the table, and I go bring dinner out. I was going to freeze all the extra, but now I have a guest to share it with.'

When he brought out the main course, arms straining under the weight of the platter, my mouth fell open. And that was just the beginning. He loaded the table with plate after plate of food: roasted chicken with a giblet stuffing; rich, creamy gravy; tossed salad with exotic greens; huge mounds of mashed potatoes; some kind of fruit preserve. He refused to answer my questions.

'I go tell you all about it after, *doux-doux*. Now is time to eat.'

It certainly was. I was so busy trying to figure out if he could have turned food bank rations into this feast, that I forgot all about calories and daily allowable grams of fat; I just ate. After the meal, though, my curiosity kicked in again.

'So, Mr Morris, tell me the truth; you snowing the food bank? Making some money on the side?' I grinned at him. He wouldn't be the first one to run a scam like that, working for cash so that he could still claim welfare.

'No, *doux-doux*.' He gave me a mischievous smile. 'I see how it look that way to you, but this meal cost me next to nothing. You just have to know where to *shop*, that is all. You see this fancy salad? You know what this is?' He pointed to a few frilly purple leaves that were all that remained of the salad.

'Yeah. Flowering kale. Rich people's cabbage.'

Mr Morris laughed. 'Yes, but I bet you see it somewhere else, besides the grocery store.'

I frowned, trying to think what he meant. He went on: 'You know the Dominion Bank? The big one at Bathurst and Queen?' I nodded, still mystified. His smile got even broader. 'You ever look at the plants they use to decorate the front?'

I almost spat the salad out. '*Ornamental cabbage*? We're eating ornamental cabbage that you *stole* from the front of a building?'

His rich laugh filled the tiny room. 'Not "ornamental cabbage", darlin': "flowering kale". And I figure, I ain't really stealin' it; I recyclin' it! They does pull it all up and throw it away when the weather turn cold. All that food. It does taste nice on a Sunday morning, fry-up with a piece of saltfish and some small-leaf thyme. I does grow the herbs—them on the windowsill, in the sun.'

Salted cod and cabbage. Flavoured with french thyme and hot pepper. My mother made that on Sunday mornings too, with big fried dumplings on the side and huge mugs of cocoa. Not the cocoa powder from the tin, either; she bought the raw chocolate in chestnut-sized lumps from the Jamaican store, and grated it into boiling water, with cinnamon and condensed milk. Sitting in Mr Morris's living room, even with the remains of dinner on the table, I could almost smell that pure chocolate aroma. Full of fat, too. I didn't let my Mom serve it to me any more when I visited. I'd spent too much money on my tight little butt.

Still, I didn't believe what Old Man Morris was telling me. 'So, you mean to say that you just . . . take stuff? From off the *street*? What about the chicken?'

He laughed. 'Chicken? *Doux-doux*, you ever see chicken with four drumstick? That is a wild rabbit I catch meself and bring home.'

'Are you crazy? Do you know what's in wild food? What kind of diseases it might carry? Why didn't you tell me what we were eating?' But he was so pleased with himself, he didn't seem to notice how upset I was.

'Nah, nah, don't worry 'bout diseases, darlin'! I been eatin' like this for five-six years now, and I healthy like hog. De doctor say he never see a seventy-four year-old man in such good shape.'

He's seventy-four! He does look pretty damned good for such an old man. I'm still not convinced, though: 'Mr Morris, this is nuts; you can't just go around helping yourself to leaves off the trees, and people's ornamental plants, and killing things and eating them! Besides, how do you catch a wild rabbit?'

'Well, that is the sweet part.' He jumped up from his chair, started rummaging around in the pockets of his old tweed jacket that was hanging in the hallway. He came back to the table, clutching a fistful of small rocks and brandishing a thick, 'Y'-shaped twig with a loose rubber strap attached. So that's what he kept in those pockets—whatever it was.

'This is a slingshot. When I was a small boy back home, I was aces with one of these!' He stretched the rubber strap tight with one hand, aimed the slingshot at one of his potted plants, and pretended to let off a shot. 'Plai! Like so. Me and the boys—them used to practise shooting at all kind of ol' tin can and thing, but I was the best. One time, I catch a coral snake in me mother kitchen, and I send one boulderstone straight through it eye with me first shot!' He chuckled. 'The stone break the window too, but me mother was only too glad that I kill the poison snake. Well, *doux-doux*, I does take me slingshot down into the ravine, and sometimes I get lucky, and catch something.'

I was horrified. 'You mean, you used that thing to kill a rabbit? And we just ate it?'

Mr Morris's face finally got serious. He sat back down at the table. 'You mus' understan', Cynthia; I is a poor man. Me and my Rita, we work hard when we come to this country, and we manage to buy this little apartment, but when the last depression hit we, I get lay off at the car plant. After that, I couldn't find no work again; I was already past 50 years old. We get by on Rita nurse work until she retire, and then hard times catch we ass. My Rita was a wonderful woman, girl; she could take a half pound of mince beef and two potatoes and make a meal that have you feelin' like you never taste food before. She used to tell me, "Never mind, Johnny; so long as I have a little meat to put in this cook pot, we not goin' to starve."

'Then them find out that Rita have cancer. She only live a few months after that, getting weaker till she waste away and gone. Lord, child; I thought my heart woulda break. I did wish to dead too. That first year after Rita pass away, I couldn't tell you how I get by; I don't even remember all of it. I let the place get dirty, dirty, and I was eatin' any ol' *caca* from the corner store, not even self goin' to the grocery. When I get the letter from the government, telling me that them cuttin' off Rita pension, I didn't know what to do. My one little pension wasn't goin' to support me. I put on me coat, and went outside, headin' for the train tracks to throw myself down, *oui*? Is must be God did make me walk through the park.'

'What happened?'

'I see a ol' woman sittin' on a bench, wearing a tear-up coat and two different one-side boots. She was feedin' stale bread to the pigeons, and smiling at them. That ol' lady with she rip-up clothes could still find something to make she happy.

'I went back home, and things start to look up a little bit from then. But pride nearly make me starve before I find meself inside the food bank to beg some bread.'

'It's not begging, Mr Morris,' I interrupted.

'I know, *doux-doux*, but in my place, I sure you woulda feel the same way. And too besides, even though I was eatin' steady from the food bank, I wasn't eatin' good, you know? You can't live all you days on tunafish and tin peas!'

I felt myself blushing. Two years in this body, and I still wasn't used to how easily blushes showed on its pale cheeks. 'So, what gave you the idea to start foraging like this?'

'I was eatin' lunch one day; cheese spread and crackers and pop. One *paipsy*, tasteless lunch, you see? And I start thinkin' about how I never woulda go hungry back home as a small boy, how even if I wasn't home to eat me mother food, it always had some kinda fruit tree or something round the place. I start to remember *Julie-mango*, how it sweet, and *chataigne* and *peewah* that me mother would boil up in a big pot a' salt water, and how my father always had he little kitchen garden, growin' dasheen leaf and pigeon peas and yam and thing. And I say to meself, "But eh-eh, Johnny, ain't this country have plants and trees and fruit and thing too? The squirrels—them always looking fat and happy; they mus' be eatin' something; and the Indian people them-self too; they must be did eat something else besides corn before the white people come and take over the place!"

'That same day, I find my ass in the library, and I tell them I want to find out about plants that you could eat. Them sit me down with all kinda book and computer, and I come to find out it have plenty to eat, right here in this city, growing wild by the roadside. Some of these books even had recipes in them, *doux-doux*!

'So I drag out all of Rita frying pan and cook spoon from the kitchen cupboard, and I teach meself to feed meself, yes!' He chuckles again. 'Now, I does eat fresh mulberries in the summer. I does dig up chicory root to take the bitterness from my coffee. I even make rowanberry jam. All these things all around we for free, and people still starving, *oui*? You have to learn to make use of what you have.

'But I still think the slingshot was a master stroke, though. Nobody ain't expect a ol' Black man to be hunting with a slingshot down in the ravine!'

I was still chuckling as I left Mr Morris's building later that evening. He'd loaded me down with a container full of stuffed rabbit and a bottle of crabapple preserves. I deactivated the screamer alarm on the car, and I was just about to open the door when I felt a hand sliding down the back of my thigh.

'Yesss, stay just like that. Ain't that pretty? We'll get to that later. Where's your money, sweetheart? In this purse here?' The press of a smelly body pinned me over the hood. I tried to turn my head, to scream, but he clamped a filthy hand across my face. I couldn't breathe. The bottle of preserves crashed to the ground. Broken glass sprayed my calf.

'Shit! What'd you do that for? Stupid bitch!'

His hand tightened over my face. I couldn't *breathe*! In fury and terror, I bit down hard, felt my teeth meet in the flesh of his palm. He swore, yanked his hand away, slammed a hard fist against my ear. Things started to go black, and I almost fell. I hung onto the car door, dragged myself to my feet, scrambled out of his reach. I didn't dare turn away to run. I backed away, screaming, '*Get away from me! Get away!*' He kept coming, and he was big and muscular, and *angry*. Suddenly, he jerked, yelled, slapped one hand to his shoulder. 'What the fuck . . .?' I could see wetness seeping through the shoulder of his grimy sweatshirt. Blood? He yelled again, clapped a hand to his knee. This time, I had seen the missile whiz through the air to strike him. Yes! I crouched down to give Mr Morris a clear shot. My teeth were bared in a fighter's grin. The mugger was still limping towards me, howling with rage. The next stone glanced by his head, leaving a deep gash on his temple. Behind him, I heard the sound of breaking glass as the stone crashed through the car window. He'd had enough. He ran, holding his injured leg.

Standing in the middle of the street, I looked up to Mr Morris's sixth floor window. He was on the balcony, waving frantically at me. In the dark, I could just see the 'Y' of the slingshot in his hand. He shouted, 'Go and stand in the entranceway, girl! I comin' down!' He disappeared inside, and I headed back towards the building. By the time I got there, I was weak-kneed and shaky; reaction was setting in, and my head was spinning from the blow I took. I didn't think I'd ever get the taste of that man's flesh out of my mouth. I leaned against the inside door, waiting for Mr Morris. It wasn't long before he came bustling out of the elevator, let me inside, and sat me down on the couch in the lobby, fussing the whole time.

'Jesus Christ, child! Is a good thing I decide to watch from the balcony to make sure you reach the car safe! Lawd, look at what happen to you, eh? Just because you had the kindness to spen' a little time with a ol' man like me! I sorry, girl; I sorry can't done!'

'It's okay, Mr Morris; it's not your fault. I'm all right, I'm just glad that you were watching.' I was getting a little hysterical. 'I come to rescue you with my food bank freeze-dried turkey dinner, and you end up rescuing me instead! I have to ask you, though, Mr Morris; how come every time you rescue a lady, you end up breaking her windows?'

That Sunday, I drove over to my parents' place for Thanksgiving dinner. I was wearing a beret, cocked at a chic angle over the cauliflower ear that the mugger had given me. No sense panicking my Mom and Dad. I had gone to the emergency hospital on Friday night, and they disinfected and bandaged me. I was all right; in fact, I was so happy, I felt giddy. So nice to know that there wouldn't be photos of my dead body on the covers of the tabloids that week.

As I pulled up in the car, I could see my parents sitting in the living room. I went inside.

'Mom! Dad! Happy Thanksgiving!' I gave my mother a kiss, smiled at my dad. 'Cynthia, child,' he said, 'I glad you reach; I could start making the gravy now.'

'Marvin, don't be so *stupidee*,' my mother scolded. 'You know she won't eat no gravy; she mindin' she figure!'

'It's okay, Mom; it's Thanksgiving, and I'm going to eat everything you put on my plate. If I get too fat, I'm just going to have to start walking to work. You've got to work with what you've got, after all.' She looked surprised, but didn't say anything.

I poked around in the kitchen, like I always did. Dad stood at the stove, stirring the gravy. There was another saucepan on the stove, with the remains of that morning's cocoa in it. It smelt wonderful. I reached around my father to turn on the burner under the cocoa. He frowned at me.

'Is cocoa-tea, Cyn-Cyn, You don't drink that no more.'

'I just want to finish what's left in the pot, Dad. I mean, you don't want it to go to waste, do you?'

Ashok Mathur *b.* 1961

BHOPAL, INDIA

'I focus on language as a site of resistance,' says Ashok Mathur. As a writer, cultural worker, editor, and publisher, he sees his work as 'challenging a status quo that is extremely conservative and resistant to effective change, particularly in terms of race, but including gender, class, and sexuality'. Born in Bhopal, India, Mathur moved to Canada at a young age. He received a BA in English (1988) and an MA in Postcolonial Studies (1990), and completed his doctoral dissertation on Pedagogy and South Asian Writing in Canada in 1999, all at the University of Calgary. While a member of the editorial collective of *absinthe*, Mathur co-edited, with Hiromi Goto and Suzette Mayr, *The Skin On Our Tongues* (1993), a special issue of writers of colour and aboriginal writers conceived at 'The Appropriate Voice' session that was part of the gathering of writers of colour and aboriginal writers at Geneva Park in Orillia, Ontario, in 1993. He was also the publisher and editor, together with Nicole Marcotic, of DisOrientation Chapbooks, an alternative poetry publication series that has published such writers as Erin Mouré, Roy Miki, Robert Kroetsch, Ian Iqbal Rashid, and Hiromi Goto. 'Our books', he says, 'are bound in radically unconventional formats, the intent being to disrupt the normative reading patterns which are culturally

induced and restrictive.' While Head of Critical and Cultural Studies at the Emily Carr College of Art + Design (1998–2005), he directed and curated the IntraNation Project, a series of interrelated symposia, residences and exhibitions about the relationship of nation-states and globalization. As Canada Research Chair in Cultural and Artistic Inquiry at Thomson Rivers University, Kamloops, he continues to investigate—critically, politically, and aesthetically—how cultural practices offer 'implicit and explicit critiques of the workings and failings' of multiculturalism. He has lectured widely in Canada and around the world.

Mathur's writing reflects a desire at once to locate language in the cultural and social contexts that inform it and to resist the strictures of literary conventions, a resistance that he sees as being 'an actual discontinuance of a formal (read: normal) approach, an out and out desistance'. As he stresses, desistance is 'not a refusal to read the page but a desisting insistence to stop and remake the page. This is turning left on a red light, reading right to left, cutting of the impulse to orient myself by the north star turning my back on the balcony and saying, "I is the West, and Juliet is . . . not there." This desistance is disOrientation. A stopping and restarting. Beginning again.' This is reflected in his first book, *Loveruage: A Dance in Three Parts* (1994), a narrative that challenges generic conventions. His novel, *Once Upon an Elephant* (1998), in part, an ironic take on Judge Allan McEachern who presided over the Delgamuukw land-claims case of the Gitxsan Nation in British Columbia and, in part, about the elephant-headed Hindu deity Ganesh, is a murder mystery with a twist. Satire, humour, and intertextual references are the tools Mathur employs in his second novel as well. In *The Short, Happy Life of Harry Kumar* (2001), Harry is a frustrated bank employee who travels around the globe in search of the missing Sita (of the Hindu *Ramayana* epic) accompanied by his dog Hanuman (the name of a monkey Hindu deity). Mathur's deconstruction of the normative values of stereotypes and identity politics also characterizes his multimedia novel, *A Little Distillery in Nowgong* (forthcoming) that focuses on the Parsi diaspora.

Into Skin

Ho and the story begin to here. No story to beginning there before. But cause this is the way it happened, and I can't make it up if I try. It was happening this sort long ago but cause ten years back least that and when I would have kill my own self if wasn't for the sing. Ready to go as was but cause for the sing and the sleep and the branch but but but cause. Happened so fast so ago so I'm here try to telling this story but the words caughting but cause up up in the high highing branches which did saving my life. And so that look. Yes yeahyes I've been see that looking before always always when I begin of talking but cause no one can see be seeing what I say oh say now. When I first begin to speaking so in this way this new way in this new place from far far from where I being child, I yes but cause be get looking from all you all you just as now. But cause but you sit and wait for me I be changing changing all the time and soon you hearing the language you wait but cause for so long oh yeah. When I look forward seeing, look forward my talk and talking all of this but cause, but, so I have to be shift-like and look back when it was now and all different and not so hard as then. When it was now, ten years after.

When it was now, after years of learning and speaking and writing.

When it was now, a full decade after.

When it was now, and here I am, ten years older and growing older still, thanks to what happened those long years ago. And words are so different for me now.

Standing. Stilling. Swaying. Breezing. Standstillswaybreeze. Leaves filling. Sap slowing. Air cooling. Leavesfall sapslow aircool. Rope burn cut slice. Standing. Still.

Back then, when I was new here, everything seemed new here. So much action and speed. What a picture I was, dowdy and dazed, standing on the bus platform like I'd just stepped out of a Unesco postcard. My cousin said she'd be there but she wasn't. This was the new world. My new world. Everything full of action and speed and I was dazzled by the Whiteness of it all.

'Say man, you lost?'

'?'

'I mean, ma'am—?'

'Gnugh!?'

'Cuz if you're lost or somethin' . . .'

'*Uj'ana sudhana.*' River flowing river river current up against, this is what I mean, this is my voice, choose the path of resistance, up against the current, swimming hard, banging off the waves, bouncing off the rocks, and make the path my own.

'I'm sorry? Well, take it easy ma'am—or, I mean . . .'

The young man was only trying to be helpful. He was my introduction to a spotless, unscented world. It wasn't his fault that he didn't know whether I was man or woman. At home I was—but no, that was there, the past, the dead past, and this was the here and now and I was whatever this new world gave me. I was greeted on the platform with a man-ma'am and I took the first step, first stroke, *ujana sudhana*, against the current. At home I was—but here I was newnamed and I became Manam. My cousin never did come that day and I left the platform by myself.

You left the platform by yourself. And you were by yourself for so many years. You were oogyana sa-dana? is that right? fighting against the current, going against the flow. To have known you then, to have met you then. When you were coming off that platform. Before everything happened. It must have been awful. Feel for you, really do. You were so fresh, as you say, a photograph come to life from a third world postcard. You must have been so beautiful. Must have been, huh. You are, you are beautiful, see it in you, emanating from you. Knew it when first saw you. Standing there, you were alone again, and your eyes were full of sorrow and love and couldn't help but fall in love. Watching you standing there; said:

'Couldn't help noticing you, sorrysorry, don't mean to be rude, but areyou areyou waiting for somebody?'

And you said: 'Uh-uh. Jus' standin' here.' Just like that, you said that jus' standin' here, and couldn't help (couldanyone?) couldn't help but fall in love with that sorrow in your eyes. Had to be with you. Had to love you. You, such a beautiful . . . beautiful . . . beautiful Manam . . . .

I floated for a long time. Uglily. A spotted and darkened blot on a frothy white sea, pristine white sea, clean oh so clean that's what it was, the world I was in. And I was an aberration, an abomination on this frothy surface. And I floated uglily for a long time.

'Do you have any skills?'

'Scellz?'

'Skills. Abilities. What can you do?'

'Do? Do. I can doing anything all sorts. Work in all sorts all sorts, all have. All can doing but cause if any help help . . .'

'All sorts? Like a handy-person? Well, that would come in . . . handy. Sure. Uh, do you have any education?'

'?'

'EDuCAtion? Training. School?'

'Ah school, but cause no good teacher if to teach the small childs with speak speaking this very very hard.'

'No, have you *had* any training, formal training as a handy, or whatever, anything. Ms . . . ter? I'm sorry, it doesn't say here whether you're, well . . .'

'Manam.'

'Yes, well, M-anam, then. It's very difficult for us to place someone without knowing exactly what they can do.'

'Work hard but cause need knowing how to speak then all will be righting all will be.'

'Yes. It will be.'

'Yes.'

But no. It was hardly an easy road. I floated in and out of the froth, working where I could and playing the roles asked of me. I had come from a world where nothing was asked and I had chosen to come here. And here they asked me to cleanse myself, to cleanse myself and purify the world I had come into. They asked this of me.

They asked this of you. You have told of this. How you floated between jobs as a man-thenawoman but always as Manam. They asked you to clean yourself, you said, clean yourself and the world you were in. You tell, laughing now, how you began cleaning toilets at the bus station, the same station you first came to. And you went from there to cleaning floors. Then you cleaned windows. Then you moved to an office building, and late at night, when all the office workers were safely sleeping, you told how you'd clean from floor to floor. And that's where you were written, wasn't it? that's where you said it happened and kept on happening and hearing that, you telling that, there were tears here so many tears. Nothing to do.

> *Whisperly rustle. Tenderly twirling. Autumnly waiting.*
> *Desperately dormant.*
> *Whisperhiss. Tendertensed. Autumnugly. Desperatedying.*
> *Whispertenderautumndesperate. Ropely sweet sensation*
> *undercutly into bark.*

I would work there in the office tower, darkened but for the perpetual light from the tubing in the hall. Work hard. And in the days I'd read the books I'd find, a glutton for the words that would one day wash away the smell of vinegar and lye. And yes I learned. Learned to speak the way the new world wanted me to speak. Learned to forget that *ujana sudhana* was my mentor, and that my true learning came as I soaped and scrubbed the floors walls desks doors. And when I met Him who would teach me more than I ever wished to know. . . . He was tall and large and His eyes were a smoggy grey and when I looked at them I was looking through Him. My shift was nearly over that morning. I was on my last floor, emptying waste paper baskets and, as I always did, seizing wads of computer sheets to practise my writing. I had a box of paper in my hands when I felt His presence.

'Wht th hll r y'dng?'

'Nothing, sir no sir nothing but cause going throw 'way and all so put for using in.'

'Tht's cmpny prprty, ya stpd ful.'

'Sir, yesyes sorry nothing but cause . . .'

'Gdm thf, shd kc sm sns'n tayou.'

I couldn't protect myself against the butterfly quickness and unpredictability of His words. They flew at me, landed angrily, then before I could grasp them they were replaced by new, yet more unfamiliar sounds.

'Foreigner, gv nch tk mile, tch a lsn, tch ya gd.' His face was pink and hot and so close I could feel the sweat leech from his pores; and my face, brown and smooth, passively bore his exhaustive torrent of verbal violence. Acquiescing, I bowed my head, to show respect, to acknowledge defeat and wrongness. And that's when words grew louder and blastier and when they stopped the silence was worse, for there He stood, breathing hate and closeness into my flesh my mind my

He was there forever and when He left I eased my body to the floor. He was gone. I could still hear and fear his words in my head. Banging and insistent. Compared to those words inside my body, his silence was nothing. But it stayed with me, shrouded around me. I rose. There were bootmarks, his, on the computer paper. I took that with me and, later that afternoon, over the stained, warped surface, copied neat lines of verse from a damaged and discarded book of modernist verse I had found in the garbage of a second-hand bookstore. My letters were neat and perfectly formed that afternoon.

Your letters were perfectly formed that day. And you continued to copy lines of poetry and prose from thrown-out books you had found. And you got better at writing on thrown-out computer paper from the office tower where you still worked. And every night, or almost every night, he was there and he would attack you with his words and then his breath and awful silence, and then his mouth would ooze more spit and filth upon you. But you kept going to work. You kept going and he kept coming. You said he was enjoying it now, unleashing those words on you like he could do to no one else. You said the standing silent, the breathy quiet, was not so bad, would not have been so bad, if it hadn't been preceded, always, by those words. Words tongued into your skin, welted into your body. But you kept going back. Going back. Why did you keep going back?

> Braided branded sucked stucked rope into limb into side into
> skin. Wrapped warped corpsed cutted. Into

I. I remember. I remember that night. I remember that night He came and He cut and He wrote.

'Thr y r s-hole, cm here so'i cn shw y smthng spshl.'

'But cause this is nevernever bad thing, I working so good and cannot bear very much reality but cause.'

He turned out the light so the office was dark and all I could see was the pinky glow from His face and a grey light from His eyes. In His hand was a letter opener with a grey blade and I knew this time there would be no standing there silence, no quiet after the words.

'Dm bch. Bch? r y mn or wmn? Hrd t tl wth those clothes on.' And in the pinkgrey light from His face the blade came toward me and His hand reached out ripping tearing and the knife ripping tearing dully pulling shredding and and and He stood above me laughing spitting words and letters incomprehensible unconnected and then the letter opener coming closer to my body naked body open body blank unwritten body. And in the dark, lit only by the pinkgrey of his face, he began to write upon my skin with that dull blade words full words no mistaking them now, words I remembered painfully writing myself on bootstamped sheets of stolen computer paper and I could hear these words well, I could read these words in my body well, the vowels and consonants and carefully scribed syllables, written into me, and me, stonestill fascinated, the bloodly ink obscuring obfuscating then revealing letters in my skin. He wrote my death into my body.

He wrote your death into your body. But he did not write you into death. He did not write you to death. He left you alone, ashamed, writhing with the writing or your bloody skin. The morning light was pinkgrey, too, but brighter than his face and horrified workers saw you written on the office floor. You stood and clothed yourself, covered the words, and forever left the building of your learning. You walked to your home and you filled a bag with doubly inscribed computer paper. You took a rope. You walked far far and through the day and no words came to you except what words were with you and then it was evening and the city was behind. You saw the grove and you saw the tree. You touched its bark its coarsely written skin. You began to climb.

Stroke and stride. Cleave and climb. Breathe and brush. Rush
and rope.
strokecleavebreatherush
strideclimbbrushrope

I ascended with the rope. I touched the hoary bark and clawed words into the cracks; written bark clawed back and overwrote upon my skin. I reached the topmost branch and sat with words in me and over me. I tied the rope around the limb, tied it tight, and let the rope hang loose below. In setting sun the rope was silhouetted, a hanging silent O. I touched the coarseness of the rope the roughness of the bark the toughness of my skin and lay my head to rest upon the tree.

Sleepdreamriserest wordless wondrous dream a dream of life
dream a dream of wordless wondrousity dream a dream of
dreams dream into a life dream away from death undeathed
dream

You lay your head to rest upon the tree and when you woke the sky was dark and words had come and gone and would not hurt you now. You say the tree began to sing, a wordless song, singing to you in your sleep, song and sing and soft inside your ear. You came down from the tree and looked up at the O and smiled your gratitude. You burned the words you had so carefully inscribed on computer paper and left the ashes as an offering for your life. And two days later you were standing there, saw you standing there and you were beautiful, full of sorrow, but beautiful, too beautiful for words and who could not love you?

The words inside my skin are softer now. They fade and fall away with every passing day. We go back to the tree now. I see her in the grove and know that she is taller now. Up up so high silhouetted by the sky I see the O, still there, speaking to me wordlessly. O. O. O. I touch her written skin and sing the song she sang to me and then begin to climb her slowly stilly. I have no words I have no sex I have no song but what she sang to me singing softly Manam Manam Manam

> *Manam ma'am, no man wo man curl unfurl me let me breathe*
> *untie me sift me sing me touch and tinge me manam manam*
> *manam*

Singing softly Manam manam manam, you fall asleep upon the branch, the singing limb, and breathe and listen wordlessly and under watchful eye you wake and wonder touch the aged O.

The rope is old and weathered but hangs there still. The limb is written into by the loop, the rope writes words upon the branch and I say O. I try untie the rope but fast it holds, imprinted on the tree I work unwork pull push try hard but cause no way grows there inside no way is buried so so but cause not worked and words worded in the tree unsinged pull but never never but cause and I say yes this happening just so but cause you never gonna believe this when I tell you, but I can't never make it up if I try. Never.

Tess Fragoulis *b.* 1964

HERAKLION, CRETE, GREECE

Born in Heraklion, on the island of Crete, Greece, Tess Fragoulis moved to Montreal, where she has lived for most of her life, with her family when she was one year old. Steeped in the world of Greek myths since the age of six—'My father told me they belonged to me'—she grew up taking 'her heritage for granted': 'It's part of that immigrant mentality—that you need to throw away, leave behind whatever your roots are and just be part of the society you are living in. You grow up not wanting to be Greek, not wanting to be part of those stories.' Her first book, *Stories to Hide from Your Mother* (1997), nominated for the Quebec Writers' Federation First Book Award, does exactly that. Hailed for its 'assured and accomplished prose, and for the range, depth, and inventiveness of [the stories']

imaginative insights', the collection lives up to its title. In the words of the narrator in 'Exhortations', 'the stories are a series of random outpourings that nobody's mother should read, let alone mine'; their '[n]ewness and risk are good for the soul, for the collective unconscious of a culture.' Urban and tense, and often resisting the principles of conventional realism, these stories draw the reader into an intimate and edgy world.

Fragoulis holds a BA (1989) and an MA (1999) in English from Concordia University, where she has been teaching Creative Writing since 2000. The granddaughter of the celebrated Cretan writer, Constantine Fragoulis, a novelist, poet, and journalist, she started writing when she was in grade three. Prior to dedicating herself to writing (1993), she worked in an array of jobs in Toronto, and continues to work as a journalist, reviewer, and freelance editor. She has edited, with Helen Tsiriotakis and Steven Heighton, the first Greek Canadian anthology, *Musings: An Anthology of Greek-Canadian Literature* (2004). Fragoulis is one of the writers featured in the documentary series *The Writing Life* (produced by Michael Glassbourge, 2004). The same edginess that marks her stories also characterizes her first novel, *Ariadne's Dream* (2001), only here Fragoulis confronts the Greek mythological figures she ran away from earlier in her writing life. Non-episodic, mythological, and contemporary in its sensibility, it tells the story of Ariadne, a Greek Canadian who, while trying to come to terms with her dejection, the result of an unhappy relationship, goes to Greece to work on an island known for its wild lifestyle. It was nominated for the IMPAC International Dublin Literary Prize and given an honourable mention for the Books in Canada/Amazon First Novel Award. Fragoulis has just completed her second novel, *The Goodtime Girl*, a historical narrative about music, drugs, and warfare set in Asia Minor and Greece in the 1920s.

It was a rainy spring day in Toronto in the early 1990s, when she came upon a paperback book, face down in a puddle, run over by cars, scratched. It was Murray Bail's *The Drover's Wife*, a book and author she had never read. She loved it so much that she wrote the story that follows, which she sent as a letter to Bail. He wrote back, sending her in appreciation one of his books, calling it 'scraps'.

Dear Mr Bail

There has been a mistake—but of no great importance—made in the denomination of this picture. The woman depicted is not 'The Drover's Wife.' She is my wife. We have not seen each other now . . . it must be getting on thirty years.

—Murray Bail, *The Drover's Wife*

Dear Mr Bail,

I would like to report that I found the Drover's wife lying face down in a puddle on the street, here in Toronto. This was on College Street, to be exact, in Little Italy. I don't know whether she tried to get directions back to Australia, but with the glut of Italians in the neighbourhood, she probably had a hard time communicating. And they, I'm sure, had a hard time understanding her accent. They are not unfriendly here in Little Italy, just suspicious of strangers.

How she got into the street, and who was the first to run her over, I don't know. But her skirt was up over her hips and there were tire tracks criss-crossing her back, not a pretty sight. Okay, I admit I ran her over, too. But just with my bike, and at least I stopped. Okay, not immediately. I got to the sidewalk and then turned back. I looked around to see if anyone else might help her, take the responsibility, but all I saw were numb stares and noses grazing the sky or the sidewalk, depending on the degree of ennui and self-esteem.

Yes, I hesitated, but with good reason. You see, I've had a similar experience in the past, at a corner near a church on Carlton Street. A man with the face of petrified, grey horror, who smelled of old socks, festering meat and gin, fell face first into the street. I saw him fall and heard the smack of bone on cement. It was surprisingly loud and distinct, considering traffic, as if everything stood still for a moment. This was the man's standing ovation, and he was missing it.

No one would help me lift him off the pavement. I have been described as small-boned, and he could be described as dead weight, so I couldn't even drag him an inch by myself, let alone lift him. I looked towards a black woman at the bus shelter with that desperate expression reserved for long bathroom lines at the movies, but she recoiled, shaking her head as if I'd asked her to abort Jesus.

Four men with Humpty Dumpty waistlines appeared out of nowhere, as if they'd rehearsed for this moment for weeks, and rolled him over. I looked into the man's face and locked onto his eyes, icy blue. A trickle of blood slithered down his forehead and over his right eyebrow, a red tributary emptying into his eye.

I offered to find a phone, and the rotund men nodded in unison. The phone booths were a right angle away from where I was standing, on the other side of the street, so I went into the church instead. Later, when I went over that choice, closer to the event in question, I concluded that I chose the church because I didn't want to cross at two different intersections (I don't like cars, they scare me). But now, in writing this letter, I realize that I chose the church because somewhere, deep down in my heathen psyche, the archetype for God still resides, and as an extension (like bunga-lows), the recognition of priests as caring, and the house of God as a safe and charit-able haven open to all who need help. The right place to go and yell in a voice loud and desperate, tinged with a Southern accent, 'Father, there's an angel fallen in the streets, come quickly.' The priest would look at me in a combination of pained dis-belief and alarm, realizing that his moment had come. That the big test they'd prepared him for at the seminary, that he'd prepared himself for since childhood through devotion, fasting, meditation, and abstinence from sex was finally here. And this was the day that, if he were good enough, he'd get his wings.

Of course my priest didn't have wings, just Hush Puppies and a limp. He wasn't even on the shortlist for wings. I explained that a man had fallen in the street, face first, crunch, using sophisticated hand gestures to demonstrate precisely the occurrence and my point, which was that he should call an ambulance immediately because the man didn't look like he had long for this earth, and his audience was starting to thin.

The priest stared at me blankly and then consulted Igor, the overgrown altar boy (they have push buttons for bell tolling in this church, but they sound like synthesiz-ers, weak and hollow, as if they've been castrated). They both looked me over at the same time: first my rumpled hat, then my boots, their gaze finally resting on my naked knee peeking out of my torn jeans. 'Show me where,' the priest said, leading the way down the hall. I did not mention the doctrine he swears by that requires him to believe in exactly that which he does not see. I just followed his sticky brown shoes down the hall. Igor followed at a skittish pace, like those seabirds at Biloxi Beach in Mississippi that move like overgrown gnats with feathers.

When we got to the front door and opened it towards the light, the whole scene had disappeared, including the victim, the rotund men, and the black Virgin Mary. The priest and Igor scowled at me, then pushed me down the stairs. The priest wiped his hands clean of me with that rhythmic, clapping back and forth dance step motion, which also turns old people's lights on and off. Igor spat his bubble gum in my general direction, and then they disappeared inside, slamming the heavy door behind them, leaving me sprawled on my butt on the sidewalk. I looked around for the Humpty Dumpty men, but I guess they had already gone home to celebrate the arrival of their big moment, so I got up, dusted myself off, and left.

The bad thing about that happening, and all other happenings, is that it began to fade once the objects of the happening were taken away. It shrank like a dream, until there is no way left to prove it even happened. Unless someone took a picture, and even that might not help. Everything eventually disappears.

Imagine an old woman rocking back and forth, muttering to herself in the cramped attic where she's been relegated along with boxes of old clothes, broken furniture, and mouldy stacks of newspapers. Everything she owned, all the objects that defined her existence—her religious icons, her orange straw sewing basket, her mink hat—have been given away to charity, or plundered by greedy relatives. She has fallen out of context, and no one has much use for her anymore, though they sometimes reminisce about the pies she used to bake and smack their lips. She sits up there alone in the near-dark, rummaging through a box of family photos. She smiles at the children in sailor suits and cowboy hats, at the charming young bride with her handsome groom. Her eyes glaze over as she stares at the elegant blue script that covers the yellowed pages of her diary. She tears the brittle pages into tiny pieces and eats them, then disposes of the photos in the same manner. She grins at me when I bring up her dinner, shreds of memory poking out between her teeth like feathers. She bites my fingers when I try to pluck them out.

The rest of her family does not understand; they are annoyed and resentful and sigh harshly at her every coo. You see, Mr Bail, they have been counting on her as the repository of their life, the place where they can be the protagonist whenever they feel unappreciated by the rest of the world. How dare she forget? They quiz her for the whole thirty minutes of their quarterly visit, and she isn't pretending, she truly can't answer any of their questions. 'Come now, don't you remember me? It's Pete, Auntie. Peter. Remember how you used to tie me to the sofa leg so I wouldn't break your porcelain figurines, Auntie?' She isn't even sure who the people asking the questions are, or what some of the words mean. So she starts talking to mirrors instead of people because people make her feel crazy with all of their questions, expectations, and condescending smiles. She goes to the mirror to ask it what she still knows, and before it can answer, these strangers have put her, for her own good, into an institution with white walls, puréed green food, plenty of mirrors, and no taboo about talking into them. 'Mirror, mirror on the wall, did I ever exist at all?'

There are three mirrors in her room, side by side, positioned so she can even talk to the back of her head. She can see three images of herself at once and gives each one a different name. On some days she knows all three, though the middle one won't stop crying, the one on the right is either Lucy or Catherine depending on the weather, and she's not on speaking terms with the one on the left, though they grimace at each other from time to time and then turn their backs.

One day they hatch a plan, and she escapes with the other three hiding under her coat. Once outside, she directs them to spread out, ''Cause they can't take all of us at the same time.' She wanders the streets of Toronto on her own, wearing a trenchcoat, a blue hospital gown, and paper slippers soggy with rain and dirt. She tugs on her crazy hair, mutters to herself, and screams in a language that only she and her cohorts understand. People on the sidewalk veer around her, afraid that they'll catch whatever it is she has. Old age, senility, insanity, uselessness—they aren't sure what. 'Where did you come from, where do you live?' a young policeman asks, but she just grabs his face with her hands, hisses in his ear like a deflating balloon, and laughs. Tells him she loves him and kisses him on his thin, bloodless lips. She then spots Lucy out of the corner of her eye and runs across the street to give her a bus ticket, since she knows Lucy's off to visit her daughter to make her miserable. And she gets hit by a car just when she's about to reach her. She didn't check the traffic lights because she doesn't remember anything like that ever existed, let alone that there is some use for such a thing other than pretty flashing lights to dance to. Memories of such things are without importance in the institution. As unimportant as the fact that she's forgotten her name.

I go by that corner and that church every once in a while. I stare at that piece of pavement, and for the time being, the fallen man always reappears. Maybe I should have brought him home with me, too. Maybe I did.

I don't stop much anymore except to toss a quarter to a musician, or a dollar to the older men who look as if they might be someone's grandfather who escaped from the circus wearing red-striped flood pants and a gangly purple sweater. There's no more room left in my apartment. I even have to do all my writing at my kitchen table. But they still follow me, on the streets, down hallways, to the elevator, pleading with me to take them home, clawing at the doors until their fingers bleed, until the nurse takes them back to their beds and straps them down. I can see them, even with my back turned. And then I cry. There just isn't enough room.

So as you can see, Mr Bail, I have very good reasons for hesitating when I see someone laying face first on the street. I need some time to work out my dilemma. Should I bother at all with a good deed since no memory of it will comfort me in my old age? Or is it like Vladimir said in *Waiting for Godot*: 'Let us do something while we have the chance. It is not every day that we are needed.' I usually opt for the latter, to remain in the present, to do my share, and that's how I came to pick up the Drover's wife. I wiped the rain off her with my sleeve, smoothed down her hair, then perched her on the back of my bike and brought her home with me.

Though a little crumpled and warped, and starting to show her age around the edges, she's happy here with me. We drink raspberry tea in the afternoons and ride the streetcar back and forth without a destination to eavesdrop on other lives. Mostly they're boring, but every once in a while we hear a gem and write it down in a small black and red notebook. I don't think the scars across her back will ever really heal, though they did prove to be an interesting conversation piece at a recent cocktail party where I dared her to wear a backless cocktail dress, and she did. She's still feisty, for all the wear and tear.

She says she likes it here because no one asks her any questions about her past. As for me, I only know her as she is now, and have never been to Australia, so she can tell me anything she wants and I'll believe her. I think I'm even beginning to pick up a bit of her accent, as well as a few strange words that she may or may not have made up. This has caused some eye-rolling in the neighbourhood, but I never attempt to explain. Most people don't recognize truth when they hear it, so what harm could a few made-up words do to my vocabulary, anyway? When they do ask, I tell them I'm speaking in tongues.

Before I forget, a message to the Drover: stop searching for her. She doesn't look like her picture anymore. I've cut her hair into a 'bob' and have given her a pair of my cat's eye sunglasses. She's considered quite eccentric in the neighbourhood, and she enjoys that. She's not coming back. She doesn't even remember that she had a husband, and I think it's best for all concerned that it stays that way. If it weren't for my chancing upon your report, Mr Bail, I wouldn't even know what a Drover was. She didn't look very happy in the picture. She answers to Peggy here in Toronto, and laughs whenever she hears me call her by name. She thinks it's a funny name, one you'd give to a cow. I've grown used to her and can't imagine living without her now that we've found each other. (Do you believe in karma? I do.) I need her here. She has been an inspiration and a comfort.

Mr Bail, I leave the decision of whether to pass this information on to the proper authorities up to you. I just thought you'd be interested in her whereabouts. Yours was the only name in her shirt pocket.

(Inspired by the discovery of Murray Bail's book, The Drover's Wife, *on the wet and indifferent streets of Toronto.)*

Miriam Toews *b.* 1964

STEINBACH, MANITOBA

'The understatement, the subtlety, the emotional honesty without giant flash cards and neon signs . . . that is what I would be trying to do as a writer and what most writers are trying to do,' says Miriam Toews. Indeed, her writing is built on these qualities, as well as a sense of humour. Born in Steinbach, in the heart of Mennonite country in Manitoba, she grew up in an educated and progressive-thinking family (both her parents had graduate degrees). Yet, she says, 'There was this weird disparity,' as her tolerant family belonged to 'the most conservative congregation in town'. Toews's writing revolves mostly around this disparity. Her first two novels, *Summer of My Amazing Luck* (1996), which was nominated for the Stephen Leacock Medal for humour and won the John Hirsch Award, and *A Boy of Good Breeding* (1998), winner of the McNally Robinson Book of the Year award, rely on Toews's zany humour to tell the stories, respectively, of young single mothers on welfare and of the familial and community politics about keeping a small town the smallest town in Canada. In contrast, *Swing Low: A Life* (2000), though marked by the same compassion through which she creates her characters, features humorous elements that are gracefully tempered by the sadness and bravery of her father's life-long struggle with manic depression that led him to commit suicide. A first-person narrative about her father's experiences, it is at once an audacious tour de force as Toews imagines what it was like for her father, a loved school teacher and a pillar in his Mennonite community, to hide his condition, and a narrative that challenges the conventional distinctions between autobiography and fiction, between life-writing and biography. *Swing Low* won the Alexander Kennedy Isbister Award for non-fiction.

Toews, who left Steinback at the age of eighteen to live in Montreal and London, England, holds an MA in Film Studies from the University of Manitoba and a BA in Journalism from King's College, Halifax. Since 1991 she has lived with her husband and children in Winnipeg, where she works as a documentary writer for CBC Radio and a freelance writer for various Canadian and American magazines. Her most recent novel, *A Complicated Kindness* (2004), which remained on the bestseller list for a full year, established her as one of the most important and popular novelists of her generation. The winner of many awards, including the Governor General's Award, it articulates the disparity that affects the life of a teenage girl in a Mennonite community, a girl who hopes, following at her mother's and sister's footsteps, to escape. Funny yet disturbing, it reflects Toews's attempt to come to terms with a culture that she both feels close to and critiques. As she says, 'Sometimes I am bugged by my own tendency to continuously go for the laughs, but I am trying to be genuinely funny even if it's in a dry, tragic way. . . . I have seen the damage that fundamentalism can do. The way the religion is being interpreted, it's a culture of control and that emphasis on shame and punishment and guilt is not conducive to robust mental health.'

A Father's Faith

On the morning on May 13, 1998, my father woke up, had breakfast, got dressed and walked away from the Steinbach Bethesda Hospital, where he had been a patient for two and a half weeks. He walked through his beloved hometown, along Hespeler Road, past the old farmhouse where his mother had lived with her second husband, past the water tower, greeting folks in his loud, friendly voice, wishing them well. He passed the site on First Street where the house in which my sister and I grew up once stood. He walked down Main Street, past the Mennonite church where, throughout his life, he had received countless certificates for perfect attendance, past Elmdale School where he had taught grade six for forty years.

As he walked by his home on Brandt Road, he saw his old neighbour Bill sitting in his lawn chair. He waved and smiled again, then he continued on past the cemetery where his parents were buried, and the high school his daughters had attended, and down Highway 52, out of town, past the Frantz Motor Inn, which is just outside the town limits because it serves alcohol and Steinbach is a dry town. He kept walking until he got too tired, so he hitched a ride with a couple of guys who were on their way to buy a fishing licence in the small village of Woodridge on the edge of the Sandilands Forest.

The sun would have been very warm by the time they dropped him off, and he would have taken off his stylish cap and wiped his brow with the back of his hand. I'm sure he thanked them profusely, perhaps offering them ten dollars for their trouble, and then he walked the short distance to the café near the railroad tracks, the place he and my mom would sometimes go for a quiet coffee and a change of scenery. He would have been able to smell the clover growing in the ditches beside the tracks and between the ties. He may have looked down the line and remembered that the train would be coming from Ontario, through Warroad, Minnesota, on its way to Winnipeg.

A beautiful young woman named Stephanie was just beginning her shift and she spoke to him through the screen door at the side of the restaurant. Yes, she said, the train will be here soon. And my dad smiled and thanked her, and mentioned that he could hear the whistle. Moments later, he was dead.

Steinbach is an easy forty-minute drive from Winnipeg, east on the Trans-Canada, then south on Highway 12. On the way into town there's a sign proclaiming 'Jesus Saves.' On the way back to the city just off Highway 12 there's another that says, 'Satan is Real. You Can't Be Neutral. Choose Now.' The town has recently become a city of 8,500 people, two-thirds of whom are Mennonite, so it's not surprising that about half of the twenty-four churches are Mennonite and conservative. There is a Catholic church too, but it's new and I'm not sure exactly where it is. A little way down from the bowling alley I can still make out my name on the sidewalk, carved in big bold letters when I was ten and marking my territory.

My town made sense to me then. For me it was a giant playground where my friends and I roamed freely, using the entire town in a game of arrows—something like hide-and-seek—for which my dad, the teacher, provided boxes and boxes of fresh new chalk and invaluable tips. He had, after all, played the same game in the same town many years before.

At six p.m. the siren would go off at the firehall, reminding all the kids to go home for supper, and at nine p.m. it was set off again, reminding us to go home to bed. I had no worries, and no desire ever to leave this place where everyone knew me. If they couldn't remember my name, they knew I was the younger daughter of Mel and Elvira Toews, granddaughter of C.T. Loewen and Henry Toews, from the Kleine Gemeinde congregation, and so on and so on. All the kids in town, other than the church-sponsored Laotians who came over in the seventies, could be traced all the way back to the precise Russian veldt their great-grandparents had emigrated from. They were some of the thousands of Mennonites who came to Manitoba in the late 1800s to escape religious persecution. They were given free land and a promise that they could, essentially, do their own thing without interference. They wanted to keep the world away from their children and their children away from the world. Naturally it was an impossible ideal.

As I grew older, I became suspicious and critical and restless and angry. Every night I plotted my escape. I imagined that Barkman's giant feed mill on Main Street, partially visible from my bedroom window, was a tall ship that would take me away some day. I looked up places like Hollywood and Manhattan and Venice and Montreal in my Childcraft encyclopedias. I begged my sister to play, over and over, the sad songs from her Jacques Brel piano book, and I'd light candles and sing along, wearing a Pioneer Girls tam on my head, using a chopstick as a cigarette holder, pretending I was Jackie Brel, Jacques's long-lost but just as world-weary Mennonite twin. I couldn't believe that I was stuck in a town like Steinbach, where dancing was a sin and a serving beer a felony.

There were other things I became aware of as well. That my grandmother was a vanilla alcoholic who believed she was a teetotaller. That seventy-five-year-old women who had borne thirteen children weren't allowed to speak to the church congregation, but that fifteen-year-old boys were. That every family had a secret. And I learned that my dad had been depressed all his life.

I had wondered, when I was a kid, why he spent so much of the weekend in bed and why he didn't talk much at home. Occasionally he'd tell me, sometimes in tears, that he loved me very much and that he wished he were a better father, that he were more involved in my life. But I never felt the need for an apology. It made me happy and a bit envious to know that my dad's students were able to witness his humour and intelligence firsthand, to hear him expound on his favourite subjects: Canadian history, Canadian politics, and Canadian newspapers. I remember watching him at work and marvelling at his energy and enthusiasm. I thought he looked very handsome when he rolled up his sleeves and tucked his tie in between the buttons of his shirt, his hands on his hips, all ready for business and hard work.

Teaching school—helping others make sense of the world—was a good profession for a man who was continuously struggling to find meaning in life. I think he needed his students as much as they needed him. By fulfilling his duties, he was also shoring up a psyche at risk of erosion.

Four years before his death he was forced to retire from teaching because of a heart attack and some small strokes. He managed to finish the book he was writing on Canada's prime ministers, but then he seemed to fade away. He spent more and more of his time in bed, in the dark, not getting up even to eat or wash, not interested in watching TV or listening to the radio. Despite our pleading and cajoling, despite the medication and visits to various doctors' offices, appointments he dutifully kept, and despite my mother's unwavering love, we felt we were losing him.

I know about brain chemistry and depression, but there's still a part of me that blames my dad's death on being Mennonite and living in that freaky, austere place where this world isn't good enough and admission into the next one, the perfect one, means everything, where every word and deed gets you closer to or farther away from eternal life. If you don't believe that then nothing Steinbach stands for will make sense. And if life doesn't make sense you lose yourself in it, your spirit decays. That's what I believed had happened to my dad, and that's why I hated my town.

In the weeks and months after his death, my mom and my sister and I tried to piece things together. William Ashdown, the executive director of the Mood Disorders Association of Manitoba, told us the number of mentally ill Mennonites is abnormally high. 'We don't know if it's genetic or cultural,' he said, 'but the Steinbach area is one that we're vitally concerned about.'

'It's the way the church delivers the message,' says a Mennonite friend of mine, 'the message of sin and accountability. To be human, basically, is to be a sinner. So a person, a real believer, starts to get down on himself, and where does it end? They say self-loathing is the cornerstone of depression, right?'

Years ago, the Mennonite Church practised something called 'shunning', whereby if you were to leave your husband, or marry outside the Church, or elope, or drink, or in some way contravene the Church's laws or act 'out of faith', you could be expelled from the Church and ignored, shunned by the entire community, including your own family. Depression or despair, as it would have been referred to then, was considered to be the result of a lack of faith and therefore could be another reason for shunning.

These days most Mennonites don't officially practise shunning, although William Ashdown claims there are still Mennonites from extreme conservative sects who are being shunned and shamed into silence within their communities for being mentally ill. Certainly Arden Thiessen, the minister of my dad's church, and a long-time friend of his, is aware of the causes of depression and the pain experienced by those who suffer from it. He doesn't see it as a lack of faith, but as an awful sickness.

But I can't help thinking that that history had just a little to do with my alcoholic grandmother's insisting that she was a non-drinker, and my dad's telling his doctors, smiling that beautiful smile of his, that he was fine, just fine.

Not long before he died my dad told me about the time he was five and was having his tonsils out. Just before the operation began he was knocked out with ether and he had a dream that he was somersaulting through the hospital walls, right through, easily, he said, moving his hands in circles through the air. It was wonderful. He told me he would never forget that feeling.

But mostly, the world was a sad and unsafe place for him, and his town provided shelter from it. Maybe he saw this as a gift, while I came to see it as oppression. He could peel back the layers of hypocrisy and intolerance and see what was good, and I couldn't. He believed that it mattered what he did in life, and he believed in the next world, one that's better. He kept the faith of his Mennonite forebears to the very end, or what he might call the beginning, and removed himself from this world entirely.

Stephanie, the waitress in the café in Woodridge, told my mother that my dad was calm and polite when he spoke to her, as if he were about to sit down to a cup of tea. She told her that he hadn't seemed at all afraid. But why would you be if you believed you were going to a place where there is no more sadness?

My dad never talked to us about God or religion. We didn't have family devotion like everybody else. He never quoted out loud from the Bible or lectured us about not going to church. In fact his only two pieces of advice to me were 'Be yourself' and 'You can do anything.'

But he still went to church. It didn't matter how low he felt, or how cold it was outside. He would put on his suit and tie and stylish cap and walk the seven or eight blocks to church. He always walked, through searing heat or sub-arctic chill. If he was away on holidays he would find a church and go to it. At the lake he drove forty miles down gravel roads to attend an outdoor church in the bush. I think he needed church like a junkie needs a fix: to get him through another day in a world of pain.

What I love about my town is that it gave my dad the faith that stopped him from being afraid in those last violent seconds he spent on earth. And the place in my mind where we meet is on the front steps of my dad's church, the big one on Main Street across from Don's Bakery and the Goodwill store. We smile and talk for a few minutes outside, basking in the warmth of the summer sun he loved so much. Then he goes in and I stay outside, and we're both happy where we are.

David Odhiambo *b.* 1965

NAIROBI, KENYA

Born two years after Kenya gained its independence from Britain, David (Nandi) Odhiambo grew up aware of his responsibility 'to honor' his parents' struggle for freedom, 'namely, by writing as freely as I desire'. This intellectual and political heritage, what he calls a 'territory', is the subject of *Pillar to Post*, a novel he is currently writing while living in Philadelphia; it will be his third. Having been sent to a boarding school in western Kenya at the age of five, he had his 'first foray' into writing through his correspondence with his parents. At the age of twelve, Odhiambo moved from his birthplace, Nairobi, to Winnipeg to attend a prestigious boarding school. A loner during those years, and nicknamed Kunta Kinte, after the character in Alex Haley's *Roots*, he was accosted with stories about famous Kenyan distance runners that inspired him to run his first marathon (1979). He was a competitive track athlete—participating in the Quebec University Championships, where he won the 600-metre event, and the Canadian Interuniversity Athletic Union games—but following an injury, 'writing took the place that running previously held' in his life.

After studying classics at McGill University (BA, 1986), Odhiambo moved first to Ottawa and then to Vancouver, where his work with street youth and teens with disabilities—work that, for him, is 'a form of activism' —provided him with the setting for his first novel, *diss/ed banded nation* (1988), an excerpt

from which appears below. It is a multilayered narrative about Benedict Ochieng, an illegal immigrant who is hiding from the immigration authorities in a seedy flop house in Vancouver. He is an accomplished jazz singer whose first-person, non-linear narrative echoes the rhythms of jazz and of African music, 'mostly drums in conversation with vocals', the music Odhiambo listened to while writing the novel. The author acknowledges that 'both Dizzy Gillespie and Thelonius Monk were major influences on the way I approached my writing. . . . I learnt to give myself permission to use language in a similar way. [The] structure of *diss/ed banded nation* evolved out of the way rhythm and language related on the blank page . . . a musical composition broken up into pieces that flow seamlessly into one another.' Jazz is just one of a number of cultural influences reflected in Odhiambo's work; others include the English and Swahili languages he was brought up on and writers ranging from James Baldwin and Ralph Ellison to Imamu Baraka and Toni Morrison.

Odhiambo's second novel, *Kipligat's Chance* (2003), inspired by Brian Granville's novel *The Olympian*, is a coming-of-age narrative about the ambition of two young Kenyan immigrants, the black John 'Leeds' Kipligat and his Indian friend Kulvinder, to become track stars in order to escape the poverty of their lives. Set in Vancouver in the 1970s and written in Odhiambo's jazzy voice, it explores their adolescent angst and interracial gender relations, but also deals with the young men's difficulty coming to terms with their loss of social status after arriving in Canada, a common experience for immigrants. Odhiambo has also written a

play, *afrocentric*, produced by Theatre Passe Muraille in Toronto, and collaborated with Suzanne Buffam and Joelle Hann to produce *mouth to mouth* (1995).

from *diss/ed banded nation*

`1a. (sunday october 5/97, 11.52 p.m.)`

acid rain slithers slatternly through the shutters of the strip-joint on richards street in which benedict ochieng sits suckling the teat of his sixth beer. porcelain mist hurdling the city's northern perimeter. a dank and moldy traipse over velvet knuckles of clear-cut mountain. this as chafing frothy ocean—the pacific—moshes impervious.

he'd quit drinking that morning. another uneventful vancouver morning stapled grey by grumbling cloud. but . . . finds himself, late evening, having lost track of the number of times he's said. enough. no more. failing, like before, to meet another commitment misplaced in the maze of this perpetual haze he's become. leading, once again, to imbibing, yet again, on the medication he's prescribed himself—heineken washed down with shots of lemon gin. this to take the edge off his latest catalogue of regret: the student visa having long ago expired; low on cash; now hiding out in a room on the east side.

he tries to focus . . . the upcoming gig. the a/saxxy fro crew at the azure. focus on all that has been sacrificed for another moment up on stage. kicking it. doing what it is he wants to do. what he feels compelled to do—which is sing.

but . . . he's stuck. a tractor tire wedged in and spitting up rank muck. unable to find the fix. make the mix. that'll give him back his chops. stringing together a mesh of phat tones. instead of all this clumpy . . . couldn't-much-care/thrombosis of drabness.

a piss-ass glaze of smoke rusts away his lungs as he surveys the room. trying to locate . . . another beer. attempting to find . . . a waitress. one who'll ripple the surface of yellowing eyes. buckling corneas until they snap moping muscle in shackles. shoulders. releasing him into . . . mint-scented entrails/forgetting.

his body is weak—countless experimentations with an arsenal of designer drugs. and he peels the label off his heineken hoping for the day this infernal funk will vanish like ivory blossoms wilting in heat.

he hasn't had a decent night's rest since the previous gig; another indifferent audience. the experience having left him . . . in the zone—the hasn't-slept-in-days zone; an aimless meander from bar to café; the chameleon; level 5; joes. obsessively ruminating on the perpetual trail of has-beens packing them in on tours venturing across far flung corners of the globe; the stones; duran duran; his fallen idol, the artist formerly known as whatever it had been he once was.

mariah carey leaks from house speakers. as he . . . searches the room, once again, for . . . an oasis. stasis. yet again . . . somewhere to rest. hell, someone who'd allow him to trail the underbelly of his tongue against the veins of her neck. just until he finds the elusive formula to manufacture a solution to his woes.

downloading neon advertisements for coors dangling from walls. his overtaxed faculties sluggishly format a televisual collage of burning car n' speedboat crashes among body-crunching bodychecks. the clang of cash registers indifferently documenting the steady sale of booze.

. . . 'i'd like you all to put your hands together and give a warm pet club welcome to luuuuuuu-cy rox, lucy rox gentlemen.'

handclapping erupts to whistles n' catcalls as numbness unlocks into . . . *ripple/ ripples* . . . his eyes snagging on . . . a dancer he'd hit it up with during a too-short visit he'd made to the brick-laden streets of old montreal three humid summers before. snacking on lucy rox/anna—an unanswered question still . . . after all this time . . . cluttering up his centre.

he'd vowed to return to her then. she to wait for him. but—distance/other priorities—nothing had come of it. at least until this . . . unexpected . . . paths inexplicably crossing after weeks heaped into months of displaced hope buried in a trek of hearts unable to retrieve the two days before the blue/black night in which they'd said so long/good bye. we'll write. i'll call.

nothing . . . until this serendipitous opening/glimpsed—all ankles n' knees; hair of dark brillo; ring in bellybutton n' bottom lip—saxxily descending a ladder onto centre stage.

'see-through fishnet everything!' a bloated suit bawls over a pitcher. scarlet embers sparking to life in crinkled features. his liquored-up colleague glancing up from where he decompresses with a brew. hoping to kick back after another day of paperwork n' phonecalls—cutting loose, no place else to go; hell-bent on avoiding any number of domestic chores awaiting him at home—trimming the hedge; walking the dog; lighting up the goddamn barbecue. as four gangly teens—still unable to grow beards—distract away with furtive glances towards non-existent authority figures in the direction of the front door. borrowed i.d. imbuing their evening with mawkish intrigue.

anna, wired on smack, struggles to a hip-hop beat in thigh-high stiletto boots. before lavishly pirouetting to lean with her back to a pole. quickly sliding down. downward. landing in a heap/legs splayed open in front of her. shyly covering her mouth. and . . . after thinking things through, flashing a tan buttock.

boisterous beer-guts—bodies jumping crudely about in overtaxed clothing—belch n' curse in solidarity over the right to leer at this cornucopia of elusive cunt n' evasive ass.

'take it off, bitch. take it off.'

anna winks before straddling the pole. hips seductively bucking the metal between her thighs. her eyes closed. then . . . opening to focus on . . . benedict who grips tightly at the neck of his half-empty heineken. her cortex . . . tweaked n' tweaking with where they'd been. a fucked-up weekend degenerating into an all-out coke binge. two blathering n' free, adrift. the tactical use of french in lovemaking colliding with eclectic reworkings of the kama sutra.

. . . 'can i get you anything?'

it's . . . the waitress. a sista wearing a too/too short black skirt and frilly white blouse.

'uuuumm . . . sure. what's on special?' he's speaking too fast . . . he should apologise to her for his presence here. make an off-colour reference to audre lourde. or toni morrison. or better yet, both. tell her he's read bell hooks—the academic dominatrix—n' enjoyed it too.

'the special . . . pale ale, darling.'

'a pale ale it is then.'

she moves over to the next table—an impenetrable smile playing at rubysticked lips.

. . . anna, tripped out n' finally going to work, rolls up close to the once boisterous, now studiously silent, beer-gutted pair. lingering. pouting. before rolling away again. the larger of the two greedily biting down into a knuckle as she rolls up into a one-armed handstand.

'she's native,' he shouts. 'i love native women.'

disgusting, benedict thinks. adjusting in his seat for a better look.

three blue collars—jeans stiffened with dried mud—slouch around a table, pre-occupied with hockey highlights up on a screen. the sight of them over benedict's shoulder trapping anna back into . . . rubbing her tan buttocks grandesquely up then down against the pole. music braking from frenetic to lush n' slow—boyz II men crooning out a song for mama.

she arches back, then bends forward, lime underwear dropped to knees/exposing a triangular shock of dark hair.

voyeurs locate themselves in bellows n' cheers. anna responding with delicate flicks at a pubic ring. before slowly pulling underwear to ankles then discarding the garment behind her.

'shower. shower.' it's the gangly teens. having finally relaxed into the occasion. one pointing to the glass-encased shower at the back of the stage. yearning to watch her stripped naked caressing booty n' pulling on nipples in steam n' splashing water.

she smiles. shucks. shimmies. then glides over to the shower. the numb indifference of cash registers carping nearby.

robson street suits engross themselves in a game of pool at a table in the back of the room. the taller of the two—a wrinkle-free armani—stopping to answer a cellular phone. as benedict toys with a lump behind his right ear.

could he coax anna into leaving with him—as he had once done—tempt her back to his hideaway; there to nestle up against each other—as they had once done—achily putting off straightening his itchy ass out with the folks at immigration? spending till the ends of time. finding an eternity of moments in those soap carvings for cheekbones.

he thinks this while watching . . . always and forever . . . the suits? people who get up each day and slip on ties. get into sporty hatchbacks—stick shift; auto theft device—and drive off to offices in . . . yaletown. beeping brokers. making investments on the stock market. then hitting the boardrooms before a three-martini lunch. a lifestyle which would resolve so much for him. ensuring he'd no longer reek of the need which kept the people of this city uninterested in the story his sorry-looking threads betrayed. providing the security which would keep some clingy soul stuck like lint to him.

he reaches for another snatch of brew. a sepulchral sound thudding in the base of his belly. spinning heretofore untested spindles to puke out . . . yards of remorse. as . . . another thought . . . he invests these strangers' lives with a certainty they have yet to attain. and in doing so undervalues their capacity to suffer. because they too seek the opposite of what they've become. which is what he suspects they would see if they noticed him—all they'd reluctantly given up on to become men.

the room tilts . . . loco/motion—the end of the set. as anna wraps up angles in a mustard towel. stoked. peaked. this registered in twitches at the corners of her eyes. his heart clunking . . . as she collects scattered undergarments. aware of his gaze spiked with yearning. conscious of his desire to entice her with words of lace lilted after the rain.

but . . . where would he begin? how would he start that conversation which would make sense of his under the table/on the run/below-minimum-when-he-can-get-them wages to her? all for the sake of his impractical obsession with sound strung musically to soul on bone. this dream which maroons him on an isle of uncertainty—she'll need more from him; STABILITY. thinking this as he's enticed forward . . . nevertheless . . . towards another moment in her eyes. outside, night of tree as darkened shadow shaking beneath obscuredbycloud moon.

innards burble like skin percolated by boiling oil. as . . . trying to hold on/hold on. for how long? he watches a stranger order her up a cutty sark. the elusive lover whom she will imagine has finally made her scene. the one with whom time will ripen in wrinkles on skin. as . . . looking up towards a clock . . . she finds . . . benedict—the sinewy, intense-looking cat whom she'd remembered never to forget—noticing her notice him.

there's a . . . tug . . . look away. but . . . something familiar . . . her eyes of ash/his sable cheekbones. before each quickly turns—asphyxiating on . . . at a loss for language—back to a purgatory they'd managed a brief escape from.

1b. (monday october 6, 1.16 a.m.)

benedict tips out the door. the night dour and skanky with a rhumba of traffic. warily adjusting a long s/lick multicoloured patch-leather jacket to cover ears. collecting himself before tilting forward/falling into rain's cool viola sting.

corduroy bell-bottoms clap uncomfortable at chilled flesh as he drunkenly meanders west on davie street. steam rising gently off sallow tarmac. a distant light peering green through the onset of fog.

nostrils pick up the stench of tobacco dyed into unwashed clothes. as it no longer rains. just this cold stillness that is long shadow. the lean and linger of tree. light from streetlamps and dented moon glistening in discoloured autumn leaves.

jacked on nausea he tries . . . try to . . . head up. *head up.* in a whir of bike chain n' cars struggling n' birds calling out names only they can understand. sediment gathering in puddle-water. as bush everywhere flips in phlegmatic breeze.

a heaviness descends upon him like a sudden ageing. and he gathers before another stumble south on burrard street. the prickly horizon line jittery with the flash of car brights drowsily etching his shadow. which bends in the wind.

motorists crawl along the bridge beside him like beetles half asleep. motors thunder-rolling by—dissonant symphonic pounding.

if only he had an answer—anything—for questions he'd yet to adequately formulate. thinking this as he slumps over cold railing. sick to the pit of his stomach. black water spanking eyes.

he burps up bile sputtering from a distended belly. a safety latch busting loose into a sloop of yachts. belching out clumsily on another of these vancouver nights that will not sleep. as the darksmooth inlet disturbs with the odd drop of rain. a drizzle of translucent beads drowning him in memory. high school. sweating in a boiler room, bare knuckles breaking skin against a canvas punching bag. trying to be cassius clay gone ali. maybe taking it to the golden gloves. a skinny n' scared brother who could bust your lip or blacken an eye.

he leans up against the moist metal. kicking a pebble out into brooding water. waiting for . . . PLOP. as he meanders into another yesterday still.

1975. four years old. another childhood. living on the motherland/alego district/ western kenya. cloud darkened on the edge anticipating another storm. as, shrouded in black, cloaked in it from head to toe, he stands next to grandmama. men in black suits shovelling red soil onto the wooden casket. as a part of him disappears along with his parents into a tomb. a lake of water spilling from sky. washing over them. shepherding the dearly departed into this place where his parents—whom he hasn't known for long—are now slumbering. their skin wrinkled n' black and crinkled like dry grapes. wrapped up in the white sheets they've been buried in.

their van had been struck by a truck as they'd returned from an evangelical meeting in the rift valley; the right reverend jim toshack, also dead. all crunched and crushed in the head-on collision.

grandmama, after learning of their passing, hadn't risen from bed for three days. HER daughter. her ONLY daughter now gone. when it was she who was near the end of her journey of many moons and suns and lightning storms.

benedict watches sombre men pack down damp earth with shovels. as mourners slowly begin to disperse among twigs crackling underfoot on their way back to the mission. inconsolable grandmama collapsing into the arms of other mothers. wailing. benedict shaking. afraid because he's never seen her like this. staying as close to mrs toshack as possible.

he clutches the hem of her black dress. as the widow pulls him close—lost in reminiscences of her lovely christian dish as he'd been the last time they'd spoken; elated by the progress they'd been making in the villages; his latest batch of converts having given up on an allegiance to the bush buck; now replacing it with an image of christ hanging buck-naked from a cross . . . and benedict grips folds of wet cotton. unwilling to cry . . . NOTHING. that part of him now banished in that soil. replaced with this jigging at what mrs toshack had said. about mama and baba resting in a better place. the hows of this beyond him.

 . . . what if she didn't know? what if no one knew what now happened to them and wouldn't let on . . . that no one knew?

petals of rain sluice from cheekbones into his mouth. as famished eyes feast on fields of maize and sugarcane. water running over earth cracked in places. in spaces. as he notices, the first time he really knows this, that grandmama is greying to feeble, weak.

will this also happen to him? too tired to sit up in a bed. someone coming in to clean the places one makes a life of hiding with modesty.

he squeezes the soggy hem of mrs toshack's dress. trying to forget the danger they're all in. this fear of a beyond none of them knew.

'we have a friend in jesus, my son,' she whispers. 'a friend in the lord.'

and he clutches tighter. tension abating . . .

'a friend in jesus,' he snorts. dropping another pebble into the inlet. 'fuck that noise.' . . . PLOP. and searches through pockets for a cigarette. to settle . . . anaesthetize him. KICK. afraid . . . these memories he's held at bay for so long . . . will finally devour him like the unequivocal monsoon consumes its season.

PLOP.

shaky . . . shaken into visions he's recoiled from for so long. slag heaps breaking out of silence. his creaky head drops into clammy palms. before the threat of tears— which, for so long—still will not come . . . space and time/space and rhyme. the moment slipping forward. backward. receding into . . . a hand in the small of his back startles him. sky suddenly jarred n' festooned with seeping cracks of bright lightning licks. anna . . . taking his hand. the clack following another flash . . . closer this time. as she silently pulls him north on burrard. and down/down into trails of swaying grass which slap up against outstretched fingertips. still silent as cool wind trims the fronds of her hair. shoulders touching. hands snacking on the braise of each other. a daze of electrical frays lashing deliriously out into the gloom.

rain tentatively spits/drumming against tombstones as they silently walk a cemetery. white crosses. beige slabs of stone. rain slipping sideways from rooftops out- side the bars of distant windows. a hint of ocean murmuring 'butterfly/swallow' till wind flicks water to froth at eyes so wild they bloom awkward. names. dates. as they walk on towards the seawall. old hurts momentarily shed like skin on a rattler. a tugboat hauling a ship from harbour. water crashing lickety-split. a distant lighthouse murky with graffiti/weed.

thunder draaawls/its reverberation hovering over treetops. the odd seagull chatter- ing. disappearing. as they spoon in a crevice gouged in rock. a pack of unopened players lights bobbing in the water. her sweater—thread in tatters hanging from sleeves. hair— smears of coconut oil. still silent. just staring off. salt splattering up to taste between lips. as they continue to spoon. rain falling into droplets of flavour on tongues. a fishing boat—paddles drunk at sides. as they continue to spoon.

chill descends to the belly of muscle. cutting to marrow. their names balanced between wet lips. as they continue to spoon. night passing from dark to grey to bright to day as they continue to spoon.

Shyam Selvadurai b. 1965

COLOMBO, SRI LANKA

Born in Colombo, Sri Lanka, Shyam Selvadurai grew up, as he says, 'aware of the interaction between the personal and the political'. With his parents and three siblings, Selvadurai came to Canada in 1984, after the 1983 rioting by the Tamil and Sinhalese communities. 'Being in Canada has been good,' says Selvadurai, who is a Tamil; 'it has given me a creative perspective that I might not have had otherwise.'

Selvadurai holds a BFA from York University, where he studied Creative Writing as well as Theatre Directing and Playwriting. His book *Funny Boy* (1994), the winner of the W.H. Smith–Books in Canada First Novel Award and the Lambda Literary Award for best gay men's fiction, is 'a novel in six stories' narrated from the point of view of Arjie, a young boy when the book opens. It offers a realistic portrayal of characters whose lives are shaped by the tensions holding together—and separating—collective and personal yearnings. Through Arjie's soon-to-be-lost innocence, we witness the violent and insidious confrontations between the Tamils and Sinhalese as they are dramatized through love relationships and familial ties. 'Funny', Arjie gradually learns, stands for what his society decides is queer—strange, unpredictable, unmanageable, ultimately threatening to the status quo. It also speaks of Arjie's growing sense of gay identity, an awareness that further complicates his responsibility toward his Tamil community and his family. Although not an autobiographical novel, it is an evocation of Selvadurai's background.

Though he now lives in Toronto, Selvadurai has returned to his birthplace many times and says that 'Sri Lanka is still vivid. . . . For me, life then is just a daily thing.' His second novel, *Cinnamon Gardens* (1998), is set in 1920s Sri Lanka (then Ceylon); it was shortlisted for the Trillium Book Award. His children's book *Swimming in the Monsoon Sea* (2005), also set in Sri Lanka, was nominated for the Governor General's Award. Selvadurai has also written for television and is the editor of *Storywallah! A Celebration of South Asian Fiction*.

Pigs Can't Fly

Besides Christmas and other festive occasions, spend-the-days were the days most looked forward to by all of us, cousins, aunts, and uncles.

For the adults a spend-the-day was the one Sunday of the month they were free of their progeny. The eagerness with which they anticipated these days could be seen in the way Amma woke my brother, my sister, and me extra early when they came. Unlike on school days, when Amma allowed us to dawdle a little, we were hurried through our morning preparations. Then, after a quick breakfast, we would be driven to the house of our grandparents.

The first thing that met our eyes on entering our grandparents' house, after we carefully wiped our feet on the doormat, would be the dark corridor running the length of it, on one side of which were the bedrooms and on the other the drawing and dining rooms. This corridor, with its old photographs on both walls and its ceiling so high that our footsteps echoed, scared me a little. The drawing room into which we would be ushered to pay our respects to our grandparents was also dark and smelled like old clothes that had been locked away in a suitcase for a long time. There my grandparents Ammachi and Appachi sat, enthroned in big reclining chairs. Appachi usually looked up from his paper and said vaguely, 'Ah, hello, hello,' before going back behind it, but Ammachi always called us to her with the beckoning movement of her middle and index fingers. With our legs trembling slightly, we would go to her, the thought of the big canes she kept behind her tall clothes almariah strongly imprinted upon our minds. She would grip our faces in her plump hands, and one by one kiss us wetly on both cheeks and say, 'God has blessed me with fifteen grandchildren who will look after me in my old age.' She smelled of stale coconut oil, and the diamond mukkuthi in her nose always pressed painfully against my cheek.

When the aunts and uncles eventually drove away, waving gaily at us children from car windows, we waved back at the retreating cars, with not even a pretence of sorrow. For one glorious day a month we were free of parental control and the ever-watchful eyes and tale-bearing tongues of the house servants.

We were not, alas, completely abandoned, as we would have so liked to have been. Ammachi and Janaki were supposedly in charge. Janaki, cursed with the task of having to cook for fifteen extra people, had little time for supervision and actually preferred to have nothing to do with us at all. If called upon to come and settle a dispute, she would rush out, her hands red from grinding curry paste, and box the ears of the first person who happened to be in her path. We had learned that Janaki was to be appealed to only in the most dire emergencies. The one we understood, by tacit agreement, never to appeal to was Ammachi. Like the earth-goddess in the folktales, she was not to be disturbed from her tranquillity. To do so would have been the cause of a catastrophic earthquake.

In order to minimize interference by either Ammachi or Janaki, we had developed and refined a system of handling conflict and settling disputes ourselves. Two things formed the framework of this system: territoriality and leadership.

Territorially, the area around my grandparents' house was divided into two. The front garden, the road, and the field that lay in front of the house belonged to the boys, although included in their group was my female cousin Meena. In this territory, two factions struggled for power, one led by Meena, the other by my brother, Varuna, who, because of a prevailing habit, had been renamed Diggy-Nose and then simply Diggy.

The second territory was called 'the girls', included in which, however, was myself, a boy. It was to this territory of ' the girls', confined to the back garden and the kitchen porch, that I seemed to have gravitated naturally, my earliest memories of those spend-the-days always belonging in the back garden of my grandparents' home. The pleasure the boys had standing for hours on a cricket field under the sweltering sun, watching the batsmen run from crease to crease, was incomprehensible to me.

For me, the primary attraction of the girls' territory was the potential for the free play of fantasy. Because of the force of my imagination, I was selected as leader. Whatever the game, be it the imitation of adult domestic functions or the enactment of some well-loved fairy story, it was I who discovered some new way to enliven it, some new twist to the plot of a familiar tale. Led by me, the girl cousins would conduct a raid on my grandparents' dirty-clothes basket, discovering in this odorous treasure trove saris, blouses, sheets, curtains with which we invented costumes to complement our voyages of imagination.

The reward for my leadership was that I always got to play the main part in the fantasy. If it was cooking-cooking we were playing, I was the chef; if it was Cinderella or Thumbelina, I was the much-beleaguered heroine of these tales.

Of all our varied and fascinating games, bride-bride was my favourite. In it, I was able to combine many elements of the other games I loved, and with time bride-bride, which had taken a few hours to play initially, became an event that spread out over the whole day and was planned for weeks in advance. For me the culmination of this game, and my ultimate moment of joy, was when I put on the clothes of the bride. In the late afternoon, usually after tea, I, along with the older girl cousins, would enter Janaki's room. From my sling-bag I would bring out my most prized possession, an old white sari, lightly yellow with age, its border torn and missing most of its sequins. The dressing of the bride would now begin, and then, by the transfiguration I saw taking place in Janaki's cracked full-length mirror—by the sari being wrapped around my body, the veil being pinned to my head, the rouge put on my cheeks, lipstick on my lips, kohl around my eyes—I was able to leave the constraints of myself and ascend into another, more brilliant, more beautiful self, a self to whom this day was dedicated, and around whom the world, represented by my cousins putting flowers in my hair, draping the palu, seemed to revolve. It was a self magnified, like the goddesses of the Sinhalese and Tamil cinema, larger than life; and like them, like the Malini Fonsekas and the Geetha Kumarasinghes, I was an icon, a graceful, benevolent, perfect being upon whom the adoring eyes of the world rested.

Those spend-the-days, the remembered innocence of childhood, are now coloured in the hues of the twilight sky. It is a picture made even more sentimental by the loss of all that was associated with them. By all of us having to leave Sri Lanka years later because of communal violence and forge a new home for ourselves in Canada.

Yet those Sundays, when I was seven, marked the beginning of my exile from the world I loved. Like a ship that leaves a port for the vast expanse of sea, those much looked forward to days took me away from the safe harbour of childhood towards the precarious waters of adult life.

*　　*　　*

The visits at my grandparents' began to change with the return from abroad of Kanthi Aunty, Cyril Uncle, and their daughter, Tanuja, whom we quickly renamed 'Her Fatness', in that cruelly direct way children have.

At first we had no difficulty with the newcomer in our midst. In fact we found her quite willing to accept that, by reason of her recent arrival, she must necessarily begin at the bottom.

In the hierarchy of bride-bride, the person with the least importance, less even than the priest and the page boys, was the groom. It was a role we considered stiff and boring, that held no attraction for any of us. Indeed, if we could have dispensed with that role altogether we would have, but alas it was an unfortunate feature of the marriage ceremony. My younger sister, Sonali, with her patient good nature, but also sensing that I might have a mutiny on my hands if I asked anyone else to play that role, always donned the long pants and tattered jacket, borrowed from my grandfather's clothes chest. It was now deemed fitting that Her Fatness should take over the role and thus leave Sonali free to wrap a bedsheet around her body, in the manner of a sari, and wear araliya flowers in her hair like the other bridesmaids.

For two spend-the-days, Her Fatness accepted her role without a murmur and played it with all the skilled unobtrusiveness of a bit player. The third spend-the-day, however, everything changed. That day turned out to be my grandmother's birthday. Instead of dropping the children off and driving away as usual, the aunts and uncles stayed on for lunch, a slight note of peevish displeasure in their voices.

We had been late, because etiquette (or rather my father) demanded that Amma wear a sari for the grand occasion of her mother-in-law's sixtieth birthday. Amma's tardiness and her insistence on getting her palu to fall to exactly above her knees drove us all to distraction (especially Diggy, who quite rightly feared that in his absence Meena would try to persuade the better members of his team to defect to her side). Even I, who usually loved the ritual of watching Amma get dressed, stood in her doorway with the others and fretfully asked if she was ever going to be ready.

When we finally did arrive at Ramanaygam Road, everyone else had been there almost an hour. We were ushered into the drawing room by Amma to kiss Ammachi and present her with her gift, the three of us clutching the present. All the uncles and aunts were seated. Her Fatness stood in between Kanthi Aunty's knees, next to Ammachi. When she saw us, she gave me an accusing, hostile look and pressed further between her mother's legs. Kanthi Aunty turned away from her discussion with Mala Aunty, and, seeing me, she smiled and said in a tone that was as heavily sweetened as undiluted rose-syrup, 'So, what is this I hear, aah? Nobody will play with my little daughter.'

I looked at her and then at Her Fatness, shocked by the lie. All my senses were alert.

Kanthi Aunty wagged her finger at me and said in a playful, chiding tone, 'Now, now, Arjie, you must be nice to my little daughter. After all, she's just come from abroad and everything.' Fortunately, I was prevented from having to answer. It was my turn to present my cheek to Ammachi, and, for the first time, I did so willingly, preferring the prick of the diamond mukkuthi to Kanthi Aunty's honeyed admonition.

Kanthi Aunty was the fourth oldest in my father's family. First there was my father, then Ravi Uncle, Mala Aunty, Kanthi Aunty, Babu Uncle, Seelan Uncle, and finally Radha Aunty, who was much younger than the others and was away, studying in America. Kanthi Aunty was tall and bony, and we liked her the least, in spite of the fact that she would pat our heads affectionately whenever we walked past or greeted her. We sensed that beneath her benevolence lurked a seething anger, tempered by guile, that could have deadly consequences if unleashed in our direction. I had heard Amma say to her sister, Neliya Aunty, that 'Poor Kanthi was bitter because of the humiliations she had suffered abroad. After all, darling, what a thing, forced to work as a servant in a whitey's house to make ends meet.'

Once Ammachi had opened the present, a large silver serving tray, and thanked us for it (and insisted on kissing us once again), my brother, my sister, and I were finally allowed to leave the room. Her Fatness had already disappeared. I hurried out the front door and ran around the side of the house.

When I reached the back garden I found the girl cousins squatting on the porch in a circle. They were so absorbed in what was happening in the centre that none of them even heard my greeting. Lakshmi finally became aware of my presence and beckoned me over excitedly. I reached the circle and the cause of her excitement became clear. In the middle, in front of Her Fatness, sat a long-legged doll with shiny gold hair. Her dress was like that of a fairy queen, the gauze skirt sprinkled with tiny silver stars. Next to her sat her male counterpart, dressed in a pale-blue suit. I stared in wonder at the marvellous dolls. For us cousins, who had grown up under a government that strictly limited all foreign imports, such toys were unimaginable. Her Fatness turned to the other cousins and asked them if they wanted to hold the dolls for a moment. They nodded eagerly and the dolls passed from hand to hand. I moved closer to get a better look. My gaze involuntarily rested on Her Fatness and she gave me a smug look. Immediately her scheme became evident to me. It was with these dolls that my cousin from abroad hoped to seduce the other cousins away from me.

Unfortunately for her, she had underestimated the power of bride-bride. When the other cousins had all looked at the dolls, they bestirred themselves and, without so much as a backward glance, hurried down the steps to prepare for the marriage ceremony. As I followed them, I looked triumphantly at Her Fatness, who sat on the porch, clasping her beautiful dolls to her chest.

When lunch was over, my grandparents retired to their room for a nap. The other adults settled in the drawing room to read the newspaper or doze off in the huge armchairs. We, the bride-to-be and the bridesmaids, retired to Janaki's room for the long-awaited ritual of dressing the bride.

We were soon disturbed, however, by the sound of booming laughter. At first we ignored it, but when it persisted, getting louder and more drawn out, my sister, Sonali, went to the door and looked out. Her slight gasp brought us all out onto the porch. There the groom strutted, up and down, head thrown back, stomach stuck out. She sported a huge bristly moustache (torn out of the broom) and a cigarette (of rolled paper and talcum powder), which she held between her fingers and puffed on vigorously. The younger cousins, instead of getting dressed and putting the final touches to the altar, sat along the edge of the porch and watched with great amusement.

'Aha, me hearties!' the groom cried on seeing us. She opened her hands expansively. 'Bring me my fair maiden, for I must be off to my castle before the sun setest.'

We looked at the groom, aghast at the change in her behaviour. She sauntered towards us, then stopped in front of me, winked expansively and, with her hand under my chin, tilted back my head.

'Ahhh!' she exclaimed. 'A bonny lass, a bonny lass indeed.'

'Stop it!' I cried, and slapped her hand. 'The groom is not supposed to make a noise.'

'Why not?' Her Fatness replied angrily, dropping her hearty voice and accent. 'Why can't the groom make a noise?'

'Because.'

'Because of what?'

'Because the game is called bride-bride, not groom-groom.'

Her Fatness seized her moustache and flung it to the ground dramatically. 'Well I don't want to be the groom any more. I want to be the bride.'

We stared at her in disbelief, amazed by her impudent challenge to my position. 'You can't,' I finally said.

'Why not?' Her Fatness demanded. 'Why should you always be the bride? Why can't someone else have a chance too?'

'Because . . .' Sonali said, joining in. 'Because Arjie is the bestest bride of all.'

'But he's not even a girl,' Her Fatness said, closing in on the lameness of Sonali's argument. 'A bride is a girl, not a boy.' She looked around at the other cousins and then at me. 'A boy cannot be the bride,' she said with deep conviction. 'A girl must be the bride.'

I stared at her, defenceless in the face of her logic.

Fortunately, Sonali, loyal to me as always, came to my rescue. She stepped in between us and said to Her Fatness, 'If you can't play properly, go away. We don't need you.'

'Yes!' Lakshmi, another of my supporters, cried.

The other cousins, emboldened by Sonali's fearlessness, murmured in agreement.

Her Fatness looked at all of us for a moment and then her gaze rested on me.

'You're a pansy,' she said, her lips curling in disgust.

We looked at her blankly.

'A faggot,' she said, her voice rising against our uncomprehending stares.

'A sissy!' she shouted in desperation.

It was clear by this time that these were insults.

'Give me that jacket,' Sonali said. She stepped up to Her Fatness and began to pull at it. 'We don't like you any more.'

'Yes!' Lakshmi cried. 'Go away you fatty-boom-boom!'

This was an insult we all understood, and we burst out laughing. Someone even began to chant, 'Hey fatty-boom-boom. Hey fatty-boom-boom.'

Her Fatness pulled off her coat and trousers. 'I hate you all,' she cried. 'I wish you were all dead.' She flung the groom's clothes on the ground, stalked out of the back garden, and went around the side of the house.

We returned to our bridal preparations, chuckling to ourselves over the new nickname we had found for our cousin.

When the bride was finally dressed, Lakshmi, the maid of honour, went out of Janaki's room to make sure that everything was in place. Then she gave the signal and the priest and choirboys began to sing, with a certain want of harmony and correct lyrics, 'The voice that breathed on Eeeden, the first and glorious day. . . .' Solemnly, I made my way down the steps towards the altar that had been set up at one end of the back garden. When I reached the altar, however, I heard the kitchen door open. I turned to see Her Fatness with Kanthi Aunty. The discordant singing died out.

Kanthi Aunty's benevolent smile had completely disappeared and her eyes were narrowed with anger.

'Who's calling my daughter fatty?' Kanthi Aunty said. She came to the edge of the porch.

We stared at her, no one daring to own up.

Her gaze fell on me and her eyes widened for a moment. Then a smile spread across her face.

'What's this?' she said, the honey seeping back into her voice. She came down a few steps and crooked her finger at me. I looked down at my feet and refused to go to her.

'Come here, come here,' she said.

Unable to disobey her command any longer, I went to her. She looked me up and down for a moment, and then gingerly, as if she were examining raw meat at the market, turned me around.

'What's this you're playing?' she asked.

'It's bride-bride, Aunty,' Sonali said.

'Bride-bride,' she murmured.

Her hand closed on my arm in a tight grip.

'Come with me,' she said.

I resisted, but her grip tightened, her nails digging into my elbow. She pulled me up the porch steps and towards the kitchen door.

'No,' I cried. 'No, I don't want to.'

Something about the look in her eyes terrified me so much I did the unthinkable and I hit out at her. This made her hold my arm even more firmly. She dragged me through the kitchen, past Janaki, who looked up, curious, and into the corridor and towards the drawing room. I felt a heaviness begin to build in my stomach. Instinctively I knew that Kanthi Aunty had something terrible in mind.

As we entered the drawing room, Kanthi Aunty cried out, her voice brimming over with laughter, 'See what I found!'

The other aunts and uncles looked up from their papers or bestirred themselves from their sleep. They gazed at me in amazement as if I had suddenly made myself visible, like a spirit. I glanced at them and then at Amma's face. Seeing her expression, I felt my dread deepen. I lowered my eyes. The sari suddenly felt suffocating around my body, and the hairpins, which held the veil in place, pricked at my scalp.

Then the silence was broken by the booming laugh of Cyril Uncle, Kanthi Aunty's husband. As if she had been hit, Amma swung around in his direction. The other aunts and uncles began to laugh too, and I watched as Amma looked from one to the other like a trapped animal. Her gaze finally came to rest on my father and for the first time I noticed that he was the only one not laughing. Seeing the way he kept his eyes fixed on his paper, I felt the heaviness in my stomach begin to push its way up my throat.

'Ey, Chelva,' Cyril Uncle cried out jovially to my father, 'looks like you have a funny one here.'

My father pretended he had not heard and, with an inclination of his head, indicated to Amma to get rid of me.

She waved her hand in my direction and I picked up the edges of my veil and fled to the back of the house.

That evening, on the way home, both my parents kept their eyes averted from me. Amma glanced at my father occasionally, but he refused to meet her gaze. Sonali, sensing my unease, held my hand tightly in hers.

Later, I heard my parents fighting in their room.

'How long has this been going on?' my father demanded.

'I don't know,' Amma cried defensively. 'It was as new to me as it was to you.'

'You should have known. You should have kept an eye on him.'

'What should I have done? Stood over him while he was playing?'

'If he turns out funny like that Rankotwera boy, if he turns out to be the laughing-stock of Colombo, it'll be your fault,' my father said in a tone of finality. 'You always spoil him and encourage all his nonsense.'

'What do I encourage?' Amma demanded.

'You are the one who allows him to come in here while you're dressing and play with your jewellery.'

Amma was silent in the face of the truth.

Of the three of us, I alone was allowed to enter Amma's bedroom and watch her get dressed for special occasions. It was an experience I considered almost religious, for, even though I adored the goddesses of the local cinema, Amma was the final statement in female beauty for me.

When I knew Amma was getting dressed for a special occasion, I always positioned myself outside her door. Once she had put on her underskirt and blouse, she would ring for our servant, Anula, to bring her sari, and then, while taking it from her, hold the door open so I could go in as well. Entering that room was, for me, a greater boon than that granted by any god to a mortal. There were two reasons for this. The first was the jewellery box which lay open on the dressing table. With a joy akin to ecstasy, I would lean over and gaze inside, the faint smell of perfume rising out of the box each time I picked up a piece of jewellery and held it against my nose or ears or throat. The second was the pleasure of watching Amma drape her sari, watching her shake open the yards of material, which, like a Chinese banner caught by the wind, would linger in the air for a moment before drifting gently to the floor; watching her pick up one end of it, tuck it into the waistband of her skirt, make the pleats, and then with a flick of her wrists invert the pleats and tuck them into her waistband; and finally watching her drape the palu across her breasts and pin it into place with a brooch.

When Amma was finished, she would check to make sure that the back of the sari had not risen up with the pinning of the palu, then move back and look at herself in the mirror. Standing next to her or seated on the edge of the bed, I, too, would look at her reflection in the mirror, and, with the contented sigh of an artist who has finally captured the exact effect he wants, I would say, 'You should have been a film star, Amma.'

'A film star?' she would cry and lightly smack the side my head. 'What kind of a low-class-type person do you think I am?'

One day, about a week after the incident at my grandparents', I positioned myself outside my parents' bedroom door. When Anula arrived with the sari, Amma took it and quickly shut the door. I waited patiently, thinking Amma had not yet put on her blouse and skirt, but the door never opened. Finally, perplexed that Amma had forgotten, I knocked timidly on the door. She did not answer, but I could hear her moving around inside. I knocked a little louder and called out 'Amma' through the keyhole. Still no response, and I was about to call her name again when she replied gruffly, 'Go away. Can't you see I am busy?'

I stared disbelievingly at the door. Inside I could hear the rustle of the sari as it brushed along the floor. I lifted my hand to knock again when suddenly I remembered the quarrel I had heard on the night of that last spend-the-day. My hand fell limply by my side.

I crept away quietly to my bedroom, sat down on the edge of my bed, and stared at my feet for a long time. It was clear to me that I had done something wrong, but what it was I couldn't comprehend. I thought of what my father had said about turning out 'funny'. The word 'funny' as I understood it meant either humorous or strange, as in the expression, 'that's funny'. Neither of these fitted the sense in which my father had used the word, for there had been a hint of disgust in his tone.

Later, Amma came out of her room and called Anula to give her instructions for the evening. As I listened to the sound of her voice, I realized that something had changed forever between us.

A little while after my parents had left for their dinner party, Sonali came looking for me. Seeing my downcast expression, she sat next to me, and, though unaware of anything that had passed, slipped her hand in mine. I pushed it away roughly, afraid that if I let her squeeze my hand I would start to cry.

The next morning Amma and I were like two people who had had a terrible fight the night before. I found it hard to look her in the eye and she seemed in an unusually gay mood.

The following spend-the-day, when Amma came to awaken us, I was already seated in bed and folding my bride-bride sari. Something in her expression, however, made me hurriedly return the sari to the bag.

'What's that?' she said, coming towards me, her hand outstretched. After a moment I gave her the bag. She glanced at its contents briefly. 'Get up, it's spend-the-day,' she said. Then, with the bag in her hand, she went to the window and looked out into the driveway. The seriousness of her expression, as if I had done something so awful that even the usual punishment of a caning would not suffice, frightened me.

I was brushing my teeth after breakfast when Anula came to the bathroom door, peered inside, and said with a sort of grim pleasure, 'Missie wants to talk to you in her room.' Seeing the alarm in my face, she nodded and said sagely, 'Up to some kind of mischief as usual. Good-for-nothing child.'

My brother, Diggy, was standing in the doorway of our parents' room, one foot scratching impatiently against the other. Amma was putting on her lipstick. My father had already gone for his Sunday squash game, and, as usual, she would pick him up after she had dropped us off at our grandparents'.

Amma looked up from the mirror, saw me, and indicated with her tube of lipstick for both of us to come inside and sit down on the edge of the bed. Diggy gave me a baleful look, as if it was my fault that Amma was taking such a long time to get ready. He followed me into the room, his slippers dragging along the floor.

Finally Amma closed her lipstick, pressed her lips together to even out the colour, then turned to us.

'Okay, mister,' she said to Diggy, 'I am going to tell you something and this is an order.'

We watched her carefully.

'I want you to include your younger brother on your cricket team.'

Diggy and I looked at her in shocked silence, then he cried, 'Ah! Come on, Amma!'

And I, too, cried out, 'I don't want to play with them. I hate cricket!'

'I don't care what you want,' Amma said. 'It's good for you.'

'Arjie's useless,' Diggy said. 'We'll never win if he's on our team.'

Amma held up her hand to silence us. 'That's an order,' she said.

'Why?' I asked, ignoring her gesture. 'Why do I have to play with the boys?'

'Why?' Amma said. 'Because the sky is so high and pigs can't fly, that's why.'

'Please, Amma! Please!' I held out my arms to her.

Amma turned away quickly, picked up the handbag from the dressing table, and said, almost to herself, 'If the child turns out wrong, it's the mother they always blame, never the father.' She clicked the handbag shut.

I put my head in my hands and began to cry. 'Please, Amma, please,' I said through my sobs.

She continued to face the window.

I flung myself on the bed with a wail of anguish. I waited for her to come to me as she always did when I cried, waited for her to take me in her arms, rest my head against her breasts, and say in her special voice, 'What's this, now? Who's the little man who's crying?'

But she didn't heed my weeping any more than she had heeded my cries when I knocked on her door.

Finally I stopped crying and rolled over on my back. Diggy had left the room.

Amma turned to me, now that I had become quiet, and said cheerfully, 'You'll have a good time, just wait and see.'

'Why can't I play with the girls?' I replied.

'You can't, that's all.'

'But why?'

She shifted uneasily.

'You're a big boy now. And big boys must play with other boys.'

'That's stupid.'

'It doesn't matter,' she said. 'Life is full of stupid things and sometimes we just have to do them.'

'I won't,' I said defiantly. 'I won't play with the boys.'

Her face reddened with anger. She reached down, caught me by the shoulders, and shook me hard. Then she turned away and ran her hand through her hair. I watched her, gloating. I had broken her cheerful façade, forced her to show how much it pained her to do what she was doing, how little she actually believed in the justness of her actions.

After a moment she turned back to me and said in an almost pleading tone, 'You'll have a good time.'

I looked at her and said, 'No I won't.'

Her back straightened. She crossed to the door and stopped. Without looking at me she said, stiffly, 'The car leaves in five minutes. If you're not in it by then, watch out.'

I lay back on the bed and gazed at the mosquito net swinging gently in the breeze. In my mind's eye, I saw the day that stretched ahead of me. At the thought of having to waste the most precious day of the month in that field in front of my grandparents' house, the hot sun beating on my head, the perspiration running down the sides of my face, I felt a sense of despair begin to take hold of me. The picture of what would take place in the back garden became clear. I saw Her Fatness seizing my place as leader of the girls, claiming for herself the rituals I had so carefully invented and planned. I saw her standing in front of Janaki's mirror as the other girls fixed her hair, pinned her veil, and draped her sari. The thought was terrible. Something had to be done. I could not give up that easily, could not let Her Fatness, whose sneaking to Kanthi Aunty had forced me into the position I was now in, so easily take my place. But what could I do?

As if in answer, an object which rested just at the periphery of my vision claimed my attention. I turned my head slightly and saw my sling-bag. Then a thought came to me. I reached out, picked up the bag, and hugged it close to my chest. Without the sari in that bag, it was impossible for the girls to play bride-bride. I thought of Her Fatness with triumph. What would she drape around her body? A bedsheet like the brides-maids? No! Without me and my sari she would not be able to play bride-bride properly.

There was, I realized, an obstacle that had to be overcome first. I would have to get out of playing cricket. Amma had laid down an order and I knew Diggy well enough to know that, in spite of all his boldness, he would never dare to disobey an order from Amma.

I heard the car start up, and its sound reminded me of another problem that I had not considered. How was I going to smuggle the sari into the car? Amma would be waiting in the car for me, and if I arrived with the sling-bag she would make me take it back. I could not slip it in without her noticing. I sat still, listening to the whir of the engine at counterpoint to the clatter of Anula clearing the breakfast table, and suddenly a plan revealed itself to me.

I took the sari out of the bag and folded the bag so that it looked like there was something in it and left it on the bed. Taking the sari with me, I went to the bedroom door and peered out. The hall was empty. I went into Sonali's room, which was next to my parents', and I crouched down on one side of the doorway. I took off my slip-pers and held them with the sari in my arms. The curtain in the open doorway of Sonali's room blew slightly in the breeze and I moved further away from it so that I would not be seen. After what seemed like an interminable amount of time, I heard

Amma coming down the hallway to fetch me from her room. I crouched even lower as the sound of her footsteps got closer. From below the curtain, I saw her go into her room. As she entered, I stood up, pushed aside the curtain, and darted down the hallway. She came out of her room and called to me, but I didn't stop, and ran outside.

Thankfully the rear door of the car was open. I jumped in, quickly stuffed the sari into Sonali's sling-bag, and lay back against the seat, panting. Diggy and Sonali were looking at me strangely but they said nothing.

Soon Amma came out and got into the car. She glared at me and I gave her an innocent look. I smiled at Sonali conspiratorially. Sonali, my strongest ally, was doing her best to keep the bewilderment out of her face. By way of explanation, I said, with pretend gloominess, 'I can't play with you today. Amma says that I must play with the boys.'

Sonali looked at me in amazement and then turned to Amma. 'Why can't he play with the girls?' she said.

'Why?' Amma said and started up the car. 'Because the sky is so high and pigs can't fly.'

Amma sounded less sure of herself this time and a little weary. Looking in front, I saw that Diggy had turned in his seat and was regarding me morosely. I was reminded that the sari in the bag was worth nothing if I couldn't get out of the long day of cricket that lay ahead of me.

All the way to my grandparents' house, I gazed at the back of Diggy's head, hoping inspiration would come. The sound of his feet kicking irritably against the underside of the glove compartment confirmed that, however bad the consequences, he would follow Amma's orders. The sound of that ill-natured kicking made me search my mind all the more desperately for a way to escape playing cricket with the boys.

When the car turned down Ramanaygam Road, I still had not thought of anything. Meena was standing on top of the garden wall, her legs apart, her hands on her hips, her panties already dirty underneath her short dress. The boy cousins were on the wall on either side of her.

As we walked up the path to pay our respects to Ammachi and Appachi, I whispered to Sonali to keep the sari hidden and to tell no one about it. When we went into the drawing room, Her Fatness, who was as usual between Kanthi Aunty's knees, gave me a victorious look. A feeling of panic began to rise in me that no plan of escape had yet presented itself.

Once we had gone through the ritual of presenting our cheeks to our grandparents, we followed Amma outside to say goodbye.

'You children be good,' Amma said before she got into the car. She looked pointedly at me. 'I don't want to hear that you've given Ammachi and Appachi any trouble.'

I watched her departing car with a sense of sorrow.

Diggy grabbed my arm. I followed reluctantly as he hurried across the road, still holding on to me, as if afraid I would run away.

The wickets had already been set up in the field in front of the house and the boys and Meena were seated under a guava tree. When they saw us come towards them, they stopped talking and stared at us.

Muruges, who was on Diggy's team, stood up.

'What's he doing here?' he demanded, waving his half-eaten guava at me.

'He's going to play.'

'What?' the others cried in amazement.

They looked at Diggy as if he had lost his mind.

'He's not going to play on our team, is he?' Muruges said, more a threat than a question.

'He's quite good,' Diggy answered halfheartedly.

'If he's going to be on our team, I'm changing sides,' Muruges declared, and some of the others murmured in agreement.

'Come on, guys,' Diggy said with desperation in his voice, but they remained stern.

Diggy turned to Meena. 'I'll trade you Arjie for Sanjay.'

Meena spat out the seeds of the guava she was eating. 'Do you think I'm mad or something?'

'Ah, come on,' Diggy said in a wheedling tone, 'he's good. We've been practising the whole week.'

'If he's so good, why don't you keep him yourself. Maybe with him on your team you might actually win.'

'Yeah,' Sanjay cried, insulted that I was considered an equal trade for him. 'Why don't you keep the girlie-boy?'

At the new nickname 'girlie-boy', everyone roared with laughter, and even Diggy grinned.

I should have felt humiliated and dejected that nobody wanted me on their team but instead I felt the joy of relief begin to dance inside of me. The escape I had searched for was offering itself without any effort on my part. If Diggy's best team members were threatening to abandon him he would have no alternative but to let me go. I looked at my feet so that no one would see the hope in my eyes.

Unfortunately, the nickname 'girlie-boy' had an effect which I had not predicted. The joke at my expense seemed to clear the air. After laughing heartily, Muruges withdrew his threat. 'What the hell,' he said benevolently. 'It can't hurt to have another fielder. But,' he added, as a warning to Diggy, 'he can't bat.'

Diggy nodded as if he had never even considered letting me bat. Since each side had only fifty overs, it was vital to send the best batsmen in first, and often the younger cousins never got a chance.

I glared at Muruges, and he, thinking that my look was a reaction to the new nickname, said 'girlie-boy' again.

Diggy now laughed loudly, but in his laugh I detected a slight note of servility and also relief that the catastrophe of losing his team had been averted. I saw that the balance he was trying to maintain between following Amma's orders and keeping his team members happy was extremely precarious. All was not lost. Such a fragile balance would be easy to upset.

The opportunity to do this arose almost immediately.

Our team was to go first. In deciding the batting order, there was a certain system that the boys always followed. The captain would mark numbers in the sand with hyphens next to each and then cover the numbers with a bat. The players, who had been asked to turn their backs, would then come over and choose a hyphen. What was strange to me about this exercise was its redundancy, for, when the numbers were uncovered, no matter what the batting order, the older and better players always went first, the younger cousins assenting without a murmur.

When Diggy uncovered the numbers, I was first, Diggy was second. Muruges had one of the highest numbers and would bat towards the end, if at all. 'Well,' Muruges said to Diggy in a tone that spoke of promises already made, 'I'll take Arjie's place.'

Diggy nodded vigorously as if Muruges had read his very thoughts.

Unfortunately for him, I had other plans.

'I want to go first,' I said firmly, and waited for my request to produce the necessary consequences.

Muruges was crouched down, fixing his pads, and he straightened up slowly. The slowness of his action conveyed his anger at my daring to make such a suggestion and at the same time challenged Diggy to change the batting order.

Meena, unexpectedly, came to my defence. 'He is the first!' she said. 'Fair is fair!' In a game of only fifty overs, a bad opening bat would be ideal for her team.

'Fair is fair,' I echoed Meena. 'I picked first place and I should be allowed to play!'

'You can't,' Diggy said desperately, 'Muruges always goes first.'

Meena's team, encouraged by her, also began to cry out, 'Fair is fair!'

Diggy quickly crossed over to Muruges, put his arm around his shoulder, turned him away from the others, and talked earnestly to him. But Muruges shook his head, unconvinced by whatever Diggy was saying. Finally Diggy dropped his hand from Muruges's shoulder and cried out in exasperation at him, 'Come on, men!' In response, Muruges began to unbuckle his pads. Diggy put his hand on his shoulder, but he shrugged it off. Diggy, seeing that Muruges was determined, turned to me.

'Come on, Arjie,' he said, pleading, 'you can go later in the game.'

'No,' I said stubbornly, and, just to show how determined I was, I picked up the bat. 'I'm on your team now,' he announced to Meena.

'Ah, no! Come on men!' Diggy shouted in protest.

Muruges began to cross over to where Meena's team was gathered.

Diggy turned towards me now and grabbed the bat.

'*You* go!' he cried. 'We don't need *you*.' He pulled the bat out of my hands and started to walk with it towards Muruges.

'You're a cheater, cheater pumpkin-eater! I chose to bat first!' I yelled.

But I had gone too far. Diggy turned and looked at me. Then he howled as he realized how he had been tricked. Instead of giving Muruges the bat, he lifted it above his head and ran towards me. I turned and fled across the field towards my grandparents' gate. When I reached it, I lifted the latch, went inside the garden, and quickly put the latch back into place. Diggy stopped when he reached the gate. Safe on my side, I made a face at him through the slats. He came close and I retreated a little. Putting his head through the slats, he hissed at me, 'If you ever come near the field again, you'll be sorry.'

'Don't worry,' I replied tartly, 'I never will.'

And with that, I forever closed any possibility of entering the boys' world again. But I didn't care, and just to show how much I didn't care I made another face, turned my back on Diggy, and walked up the front path to the house. As I went through the narrow passageway between the house and the side wall that led to the back, I could hear the girls' voices as they prepared for bride-bride, and especially Her Fatness's, ordering everyone around. When I reached the back garden, I stopped when I saw the wedding cake. The bottom layer consisted of mud pies moulded from half a coconut shell. They supported the lid of a biscuit tin, which had three mud pies on it. On these rested the cover of a condensed-milk tin with a single mud pie on top. This was the three-tiered design that *I* had invented. Her Fatness had copied my design exactly. Further, she had taken upon herself the sole honour of decorating it with florets of grandapahana flowers and trails of antigonon, in the same way I had always done.

Sonali was the first to become aware of my presence. 'Arjie!' she said, pleased.

The other cousins now noticed me and they also exclaimed in delight. Lakshmi called out to me to come and join them, but before I could do so Her Fatness rose to her feet.

'What do you want?' she said.

I came forward a bit and she immediately stepped towards me, like a female mongoose defending her young against a cobra. 'Go away!' she cried, holding up her hand. 'Boys are not allowed here.'

I didn't heed her command.

'Go away,' she cried again. 'Otherwise I'm going to tell Ammachi!'

I looked at her for a moment, but fearing that she would see the hatred in my eyes, I glanced down at the ground.

'I want to play bride-bride, please,' I said, trying to sound as pathetic and inoffensive as possible.

'Bride-bride,' Her Fatness repeated mockingly.

'Yes,' I said, in a shy whisper.

Sonali stood up. 'Can't he play?' she said to Her Fatness. 'He'll be very good.'

'Yes, he'll be very good,' the others murmured in agreement.

Her Fatness considered their request.

'I have something that you don't have,' I said quickly, hoping to sway her decision.

'Oh, what is that?'

'The sari!'

'The sari?' she echoed. A look of malicious slyness flickered across her face.

'Yes,' I said. 'Without the sari you can't play bride-bride.'

'Why not?' Her Fatness said with indifference.

Her lack of concern about the sari puzzled me. Fearing that it might not have the same importance for her as it did for me, I cried out, 'Why not?' and pretended to be amazed that she would ask such a question. 'What is the bride going to wear, then? A bedsheet?'

Her Fatness played with a button on her dress. 'Where is the sari?' she asked very casually.

'It's a secret,' I said. I was not going to give it to her until I was firmly entrenched in the girls' world again. 'If you let me play, I will give it to you when it's time for the bride to get ready.'

A smile crossed her face. 'The thing is, Arjie,' she said in a very reasonable tone, 'we've already decided what everyone is going to be for bride-bride and we don't need anyone else.'

'But there must be some parts you need people for,' I said and then added, 'I'll play *any* part.'

'Any part,' Her Fatness repeated. Her eyes narrowed and she looked at me appraisingly.

'Let him play,' Sonali and the others said.

'I'll play any part,' I reiterated.

'You know what?' Her Fatness said suddenly, as if the idea had just dawned on her. 'We don't have a groom.'

That Her Fatness wanted me to swallow the bitter pill of humiliation was clear, and so great was my longing to be part of the girls' world again that I swallowed it.

'I'll take it,' I said.

'Okay,' Her Fatness said as if it mattered little to her whether I did or not.

The others cried out in delight and I smiled, happy that my goal had been at least partially achieved. Sonali beckoned to me to come and help them. I went towards where the preparations were being made for the wedding feast, but Her Fatness quickly stepped in front of me.

'The groom cannot help with the cooking.'

'Why not?' I protested.

'Because grooms don't do that.'

'They do.'

'Have you ever heard of a groom doing that?'

I couldn't say I had, so I demanded with angry sarcasm, 'What do grooms do then?'

'They go to office.'

'Office?' I said.

Her Fatness nodded and pointed to the table on the back porch. The look on her face told me she would not tolerate any argument.

'I can't go to office,' I said quickly. 'It's Sunday.'

'We're pretending it's Monday,' Her Fatness replied glibly.

I glared at her. Not satisfied with the humiliation she had forced me to accept, she was determined to keep my participation in bride-bride to a minimum. For an instant I thought to refuse her, but, seeing the warning look in her eyes, I finally acquiesced and went up the porch steps.

From there, I watched the other cousins getting ready for the wedding. Using a stone, I began to bang on the table as if stamping papers. I noted, with pleasure, that the sound irritated Her Fatness. I pressed an imaginary buzzer and made a loud noise. Getting no response from anyone, I did so again. Finally the other cousins looked up. 'Boy,' I called out imperiously to Sonali, 'come here, boy.'

Sonali left her cooking and came up the steps with the cringing attitude of the office peons at my father's bank.

'Yes sir, yes sir,' she said breathlessly. Her performance was so accurate that the cousins stopped to observe her.

'Take this to the bank manager in Bambalapitiya,' I said. Bowing again she took the imaginary letter and hurried down the steps. I pressed my buzzer again. 'Miss,' I called to Lakshmi. 'Miss, can you come here and take some dictation.'

'Yes, sir, coming sir,' Lakshmi said, fluttering her eyelashes, with the exaggerated coyness of a Sinhala comic actress. She came up the steps, wriggling her hips for the amusement of her audience. Everyone laughed except Her Fatness.

When Lakshmi finished the dictation and went down the steps, the other cousins cried out, 'Me! Me!' and clamoured to be the peon I would call next. But, before I could choose one of them, Her Fatness stormed up the steps.

'Stop that!' she shouted at me. 'You're disturbing us.'

'No!' I cried back, now that I had the support of everyone else.

'If you can't behave, go away.'

'If I go away, you won't get the sari.'

Her Fatness looked at me a long moment and then smiled.

'What sari?' she said. 'I bet you don't even have the sari.'

'Yes, I do,' I said in an earnest tone.

'Where?'

'It's a secret.'

'You are lying. I know you don't have it.'

'I do! I do!'

'Show me.'

'No.'

'You don't have it and I'm going to tell Janaki you are disturbing us.'

I didn't move, wanting to see if she would carry out her threat. She crossed behind the table and walked towards the kitchen door. When she got to the door and I was sure she was serious, I jumped up.

'Where is it?' I said urgently to Sonali.

She pointed to Janaki's room.

I ran to Janaki's door, opened it, and went inside. Sonali's bag was lying on the bed, and I picked it up and rushed back out onto the porch. Her Fatness had come away from the kitchen door.

'Here!' I cried.

Her Fatness folded her arms. 'Where?' she said tauntingly. I opened the bag, put my hand inside, and felt around for the sari. I touched a piece of clothing and drew it out. It was only Sonali's change of clothes. I put my hand inside again and this time brought out an Enid Blyton book. There was nothing else in the bag.

'Where is the sari?' Her Fatness demanded.

I glanced at Sonali and she gave me a puzzled look.

'Liar, liar on the wall, who's the liarest one of all!' Her Fatness cried.

I turned towards Janaki's door, wondering if the sari had fallen out. Then I saw a slight smirk on Her Fatness's face and the truth came to me. She'd known all along about the sari. She must have discovered it earlier and hidden it. I realized I had been duped and felt a sudden rush of anger. Her Fatness saw the comprehension in my eyes and her arms dropped by her sides as if in readiness. She inched back towards the kitchen door for safety. But I was not interested in her for the moment. What I wanted was the sari.

I rushed into Janaki's room.

'I'm going to tell Janaki you're in her room!' Her Fatness cried.

'Tell and catch my long fat tail!' I shouted back.

I looked around Janaki's room. Her Fatness must have hidden it here. There was no other place. I lifted Janaki's mattress. There was nothing under it, save a few Sinhala love-comics. I went to Janaki's suitcase and began to go through the clothes she kept neatly folded inside it. As silent as a shadow, Her Fatness slipped into the room. I became aware of her presence and turned. But too late. She took the sari from the shelf where she had hidden it and ran out the door. Leaving the suitcase still open, I ran after her. The sari clutched to her chest, she rushed for the kitchen door. Luckily Sonali and Lakshmi were blocking her way. Seeing me coming at her, she jumped off the porch and began to head towards the front of the house. I leapt off the porch and chased after her. If she got to the front of the house, she would go straight to Ammachi.

Just as she reached the passageway, I managed to get hold of her arm. She turned, desperate, and struck out at me. Ducking her blow, I reached for the sari and managed to get some of it in my hand. She tried to take it back from me, but I held on tightly. Crying out, she jerked away from me with her whole body, hoping to wrest the sari from my grip. With a rasping sound, the sari began to tear. I yelled at her to stop pulling, but she jerked away again and the sari tore all the way down. There was a moment of stunned silence. I gazed at the torn sari in my hand, at the long threads that hung from it. Then, with a wail of anguish, I rushed at Her Fatness and grabbed hold of her hair. She screamed and flailed at me. I yanked her head so far to one side that it almost touched her shoulder. She let out a guttural sound and struck out desperately at me. Her fist caught me in the stomach and she managed to loosen my grip.

She began to run towards the porch steps, crying out for Ammachi and Janaki. I ran after her and grabbed the sleeve of her dress before she went up the porch steps. She struggled against my grip and the sleeve ripped open and hung down her arm like a broken limb. Free once again, she stumbled up the steps towards the kitchen door, shouting at the top of her voice.

Janaki rushed out of the kitchen. She raised her hand and looked around for the first person to wallop, but when she saw Her Fatness with her torn dress, she held ner raised hand to her cheek and cried out in consternation, 'Buddu Ammo!'

Now Her Fatness began to call out only for Ammachi.

Janaki came hurriedly towards her. 'Shhh! Shhhh!' she said, but Her Fatness only increased the volume of her cry.

'What's wrong? What's wrong?' Janaki cried impatiently.

Her Fatness pointed to me.

'Janakiii! See what that boy did,' she replied.

'I didn't do anything,' I yelled, enraged that she was trying to push the blame onto me.

I ran back to where I had dropped the sari, picked it up, and held it out to Janaki.

'Yes!' Sonali cried, coming to my defence. 'She did it and now she's blaming him.'

'It's her fault!' Lakshmi said, also taking my side.

Now all the voices of the girl cousins rose in a babble supporting my case and accusing Her Fatness.

'Quiet!' Janaki shouted in desperation. 'Quiet!'

But nobody heeded her. We all crowded around her, so determined to give our version of the story that it was a while before we became aware of Ammachi's presence in the kitchen doorway. Gradually, like the hush that descends on a garrison town at the sound of enemy guns, we all became quiet. Even Her Fatness stopped her wailing.

Ammachi looked at all of us and then her gaze came to rest on Janaki. 'How many times have I told you to keep these children quiet?' she said, her tone awful.

Janaki, always so full of anger, now wrung her hands like a child in fear of punishment. 'I told them . . .' she started to say, but Ammachi raised her hand for silence. Her Fatness began to cry again, more out of fear than anything else. Ammachi glared at her, and, as if to deflect the look, Her Fatness held up her arm with the ripped sleeve.

'Who did that?' Ammachi said after a moment.

Her Fatness pointed at me and her crying got even louder.

Ammachi looked at me sternly and then beckoned me with her index finger.

'Look!' I cried and held out the sari as if in supplication. 'Look at what she did!'

But Ammachi was unmoved by the sight of the sari and continued to beckon me.

As I looked at her, I could almost hear the singing of the cane as it came down through the air, and then the sharp crack, which would be followed by searing pain. The time Diggy had been caned for climbing the roof came back to me, his pleas for mercy, his shouts of agony and loud sobs.

Before I could stop myself, I cried out angrily at Ammachi, 'It's not fair! Why should I be punished?'

'Come here,' Ammachi said.

'No. I won't.'

Ammachi came to the edge of the porch, but rather than backing away I remained where I was.

'Come here, you vamban,' she said to me sharply.

'No!' I cried back. 'I hate you, you old fatty.'

The other cousins and even Janaki gasped at my audacity. Ammachi began to come down the steps. I stood my ground for a few moments but then my courage gave out. I turned, and, with the sari still in my hands, I fled. I ran from the back garden to the front gate and out. In the field across the way, the boys were still at their cricket game. I hurried down the road towards the sea. At the railway lines I paused briefly, went across, then scrambled over the rocks to the beach. Once there, I sat on a rock and flung the sari down next to me. 'I hate them, I hate them all,' I whispered to myself. 'I wish I was dead.'

I put my head down and felt the first tears begin to wet my knees.

After a while I was still. The sound of the waves, their regular rhythm, had a calming effect on me. I leaned back against the rock behind me, watching them come in and go out. Soon the heat of the rocks became unbearable and I stood up, removed my slippers, and went down the beach to the edge of the water.

I had never seen the sea this colour before. Our visits to the beach were usually in the early evening when the sea was a turquoise blue. Now, under the mid-day sun, it had become hard silver, so bright that it hurt my eyes.

The sand burned my feet, and I moved closer to the waves to cool them. I looked down the deserted beach, whose white sand almost matched the colour of the sea, and saw tall buildings shimmering in the distance like a mirage. This daytime beach seemed foreign compared with the beach of the early evening, which was always crowded with strollers and joggers and vendors. Now both the beach and the sea, once so familiar, were like an unknown country into which I had journeyed by chance.

I knew then that something had changed. But how, I didn't altogether know.

The large waves, impersonal and oblivious to my despair, threw themselves against the beach, their crests frothing and hissing. Soon I would have to turn around and go back to my grandparents' house, where Ammachi awaited me with her thinnest cane, the one that left deep impressions on the backs of our thighs, so deep that sometimes they had to be treated with Gentian Violet. The thought of that cane as it cut through the air, humming like a mosquito, made me wince even now, so far away from it.

I glanced at the sari lying on the rock where I had thrown it and I knew that I would never enter the girls' world again. Never stand in front of Janaki's mirror, watching a transformation take place before my eyes. No more would I step out of that room and make my way down the porch steps to the altar, a creature beautiful and adored, the personification of all that was good and perfect in the world. The future spend-the-days were no longer to be enjoyed, no longer to be looked forward to. And then there would be the loneliness. I would be caught between the boys' and the girls' worlds, not belonging or wanted in either. I would have to think of things with which to amuse myself, find ways to endure the lunches and teas when the cousins would talk to one another about what they had done and what they planned to do for the rest of the day.

The bell of St Fatima's Church rang out the angelus, and its melancholy sound seemed like a summoning. It was time to return to my grandparents' house. My absence at the lunchtable would be construed as another act of defiance and eventually Janaki would be sent to fetch me. Then the punishment I received would be even more severe.

With a heavy heart, I slowly went back up the beach, not caring that the sand burned the soles of my feet. I put my slippers on, picked up my sari, and climbed up the rocks. I paused and looked at the sea one last time. Then I turned, crossed the railway lines, and began my walk up Ramanaygam Road to the future that awaited me.

Warren Cariou *b.* 1966

MEADOW LAKE, SASKATCHEWAN

'We are faced, as writers,' Warren Cariou writes, 'with the problems and possibly the opportunities of multiple cultural narratives co-existing within a political entity that we may or may not call our own. For many people, this situation leads to questions about who they are and where they belong. I think this might partly explain our current mania for tracing our family roots: we are searching for a stable identity to cling onto.' *Lake of the Prairies: A Story of Belonging* (2003), his own search for such roots, brought to light that he belongs, in part, to what he calls the 'Métis diaspora', but that above all he is 'many things, . . . "a child of the heterogeneous multitudes"'. The winner of the Drainie-Taylor Prize and short-listed for the Charles Taylor Prize, it is narrative that is at once memoir and social commentary.

Cariou, raised on a farm near Meadow Lake, Saskatchewan, holds a BA in English (1988) from the University of Saskatchewan, and an MA (1992) and PhD (1998)—a study of William Blake's composite art—from the University of Toronto. He has taught Aboriginal literature at the Universities of British Columbia and Greifswald (Germany), and has been on the faculty of the English department at the University of Manitoba since 2002. As a critic, he writes both about Canadian literature and Romanticism. Nominated for the First Book Award in Saskatchewan, the two novellas that comprise his first book, *The Exalted Company of Roadside Martyrs* (1999), address the frailties of human nature in relation to power and positions of authority, more specifically, the church and state. His forthcoming novel, *Exhaust*, set against the backdrop of conflict in Iraq but focusing on the conflict between a Calgary Oil company and Native protesters in a nearby reserve, has been announced as an 'allegory of a global culture hovering at the brink of catastrophe'.

from *Lake of the Prairies*

Remembering Clayton

Less than a year after the blockade, Meadow Lake was in the news again, but this time I got no advance warning. The first thing I heard was a familiar name on the radio— a name that didn't belong there, a name from my childhood. I was living in Saskatoon again by this time, making my first concerted effort at full-time writing, and I used to leave the radio on in the other room while I wrote, to trick myself into thinking I wasn't alone. Usually it was just on the edge of intelligibility, a pleasant droning in the background, a patter of simulated companionship. But sometimes, despite my concentration on the writing, I heard bits of conversation, song lyrics, news highlights. On the afternoon I'm thinking of now, I heard only that name, one that was so out of place on the national airwaves that I didn't really register it for several seconds, and I didn't walk out to the other room for another half a minute. By that time the news piece was over, and I was left wondering why they were talking about Clayton Matchee, the skinny Native kid who had clung to the outskirts of my social group in Meadow Lake for years. Clayton had done well for himself against the odds, had got married and had landed a good job with the army. What had happened to him, that he would make the national news?

I found out in the next broadcast. The announcer said that Master Corporal Clayton Matchee of the Fifth Airborne Division had been found hanging by a bootlace in a prison cell at the Canadian Forces peacekeeping base at Belet Huen, Somalia. He had been evacuated to a medical facility in that country but was expected to be returned to Canada for further treatment. Investigations had begun into the circumstances surrounding his injury.

As I listened, a slow tremor passed through my cluttered living room, like when distant bombs used to shake the ground at our cabin. I knew suddenly that on the edges of my happy childhood there had always been something else, some ominous possibility that would only become manifest when each of us went out into the world. I remembered the giggly eight-year-old I had played hockey against, the smart-ass kid in junior high school. Clayton had never been exactly my friend, but I had known him for many years, and his family was famous in Meadow Lake. He was the grandson of the Flying Dust Nation's most illustrious and long-lived hereditary chief, Gregoire Matchee. There was even a place called Matchee east of Meadow Lake, named after Chief Gregoire.

The first news about Clayton was devastating enough, but of course it was only the beginning. In the following weeks and months, there were many more revelations. The information arrived in bursts from my relentless radio, each requiring a separate observance of shock, of horror. Eventually a story emerged of what had happened the day before Clayton's injury. A Somali boy named Shidane Arone was apprehended by the peacekeepers after he entered the Canadian military compound at Belet Huen in search of food. The soldiers, one of whom was Master Corporal Clayton Matchee, held Atone under armed guard while they kicked him and beat him with a metal bar. His cries of pain and his pleas for mercy echoed across the compound, but no one intervened in the attack. Eventually the cruelty escalated even further: Arone's captors burned the soles of his feet with cigarettes, and they posed with his semiconscious body for trophy-hunter-style photographs. And after more than three hours of torture, they killed him.

It seems clear to me and to many others that the attack was racially motivated, that Shidane Atone was systematically dehumanized, tortured, and murdered not because he was an interloper in the military compound but because he was black. In the days before the murder, soldiers of the Airborne were heard calling the local Somalis 'nignogs', and making jokes about hunting them as trophies. In this context, Arone became a scapegoat in an almost ritualistic act of racism, an act that was preserved on the film of Private Kyle Brown's camera and later published in several Canadian newspapers. Clayton was the main figure in many of those photographs, and because I knew this, I couldn't bring myself to look at them for a long time. I had shared a playground with him, and a classroom, and a town. It seemed impossible that he could be present at the scene of such monumental depravity. Yet he was.

Along with everyone else, I wondered: where did these actions come from?

Millions of dollars were spent trying to answer that question. After the reports, the testimonies, and the trials, a consensus seems to have emerged that the Canadian military—rife with racism, poor leadership, and morale problems—provided the catalyst for the soldiers' acts of brutality. I have no doubt that this is true. But it is not the whole story. Each of these soldiers came from somewhere before they joined the Airborne. I don't know about the other men, but I can't help remembering that Clayton had learned all about racism and power during his childhood and youth in Meadow Lake. To see him portrayed as the aggressor in a racist attack is like the fulfillment of some nightmare prophecy. It makes no sense, and yet there is a murky symmetry to it that makes me think that racism—in Meadow Lake and elsewhere—is even more insidious than I had ever imagined.

I wish I could ask Clayton what he was doing there, but that's impossible now. He has never recovered from the injuries he sustained in the prison cell. It was ruled an attempted suicide and was interpreted by some as an admission of guilt, but no one really knows how it happened or what it might have meant. All we know is that the prison guards cut him down before the bootlace had finished its job, and since that time, Clayton has been one of the undead. He remains in a state of brain-damaged limbo, suspended between this world and the next, between guilty and innocent. He is unable to speak coherently, unable to understand the consequences of his actions, unfit to stand trial. And as the inquiries and the courts martial made their various reports, he became the *tabula rasa* upon which much of the blame was written. Some of the other soldiers testified that he was the instigator of the attack, the one who pushed it to its conclusion. One of the courts martial identified Clayton as 'the main perpetrator' of the crimes against Shidane Arone. Everyone else has made their explanations, and to a large degree, Clayton is the explanation. But he will never be able to do any explaining of his own, and he will never be tried in a court of law to determine the true extent of his culpability.

Clayton's silence has been weighing on me almost as much as the possibility of his guilt. I know I can't speak for him here. I'm not trying to vindicate him, or to make excuses, or to cast blame. I only want to understand, even in the most rudimentary way, how he could have taken part in the crime that left a boy dead and a world in shock. I do believe that he was caught up in something larger than himself, something that belongs not only to the military but also to the culture in which he was raised. I can see something of this in the reaction to the initial publicity back home in Meadow Lake. Some townspeople were stunned to hear the news, and others were angry at Clayton for bringing shame upon the town. There were a few people, mostly from the Native community, who spoke in Clayton's defence early on, saying that he was not the kind of person who would willingly take part in such activities, and reminding everyone that none of the allegations had been proven. But there were also some people who claimed to have been expecting it. 'I knew he'd fuck things up somehow,' they said. They had been surprised earlier when Clayton seemed to be making something of himself, and now they were almost comforted to learn that it wasn't true after all.

But I understood that this was not just a character judgment. What they meant was: he's not an exception after all; he's just like all the other Indians. They wanted to see him as a born savage, a symbol of his people.

Later, when the Somalia photographs were published, that sentiment was expressed even more blatantly. Clayton's family in Meadow Lake received a barrage of anonymous death threats and hate mail. His father, Leon Matchee, described the attacks as 'mostly a lot of swear words and very poorly written—"Indian, welfare bum, you deserve to die, you should be dead."' It is instructive to compare these comments with the racist aspects of the crime Clayton was accused of.

Nothing I knew about Clayton could have led me to expect that he might be involved in anything like the Somalia scandal. As a boy, he was not extraordinarily violent or depraved or dissolute—not a monster in the making, as some people now might want to believe. He got into trouble regularly, and he was known to be someone you didn't want to pick a fight with, but I never saw him do anything cruel. What I remember most about him was that he wanted desperately to fit in. I could sense this in the way he haunted the hallways at recess, listening in on the conversations of more popular kids, tossing in comments from the sidelines.

Clayton was different from Billy Tootoosis and the Fiddler boys, who sometimes seemed to enjoy intimidation. He didn't belong to a gang, and as far as I can remember he didn't make a pastime out of terrorizing the white kids. I think it was because he wanted to be one of them. He was part white, after all—though none of the white kids knew this at the time. His mother was of mixed European ancestry, and she had moved out to the Flying Dust Reserve only after marrying Leon Matchee. But Clayton's skin was as dark as any Native person's, and he lived on the reserve, so nobody in Meadow Lake bothered to think of him as anything other than an Indian. And so he was treated like they were.

There were exceptions to the town's division between Native and white roles, but they were always invoked with the knowledge that they were exceptions. Gilbert Lachance was welcomed among the white kids because he was a talented athlete, and Frankie Caplette was tolerated because his parents had given him a motorcycle for his thirteenth birthday. But Clayton was not an exception, at least not then, much as he may have wanted to be. It was only years later, when he married a white woman from town and got a good job in the army, that people started thinking of him as an exception.

It must have been hard work, being an exception. Even for those Native kids who *were* welcomed into the white crowd, the trial was never over. If they made the football or basketball or volleyball teams, they crossed over into a certain kind of respectability in school, but they always had to continue proving themselves, and the price of such proof was often horrendous. I remember on the volleyball team in high school there was an aboriginal guy named Gary. He was a strong power-hitter and a pretty fast digger in the backcourt, but no one looked up to him. He was treated as the team's jester instead, and he played along with this role, perhaps realizing that it was the only one he was likely to get. We called him Tomahawk, and he went along with it. If he wanted to feel like part of the team, he had no choice in the matter. At practice someone would say, 'Hey, Tomahawk, you scalping bastard, you,' and he would laugh with the rest of us. Sometimes he would brandish an imaginary tomahawk or give a ridiculous war whoop, as if he could efface his nativeness by ridiculing it like everyone else did. After a while he began making racist comments about the Indians on the teams we played against. He ranted about them, stringing together curses and racist insults that he had certainly learned the hard way. This was the zenith of Gary's belonging. When he had learned to act out the racism of the team and project it onto our rivals, he was as close to being an honorary white man as he was going to get. Gary had learned two things in his search for approval: that whiteness is power, and that the way to become white is to be a racist.

I don't remember exactly what terrible things we said to Clayton, but I know he got the same treatment as every other dark-skinned person in the school. Nobody was immune to it. Even the tough kids like Clayton were subject to taunting and verbal abuse, especially at school, when the perpetrators could run to the teachers for protection whenever necessary. This was probably one of the reasons Clayton was always getting into trouble. And even when he wasn't being taunted himself, he would have witnessed the attacks on other Native kids. Seeing all this, day after day, would be enough to make anyone wish they were white, just as a matter of survival.

Clayton left school after grade ten, and I lost track of him for a few years. I can't say that I thought about him much. By the time I finished high school I heard he was working in the bush, cutting trees or operating a skidder. Two years after that I bumped into him and his friend Jeremy on the banks of the Green River, where they were fishing and I was looking for a spot to fish. They were bigger and more muscular now, but essentially they hadn't changed since grade nine: still goofy and hyperactive, still fond of shoulder-punching and fart jokes. They didn't ask me anything about myself, but when I inquired about the fishing Jeremy showed me a string of walleye laid out in the grass beside half a dozen empty bottles of beer. Clayton started razzing him about the little pickerel he had kept. I remember his laugh: a high-pitched, theatrical giggle that sounded like someone was tickling him. The two of them were wrestling over the last beer when I left, so none of us said goodbye.

That was the last time I ever heard from Clayton. His unlikely changes occurred shortly after. He married the daughter of a respected family in Meadow Lake and then he enlisted in the Canadian Armed Forces. It's hard to believe that any Native people would willingly join the same institution that the government has repeatedly used to repress indigenous people in this country. But many other Native people before Clayton and after him also joined the army, simply because it's a respectable job, a place where their skills and dedication might be valued. Perhaps no other employer will give them a chance. In any case, Clayton was very successful as a soldier, so perhaps he felt he had found his vocation. Still, I wonder what he thought in the summer of 1990, when the Canadian government sent troops to the barricades at Oka, to put down an Indian uprising once again. Clayton's own reserve and his own army division weren't involved, so maybe he didn't worry much about it. He might have had other things to think about, because the Third Airborne Division, in which he was stationed, was a hotbed of racist activities.

Any reports about Clayton's behaviour in the army during his pre-Somalia days are probably tainted by what happened later, so it's difficult to know exactly what role he played in the Airborne's now-notorious racism. Official and unofficial investigations have revealed that several members of the division openly espoused neo-Nazi and white supremacist beliefs. There were horrifyingly degrading initiation rituals, during which visible minorities were singled out for the most extreme humiliation. They were beaten, insulted, smeared with excrement. If they wanted to be part of the group, they had to suffer this abuse without complaint. Once they had gotten through the ordeal, they were accepted into the group—and a sign of their belonging was that, in the next year's initiation, they got to be the aggressors.

Clayton must have undergone an initiation of this sort. It's the nature of these rituals that no exceptions are allowed. There is no record of his initiation, nor of course his reaction to it, but I imagine the ordeal itself wouldn't have come as a surprise to him. He would have already known the rules from his youth in Meadow Lake, where almost every sports team practised some variation of this vicious rite of passage. I can only speculate about this, but it seems probable that during his time in the Airborne, Clayton learned something very similar to what my teammate Gary had learned on the Carpenter High School volleyball team: that in order to be accepted by a racist white majority, he had to adopt their prejudices himself.

There is some evidence that Clayton was indeed accepted among his peers at the Airborne, but he didn't have to play the role of the jester like Gary had done. In fact, he was something of a leader. He was promoted rapidly, to corporal and then to master corporal. At the same time, his once-skinny body began to fill out, and he became an imposing man: muscular, self-assured, seemingly fearless. There are rumours that other soldiers in the division were afraid of him because of his strength and his ferocity during training exercises. This is one explanation of how Clayton came to be the instigator of the attack on Shidane Arone. The other participants said they were scared to stop him.

I fear him too, now that I have seen him in the terrible photographs, the ones that caused a national furor when they were published in Canadian newspapers. I couldn't bring myself to look at them then, but years later I realized I had to face them if I was to come to terms with Clayton's actions. I looked them up on microfilm, clenching my teeth as I scrolled back through the myriad calamities of yesterday's news. There they were. The scratches and distortions of the microfilm did nothing to disguise the brutality of the images. I looked away, at the cool orderliness of the library reading room, then back into Clayton's face. It was almost impossible to reconcile those vicious poses with my memories of the boy I knew, and yet it *was* unmistakably Clayton, there at the scene of horror.

In one of the photos he points with his index finger at Shidane Arone's swollen and bloodied head, perhaps mimicking a handgun, or maybe just pointing out the damage that has already been done. On Clayton's face is a smirk, a cocksure expression, perhaps even a show of pride. In the most horrific of the published photographs, Shidane Arone leans forward, bound by two thick ropes, blindfolded with a piece of plaid cloth that drapes from his head onto his right shoulder. The cloth is Clayton's shirt, which he has removed sometime during the torture. Clayton stands above Arone's shoulders, almost riding on the prisoner's back, and he holds a long metal bar between his outstretched hands. He has forced the bar into Shidane Arone's bloodied mouth, and now he holds it there, looking up into the camera with an expression that is a mixture of solemnity, questioning, and pride. His face is like that of a small boy looking up at his father for affirmation. His bare chest almost touches the back of Arone's head, and the powerful muscles of his arms and shoulders are outlined against the white of his pants. It's a pure display of strength, like the poses in bodybuilding magazines. But something else is also on display here, something that Clayton had usually taken pains to cover up.

Look, he seems to be saying. *My skin is lighter than his.*

Almost two years after the murder of Shidane Arone, Clayton returned home—or as near to home as institutional facilities would allow. He is now a patient in the mental hospital in North Battleford, ninety miles south of Meadow Lake. It's the place we all used to joke about as kids: the loony bin, the funny farm, the zoo. The way we talked, half of our friends were either recent escapees or were soon to be patients. If we had believed that any of us might actually end up there, the jokes wouldn't have been so funny.

Even as it was, the very idea of the place made me queasy. Our grade seven teacher once told us about a patient he had seen there: a teenage boy who had sniffed so much gasoline that he became a vegetable. This boy's mind, the teacher said, was so completely vacant that all he could do, day in and day out, was stare up into the corner of his room. The only thing the staff could do for him was to hang a balloon up there in the corner so he had something pretty to look at. Every few days, as a favour to him, they changed the colour of the balloon.

In my imagination, Clayton became that lost boy. I often thought of him up there, alone in his room, sitting in a low vinyl chair with his head leaned back against the wall, his mouth partly open. I pictured a whole ward full of people like him, and dozens of other silent patients shuffling in the halls, trembling to the rhythms of their medications.

I knew that Clayton was no longer Clayton. But still there was a body that occupied his space in the world, and his family called that body by his name. So did the nurses in the hospital. I supposed they didn't hold his reputation against him. To them, he would be just another body to shepherd through the cycles of eating, shitting, sleeping, walking.

The official reports were never very clear about Clayton's level of mental functioning. Sometimes I wondered: does he have any memory of Somalia? Of his wife and daughter? His hometown? Can he express love, or remorse, or anger? Does he dream?

He had been up there in his room for years already when I went to visit him. I went there not to ask questions but simply to look into his face, to remind myself that part of him, at least, lived on. There was also something I felt I had to tell him about myself, something he might have found funny or tragic or ironic if he could understand me. So one September afternoon when I was visiting Meadow Lake, I drove down to the outskirts of North Battleford, where the Mental Health Centre looks out on the magnificent Battle River valley. It was a far more beautiful place than any of my imaginings had prepared me for.

'I'm here to visit someone I used to know,' I said at the front desk where two nurses were sorting through a sheaf of papers. 'Clayton Matchee.'

Both of them stopped, looked at each other. I wondered if such a request was unusual, or if Clayton still received death threats even now.

'What relation are you?' the nearest one asked.

'We went to school together in Meadow Lake.'

She informed me that Clayton had a restricted visitors' list, but still, they would see what they could do. I was told to fill out a form indicating my connection to the patient, and then one of the nurses made a cryptic phone call while the other one disappeared down the corridor.

I waited for a long time in that hallway. Patients and nurses and doctors strode past, each of them glancing at me appraisingly, as if to decide what category I belonged in. Somewhere, probably only a few feet away, Clayton would be waiting. I tried not to think about what he had once been; tried to focus on what he might be now, though that wasn't much of a diversion. By the time I saw the nurse coming back down the hallway I could feel my pulse in my palms, my ears.

But they didn't let me in. She was shaking her head as she approached, and the apprehension had almost drained out of me when she finally spoke.

'I'm sorry,' she said. 'He doesn't remember you.'

Hiromi Goto *b.* 1966

CHIBA-KEN, JAPAN

'Inscribing a place. A sensitivity, a sensibility which resists commonality,' says Hiromi Goto by way of explaining what motivates and informs her writing. 'Defining my position through language. The intensely personal becomes public in the process of addressing issues of racism and sexism as a woman of colour writing in Canada.'

Born in Chiba-ken, Japan, in 1966, she immigrated to Canada at the age of three with her family. After a short time on the West Coast, they settled in Nanton in southern Alberta. Goto received a BA in English (1989) from the University of Calgary, where she studied creative writing with Aritha Van Herk and Fred Wah, and has had her short stories and poetry published in many literary magazines and anthologies. A resident of Vancouver, she was writer-in-residence at the Emily Carr College of Art and Design (2003–4).

A member of the editorial collective of *absinthe* magazine, Goto was one of the co-editors of *The Skin On Our Tongues* (1993), a special issue on writers of colour and aboriginal writers. In her editorial statement accompanying that issue, she expresses a 'certain mistrust of . . . anthologies which highlight writers from a specific racial/cultural background.' Still, while agreeing 'on the surface' that such anthologies tend to 'segregate "ethnic writing" from the mainstream', she believes it is important to resist the 'ingrained canon of literary acceptance which excludes most writing that does not adhere to a Western (Eurocentric) standard'. As she says, writing 'that steps outside of this category is immediately "othered" as *ethnic*, thereby creating a division between what is deemed literary and what is not'.

Goto has published a full colour postcard poem, *Tea* (1992), with DisOrientation Chapbooks, and a young adult novel, *The Water of Possibility* (2001). Her first novel, *Chorus of Mushrooms* (1994), which has appeared in a

Hebrew translation and won the Commonwealth Prize for Best First Novel in the region of North America and the Japan–Canada Book Award, has been widely read and taught. Through humour and Japanese folktales, memory and engagement with food, it is a narrative that employs elements of postmodernism and magic realism to tell the story of three generations of women in the same family. The same interplay of realism and fantasy characterizes her second novel, *The Kappa Child* (2001), which was awarded the James Jr Tiptree Award and short-listed for the Sunburst Award for Literature of the Fantastic and the Spectrum Award. Through the point of view of an anonymous, and androgynous-looking young Japanese Canadian and that of a Kappa egg growing in her body, the novel, set in Calgary, explores the ways in which cultural difference is often misconstrued as monstrosity, a theme she also takes up in her collection of short stories, *Hopeful Monsters* (2004). A trickster-like creature in Japanese folklore, Kappa is an 'aquatic' figure with webbed hands and feet; it is its bowl-shaped head that endows it with supernatural powers that the human narrator is both troubled by and benefits from. Goto is not so much interested in depicting the day-to-day experiences of immigrants; rather, her powerful, and often self-reflexive, narratives, are concerned with ambivalence and with deconstructing paradigms of normalcy.

Stinky Girl

One is never certain when one becomes a stinky girl. I am almost positive I wasn't stinky when I slid out from between my mother's legs, fresh as blood and just as sweet. What could be stinkier, messier, grosser than that? one might be asked, but I'm certain I must have smelled rich like yeast and liver. Not the stink of I-don't-know-what that pervades me now.

Mother has just looked over my shoulder to see what I try to cover up with my hand and arm, while I meditatively write at the kitchen table.

'Jesus!' She rolls her eyes like a whale. 'Jesus Christ!' she yells. 'Don't talk about yourself as "one"! One what, for God's sake? One asshole? One snivelling stinky girl?' She stomps off. Thank goodness. It's very difficult having a mother. It's even more difficult having a loud and coarse one.

Where was I? Oh, yes. I am not troubled by many things. My weight, my mother, my dead father's ghost and a pet dog that despises me do not bother me so very much. Well, perhaps on an off-day they might bring a few tears to my eyes, but no one will notice a fat stinky mall rat weeping. People generally believe that fatties secrete all sorts of noxious substances from their body. But regardless, the one bane of my life, the one cloud of doom that circumscribes my life is the odour of myself.

There's no trying to pinpoint it. The usual sniff under the armpits or cupping of palms in front of my mouth to catch the smell of my breath is like trying to scoop up an iceberg with a goldfish net. And it's not a simple condition of typical body odour. I mean, everybody has some natural scents and even the prettiest cover girls wear deodorant and perfume. It's not because I am fat that foul odours are trapped in the folds of my body. No, my problem is not a causal phenomenon and there are no simple answers.

Perhaps I am being misleading, calling myself a mall rat. It's true, I spend much of my time wandering in the subculture of gross material consumerism. I meander from store to store in the wake of my odour, but I seldom actually purchase anything I see inside the malls. Think, if you will, upon the word 'rat'. Instantly, you'll picture a sharp whiskered nose, beady black eyes, an unsavoury disposition, grubby hands with dirty nails, perhaps, and a waxy tail. You never actually think fat rat. No, what comes to mind is a more sneaky and thinner rodent. If I am a rat, think of, perhaps, the queen of all rats in the sewer of her dreams, being fed the most tender morsels of garbage flesh her minions bring her. Think of a well-fed rat with three mighty chins and smooth, smooth skin, pink and fine. No need for a fur covering when all your needs are met. A mighty rodent with more belly than breath, more girth than the diameter of the septic drains. If you think of such a rat, then I am that mighty beast.

Actually, I always thought of myself more in terms of a vole or perhaps a wise fat toad, or maybe even a manatee, mistaken by superstitious sailors as a bewitching mermaid. But, no, Mother tells me I was born in the Year of the Rat and that is that. No choice there, I'm afraid, and I can't argue with what I can't remember. Mother isn't one for prolonged arguments and contemplative discussions. More often than not, all I'll get is a 'Jesus Christ!' for all my intellectual and moral efforts. I hope I don't sound judgmental. Mother is a creature unto herself and there is no ground for arbitrary comparison. 'Each to their own' is a common phrase, but not without a tidbit of truth.

Perhaps I mislead you by calling myself a stinky girl. I am not a girl in the commonly held chronological sense of time. I've existed outside my mother's body for three and thirty years. Some might even go so far as to say that I'm an emotionally crippled and mutually dependent member of a dysfunctional family. Let's not quibble. In the measure of myself, and my sense of who I am, I am definitely a girl. Albeit a stinky one.

When people see obesity, they are amazed. Fascinated. Attracted and repulsed simultaneously. Now if we could harness all the emotions my scale inspires, who knows how many homes we could heat, how many trains we could move? People always think there is a why to being grand, that there is some sort of glandular problem, an eating disorder, a symptom of some childhood trauma . . . All I can say is, not to my knowledge. I have always been fat, and, if I must say so myself, I eat a lot less than my tiny mother. I wasn't adopted, either. Mother is always bringing up how painful her labour was to eject me from her body. How she had to be tied down and how she pushed and screamed and pushed and cursed for three days running. Perhaps that's the reason for her slightly antagonistic demeanour. She didn't have any more children after I was born, and I must say, this birthing thing sounds like a nasty business what with all the tying down and screaming.

Oh, yes. I do have siblings, but they are much older than I. Three sisters and a brother who became women and men long before their due. Cherry was born in the Year of the Rabbit, Ginger, the Year of the Dragon, Sushi, the Year of the Horse, and Bonus, the Year of the Sheep. Mother was feeling quite tired of the whole affair by the time her second-last child was born. Bonus was so named because he came out of her body with such ease, she couldn't believe her luck. There was a seventeen-year stretch with no other pregnancies and she must have thought that her cycles were finished. And what better way than to end on a bonus?

But Mother wasn't fated to an easy existence. She wasn't going to inhabit the autumn years of her life without considerable trials and tribulations. At the age of fifty-one, she became pregnant with me. Promptly thereafter, my father died and she was left in a trailer, huge and growing, her children all moved away. A tragic life, really, but I shouldn't romanticize. One is easily led toward a tragic conclusion, and one must fight the natural human tendency to dramatize the conditions of one's life. One must be level-headed. A fat girl especially. When one is fat, one is seldom seen as a stable and steadying force in an otherwise chaotic world. Fat people embody the disruptive forces in action and this inspires people to lay blame. Where else to point their fingers but at the fat girl in striped trousers?

Did I mention I am also coloured?

I can't remember my very first memory. No one can, of course. I must remember what others have told me before I can remember on my own. Of my living father I have no recollections, but his ghost is all too present in my daily life. I wouldn't be one to complain if he was a helpful and cheerful ghost, prone to telling me where there are hidden crocks of gold or if the weather will be fine for the picnic. But no. He is a dreadfully doleful one, following me around the small spaces in our trailer, leaning mournfully on my shoulder and telling me to watch my step *after* I've stepped in a pile of dog excrement. And such a pitiful apparition! All that there is of him is his sad and sorry face. Just his head, bobbing around in the air, sometimes at the level of a man walking but, more often than not, down around the ankles, weaving heavily around one's steps. It's enough to make one want to kick him, but I am not one who is compelled to exhibit unseemly aggressive behaviour.

Mother, on the other hand, is not above a swift 'kick in the can' as she calls it, or a sudden cuff to the back of the head. I would not be exaggerating if I said I had no idea how she can reach my buttocks, let alone high enough to cuff my head, for I am not only very fat, but big and tall. Well, tall might be misleading. It would make one imagine that height is greater than girth. Let there be no doubt as to my being rounder than I would ever be considered tall. However, I am at least two feet taller than my mother, who stands four foot eight. She is not a dwarf, and I am not a giant. But we are not normal in the commonly held sense of the word.

No, my mother is not a dwarf, but she is the centre of the universe. Well, at least the centre of this trailer park, and she leaves no doubt as to who 'kicks the cabbage around this joint', as she is so fond of reminding me. It gives me quite a chuckle on occasion, because Father's ghost often looks much like a cabbage, rolling around the gritty floor of our trailer. And even though Mother cannot see him, she has booted his head many times, when she punctuates her sayings with savage kicks to what she can only see as empty air. It doesn't hurt him, of course, but it does seem uncomfortable. He rolls his sorry eyes as he is *tha-klunked, tha-klunked* across the kitchen.

'What are you sniggling at, Mall Rat?' Mother snaps at me.

'Nothing,' I say, sniggling so hard that my body ripples like tides.

Mother kicks me in the can for lying and stomps off to her bedroom to smoke her cigars. I feel sorry for my father and right his head, brushing off some ghostly dust.

'See what happens when you inhabit this worldly prison? Why don't you float up to the heavens or at least a waiting room?' I scold. 'There's nothing left for you here except kicks in the head and a daughter who doesn't want to hear your depressing talk of dog excrement and all the pains you still feel in your phantom body that isn't there.'

'As if I'm here by choice!' he moans. 'As if any ghost would choose to remain in this sorry purgatory of a trailer! Finally dead and I get the nice light show, the tunnel thing and a lovely floating body. I think that I might be hearing a chorus of singing mermaids when an unsympathetic voice utters, "You have not finished doing time," and I find my head bobbing in a yellow stained toilet bowl. It takes me a couple of minutes to figure out it's my own toilet bowl, in my old washroom, because I'd never seen the bathroom from that perspective before. Imagine my shock! What's a poor ghost to do? Oh woe, oh woe,' he sobs. Because ghosts have ghostly licence to say things like that.

Frankly, his lamenting and 'woeing' is terribly depressing and I have plenty of my own woes without having to deal with his. I might not give in to excessive displays of violence, but I am not above stuffing him in the flour bin to make my escape.

I suppose calling oneself a rat might seem gender-specific. 'Rat,' I'll say and instantly a man or a nasty boy is conjured up.

There are female rats as well, don't you know? His and hers rat towels. Rat breasts and rat wombs. Rat washrooms where you squat instead of peeing standing up. A girl can grow up to become a doctor or a lawyer, now. Why not become a rat? Albeit a stinky one.

Yes, yes, the odour of my life. It is large as myth and uglier than truth.

There are many unpleasant scents as you twiddle twaddle through the grey felt tunnels of life. Actually, smells hinge the past to the clutter of memory. Nothing is comparable to the olfactory when it comes to distorting your life. To jar a missing thought. Or transmute into an obsession. The dog excrement smell that's trapped in the runnels of the bottom of a sneaker, following you around all day no matter how fast you flee. That high-pitched whine of dog shit, pardon my language. Mother is a terrible influence and one must always guard against common usage and base displays of aggression. Yes, there is nothing like stepping in a pile of doggy dung to ruin your entire day. It is especially bad when the dog is supposedly your own.

Mother found the dog in the trailer-park dumpster, and as it was close to my 'sorry birthday', as she called it, she brought the dirt-coloured wall-eyed creature home as a gift for me. I was touched, really, because she had forgotten to give me a present for the last twenty-seven years and I had always wanted a dog as a devoted friend.

The dog started whining as soon as Mother dragged it into the trailer by the scruff of its mangy neck. It cringed against the floor, curling its lip back three times over. Then the dog started chasing itself, tried to catch up with its stumpy tail so it could eat itself out of existence. I was concerned.

'Mother, perhaps the dog has rabies.'

'Arrghh.' (This is the closest I can get in writing to the sound of my mother's laughter.) 'Damn dog's not rabid, it's going crazy from your infernal stink. Lookit! It's hyperventilating! Aaaaaarrggghhh!'

The poor beast was frothing at the mouth, chest heaving, smearing itself into the kitchen linoleum. It gave a sudden convulsive shake, then fainted. It was the first time I had ever seen a dog faint. Needless to say, my 'sorry birthday' was ruined. I actually thought the dog would die, or at least flee from my home as soon as it regained consciousness. But surprisingly, the animal stayed around. There is no accounting for dog sense. Perhaps it's a puerile addiction to horrible smells. Like after one has cut up some slightly going-off ocean fish and raises one's fishy fingers to one's nostrils throughout the day and night until the smell has been totally inhaled. Or sitting down in a chair and crossing an ankle over the knee, clutching the ankle with a hand, twisting so the bottom of the runner is facing upward. The nose descending to sniff, sniff, sniff again. There is an unborn addict in all of us, and it often reveals itself in the things we choose to smell.

I must admit, I cannot smell myself because I have smelled my scent into normality. I only know that I still emit a tremendous odour because my mother tells me so. Also, I have no friends, and people give me a wide berth when I take my trips to the mall. There is a certain look people cannot control when they smell an awful stink. The lips curl back, the nose wrinkles toward the forehead, trying to close itself. (Actually, if one thinks about it, the nostrils seem more greatly exposed when in this position than when at rest, but I needn't linger on that thought just now. Later, I'll ponder it at my leisure.) People cannot control this reaction. I have seen it the whole of my life and can interpret the fine sneer in the corner of an eye, a cheek twitching with the sudden sour bile rising from the bottom of the tongue.

Let me reassure you, I am not some obsessive fecal compulsive who is actually pleasured by foul odours. I am not in the league of people who get perverted thrills from the filth of metabolic processes. I bathe twice a day, despite the discomfort of squeezing my body into a tiny shower stall. Not to mention all the commotion Mother makes about how much hot water I use. I must say, though, that Mother would be wise to take greater care with her personal hygiene, what with her cigars and her general disregard for appearance and decorum.

In the summertime, I can bathe myself in my shower garden. I planted a hedge of caragana for some privacy and I only clip it in width, so it doesn't invade the yard. It stands over ten feet in height and inside the scratchy walls, when it is heady with yellow blossoms, I can stand beneath an icy stream of hose water and feel almost beautiful. Mother always threatens to burn my beautiful bush to the ground.

'It's like a damn scrub prison in here! We get no bloody sunlight in the yard. Nothing grows. Just mud and fungus, and you muck it up with water and wallow there like some kind of pig. Burn the thing to the ground,' she smacks me with her words. But Mother isn't as cruel as her words may sometimes seem. She does not reveal her inner spirit to those who are looking; instead, she throws verbal daggers in order not to be seen. Regardless, I know she will never burn down my summer shower because, sometimes, I catch her standing inside the bower of caragana. When the days are summer long into night and the heat is unbearable, the humble yellow blossoms turn into brittle brown pods. The shells crack with tiny explosions of minute seeds that bounce and scatter on the parched ground. They roll to where my mother douses herself with icy water. I catch her when she thinks I'm still at the mall. I catch her hosing down her scrawny old woman body, a smile on her normally scowling face, and a cigar burning between her lips. I never let on that I see her in these moments. She is more vulnerable than I.

The dog decided to remain in the confines of our trailer, and it made me realize that one can never foretell the life choices that others will enact. That first day, Mother named the dog 'Rabies', and dragged his floppy body outside. She hosed him off in the caragana shower and he came to, shook himself off like dogs will do, slunk into the kitchen and hunkered beneath the table.

Mother laughed once: 'Aaarrrrgh,' reached inside the refrigerator, and threw him the first thing her hand came in contact with. It was father's head. I had tucked him there to keep him from being underfoot, and he must have fallen asleep. The starving dog clamped down on an ear and gnawed with stumpy teeth. Father screamed in outrage.

'What you say, Stink-O? Speak up. Fat girls shouldn't whisper.'

'Nothing, Mother. I think you tossed Rabies a cabbage. I'll just take it back and feed him something more suitable. Perhaps that beef knuckle we used to make soup yesterday.'

'Suit yourself. But don't say "perhaps".' Mother stomped off 'to sit on the can', as she calls it.

'A dog. Your mother fed me to a dog. Haven't I been tormented enough? When will this suffering end?' Father started weeping, the dog keening. I sighed. I am not one who gives in easily to the woes of this world. Sighing is an expression of defeat, or at least weakness that reveals a lack of toughness or that certain get-up-and-go attitude. But Father is a sorry shade, a cloud of perpetual doom and defeat. I don't even want to know what sort of man he was before he fell to this. It would only make a tragic comedy out of what was probably a pathetic life. I swooped down, scooped Father's head out from between Rabies' paws and set him on the table, right side up. I dug through the garbage for the dry soup bone and tossed it to the dog.

Yes, a fat girl can swoop. I am remarkably light on my feet, I almost float on the tips of my toes. Certainly, one may be fat and stinky, but it doesn't necessitate stumbling awkwardness. I never drag my feet and I never stomp fit to bring down the roof. It is Mother who is the stomper in this house and many a time I have whipped up the ladder to tap another layer of tar paper on the rusty roof. I may be grand, stinky and hated by dogs, but I have a dancer's feet and the endurance of a rice-planter's thighs.

Did I mention that I'm also coloured? One is led to say 'also' in a long list of things I am that are not commonly perceived as complimentary. One cannot say, 'I'm coloured,' and expect: 'You know, I've always wanted to be coloured myself,' as a standard reaction. Not that I would rather be a stinky, fat white girl. Perhaps mauve or plum. Plum . . . now that's a colour!

A fat coloured rat girl has to look out for herself and never reveal her cards. Lucky for me, I must say I'm blessed with a certain amount of higher intelligence, a certain sensitivity that enables me to more than endure the trials of this existence. On my better days, I can leap and soar above the patchy roof of the trailer house. On my better days, the stars sing closer to my ears. I may be fat, I may stink larger than life, I may be a coloured mall rat in striped trousers, but I am coyly so.

Ah, yes, the mall. Now why would a clever girl like myself bother to habit such a gross manifestation of consumer greed? Is it some puerile addiction, a dysfunction I cannot control? Ahh, many a time I've pondered on this, but it is not as an active consumer that I return to the mall as I oft do. My forays there are part of an ongoing study of the plight of human existence in a modern colonized country. A mall is the microcosm, the centrifugal force in a cold country where much of the year is sub-zero in temperature. The mall reveals the dynamics of the surrounding inhabitants. Yes, the traits of the masses can be revealed in the Hudson's Bay department store and in the vast expanses of a Toys 'R Us, where hideously greedy children manipulate TV dinner divorcées into making purchases with the equivalent monetary value of feeding a small village for a week.

When I have fully understood the human mall condition, it will become a doorway to a higher level of existence. One must understand one's limitations, the shackles of social norms, in order to overcome them. And when I have accomplished this, I will cast aside my mantle of foul odour and float to the outer limits of time and space. Alas, one must always take care not to steep oneself too deeply in theoretical thought. It would only lead to the sin created by the Greeks and taught in every Western educational institution today: hubris, dreaded hubris.

Luckily for me, my father's pale and pathetic head is confined to the parameters of our trailer lot. Imagine what a hindrance he'd be in my pursuit of higher consciousness! I slip into my gymnast's slippers and chassé through my caragana bowers and out the tattered back gate. Father's head rolls down the walk after me as far as the last concrete slab, then teeters back and forth in what I assume is a head wave. Feeling extra generous, I throw back a kiss, and he levitates a few feet in pleasure. There is neither sight nor sound of Rabies, much to my father's relief.

'Arrr! Stink-O! Pick me up a box of cigars. Don't cheap out on me and buy those candy-flavoured Colts, you hear!' Mother snarls from the tiny bathroom window. I blow kisses, five, six, seven and flutter down the sidewalk. Mother or her bowels growl from the dark recesses of our tinny home.

As I traipse between the rows of identical rectangular homes highlighted with large, colourful butterflies and plastic petunias, I hear the slamming of doors and the snap of windows closing. My odour precedes me. I never need an introduction; my signature prevails. Alas, a thought. If one smells a smell and was never taught to like it, would not one find it distasteful as a result of ignorance? Let me pursue the opposite line of thought. If one were taught as a very small child that roses were disgusting, that they were vile, noxious and ugly, to boot, would one not despise the very thought of their scent? It may be that I smell beautiful beyond the capacity of human recognition: the scent of angels and salamanders. There's just no one capable of appreciating the loveliness.

The mall. The mall. It is Saturday and the mall is a virtual hub of hustle and bustle. Infants cry and old women smoke. Unisex teens sprout rings from every inch of revealed skin and the mind boggles thinking about what's not revealed. Fake and real potato french fried into greasy sticks, stand-in-line Chinese food, trendy café au laits and iced coffees. It is crowded but I always have a wide path. A minimum ten-foot radius circumscribes my epicentre. No one dares come any closer, I'm afraid. Like a diver in a shark-protection cage. No, that's not quite right. Regardless.

I have a daily route I take and even if my eyes were put out, I could wind my way through the blind corners and dead-end halls of this mall. Like the tragic Shakespearean kings, I would prevail with an uncanny sense of despair and enlightenment. The merchants all know me by smell, and sometimes, a wave or a brief nod of a head is offered. There was a time when most of the merchants convened to put an end to my forays, to banish me from my chosen road of human contemplation. But legally there was nothing they could do as long as I bought an item now and again, like mother's cigars, or a soup bone from the butcher. They couldn't evict me for the way I smell, or how I looked in my striped trousers. There was a time when I could have been evicted for being coloured, but at the present time in history, in this geographical location, I am lawfully tolerated.

Alas, no one wants to be merely tolerated, like a whining child or an ugly dog. Such human arrogance. We dare to assume that some are meant to be merely tolerated while others are sought out to be idolized, glorified, even to have their dainty asses wiped. Have a care! I mustn't fall into the pit of baseness like my mother before me! The utter unfairness of it all is enough to make one want to bite one's own tongue off, a mute supplication to the evils of this world, but that's the other end of the stick. Father's end of misery and woe. It is my chosen path to seek another . . .

I glide into Holy Smoke to pick out a box of cigars. If I wait until I have done my daily study of the machinations of mall existence, I may very well forget and Mother would be sorely vexed in a manner that would be audible for several square miles.

'Good afternoon.' Adib nods politely, from behind his pastel handkerchief.

'Lovely.' I breezily smile as I step up to the marble counter.

'A box of the usual for you?' he asks, backing up a pace and smiling behind the cover of his handkerchief to make up for his instinctual retreat.

'Please,' I say, bobbing my head and leaning my arm against the cool grey rock slab that runs the length of the entire store. Men on stools on either side of me hop off, stuff burning pipes in trouser pockets in their haste to escape me.

Adib sighs, even though he has his back to the mass exodus. He turns around with a box filled with cigars as thick as my thumb, individually wrapped and sealed with a red sticker. He has thrown five extra ones on top, so it will take that much longer before I have to return.

'Your generosity is so greatly appreciated.' I bow, clicking my heels like some military personage and pay him with bills sweating wetly from the pocket of my striped pants.

Adib accepts them as graciously as a man extending a pair of tweezers can. No, I am not angered by his reticence to come into direct contact with me. Indeed, I find his manner refreshingly honest. He never hurls abuse like some are apt to do.

'My best to your mother.' Adib hands me my change via the tweezers. 'By the way,' he adds, 'you might want to take in the new children's play area in the west wing of the mall. I heard that it's quite the development.'

'Why, thank you,' I beam. Then frown. 'But how is it that I am not acquainted with this wonder of childish bliss?'

Adib just shrugs, breathing shallowly from behind his lavender-scented hanky. I thank him again. Glissade en avant gracefully through the door and, toes pointed, leap excitedly to the West wing.

The sign reads: FRIENDZIES!

It's one of those obscure word conflations that means almost nothing at all. Like a joke told with a punchline from another, one realizes an attempt at humour has been made, but there is nothing to get. It does not bode well.

Grand-opening balloons, limp and wrinkled, dangle from pastel walls. Streamers trail limply from golden pillars and curl in the dust on the cold floor. There's a table with free coffee and donuts and Coke-flavoured pop made out of syrup. I walk up to the gate, disheartened, but must enter for study purposes. One must not let first impressions alter one's methodology, one's code of ethics.

'One adult please,' I say, smiling courteously.

'Where's your kid?' a girl chews out with an unseemly quantity of gum.

I am amazed. She does not curl her nose in disgust at the stench that permeates my being. Her eyes do not water and she doesn't gape at my size.

'I have no children,' I say. 'I just want to see the newly constructed premises.' How is it that she doesn't seem to notice? Perhaps her nose has been decimated from smoking or, perhaps, lines of cocaine.

'Ya can't go in without a kid, because adults go in free but a kid costs eight bucks.' The girl tips forward on her stool to rest her chin in her hands, elbows splayed sloppily on the countertop before me.

'My goodness! Eight dollars for a child!' I am shocked. Who could possibly afford to entertain their children here, and what could possibly be worth the price? 'What if one were to tell you that the child is inside already, that one has only come to join her?'

The young woman kicks a button with her foot and the gate swings open. 'Don't forget to take off your shoes and keep valuables on your person,' she intones, bored to insensibility.

She is from a generation where nothing seems to matter. She is so bored of the world and of herself that even my anomalous presence doesn't measure on her radar. Is there no hope for our next generation? Will the non-starving members of our species perish from ennui even before we've polluted our environment to the point of no return?

This turn of thought does nothing to advance my research. It only makes me weary. Ever weary. I adjust my mental clipboard and focus on the task at hand.

Plastic tubing runs crazily throughout the room, like a diseased mind twisting and turning back on itself with no end, no beginning. Plastic balls fill a pit of doom, three toddlers drown to the chorus of their parents' snap-shotting delight. Primary reds, blues and yellows clash horribly with khaki, lavender and peach. Children, fat children, skinny children and coloured children, pale from too much TV, run half-heartedly through the plastic pipes, their stocking feet pad-padding in the tubes above my head. They squeal listlessly from expectation rather than delight. A playground for children constructed from a culture of decay. There is enough plastic here to make Tupperware for a whole continent and I am too stunned to even drop my mouth in horrified dismay.

Mother would think that this is some kind of grandiose joke. She would laugh in her cigar-breath way, her ever-present stogie clenched between her molars in a way that would make Clint Eastwood envious. Mother would enjoy this place to no end, but I am stricken. I am an urban rat, but I still recognize the forces of the sun, the moon, the patterns of wind that guide me. Albeit through a film of pollution. These tragic children who are taught to play in an artificial world can only follow the route to an artificial death. Their spirits will be trapped forever with a shelf-life of an eternity.

I wander, dazed, dismayed, my dancer's feet dragging heavily on the Astroturf. Some of the older, anaemic children stop and stare, whisper to each other from behind covered mouths. I take no heed. I continue through the cultural maze of hyper-artificiality.

There is no hope, my mind mutters incessantly. My steps slow, motion is stilled, all joie de vivre leached through the bottom of my feet.

Stone.

A toddler toppes backward out of a chute. A milisecond of silence. Then she bawls like the world has ended. Red, yellow and blue balls fly fitfully through the air. Children gulp from tubs of simulated Coke while waiting for their microwave-heated pizzas. A boy bends over and, splat!, vomits a soft pink mound of hotdogs.

Horrible humanity. How can I bear this? How can anyone bear it?

No! I must not waver from my calling. I will not follow the path of my father into woe and I won't encrust my airy spirit within a coarse mantle like my mother. It is not enough to simply stand on the outside and gape, albeit with a closed mouth. It is not enough that only I fully understand the human mall condition. What if I am to overcome the shackles of social norms and, thus, reach the outer limits of time and space? Do I want to survey the vista alone? I must join the epicentre of humanity.

I must enter the maze.

'Watch your fat can,' I can hear my mother's raspy voice all around me. 'Don't come crying to me. I'll only say "I told you so" and kick you in the butt.'

Mother, oh, Mother.

I circle the strange man-made maze, thinking to myself that a woman never would. I circle thrice before I spot a young child scurrying up a hot pink pipe like a rabbit with a watch. I squelch my body into the mouth of the tube, wishing for a ball of thread.

Fat rat in a sewer pipe. The thought bubbles hysterically to the surface of my mind, but I kick it in the can just like my mother.

What is strangely interesting is that instead of getting stuck like an egg in the throat of an overly greedy snake, my body elongates. It spreads towards the ends. All I need to do is flutter my toes to initiate a forward motion.

I slide, glide smoothly through the twisting tubing. The only impediments are the large metal heads of bolts that are used to fasten the portions of pipe together. The friction of my clothing rubbing against the plastic raises such electricity that I am periodically zapped with great sparks and frazzle. Definitely a design flaw. Children in neighbouring tubes pad, pad, twirl down spiral slides. Their small muffled noises are only broken with intermittent zaps and small exclamations of pain.

I have never taken care of children, although I've cared about them in theory . . .

Something pokes the bottom of my foot. Of course, I cannot turn around to look. A barely discernible voice squeaks in protest and the single voice is joined with another, another. For in my contemplation I've ceased my inching progress and I've blocked the tube like a clot of fat in an artery. Their small mouse-like rustlings unsettle my philosophical and scientific musings. I flap my foot at them to go back the other way.

Then I notice, for the first time in my life, something that has always been with me. I am so completely encased in plastic that it cannot be diluted by outer forces.

I can smell myself.

The wonder! My odour is not smell, but sound . . . It's the voices of mythic manatees, the cry of the phoenix, the whispers of kappa lovers beside a gurgling stream, the voice of the moon turning away from our gaze, the song of suns colliding. The sounds that emanate from my skin are so intense that mortal senses recoil, deflect beauty into ugliness as a way of coping. Unable to bear hearing such unearthly sounds, they transmute it into stench.

And my joy! Such incredible joy. The hairs on my arms stand electric, the static energy and my smell/sound mix with such dizzying intensity that the plastic surrounding me bursts apart, falls away from my being like an artificial cocoon.

I hover, twenty feet in the air.

The children who were stuck behind me tumble to the ground. They fall silently, too shocked to scream, but the pitch of sound that seeps from my skin intensifies, like beams of coloured light. The sound catches the children from their downward plummet and they bob, rise slowly up to where I float. I extend my hands and the children grab hold, hold each others' hands as well, smile with wonder.

'Oh my God!' someone finally gasps, from far beneath us. Another person screams. Fathers faint and an enterprising teenager grabs a camera from a supine parent and begins to snap pictures. None of it matters. This moment. Tears drip from my eyes and the liquid jewels float alongside us like diamonds in outer space. I burst out laughing and the children laugh too. I don't know what will happen tomorrow or the day that follows, but the possibilities are immense.

We float, the rest of the plastic pipes shimmer, buckle beneath our voices then burst into soft confetti.

Gregory Scofield *b.* 1966

MAPLE RIDGE, BRITISH COLUMBIA

'I am called a poet—a political poet, an angry poet, a Métis poet, an ex-street-involved poet, a gay poet—yet I think of myself as a community worker, a teller of stories, a singer of songs.' Gregory Scofield's self-definition is an accurate description of the composite profile that emerges from his work. He writes through a voice that is 'the voice of many communities, the voice of ancient speakers, the voice of contemporary nomads—though always it is the voice of my "Grandmothers and Grandfathers", a voice that sings one small song in a community of powerful singers.' These voices, and the intricate stories they tell about the displacement of the Métis people, speak powerfully through Scofield's poetry. *The Gathering: Stones for the Medicine Wheel* (1993), which won the Dorothy Livesay Poetry Prize, and *Native Canadiana: Songs from the Urban Rez* (1996), which won Scofield the Canadian Authors Association Air Canada Award for the most promising young writer, have established him as a poet who writes, in a lyrical voice that captures both the cultural and spiritual tenor of his Cree heritage and the search for self-expression, about the gritty life on the street and the traumas of growing up in foster homes.

Scofield was born in Maple Ridge, British Columbia, and grew up in Vancouver, northern Saskatchewan, northern Manitoba, and the Yukon. Of Cree, Scottish, English, and French descent, Scofield has traced his ancestry to the Métis Red River Settlement and Kinesota, Manitoba. *Thunder through My Veins: Memories of a Métis Childhood* (1999), an autobiographical prose narrative punctuated with poetry, has allowed him to take ownership of his life of dispossession and turn the vulnerability of his early years into personal and spiritual strength. This book also pays homage to the two important figures in his life, his late mother, Dorothy Scofield, and his aunt Georgina Houle Young, not a relative, but a neighbour who was instrumental in his discovery, and appreciation, of his Native heritage. *I Knew Two Métis Women* (1999), inspired by and dedicated to these two women, is a book of often comic poems 'fused with old time country music', the songs Dorothy and Georgina were fond of. *Sakihtowin-Maskihkiy Ekwa Peyak Nikamowin / Love Medicine and One Song* (1997) is a series of candid erotic poems that speak of Scofield's 'two-spirited' sexual identity. Scofield's writing, which includes CBC radio dramas, has been widely anthologized.

Offering: 1996

This long drought
scorches the skin,
blisters me in places

most vulnerable; inner thighs,
tailbone, nape of neck—
the sacred temples.

5

Since your body eclipsed
I've swallowed the moon,
pretended light from others

and my bones did crack   10
and from my mouth
grew many unhappy weeds.

Where once were drums
and flutes and songs
there is silence,   15

incurable as the heart, hopeless
like your resurrection
I breathe all my breath

to conjure
what I hold most sacred: 20

your full, coaxing mouth,
the two perfect moles
I've named and kissed
the back of your legs,

that smooth dip   25
between your cheeks, the musk
from the shell of your arms

which left underwater
is a potion, a drug
lulling me to dizziness,   30

lifting me upward
like sage and cedar
singing to the heavens, singing

to guide you home.

from *Thunder Through My Veins*

Ta-pa-koo-Me-way-win (Making Relations)

It was the same moon
glowing hot
from my aunty's mouth
while drinking.
Those demon fire-balls   5
bounced in my head
and became stories.
Mornings
I thought I heard them
rumbling her guts   10
behind the bathroom door.

Years later
I met others downtown,
all piss-moon talkers.
The yellow lines   15
dividing the road
said which side
we belonged on.
The alley or ditch
was where we pissed,   20
all swapping coyote scents,
charming
the scarred moon face
out of her
shameful silence.   25

Haw, ne-kis-key-sin

the language was spoken,
always spoken.

Ekwa ekose ke-toh-ta!

Haw, ne-kis-key-sin: Now, I remember   30
Ekwa ekose ke-toh-ta: And so, listen

Mom got out of treatment two months later, and for the first time since coming back to Maple Ridge, she seemed happy. She started going to AA and began to meet all kinds of people, most of whom were recovering alcoholics with one common purpose: to stay sober. Sometimes she took me along to meetings, and I'd hear stories about them losing their homes, partners, and children. It was so depressing, and I wondered if any of them had lived in our building.

Abby and I continued to play together in spite of the hurtful things she said. When our regular games of hide-and-seek, river combing, and sitting in our old rusted jalopies grew boring, she got the idea to sneak around people's suites in the hopes of catching them at something—what, I didn't know, but it seemed thrilling at the time. One afternoon we were snooping around the back of the building when suddenly Abby grabbed my arm and hushed me. 'Ho-ly fuck!' she burst out, pointing to one of the suites where the drapes were open. 'That guy's playing with his dink.' I was so shocked, I couldn't speak. Abby was grinning from ear to ear and she had a terrible twinkle in her eyes.

'Let's bang on his door and run away,' she exclaimed gleefully.

'No,' I said, disgusted that she would even suggest it.

'Oh, come on,' she coaxed. 'You're such a chicken shit.'

Before I knew it, we crept to his front door, knocked loudly, and took off. As if that wasn't enough, Abby insisted we do it again. Only the second time, we got caught. The man threw open the door and stood there completely naked. He invited us in and Abby pulled me inside. He wanted us to take our clothes off and asked me to lie on top of Abby. He said he would give us each twenty dollars (which seemed like a lot of money) and made us promise not to tell anyone. Abby started to giggle and told him we were too young to fuck. I was so mortified I bolted out the door and ran home. A few moments later Abby came to get me, laughing so hard tears were streaming down her face. But later on we told her mother who immediately called the police. The man was arrested, and we never saw him again.

In spite of the severe warning we received from our mothers not to talk to anyone in the building, Abby and I continued to visit the tenants we knew. One tenant in particular was a retired teacher named Phil, whom our mothers trusted implicitly and whom we called Uncle Phil. He often took us to the lake or out for ice cream, and sometimes we even slept overnight. Uncle Phil didn't have any children of his own, and so our mothers encouraged us to spend time with him. He was loving and gentle, and treated us like nieces and nephews. But after a while he started to change. He would slip his hands down our swim trunks or ask us to sit in his lap and rock back and forth. We didn't tell our mothers for fear of breaking our promise to him. But then one night Billy came home crying, saying that Uncle Phil had tried to suck his penis.

I'll never forget the utter chaos of that night. Abby's mother woke Mom up and they stormed upstairs to Uncle Phil's and dragged him out of his apartment. They yelled and hit him as if they were going to kill him. The entire building was awake and everyone was watching. After the police came, and we were questioned, Uncle Phil was taken away. I remember watching him being escorted down the stairs and into the car, his hysterical sobs filling my ears like sharp knives. Abby, Billy, and I were told: '*Never talk to anyone in the building again.*' Mom then warned me she didn't want me playing with Abby any more, which made no difference because a short time later Abby's mother got back with her father. She quit her job, they left town, and I never saw Abby again.

With Abby gone, bad as she was, I didn't have a friend in the world. I wasn't interested in anyone at school, nor was anyone interested in me. I was just as happy to be alone, wandering off down to the river or losing myself in books. To me, no one could be as interesting as watching the river flow by with its massive log booms or reading about the great chiefs like Sitting Bull, Red Cloud, Geronimo, and Chief Joseph.

One afternoon, on the way home from school, I remembered the Indian woman. I hadn't seen her and wondered if maybe she had moved. I rushed home, threw my schoolbooks down and was already halfway up the stairs to her suite when I remembered Abby's words, 'Indians are all drunks.' I also remembered Mom's warning, but I had to know if she was still there. I crept around to her living-room window and sure enough she was busy at her sewing machine. She must have felt me watching her because she suddenly turned around. I froze on the spot. She came to the door, opened it, and looked at me inquisitively.

'You're Dorothy's boy, uh?' she asked, squinting through her glasses.

'Yes,' I nodded, feeling ashamed for spying on her.

'Ah, den how's your mama?'

'Fine.' She caught me looking into her suite and smiled.

'I'm jist doin' some sewing in here,' she said. 'Dis guy wants his slacks hemmed up. You wanna come inside?'

'I'm not supposed to,' I said feebly. 'My mom told me not to talk to anyone.'

She looked at me thoughtfully, nodding her head. 'Well, in dat case maybe it's not a good idea,' she concluded. 'Maybe first ask your mama, den you can come back to visit.'

'Okay,' I mumbled and shot off down the stairs before she even had a chance to close her door.

Oddly enough, I wasn't sure if she was even an Indian. She didn't really look like one, not like the Indians in my picture books. She had shoulder-length auburn hair which she wore tied back in a ponytail and had a small, narrow face with sharp features and light brown eyes. She wore large-framed glasses, a pink jogging suit, and matching slippers. She sort of looked like Mom, only older. But she talked funny, pronouncing her *t*'s as *d*'s, and I thought she might be from Europe—maybe even Italy.

That night I told Mom about meeting her. At first she didn't have a clue who she was, but then she suddenly remembered. 'Oh, yes! That's Georgie. I've spoken to her in the laundry room. She seems like a very nice lady.'

'Can I visit her then?' I asked hopefully.

'Only if you promise not to make a nuisance of yourself.'

I was so excited, I could barely sleep. The next day, after school, I ran home and went straight up to see Georgie. When I peeked in the window she was busy at the sewing machine. I tapped on the glass and she came to the door.

'So you come back to visit me, uh?' she said. 'You ask your mama?'

'Yes.'

'Well den, *ke-pe-tah-kway*,' she said, gesturing me inside. What language was that? I wondered.

Her suite was small and immaculate, smelling of pine-sol and freshly baked bread. The furniture was old and tattered, but it gleamed in the sunshine. There were piles of clothes, all neatly folded in baskets by the sewing machine. In one corner of the living room were stacks of old records, a stereo, and a guitar. A homemade quilt and richly coloured pillows covered the couch. In another corner stood or sat dolls of various sizes and shapes, all of them dressed in old-fashioned clothes and wearing miniature moccasins. Above the dining-room table hung pictures of the Virgin Mary and of a dark-haired man, smiling tenderly in a beaded picture frame.

'Dat's my boy, Danny,' she said, pointing to the picture. 'He's not wit us any more.' I wasn't sure if that meant he was dead, but she looked sad and I didn't want to pry.

'What about school today?' she asked, changing the subject.

'It was okay.'

'I bet you got all gold stars, uh?'

'That's only in kindergarten!' I laughed.

'Is dat so!' she teased, grinning through her glasses. 'I taught maybe you were only tree years olt.'

'I'm almost eight!' I exclaimed, grinning at her silliness.

'But not too olt for milk and cookies, I bet!' She went to the kitchen and started to fix me a plate. Her back was to me, and without thinking I suddenly blurted out my question: 'Are you an Indian?'

'Sure,' she said, turning around and smiling. 'I'm a Cree—a *Nay-he-yow*!'

'Who?'

'A *Nay-he-yow*,' she said, slowly pronouncing the word. 'Dat means a Cree Indian. And what about you?' she asked.

I shrugged my shoulders, suddenly aware that I didn't know anything about my background.

'Well, den let's see,' she said, coming over to look at me. 'Hmm,' she began, bending down to examine my face. 'You got grey iyz and light hair, but you also got a big nose, high cheekbones, and big fat lips.' I felt my face going red and she started to laugh. 'I tink you must be an *Awp-pee-tow-koosan*, like me,' she concluded. 'I see it, too, in your mama.'

'What's that?'

'Dat's a half-breed. Half dis and half dat.'

'Half what?' I asked, afraid of the answer.

'You know, half devil and half angel,' she teased.

'I don't think so,' I politely answered. 'I think I'm a great chief like Sitting Bull and Red Cloud.'

'Is dat so!' she called out, looking at me closely, a smile breaking across her lips. 'Oh, yes, now I can see it.'

I sat back proudly on the couch and dug into the milk and cookies, pondering what she had just said about being a half-breed.

'But I heard you singing an Indian song,' I suddenly blurted. She thought for a moment and then said, 'Oh, yeah. My mudder taught me dat song. She was da *Nay-he-yow* and my fadder, he was French. I can sing in French, too!' she exclaimed proudly, rolling her *r* drastically.

Georgie was smart and funny, kind and wise, and I spent every available moment I had with her. She had lost all three of her children, two of them as babies to pneumonia, and Danny when he was thirty-three. He was coming home from Alberta for Christmas and was killed in a car accident. She seldom talked about her first two sons, but she talked about Danny all the time. She told me that he was a wonderful musician and that he knew how to play and sing every Hank Williams song. He was also a gifted artist, and sometimes she brought out his drawings to show me. I remember looking at them and touching them as if they were fragile, as if I were beholding a piece of him.

Sometimes, when I stayed overnight with Georgie, she told me stories about her childhood in northern Alberta, and how her mother had taught her to hunt and trap. She told me stories about the convent school she attended, the nuns and priests, and all of the mischief she and her chum Agnes got into. I spent hours at her table, wide-eyed and curious, drinking mugs of hot tea (she said tea was the only good thing to ever come out of England), while she transported me to another time and place. My favourite stories were the ones about *We-sak-e-jack*, the First Man, the Trickster, and how he forever tried to trick the birds and animals. She also told me about *We-tik-koow*, the cannibal monster who roamed in the bush at night, looking for unsuspecting children to eat. Sometimes she would be doing beadwork or making a beautiful pair of moccasins or vest for someone. Her floral patterns and brightly-coloured beads were the most exquisite things I'd ever seen. In time, she taught me to do beadwork, giving me a little piece of moosehide to practise on. We sewed for hours on end, over tea and stories, and I gradually became a skilled beadworker. I recall how satisfied I felt finishing my very first pair of moccasins. She said that my work was much better than a lot of the old ladies back home, and her praise made me feel all the more special.

But there were also times when I wasn't allowed to see Georgie. Mom would say that she was busy and not to bother her, although I knew the truth. The drapes would be drawn and everything looked dark. Sometimes I could hear strains of the Carter Family or Hank Williams coming from her suite. Other times I would see her leaning out her bedroom window and she would call down, 'How's my boy doing?' I knew she was drinking. I always felt sad when I saw her drunk, because I knew she missed Danny.

I never told Mom that Georgie called us half-breeds. I still wasn't sure what it actually meant, only that we were sort-of-Indians. But I told her everything else Georgie said and taught me. Mom never said much, only that she liked her a great deal and that she was happy I'd found such a good friend. And as always, she made me promise not to make a nuisance of myself.

A short time later, Georgie verbally adopted me in the Indian way, and from then on I called her *Ne-ma-sis* (my little mother; Aunty). She said the Creator had sent me to her and that I was meant to take the place of Danny. By now Mom and Georgie had become friends, and Mom was pleased to share me with her. Aunty began to teach me Cree, and I picked it up quickly, as if I'd heard it before, as if the words were buried somewhere within me. She taught me about the old-time medicines: how to prepare and use them, what their names were in Cree, the need to be quiet and respectful when I used them. The medicines, like *che-stay-maw* (tobacco) and *we-ke-mah-kah-sekun* (willow fungus) were used for 'smudging' or praying, while the medicines like *muskeeg-ke-wapoy* (muskeg tea) and *a-cha-cha-moon* (sneezing root) were ground up and boiled into a strong tea and used for various ailments such as colds or fevers. And she told me about *Ke-chee-manitow*, the Creator, explaining that the Indian religion was the same as Christianity, and that the white people had no business telling the Indians how to pray; that they did so because they were afraid of what they couldn't see or understand.

The more Aunty taught me about the medicines and the old-time ways, the more I felt connected to something. I felt as if she had given me special knowledge that none of the other kids at school had. I felt a new and powerful connection with God, *Ke-chee-manitow*, who, unlike Grandma's Bible pictures, became the Great Spirit without a face: the Spirit that lived in the river and trees, mountains and rocks.

Mom seemed happy. She met someone at an AA meeting and began to date him. His name was Don and he lived in our building. He was tall and slim, had black hair and eyes, and he seemed like a nice man. Mom was head over heels for him and she acted like a schoolgirl, laughing and giggling. She started wearing make-up and jewellery, nice clothes, and even traded in her flip-flops for high heels.

At first I liked Don because he treated me kindly and listened to all of my Indian stories. He laughed and said I had a great imagination. I couldn't understand what he found so funny, because he was obviously part Indian. I wasn't sure about me or Mom, but I figured we must be Indians—like Aunty—she had said so. Then one day when Don and I were alone in my room, I showed him some of the medicines Aunty gave me. He seemed uncomfortable and impatient. I assumed he would be interested, and without giving it a second thought, I said, 'But you're an Indian.' His face went about twenty shades of red. He grabbed my arm and squeezed it so tightly, I began to cry. 'Don't ever fucking call me that again!' he hissed. He let go of me and went upstairs to see Mom. I was stunned by his response. I didn't tell Mom for fear of being called a liar or, worse yet, spoiling her newfound happiness.

Mom and Don continued dating and attending meetings together. By now he was having dinner with us and spending the night. Secretly I hoped he would go away, but he only seemed to come around more and more. I spent as much time as possible with Aunty, and told her what Don had done. 'Dat bastard!' she roared. 'You come stay wit Aunty whenever you want, my boy.'

Now Don made no attempt to hide his dislike for me. I often overheard him talking to Mom, telling her I was spoiled, and that if she wasn't careful, I'd turn out to be one of those 'poofters'. I had no idea what that meant, but it sounded bad. He also told her that I was jealous of him and that I would do anything to split them up. He said that I needed strong but *loving* discipline, and to my surprise, Mom believed him. She turned the discipline over to him, and he used every opportunity to 'show me the right way'.

In the beginning Don would march me downstairs, force me to pull my pants down, and spank me. But then he started to use belts or whatever else he could find, like coat hangers or pieces of wood. Still, when that wasn't enough, he would hit me in the face or stomach. Sometimes he even threw me down the stairs. He would march down after me, grab me by the scruff of the neck, and shake me until I went limp. Mom knew he was getting carried away and tried to stop him, but he would hit her, too, all the while screaming, 'Do you want a God damn brat on your hands!'

I had bruises and marks all over my body, and the teacher began to ask me questions. I always lied, telling her that I'd slipped or fallen. Once, when she asked me outright if someone was hitting me, I looked her straight in the eye and said no. Mom's social worker also came by, but nothing came of it. As usual, I stuck to my story, more for Mom than anything. I just couldn't bear to leave her again.

The only one who knew the truth was Aunty. How I loved and trusted her, even more than Mom! After my 'punishments', I'd run up to her place and bury my face in her lap and cry. 'Never mind, my boy,' she'd soothe. 'One day you'll show dat bastard whose boss—if not wit a good licking, den in udder ways.'

Then came the blackest day. Mom announced that she and Don were getting married. I was so panic-stricken, I couldn't see straight. How could she? He hit her! He hit me! But she was determined and promised me he would change. All I had to do was behave and mind my manners. Everything, or so she wanted to believe, would turn out just fine. Later, Don sat me down and told me the new rules:

1. No more Indian stuff in the house.
2. No more sassing him or giving him dirty looks.
3. No more asking Mom for favours like staying up late to watch TV or read, I was to go directly to him.
4. No more wasting time after school, I was to come home every day and do my chores and homework.
5. No more Aunty.

Even before he got to the last rule I knew what it would be. He knew that I loved Aunty more than anything in the world and that I went to her whenever I had problems. I looked to Mom for help, but she looked away. After Don excused me, I ran as fast as I could down to the river where I sat and watched the murky water. I felt betrayed, as if my heart had been yanked out, as if a vital part of me had been killed. For the very first time I thought about my father and wished he was with me. Like Mom, I didn't know if I should love or hate him. But it was clear I hated Don. *Ke-chee-manitow* had given me Aunty—and now the Devil was taking her away.

Phinder Dulai *b.* 1967

PUNJAB, INDIA

As the title of his poetry book, *Basmati Brown: Paths, Passages, Cross and Open* (2000) suggests, Phinder Dulai is a poet journeying through the different spaces—real spaces and those existing only in memory that tend to preoccupy diasporic writing. While his poems in this collection 'speak of home and homeland', they do so 'without nostalgia, and with a clear place of connection'. As he says, 'one can never turn away from family lineage.' His own lineage hails from the state of the Punjab, India, where he has returned a number of times. His writing has been published in many literary magazines and he has performed his work and talked about migrant voices in schools and universities across Canada and overseas. The author of a second poetry book, *Ragas from the Periphery* (2002), Dulai has worked as a journalist in Vancouver's South Asian media, and was associate producer for CBC's *Gabereau Live*. He lives in Burnaby, British Columbia, and works for the BC government.

basmati brown

(confession of a punjabi breeder)

i'm coming out
i shall say
i'm outing my self
declaring:
hey, and by the way i'm brown baby   5
and though i know the
low (g)lass achievement
will not change
i want the world to know i'm brown
like a dark cup of coffee   10
dollops of cream
lots of succour
dark green brown
an oak tree in full bloom
marigolds ripple with velvet flesh   15
an instant when you squint
hues exploding into each other
in glorious fluidity

i want you to know i'm as brown
as the earth that once shaped the way my mother ran   20
how she whispered of her life, future and husband
thinking that he would be the oldest and wisest

when she knew she would have to be the oldest and wisest
in a new land that ate up dads 16 hours a day
stumped out souls   25
no wonder she lost her mind
a child's mind, wise beyond her manic laugh
that still raised five kids
sits broken
like a raggedy doll   30
doing time in the playhouse
wondering
where did they all go
and laughs when her punjabi radio station
allows her sometimes to phone in   35
and offer the world her views and thoughts

i'm basmati brown, feeding into you into me
as silver streaks, and glory follows me
folding around
a ghostly cloth   40
dirty with age
maybe an outline
the bearded one
saviour as you called it

and the world listens   45
to the way my foam
reaches the shoreline
and vanishes into the roots of the sand

i'm coming out
through the rail that hugs   50
dry sediment
when it dies out from under
the tracks, while a line changes
a brother
at the cpr   55
switches miles
thinking maybe that mile
could bring him someone who will fix him
i'm brown and broken

. . . i get   60
. . . the job
. . . done

love
i'm broken, don't know how to fix me
fixed me   65
frozen in the blistering heat
i'm broken
let me be right
open me up
the way i opened   70
i had friends and soul,
i knew how to love between lines
enemy/friend
a clock turns heavy in my heart

i want to declare to the world   75
it will mean nothing to say this
cause it means everything
when i out myself to my beloved
she will tilt her head and say
'i know already, i know already'   80
and i will say
i never knew how brown i was
until i saw it in people's faces
cool amusement
asexual nighttime tryst of fear and lust   85
curse and cradling head
lines of fixation
oh how brown
fevered paws in the dirt
vats full of strawberries and blueberries   90
broken smile
brow fretting upon brown
not so pretty eh?
wife beater
illiterate   95
dirty
small
limited corporate mobility
too good of an employee
shitty worker, does nothing   100
doesn't even speak english
too smart for his own good
better keep an eye on that one
a real r-a-d-i-c-a-l, shit disturber, activist
shit like brown the way you shit   105

stinks of curry
should put on deodorant
funny how he doesn't wear a turban, i thought they all did?
hey how come you don't wear a turban?

brown baby,   110
brown like the *pind*
the way the cow shits it out
life . . . matter . . .
all life matters
but it is nothing for me   115
to say this
and everything for you

Larissa Lai *b.* 1967

LA JOLLA, CALIFORNIA

'In my fiction writing,' Larissa Lai says, 'I have been focusing on trying to create a sort of historical launch pad for hybrid flowers like myself. I have been trying to foster the germination of a culture of identified women of Chinese descent living in the West.' This is clearly the case with her first novel, *When Fox Is a Thousand* (1995, 2004), which won her the Astraea Foundation Emerging Writers Award, and was shortlisted for the Chapters/Books in Canada First Novel Award. The novel, inspired in part by the traditional Chinese stories about supernatural experiences collected by the sixteenth-century writer Pu Songling, revolves around a Fox, a recurring trickster-like figure in Songling's books. Capable of metamorphosing and of 'travel[ling] both beneath the surface of the earth and above it', the Fox is a 'wily' character that transcends time. A mischievous figure that embodies 'the power of seduction', it enables Lai to construct a beguiling narrative that asks difficult questions about sexuality and feminist politics.

Lai's desire 'to rediscover a selfhood that does not rely on either white and/or patriarchal expectations of what I/we should be', and to do so in ways that challenge realism or engage with speculative fiction, motivates the narrative of her second novel, *Salt Fish Girl* (2002). Shortlisted for the Sunburst Award, the Tiptree Award, and the W.O. Mitchell Award, it presents the female body as a site of cultural, racial, sexual, and economic conflicts. Oscillating between Chinese mythic time and a future time when transnational corporations have rendered nation-states obsolete, it is a compelling narrative that denaturalizes many inherited assumptions about origins—those of families, nations, and myths, but also those of the human body. The limits as well as limitless potential of human subjects and cyborgs are at the centre of this book.

These two novels, along with Lai's other writings, including her 2004 poetry chapbooks, *Rachel*, *Nascent Fashion*, and *Sibyl Unrest* (the latter co-authored with Rita Wong), show that Lai's literary imagination is inextricably related to her political consciousness. 'I love the power and the romance of confrontational politics,' she says, 'because there is a purity in that refusal to back down, that refusal to take shit, or to compromise. But in another way, I found increasingly that to engage politically in that manner also confirmed and validated precisely those liberal racist politics we meant to dismantle, by always placing ourselves in opposition to them. In other words, to claim the opposite was to affirm and validate as original and meaningful precisely those insipid ways of seeing and behaving that I found most offensive.'

The daughter of academic parents, born in La Jolla, California, Lai grew up in Newfoundland, and has lived in Vancouver and Calgary. She holds a BA (Hon.) in Sociology from the University of British Columbia (1990), an MA in Creative Writing from the University of East Anglia (2001), and a PhD in English from the University of Calgary (2006). Her dissertation, a study of 'Strategies of Liberation after Identity Politics,' reflects her own activism. Involved in anti-racist work since the early 1990s, Lai worked with Paul Wong and Elspeth Sage on *Yellow Peril: Reconsidered*, and helped organize 'that madcap conference Writing Thru Race that sent a bunch of injured white men howling on the pages of the *Globe and Mail* about how they were being silenced and marginalized'. Empowering and enabling in many ways, these events also made Lai realize 'the way people tend to reduce activists to their politics'. Though her creative and critical work challenges the history of racialization, aware of the 'irretrievability of history', of 'how historical writings must always necessarily be about the present', Lai is 'trying to escape writing from a racialized space'.

Named one of the Top Ten Writers to Watch Under 40 by TVO's *Imprint*, Lai has just been hired as a professor of English at the University of British Columbia. She is presently at work on a new novel, called *The Corrupted Text*.

The Salt Fish Girl

La senteur du poisson salé évoque plusieurs tensions complexes autour de l'amour et du ressentiment. Ayant dans sa tendre enfance été nourrie au poisson salé, une jeune fille voit son estomac réclamer ce goût et ses narines rechercher cette odeur. La senteur la conduit au marché, vers la fille du marchand de poisson salé. Défiant sa mère entremetteuse et se dérobant de ses devoirs domestiques, elle retourne semaine après semaine au kiosque de la fille au poisson sale—pour acheter son poisson, pour la sentir, pour l'aimer. Elle est accrochée, saisie par la senteur et fini par établir un plan audacieux et désespéré pour s'échapper avec son amante.

When I was fifteen and still many years from marriage, I fell in love with a girl from the Coast. She was the daughter of a dry goods merchant who specialized primarily in salt fish. It was, in fact, her father's trade that brought her to my attention. She stank of that putrid, but nonetheless enticing, smell that all good South Chinese children are weened on, its flavour being the first to replace that of mother's milk. They feed it to us in a milk-coloured rice gruel, lumpier than the real thing and spiked up good with salt for strength.

You might say saltiness is the source of our tension. Stinky saltiness, nothing like mother's milk. The scent calls all kinds of complicated tensions having to do with love and resentment, the passive-aggressive push-pull emotions of a loving mother who nonetheless eventually wants her breasts to herself, not to be forever on tap to the mewling, sucking creatures that come so strangely from her body and take over her life.

Especially knowing from keen observation of her mother before her, that we eventually grow too monstrously huge for the memory of our births, and that we will eventually leave. Why give away too much of yourself, especially intimate bodily fluids, when you know you'll be abandoned, with or without gratitude depending on luck? Give 'em salt fish congee early and you'll forget about 'em sooner and vice versa.

That's the problem with girls. They leave. You can't rely on them. Of course, in these modern times of difficulty and poverty, you can't rely on boys either. Who knows if or when their overseas uncles will call for them, change their names, call them 'son' instead of 'nephew', and leave you in the dirt. The red earth, I mean, that's the classical term, isn't it, so bloody and morbid, those old sages. So my mother started me on salt fish congee early. Who could blame her? She was never the type meant for motherhood. If it hadn't been expected of her, if she had had other options, she'd have been an empress or a poet or a martyr. Something grand, and perhaps a bit tragic. She loved those old sages, with their subtle cleverness and sad girl stories. But leave those to me. I didn't ask for them mind you, I'm as much a puppet of fate as anyone else.

I noticed the salt fish girl on market day. My mother had bribed me with a promise of sweet sesame pudding to do the shopping. Trying to make up for lost time, I guess. But why bother offering me sweet now, when it's salt I'm hooked on? She thought she could change me, but it was a bit late for that. Besides, while the sticky pot may be a great place for drowning spirits, its dark thickness doesn't entice. Perhaps later, when I've learned to love my dark self, thick and heavy, but sweet as sugar in spite of everything. Until then, it's stinky salt fish I'm after.

I went to the market more because I wanted to get out of the house than because sesame pudding does anything for me. Little did I know that my mother's intentions behind the black sesame pudding had nothing to do with making up for any neurotic, return-to-infancy, childhood-deprivation fantasies on my part. That she had something infinitely more immediate and material in mind.

I'm not saying that my take on the matter was entirely fabricated, mind you. My mother *was* thinking about abandonment. She wanted me out of the house that day so she could invite nosy Old Lady Liu the go-between over to talk behind my back about matters matrimonial. I know some girls are betrothed at ages much more tender than mine, but still! I was only fifteen. Wouldn't there be plenty of time for that later?! Talk about morbid, self-fulfilling fantasies! Oh sure, I know it's tradition. I know my mother isn't personally to blame, that she was just doing what all good mothers are supposed to do if they want their daughters to live respectable lives. Note I didn't say happy. We all know that joy and sorrow are entirely matters of fate and have nothing whatsoever to do with planning.

So she had only my welfare in mind, but did she have to start so early? It was a cruel trick of patriarchy to make her the agent of our separation which she so dreaded. Dreaded and longed for, just to have it over with. It was a complicated black sesame pudding she stirred up that afternoon.

As for me, I went to the market with my baby brother strapped to my back and a belly clamouring for something savory.

As we approached the market, a young woman turned the corner down a dark alley, one strong brown arm bracing a basket of salted dainties atop her lovely head. The scent of the fish, or perhaps her scent, or more likely still, some heady combination of the two wafted under my nose and caused a warmth to spread in the pit of my belly. I followed her right to the entrance of the market, ignoring the rice-wrap and sweet potato seller whose wares I otherwise would have paused to ponder over.

I followed her right to the salt fish stall that she ran with her father. She set the basket down among numerous others filled with tiny blue-veined fish so small it would take twenty to make a modest mouthful, and others filled with long dry flats of deep ocean fish the length of my forearm and half again. I bought enough to flavour a good-sized vat of congee and then breathed deeply to still my mind for the rest of the shopping.

After that I was hooked. The recollection of her bright eyes and lean muscular arms reeled me in as surely as any live fish seduced by worms, or perhaps more accurately by shreds of the flesh of their own kind. I made it my job to do the family's marketing in spite of the fact that it fell on top of all my regular chores, of which there were many—fetching water, feeding the chickens, sweeping the courtyard, taking care of my baby brother and chopping all the meat and vegetables for every meal. I was frugal, had an eye for fresh goods, and was a good bargainer, so my mother was happy to send me. Besides, my Saturday morning absences were a perfect time for the go-between to visit.

So while my mother secretly sweetened-up that meddling old nanny-goat, I managed to see the salt fish girl once a week, except when she went back to the Coast with her father for more supplies. At first she took little notice of me—just another skinny village girl with bad skin and bony fingers. She sold me my fish without a word beyond the few necessary numbers and then turned to the impatient aunties eager to get home for their morning congee.

Whether it was because I was such a staunch regular, or whether it was because of the way I gazed at her above the smelly baskets over which black flies hovered and dirty hands exchanged coins, I don't know, but she began to recognize me and put aside choice bits of merchandise in anticipation of my arrival. As she passed me the pungent preserves and took my coins, she stole a quick glance or two and flashed a shy smile through which her crooked teeth peeked endearingly.

A number of months passed in this manner before I worked up the gall to invite her to come with me when market day was over. Of course I would catch a scolding for shirking my day's duties when I got home, but the adventure would be well worth the bother. In the late afternoon, we walked down to the river together, lay down in the tall grass and played tickling games until the stars sprinkled down from the night sky and covered us like bright, hungry kisses.

Then we separated. I walked home reeking of salt fish, took my anxious mother's scolding with a brave and defiant face, went to bed and tumbled into a deep and contented slumber.

The following week, I announced my decision to become a spinster. Tradition allows this, if the family is agreeable and there is no protest from the local magistrate. My mother was furious. The go-between had found a suitable husband for me in the neighbouring village. He was the youngest son of a silk farmer, which was a common but respectable trade in these parts. He was blind in one eye, and ugly as sin. He was the only one of his brothers who had been sent to school and rumour had it that his father wanted to find him a position with the government. My mother had been making arrangements for us to meet that week.

'Forget it,' I said. 'I've got arrangements of my own.'

'I never raised you to be so cheeky, I'm sure,' she said.

'True. But aren't you glad I'll be here with you when you grow old, rather than scrubbing undies for my mother-in-law?'

I showed her all the money I had saved spinning silk for other village families, and announced that I would pay for my spinsterhood ceremony myself. I refused to eat until she acquiesced to my will.

It was harder for the salt fish girl. No spinsterhood tradition was observed on the coast and her father was dead set against her picking up the nasty customs of the locals. He forbade her to see me.

I hadn't expected this little difficulty. I had assumed she would follow my example. I hadn't asked myself what I would do if she wasn't able to. Did I still want to enter the sisterhood on my own? It is hard to retract such a grave decision as I had made without losing clout to make further autonomous decisions regarding one's life. Worse still, some of my sisters were upset with me for choosing spinsterhood for less than spiritual reasons. I sat tight and continued to see it through even as I plotted how to rescue the salt fish girl.

Her father could not stop me from coming to the market. I continued to buy fish from her until one afternoon, in a fury, he closed his stand early and marched her to the mud hut on the edge of the market district which was their home when they were doing trade in town.

Desperation made me bold. I went to his stall the following market day, hoping to see her. I didn't, but the pungent odour of salt fish inspired a plan. Pumped full of fool's courage, I went up to him.

'Where is your daughter?'

'Thank-you for your concern, but if you don't mind my saying, it's none of your business.'

'That may or may not be the case,' I said, more boldly still, 'but won't you tell me anyway?'

'She's sick at home, no thanks to you.'

'Then tell her I wish from the depths of my heart that she would get well soon and come to see me,' I responded politely.

If there had been fewer people standing around watching, he would have reached out and slugged me. I could read the restraint in his eyes. As it was, he refused to sell me any salt fish, but pointed me in the direction of the butcher instead and said perhaps the man with the bloody apron could do something for me.

I thought to stay and argue, but decided I'd better back off for the time being.

The next market day, I passed by his house just as he was leaving. I heard his daughter pleading with him to be allowed out, to be taken along to the market. He refused sternly and locked her in the back room where she wailed loudly long after he was beyond earshot.

An hour later, I approached him at his stall.

'Where is your daughter on this auspicious market day?'

'She's at home with a fever, no thanks to you.'

'Tell her I am praying to the Goddess of Mercy for her health and hope that she will come and see me soon.'

He grunted.

I tried to buy some fish, but he said I didn't deserve it and would find what I deserved at the execution grounds on the other side of town. I would have spat at him, but there were too many people watching.

The following market day, when I approached him, he lunged at me in sheer fury, grabbed me around the neck and squeezed as hard as he could. I choked desperately. It took five big men, including the bloody-aproned butcher, to pull him off me. The first thing I could smell when I could breathe again was salt fish. The stink of it made me want to live more than ever.

I walked around the marketplace at a furious pace, contemplating. The sky grew dark and the vendors one by one began to close their stalls. My stomach started to grumble. I hadn't eaten since early that morning. I circled the market place looking for a cooked food vendor, but they had all packed up and gone home. The poultry man was busy with his fowl. He had three unsold chickens which he was trying to pack into the same basket, but they squawked and pecked at each other, as though each was to blame for her sister's unhappy fate. Suddenly the basket burst and the chickens ran about clucking madly. One ran farther afield than the rest. On an impulse I took off after it. The poultry vendor, in a hurry to get home, yelled after me, 'If you can catch it, it's yours.' The chicken led me right to the salt fish girl's back window, where I pounced on it and clutched it, squawking, in my arms.

She leaned out the window dangling a heavy fish hook. Expertly, she hooked me by the scruff of my collar and pulled me, chicken and all, into the house. 'You could try to be a little more subtle,' she said.

The chicken kept squawking. She drew a fish gutting knife from her skirt and solemnly slit its throat. Blood spurted up in a long arc, and drenched me in a dark shower.

In the downpour I hatched a plan. 'Pack a bag,' I said. 'We're going to escape.'

She gave me a mop and some clean clothes. I sopped the blood up quickly, put on the clean clothes and helped her out the window. With the chicken in one hand and the bloody clothes in the other, I jumped out after her.

We dug a shallow hole in the backyard, buried the bloody clothes and then ran to the river. There, we stole a skiff and floated downstream.

In the morning, finding his daughter missing, the old merchant ran to the police and accused me of kidnapping. The police searched my parents' house and found nothing. They said I had not come home since setting out for market the previous day. Eventually, questioning led the police to the bloody-aproned butcher and the other four men who had dragged the salt fish merchant off me the day before.

'Perhaps,' said the butcher, 'he's accusing the girl to conceal something terrible he's done to her. Surely it's at least worth searching his house.'

The police made a careful search of the merchant's house and found nothing but baskets and baskets of sweet and pungent salt fish. The merchant shot a scornful look to the butcher, who stood in the doorway. The police were just about to call off the search for the day, when the youngest of them noticed some newly turned soil behind the house. As I had hoped, the bloody clothes were unearthed and identified by both my parents and the butcher as mine. The poor old salt fish merchant stood accused of murder.

Many miles downstream, munching on boiled chicken, I chuckled at the thought.

The salt fish girl asked me why I was laughing and so I told her. But instead of laughing with me, she pulled a long face.

'What's wrong?' I asked.

'I don't want my father to die,' she whispered, and began to cry.

It's a bit late for that, I thought. *You should have said so a long time ago.* But I said nothing and put my arms around her. I could feel her heart pounding inside her ribcage. She sobbed and howled so desperately that I said, 'We could go back. We'd still be in time to save him.'

But she shook her head through her tears. 'What's done is done,' she said. 'What happens is what's meant to be.'

I held her and said nothing. She continued to weep and eventually sobbed herself to sleep. And that, I suppose, was the beginning of our quarrels.

Suzette Mayr *b.* 1967

CALGARY, ALBERTA

'I'm . . . interested in talking about the second and third generation Canadians of colour who can't be categorized as immigrants,' says Suzette Mayr; 'this makes them trouble, and for me trouble is a great place to start writing fiction.' Highly adept at writing as much realistic prose beaming with energy as prose that fuses surrealism and cultural mythologies with sharp wit and humour, Mayr is one of the most original writers of her generation. Of German and Afro-Caribbean origins, she was born and raised in Calgary, where she worked as a waitress and night-shift sandwich maker before she took up writing and became actively involved in the city's literary community. She holds an Honours BA in English from the University of

Calgary and an MA in Creative Writing from the University of Alberta. The Markin-Flanagan Writer in Residence at the University of Calgary in 2002–3, she has been on the faculty of the English Department at the University of Calgary since 2003, teaching Creative Writing and twentieth-century Canadian literature focusing on representations of race and ethnicity.

Mayr was already widely anthologized by the time she published her highly acclaimed first novel, *Moon Honey* (1995). Nominated for the Georges Bugnet Award for best novel and the Henry Kreisel Award for best first book, it revolves around one of Mayr's major preoccupations, mixed-raced subjectivity. Its protagonist,

Carmen, a young white woman who 'has known few coloured women', metamorphoses, virtually in the middle of a sentence, into a black woman. But while her blackness seems to thrill her white boyfriend's hunger for the exotic, it brings out the worst in his mother, Fran, whose racism is already known. Relying on Ovid's tales of metamorphosis, Mayr constructs a unique parable of racial transformation and racialization as Carmen comes to feel at home in her newly changed body: 'Being a brown girl almost feels like being drunk. . . . A reverse Oreo cookie, an inside-out coconut, the juice running down the sides . . . She's sipped and gulped so much she's drunk. . . . That's what being a white girl turned brown girl is all about. Or a brown girl who was brown all along but nobody knew, not even herself.'

Interracial relations, and the conflict of cultural and national traditions, also feature prominently in Mayr's second novel, *The Widows* (1998), translated into German and shortlisted for the Commonwealth Prize for best book in the Canadian–Caribbean region. In her third novel, *Venous Hum* (2004), about a high school reunion and the racial and gender tensions it gives rise to, Mayr's wit turns to satire. Irony and humour help to mediate Mayr's concern about the perception that her writing is not 'black enough'. As she says, 'race and the representation of race are complicated, and people of colour can also be dinks, and talking about these things shouldn't be a bad thing. It becomes a bad thing, though, when there are so few people of colour being noticed and only "good" representations are wanted.' The co-editor of *The Broadview Anthology of Short Fiction* (2004), Mayr has also published two poetry chapbooks, *Tale* (2001), with Geoffrey Hunter and Robin Arsenaeault, and *Zebra Talk* (1991).

The Education of Carmen

> *My purpose is to tell of bodies which have*
> *been transformed into shapes of a different kind.*
> —Ovid, *Metamorphoses*

Carmen and Griffin begin dating the day she turns eighteen, back when she is still a white girl. When she is eighteen and a half they make love for the third time under the pool table in his parents' basement; she knocks her head on the table leg, and her skull roars with pain while Griffin pumps, his eyes closed. Her eyes roll back until the whites gleam pearl, her bottom jaw drops, and when she comes to she figures she's been unconscious for about a minute and a half. Griffin takes about fifty-eight seconds. Carmen's timed him. They've timed each other. Griffin fifty-eight seconds, Carmen ten minutes—they've learned that orgasm speed relies on biology, the difference between men and women. Some of her girlfriends never have orgasms. Griffin's buddies, on the other hand, have no problem. Men and women.

They have concussive sex in the same room as the wooden inlay picture of three happy black people, Africans she supposes, with long thin necks, baskets on their heads, thick red lips and gold hoops in their ears. Under the pool table they can lie relaxed and sweaty, side by side, and look up at the picture, the only decoration on any of the walls. A souvenir, Griffin says, a souvenir his mother picked up on one of her business trips.

Where? asks Carmen.

I don't know, some place where blacks live, obviously.

His mother, Fran, doesn't like Carmen at all. Carmen is not the kind of girl Fran would choose for her son, not the kind of girl Fran wants included in her family's blood-line. Carmen doesn't talk, slides in and out of Fran's house without so much as a hello or goodbye, as though Fran were invisible or merely a servant. Fran only ever knows if Carmen is somewhere in the house from her grimy sneakers parked in the front hall, or the normally immaculate ashtrays crammed with lipsticked cigarette butts. Griffin and Carmen disappear for hours, the entire day sometimes, slam the front door or the back door or the patio door when they're back from wherever they go. 6 PM, a door slams and Griffin asks, when's supper, Mom? just like nothing's happened, and the next thing Fran knows, Griffin is stuffing an entire bowl of green salad into his mouth and Carmen's beside him at the dinner table holding out her plate as if Fran owes her food. Fran's mother would have slapped that plate out of Carmen's hand, then slapped Carmen hard in the face. The least Carmen can do is help clear up. Fran is tired of being her servant.

Have some more green salad, Carmen, Fran says, and whips the bowl of salad across the table.

Fran also disapproves of the premarital sex she knows Carmen and her son are having. Fran isn't stupid, she wasn't born yesterday. Sex is for people mature enough, financially stable enough, to handle an accident. She wouldn't put it past Carmen to get pregnant just to get her bitten nails into Griffin now, while he's still young, with so much promise. Oh yes, Fran's laid down the rules, no Carmen in the bedroom, no closed doors in the house, all the lights on the moment the sun goes down. She doesn't approve of the two of them disappearing for entire days, or Griffin arriving home at four o'clock in the morning, but she refrains from commenting because even if Fran doesn't like Carmen, at least Griffin isn't homosexual. At least he's sticking to girls, whorish and unmannered as Carmen may be.

Now if he was out until four o'clock in the morning with some strange boy, she'd certainly have something to say. Ida Sorensen down the street found out her son was homosexual, walked in on him and some young fella kissing for God's sake. God knows what would've happened if Ida'd walked in just ten minutes later. God knows. Fran would kill herself first. Carmen is a quiet and devious little tart, but maybe Carmen can learn. Be changed. Converted.

When Carmen turns twenty, Fran hints during Sunday dinner that they should be thinking about marriage. She wants to see grandchildren before she dies. St Francis, she says, is a beautiful chuch. Carmen doesn't say anything—she doesn't believe in God or St Francis or church or marriage—and Griffin chomps with his lips drawn back on the tail of his steak. He's a vegetarian when he's not in his mother's house; he doesn't become a meat-eater until he goes home at night. Fran sulks if he doesn't eat her dinners.

We were thinking maybe we'd just live together eventually, Ma. He chews the steak slowly, doesn't eat the fat, doesn't suck at the juice, doesn't let the bloody flesh touch his lips.

Oh, well, if that's what you want, says Fran, stacks the dishes loudly, one on top of the other so that long cords of fat lop down over the rims. If that's what you want, but her face says Closed For Business. If her body were a section of land, she would be surrounded by coils of barbed wire, protected by Doberman pinschers snarling. No Trespassing. No Ingrate Sons Allowed.

When Carmen and Griffin are together they are so much in love. These are the kind of dishes we'll buy, says Carmen. Brown ceramic. That's my favourite. Earthy. I just can't do porcelain.

Mine, too, he says, surprised. And I've always liked the name Italo for a boy.

Hmm, says Carmen. I won't breastfeed, so you and the baby will have a chance to bond via the feeding experience.

I could be a superior househusband, he says doubtfully. Griffin doesn't know anything about children. Neither does his mother. Fran wrinkles her nose in disgust at the masturbation stains on his bed when she changes the sheets.

Anyway, how can they live together, let alone get married; it's a great big joke what with both of them still in school and no real money to live on except from rotten summer jobs, landscaping for Griffin and waitressing for Carmen.

There is always more opportunity for sex in the summer, though, since the warm weather lets them use the car or the shelter of trees in city parks. Their bones clash rhythmically in the dark, bodies pale and pasted together, a four-legged, two-headed amoeba. Because they have no privacy, they rely on masturbatory short cuts, their uniforms clothes that fall open but stay on. Most of all, they rely on speed. Carmen scuttles for cover when headlights peer through the dripping windshield, or the beam of a flashlight skips through the trees. She is an expert at pulling her jeans up, or her skirt down, her cheeks bright red but her mouth bland and virginal, her hair, the colour of blades of wheat, falling smoothly into place. Griffin just takes a flip to his fly, lies serenely in the half-dark of the car seat, or propped against a tree trunk, arms crossed behind his head, his skin opal.

It's not like we're committing a crime, says Carmen. Next time we should just keep going. Too bad for whoever walks in on us.

One day they will live together like a real couple. Not necessarily get married, Carmen sees marriage as territorial and possessive. Why, once she tried to find a married friend in the phone book and couldn't because she didn't know the husband's last name.

Sometimes bits of gravel and dust on the floor of Griffin's parents' car get stuck in her underpants. One day she will stop lying and tell her parents she and Griffin are spending the night together. She will just *tell* them.

Screwing in the car and getting gravel in her pants is preferable to winter sex. Winters they have to resort to a dangerous game of tag with Fran, grabbing sex in whatever room of the house they're sure she's not in. If she's upstairs they skitter downstairs to the room with the pool table, or the laundry room. If she's downstairs they spill their juices in his bedroom (not on the bed, for God's sake—the springs! the springs!) or on the kitchen floor, or upright in the dark front hallway. What can they do, they're so much in love, the urge just takes them and they can't help themselves.

For now, since it's summer, they use Fran and Godfrey's car floor, Carmen's parents' car, Fish Creek park, or if they're lucky, her best friend Joan's apartment. Do it on top of a sleeping bag on the living room floor. Carmen gets nervous about having sex in other people's beds. Profane somehow. Embarrassing when there's a mess.

Carmen works mostly the morning shifts and then leaves for home in the middle of the afternoon. Her uniform is a pair of navy blue cotton shorts with a white cotton shirt and an apron she folds over and ties around her waist. She carries menus in her left hand, swiftly pours coffee with her right, and can carry up to six full plates of food at a time. Most days she combs her hair into an orderly ponytail, barrettes the sides so the long straight strands don't drag in the food, and sprays her bangs until they crackle. If she wakes up early enough she can French-braid her hair, spray it, then curl the bangs into a springy slope across her forehead. Ringlets are her favourite, ringlets on both sides of her face, and her back hair in a bun. She looks dynamite with ringlets, Griffin says so, the other waitresses say so, *Carmen* says so, but ringlets drag in the plates of food and by the end of the shift have transformed into long, greasy, eggy, jam-encrusted strands tucked behind her ears anyway. Bangs scraped back and a bun at the back of her head are the most sanitary way to go, but really, what is she? A nurse? Or worse, a nun? She has to feel proud of herself.

The more tables she has the more challenged she feels, the better she performs; she moves with figure-skating speed and grace as she whirls out coffee, menus, food, keeps her customers happy, and chatters in a friendly but business-like manner.

White or brown? Apple or orange? Overeasy or sunnyside up? Cash or charge?

She is, undoubtedly, the best waitress in the world. But being the best waitress isn't necessarily the best career choice.

Waitressing is the job she resigns herself to every summer. Every year she swears she'll find a job more suitable to her area of university study, a job less demeaning, a job less *high schoolish.*

We have unlimited potential! she insists to Griffin. We can do better than this!

But the wage improves every year and so does she; she has to be realistic. She will keep waitressing until she is offered a better-paying, more meaningful alternative. This year her manager, Rama, is a woman, originally from India or somewhere, and so sensitive. Rama unbalances all the waitresses, not only because she is so strict but also because she is the most beautiful woman in the world.

You know, says Luce, a waitress who's been at the restaurant even longer than Carmen, these Pakistani-types have such beautiful complexions. Smooth as babies' butts. And big brown puppy eyes to boot. Amazing.

Uh-huh, says Carmen.

Although, you know, continues Luce, my second cousin's married to a man who's black as the ace of spades and his complexion isn't the greatest, I have to say. So some of these coloured people don't have the best skin. Rama has beautiful skin. She's one of the lucky ones.

Uh-huh.

Because what else is there to say. Carmen is afraid to say anything else, she has never worked so closely with a coloured person before. Rama smells different. Spicy, or flowery, some strange brown-skin perfume. The distinctly gritty smell of armpits when Rama sweats. She's seen Rama spread hand lotion on. Standard hand lotion. It's the chemistry of a person's skin, she's heard, that can make a perfume change its smell. Rama must have a certain chemical makeup to make her body smell this way with just a bit of hand lotion. Or maybe it's what Rama eats at home, although Rama eats restaurant food just like everyone else during breaks. She's heard East Indians eat a lot of curry in their food. Is it curry? Carmen likes curry. Maybe it's just the combination of hand lotion and brown skin and sweat. Pigment transforming smell.

Carmen has known few coloured women, so Rama makes her nervous; she would never ask Rama what she eats at home or what perfume she wears. All the coloured women Carmen meets are so *angry*, not that Carmen's really met any—well, she's been in the same classes as some but they don't really talk that much generally. She's seen them on television at demonstrations and riots and things in the States. Always in packs. Carmen is afraid to speak in front of Rama, afraid to say something that will offend. What if Carmen causes a riot by saying something racist? Carmen knows how different races stick together, she's seen ethnic gangs on the news.

Rama's hair, long, shiny, black hair cut so perfect and make-up matched to her skin. Carmen tells Griffin that Rama's skin is like cinnamon, or no, like cappuccino. Carmen would like a tan halfway between her own skin colour and Rama's. That would be the perfect colour.

Customers naturally ask Rama where she comes from, and Rama says CANADA like she's offended. Carmen and the other waitresses hang out in the kitchen, gossip and flirt with the prep cooks whenever Rama's out of the way. Rama's too uptight, she'll never last, they say. Is she even qualified to be a restaurant manager? Heard she's sleeping with the owner.

Get your asses back to work, yells the chef, he's a grouchy little man, and the prep cooks mutter about how they work their asses off, work like niggers, do most of the work in fact—why's a Chinese guy cooking hamburgers anyway? Stick to egg foo yung at the Long Duck Dong.

Yeah, Long Duck Dong, Long Duck's Dong, Duck's Long Dong, echo the waitresses, and they scatter. Carmen doesn't ever say this out loud, but Duck's Long Dong is what pops into her head whenever the chef screws up an order. Long Dong Duck. Long Dong Duck.

Norm, yells Luce. I can't serve this bacon! This bacon's still squealing!

Luce skewers the bacon on a small plate with a fork, takes a bite out of it.

Maybe in China people are happy with raw meat, but welcome to the Western world!

Norm pushes a small plate of bacon towards Luce, doesn't speak, only keeps cooking, sweat dripping from his forehead, soaking into the rim of his chef's hat.

Stick to making chop suey, mutters Luce. Ching chong duck damn dong. She pops a piece of butter on her plate of food.

What did you say? says Rama.

Nothing, I didn't say anything. Just talking to Norm.

What did you say?

Nothing. Jesus.

Rama goes into her office and closes the door. Luce serves her customers their breakfasts, passes the office on the way to the coffee station.

Rama opens the door slightly and gestures to Luce with a long, shiny fingernail, the inside of her finger pink and the outside dark, coffee-flavoured brown. The office door closes behind them.

Carmen and the other waitresses do their jobs, keep their ears toward the office door in case either Luce or Rama says something loud enough to penetrate. The waitresses change ashtrays that contain only a smidgen of ash, pour coffee for their tables over and over until customers become annoyed by the excessive attention. Could I have the bill, miss, please? I don't need any more coffee.

Carmen's bangs droop and feather into her face from the nervous sweat on her forehead. She takes over Luce's tables.

Luce stays in Rama's office until the restaurant is closed. Luce's voice pierces through the door, shrill and constant. The waitresses cluster, waiting for their tips to be collected and distributed. They stand close to the office door, but not too close in case either Rama or Luce behind the door lashes out and burns them.

Luce steps out of the office and closes the door behind her. She stands facing the other waitresses, swaying a little, her face carved from wax. She stands and sways under the fluorescent lighting of the restaurant, her skin shiny from sweat and oil, her lipstick bitten off and the exposed skin on her lips chapped and raw. Luce's body suddenly shrinks, crouches as she gathers breath into her lungs. She screams. Screams and screams and screams, her face blossoming into a bright and rabid pink. She twirls around and gives Rama's door the violent middle finger of her right hand, then her left hand, then kicks the fake wooden panelling, left foot, right foot, left food, right foot.

Everyone says that, shrieks Luce between kicks, everyone does! We say it to his face, he doesn't mind, he likes it, he's used to it! What does he expect coming to this country, that he'll *fit in*? I was going to quit this job anyway! You wouldn't know how to run a fucking restaurant if your fucking life depended on it!

Luce holds a pink slip, the same colour as her face. Blood gone from her knuckles, she crumples the slip in her hand, and throws it on the floor. Rama doesn't answer, doesn't even watch Luce run out of the restaurant and down the street still in her uniform, just opens the door to her office, then sits back down behind her desk. Rama counts out the waitresses' tips into even piles of ten-, five-, two-dollar bills and loonies with her dark brown fingers, her fingernails polished and pinky-brown as seashells on a tropical beach. Her fingernails brush and tap the surface of her desk. The door to the office now wide open, Carmen and the other waitresses line up at Rama's desk, listen to the fine clicks of her fingernails, the snap of money in her hands. Rama counts out money, writes down numbers, lightly swivels her body in her chair as she reaches from one part of the desk to the other. The waitresses stand around the desk in a semicircle, simmering, resentful, afraid. Rama lifts her face, wrings them all dry with a *look*.

Carmen's stomach sinks whenever Rama approaches her, whenever Rama swishes past, long black hair spread fan-like across her shoulders, make-up always dark and perfect. Rama the thundercloud. She tells Carmen not to forget to water table eight, or that table one needs their ashtray changed—as if Carmen needs someone to tell her how to do her job. Carmen speaks to Rama not at all if she can get away with it.

Hi, Rama, bye, Rama. This is all she would say if she could get away with it.

The prep cooks, one by one, are replaced.

Not too busy today, eh, says Rama.

No. No it's not, says Carmen. She looks down to make sure her apron's on straight. She left a little note for Rama asking for tomorrow off, she hopes and prays that Rama will give her tomorrow off, tomorrow Griffin has promised to take her to the mountains.

Guess we won't be needing you tomorrow morning then. Hasn't been busy lately.

Thanks!

Carmen feels a tear-pricking surge of gratitude and fondness for Rama. Carmen wants to hug Rama until she cracks. Rama smiles.

Where do you come from Rama, Carmen ventures, feeling chummy and happy, I mean originally you know?

Well, Rama hesitates, I was born in Winnipeg. That's where my parents come from.

Rama isn't so frightening after all, maybe they could even be friends.

Winnipeg. Well. I guess I mean where does your family really come from. My boyfriend's Scottish all the way back and his dad even has a *kilt* stashed away. You speak without an accent, just like you're Canadian. You know, with Canadian parents.

The air around Rama's body glints polished slate. Carmen, unable to stop, finds herself saying: You're not like other coloured people of course. You don't *act* coloured. A lot of time I don't even notice. Your skin, I mean. Maybe it's none of my business.

Maybe it's not, answers Rama softly.

I'm sorry. But I don't understand, I don't understand what the big deal is. I mean we're all the same underneath aren't we? I would never say anything racist intentionally, but wouldn't it be better for me to know just in case I make a mistake? Why can't you just tell me why it bugs you so much when people ask you where you come from? Why are you so angry all the time? What d'you have against white people anyway? This isn't a racist town, it's not like the KKK goes galloping up and down the streets or something. You've got a good job. I don't know why people have to be sensitive all the time. Why not just integrate? Why try to stick out all the time? People don't mean to be mean. Surely you understand *that*. Don't set yourself up as a target —be more casual.

The sound of her own voice sounds off-key to Carmen, too high or too low, strings snapped from a violin under a rigidly-applied bow. The words that come from her mouth don't belong to anyone she knows. Belong to the other, another Carmen.

Carmen sees Rama's hands start to shake, the blood rush to Rama's face, Rama's mouth about to say something, but her voice is eclipsed by Carmen's questions. Carmen sounds like a drunk person, slurs her words in a tipsy monologue.

Educate me, says Carmen. Show me where all this racism is, why you're so angry and bitchy all the time. Show me. If I cut you you bleed, if I cut me I bleed, we're all the same underneath. Show me the difference. Show me the difference!

Carmen's lips can't stop stretching and singing: Luce calling Norm Long Duck Dong is the same as you calling us Canucks. Being called a Canuck may hurt my feelings but I don't let it get to me. I have more important problems.

Carmen flinches at the backfire crack in Rama's back, Carmen having laid on the last precious straw and at last, Carmen is going to lose her job, she's going to end up like Luce, broke and with no reference and her work history ruined. Now she won't be able to pay for school and she'll have to ask her parents for money and they'll want to know why and what if they don't have enough money to put her through school this year? She'll have to take out a loan, she knows all about loans, her cousin Josepha got a loan and she's *still* paying for it, $25,000 in debt and only twenty-six years old. Carmen closes her eyes. I am not going to cry I am not going to cry dear God please don't let me cry, dear God please don't let me lose this job I'll do anything, and she prays oh she prays even though she doesn't believe in God, up until now she hasn't believed in anything anything anything. Her mouth opens and closes, opens and closes, her instrument wound to the breaking point.

Three veins in Rama's forehead stretch upward in the shape of a trident. She gives Carmen a *look*, but this time the look pulls apart Carmen's face, peels off Carmen's skin. *I cut you you bleed I cut me I bleed*, burrows through the layer of subcutaneous fat and splays out her veins and nerves, frayed electrical wires, snaps apart Carmen's muscles and scrapes Carmen's bones, digs and gouges away Carmen's life.

The colour of Carmen's pink and freckled fingers and forearms deepens, darkens to freckled chocolate brown and beige pink on the palms of her hands. Her hair curls and frizzes, shortens. Hairs dropped into a frying pan kink up around her face, curl into tight balls on the back of her neck. Her skin, covered in a thin layer of dry skin, flakes from where she missed with the skin lotion this morning. Her hair is drier, finer; irises freshly dipped in dark brown cradle her pupils. And her scars, old knotted scars from childhood, from last year, from last week when she touched the hot oven with the back of her hand, open their eyes and glare pale against her skin. Her history is etched out in negative.

The hot slab of granite that is Rama's face dissolves as Carmen changes and Rama suddenly laughs. Laughs and says, Yeah, some of my best friends are coloured people too. I even know some okay white people. And Carmen lets out a breath.

Carmen, now a brown girl, keeps her job *and* gets tomorrow off to go to the mountains with her one true love.

Carmen also starts to laugh, the bridges of the two women's noses wrinkle meanly as they laugh, and Carmen goes back to her station. Waters the customers and fetches more buns and whipped butter from the kitchen to stop the rumble of hunger, the questions: Where do you come from? How long have you been in Canada? Is the seafood here fresh?

Part of the job, part of the job, the customer is always right.

One of these days, I swear Rama, Carmen says, I'm going to give these dumb white people what-for.

This is how metamorphoses work. They happen all the time. Women turn into trees, birds, flowers, disembodied voices at the moment of crisis, just before anger, grief, desperation eats them alive. Daphne twists and stumbles before Apollo until she gnarls into a tree, her smooth skin rough and impenetrable, forever a virgin. Echo's love unrequited, she withers into her name. Loses herself to love instead of cutting her losses and finding a new lover. Other fish in the sea—she should have asked to be a trout instead. Women who've lost their mothers grow poplar bark and weep sap, as though tears of sugar instead of salt make the sadness less. Or attractively more. The more charming you are in your sadness the more likely you are to be saved. The more desperate the more likely you will be saved. Take a second look and become a pillar of salt.

At the most terrible moment bodies transform into bears, nightingales, bats. But which bodies? Who's so lucky? White girls in a blasted moment grow the bark and flow with the sap of coloured girls. But this is only one moment.

I've never seen lips on a vagina so brown, says Griffin. I've never touched black hair, can I touch it? So soft.

Stupid question, Carmen says. What a stupid question.

Well, you know what they say, says Griffin, as he strokes her black hair, pushes in her dark brown nipples. Once you sleep with black, you never go back. Something like that.

Carmen and Griffin cover their mouths with their hands, giggle at his naughtiness.

I've always wanted to sleep with a black woman.

Oh, yeah? Why's that?

But she is more concerned that he is leaving, going to Europe, than she is about her new *pelt*, as Griffin calls it. Her *pelt*, he says and strokes the skin all over her body. She, knows Griffin has always wanted to travel to Europe, *has* to. It's his dream, he's planned to go all his life, still it's hard not to want him to stay with her, it's hard to give him up for so long. She thought of going, long ago when he first mentioned Europe, but he never *asked* her.

Of course she never asked him to ask her. Her priorities are different. What's the big deal anyway, meet more people, meet more problems. She works in the public service field—she knows. And money. What about the money? She wants to finish school first, she's not a stupid girl. Europe is all fine and dandy but afterwards, then what?

It's the experience, Griffin says. I want to see other places, other people. Get a better sense of how I fit in the world. See Buckingham Palace before I settle down.

One of them has to be practical, experience won't pay the rent, won't free them from living in their parents' houses. She doesn't mind being the practical one. If they both went to Europe they couldn't afford to move in together until they were both in their fifties! She loves Griffin, but sometimes he can be so unmotivated, so shortsighted, so live-for-the-moment.

Don't spend all your money over there, she pleads, Save some for when you get back, remember our moving-in-together fund!

Maybe his spontaneity is why she loves him, so different from herself. She'll miss him so much, like having roots ripped out of her soil.

Do you love me? she asks.

Of course.

If you love me then why are you going to Europe?

Umm. Uhh.

She sees the sweat spring out on to his forehead as he scampers in his little brain for an answer. Poor sweet thing.

I'm just kidding, she says. Just testing.

They walk in the park together. She admires her long brown legs in the sun, smells the lemon-scented laundry detergent of her clean cotton t-shirt. She puts her arm around his waist. A beautiful day. *They* are not as beautiful as usual, though, she isn't wearing make-up today. Hasn't worn make-up for almost two weeks, her make-up from before no longer fits her brown skin. She never realized how vital make-up is to making a girl feel good about herself. Just a little something to brighten up her face, her heart. She even catches herself avoiding mirrors now. But at least she has Griffin, and Griffin doesn't seem to mind her naked face. Griffin thinks she's beautiful no matter what. He is wearing the nice blue shirt she bought him last Christmas, 100 per cent cotton. She slides her hand under the shirt, feels the indented small of his back, the shifting muscles with each step. Notices how people stare.

Haven't you noticed? she asks. Strange, isn't it?

I guess that's because we're a mixed couple now, he says. Just like John Lennon and Yoko Ono. He squeezes her hand. He's so smart.

I guess we'll have cocoa babies, he says, and Carmen smiles. She has always liked the look and smell of cocoa. Hot chocolate is her favourite drink. Hot chocolate in winter, chocolate milk in summer. Small brown babies, hers and Griffin's. Maybe if they have a boy, the baby's middle name could be Italo.

Pushing her little chocolate Italo in a carriage through a park.

Rita Wong *b.* 1968

CALGARY, ALBERTA

A 'large tradition of social and political movements for justice, a hidden tradition of women's writing, a well-known tradition of love poetry, a long tradition of travel writing'—these are the cultural and political sites that inform and shape Rita Wong's poetry. *monkeypuzzle* (1988), her first poetry book, is the result of an intense dialogue between the political and lyrical forces that take this poet across real and imagined landscapes—into the intimacy and energy of a kitchen, the sweat floor of a factory, a dark cave with wall paintings. Written from the perspective of a woman trying to reconcile her Chinese background with her North American vantage point, these poems reveal Wong's interest in straightening out the vagaries of history and of the present moment.

For Wong, trying to find the tradition she comes from as a writer entails unwriting and rewriting received knowledge and wisdom, as is the case, for example, with her family tree, which '[goes] back 20 generations' but lists only 'the oldest son of each generation': 'none of us [women and younger sons] would be on that tree if we followed its rules.' Her many poems anthologized and published in literary magazines also show Wong's profound concern for those suffering as a result of global capitalism, as well as her commitment to fighting racism. 'I grew up during an era of multiculturalism,' she says, 'which is not necessarily as progressive as one might think. . . . When we get beyond song, dance and food, a lot of serious issues around institutional access and genuine social equality still need to be addressed.'

A resident of Vancouver, where she has lived for a number of years, Wong was born and raised in Calgary and holds an Honours BA from the University of Calgary (English, with a minor in East Asian Studies, 1990) and an MA from the University of Alberta (English, 1992). Her PhD thesis, written while attending Simon Fraser University (English, 2002), is a study of labour and racialization in literature. A critic, editor, and reviewer, Wong has been on the faculty in the Department of Critical and Cultural Studies at the Emily Carr Institute of Art and Design since 2004. She is an active member in the Asian Canadian writing community, and received the Asian Canadian Writers' Workshop Emerging Writer Award for *monkeypuzzle*. She is currently at work on her second book, tentatively titled *present imperfect*, and is the co-author, with Larissa Lai, of the chapbook *Sybil Unrest* (2004).

lips shape yangtze, <u>chang jiang</u>, river longing

three gorges, you whisper,
the sound of rocks filling your mouth:
we who have always been displaced by poverty
sent across the ocean to find rice

i look for the big sky, but the clouds suffocate me,   5
rain defeat for the dispossessed, over a million mouths gape hunger
stone soup, stone face, cracking as earth reveals herself through us

throat. gorges. the glottal stop rising into my nose
pressure on my lungs one hair away from unbearable
the heaviness of signing on the black dotted line   10
when you cannot read what you've signed

without memory, we die fast and brutal
flooded by greed
the drowned, bloated arm waves
and who will wave back?   15

the sound of rock breath
falls, empty into the diasporic spray
light wet on black hair

missed the boat, even as we step off it

cites of disturbance

'colonialism is even more active now in the form of transnational
corporatism' mm

commercial arteries

the top five arms manufacturers—lockheed martin, boeing, raytheon,
british aerospace and GEC—are all based in either the united states or   5
britain ni

'only a rat can win a rat race' mf

a calculated offensive

'i hear ocean sounds and a history of rain' ll

rupture@rapture   10

'he soon became convinced that the problems treated by psychoanalysis
were at their roots social problems' rh

red butterfly

'a Canadian government programme of subsidies for the military and
civilian aerospace industries was ruled illegal by the WTO, so it was   15
restructured to cover only military equipment and duly went through' ni

vancouver boasts 23 public libraries & 26 McDonald's

'ethics is probably something that surrounds you like your house it's where
you live' fw

'would you like fries with that?' *no, just a copy of* Stolen Life yj   20

mm masao miyoshi, 'a borderless world?' *asian american studies: a reader*
ni 'brute force: the facts' *new internationalist* 330, december 2000
mf michael franti, *live at the baobab*
ll li-young lee, *the city in which i love you*
rh rosemary hennessy, *profit and pleasure: sexual identities in late capitalism*
ni gideon burrows, 'a tawdry trade,' *new internationalist* 330, december 2000
fw fred wah, *music at the heart of thinking*
yj by yvonne johnson and rudy wiebe

'but the words she had. the language wasn't built for truth. it was a lying
tongue. the only one she had. it made separations. divided against itself.
it could not allow enwholement. only fragmentation. and it was the only
language they all knew together—the people in her world. the tongue that
only knew how to lie. the only words she had. the only containers for the   25
food, the water, the soil of recovery, uncovery, discovery. to re learn. to re
member.' pga

open why

clenched heart fist

'the city itself, perhaps the whole country, was a palimpsest, Under World   30
beneath Over World, black market beneath white' sr

chips in a casino economy

do mass denials return as mass addictions?

'arms exports account for more than half of the combined trade surplus
of the developed economies' mw   35

tokens of inspection, manufactured infection

'what you risk reveals what you value' jw

what you repress will return to haunt you

whoring in a liberal hegemony, commercial interludes second nature

the *deprive* in privatization   40

'it is not an exaggeration to say that it is clearly in the interests of the world's leading
arms exporters to make sure there is always a war going on somewhere' mw

a ghostly limb of labour in your sweatpants

from 1995 to 2000, texas governor george bush presided over 138 executions
of poor, unlucky people. gore also supports the death penalty.   45

pga paula gunn allen, *the woman who owned the shadows*
sr salman rushdie, *the moor's last sigh*
mw marilyn waring, *if women counted*
jw jeanette winterson, *the passion*
mw marilyn waring, *if women counted*

'i cannot go on strike, nor can i unionize . . . . i earn one dollar a month. i
cannot even voice grievances or complaints, except at the risk of incurring
arbitrary discipline or some covert retaliation. you need not worry about
NAFTA and your jobs going to Mexico and other Third World countries. i
will have at least five percent of your jobs by the end of this decade. i am   50
called prison labor. i am The New American Worker.' ᵐˡᵖ

'the body shuts down when it has too much to bear, leaving you numb
and half alive' ʲʷ

federal became feudal at the speed of corporations

'poverty kills. it kills faster and, currently, on a higher level than war and   55
nuclear militarization.' ᵐʷ

reinventing the enemy's language ʲʰᵍᵇ

substantive freedom has an economic backbone

a pocketful of music, a stomachful of nightmares masquerading as dreams

ᵐˡᵖ michael lamar powell, a prisoner in capshaw, alabama, quoted by angela davis in *the angela davis reader*
ʲʷ jeanette winterson, *the passion*
ᵐʷ marilyn waring, *if women counted*
ʲʰᵍᵇ title of anthology edited by joy harjo & gloria bird

puzzlinen

                                        blood red dye #3
                                    iron chink fish gutter
                                    tins   rust

              put into knit penguin purl two & woven baskets
strandmade   berry-dyed in woof cones weft china   5
              thread proceeds to east timorese rebels
chinese students grassroots africville   doing
language slow consciousness juggle   fishgasp & leap
struggle with what   put your toe on   slid—
    grasp for rail   de-railed   juggle jaguar grin bear   10
children & stories   maybe this that ribbon other or sprigs
on crazyquilt patch   sprigs on underwear before rip

fury channel
push

to oceans jump　　　to mountains track　　　over over over　　　15
not yet　　　　　to photographs tell　　　to trunk open over
only　　　laundromats always open　　　sundays even
　　　punch the cash register over　　　cheap food
pull the door　　it won't open　　　for you
　　　　what's wrong　　　you　　　20
　　　　everyone else　　　can
　　　they don't see it　　　laugh
　　　　basket　　　case
　　　　re　　　run
　　　suzy wongs　　　pocahontas! run!　　　25
　　　give them　　　hot food
　　　rotsa raffs　　　voice? what voice?
　　　you must　　　make this up

Tamas Dobozy *b.* 1969

NANAIMO, BRITISH COLUMBIA

Though Tamas Dobozy has 'trouble seeing himself as an immigrant writer,' since only three of his short stories in his book *Last Notes* (2005) deal with the immigrant experience, he thinks that 'in many cases' 'all writing in North America is to some degree a kind of diasporic writing'. The 'immigrant condition', he says, 'is far more widespread in North American writing than most people would admit. That being said, I write about a very specific kind of immigrant writing, and that is Hungarian immigration, and especially second-generation experiences. The stories that do deal with immigration are . . . about . . . negotiating one's existence in what is sometimes a . . . hostile situation, usually because the immigrant has made that situation hostile through some inability to conform.' While he does not 'feel [him]self connected in any way to other writers of immigration', the diasporic condition 'certainly inform[s his] sense of being a writer'. But his immersion into European literature while he was growing up and his academic background in American literature suggest that he 'come[s] at writing from a series of traditions, not just one'. He sees his writing, then, as a 'transnational writing, a writing that crosses borders, . . . that engages with many national experiences, and is not reduced to one nation'.

Dobozy was born in Nanaimo, but grew up in Powell River, British Columbia. He studied English at the University of Victoria (BA and BFA, 1991), at Concordia University (MA, 1993), and at the University of British Columbia (PhD, 2000). A specialist in American literature, and interested in the concept of hypocrisy in twentieth-century American writing, as well as the relationship of textuality and prayer, he teaches at Wilfrid Laurier University. His first book, *Doggone* (1998), a novel about the son of first-generation Hungarian immigrants who obsesses with killing the family's dog and finding his ex-girlfriend believed to have committed suicide, announces Dobozy's interest in irony, deadpan humor, and in stretching the limits of realism and narration. Influenced mostly by the way the European and Canadian sensibilities are fused in Mavis Gallant's short fiction, Dobozy's stories articulate a strong sense of 'detachment from place'. His characters, both those in his recent book and those in his first collection, *When X Equals Marylou* (2002), tend to inhabit an array of spaces ranging from Russia to Canada, from the Library of Alexandria to Alcoholics Anonymous meetings, from the interior space of dreams to the absurd yet multifarious spaces that suburbs can be. How to come to terms with 'not belonging' appears to be the overarching theme in his writing, a concern that mirrors his own experience as a second-generation Hungarian who has lived in different places in Canada, but has also spent considerable time in Budapest, Hungary, where he taught and wrote.

Four Uncles

Though Krisztina wondered at my loyalties, I buried them all: Uncle Gyuri, who, having emigrated from Hungary in the early 1950s, and having watched his taxes go to social programs, insisted he'd 'left one communist country only to end up in another', and who, in a fit of apoplectic rage one election night, refused to let his daughters out of the house, barring them with a shotgun because they threatened to vote for the Left; Uncle Pál, who wore scars on his back from the barbed wire he crawled under to escape a POW camp in 1946, and who, in defence of his Roman Catholicism and anti-Semitism, refuted the argument that Jesus was a Jew by saying, 'Technically speaking, Christ could not be Jewish since his father was God—a non-racial entity—and his mother, Mary—a being conceived without original sin and thus not human in the classical sense either'; Uncle Ottó, who, as a boy, trapped crows for his starving family to eat during the famine that accompanied the Soviet Army into Hungary at the end of World War II, and who had no time for unemployed Quebecers and Newfoundlanders refusing to move to where the work was, saying he'd left behind not only his region and culture, but also his country, language, and family, and had arrived in Canada with nothing, working his ass off in the face of considerable obstacles to build himself a fortune, and if he could do it, then damn it they could too and with a whole lot less sacrifice and pain.

I buried them all.

I'd come out at the start of 1958, having spent the previous year in root cellars and attics. Friends would show up now and again, either with food, or directions to the next hiding place and the exact dates and times when I should move. Mostly, though, I was alone in places without running water, or electricity, or heat, at the mercy of shivering fears—of capture and interrogation, of being sent to a Soviet work camp—glancing between the curtains, jumping at every creak in the architecture, and reaching the point of ravening hunger before I dared go into the street, in the dead of night, to scrounge in garbage cans. Invariably, once down there, I would become so frightened of the noise I was making in my haste to find something to eat—so scared it would give me away—that I'd sprint back empty-handed to my hiding place. Within two months I'd lost fifty pounds, and was a twitchy mess.

In my solitude I began reading every book, magazine, and newspaper at hand, their content increasingly irrelevant as my situation worsened, until only words mattered, the thought that someone out there was writing against my solitude. And as minutes turned to hours and hours to days and days to weeks and weeks to months, ever more noises broke the silence of my hiding places, or, rather, what sounds there were—the ticking of walls, muffled voices from above or below, gargle of pipes— became magnified, and began to make sense, forming intelligible rhythms; until I found myself imagining that somewhere in that intelligence—both on the page and in the air—were messages from the people I'd known. And when my associates came around, once every six weeks, they'd find me eating the rot I'd scrounged on some midnight run, or drinking rainwater from the pots I dangled out the windows during thundershowers, or sitting in my room with an idiotic grin and a mass of writing spread across every surface, as though I had all the company I needed.

But when opportunity came at last—when a friend burst into the room to tell me that the time was right, that a blizzard was blanketing the western half of the country which would help me cross the border unnoticed, that there was a driver waiting to take me—there was only one person I had time for: my mother. I had kept track of her in my seclusion, relying on outside reports, in the hopes that I could bring her with me when I escaped. Things had not gone well for my mother after 1956, as they had not gone well for anyone whose immediate relatives were involved in the uprising. Denied all assistance by the state, and having no other resources, she moved in with her sister; and it was there I went that night, rushing so I would still have time to meet the driver, slipping through the heavy snows that hid me from policemen into my aunt's house, skinny as a stray dog, sneaking from room to room until I came upon the tiny broom closet where she lay in bed.

'Mother!' I hissed, leaning over her. I'll never forget it: the room so quiet you could hear snow falling beyond the open window, a clock ticking somewhere far off; and, instead of the closed eyes and sleeping face I'd expected, I saw my mother staring at me as though she'd been awake all night. And in response to my quiet cry she began to hum, and to hum, and to hum, a tune I'd never heard before. 'Mother!' I hissed again. 'Mother, it's me. I'm alive.'

She hummed on.

And for a moment longer I stared into her eyes, thinking insane thoughts—that I might bundle her up, lead her into the blizzard, get her to ride in the truck to the border and keep quiet as we crawled past the fences and dogs and snipers. Then I gently took her hand, realizing there was no point, that she was already released, having hummed herself free of history: free of her father's death at the battle of the Don; of her mother's murder at the hands of Soviet soldiers who discovered them—her and the children—hidden in a cellar in Budapest, and who decided on a kind of R and R not at all entertaining to the children, and only entertaining to the soldiers because they'd spent two years throwing themselves in front of bullets and marching through Russian winters in boots flapping at the soles; free of her three brothers' disappearance into fates she obsessed about, bolting up in bed or in the middle of lacing her shoes, as one tormented by waking nightmares; and, finally, of the apparent deaths of her husband and her one and only son, who'd both been too active in the cause of 1956.

I do not remember how I felt, sitting by her bed that night, though I recall consoling myself with the thought that she was beyond loss; for she said nothing as I described how I'd passed the year since the uprising—how afraid I'd been to compromise her by making contact (even to say I was alive), why I was running, and from whom, and what would happen if they caught me—because she seemed not to be listening, neither replying nor glancing in my direction nor hardly breathing.

Instead, she simply looked around the room as if its walls formed the limits of her world, beyond which there was nothing to speak or hear of. It was as if the year I'd spent in similar confines demanded—in an inverted logic—another person, my mother, to be driven crazy for reasons opposite to those that had nearly claimed my sanity: the sight of all that space—trees and lakes and mountains and sky and whole nations—into which her family had vanished; the proximity of people in the cities she'd searched, crowds upon crowds upon crowds, everyone in the world but the one she desperately wanted to see; all that language forced into her ears and eyes by people who demanded dialogue: the local workers council who expelled her from her job for having 'harboured' (that is, given birth to) a counter-revolutionary; neighbours who scolded her for raising a son of dubious character; policemen who'd come by, day after day, demanding she tell them who my 'friends' were; and, finally, the only person she could rely upon, her older sister, who took her in but spent the days disguising her anxiety with long sighs. All those noises except the few words she needed to hear. Until it was not so much what she'd lost that my mother battled against, but the sense of loss itself, a battle she could only win—or so my aunt told me later that night, handing me a bag of clothes and food for the journey—by turning from the agents who followed wherever she went (in the hopes that she'd lead them to others like me); twisting away from the mailbox (word never arrived) toward a small room at the back of the house where she made her bed one night; by avoiding all language that was either a response or which required one, and humming, instead, quiet songs in a place so little, so *already a prison*, that no one could ever take it away.

I have added her—my mother as she was on the night I last saw her—to my teetering tower of guilt, though even after all this (indeed, perhaps because of it) I am not sure she still wouldn't have wanted me to fight, to take part in the suicide that was our October of 1956. I do not know whether my escape from Hungary was enough— *finally enough*—to kill her, but I too wake at night, bent on the sheets, imagining that room she chose for herself, to which the price of entry was dereliction of self, a dropping of everything that defined you like a worn coat in the doorway.

You would not believe the network of refugees they had in the 1950s. You could head over to the Arany Tyúk in Toronto and mention to a waitress the name of some relative you'd last seen in 1944, and whom you thought may have come to Canada, though perhaps Australia, and within months she'd introduce you to some old guy in a leather hunting cap (which made him the laughingstock of everyone on the street), who'd tell you he'd shared a shack in an Austrian refugee camp with your long-lost relative, and had recently received a postcard from Vancouver with his signature at the bottom. In those days, we specialized in everything, including coincidence.

So by 1965, a short seven years after my escape, I had made contact with all three of my uncles.

Gyuri died first, on a bitter February day when he realized that, despite the corruption everywhere evident in the Liberal government, the Conservatives were not going to win the next election. I was there a few days before he died—along with his émigré wife and three daughters—when Gyuri rose from the sickbed and pointed emphatically at the mantelpiece, continuing to rise and grunt and point, wasting his remaining strength, until they brought everything on it down to him: a vase, a picture of himself as a young soldier, a ring that had belonged to my grandmother, and, finally, the item that calmed him—an envelope containing his official membership in the Conservative party. He died holding that paper to his heart.

And here's where my troubles began. Krisztina, Gyuri's eldest daughter, only five years younger than I, recalled to me our family tradition, which I knew little about, having left Hungary before being fully introduced to ancestral lore. It was she who came to visit me a few days after we'd sat around Gyuri's bedside, watching the respirator rise and fall.

She was carrying a letter, old and creased from having been folded and refolded, as though the sender had been unsure of the writing he'd placed upon it, or to whom it should be addressed. It was Gyuri's will. 'In accordance with the tradition of the Kassai family, I would like my remains to be buried by my nearest male blood relatives.' Frowning, Krisztina fanned the letter in my face. 'That's you,' she said.

I looked at the clumsy handwriting, the left-out or misplaced accents, the interruption of the flow of Hungarian by the occasional English word conjugated to fit, and then gazed at Kristzina with an expression that indicated how far we'd come from Hungary (she and her sisters had never even been there!), as well as the obligation I felt to the history we'd suffered through. 'You know,' she said quietly, looking at me, 'I thought you would be happy to ignore this.' She glanced at the letter as if she wished she'd never brought it to my attention. 'I loved my father,' she continued, the softness of her tone edged with a bitterness verging on hostility, 'but I can't say I liked him. He never had time to listen to us. We were women. Pegged us even before we were born. And, you know, that's the main thing he instilled into us: loyalty to principles first, loyalty to people second.' Krisztina laughed humourlessly, 'I wonder what he'd think if he knew that *my principles* say we—my sisters and I—should be the ones to bury him. And *him* and *his wishes* can come second.' She looked at me and smiled then, putting the heel of one hand up to her eyes. 'Why weren't we good enough to bury him? Can't women hold shovels as good as anybody?'

I looked at the paper, recalling how Gyuri had treated his daughters, a bear of a man, stained sweaters and emphysema, the way he could slam a door or stare at the boyfriends they brought home, standing at the kitchen table glaring at them as though they were strangers come into the house uninvited, utterly silent, before finally asking, 'Are you Hungarian? Are you, at least, German?' They never were; and when his youngest, Gyöngyi, took up with a foreign exchange student from China, Gyuri once again went into the envelope I was holding, and made another of his thousand emendations.

'A Chinaman!' roared Gyuri (in Hungarian, of course) that day in the office of the transmission repair shop I'd managed to scrape out of the earth and pile up on a corner of Kingsway. 'I've always told my daughters! Always!' he continued, 'One of the beautiful things about this world is all the different races in it. A wonder—all these races!' he shook his finger at me. 'And we have a duty and responsibility to keep it that way!'

While he was staring out the window in a rage, I reached forward carefully and plucked from his grasp the wedding invitation sent by Gyöngyi and her fiancé.

I tried very hard not to think badly of Gyuri then, watching the stillness of the fingers I'd taken the invitation from, quivering as though they'd lost their grip on something, though he refused to believe it, thinking this something just beyond reach, as if the right strings were dangling just millimetres above, though of course he gave himself reason upon reason for not reaching up, since he did not want to risk the fact that everything that had defined his life—that he *still* defined it by—was not only out of range but out of existence.

I waited in a chair, the smell of carbolic on my hands, trying to find some way to present my thoughts in the form of praise, though in truth I had little to say, wanting only to point out that by turning his daughters into mementoes of the country he'd left he'd also turned them into reminders of the consequences of leaving, so that every time he looked at them, they rubbed his nose into a soil he'd risked life and limb for them to walk upon. And while he prided himself on this, he had never once, really, touched down on Canadian earth, moving along as if he were somehow insulated from it by the layer of Hungarian dust he'd been so careful not to kick from his heels. It was, perhaps, time for him to look down.

And, in the end, this bit of equivocation, this 'perhaps', was the only concession I could make to Gyuri, and he reacted to it exactly as expected, turning from the window to shout that he had escaped Hungary, he really had, and I was a *seggfej* for suggesting he hadn't. Moreover, he was more than 'man enough' to take Canada on its own terms.

Within months, Gyöngyi and Li Peng were married at the Vancouver Hungarian Cultural Centre, the whole thing paid for by Gyuri, who walked among the milling crowds of confused Asians and Hungarians as a holy man might along a path of nails, the difference being that Gyuri's coolness was the result of such self-control it was not coolness at all but rather a kind of psychological fascism. For if holy men transcend the self, achieving a plane above, Gyuri had liquidated it, and was thus nowhere. He walked as if his insides had gone dead and grey, and when I followed him into the alley outside the hall I found him leaning against a wall and weeping; and he, turning to see me, said, 'I have escaped! I have!' and waved me back inside.

Krisztina and Cili had it easier than Gyöngyi, but since neither of them married a Hungarian or German, Gyuri was not much more natural at their ceremonies either, especially after learning that Jason, Krisztina's fiancé, had distant Jewish blood, and that Ed, Cili's husband, belonged to a family with historical connections to the labour movement. The only thing worse than being of the wrong race was being of the wrong political persuasion.

The three daughters, of course, had little admiration for Gyuri's discipline. They saw only the beads of sweat on his face, the fingers digging at his armpits, the utter lack of grace, and resented him for never being able to relax around their husbands and kids (his own grandchildren!), whom he patted as if there were handprints telling him exactly where to place his palm and fingers. Unlike me, the three daughters had never had Gyuri's image before their eyes, guiding them when everything else was lost; and I was incapable of explaining to them the connection between this image and the bully who'd raised them.

By the time I buried Gyuri, Pál and Ottó were geriatrics, the former leaning on two canes, the latter with a private nurse to hold up his IV pole. I saw them from where I stood, both men having to be forcibly restrained (which wasn't too difficult, given their infirmities) from grabbing and wielding one of the shovels struck into the dirt by the grave. Gyuri, being naturally lazy, was easy to dissuade, but Ottó was a different case, and his language became ever more colourful as he tried to shake off the nurse and me—cursing up and down about how he was a 'free man', how he'd overcome physical extremes 'far worse' than old age and heart disease and encroaching mortality, and how 'by Christ' there wasn't a man alive, 'not one', with the strength to prevent him 'doing right by family tradition'—in a tug-of-war that went on for twenty minutes before Krisztina finally had to step forth, lay a gentle hand on the old man's tailored sleeve, and stare him down. The intensity of her tear-stained eyes forced him to relinquish the shovel and gaze at the ground in shame.

And so, as I dug, and despite how obviously infirm Pál and Ottó were, I couldn't help but see two men whose escapes, by the summer of 1954—because we had no information, because their letters could not get to us, because no one who'd seen them go had returned to tell of it—had become legendary. The two men looked so faint on the afternoon I buried Gyuri—their outlines chalk traces upon the day—that it made me thankful I was so young at the time of my escape, not because it meant I was healthy, but because of youth's idealism and its accompanying amnesia, because if I'd really known what my uncles were like they would not have been there to guide my steps. For if history is determined by the quality of the explanations we offer for events, then the luck of youth is not to inquire too deeply into that quality, even when it carves its saints out of reactionaries. But perhaps I am only making excuses, because even later, once their characters came clear, I always tried to support them. And I suppose if this story is anything then it is the confession of an accessory who, while recognizing his sin, continued to help the men with whom he's been condemned.

Because they lost their lives. I'm not speaking biologically, of course, but I knew, even in the autumn of 1956, that to stay in Hungary and die was not to fight as they had, as only a single person *can* fight: by leaving. Theirs was the type of battle where you are always a casualty, a battle in which—rather than watering your country with your blood, making it fertile through martyrdom—you leave it worse for your absence. This was their paradox: that, when they left, they did not go for reasons of a better life elsewhere, but because dissent demanded it, because they wanted to strike some kind of blow, even while knowing that exile was a relinquishing, not only of a country but also of the only life that mattered. It was this I thought of, often, in the year following 1956, when the things that had once provided warmth—my country, my village, my home, my people—lost all worth the second I went into hiding, the second I could no longer share them with anyone; so that no matter how I concentrated, struggling to remember every detail, they were as little use to me as a secret that cannot be told, a love letter without a recipient.

Uncle Pál, like Uncle Ottó, did not have any children. He loved keeping tin goods unopened, stacked in tall columns in the kitchen, until whatever was inside began to rot, expelling gasses that bent the tops and bottoms of the cans convex, making them even more precious to Pál, who hoarded them in the absence of all usefulness, treasuring them though their contents were spoiled, inedible, a testament to a hunger so great you'll stack rot against the fear of experiencing it again. As I learned after Pál died, he spent most of his life writing for right-wing periodicals published by Orthodox Catholics, radical Hungarians, and other fascist nostalgics in Australia, who sent him money to supplement his UI and welfare cheques, and (when things got bad) the money I gave him for helping sort nuts and bolts, steam clean engines, and—when he didn't find it too demeaning—make coffee and stroll down Kingsway to pick up lunch for my mechanics.

Pál often spoke about having children, lamenting not his own failure in this regard but mine. 'You need to get yourself a wife,' he'd say. 'A Catholic. One who'll go around and clap your kids' hands together to pray.' And on those nights when I was unable to sleep, I would move around my apartment and look down at my slack, skinny belly (loss of appetite was only one legacy of my time in hiding), pacing in circles, thinking how little difference there was between Pál and me, both of us so afraid of bringing children into the world we were awkward in the company of women, flinching involuntarily from images of suffering, whether in magazines, or on TV, or in our imaginations, as if what we'd endured made us incapable of considering anyone else—much less a child—having to face even a tenth of it. We'd lost our faith not only in humanity but also in the process of being human, though I hope that I, at least, was not stuck in a holding pattern, hanging onto the days until one finally came along that defied my grip. And on these sleepless nights I knew I could call him, no matter how late, that he would be up when no one else was, and that while the conversation would be stilted and halting there was at least something to listen to other than the ticking of the clock and the relentless churn of memory.

We had quiet arguments whenever he came to the garage. During these, my responses were always silent. He'd make a remark about the shape of one of the mechanic's noses, or about some customer who'd tried to shortchange us, and I would

simply stare at him, or off to one side, leaving him unsure of whether my unrespon-
siveness was agreement or dissent. Afterwards, he'd disappear for a few days, though he
always came back, saying he needed the money.

I remember Krisztina coming to see me the night after the police entered Pál's apartment. He'd passed away days earlier in the solitude of his home, meaning that his body
had begun stinking up the corridor between suites before anyone noticed. 'The police
came to see me,' she said. 'They had a boxful of books and papers. You should have
seen this stuff!' She shook her head. I didn't ask Krisztina what Pál's writing was about
because I already knew, thinking back to those nights when we'd spoken on the telephone, back to the things he'd admitted, both of us speaking through the fevers of
insomnia. 'The policeman wanted to launch an investigation, but there didn't seem to
be any collaborators.'
   'He didn't have anyone,' I said, answering a different question.
   'You know that he made me and my sisters his principal beneficiaries? We don't
want any of that money!'
   'He didn't have any money,' I said.
   'Are you kidding?' Krisztina replied, pulling out a file prepared by the lawyer for
Pál's estate. 'He had it squirrelled away everywhere!' I held the bank books, squinting
down the neat columns of deposits, which Pál apparently made on regular dates,
times when he'd come begging to me for work, and during which he'd received the
money I'd given him (he insisted on being paid in cash) in cupped hands, as if receiving the Eucharist. But where had the rest come from? (Surely, hate literature didn't
sell *that* well?)
   'I've spoken to Cili and Gyöngyi. None of us wants the money. There are organizations. Jewish museums. Holocaust education. We could donate it. . . .'
   'That would be a good idea,' I said, quietly.
   'You're not . . .' Krisztina looked out the window. 'I mean you wouldn't contest it
if we did that . . . ?'
   I turned my eyes to her, stunned. 'You think I would mind?' I couldn't help it, I was
shouting. 'I knew he hated Jews, but I didn't know he wrote that—' I waved my hand
at her, though she wasn't holding anything other than the file, '—that garbage!'
   'Well.' Krisztina smiled carefully, neither out of amusement nor happiness, but
rather in defence of my aggression. 'I know you were close to Pál bácsi, and I thought
maybe . . .'
   'You think I was sympathetic to that?'
   Krisztina looked at the ground. 'My father spoke highly of you. I can't see him
doing that unless the person he spoke about was like him. . . . He and Pál bácsi got
along, you know.'
   I opened my mouth to yell some more, then closed it, at a loss as to how to justify
myself to Krisztina, to explain my devotion to her father, to Pál, to Ottó, without at
the same time implicating myself in their insanity. Anyhow, I couldn't be sure I *wasn't*
implicated, since the trauma that had warped and ossified their thinking, that had
made of them brutal and twitchy obsessive-compulsives, was also *my* trauma, though I

would have liked to think I was not a fascist, and that Krisztina and her sisters knew it. And yet, how else could I explain an affection for the three men that was prepared to overlook almost anything (though that was wrong, too, for I certainly would not have given money to Pál had I known of his stash, nor tolerated the publication of his anti-Semitic rants)? Instead, I asked, 'Did your father really hurt you that badly?'

'I didn't have much of a father,' said Krisztina, after a moment of silence. 'He was never really here. I think history ended for him the moment he left Hungary. I don't know what kind of truths they had then, but it seemed like he held on to them long after they'd become the worst kind of lies.'

And to that, really, there was no response.

The priest and I buried Pál. I suppose Father Conklin pitied me that overcast day, grabbing an extra shovel the minute he'd finished with the service, the two of us working in silence as a warm wind blew in from offshore, carrying a spring rain so gentle it felt as if we were passing through spiders' webs. There was nobody else willing to come to the funeral, not even Ottó, who claimed to be too sick, though I knew for a fact that Pál had disgusted him, and that, for Ottó, Gyuri's funeral had been a happy occasion, since it was the last time he would ever have to see Pál again or acknowledge their relation. On hearing I was burying Pál, he'd said, 'I hope he left you something in return!' Well, he *has* left me something, I thought at the time, though both Ottó and I knew that neither Gyuri nor Pál (nor Ottó himself, for that matter) were inclined to financially reward the duties of tradition.

It took the priest and me twenty minutes to pile all the dirt on Pál's casket, and maybe another five for the priest to utter a few parting remarks.

And then it was over, an entire life done with, and not a soul except me to acknowledge or weigh it against Krisztina's condemnation, which, it seemed to me, was relevant not because it addressed Gyuri and Pál's failure to escape the truths of their times—to acknowledge the contradiction between its Christianity and hate—since, let's face it, very few are capable of this, but because it addressed their failure—both of them having outlived those times—to gaze back in recognition, and use the remorse that gaze *should have* occasioned against the illusions that comforted and rotted them for the rest of their lives.

Upon leaving the cemetery I thought I saw Krisztina's car moving off the avenue that led from the cemetery to the freeway, but there are too many red cars in the world for me to be sure, and it was probably just an illusion of my own, a hope that Krisztina's presence at the funeral in some way signified an awareness of the failure, this time mine, that demanded I be present at Pál's funeral.

But if she was there, she never mentioned it.

Of all my uncles, Ottó's was the only death at which I was actually present. Unlike Gyuri—whom he liked but didn't have a lot in common with—or Pál—whom he hated—Ottó had never seen me as a confidant, never come to me in moments of familial or financial crisis, though we met often enough, sitting on his back verandah and telling jokes, talking politics, reminiscing, our brains awash in more than a few shots of pear brandy. Our relationship consisted of maintaining the distance required by politeness, like waltzing partners determined to keep a full twelve inches between their bodies, so that when one of us moved forward (metaphorically of course, say by asking a personal question), the other would move back (answering with another question, or with an impersonal reference, bringing up a historical or political reason for why they had broken off with this or that woman). Ottó always wore a suit, often of linen, and his shirts were crisply pressed, his style so impeccable that it dominated his personality and made it impossible to think of either Gyuri or Pál as his siblings. Ottó was a member of not just the local Hungarian club, but was a 'friend' (financial contributor) to the Vancouver Symphony, as well as a host of other cultural institutions. He was the sort of man who received invitations to formal functions, and nods in the hallways when business took him to city hall.

'You know,' he said as I sat by his bed the night he died, 'Pál was an idiot. Really! I shouldn't talk about him that way,' he interrupted his confession with an extended period of wheezing, and I saw the fear in his eyes afterwards, as if—for reasons of death, and whatever might lie beyond it—he was considering not making fun of his brother, though a second later he shrugged and continued, 'but what else can you say about a man who smokes two packs a day, doesn't exercise, eats mouthfuls of lard, and then tells you, because he doesn't like to bathe, that a lot of our health problems today can be traced to the fact that our society showers too much? "Washing away all of our natural oils," he'd say! "That's why we're all so sick and allergic to everything." You know what my response was? "You stink!" That's what I'd say. "You stink!" And he'd reply, "It's a manly smell." A manly smell! Can you believe it?' Ottó shook his head, smiling at the memory.

'And then there was Gyuri,' he grimaced. 'Pig-headed, that's what! You could have used his skull to hammer nails! I can't believe that his daughters didn't poison him.' He began laughing now, as the pain of the cancer and the euphoria of morphine confused his responses. 'Maybe they did, maybe they did,' he said, growing thoughtful and quiet, and taking his eyes from mine to let them wander in sudden fits and starts along the pictures mounted on the walls, the collection of leather-bound books on the mantelpiece, as if whatever he was looking at wavered before him; and when he spoke next it was exclusively to these flitting spirits.

'Stop it! Both of you,' Ottó shouted. 'You—neither of you!—don't know what it was like. You only complained.' Ottó's voice faltered now, and when he spoke again it was lower than a whisper. 'You only knew what it was like to wake up with teeth inside your stomach. Staring at the dark. You knew the coldness of the room but not what it was like to step into those boots. It was like putting your feet into blocks of ice. Then out, while it was still night. Along the fences, under them, every step in fear of unexploded shells. I was only twelve years old! And what kept me moving were those teeth, gnawing upwards from my stomach, burning in my throat. Twelve years old: the oldest boy, but smaller than a man. Under the fences, in the fields. Sometimes hiding for hours beneath a bridge, in empty pigpens and henhouses, anywhere the Russians might not look. With Grandfather's watch in my pocket—something to give them if they caught me. My fingers so stiff with cold I was afraid to bend them.

'Then to the traps, the crows, some already frozen, some feeble, gone the whole night squawking, flapping their wings, losing heat. One twist of the neck with my child's hands, then into the bag. Baiting the traps again. And then back home after being out in that winter—why was it so cold then?—sometimes four hours, back home, on a good day, with one, maybe two, standing in the kitchen with my hands in my armpits, trembling with cold. I had to pluck the birds. Mother refused to. Refused to kiss me until I put my cold hands in the cold water to wash them.

'And then the two of you and father at the table. Mother ladling out the soup. The smallest amount of grease on its surface. Twiglike bones coming to the surface. Wrinkling your noses, eating only out of the most desperate hunger, pausing to catch your breath between each spoonful, looking at me accusingly. "Couldn't you catch a sparrow?" father said. "There are better birds out there than crows." "A crow belongs to the songbird family," mother always replied.

'It tasted like shit. That's what crows ate in those days. The shit in the fields, the manure, the bugs, rotting leaves falling from the trees, the mud packed up on the sides of the ditches along the road, crumbs of bread fallen between the prints left by the soles of marching soldiers, rotted meat of fallen horses, broken eggshells on the floors of chicken coops, the grubs and offal from where the slaughter went on, both in the yards and elsewhere, out there, in the forest, where the Germans had marched those people from our village, out there from where the ringing shots could be heard, one volley, a pause, then another, wave upon wave, out there in the forest where we were forbidden to go—the crows eating it all up, whatever could be scavenged, whatever fit inside their beaks, until it was like they'd swallowed everything, from the dirt to the blood, until the crows seemed composed of the earth under the frost and snow and slush and our feet—composed of the country itself—bits and pieces torn away from the ground, flung up into the sky to land in my traps.

'That's what we ate. And you complained and complained and complained, forcing it down past the tightening in your throat. Mother spoke of songbirds.'

And now, Ottó, in a spasm, forced his eyes away from the patterns they were weaving upon, or seeing within, the air; and with a supreme effort—as if by sheer will he could push himself one last time between the walls of pain that separated us—met my eyes with such intensity, I felt as though it would throw me from my chair.

'And how many times,' he said, his voice almost at a conversational level, 'how many times, in all the thirty years since, would we have murdered for that taste, killed for it—betrayed everything for just one more bite?'

And with that he closed his eyes and died.

Krisztina, Cili, and Gyöngyi came to Ottó's funeral, along with half the city. It was disconcerting to stand before what was easily five hundred people, most of whom were extremely uncomfortable watching me work the shovel alone, and would have gladly joined in had Ottó's strictly worded testament permitted it. But I dug the shovel in, dropping dirt on the casket, until it was over, the crowd waiting patiently for me to finish, at which point they came and shook my hand, some of whom—not realizing I was Ottó's blood relation—even stuffing money into my pockets.

The three women and I were strangers in the reception hall, where it seemed everyone but us knew everyone else, as if the businessmen and politicians, lawyers and accountants, and members of private clubs were Ottó's true family, and the three girls and me only hired help.

'I wonder if any of these people knew who Ottó's brothers were?' asked Krisztina, punching her fork into the roast beef.

I picked at the potato salad, thinking of the soup Ottó had described, before pushing my plate away. I sat for a minute more, watching the girls eat, then rose abruptly—a man jerked up, something biting at his spine—and staggered outside into the parking lot, where I wandered in a daze, back and forth between the bumpers and fenders, my jacket catching on side-view mirrors, my pants rubbing on dirty tires, feeling as if there were something out here, a place I might get to where I could alleviate this sense of loss; though there was only the endless parking lot, in which—no matter how I moved, left or right—I came no nearer to the perimeter, as if the cars had been parked there to perpetuate a maze without exit.

By the time Krisztina found me, I was nearly in tears with desperation, and she folded her arms around me, whispering, 'You really loved those old men.' And though her tone and touch expressed sympathy, it was entirely without understanding, done out of love for the griever rather than in recognition of the grief, a comfort no different from what you might give a child on the death of a goldfish.

And how would I have explained it to her, had I lifted my head and managed to get the words out? 'They were afraid—' I might have said '—afraid all their lives.' But I was not looking to excuse them, to chart their offences as if every step had been decided by what they'd survived, as if those horrors determined, for the rest their lives, what they would never again willingly face. For there is nothing like trauma to make one rage for certainty, to make one invest one's belief in the ugliest of securities—fascism and greed—and to mistake the form this belief takes for reality, when the truth is you are too frightened, too demoralized, to cope with a world that does not accommodate faith. Thinking back now, I know this is what I should have said, not on behalf of those three men—they were too far gone to be helped—but on behalf of those who had lived with them, who had spent all those years trying to get them to negotiate the terms of a relationship, when any form of negotiation—and the compromise it entailed—would have forced them back to a world they could not abide, far from that nowhere untouched by change or violence or unpredictability that they'd invented to make the running easier. Their principal mistake was thinking they were in exile when they'd always been home.

But, in truth, the only thing that occurred to me, the only images that came to mind, the only words I might have articulated, were exactly the ones Krisztina would not have understood. Her anger, and her suffering under Gyuri, were too strong for her to comprehend my debt to these three men. Or, rather, she would have understood, but without experiencing, what it was like to wait weeks and weeks in absolute silence, listening to the ticking of a house and the rumbling of your stomach; rationing your remaining food in ever tinier portions, halving and halving and halving what remains until you seem to be splitting atoms; wondering who will deliver the next knock at the door: the man with the fresh bread and safe addresses, or the guards too happy to hammer your fingers from the table leg as they drag you away; and, finally, risking capture to make one last visit to your mother, to the one person not defaced by absence and isolation, only to realize she said goodbye to you a lifetime ago, and because she is no loner part of this world, neither are you, having lost so much in those tiny rooms that flight is not a risk but an admission that you've survived all you care to survive, stumbling by night through the driving snow, having said goodbye, crawling west across an almost unprotected stretch of border knowing that even before the first step you have already gone much farther than you wanted, along a journey from which none of us returned.

Because the tragedy was this: during that winter trek, there was only one light strong enough to blot out the memory of my mother—or strong enough to redeem what had happened to her, to my father, to me—and it was the faces of my uncles glimmering through the snow and trees in defiance of the distance ahead and the greater distance behind, assuring me that certain acts of resistance require you to run not to save your life but to lose it, and in losing add another corpse to the dead piled on the doorstep of those responsible. I was, in a sense, joining them and my mother in the only form of dissent left us. And I realized then that what I had been looking for in the parking lot—and even from Krisztina—was forgiveness, when the only thing I had any right to truly expect was condemnation. For if in the moment of defeat I had been drawn to my uncles as to a light, then it was my failure, and crime, that nothing they did or said after that terrible winter of 1958 had ever really been able to diminish it.

Richard Van Camp *b.* 1971

FORT SMITH, NORTHWEST TERRITORIES

The first Dogrib (Tlicho) writer to be published, Richard Van Camp was born in Fort Smith, Northwest Territories. Brought up in the midst of traditional storytellers—'I was privy to the best storytelling in the world . . . because northerners love stories. . . . Stories for us are the best medicine'—he also belongs to the generation that has grown up steeped in television, music, graphic novels, and comic strips, elements that inform his own stories. As a child he loved to create visual stories, drawings with titles, but gradually, he says, 'my drawings became smaller and my titles got longer, and they started to wrap around the page. . . . The titles turned into stories. That's how I became a writer.' And the stories he began telling were the stories he 'wanted to read'. As he says, 'Nobody was writing the stories about my life and my experience, what I saw, what I felt, what I heard, what I sensed. So I sat down and I wrote for five years, a story that turned into a novel.' That novel is *The Lesser Blessed* (1996), a narrative set in Fort Simmer, a composite of his native Fort Smith and other northern communities. Often categorized as juvenile fiction and translated into German and French, it is a coming-of-age story about the social hardships and personal heartaches faced by its male protagonist. It won Van Camp the Canadian Authors Association Air Canada Award for promising writers under thirty.

Van Camp began his studies at the En'owkin International School of Writing before obtaining a BA from the University of Victoria and an MA from the University of British Columbia, both in Creative Writing. A participant in many literary festivals both in Canada and abroad, he has also written two children's novels, *A Man Called Raven* (1997) and *What's the Most Beautiful Thing You Know about Horses?* (1998), both illustrated by Cree artist George Littlechild. He has taught creative writing workshops in various places, including one designed specifically for Aboriginal students at the University of British Columbia (2001), and a storytelling workshop on the Musqueam Indian Reserve in south Vancouver. He also co-authored the script for *The Promise*, a film entered in the 2004 Sundance Film Festival, and wrote for the CBC television show *North of 60*. His most recent book is *Angel Wing Splash Pattern* (2002), a collection of his best short stories, including the one that follows.

Sky Burial

Pain seared up Icabus' leg forcing him to stop and wince. He wheezed through one lung, and the mall blurred around him. Each heartbeat drove a long hot metal blade through his skull over and over. He coughed and his chest sounded and felt as if it were stuffed with the broken glass of gray light bulbs. This was it: he was dying. The Cree medicine had him.

In his reflection, Icabus hated what he saw. *I'm not that skinny, am I?* He was bleeding inside and felt so weak. 'I seen better lookin' corpses.' Something had blown behind his left eye earlier that morning, causing his ears to ring.

The bird. It was dying in front of him. He didn't know what the bird was called but was awed at how bright and blue the feathers were.

Parakeet? Parrot? No, he knew it wasn't the true name of the bird's tribe, and he wished he knew. He thought of all the shampoo bottles his daughter Augustine used and chose the one that smelled the best. 'Papaya,' he said. 'That's your Dogrib name now: Papaya.'

The pet store, which showcased the bird, had it in a cage. The bird measured three feet from black beak to bright blue tail, yet the cage only offered four. A sign read: 'Do Not Tap Cage.' The bird was upside down, shitting on itself and biting at the chain that sliced into its leg.

The bird deserved something far better than this, he thought.

Oh, how Icabus wished to be around fire. He was sure the bird was a woman. She panted; her black tongue licked at her swollen ankle. She hung awkwardly, rested, shivered, tried to bite at the chain, fell back, shivered again. It looked as if she were drowning. Icabus watched the bird and felt under his shirt where he was bleeding inside. It was if he had been force-fed thousands of porcupine quills that were growing with each breath. He pressed into his left rib cage as he strained to open the cage.

'Macaw,' a voice said suddenly behind him.

'Huh?'

'It's a Macaw.'

Icabus turned to look at the wielder of such a firm voice. It was a child. An Indian girl. Tall, slim. She was beautiful. Her eyes were large and round. She wore a T-shirt boasting a huge white owl with yellow eyes on it. A younger white boy with a runny nose came up and started banging on the cage. The girl left as fast as she had appeared. Icabus wanted to talk to her, but he was hit again with pain. He coughed and coughed and coughed. He held himself up against the glass and looked down until the reddest blood dripped from his mouth. He had to hurry, but where was the sign?

Icabus bought a coffee and a doughnut at Grandma Lee's. As he sat, the pain bit again as if the quills inside him were starting to burrow and grind inside his guts, shredding everything inside him. He put his head down and focused on his shoes. He took a breath, biting the tip of his tongue. 'Chinaman did a good job on polishing them up,' he wiggled his toes. 'Too bad the bitches got me.'

Any other man, he coughed, *any other man would not have woken up from last night's sleep.* This was not the flu. It was a death sentence for what he and the boy had done to the sweat lodges in Rae.

Together he and Morris had burned them all. Icabus wanted to teach the Crees not to charge money for their sweat lodges on Dogrib soil, but the lesson had cost him everything—or had it? Was there still time? He'd thought last night about passing on his medicine to Morris, but Icabus had seen black around him before he left, and he knew Morris' days were numbered.

If he thought about it, he'd start to cry and if he started to cry here he'd never stop. The boy would have to look after himself. Their time was getting closer, and he knew it.

No more sunrises, no more northern lights, no more snow or cold or anything . . . and it had to be here, in a mall of strangers in Edmonton. All he could do was look down and think. His shoes were so polished they looked like black ice. In the reflection he watched the shadows and saw a man walking towards him. *Morris?* He wanted to ask. *My adopted son?*

'There you are,' Harold said and sat beside him.

The pain struck again. Icabus bit into his doughnut. The dough would soak up the blood inside him. The noise of the mall rose around him: the metal-whine of blenders, children hollering for toys. Harold had a tray of Cokes and tacos and the smell was thick and sweet.

'We were looking for you. God, you look sick.'

Icabus stared out the window to the mall parking lot. His ear began to ring again. A blonde child stood crying in the middle of the pavement, her red balloon flying away. One of her shoes was off. Behind her, the Edmonton sunset tore the sky in half. Icabus squinted but couldn't see a parent for the girl. He leaned forward, tracking the balloon as far as he could, and he wanted so desperately to follow it.

'I see you got your shoes fixed.' Harold took the paper bag and looked inside. 'What else?'

Icabus glared at him for not asking first. 'Safes,' he grumbled. 'Suzy Muktuck's in town.' He studied Harold's throat and hated how white it was.

'Icabus,' Harold blushed. 'Nobody calls them *safes* anymore. Did Augy say you could afford these?'

Icabus ignored the question and wiped cold sweat from his forehead. *I'm dying. They got me bleeding to death inside.*

'I don't understand why you got those fixed up,' Harold scoffed. 'You don't even have enough money for next week. Christ, you've been eating at our place the last four days . . .'

'Gotta look good at my funeral,' Icabus explained.

Harold missed it. 'If I hear another trapping story, I don't know what I'll do.'

'Our family comes from the land. You need to remember this.'

Harold rolled his eyes and bit into the taco. Tomato sauce gushed out the bottom. Icabus closed his eyes. The sauce was blood. Augustine's blood every time she tried to have a baby. The blood in his piss and spit. The blood of his son who had killed himself.

Harold went on talking with a full mouth. Icabus nodded, pretending to pay attention. He sipped his coffee and waited for a sign. 'Where's Augy?' he asked.

'Looking for you.' Harold bit into the taco again and Icabus looked for the little girl. She was gone.

'There you are,' an exhausted voice heaved. Augustine huffed towards them: her bad perm, pink track pants, Jean jacket, dusty runners. She sat down, grabbed the other taco, and elbowed Harold. 'And you!' she scolded, 'this is cold.' She bit into it anyway. Icabus studied his daughter and her husband. He looked into her black, dreadful perm, and thought, 'Spider legs, thousands of spider legs.'

The couple gabbed. Food toppled out of their mouths. Their noise was muffled and lost to the crowd. It will be okay, he thought. He'd left his wedding band by his bed. The day before, when Harold had assumed he was at the dentist's, Icabus had emptied his account and left his money in his wallet under his pillow. Three thousand dollars in thirty 100 dollar bills would go far for them. As for his clothes, they would all be burned once he left. Icabus looked around.

To his right, a table away, sat a family of ruined Indians. They had all let themselves go. They fed on burgers, fries, shakes. The mother had cut her hair. The kids were pudgy. The man was soft. *Where are the warriors?* Icabus had been waiting for a nod or a sign of acknowledgment, but the Indians wouldn't meet his eyes. *What's happened to us?* he thought. *What the hell has happened to all of us?*

'*Oh,*' a breath lit from his mouth. It was the young girl he saw, the one with the owl shirt. Augy and Harold kept talking, taking turns sucking the straw, biting into more tacos.

Her long black hair was what caught him. She was as slender as a diamond willow. She moved with a white woman across the perimeter. *What the hell was she doing with a white woman?* They carried hot dogs and drinks. The girl sat down quickly out of his view. He shifted to see her better.

'. . . and the lady, Dad. The lady said we could visit Sundays and we could bring you home cooked food. It'll be good for you to be with others your own age.' Augy ate while Harold listened and nodded. 'You'll love it.'

'The move will be good for you.' Harold added. 'Think of all the French Safes you could use over there.'

Augy elbowed her husband and laughed. 'Ischa!'

Icabus nodded again and looked for the young girl. A young couple was in his way. They had their lower lips pierced and whenever they kissed Icabus could hear metals clicking, clicking. '*Savages*,' he thought. He squinted and saw her. She was nodding, listening to the white woman speak.

Icabus sat straight up and almost spilled his drink. He brought his hand up over his lip and caressed the whiskers on his chin. *She's the one*, he thought. It was her shirt that did it. The white owl was the sign he'd been looking for.

'I'm Stan the man with the nine!' Stan would yell to the women who drank with them. 'When I die, there's gonna be two boxes: one for Stan and one for the nine!' The women would giggle and Stan would always throw Icabus a wink.

It was the winter of '79. They were drinking at Stan's. Icabus was taking a leak outside a party when he looked up and saw a huge white owl looking down at him. What he remembered most was the eyes. Yellow eyes, with fire and power behind them. They were eyes he couldn't lie to; eyes he couldn't tame. The eyes saw him for what he really was: a drunk.

The owl hissed at him as he ran back to his shack. He grabbed his .410 and Stan ran after him. 'Lookit' this fuckin' owl!' Icabus hooted. 'Look!'

They were both drunk and Stan made the sign of the cross when he saw the owl.

Stan yelled, 'Someone's gonna die! Don't shoot it!' but Icabus aimed and fired. *I didn't mean to hit it*, he would say later, but they saw an explosion of white feathers. Stan punched him hard, catching his ear. Icabus fell down. Stan ran into the snow to help the bird. It was dead.

Neither of them buried the bird, and Icabus never spoke to Stan ever again.

The next time Icabus saw the owl, it was in a dream. He dreamt he was walking in the snow to the old trapline he and Stan shared when they were kids when the owl landed in front of him. The eyes of the owl had changed. They were Stan's.

Icabus woke as Augy ran into his room saying that Stan had died. Family had called from Rae. A stroke had taken Stan during the night.

The pain hit again. Icabus bit his cheek so he wouldn't scream. 'It's gettin' closer,' he whispered. He thought of his wife who had died far too young from the cancer. *Delphine*. He thought of her grace, her elegance. The community thought she was so shy, but Icabus knew that she saved the very best of herself for him. Oh, they had argued; they had yelled, but the passion and the peace between them grew every year they had together. He missed her love and was sad at the thought of losing her. *God took you*, he thought, *and I never got to hear everything you had to say.*

After her funeral, whenever he saw a butterfly, he would call her name. And whenever he saw a red fox, he would whisper 'Justin', his son's name, and weep with guilt because his son died alone and ashamed.

It will be something, he thought, *to see you both again: young, alive and radiant.* In his dreams, Icabus walked into the Great Slave Lake by his home in Rae as he died, releasing himself to it, and disappearing.

On CBC, before he left Rae, the Dogrib leaders were telling everybody to boil the water twice before drinking it. They never said why. He shook his head. 'We can't drink it, but we bathe in it.' He took a long breath. Using the table, he pulled himself up slowly and stood still as the blood roared in his ears. He could taste blood in his saliva.

'Where are you goin'?' Harold asked.

'To sing for the last time,' Icabus answered.

'What?'

Icabus began to sing under his breath. He walked carefully, cautiously. His lips moved and he felt the wind gather around him. He walked slowly in his polished shoes, almost as if making a deal with the pain to give him just a little more time, just a little more, and there she was. She and the white woman were eating their hot dogs. The girl was the first to see him. 'Mommy,' she said. 'Look at the Indian.'

The mother gawked towards him and warned, 'Now, honey . . .'

' 'Scuse me,' Icabus said, all the while hoping he'd have enough time. The mother looked around, perhaps for Security, but the girl watched him. 'There's something in your daughter's hair.'

'What!' the mother squawked. 'Where?' She went through her daughter's hair. 'Oh, Mindy . . .'

Mindy wouldn't stop looking at him.

Icabus tried to smile through all of the pain inside of him. 'I'm a Dogrib Indian. Have you ever heard of us?'

The mother stopped briefly looking through Mindy's hair and watched him. 'Please have a seat. My daughter is Cree.'

He held his back, leaned into the table, careful of his knees, and sat slowly across from them. He winced and bit his lip. 'It's okay if you haven't.'

'But your hair is short,' Mindy said.

Icabus laughed, surprised with the observation. 'Our hair is short. We're different, that way, from the Crees, but we pray the same way . . .'

Icabus began singing inside and could feel the power rising around him. He ran his fingers through his hair and pulled three hairs from his scalp. From the inside of his jacket, he pulled out his gift for the girl.

'Well,' Mindy's mother exhaled, 'I can't find anything.'

'It's right here.' Icabus explained. He leaned forward, passing the gift from one hand to the other, before feeling through Mindy's hair. He felt the waves of a hot lake, the down on a duck's belly, the underflesh of a thousand petals.

'Can I give you something?' he asked.

She smiled and nodded.

'Look!' he said and brought back a bright blue feather. He pulled a few hairs from her head when he pulled back the feather.

'Oh my,' the mother grinned. 'Oh my!'

'Oh, Mommy,' Mindy clapped, 'it's beautiful!'

'For you.' Icabus offered to Mindy. 'From the bird.'

'The Macaw!' Mindy beamed.

'When a woman gives birth to a girl,' he offered, 'the girl is the father's teacher.'

Under the table, he wrapped her hair around his fingers.

'I'm my daddy's teacher?' Mindy asked.

'You're the one,' he finished. Yes, he would teach her. He sang. He called it forth and it came. The young girl giggled and covered her mouth. A hand grabbed onto Icabus' shoulder almost snapping the song.

'Here he is!' Harold called. 'Over here, Augy!'

Icabus looked down.

'*Dye aye kae khlee nee*,' he whispered and looked over to Mindy. 'Remember me.'

'Can I keep the feather?' she asked.

He coughed and nodded. 'Do you like cats?'

Mindy shook her head. 'I'm allergic.'

'You can't use your medicine around cats,' he said. 'They'll steal it.'

'What do you mean?' the mother asked.

'In your life, you need to listen with the deepest part of you for what to do. You need to listen with your blood.'

'That is good advice,' the mother pulled out her purse. 'What tribe are you from again?'

'Dogrib,' he answered and when he spoke, he smiled. This was it.

The mother wrote this down. 'Is that one word or two?'

'Thank you,' Mindy smiled and held the feather up to the light.

Icabus was pleased.

'Dad!' Augy said and came over. 'I'm so sorry,' she apologized to the woman. 'My father wanders.' She cleared her throat and lowered her voice. 'He's . . . confused.'

Icabus sang louder now and began moving his lips. Maybe the girl would one day visit Rae with questions about him, questions that were asked by her blood and his medicine.

Icabus felt the song push against the back of his teeth and run its fingers through her hair. He thought of the lake and looked into Mindy's eyes. He sent part of himself: the best part. Mindy's eyes registered his power. She wasn't scared and that was good.

He sang and twisted her hair with his under the table. He remembered the song as best he could. It was the same song his grandmother had sung to him. He looked down to make sure his shadow covered Mindy's. The pain sliced again. He sang her name with a breath and all she heard was: '*Deeeee . . .*'

He pulled the braid of their hair until it snapped, and Icabus left his body. It was like falling skyward. Mindy received him: the Macaw's blue feather in her hand; her mother pulling Mindy close; Augy, her bad perm blocking out the sun.

'Dad? *Dad!*'

Icabus flew with an explosion of white feathers and was swallowed by the hottest lake. He could hear the most beautiful songs being sung by thousands of voices, and there was peace. He became it. Everything was so blue, and he noticed that the colors red and black were nowhere to be seen. He could see Delphine waiting for him. She was radiant, standing in her tanned moosehide dress, and beside her stood their son, Justin, who stood so proudly before him. Morris wasn't here, and that was a good sign. Icabus looked to his left. Stan walked beside him, smiled, placed his hand on Icabus' shoulder, guiding him home . . .

Evelyn Lau *b.* 1971

VANCOUVER, BRITISH COLUMBIA

'One of the reasons I so enjoy work by [John] Cheever and [John] Updike is that they write about something that I don't know,' says Evelyn Lau. 'They write about something that is very exotic to me: well-off people having affairs, going out to parties and getting drunk and behaving badly, a real moral structure, family, secure housing, job, a privileged white class. A lot of younger writers rebel against that but to me that is sort of an ideal, something I'm very attracted to, it's a landscape I wish I could explore.' This kind of social landscape, more often than not seen from the outside, characterizes Lau's writing. 'I don't have much interest in politics yet, or "the world",' she says. 'I guess I'm most interested in people's emotional states. And the emotional states of a middle-aged man are the ones I identify most with—outside of my own.' Her short stories, widely published in literary magazines and anthologies, depict this emotional terrain, usually from the point of view of young female characters involved with married men.

Born in Vancouver, Lau escaped from her strict and overprotective family by running away at fourteen. Having begun writing and publishing in literary magazines at the age of twelve, she kept a diary during the two years she spent on the street, which became her first book, *Runaway: Diary of a Street Kid* (1989). About her experiences as a drug addict and prostitute, it became an instant best seller, was translated into six languages, and turned into a film, *The Diary of Evelyn Lau* (1994). This autobiographical narrative is, as Lau says, 'the most honest thing I could do, and the best thing I could do, at the time', but she has resisted being 'treated as a spokesperson for street kids'. This reluctance is in keeping with her resistance to being seen as a Chinese Canadian writer. While she enjoys reading works by writers like Salman Rushdie and Rohinton Mistry—'I identify with the family life that's portrayed in them'— Chinese Canadian writers do not 'make any sense to' her; 'If I feel different from other people, I think of being different in terms of my background.' Along the same lines, she also feels 'horrified and outraged . . . [at the] assumption' that she should write from a specifically feminist perspective. Lau succinctly articulates the independent stance she wants to maintain: 'I hate writing about politics. . . . The writing has to be the most important, not the message, to my mind.'

Lau has published three poetry collections that reflect her fascination with desire and sexuality. *You Are Not Who You Claim* (1990), which won the Milton Acorn People's Poetry Prize, *Oedipal Dreams* (1992), a finalist for the Governor General's Award, and *In the House of Slaves* (1994)—all express the complexity of gender roles and class differences. Her short fiction, *Fresh Girls and Other Stories* (1993), which includes the story that follows, is about young women involved with usually older men, about the hard realities of prostitutes and the comfortable lives of prostitutes' middle-class clients. 'If these stories were told by the man,' Lau says, 'they would be pornography.' But, narrated as they are by the women themselves who are aware of their ambivalent and tentative positions, the stories become an exploration of split as well as complicit subjectivities. This theme is also present in her poetry collection, *In the House of Slaves* (1994), and *Choose Me* (1999), a collection of seven stories in which, as the titles suggest, the female young protagonists, in Lau's words, 'long to be chosen [by the older men] in their relationships'. But the title is also meant to convey 'the choices people have made that they have to live with'. The sensuous writing style of these stories is also present in her novel, *Other Women* (1995), but the erotic and sexual imagery that has become characteristic of her work is less evident there. *Inside Out: Reflections on a Life So Far* (2001) is a collection of autobiographical essays in which she reflects on her family background, her bulimia and depression, her past life as a prostitute and how this affects people's perceptions of her now, the origins and implications of her attraction to older men, as well as her writing practice.

As was the case with *Runaway*, turning the private 'inside out', the need to remove the boundaries that separate her personal life from the public limelight, also characterizes this book. It includes the essay 'Me and W.P.'—W.P. referring to author W.P. Kinsella with whom she lived for a number of years—which created a media controversy when it first appeared in print, and led to Kinsella initiating a lawsuit against her. Her most recent title is a collection of poetry called *Treble* (2005). The recipient of the Air Canada Prize as Most Promising Writer Under Thirty (1990), Lau resides in Vancouver.

Marriage

His gold wedding band catches the light between the two walls of flesh that are our bodies in bed. It is a wide band with a perforated design, and it fits loosely on his finger. When he draws his hand up between us to touch me, the hand seems to take on a separate entity—as though it is a stranger's hand encountered in a crowded bus or an empty alley, the ring as hard as a weapon. I feel the coldness of it branding my skin. Yet I am drawn to it compulsively, this symbol of his commitment to another, as though it is a private part of him that will derive pleasure from my touch: rubbing it, twisting it, pulling it up to his knuckle and back down again.

In the morning we go for a walk in Queen Elizabeth Park, where a wedding is taking place. There are photographers bent on one knee in the grass, children with flowers looped through their hair, a bride in her layers of misty white. We watch from a bridge over a creek nearby, and then from the top of a waterfall. From that height the members of the wedding appear toy-like, diminished by the vast green slopes, the overflowing flower beds. When I glance sideways, I see him serenely observing the activity below, his hands draped over the low rail. I want then to step behind him, put my hands between his shoulders, and push him over, if only to recognize something in his face, some anxiety or pain to correspond with what I am feeling.

The people we pass in the park see a middle-aged man in a suit with his arm around a nineteen-year-old girl. They invariably pause, look twice with curiosity. At first I look back boldly, meeting their eyes in the harsh sunlight, but as the walk wears on my gaze falters. I keep my eyes trained on the ground, my pointy white high heels keeping step with his freshly polished black leather shoes. I don't know what people are thinking; I know they don't think I am his daughter. Their stares make me feel unclean, as if there is something illicit about me. Suddenly I wonder if my skirt is too short, my lipstick too red, my hair too teased. I concentrate hard on pretending that there is something natural about my odd pairing with this man.

He is oblivious to their looks; if anything, he is pleased by them, as though people are looking because the girl his arm holds captive is particularly striking. He does not see that the looks are more often edged with pity than any degree of approval or jealousy.

He tells me afterwards that he is proud to be seen with me.

Sometimes when he visits me he is carrying his beeper. He has just completed the crawl to the foot of my bed, drawn up the comforter tent-like over his head and shoulders, and is preparing in the fuzzy dark to attack my body with his tongue. And then from deep in the grey huddle of his pants on the floor rises the berating call of the beeper, causing the anonymous bulk under the covers to jump and hit his head against the soft ceiling of the comforter. I resist the urge to reach out and rub that dome under my comforter, like it is a teddy bear or my own bunched-up knees.

Naked, he digs into the mass of material on the floor, extracts the beeper, and seats himself on the edge of the bed. I tuck my hair behind my ear and examine his back as he dials a series of numbers to access his answering service, the hospital, other doctors.

'Good afternoon,' he says. 'Is this Dr Martin? Yes . . . yes . . . how is she? All right, one milligram lorazepam to be administered at bedtime . . .' while he remains half-erect between his long white thighs, one hand groping behind him 'til it finds and begins to squeeze my breast and then its nipple. Even though he has tucked the phone between his ear and shoulder so that the hand that flaps the air is not the one that wears the ring, I still feel it belongs to someone other than him as it rounds the blank canvas of his back and pats air and pillow before touching skin. I am reminded of the card in my desk drawer: on Valentine's Day four months ago he gave me a card that read, in a floral script, 'I Love You'. He said, almost immediately, 'I hope you don't get vindictive and send that card to my wife. It's got my handwriting on it.'

It never would have occurred to me to do so if he hadn't told me. What he said inspired me to keep the card in a special drawer, where I will not lose it. I put it away feeling reassured that at last I had some power over him. I had something I could hurt him with. I now know I saved the card because it was my only proof of his love for me, it is the only part of him that belongs to me.

The night before his wife's return from the conference she's attending in Los Angeles, we drive to our usual restaurant where the Japanese waiter smiles at us in a way he interprets as friendly, while I recognize amusement dancing at the corners of his mouth. I lift my purse into my lap and politely ask permission to smoke.

'I'd rather you didn't. My wife has a good nose for tobacco.'

How much I want his wife to come home to the smell of smoke in the family car.

After she has walked off the plane and through the terminal to where her luggage revolves on the carousel, after she has picked out his face among the faces of other husbands waiting to greet their wives and take them home, I can see her leaning back in the passenger seat, rubbing her neck, tired after her flight and eager for sleep—then the trace of smoke acrid in her nostrils, mingled perhaps with my perfume. In my fantasy she turns to him, wild-eyed and tearful, she demands that he stop the car, she wrenches the perforated wedding band from her finger and throws it at him before she opens the door and leaves. *Give it to that slut*, she will say.

'Maybe I'm subconsciously trying to ruin your marriage,' I smile as I light a cigarette and watch the smoke momentarily fill up the front of the car.

'Please don't,' he says calmly. I think a man whose marriage is in my hands should sound a little more desperate, but in the dark I can only see his profile against the stores and buildings blurring outside the window, and it is unreadable. I wish afterwards that I had looked at his hands, to see if they tightened on the wheel.

He tells me that we will have lots of time together over the years but I have no concept of time. I ask him to leave the city with me.

'Would you really do that?' he asks. 'Run off with me?'

'Yes.'

'I'm very flattered.'

'Don't be. It wasn't meant to be flattering.' I pause. I want to say, *It meant more than that.* 'Why can't we just take off?'

'I can't do it right now,' he says. 'I have people depending on me—my patients. I'd love to. I can't.'

'I have just as much to lose as you do, you know,' I say, but he doesn't believe me. He has been feeding me whisky all evening, and I am swaying in a chair in front of him. He places my hands together between his own and pulls me out of the chair, collapsing me to my knees. Kneeling, I sway back and forth and squint up at him, my hands stranded in his lap.

'You should go,' I say.

'Yes, I have to work tomorrow morning.'

'And you have to pick your wife up from the airport,' I say, struggling to my feet to press the colour of my lips against his white cheek.

I do not realize I am clutching the sleeve of his suit jacket until we have reached the door, where he chuckles and pries my fingers loose. He adjusts his beeper inside his pocket and walks out into the rain-misted night.

Back inside the apartment I am intent on finishing the bottle of Chivas he left behind on the kitchen counter, but when I go to it I find an envelope next to the bottle, weighted by an ashtray. I tear it open, my heart beating painfully—it could be a letter, he could be saying that he can no longer live without me, that tonight he will finally tell his wife about us. Instead I pull out a greeting card with a picture on the front of a girl standing by a seashore. She is bare-legged, with dimpled knees, wearing a loose frock the colour of daffodils. She looks about twelve years old.

Inside are no words, just two new hundred-dollar bills.

He tries to alleviate his guilt by giving me money: cheques left folded on the kitchen table, crisp bills tucked inside cards. He takes me shopping for groceries and clothes, he never visits my apartment without bringing me some small gift, as though all this entitles him to leave afterwards and return home to his wife. But I have no similar method of striking such bargains with my conscience. The dregs of our affair stick to my body like semen. Because I do think of his wife—of the way she must sink into bed beside him in the dark, putting her face against his chest and breathing him in, his scent carried with her into her dreams. I do think of the pain she would feel if she knew, and I am frightened sometimes by the force of my desire to inflict that pain upon her—this wife who is to be pitied in her faithless marriage, this wife whom I envy.

And tonight I want more than anything to take those smooth brown bills between my fingers and tear them up. Does he think I'm like one of those teen hookers in thigh-high boots and bustiers he says he used to pick up downtown before he met me? My hands are shaking, I want so badly to get rid of his money. Instead I go over to the chest of drawers beside my bed and add this latest contribution to the growing stack of cards and cash I have hidden there.

He often says to me, 'If you were my daughter . . .' My lips twist and he has to add each time, 'You know what I mean.' If things were different, he means. If we weren't sleeping together. We cultivate fantasies for each other of what a loving, doting father he would have made me; of what a pretty, accomplished daughter I would have made him. 'I adore you,' he says to me. 'I wish I could marry you.' And then, 'I wish you were my daughter,' as he kisses my neck, my shoulders, my breasts, his fingers slipping between my thighs. As things are, I see we don't have anything that comes close to the illusion.

His cologne has found places to lodge in my blankets, clothing, cushions. No matter how many loads of laundry I carry down the back stairs, the smell of him has taken up residence in the corners of my apartment, as though to stay.

He tells me little about his activities, but the spare portraits he paints grow vivid in my mind. This weekend he will visit Vancouver Island with his family. I picture them on the ferry, with the possibility of grey skies and rain, the mountains concealed by veils of fog, the treed islands rising like the backs of beasts out of the ocean. I wonder if his family will venture onto the deck and look down at the water, I imagine them falling overboard and being ground to pieces by the propellers, staining those foamy waves crimson.

He's told me about his three sons and I know they are all teenagers. I know that the oldest is stronger than his father, handsome with a thick head of red hair, and that this son's feisty girlfriend reminds him of me. I know they tease him with the eyeball-rolling exasperation and embarrassment that I've felt towards my own parents.

'Oh, Dad,' they'd groan in restaurants where he'd be teasing the waitress. 'Don't do that. She's in our class at school!'

I imagine him clambering up the grey steel ladder leading to the top deck of the ferry. He reaches down towards his wife. When she grips his hand his ring bites into her palm, a sensation she has grown used to, as though the ring is now a part of his body.

They walk together behind their children, past rows of orange plastic chairs in the non-smoking section, past the cafeteria selling sticky danishes and styrofoam cups of hot coffee, past the gift shop with the little Canadian flags and sweatshirts in the window. They wrestle open the heavy door leading onto the deck and the blast of air sucking them out separates his hair into pieces plastering forward, backward, tight against his cheek.

His family races in their sneakers and jeans towards the edges of the ferry, clinging to the railings, and he fights his way through the wind towards them, laughing and shouting. I know for certain that, for once, he is not thinking of me.

Wayde Compton *b.* 1972

VANCOUVER, BRITISH COLUMBIA

One of the most important writers of his generation, Wayde Compton has been instrumental in bringing to light black history and writing in British Columbia. His first poetry book, *49th Parallel Psalm* (1999, 2005), shortlisted for the Dorothy Livesay Prize, announces his poetics with great force, a poetics that explores the sound and ideological particularities of 'black North America', while also composing, through orature and hip hop, the history of the first blacks who arrived in British Columbia in the nineteenth century. Inspired by DJ Kool Herc, Compton sees hip hop as 'the conduit of a new kind of black American voice, . . . globally-known', a voice through which he also records the present tense, in particular that of the culture of his 'black and mulatto friends'. The orality and 'seething aggravation' that characterize hip hop enables him to write in a new idiom—'broken English' or 'black Englishes', he calls it—that speaks at once of 'a creeping nihilism' and of a 'freedom-of-speech' and 'the passing of communal renewals'. Distinguished from the 'masked complaints of the blues', hip hop becomes in Compton's writing 'lit-hop', a powerful mélange of contemporary sensibilities, historical echoes, voodoo, and biblical language.

Born in Vancouver, Compton teaches creative writing at Simon Fraser University's Writing and Publishing Program and English at Coquitlam College. Along with Jason de Couto, he performs 'turntable-based sound poetry' through their duo *The Contact Zone Crew*. He is a co-founder of The Hogan's Alley Memorial Project, which intends to record, through publications and other means, reminiscences about the lives of the blacks that lived there (east of Main Street, between Prior and Union Streets, Vancouver). His second poetry book, *Performance Bond* (2004), accompanied by a CD entitled 'The Reinventing the Wheel' (music by Trevor Thompson and lyrics by Compton), remembers Hogan's Alley as one of the forgotten sites of the black diaspora in Vancouver, while also dealing with the legacy of slavery in the past and the tensions that mark racial politics and 'Halfricans' like him. Compton's commitment to establishing a written record of blacks in British Columbia, what he calls 'a long, varied project of redemption', is reflected in his co-founding of Commodore Books, the first press run by and for blacks and mixed-race persons in Western Canada. His anthology *Bluesprint: Black English British Columbian Literature and Orature* (2001) is yet another manifestation of his project of recovery. The first collection of its kind, it introduces not only 'new' black and mixed-race voices into the literary landscape of this province, but also includes the writing of Sir James Douglas, a formidable representative of the colonial authorities and Governor of British Columbia, who did not acknowledge publicly his black heritage.

O

O Osiris, rise up.
raise us. some say
you are the original
Christ. some say
Isis, your sister, renewed you   5
and knew you
in an obscene way. twice

Set, your nemesis (your set),
iced you. the first time
you just rose right on up like the sun.   10
so the second time the nigger got mean, cut you up
like a DJ would a groove, splintered you like a busted mirror,
razored you good, then spread

the pieces around like a drunk does money
on a Saturday night. buried a piece in the east,   15
a portion in the north, an ounce in the south,
and the rest in the west. to the four corners, as they say,
he fixed your wagon. but he didn't count

on Isis, cool Isis, who loved you right (wrong)
and sought you out and dug you up. pick and spade   20
and all. gathered your remains
in a bloody dirty pile and watched the magic work
as you got it together. she shuffled you back to osirisness
like you was a deck. and you stood up again
at last, shook your head, cussed out   25
that punk motherfucker Set, gave Isis a big wet kiss,
and asked her to fill you in
on what had gone down. and after she did, you said,
'the only question I got, sis, is
if he burried a part of me in the west, which,   30
as all of us Egyptians know, is where heaven lies,
what was heaven like?' and Isis replied

'Osiris, bro, how else would heaven be?
it was blue.'

'just bluer that's all?'   35

'you forget to put on your ears? I said it was blue.
all sorts of blue.'

Where Heaven Lies

1865 arrives
with January rain and Victoria mud,
departs
with the victory of North over
                    South. the word in *The Mirror* is: 5

Emancipation at last!

sweet baby Jesus,
do you know what this means?
sweet baby Jesus, at last. at
last. praise be. after the cacophony   10
of war, we somehow sort of won. they saying we
emancipated
and pro
claimed. I read in *The Mirror* that they

're lining up to re   15
name themselves
down south. gonna have themselves a re
construction. gonna be some changes made.
even though the Captain caught a bullet through the centre
of his stovepipe hat in that theatre.   20

I can picture them,
all the brothers and the sisters,
down there
picking up the pieces,
though I'm missing from the frame. this dis   25

orientation is diz
zying. I can't play this game
no more; the croupier keeps changing
the rules. used to
believe the air was sweeter   30
on the Brit side of the border, freer
as of 1833, 49th degree, norther, nearer
to God and the top
of the world. Lord

been here seven years.   35
left everything.
renounced America.

what I got to show
for it? handful of magic
beens.   40

how anybody supposed to know
what crazy shit white folks are capable of?
who'da thought they'd do
something as out of character as setting us free?
headlines ought to read: 45

Hell freezes over; white people discover empathy

go figure.
got to be
something better   50
than this bullshit bitterness. a bet
ter prospect
maybe two steps
back,

cause Lord knows, in this pointless dis   55
persal, we ain't even one step forward here. our moment
nothing but a stutt

er
he
re.   60

Declaration of the Halfrican Nation

hazel's so definitive. is the window
half open or half closed? is a black
rose natural? is it indigenous to this
coast? my grammar teacher said a semi-
colon is just a gutless colon; yellow. co-   5
conuts get eaten from the inside, the sweetness
and light from the milk and the flesh, not
the husk, so skull-like. one
friend said she's white except
for having this brown skin and some-   10
times she forgets it until a mirror shatters
that conclusion casting blackward glances side-

ways, askance processions of belonging, possession. mirrors walk
on two legs too sometimes, saying hello to you cause
you are brown   15
as we pass. what is britannia
to me? one three continents removed
from the scenes my mothers loved,
misty grove, english rose,
what is britannia to me?   20
ain't no negroes on the tv shows we
produced in playground theatres; now
there's so many on screen a white acquaintance of mine
thought the us population was half
black! one drop rules aside and all   25
things being equal, I'd say that signifies
an inexorable triumph of milk's dream. we number a dozen percent, in fact, south
of the border; in canada, I really couldn't
begin to guess our numbers crunching   30
through the snow on shoes of woven
koya. black hippies; black punk rockers;
black goths with white masks *literally*
multiply like flesh-eating bacteria on the west coast. racism
is a disease, the ministry decrees to me in my bus seat   35
from an ad, and I could add
that this is just the latest stage in race management. canada all
in a rush to recruit more brown whites; entre-
preneurs only, no more slaves or railroad builders,
iron chinks or tempered niggers. the wages   40
of empire have yet to be spilled. oka. all
I halfta do is spell it and the settled snow shivers. one settler,
one bullet, south africans sang, palestinians sing; the tune
is boomin. is the mention
of bullets too american? the best way   45
anyone ever referred to me as mixed-race was a jamaican
woman who said, *I notice you're touched*. to
me sounded like she meant by the hand of god
(or the god of hands), and not the tar brush. made me
feel like a motherless child a long, long way   50
from my home. feel like history got me
by the throat. sometimes I feel like frantz fanon's ghost
is kickin back with a coke and rum having
a good chuckle at all this, stirring in the tears, his work
done, lounging with the spirits. oh, all   55
my fellow mixed sisters and brothers let us mount

an offensive for our state. surely something
can be put together from the tracts, manifestoes, auto-
biographies, ten-point programs, constitutions, and historical
claims. I know more than enough who've ex-   60
pressed an interest in dying on the wire just for the victory
of being an agreed-upon proper noun

David Bezmozgis *b.* 1973

RIGA, LATVIA

Natasha and Other Stories (2004) may be David Bezmozgis's first book, but it has catapulted him into international fame. A winner of over twenty national and international prizes, including the Toronto Book Award, the Commonwealth Writers Prize for Best Fiction Book for the Caribbean and Canada, and the Jewish Quarterly Wingate Prize for Fiction (UK), and translated into twelve languages, it is a collection that reflects at once a hip contemporary sensibility and the maturity expected from a real craftsman of language. Loosely interlinked, the stories portray the array of experiences their first-person narrator, Mark, goes through as he and his family, recent Russian Latvian Jewish immigrants in Toronto, learn to negotiate their new cultural environment and language with their sense of who they are and where they have arrived from. Though mirroring his family's experiences, they are not autobiographical, Bezmozgis says: 'the autobiographical part is largely context; the plot and most everything else is fictional.'

Born in Riga, Latvia, to Jewish parents, his family immigrated to Toronto in 1980 where it took him six months to learn English. Following his BA in English from McGill University, he studied film and learned to direct at the University of Southern California. A John Simon Guggenheim Fellow in 2005, Bezmozgis is also a documentary filmmaker. His first documentary, *LA Mohel* (1999), about the 3,700-year-old ritual of Jewish circumcision, won a major award for student filmmakers and was shown at many Jewish film festivals. He has also made two other documentaries, *The Diamond Nose* (2001) and *Genuine Article: The First Trial* (2003). Presently at work on a novel, he lives (most of the time) in Toronto. 'My culture is not broadly Canadian,' he says; 'I feel a difference in tangible ways, though I don't feel like an outcast.'

An Animal to The Memory

On the railway platform in Vienna, my mother and aunt forbade my cousin and me from saying goodbye to our grandparents. Through the window of the compartment we watched as they disembarked from the train and followed an Israeli agent onto a waiting bus. The bus was bound for the airport, where an El Al plane was waiting. We were bound for somewhere else. Where exactly we didn't know—Australia, America, Canada—but someplace that was not Israel. As my mother, aunt, cousin, and I wept, my father and uncle kept an eye out for Israeli agents. These agents were known to inspect compartments. Any indication that we had close relatives on the buses would bring questions: Why were we separating the family? Why were we rejecting our Israeli visas? Why were we so ungrateful to the State of Israel, which had, after all, provided us with the means to escape the Soviet Union?

The answer to these questions, for my father and uncle, was 150 million angry Arabs.

For my grandfather, a lifelong Zionist, this was no answer. Back in Riga, packing our bags, he had decided that he would not go chasing us around the globe. At least in Israel he knew there would be a roof over his head. And at least in Israel, surrounded by 150 million angry Arabs, he would have no trouble identifying the enemy.

In the days leading up to our departure, a common argument went:

Grandfather: There, I'll never have to hear dirty Jew.

Father/Uncle: So instead you'll hear dirty Russian.

Grandfather: Maybe. But where you're going you'll hear one and the other.

Though I never heard dirty Jew, dirty Russian tended to come up. Particularly at Hebrew school. Not very often, but often enough that I felt justified in using it as an excuse when I tried to convince my parents to let me transfer to a normal public school.

This was a campaign I started in earnest in the seventh grade. The year before, we had finally moved out of the apartment building and into a semidetached house. Geographically, the move was negligible—looking out my bedroom window, I could still see our old building—but we now had a backyard, a driveway, a garage for my bicycle, and a carpeted basement. We also now had a neighborhood. Across the street, my aunt and uncle bought a similar house. In other houses lived other Russians who had succeeded in accumulating down payments. Their children became my friends: Eugene, Boris, Alex, Big Vadim, Little Vadim. In the evenings and on the weekends, we roved the streets, played wall ball, road hockey, shoplifted from the Korean's convenience store, and abused Fat Larissa, the neighborhood slut.

My new friends were all Jewish, but after my mother framed my bar mitzvah portrait—in which I wore a white tuxedo—they took me outside, held me down, and pummeled my shoulders until my arms went numb.

My mother was categorically against me leaving Hebrew school. This was partly out of deference to my grandfather, but also because of a deep personal conviction. There were reasons why we had left the Soviet Union. She believed that in Canada I should get what I could never have gotten in Latvia. As far as she was concerned, I wasn't leaving Hebrew school until I learned what it was to be a Jew.

My father, I knew, was more sympathetic. For years, because of special considerations made for the poor Russian Jews, the Hebrew school had subsidized my tuition, but after we bought the house, the subsidy was revoked. And even though my mother had secured a better job and my father's business had improved, I saw the irritation on his face every time I started complaining about the school.

—He knows the language. He can read all the prayers. If he wants to leave maybe we should let him leave already?

—Take the money from my salary.

—I didn't say it was the money.

—Take the money from my salary.

—You want to redo the kitchen. That's also from your salary.

—If that's my choice, I can live without the kitchen.

My mother was resolute. Nothing I said helped my case. So that April, just after Passover, I put Jerry Ackerman in the hospital.

Most days, on his way to the office, my father would drop me off at school in his red 1970 Volvo. On a Friday, after gym, Jerry Ackerman said something about Solly Birnbaum's small hairless penis and Solly started to cry. Solly was fat, had webbed toes, and was reduced to tears at the end of every gym class. I had never defended him before but I seized my chance.

—Ackerman, if I had your tweezer-dick I wouldn't talk.

—Why are you looking at my dick, faggot?

—Ackerman thought he had a pubic hair until he pissed out of it.

—Fuck you, Berman, and that red shitbox your father drives.

In Rabbi Gurvich's office, Dr Ackerman said that I had banged Jerry's head so hard against the wall that I had given him a concussion. Dr Ackerman said that Jerry had vomited three times that night and that they'd had to drive him to the hospital at two in the morning. Dr Ackerman asked, What kind of sick person, what kind of animal would do this? When I refused to answer, my mother apologized to Dr and Mrs Ackerman and also to Jerry.

This wasn't the first time my mother and I had been called into Gurvich's office. After our move into the new neighborhood I had begun to affect a hoodlum persona. At school, I kept to myself, glowered in the hallways, and, with the right kind of provocation, punched people in the face. Less than a month before I gave Jerry Ackerman his concussion, I'd gotten into a fight with two eighth graders. Because of dietary laws, the school prohibited bringing meat for lunch. Other students brought peanut butter or tuna fish, but I—and most of the other Russians—would invariably arrive at school with smoked Hungarian salami, Polish bologna, roast turkey. Our mothers couldn't comprehend why anyone would choose to eat peanuts in a country that didn't know what it meant to have a shortage of smoked meat. And so, I was already sensitive about my lunch when the two eighth graders stopped by my table and asked me how I liked my pork sandwich.

For my fight with Jerry Ackerman, I received a two-day suspension. Sparing words, Gurvich made it clear that this was never to happen again. The next time he saw me in his office would be the last. To hit someone's head against a wall—did I ever think what that could do? If I got so much as within ten feet of Ackerman he didn't want to say what would happen. He asked me if I understood. My mother said I understood. He asked me if I had anything to say. I knew that what I had to say was not what he wanted to hear.

On the drive home my mother asked me what I was trying to do, and when my father got home he came as close as he ever had to hitting me.

—Don't think you're so smart. What do you think happens if you get expelled? You want to repeat the grade? We already paid for the entire year.

On the street, I told Boris, Alex, and Eugene, but they weren't impressed.

—Congratulations, you're the toughest kid in Hebrew school.

I returned to school the week of Holocaust Remembrance Day—which we called Holocaust Day for short. It was one of a series of occasions that punctuated the school year beginning with Rosh Hashanah in September and ending with Israeli Independence Day in May. For Chanukah, the school provided jelly donuts and art class was spent making swords and shields out of papier-mâché; for Purim, everyone dressed up in costume and a pageant was organized during which we all cheered the hanging of evil Hamman and his ten evil sons; for Passover, every class held a preparatory seder and took a field trip to the matzoh bakery; for Israeli Independence Day, we dressed in blue and white and marched around the school yard waving flags and singing the *Hatikvah*, our national anthem.

Holocaust Day was different. Preparations were made days in advance. The long basement hallway, from the gymnasium to the pool, was converted into a Holocaust museum. Out of storage came the pictures pasted on bristol board. There were photocopies of Jewish passports, there were archival photos of Jews in cattle cars, starving Jews in ghettos, naked Ukrainian Jews waiting at the edge of an open trench, Jews with their hands on barbed wire waiting to be liberated, ovens, schematic drawings of the gas chambers, pictures of empty cans of Zyklon B. Other bristol boards had Yiddish songs written in the ghettos, in the camps. We had crayon drawings done by children in Theresienstadt. We had a big map of Europe with multicolored pins and accurate statistics. Someone's grandfather donated his striped Auschwitz pajamas, someone else's grandmother contributed a jacket with a yellow star on it. There were also sculptures. A woman kneeling with a baby in her arms in bronze. A tin reproduction of the gates of Birkenau with the words *Arbeit Macht Frei*. Sculptures of flaming Stars of David, sculptures of piles of shoes, sculptures of sad bearded Polish rabbis. In the center of the hallway was a large menorah, and all along the walls were smaller memorial candles—one candle for each European country. On Holocaust Day, the fluorescents were extinguished and we moved through the basement by dim candlelight.

Holocaust Day was also the one day that Rabbi Gurvich supervised personally. Gurvich's father was a Holocaust survivor and had, that year, published his memoirs. We were all encouraged to buy the book. When the copies arrived, Gurvich led his father from class to class so that the old man could sign them. Whereas Gurvich was imposing—dark, unsmiling, possessing a gruff seismic voice—his father was frail and mild. In our class, the old man perched himself behind the teacher's desk and smiled benignly as he inked each copy with the double imperative: *Yizkor; al tishkach!* Remember; don't forget!

Even though I had spent the two days of my suspension fantasizing about killing Gurvich and Ackerman, I returned to school and avoided them both. Gurvich was easy to avoid. With the exception of Holocaust Day, his primary role was that of disciplinarian and—unless you were called into his office—he was rarely seen. Ackerman was different. The only class we shared was gym, but in the mornings I saw him grinning as I got my books from my locker; at lunch I sat across the cafeteria as he conspired against me; and at recess, if he was playing, then I abstained from tennis-ball soccer.

For Holocaust Day we were called down into the basement by grades. The hallway was long and, arranged in orderly columns, an entire grade could fit into the basement at one time. After Gurvich made the announcement over the intercom, we followed our teachers down. We were quiet on the way and silent once we got there. Some people started crying before we entered the basement; others started to cry when we reached the dimness and saw the photos on the walls. As we filed in, Gurvich stood waiting for us beside the menorah. When everyone was in the basement, the double doors were closed behind us and we waited for Gurvich to begin. Because the hallway was extremely reverberant, Gurvich's deliberate pause was filled with the echo of stifled sobs, and because there were no windows and the pool was so close, the basement was stuffy and reeked of chlorine.

Gurvich began the service by telling us about the six million, about the vicious Nazis, about our history of oppression. His heavy voice occupied the entire space, and when he intoned the *El Maleh Rachamim*, I felt his voice reach into me, down into that place where my mother said I was supposed to have the thing called my 'Jewish soul'. Gurvich sang: O God, full of compassion, who dwells on high, grant true rest upon the wings of the Divine Presence. And when he sang this, his harsh baritone filled with grief so that his voice seemed no longer his own; his voice belonged to the six million. Every syllable that came out of his mouth was important. The sounds he made were dictated by centuries of ancestral mourning. I couldn't understand how it was possible for Gurvich not to cry when his voice sounded the way it did.

After Gurvich finished the prayer, we slowly made our way through the memorial. I stopped by photos of the Warsaw ghetto during the uprising and then beside a portrait of Mordecai Anilewicz, the leader of the ghetto resistance. I noticed Ackerman behind me. He was with two friends and I turned my head to look.

—What are you looking at, assface?

I turned away. I concentrated on moving down the hallway but felt a shove from behind and lost my balance. I managed to catch myself along the wall. My hand landed safely on top of a child's crayon drawing, but my foot accidentally knocked over the Czech memorial candle. Everybody in the hallway froze at the sound of the breaking glass. I turned around and saw Ackerman snickering. Matthew Wise, Ackerman's friend, stood between me and Ackerman. Wise was bigger than Ackerman, and I was sure he was the one who had pushed me. Instinctively, I lunged at Wise and tackled him to the ground. I was on top and choking him when Gurvich grabbed the back of my shirt and tried to pull me off. Even as Gurvich pulled me away I held on to Wise's throat. And when Gurvich finally yanked me clear, I saw that Wise was still on the floor, trembling.

While the rest of my class finished going through the memorial, I waited upstairs in Gurvich's office. I waited, also, until the sixth grade went down to the memorial, before Gurvich returned.

I sat for half an hour, maybe longer. I imagined the horrible consequences. I foresaw my mother's reaction and, even worse, my father's reaction. I didn't regret what I had done, but the fear of squandering so much of my parents' money made me physically sick.

When Gurvich finally walked into his office, he didn't sit down. Without looking at me, he told me to get up out of my goddamn chair and go back downstairs. I was not to touch anything, I was not to move, I was to stay there until he came.

Back in the basement I waited for Gurvich by the menorah. I didn't know where else to stand. I didn't know where in the memorial my presence would be the least offensive to Gurvich. I stood in one place beside a picture of Jews looking out of their bunks, and somehow I felt that my standing there would anger Gurvich. I moved over to the sculptures and felt the same way. I wanted to strike some sort of anodyne pose, to make myself look like someone who didn't deserve to be expelled.

I was tracing the ironwork on the menorah when Gurvich pushed the double doors open and entered. Very deliberately, as if he didn't know what to say first, Gurvich walked over to where I stood. I took my hands off the menorah.

—How is it that all of this doesn't mean anything to you, Berman? Can you tell me that?

—It means something.

—It means something? It means something when you jump on another Jew in this place, on Holocaust Day? This is how you demonstrate it means something?

He raised his voice.

—It means something when you act like an animal to the memory of everyone who died?

—What about Wise? He pushed me into the wall.

—Wise had to go home because of what you did, so don't ask me about Wise. Wise wasn't the one choking another Jew at a memorial for the Holocaust.

I didn't say anything. Gurvich tugged at his beard.

—Look around this, Berman, what do you see?

I looked.

—The Holocaust.

—And does this make you feel anything?

—Yes.

—Yes? It does?

—Yes.

—I don't believe you. I don't believe you feel anything.

He put his hand on my shoulder. He leaned in closer.

—Berman, a Nazi wouldn't do here what you did today. Don't tell me about how you feel.

—I'm not a Nazi.

—No, you're not a Nazi? What are you?

—A Jew.

—What?

—A Jew.

—I can't hear you.

—I'm a Jew.

—Why so quiet, Berman? It's just us here. Don't be so ashamed to say it.

—I'm a Jew, I said into my shoes.

He turned me around by my shoulder. I may have considered myself a tough little bastard, but when Gurvich gripped me I understood that mine was a boy's shoulder and that his was a man's hand. He put his face very close to mine and made me look at him. I could smell the musky staleness of his beard. For the first time, I felt I was going to cry.

—So that my uncles hear you in Treblinka! he commanded.

He tightened his grip on my shoulder until he saw it hurt. I was convinced he was going to hit me. The last thing I wanted to do was start crying, so I started crying.

—I'm a Jew! I shouted into his face.

My voice rang off the walls, and off the sculptures and the pictures and the candles. I had screamed it in his face wishing to kill him, but he only nodded his head. He kept his hand on my shoulder and waited until I really started to sob. My shoulder shuddered under his hand and I heard the repulsive sound of my own whimpering. Finally, Gurvich removed his hand and backed away a half step. As soon as he did, I wanted him to put his hand back. I was standing in the middle of the hallway, shaking. I wanted to sit down on the floor, or lean against a wall, something. Anything but stand in the middle of that hallway while Gurvich nodded his rabbinical head at me. When he was done nodding, he turned away and opened the double doors leading up to the stairs. Halfway out, before closing the doors, Gurvich looked back to where I hadn't moved.

—Now, Berman, he said, now maybe you understand what it is to be a Jew.

Texts Cited

Quotations in the headnotes that are from personal, telephone, or e-mail communications between the editor and the authors are not referenced here.

Act Against Slavery, Upper Canada. 9 July 1793.

Allen, Lillian. 'Preface' and 'Introduction'. *Women Do This Every Day: Selected Poems* (Toronto: Women's Press, 1993), 9–21.

Armstrong, Jeannette. 'The Body of Our People', interview by Victoria Freeman. *Paragraph* 14, 3 (1992): 9–12.

———. 'Deconstructing Race, Deconstructing Racism', conversation with Roxana Ng. *Situating "Race" and Racism in Time, Space, and Theory: Critical Essays for Activists and Scholars*, ed. Jo-Anne Lee and John Lutz (Montreal and Kingston: McGill-Queens University Press, 2005), 30–45.

———. Interview by Hartmut Lutz. *Contemporary Challenges: Conversations with Canadian Native Authors*, ed. Hartmut Lutz (Saskatoon: Fifth House Publishing, 1991), 13–32.

———. 'Natural Knowing: Schooling and Sharing the Okanagan Way', *Resurgence* 226 (2004). 17 July 2006 <www.resurgence.org/contents/226.htm>.

Arnason, David. 'Arnason Prefers Storytelling'. *Winnipeg Free Press* (29 August 1992): B21.

———. 'Introduction'. *Isolation in Canadian Literature*, ed. David Arnason (Toronto: Macmillan, 1975), 1–2.

Bailey Nurse, Donna. *What's a Black Critic to Do? Interviews, Profiles and Reviews of Black Writers* (Toronto: Insomniac Press, 2003).

Bannerji, Himani. Interview by Arun Mukherjee. *Other Solitudes: Canadian Multicultural Fictions*, ed. Linda Hutcheon and Marion Richmond (Toronto: Oxford University Press, 1990), 145–52.

———. 'Returning the Gaze: An Introduction'. *Returning the Gaze: Essays on Racism, Feminism and Politics*, ed. Himani Bannerji (Toronto: Sister Vision Press, 1993), ix–xxiv.

Begamudre, Ven. 'A Life in Revolution', profile by Allan Casey. *Books in Canada* 20, 9 (December 1991): 16–18.

———. 'Process, Politics and Plurality', interview by Zool Suleman. *Rungh* 2, 3 (1994): 14–18.

———. 'Racial Bigotry in Aisle 66'. *Globe and Mail* (16 June 2005): A22.

Bezmozgis, David. 'First Time Author Copes with Sudden Literary Fame', interview by Sheldon Kirshner. *Canadian Jewish News* 34, 31 (5 August 2004): 33.

Binning, Sadhu. 'Canada's Federal Election and the Punjabi Language'. *Academy of the Punjab in North America* 17 July 2006 <www.apnaorg.com/articles/binning1/>.

Bissoondath, Neil. 'Escaping the Cultural Imperative', interview by Ali Lakhani. *Rungh* 1, 4 (1993): 8–13.

———. 'Interview', by P. Scott Lawrence. *Matrix* (Autumn 1994): 2–7.

Brand, Dionne. Interview by Dagmar Novak. *Other Solitudes*, 271–7.

———. 'In the company of my work', interview by Makeda Silvera. *The Other Woman: Women of Colour in Contemporary Canadian Literature*, ed. Makeda Silvera (Toronto: Sister Vision Press, 1995), 356–80.

———. 'Unredeemed Grace: Eva Tihanyi Speaks with Dionne Brand'. *Books in Canada* 26, 2 (March 1997): 8.

Brandt, Di. 'letting the silence speak'. *Language in Her Eye: Views on Writing and Gender by Canadian Women Writing in English*, ed. Libby Scheier, Sarah Sheard, and Eleanor Wachtel (Toronto: Coach House Press, 1990), 54–8.

————. 'The sadness in this book is that I'm reaching for this story . . .'. *Sounding Differences: Conversations with Seventeen Canadian Women Writers*, ed. Janice Williamson (Toronto: University of Toronto Press, 1993), 31–45.

Brant, Beth. 'Preface: Telling'. *Food and Spirits*, by Brant (Vancouver: Press Gang, 1991), 11–17.

————. Statement cited in *An Anthology of Canadian Native Literature in English*, ed. Daniel David Moses and Terry Goldie (Toronto: Oxford University Press, 1992), 369.

————. *Writing as Witness: Essay and Talk* (Toronto: Women's Press, 1994).

Caldwell, Rebecca. 'Dancing with Skeletons'. *Globe and Mail* (7 February 2005): R3.

Cameron, Elspeth. *Irving Layton: A Portrait* (Toronto: Stoddart, 1985).

Clarke, Austin. 'A Black Man Talks about Race Prejudice in White Canada'. *Maclean's* (20 April 1963): 18, 55–8.

————. Interview by Linda Richards. *January Magazine* (November 2002). 17 July 2006 <www.janmag.com/profiles/aclarke.html>.

————. Interview for York University Television Series 'Counterparts'. July 1980. As cited in Leslie Sanders, 'Austin Clarke'. *Profiles in Canadian Literature*, ed. Jeffrey M. Heath, vol. 4 (Toronto: Dundurn, 1982), 100.

————. 'Introduction'. *Nine Men Who Laughed*, by Clarke (Markham, Ont.: Penguin, 1986), 1–7.

————. *Love and Sweet Food: A Culinary Memoir* (Toronto: Thomas Allen, 2004).

Clarke, George Elliott. 'Fire on the Water: A First Portrait of Africadian Literature'. *An Anthology of Black Nova Scotian Writing*, ed. George Elliott Clarke, vol 1 (Lawrencetown Beach, NS: Pottersfield Press, 1991), 11–29.

Compton, Wayde. 'The Reinventing Wheel: On Blending the Poetry of Cultures through Hip Hop Turntablism'. *In Horizon: Digital Art and Culture in Canada* 08 (April/May 2003). 17 July 2006 <www.horizonzero.ca/textsite/remix>.

————. with Esi Edugyan and Karina Vernon. 'Black Writers in Search of Place. A Three-Way Conversation about History, Role Models, and Inventing "The Black Atlantis"'. *The Tyee* (28 February 2005): 24–52. 17 July 2006 <www.thetyee.ca/Life/2005/02/28/BlackWriters>.

Crusz, Rienzi. *Oppositional Aesthetics: Readings from a Hyphenated Space*, ed. Arun Mukherjee (Toronto: TSAR, 1994).

D'Alfonso, Antonio. 'Biography'. *antonio-d'alfonso.com* 18 July 2006 <www.guernicaeditions.com/antonio/bio.html>.

————. 'The Road Between: Essentialism. For an Italian Culture in Quebec and Canada'. *Contrasts: Comparative Essays on Italian-Canadian Writing*, ed. Joseph Pivato (Montreal: Guernica, 1985), 207–29.

Di Michele, Mary. 'Conversations with the Living and the Dead'. *Language in Her Eye*, ed. Libby Scheier, Sarah Sheard, Eleanor Wachtel (Toronto: Coach House Press: 1990), 100–6.

————. 'Stealing the Language: An Interview with Mary di Michele', by Ken Norris. *Essays on Canadian Writing* 43 (Spring 1991): 2–13.

Dobozy, Tamas. 'The Immigrant Experience'. 2005. *HarperCollinsCanada* 17 July 2006. <www.harpercanada.com/dobozy>.

Drew, Benjamin, ed. *A North-Side View of Slavery. The Refugee: Or The Narratives of Fugitive Slaves in Canada* (Boston: John P. Jewett, 1856).

Dulai, Phinder. 'Preface'. *Basmati Brown*, by Duali (Madeira Park, BC: Nightwood Editions, 2000).

Friesen, Patrick. Cited in 'Closing Panel'. *Acts of Concealment: Mennonite/s Writing in Canada*, ed. Hildi Froese Tiessen and Peter Hinchcliffe (Waterloo: University of Waterloo Press, 1992), 223–42.

————. '*hooked, but not landed:* A Conversation with Patrick Friesen, part II', by Hildi Froese Tiessen. Prairie Fire 11, 2 (Summer 1990): 152–9.

Grove, Frederick Philip. 'Assimilation'. A *Stranger to My Time: Essays by and About Frederick Philip Grove*, ed. Paul Hjartarson (Edmonton: NeWest, 1986), 177–87.

———. 'Canadians Old and New'. *A Stranger to My Time*, 169–76.

Gunnars, Kristjana. 'Myriads of Stars', interview by Jennifer Eagle. *Prairie Fire* 15, 1 (Spring 1994): 22–6.

Harris, Claire. 'Choosing Control: An Interview with Claire Harris', by Monty Reid. *Waves* 13, 1 (Fall 1984): 37–41.

———. *Dipped in Shadow* (Fredericton: Goose Lane, 1996).

———. 'Why Do I Write?' *Grammar of Dissent: Poetry and Prose by Claire Harris, M. Nourbese Philip and Dionne Brand*, ed. Carol Morrell (Fredericton, NB: Goose Lane, 1991), 26–33. Cited here from an unedited version entitled 'Why I Write'.

Heble, Ajay. 'Letters in Canada: Fiction'. *University of Toronto Quarterly* 68, 1 (Winter 1998–9): 235–54.

Highway, Tomson. 'Interview', by Susannah Schmidt. *Playwright's Workshop Montreal* (May 1998). 17 July 2006 <www.playwrights.ca/portfolios/tomsonint.html>.

Hill, Lawrence. 'Colour Has to Count'. *Globe and Mail* (14 June 2001): A17.

Hopkinson, Nalo. 'An Interview with Nalo Hopkinson', by Dianne D. Glave. *Callaloo* 26, 1 (2003): 146–59.

———. 'Micro-Biography: Who (and Where) I Am'. *Nalo Hopkinson* 18 July 2006 <www.sff.net/people/nalo/writing/whome.html>.

Ipellie, Alootook. 'Alootook Ipellie: The Voice of an Inuk Artist', Interview by Michael P.J. Kennedy. *Studies in Canadian Literature* 21, 2 (1996): 155–64.

King, Thomas. 'Interview with Thomas King', by Jeffrey Canton. *Paragraph* 16, 1 (1994): 2–6.

Kiyooka, Roy. Cited in 'Coruscations, Plangencies, and the Syllibant: After Words to Roy Kiyooka's *Pacific Windows*', by Roy Miki. *Pacific Windows: Collected Poems of Roy K. Kiyooka*, ed. Roy Miki (Burnaby: Talonbooks, 1997), 301–20.

———. Cited in 'Inter-Face: Roy Kiyooka's Writing, A Commentary/Interview', by Roy Miki. *Roy Kiyooka* (Vancouver: Artspeak Gallery and Or Gallery, 1991), 41–54.

———. 'Dear Lucy Fumi: c/o Japanese Canadian Redress Secretariat'. *West Coast Line* 3 (Winter 1990): 125–6.

———. 'We Asian North Americanos: An unhistorical "take" on growing up yellow in a white world'. *West Coast Line* 3 (Winter 1990): 116–18.

Klein, A.M. 'The Bible's Archetypal Poet'. *A.M. Klein: Literary Essays and Reviews*, ed. Usher Caplan and M.W. Steinberg (Toronto: University of Toronto Press, 1987), 143–8.

———. (On Quebec.) Cited in *Like One That Dreamed: A Portrait of A.M. Klein*, by Usher Caplan (Toronto: McGraw-Hill Ryerson, 1982), 149.

Kogawa, Joy. 'The Literary Politics of the Victim', interview by Magdalene Redekop. *Canadian Forum* (November 1989): 14–17.

Kroetsch, Robert. 'Preface'. *Dreaming Backwards: The Selected Poetry of Eli Mandel* (Don Mills, ON: General Publishing, 1981), 9–12.

Kulyk Keefer, Janice. Interview by Jars Balan. *Other Solitudes*, 290–6.

———. 'From Mosaic to Kaleidoscope: Out of the Multicultural Past Comes a Vision of a Transcultural Future'. *Books in Canada* 20, 6 (September 1991): 13–16.

Ladha, Yasmin. 'Circum the Gesture'. *Open Letter* 9, 3 (Summer 1995): 53–73.

Lau, Evelyn. 'The Economies of Language', interview by Brian Fawcett. *Books in Canada* 22, 4 (May 1993): 13–16.

———. Interview by Linda Richards. *January Magazine* (October 1999). 17 July 2006 <http://www.janmag.com/profiles/lau.html>.

———. As cited in 'Reading Evelyn Right', by Misao Dean. *Canadian Forum* LXXIV, 837 (March 1995): 22–6.

la Vonne Brown Ruoff, A. 'E. Pauline Johnson (Tekahionwake).' *Dictionary of Literary Biography*, ed. Kenneth M. Roemer, vol. 175 (Detroit: Gale Research, 1997), 131–6.

Layton, Irving. 'The Graveyard.' *The Shattered Plinths*, by Layton. (Toronto: McClelland Stewart, 1968), 90.

Lee, SKY (Sharon Lee). 'Is there a mind without media any more?', a talk with C. Allyson Lee. *The Other Woman*, 382–403.

———.Untitled. *Jin Guo: Voices if Chinese Canadian Women*, ed. The Women's Book Collective, Chinese Canadian National Council (Toronto: Women's Press, 1992), 91–8.

Mandel, Eli. 'Ethnic Voice in Canadian Writing.' *Another Time*, by Mandel. (Erin, ON: Porcepic, 1977), 91–102.

———. 'Criticism as Ghost Story.' *Another Time*, by Mandel. (Erin, ON: Porcepic, 1977), 146–50.

Maracle, Lee. 'an infinite number of pathways to the centre of the circle', interview by Janice Williamson. *Sounding Differences*, 166–78.

———. 'Just Get in Front of a Typewriter and Bleed'. *Telling It: Women and Language Across Cultures*, ed. The Telling It Book Collective (SKY Lee, Lee Maracle, Daphne Marlatt, and Betsy Warland) (Vancouver: Press Gang, 1990), 37–41.

———. 'Native Myths: Trickster Alive and Crowing'. *Fuse* 13, 1/2 (Fall 1989): 29–31.

———. 'The "Post-Colonial" Imagination'. *Fuse* 16, 1 (Fall 1992): 12–15.

———. 'Preface: You Become the Trickster'. *Sojourner's Truth & Other Stories*, by Maracle (Vancouver: Press Gang, 1990), 11–13.

Marlatt, Daphne. 'Meeting on Fractured Margins'. *Telling It: Women and Language across Cultures*, 9–18.

———. 'On *Ana Historic*', interview by George Bowering. *Line* 13 (Spring 1989): 96–105.

———. *Taken* (Concord, Ont: Anansi, 1996).

———. 'When we change language . . .', interview by Janice Williamson. *Sounding Differences*, 182–93.

Mathur, Ashok. 'Ashok Mathur Chairholder Profile'. *Canada Research Chairs* 17 July 2006 <www.chairs.gc.ca/web/chairholders/viewprofile_e.asp?id=1732&Province_ID=0&UniversityID=&SubjectID=&DisciplineID=&Researcher=mathur&Keyword=>.

———. 'The Desisting Reader'. *West Coast Line* 10, 27/1 (Spring 1993): 67–73.

———. 'Interview', by Larissa Lai. *Writers for Change: Cultural Diversity in Canadian Writing* (Spring 1999). 17 July 2006 <www.eciad.ca/~amathur/writers/ashok-int.html>.

Mayr, Suzette. Conversation with Karina Vernon. *Matrix* 58 (2000): 14–18.

———. 'Interview', by Nathaniel G. Moore. *The Danforth Review* (February 2005). 17 July 2006 <www.danforthreview.com>.

Miki, Roy. 'From Exclusion to Inclusion'. *Canadian Forum* LXXIII, 832 (September 1994): 5–8.

Mistry, Rohinton. 'An Interview with Rohinton Mistry', by Geoff Hancock. *Canadian Fiction Magazine* 65 (1989): 143–50.

———. 'Interview', by Dagmar Novak. *Other Solitudes*, 256–62.

'National Aboriginal Achievement Awards: Tomson Highway, Arts and Culture'. *First Nations Drum* (Winter 2001). 17 July 2006 <www.firstnationsdrum.com>.

Nuttall-Smith, Chris. 'One Man Shock-and-Awe: How David Bezmozgis went from Literary Unknown to Next Big Thing'. *Quill and Quire* 70, 3 (March 2004): 14–15.

Odhiambo David. 'An E-mail Interview with David Odhiambo', by Larissa Lai. *Writers for Change: Cultural Diversity in Canadian Writing* (Spring 1999). 17 July 2006 <www.eciad.bc.ca/%7Eamathur/writers/david-int.html>.

———. 'Author Interview'. *Penguin Group (Canada)* 17 July 2006 <bookclub.penguin.ca/nf/Book/BookDisplay/0,,9780143012337,00.html?sym=QUE>.

———. 'When racism is in the eye of the beholder'. *The Vancouver Sun* (20 February 1999): H1.

Ondaatje, Michael. 'An Interview with Michael Ondaatje', by Eleanor Wachtel. *Essays on Canadian Writing* 53 (Summer 1994): 250–61.

———. ' "The Germ of Document": An Interview with Michael Ondaatje', by Gerry Turcotte. *Australian–Canadian Studies* 12, 2 (1994): 49–58.

———. 'Michael Ondaatje: An Interview', by Catherine Bush. *Essays on Canadian Writing* 53 (Summer 1994): 238–49.

Petrone, Penny. *Native Literature in Canada: From the Oral Tradition to the Present* (Toronto: Oxford University Press, 1990).

Philip, Marlene NourbeSe. 'Zong! Zong!'. *Fascicle* 1 (Summer 2005). 18 July 2006 <www.fascicle.com/issue01/Poets/philip1.htm>.

———, with Thierry Hentsch, Amin Maalouf, Sara Suleri, and Julian Samuel. 'The Raft of the Medusa: Five Voices on Colonies, Nations and Histories'. *The Raft of the Medusa: Five Voices on Colonies, Nations and Histories*, 1–85.

Redekop, Magdalene. 'The Pickling of the Mennonite Madonna'. *Acts of Concealment: Mennonite Writing in Canada*, ed. Hildi Froese Tiessen and Peter Hinchcliffe (Waterloo, University of Waterloo Press, 1992), 100–28.

Ricci, Nino. 'A Big Canvas', interview by Mary Rimmer. *Studies in Canadian Literature* 18, 2 (1993): 168–84.

———. 'Recreating Paradise', interview by Jeffrey Canton. *Paragraph* 13, 3 (1991): 2–5.

Rodriguez, Nice. 'Innocent Lust'. *Piece of My Heart*, 82–7.

Scofield, Gregory. 'Artist's Statement'. *Faculty Profiles, Alberta College of Art and Design* 17 July 2006 <www.acad.ab.ca/faculty>.

———. 'Interview', by Linda Roberts. *January Magazine* (September 1999). 17 July 2006 <www.januarymagazine.com/profiles/scofield>.

Selvadurai, Shyam. Cited in 'Personal and Political', by Leona Gom, Joyce Marshall, and John Steffler. *Books in Canada* 24, 3 (April 1995): 9.

———. Cited in 'A Tale of Two Prizes', *Globe and Mail* (29 October 1994): C7.

Sekora, John. 'Black Message White Envelope: Genre, Authenticity, and Authority in the Antebellum Slave Narrative'. *Callaloo* 10 (Summer 1987): 44–54.

Silvera, Makeda. 'The Characters would not have it'. *The Other Woman*, 405–19.

Smedman, Lisa. 'Hogan's Alley Heart of Black Community.' *Vancouver Courier* (23 February 2005): 40.

Spettigue, Douglas O. *FPG: The European Years* (Ottawa: Oberon, 1973).

Steinfeld, J.J. Interview by Michael Bryson. *The Danforth Review* (August 2003) 18 July 2006 <www.danforthreview.com/features/interviews/jj_steinfeld.htm>.

Stobie, Margaret R. *Frederick Philip Grove* (New York: Twayne, 1973).

Suknaski, Andrew. 'Rose Far in the East'. An envelope of nine *Poem/Drawings* (1971).

Thomas, H. Nigel. 'Biographical Note'. *Bequia Marketing* 18 July 2006 <www.bequiamarketing.com/literature_nigel_bio.htm>.

———. 'Memories of Caribbean Nurtured in Quebec City', Interview by Robert Edison Sandiford. *The Gazette* (30 April 1994): 14.

———. 'You Belong to the Village or You Don't: Isolation Is a Reality, Professor Says'. *The Gazette* (24 September 2002): A21.

Van Camp, Richard. 'Interview', by Judi Saltman. *Canadian Children's Illustrated Book Project* (29 September 2003). 17 July 2006 <www.richardvancamp.org/JSaltman.html>.

Vassanji, M.G. ' "Broadening the Substrata": An Interview with M.G. Vassanji', by Chelva Kanaganaykam. *World Literature Written in English* 31, 2 (1991): 19–35.

———. 'An Interview' by John Clement Ball. *Paragraph* 15, 3&4 (Winter 1993–Spring 1994): 3–8.

Waddington, Miriam. 'Rochl Korn: Remembering a Poet'. In *Apartment Seven: Essays Selected and New* by Waddington (Toronto: Oxford University Press, 1989), 190–9.

Wiebe, Rudy. '"Looking at our Particular World": An Interview with Rudy Wiebe', by Om P. Juneja, M.F. Salat, and Chandra Mohan. *World Literature Written in English* 31, 2 (Autumn 1991): 1–18.

Winks, Robin W. *The Black in Canada: A History*, 1971. (Montreal and Kingston: McGill-Queen's UP, 1977).

Wong, Rita. 'Interview', by Larissa Lai. *Writers for Change: Cultural Diversity in Canadian Writing* (Spring 1999). 17 July 2006 <www.eciad.ca/~amathur/writers/rita-int.html>.

Yanofsky, Joel. "Booze, Sun, Sex and Mythology: Tess Fragoulis Rides a Mediterranean Wave with her New Novel". *Montreal Review of Books* Ninth Issue, 5, 1 (Fall and Winter 2001–2). 17 July 2006 <www.aelaq.org/mrb/>.

Acknowledgements

JEANETTE ARMSTRONG 'History Lesson' and 'Indian Woman' from *Breathtracks* by Jeannette Armstrong. Thank you to Theytus Books Ltd and Jeannette Armstrong for the use of these poems.

DAVID ARNASON 'The Sunfish' by David Arnason. From *Fifty Stories and a Piece of Advice* (Turnstone Press 1987). Copyright © David Arnason. Reprinted by permission of the author.

VEN BEGAMUDRÉ 'Mosaic' by Ven Begamudré. Reprinted by permission of the author.

DAVID BEZMOZGIS 'An Animal to The Memory' from *Natasha and Other Stories* by David Bezmozgis. Published by HarperCollins Publishers Ltd. Copyright © 2004 by Nada Films, Inc. All rights reserved.

SADHU BINNING 'The Symptoms' and 'To Mother' Teresa' from *No More Watno Dur* by Sadhu Binning. Reprinted by permission of the author and TSAR Publications. Vancouver writer Sadhu Binning's published works include a novel, three poetry and two short fiction collections and a bilingual volume of poetry. He has also co-authored and produced a number of plays about the local South Asian community.

NEIL BISOONDATH From *Selling Illusions* by Neil Bissoondath. Copyright © Neil Bissoondath, 1994. Reprinted by permission of Penguin Group (Canada), a Division of Pearson Canada Inc.

DIONNE BRAND Excerpts from *No Language Is Neutral* by Dionne Brand. Used by permission of McClelland & Stewart Ltd. Excerpts from *Land to Light On* by Dionne Brand. Used by permission of McClelland & Stewart Ltd.

DI BRANDT 'foreword' by Di Brandt. From *questions i asked by mother* (Turnstone Press 1987). Copyright © Di Brandt. Reprinted by permission of Turnstone Press. 'Zone: <le Detroit>' by Di Brandt, from *Now You Care* (Coach House Books, 2003). Reprinted by permission of the publisher.

BETH BRANT 'This is History' from *Food & Spirits* by Beth Brant (Vancouver: Press Gang Publishers, 1997)

WARREN CARIOU Extracted from *Lake of the Prairies* by Warren Cariou. Copyright © Warren Cariou 2002. Reprinted by permission of Doubleday Canada.

WAYSON CHOY From *Paper Shadows* by Wayson Choy. Copyright © Wayson Choy, 1999. Reprinted by permission of Penguin Group (Canada), a Division of Pearson Canada Inc.

AUSTIN CLARKE 'When He Was Free and Young and He Used to Wear Silks' copyright © 1971 by Austin Clarke from *Choosing His Coffin*, published by Thomas Allen Publishers, 2003. Reprinted by permission of the author.

GEORGE ELLIOTT CLARKE 'Look Homeward, Exile' and 'The Symposium' from *Whylah Falls* by George Elliott Clarke. Reprinted with permission from Raincoast Books. First published by Polestar, an imprint of Raincoast Books in 1990.

WAYDE COMPTON 'O' and 'Where Heaven Lies', from *49th Parallel Psalm* by Wayde Compton (Arsenal Pulp Press, 2000). Reprinted with permission of the publisher. 'Declaration of the Halfrican Nation', from *Performance Bond* by Wayde Compton (Arsenal Pulp Press, 2004). Reprinted with permission of the publisher.

RIENZL CRUSZ 'Civilization', Interpreting the Clothesline', and 'Roots' from *Insurgent Rain: Selected Poems 1974–1996* by Rienzi Crusz. Reprinted with permission from TSAR Publications.

ATONIO D'ALFONSO 'Im Sachsenhausen', 'The Loss of a Culture', 'The Family', and 'On Being a Wop' from *The Other Shore* by Antonio D'Alfonso (Toronto: Guernica, 1988). Reprinted by permission of the publisher.

MARY DI MICHELE 'Life is Theatre, Or O to Be an Italian in Toronto Drinking Cappuccino on Bloor Street at Bersani & Carlevale's' and 'Afterword: Trading In On The American Dream' by Mary di Michele. Reprinted by permission of the author.

TAMAS DOBOZY 'Four Uncles' from *Last Notes and Other Stories* by Tamas Dobozy. Published by HarperCollins Publishers Ltd. Copyright © 2005 by Tamas Dobozy. All rights reserved.

PHINDER DULAI 'basmati brown (confessions of a Punjabi breeder' from *basmati brown* by Phinder Dulai (Madeira Park, BC: Nightwood Editions, 2000). Reprinted by permission of the author and Nightwood Editions.

MARILYN DUMONT 'Letter to Sir John A. MacDonald', 'Still Unsaved Soul', and 'The Devil's Language' from *A Really Good Brown Girl* by Marilyn Dumont (London, ON: Brick Books, 1996). Reprinted by permission of the publisher.

TESS FRAGOULIS 'Dear Mr Bail' from *Stories to Hide from Your Mother* by Tess Fragoulis (Arsenal Pulp Press, 1997). Reprinted with permission of the publisher.

PATRICK FRIESEN 'Sunday afternoon', 'bible', and 'evisceration' by Patrick Friesen. From *Flicker and Hawk* (Turnstone Press 1987). Copyright © Patrick Friesen. Reprinted by permission of Turnstone Press.

HIROMO GOTO 'Stinky Girl' from *Hopeful Monsters* by Hiromi Goto (Arsenal Pulp Press, 2004). Reprinted with permission of the publisher.

KRISTJANA GUNNARS 'Mass and a Dance' from *The Guest House and Other Stories* copyright © 1992 Kristjana Gunnars. Reprinted by permission of House of Anansi Press.

CLAIRE HARRIS 'No God Waits on Incense' from *The Conception of Winter* by Claire Harris (Fredericton, NB: Goose Lane Editions, 1995). 'Black Sisyphus' from *Travelling to Find a Remedy* by Claire Harris (Fredericton, NB: Goose Lane Editions, 2001).

TOMSON HIGHWAY 'My Canada' from *Imperial Oil Review* (Spring 2000). With permission of the author: Tomson Highway.

LAWRENCE HILL From *Any Known Blood* by Lawrence Hill. Published by HarperCollins Publishers Ltd. Copyright © 1997 by Lawrence Hill. All rights reserved.

NALO HOPKINSON 'A Habit of Waste' by Nalo Hopkinson, *Fireweed* 53 (1996): 28–43. Reprinted by permission of the author.

ALOOTOOK IPELLIE 'Love Triangle' by Alootook Ipellie. Reprinted by permission of the author. Alootook Ipellie grew up in Iqaluit, Nunavut and currently lives in Ottawa. He is pursuing a multifaceted career in the fine arts. As graphic artist, cartoonist, photographer, and writer, he contributes to many Inuit publications in the Canadian Arctic.

JANICE KULYK KEEFER 'Nach Unten' by Janice Kulyk Keefer. Reprinted by permission of the author.

THOMAS KING From *One Good Story, That One* by Thomas King (HarperPerennial, 1993). Copyright © 1993 Dead Dog Café Productions Inc. With permission of the author.

ROY KIYOOKA From *Pacific Rim Letters* (2005) by Roy Kiyooka. Reprinted by permission of NeWest Publishers Ltd.

A.M. KLEIN 'Autobiographical' and 'Doctor Drummond' from *Complete Poems* by A.M. Klein, Zaig Pollock, ed. (Toronto: University of Toronto Press, 1990). Reprinted by permission of the publisher.

JOY KOGAWA Excerpt from *Obasan* by Joy Kogawa. Reprinted by permission of the author.

YASMIN LADHA 'Beena' from *The Lion's Granddaughter and Other Stories* by Yasmin Ladha. Reprinted by permission of the author.

LARISSA LAI 'The Salt Fish Girl' by Larissa Lai. Reprinted by permission of the author.

IRVING LAYTON 'Whom I Write For' from *The Collected Poems of Irving Layton* by Irving Layton. Used by permission of McClelland & Stewart Ltd. 'The Search' from *A Wild Peculiar Joy: the Selected Poems* by Irving Layton. Used by permission of McClelland & Stewart Ltd.

SKY LEE Excerpt from *Disappearing Moon Café* by SKY Lee, published 1990 by Douglas & McIntyre Ltd. Reprinted by permission of the publisher.

ELI MANDEL 'estevan, 1934:' and 'the return' by Eli Mandel from *Out of Place* (Toronto: Musson Book Company, 1977). Reprinted by permission of the Estate of Eli Mandel.

LEE MARACLE 'Bertha' from *Sojourners and Sundogs: First Nations Fiction* by Lee Maracle. Reprinted by permission of the author.

DAPHNE MARLATT 'Month of Hungry Ghosts' from *Ghost Works* (1993) by Daphne Marlatt. Reprinted by permission of NeWest Publishers Ltd.

ASHOK MATHUR 'Into Skin', by Ashok Mathur. Reprinted by permission of the author.

SUZETTE MAYR From *Moon Honey* (1995) by Suzette Mayr. Reprinted by permission of NeWest Publishers Ltd.

ROY MIKI All selections from *Surrender* (The Mercury Press, 2001). Reprinted by permission of the author.

ROHINTON MISTRY From *Tales Firozsha Baag* by Rohinton Mistry (McClelland & Stewart, 1992). Copyright © 1987 Rohinton Mistry. With permission of the author.

SHANI MOOTOO 'Denudation' from *Urban Fictions* by Shani Mootoo; 'For Naan' from *The Predicament of Or* by Shani Mootoo. Published by Polestar Books, 2001. Reprinted with permission from Raincoast Books.

DAVID ODHIAMBO Excerpt from *dissed/banded* by David Odhiambo. Published by Polestar Books, 1998. Reprinted with permission from Raincoast Books.

MICHAEL ONDAATJE Excerpt from *In The Skin of a Lion*, by Michael Ondaatje (Toronto: Vintage Canada, 1996). Reprinted by permission of the author.

MARLENE NOURBESE PHILIP 'Discourse on the Logic of Language' by M. NourbeSe Philip. Reprinted by permission of the author.

NINO RICCI 'Going to the Moon' by Nino Ricci. Reprinted by permission of the author.

NICE RODRIGUEZ 'Big Nipple of the North' from *Throw It To the River* by Nice Rodriguez © Women's Press 2003. Reprinted by permission of Canadian Scholars' Press Inc./Women's Press.

ARMAND GARNET RUFFO 'Power', 'At Geronimo's Grave', and 'Detour' from *At Geronimo's Grave* by Armand Garnet Ruffo (Regina, SK: Coteau Books, 2001). Reprinted by permission of the publisher.

GREGORY SCOFIELD 'Offering: 1996' from *Love Medicine and One Song* by Gregory Scofield. Published by Polestar Books, 1997. Reprinted with permission from Raincoast Books. From *Thunder Through My Veins*, by Gregory Scofield. Published by HarperCollins Publishers Ltd. Copyright © 1999 by Gregory Scofield. All rights reserved.

SHYAM SELVADURAI From *Funny Boy* by Shyam Selvadurai (McClelland & Stewart, 1994). Copyright © 1994 Shyam Selvadurai. With permission of the author.

GERRY SHIKATANI Excerpt from 'mortar rake glove or sausan broom basin sansui First Book, Three Gardens of Andalucía' (Capilano Review Society) is reprinted by permission of the author.

MAKEDA SILVERA 'Her Head a Village' from *Her Head a Village* by Makeda Silvera (Vancouver: Press Gang Publishers, 1994). Reprinted by permission of the author.

J.J. STEINFELD 'Ida Solomon's Play' was first published in *Forms of Captivity and Escape* (Thistledown Press, 1988) by J.J. Steinfeld, copyright © 1988 by J. J. Steinfeld, and reprinted in *Dancing at the Club Holocaust: Stories New & Selected* (Ragweed Press, 1993) by J.J. Steinfeld, copyright © 1993 by J.J. Steinfeld. Reprinted by permission of the author.

ANDREW SUKNASKI 'Philip Well' from *Wood Mountain Poems*, 'West to Tolstoi, Manitoba (circa 1900)', 'Vasylyna's Retreat', 'In the Beginning was The', 'Letter to Big Bear', and 'The Faceless Goodbyes' by Andrew Suknaski. All poems © Andrew Suknaski. Reprinted by permission of the author.

H. NIGEL THOMAS 'The Village Ram' by H. Nigel Thomas. Reprinted from *How Loud Can the Cock Crow? And Other Stories* (St-Laurent, QC: Afo Enterprises, 1995) with permission of the author.

MIRIAM TOEWS 'A Father's Faith' by Miriam Toews, from *Dropped Threads: What we aren't told* (Toronto: Vintage Canada, 2001). Reprinted by permission of the author. Miriam Toews's most recent novel is *A Complicated Kindness*, winner of the 2004 Governor General's award for fiction.

RICHARD VAN CAMP 'Sky Burial' from *Angel Wing Splash Pattern* by Richard Van Camp. Reprinted by permission of the author. Richard Van Camp is a Dogrib author living in Vancouver, BC, where he teaches Creative Writing for Aboriginal Students at UBC.

ARITHA VAN HERK 'Of Dykes and Boers and Drowning' by Aritha van Herk. Reprinted by permission of the author.

M.G. VASSANJI 'The London-returned' from *Uhuru Street* by M.G. Vassanji. Used by permission of McClelland & Stewart Ltd.

FRED WAH 'waiting for saskatchewan' and 'Father/Mother Haibun #4' from *Waiting for Saskatchewan* by Fred Wah (Turnstone, 1985). Excerpts from *Music at the Heart of Thinking* (2, 10, 50, 51, 52, 55) by Fred Wah (Red Deer College Press, 1987). Reprinted by permission of the author.

RUDY WIEBE 'A Night in Fort Pitt or (if you prefer) The Only Perfect Communicsts in the World', extracted from *River of Stone* by Rudy Wiebe. Copyright © 1995 Jackpine House Inc. Reprinted by permission of Knopf Canada.

RITA WONG 'puzzlinen', 'cities of disturbance', and 'lips shape Yangtze, <u>chang jiang</u>, river longing' by Rita Wong. Reprinted by permission of the author.

Index

33